The Michigan Historical Reprint Series

Reprints from the collection of the University of Michigan University Library

The Scholarly Publishing Office
the University of Michigan
University Library

LAND LAWS,

REGULATIONS AND DECISIONS.

BEING A

CONTINUATION OF ACTS OF CONGRESS RESPECTING THE SALE AND DISPOSITION OF PUBLIC LANDS;

AND EMBRACING

LAND LAWS

PASSED SINCE THE PUBLICATION OF VOL. I.

FROM DECEMBER, 1859, TO JANUARY 1, 1870;

TOGETHER WITH

SELECTED DECISIONS OF THE INTERIOR DEPARTMENT, AND REGULATIONS AND RULINGS OF THE GENERAL LAND OFFICE.

BY

W. W. LESTER,

ATTORNEY AT LAW, WASHINGTON, D. C.

VOLUME II.

PHILADELPHIA:

KAY & BROTHER,

LAW BOOKSELLERS, PUBLISHERS, AND IMPORTERS,

NO. 19 SOUTH SIXTH STREET.

1870.

PHILADELPHIA:
COLLINS, PRINTER.

INTRODUCTION.

THE same system and order of arrangement adopted in the first volume, have been continued in this.

A new series of numbers has, however, been commenced, and the letter "B" has been attached to them, in order that they may be distinguished from corresponding numbers in the original work.

The annual reports of the present distinguished Commissioner of the General Land Office, Hon. Joseph S. Wilson, which, as most interesting and valuable contributions to the geographical, statistical, scientific, and legal literature of the day, are universally acknowledged and appreciated, have for several years past embraced rulings of his Bureau and of the Interior Department upon land questions, in a brief and compendious form. Those rulings, in addition to other important decisions, have been inserted in this volume.

The compiler has to express his acknowledgments to the editors of the "American Law Times," published in the city of Washington, from which periodical he has extracted a number of valuable papers, collected in accordance with the plan adopted by them of obtaining and publishing all important recent decisions of the Courts, State and Federal, and of the Departments of the General Government, thus furnishing the profession with reports and other legal information which could not be procured in another form, except at great labor and expense.

He is also greatly indebted to Henry Beard, Esq., of Washington city, for the use of his law library and for access to his ample collection of documents pertaining to public lands, and also for advice and suggestions rendered particularly valuable by reason of his extensive experience and thorough knowledge of the subject.

The land laws are given in full in the exact words of the statutes, and are inserted in chronological order.

The case relating to the Soscol Rancho in California, embracing an opinion of the Attorney-General, the decision of the Secretary of the Interior, and of Judge Wylie, of the Supreme Court of the District of Columbia (page 280), has furnished the occasion for a full and exhaustive discussion of the pre-emption system, which will be found of great interest and importance in the investigation of rights arising under those laws. The Supreme Court of the United States, at the December term, 1869, finally determined the questions involved, sustaining, in the main, the opinions of Attorney-Generals Bates and Speed, referred to in the note on page 388 of this volume.

CONTENTS.

PART III.

PART IV.

GENERAL

PUBLIC ACTS OF CONGRESS

RESPECTING THE

SALE AND DISPOSITION OF PUBLIC LANDS.

No. 1 B.—An Act to extend the provisions of "An Act to enable the State of Arkansas and other States to reclaim the swamp lands within their limits,"* to Minnesota and Oregon, and for other purposes.

Be it enacted by the Senate and House of Representatives of the United States of America in Congress assembled, That the provisions of the act of Congress entitled "An act to enable the State of Arkansas and other States to reclaim the 'swamp lands' within their limits," approved September twenty-eight, eighteen hundred and fifty, be, and the same are hereby, extended to the States of Minnesota and Oregon: *Provided,* That the grant hereby made shall not include any lands which the government of the United States may have reserved, sold, or disposed of (in pursuance of any law heretofore enacted) prior to the confirmation of title to be made under the authority of the said act.

SEC. 2. *And be it further enacted,* That the selection to be made from lands already surveyed in each of the States including Minnesota and Oregon, under the authority of the act aforesaid and of the act to aid the State of Louisiana in draining the swamp lands therein, approved March second, one thousand eight hundred and forty-nine, shall be made within two years from the adjournment of the Legislature of each State at its next session after the date of this act; and, as to all lands hereafter to be surveyed, within two years from such adjournment, at the next session, after notice by the Secretary of the Interior to the Governor of the State, that the surveys have been completed and confirmed.

Approved, March 12, 1860.

No. 2 B.—An Act to settle the titles to lands along the boundary line between the States of Georgia and Florida.

Be it enacted by the Senate and House of Representatives of the United States of America in Congress assembled, That whenever the dividing line

* Vol. I. No. 182.

between the States of Georgia and Florida shall have been finally surveyed, approved, ratified, and confirmed, as the boundary between those States, the Secretary of the Interior shall be, and is hereby, authorized to adjudicate, upon principles of equity and justice, all claims under sales or grants by the State of Georgia, to lands which may fall within the State of Florida, and all of said claims which may be approved by him shall be and are hereby ratified and confirmed: *Provided, however*, That the State of Georgia shall first ratify and confirm all sales and grants made by the United States of lands in Florida which may fall within the limits of the State of Georgia under the final adjustment of the boundary line aforesaid.

Approved, April 13, 1860.

No. 3 B.—An Act to create an additional Land District in Washington Territory.

Be it enacted by the Senate and House of Representatives of the United States of America in Congress assembled, That, when in the opinion of the President it may be expedient, all the public lands in the Territory of Washington, to which the Indian title shall have been extinguished, or may hereafter be extinguished, lying east and south of the following boundaries, shall constitute a new land district to be called the "Columbia River District," viz: Beginning on the boundary line between the United States and the British possessions, and on the summit of the Cascade Mountains, at the nearest range line to the east line of range twelve, thence south on the nearest range lines on the summit of said mountains to the line dividing townships ten and eleven north, thence west to the line dividing ranges six and seven west, thence north on said line to the third standard parallel, thence west to "Shoal Water Bay," thence with the Shoal Water Bay, including any islands therein, to the Pacific—the western boundary of said district above the line dividing ranges ten and eleven, and on the summit of the Cascade Mountains, to be adjusted by the Department of the Interior as near the points before given as is consistent with the lines of the public surveys—and the President shall be authorized hereafter, from time to time, as circumstances may require, to adjust the boundaries of the land districts in said territory, and remove the offices when the same shall be expedient.

SEC. 2. *And be it further enacted*, That the President be, and he is hereby, authorized to appoint by and with the advice and consent of the Senate or during the recess thereof, and until the end of the next session after such appointment, a register and receiver for said district, who shall be required to reside at the site of the land office, be subject to the same laws, and entitled to the same compensation as is or may hereafter be prescribed by the law in relation to the existing land office and officers in said territory.

Approved, May 16, 1860.

No. 4 B.—An Act to settle the titles to certain lands set apart for the use of certain half-breed Kansas Indians, in Kansas Territory.

Whereas by the sixth article of a treaty made and concluded at the city of St. Louis, in the State of Missouri, on the third day of June, eigh teen hundred and twenty-five, between the United States of America and the Kansas nation of Indians, there was reserved from the lands ceded by said treaty to the United States by said Kansas nation of Indians, one mile square of land for each of the half-breeds of the Kansas nation named in the said sixth article, which land has been surveyed and allotted to each of the said half-breeds in the order in which they are named in, and in accordance with, the provisions of the said sixth article of said treaty: Therefore—

Be it enacted by the Senate and House of Representatives of the United States of America in Congress assembled, That all the title, interest and estate of the United States is hereby vested in the said reservees who are now living, to the land reserved, set apart and allotted to them respectively, by the said sixth article of said treaty; and in case any of the said reservees named in the said sixth article are deceased, and leaving heirs, then all the title, interest of the United States to the land allotted to such deceased reservees is hereby vested and confirmed in such persons as shall by the Secretary of the Interior be decided to be the heirs of such deceased reservees; but nothing herein contained shall be construed to give any force, efficacy, or binding effect to any contract, in writing or otherwise, for the sale or disposition of any lands named in this act, heretofore made by any of said reservees, or their heirs.

SEC. 2.* *And be it further enacted*, That in case of any of the reservees now living, or the heirs of any deceased reservees, shall not desire to reside upon, or occupy the lands to which such reservees or such heirs are entitled by the provisions of this act, the Secretary of the Interior, when requested by them, or either of them, so to do, is hereby authorized to sell such lands belonging to those so requesting him, for the benefit of such reservees, or such heirs; and the Secretary of the Interior is also authorized to sell, with the assent of the Kansas nation of Indians, the lands allotted to the reservees who are deceased leaving no heirs, for the benefit of the living reservees, their heirs, and the heirs of those deceased, equally; said lands to be sold in accordance with such rules and regulations as may be prescribed by the Commissioner of Indian Affairs, and approved by [the] Secretary of the Interior; and patents in the usual form shall be issued to the purchasers of said lands, in accordance with the provisions of this act.

SEC. 3.* *And be it further enacted*, That the proceeds of the land, the sale of which is provided for by this act, shall be paid to the parties entitled thereto, or applied by the Secretary of the Interior for their benefit, in such manner as he may think most advantageous to their interest.

Approved, May 26, 1860.

No. 5 B.—An Act to authorize the President of the United States, in conjunction with the State of California, to run and mark the boundary lines between the Territories of the United States and the State of California.

Be it enacted by the Senate and House of Representatives of the United States of America in Congress assembled, That the President of the United States be, and he hereby is, authorized and empowered to appoint

* Repealed and modified by No. 61 B.

a suitable person, or persons, who, in conjunction with such person or persons as may be appointed on behalf of the State of California for the same purpose, shall run and mark the boundary lines between the Territories of the United States and the State of California, commencing at the point of intersection of the forty-second degree of north latitude with the one hundred and twentieth degree of longitude west from Greenwich, and running south on the line of said one hundred and twentieth degree of west longitude until it intersects the thirty-ninth degree of north latitude; thence running in a straight line in a southeasterly direction to the river Colorado, at a point where it intersects the thirty-fifth degree of north latitude.

SEC. 2. *And be it further enacted,* That such landmarks shall be established at the said point of beginning, and at the other corners, and on the several lines of said boundary, as may be agreed upon by the President of the United States, or those acting under his authority, and the said State of California, or those acting under its authority: *Provided,* That the person, or persons, appointed and employed on the part and behalf of the State of California are to be paid by the said State: *Provided further,* That no person except a superintendent or commissioner shall be appointed or employed in this service by the United States but such as are required to make the necessary observations and surveys to ascertain such line, and erect suitable monuments thereon, and make return of the same.

Approved, May 26, 1860.

No. 6 B.—An Act authorizing the "Domestic and Foreign Missionary Society of the Protestant Episcopal Church in the United States" to enter a certain tract of land in the State of Wisconsin.

Be it enacted by the Senate and House of Representatives of the United States of America in Congress assembled, That the "Domestic and Foreign Missionary Society of the Protestant Episcopal Church in the United States" be, and is hereby, authorized to enter, at the rate of one dollar and twenty-five cents per acre, a certain tract of land known as the "Mission Farm," and numbered as lot number eighteen, on the east bank of Fox River, near Green Bay, State of Wisconsin, having a front on Fox River of six chains, and running eastwardly back from the river, between parallel lines, one hundred and fifty-four and sixty-nine hundredths chains, and containing ninety-two and eighty-one hundredths superficial acres.

Approved, June 1, 1860.

No. 7 B.—An Act for the relief of certain settlers in the State of Iowa.

Be it enacted by the Senate and House of Representatives of the United States of America in Congress assembled, That the east half of section eight, section seventeen and the east half of section eighteen, and section thirty-three, section thirty-four, the southwest quarter of section twenty-seven, and the southeast quarter of section twenty-eight in township ninety-six north, of range nine west, in the State of Iowa, formerly reserved for Fort Atkinson and an Indian agency, and since released and abandoned, as being no longer needed for public uses, shall be, and the same are hereby declared to be, subject to the ordinary disposition of the public lands, in the same manner and on the same conditions, as are provided by law, and that such persons as may have settled thereon prior to the passage of this act, and who would have been entitled to the right of pre-emption under the act of September four, eighteen hundred and forty-one,* had the reservation not been made, shall be entitled to pre-empt their claims in accordance with the provisions of said act, by making proof, payment, and entry at the proper district office, within twelve months after its approval : *Provided,* That if two or more of such persons were actually residing upon the same quarter *quarter* section, or any smaller legal subdivision, at the date of the abandonment of said reservation, the same may be entered by them jointly : *Provided further,* That no declaratory statement shall be required of said settlers.

Approved, June 7, 1860.

No. 8 B.—An Act for the relief of John W. Taylor and certain other assignees of pre-emption land locations.

Be it enacted by the Senate and House of Representatives of the United States of America in Congress assembled, That all assignments of pre-emption bounty land warrant locations at any of the land offices in the United States, made in good faith since the nineteenth day of October, eighteen hundred and fifty-two, and prior to the twenty-first day of May, eighteen hundred and fifty-six, under instructions from the Commissioner of the General Land Office of the former date, be, and the same are hereby, declared valid ; and the Secretary of the Interior is hereby authorized to cause patents to be issued in the name of the assignee in all such locations as now remain suspended and have not been patented.

Approved, June 7, 1860.

No. 9 B.—An Act to amend an act entitled An act to define and regulate the Jurisdiction of the District Courts of the United States in California in regard to the survey and location of confirmed private land claims.†

Be it enacted by the Senate and House of Representatives of the United States of America in Congress assembled, That whenever the Surveyor-General of California shall, in compliance with the thirteenth section of an act entitled "An act to ascertain and settle [the] private land claims in the State of California," approved March three, eighteen hundred and fifty-one,‡ have caused any private land claim to be surveyed, and a plat to be made thereof, he shall give notice that the same has been done, and the plat and survey approved by him, by a publication once a week, for four weeks, in two newspapers, one published in the city of San Francisco, and one of which the place of publication is nearest the land, if the land is situated in the Northern District of California;

* Vol. I. No. 48.

† This act repealed, Sec. 8, No. 103 B.

‡ Vol. I. No. 189.

and once a week, for four weeks, in two newspapers, one published in Los Angelos, and one of which the place of publication is nearest the land, if the land is situated in the Southern District of California; and until the expiration of such time, the survey and plat shall be retained in his office, subject to inspection.

SEC. 2. *And be it further enacted*, That the district courts of the United States for the Northern and Southern Districts of California are hereby authorized, upon the application of any party interested, to make an order, requiring any survey of a private land claim within their respective districts to be returned into the District Court for examination and adjudication, and on the receipt of said order, duly certified by the clerk of either of said courts, it shall be the duty of the Surveyor-General to transmit said survey and plat forthwith to the said court.

SEC. 3. *And be it further enacted*, That said order shall be granted by said courts on the application of any party whom the district courts, or the judges thereof in vacation, shall deem to have such interest in the survey and location of a land claim as to make it just and proper that he should be allowed to take testimony and to intervene for his interest therein; and if objections to the survey and locations shall be made on the part of the United States, the order to return the survey into court shall be made on the motion of the District Attorney, founded on sufficient affidavits; and if the application for such order is made by other parties claiming to be interested in, or that their rights are affected by, such survey and location, the court, or the judge in vacation, shall proceed summarily, on affidavits or otherwise, to inquire into the facts of such interest, and shall, in its discretion, determine whether the applicant has such an interest therein as, under the circumstances of the case, to make it proper that he should be heard in opposition to the survey, and shall grant or refuse the order to return the survey and location, as shall be just: *Provided, however*, That all parties claiming interest under pre-emption, settlement, or other right derived from the United States, shall not be permitted to intervene separately; but the rights and interests of said parties shall be represented by the District Attorney of the United States, intervening in the name of the United States, aided by counsel acting for said parties jointly, if they think proper to employ such counsel: *And provided further*, That before proceeding to take testimony, or to determine on the validity of any objection so made to the survey and location, as aforesaid, the said courts shall cause notice to be given, by public advertisement, or in some other form, to be prescribed by their rules, to all parties in interest, that objection has been made to such survey and location, and admonishing all parties in interest to intervene for the protection of such interest; and the said courts shall adopt rules providing for the prompt and summary decision of all controversies on surveys and locations that may arise under the provisions of this act.

SEC. 4. *And be it further enacted*, That when on the application or applications of the parties interested, as aforesaid, in said survey and location, the same shall be returned into court, the said parties may proceed to take testimony as to any matters necessary to show the true and proper location of the claim; such testimony to be taken in such manner, by deposition or otherwise, or by commission, as the court may direct, and, on hearing the allegations and proofs, the court shall render judgment thereon; and if, in its opinion, the location and survey are erroneous, it is hereby authorized to set aside and annul the same, or correct and modify it; and it is hereby made the duty of the Surveyor-General, on being served with a certified copy of the decree of said court, forthwith to cause a new survey and location to be made, or to correct and reform the survey and location already made, so as to conform to the decree of the District Court, to whom it shall be returned for confirmation and approval.

SEC. 5. *And be it further enacted,* That when, after publication as aforesaid, no application shall be made to the said court for the said order, or when said order has been refused, or when an order shall have been obtained as aforesaid, and when the District Court by its decree shall have finally approved said survey and location, or shall have reformed or modified the same, and determined the true location of the claim, it shall be the duty of the Surveyor-General to transmit, without delay, the plat or survey of the said claim to the General Land Office, and the patent for the land as surveyed shall forthwith be issued therefor, and no appeal shall be allowed from the order or decree as aforesaid of the said District Court, unless applied for within six months from the date of the decree of said district courts, but not afterwards; and the plat and survey so finally determined by publication, order, or decree, as the case may be, shall have the same effect and validity in law as if a patent for the land so surveyed had been issued by the United States.

SEC. 6. *And be it further enacted,* That all surveys and locations heretofore made and approved by the Surveyor-General of California, which have been returned into the said district courts, or either of them, or in which proceedings are now pending for the purpose of contesting or reforming the same, are hereby made subject to the provisions of this act, except that in the cases so returned or pending no publication shall be necessary on the part of the Surveyor-General.

SEC. 7. *And be it further enacted,* That for the performance of the duties imposed by this act, and the act entitled "An Act to ascertain and settle private land claims in the State of California, passed March third, eighteen hundred and fifty-one" there shall be allowed to the judges of the Northern and Southern Districts of Calfornia, as follows: To the Judge of the Northern District such a sum as will, when added to his fixed and permanent salary allowed by law and secured by him, make his compensation amount to the sum of six thousand dollars per annum, and such additional compensation to be computed from the first day of January, eighteen hundred and fifty-two; and to the judge of the Southern District such a sum as will, when added to his fixed and permanent salary allowed by law and received by him, make his compensation amount to the sum of thirty-five hundred dollars, such compensation to be computed and allowed from the date of his appointment to said office, and to continue each for and during the performance of the additional services required to be performed by this act, but not exceeding two years from and after the passage of this act.

SEC. 8. *And be it further enacted,* That all costs of surveys and publications, under the provisions of this act, shall be charged to and paid by the United States, and costs of litigation in the district courts shall abide the result thereof, and the court in its discretion may require security therefor.

SEC. 9. *And be it further enacted,* That all acts and parts of acts inconsistent with the provisions of this act are hereby repealed.

Approved, June 14, 1860.

No. 10 B.—An Act to facilitate communication between the Atlantic and Pacific States by electric telegraph.

Be it enacted, &c., That * * * permission is hereby granted to the said parties to whom said contract may be awarded, or a majority of them, and their assigns, to use until the end of the said term,* such unoccupied public lands of the United States as may be necessary for the right of way and for the purpose of establishing stations for repairs along said line, not exceeding at any station one quarter-section of land, such stations not to exceed one in fifteen miles, on an average of the whole distance, unless said lands shall be required by the Government of the United States for railroad or other purposes: *And provided*, That no right to pre-empt any of said lands under the laws of the United States shall inure to said company, their agents, or servants, or to any other person or persons whatsoever. * * *

SEC. 2.† *And be it further enacted*, That the said contractors or their assigns * * * shall have the permanent right of way for the said line or lines, under, or over, any unappropriated public lands and waters in the said territories, by any route or routes which the said contractors may select, with the free use during the said term of such lands as may be necessary for the purpose of establishing stations for repairs along said line or lines, not exceeding, at any station, one quarter-section of land, such stations not to exceed one in fifteen miles on an average of the whole distance; but should any of said quarter-sections be deemed essential by the Government, or any company acting under its authority, for railroad purposes, the said contractors shall relinquish the occupancy of so much as may be necessary for the railroad, receiving an equal amount of land for like use in its stead.

Approved, June 16, 1860.

No. 11 B.—An Act to relinquish the title of the United States to certain lands occupied by the city of Baton Rouge, in Louisiana.

Be it enacted by the Senate and House of Representatives of the United States of America in Congress assembled, That all the right, title, interest or claim of the United States, in and to the land occupied by the city of Baton Rouge, in the State of Louisiana, lying between Florida Street on the north, and the South Boulevard on the south, as shown by an original map of said city, on file in the office of the Clerk of the Sixth Judicial District Court of Louisiana, at East Baton Rouge, on the fourteenth of March, eighteen hundred and sixty, be, and the same is hereby relinquished to the Mayor and Council of the City of Baton Rouge, in trust for the several use and benefit of the owners of lots therein, according to their respective interests: *Provided*, This act shall only be construed as quitclaim on the part of the United States, and shall not affect the interests of third parties, nor preclude a judicial investigation in relation to the title to all or any portion of the lands hereby relinquished.

Approved, June 16, 1860.

* Ten years.

† This section provides for a branch line to Oregon.

No. 12 B.—An Act recognizing the survey of the Grand Cheniere Island, State of Louisiana, as approved by the Surveyor-General, and for other purposes.

Be it enacted by the Senate and House of Representatives of the United States of America in Congress assembled, That the anomalous survey of the Grand Cheniere Island, in the Southwestern District of Louisiana, as approved by R. W. Boyd, Surveyor-General, on the twenty-eighth day of February, eighteen hundred and fifty-two, be, and the same is hereby, confirmed, and persons residing thereon at the date of this act who, according to the pre-emption laws now in force would be entitled to a pre-emption, shall be allowed such right on the lands referred to in this bill; but such preference right shall be confirmed to the single subdivision of land upon which the party may reside, and shall exceed, in no case, one hundred and sixty acres.

Approved, June 16, 1860.

No. 13 B.—An Act for the relief of congressional township number two north, of range number nine west, of the fourth principal meridian, in Adams County, State of Illinois.

Whereas section number sixteen in township number two north, of range nine west, of the fourth principal meridian, in Adams County, Illinois, is located in a lake or pond, and is in consequence thereof wholly unfit for cultivation, and is worthless to the inhabitants of said township for school purposes: Therefore—

Be it enacted by the Senate and House of Representatives of the United States of America in Congress assembled, That the school trustees for the said township be, and they are hereby authorized to select one section of land in legal subdivisions of any of the public lands of the United States subject to entry or sale, at the minimum price of one dollar and twenty-five cents per acre.

SEC. 2. *And be it further enacted,* That when the same shall have been selected by the trustees aforesaid, and a description thereof returned to and approved by the Commissioner of the General Land Office, a patent or patents shall issue therefor to the inhabitants of the said congressional township, and shall be held and disposed of by them for the use of schools within the said congressional township in the same manner as other school lands are held and disposed of.

SEC. 3. *And be it further enacted,* That the said section sixteen in the township aforesaid shall revert to and invest in the United States, and be disposed of in the same manner as other public lands.

Approved, June 16, 1860.

No. 14 B.—An Act for the relief of the Missionary Society of the Methodist Episcopal Church.

Be it enacted by the Senate and House of Representatives of the United States of America in Congress assembled, That there shall be paid, out of any money in the treasury not otherwise appropriated, to the Missionary

Society of the Methodist Episcopal Church, the sum of twenty thousand dollars, upon filing in the proper department a release to the United States, to be approved by the Attorney-General, of all claim to the land embraced within the limits of the military reservation at the Dalles, in Oregon Territory, and of all claim for damages for destruction of property on or near the said land by the United States troops or volunteers, or Indians, at any time anterior to the date of said release.

Approved, June 16, 1860.

No. 15 B.—An Act confirming certain land entries under the third [proviso to the first] section of the act of third March, eighteen hundred and fifty-five,* entitled, An Act making appropriations for the service of the Post Office Department, during the fiscal year ending the thirtieth of June, eighteen hundred and fifty-six.

Be it enacted by the Senate and House of Representatives of the United States of America in Congress assembled, That all entries which have heretofore been allowed by registers and receivers, and in regard to which no adverse claims have arisen under decisions of the Secretary of the Interior, or of the Commissioner of the General Land Office, setting aside such entries, under that portion of the third proviso to the first section of an act, approved March third, eighteen hundred and fifty-five, entitled "An Act making appropriations for the service of the Post Office Department, during the fiscal year ending the thirtieth of June, one thousand eight hundred and fifty-six," in the following words: "That each contractor, engaged or to be engaged, in carrying the mails through any of the Territories west of the Mississippi, shall have the privilege of occupying stations at the rate of not more than one for every twenty miles of the route on which he carries a mail, and shall have a pre-emption right therein when the same shall be brought into market, to the extent of six hundred and forty acres, to be taken contiguously, and to include his improvements; but no such pre-emption right shall extend to any pass in a mountain or other defile," be, and the same are hereby, confirmed, subject to any *bona fide* claim under any law of the United States, to the whole or any portion of the lands embraced in said entries or locations made prior or subsequent to the date of the selection thereof by the persons aforesaid; and the Commissioner of the General Land Office is hereby directed to issue a patent for the lands embraced in said entries, upon payment of one dollar and twenty-five cents per acre for the land embraced in such patent: *Provided,* That each contractor shall satisfy the Secretary of the Interior that he has complied with the terms of his contract, and that said entries have been used and occupied as stations on the line of the route during the existence of his contract; and that the provisions of this act shall be restricted to one and the first *bona fide* set of pre-emptors on one and the same line of route.

SEC. 2. *And be it further enacted,* That no rights, from and after the passage of this act, shall accrue under the provisions of the aforesaid act of third March, eighteen hundred and fifty-five, which provisions are hereby repealed, saving all rights heretofore acquired or those provided for in the foregoing; and that for the purpose of facilitating the transportation of the public mails of the United States west of the Mississippi

* Vol. I. No. 279.

River to the Pacific Ocean, and intermediate points, the Secretary of the Interior be, and he is hereby, authorized, upon the application of the Postmaster-General, to reserve, as mail stations, for the use and occupancy of mail contractors, during the existence of their contracts, a quantity of public lands, not exceeding the area of one section at any and all such localities as in his judgment are deemed necessary or advisable, to be taken where the public surveys have been made, according to the lines of those surveys; but where stations have been or may hereafter be designated in advance of the public surveys, such stations shall be laid off, under the direction of the Postmaster-General, in a square form, with power to order the adjustment hereafter of such boundaries, to conform to the lines of the public surveys, if such adjustment be deemed advisable, which lands thus reserved as stations shall be held as permanent mail service reservations, not subject to the operation of any existing pre-emption or other general land laws.

SEC. 3. *And be it further enacted,* That whenever, from any cause, any of the reservations made under the second section of this act, shall be no longer needed for the purposes originally intended, or the convenience of the service shall require a change of location, the reservation thus abandoned by the Postmaster-General shall be laid off into suitable lots or parcels, and sold at public sale to the highest bidder, after at least three months' public notice, under the direction of the Secretary of the Interior, and patents therefor shall issue as in case of the sale of other public lands, and all laws or parts of laws, heretofore passed, granting the pre-emption privilege to mail contractors, be, and the same are hereby, repealed; but this repeal is not to affect any rights which may have actually existed under those laws before the passage of this act.

Approved, June 21, 1860.

No. 16 B.—An Act to confirm certain private land claims in the Territory of New Mexico.*

Be it enacted by the Senate and House of Representatives of the United States of America in Congress assembled, That the private land claims in the Territory of New Mexico, as recommended for confirmation by the Surveyor-General of that Territory, and in his letter to the Commissioner of the General Land Office of the twelfth of January, eighteen hundred and fifty-eight, designated as numbers one, three, four, six, eight, nine, ten, twelve, fourteen, fifteen, sixteen, seventeen, and eighteen, and the claim of E. W. Eaton, not entered on the corrected list of numbers, but standing on the original docket and abstract returns of the Surveyor-General as number sixteen, be, and they are hereby, confirmed: *Provided,* That the claim number nine, in the name of John Scollay and others, shall not be confirmed for more than five square leagues; and that the claim number seventeen, in the name of Cornelio Vigil and Ceran St. Vrain, shall not be confirmed for more than eleven square leagues to each of said claimants.

SEC. 2. *And be it further enacted,* That in surveying the claim of said John Scollay, it shall be lawful for him to locate the five square leagues confirmed to him in a square body in any part of the tract of twenty-five

* See No. 90 B. Amended No. 227 B.

square leagues claimed by him; and that in surveying the claim of said Cornelio Vigil and Ceran St. Vrain, the location shall be made as follows, namely: The survey shall first be made of all tracts occupied by actual settlers holding possession under titles or promises to settle, which have heretofore been given by said Vigil and St. Vrain, in the tracts claimed by them, and after deducting the area of all such tracts from the area embraced in twenty-two square leagues, the remainder shall be located in two equal tracts, each of square form, in any part of the tract claimed by the said Vigil and St. Vrain, selected by them; and it shall be the duty of the Surveyor-General of New Mexico immediately to proceed to make the surveys and locations authorized and required by the terms of this section.

SEC. 3. *And be it further enacted,* That the private land claims in the Territory of New Mexico, as recommended for confirmation by said Surveyor-General in his reports and abstract marked Exhibit A, as communicated to Congress by the Secretary of the Interior in his letter dated the third of February, eighteen hundred and sixty, and numbered from twenty to thirty-eight, both inclusive, be, and the same are hereby, confirmed, with the exception of the claim numbered twenty-six, in the name of Juan B. Vigil, which claim, numbered twenty-six, is not confirmed.

SEC. 4. *And be it further enacted,* That the foregoing confirmation shall only be construed as quit claims, or relinquishments, on the part of the United States, and shall not affect the adverse rights of any other person or persons whomsoever.

SEC. 5. *And be it further enacted,* That it shall or may be lawful for the said Juan B. Vigil, or any person claiming title under him, to institute suit against the United States for the lands claimed and embraced in said claim number twenty-six, not confirmed under the provisions of the third section of this act; said suit to be instituted in the Supreme Court of the Territory of New Mexico, to be defended by the District Attorney of the United States for said Territory, under the direction of the Attorney-General of the United States, with the right of appeal to either party from the decision of said Supreme Court to the Supreme Court of the United States, if such appeal be asked for within one year from the rendition of the judgment in said Supreme Court of the Territory of New Mexico, and not thereafter: *Provided,* That if the suit authorized by this section be not instituted within two years from the passage of this act, the said claimants shall be presumed to have abandoned all right or title to the lands embraced in said claim number twenty-six, and said lands shall thenceforth be held and deemed to be public lands belonging to the United States: *And provided further,* That in the determination of the suit authorized to be instituted by the terms of this section, the courts shall be governed by the treaty of Guadalupe Hidalgo, the law of nations, the laws, usages, and customs of the government from which the claim is derived, the principles of equity, and the decisions of the Supreme Court of the United States, so far as they are applicable.

SEC. 6. *And be it further enacted,* That it shall be lawful for the heirs of Luis Maria Baca, who make claim to the said tract of land as is claimed by the town of Las Begas, to select, instead of the land claimed by them, an equal quantity of vacant land, not mineral, in the Territory of New Mexico, to be located by them in square bodies, not exceeding five in number. And it shall be the duty of the Surveyor-General of New Mexico to make survey and location of the lands so selected by said heirs of Baca when thereunto required by them: *Provided, however,*

That the right hereby granted to said heirs of Baca shall continue in force during three years from the passage of this act, and no longer.

Approved, June 21, 1860.

No. 17 B.—An Act to grant to the city of Port Huron, Michigan, a part of the military reservation of Fort Gratiot for the enlargement of the city cemetery at that place.

Be it enacted by the Senate and House of Representatives of the United States of America in Congress assembled, That the Secretary of War be, and he is hereby authorized and required to convey to the city of Port Huron, Michigan, of the military reservation of Fort Gratiot, a lot not to exceed thirty acres, to be taken from the land adjoining the city cemetery, and to be used for its enlargement and for no other purpose, so far and under such conditions and reservations as in the opinion of the Secretary of War the public interest, present or prospective, may require.

Approved, June 22, 1860.

No. 18 B.—An Act to declare the meaning of the act entitled "An Act making further provisions for the satisfaction of Virginia land warrants," passed August thirty-one, eighteen hundred and fifty-two.*

Be it enacted by the Senate and House of Representatives of the United States of America in Congress assembled, That the Secretary of the Interior, in executing the provisions of the act passed August thirty-one, eighteen hundred and fifty-two, entitled "An act making further provisions for the satisfaction of Virginia land warrants," be required so to construe the same as to authorize the satisfaction in scrip of all warrants or parts of warrants issued on allowances made by the executive of Virginia prior to the first day of March, eighteen hundred and fifty-two, coming within the principles already recognized by the Department of the Interior in the execution of the provisions of the said act, and whether issued before or since the first day of March, eighteen hundred and fifty-two: *Provided, however,* That no warrant or part of a warrant shall be satisfied in scrip, founded or issued on any allowance made by the executive of Virginia since the first day of March, eighteen hundred and fifty-two.

Approved, June 22, 1860.

No. 19 B.—An Act for the relief of congressional townships number six, south of range number eight west, in Randolph County, State of Illinois.

Whereas section number sixteen, in townships number six south, of range number eight west, in Randolph County, Illinois, is covered by a private claim number two thousand and fifty, by reason whereof the

* Vol. I. No. 211.

said section has been lost to the said congressional townships for school purposes: Therefore—

Be it enacted by the Senate and House of Representatives of the United States of America in Congress assembled, That the school trustees for the said township be, and they are hereby, authorized to select three quarter-sections of land in equal subdivisions, of any of the public lands of the United States subject to entry or sale at the minimum price of one dollar and twenty-five cents per acre.

SEC. 2. *And be it further enacted,* That when the same shall have been selected by the trustees aforesaid, and a description thereof returned to and approved by the Commissioner of the General Land Office, a patent or patents shall issue thereof to the inhabitants of the said congressional townships, and shall be held and disposed of by them for the use of the schools within the said congressional township in the same manner as other school lands are held and disposed of.

Approved, June 22, 1860.

No. 20 B.—An Act for the final adjustment of private land claims in the States of Florida, Louisiana, and Missouri, and for other purposes.*

Be it enacted by the Senate and House of Representatives of the United States of America in Congress assembled, That any person or persons, and the legal representatives of any person or persons, who claim any lands lying within the States of Florida, Louisiana, or Missouri, by virtue of grant, concession, order of survey, permission to settle, or other written evidence of title, emanating from any foreign government, bearing date prior to the cession to the United States of the territory out of which said States were formed, or during the period when any such government claimed sovereignty or had the actual possession of the district or territory in which the lands so claimed are situated, shall be, and they are hereby, authorized to make application for the confirmation of their title to the lands so claimed, in the manner following, to wit: they shall file notices in writing, together with the evidence in support of their claims, before the commissioners hereinafter designated within whose district the lands claimed may be situated, together with a brief abstract of the title of the claimant, and copies of the plats of the survey thereof, whenever such surveys have been made and are within the possession of the claimant, and accompanied with a sworn statement by the claimants of the lands supposed to be covered by his claim, according to the legal divisions and subdivisions of the surveys made by the United States, if the land claimed is included in any survey so made; and the said notices, evidence, and the decisions of the commissioners thereon, shall be recorded in a book kept for that purpose, a transcript of which shall, from time to time, be transmitted to the Commissioner of the General Land Office.

SEC. 2. *And be it further enacted,* That the registers and receivers of the several land offices in the States of Florida and Louisiana, within their respective land districts, and the recorder of land titles for the city of Saint Louis, for the State of Missouri, and their successors in office, shall be, and they are hereby, appointed commissioners to hear and decide, under such instructions as may be prescribed by the Commissioner of the

* No. 194 B.

General Land Office in conformity with this act, and according to justice and equity and the principles hereinafter established, in a summary manner, all matters respecting such claims within the districts aforesaid as come within the provisions of this act; they shall have power to administer oaths, compel the attendance of and examine witnesses, demand and obtain from the proper officers all public records in which grants of land, warrants, orders of survey, or other evidence of claims to land derived from any foreign government may have been recorded, and shall make a report to the Commissioner of the General Land Office, on the claims so presented to them for decision, dividing said claims into separate classes in the manner hereinafter provided, and giving their opinion whether such claims ought to be confirmed or rejected.

SEC. 3. *And be it further enacted,* That the claims so presented and passed upon by the commissioners, as aforesaid, shall be by them divided in their report into three distinct classes, as follows, viz:—

Number one shall contain all claims, which in their opinion, ought to be confirmed, where the lands claimed have been in possession and cultivation by the private claimants, or those under whom they derive title for a period of at least twenty years preceding the date of filing the claim, by virtue of some grant, concession, or order of survey, permission to settle, or other written evidence of title emanating from some foreign government which held or claimed sovereignty or jurisdiction over the territory in which the lands claimed are situated, and where the title emanating from such foreign government bears date anterior to the cession of said territory to the United States.

Number two shall contain all claims which, in their opinion, ought to be confirmed, where the lands are claimed under written evidence of title, as above provided in class *number one*, but where there has been no actual possession and cultivation of the land claimed for a period of at least twenty years prior to the filing of the claim.

Number three shall contain all claims, which, in their opinion, ought to be rejected, whether from defect of proof, suspicion of fraud based on probable ground, uncertainty of location, vagueness of description, or any other cause sufficient, in their opinion, to justify such rejection: *Provided,* That in no case shall such commissioners embrace in said classes *number one* and *number two* any claim which has been heretofore presented for confirmation before any board of commissioners, or other public officers acting under authority of Congress, and rejected as being fraudulent, or procured and maintained by fraudulent or improper means; nor shall any such claim be received or considered by the commissioners, which has been already twice rejected on the merits by previous boards.

SEC. 4. *And be it further enacted,* That whenever the said commissioner shall approve the report of the commissioners in cases embraced in classes *number one* or *number two,* he shall report the same to Congress for its action; and whenever the said commissioner shall approve the report in cases embraced in class *number three,* the rejection of the claim so acted on shall be final and conclusive, and the land embraced within the claim shall be considered and treated as other public lands belonging to the United States.

SEC. 5. *And be it further enacted,* That all claims comprehended within any of the three classes aforesaid, on which there shall be disapproval by the commissioner of the report made by the boards of commissioners aforesaid, shall be reported to Congress for its action and final decision thereon.

SEC. 6. *And be it further enacted,* That whenever it shall appear that lands claimed, and the title to which may be confirmed under the provisions of this act, have been sold in whole or in part by the United States prior to such confirmation, or where the Surveyor-General of the district shall ascertain that the same cannot be surveyed and located, the party in whose favor the title is confirmed shall have the right to enter upon any of the public lands of the United States a quantity of land equal in extent to that sold by the Government: *Provided*, That said entry be made only on lands subject to private entry at one dollar and twenty-five cents per acre, and as far as may be possible in legal divisions and subdivisions, according to the surveys made by the United States.

SEC. 7. *And be it further enacted*, That whenever any claim is presented for confirmation under the provisions of this act, which has heretofore been presented before any board of commissioners under authority of Congress, the facts reported as proven by the former board shall be taken as true *prima facie;* and the evidence offered before such former board, and remaining of record, shall be admitted on the examination of the claims made under the provisions of this act.

SEC. 8. *And be it further enacted*, That no land claimed under the provisions of this act shall be offered for sale, or otherwise disposed of by the officers of the United States, until the final decision shall be made on the validity of such claim, and in no case where land is possessed or cultivated by private persons shall it be entered upon or surveyed as public land, or offered for sale, without previous notice given to those in possession, requiring them to present their claims for confirmation; and if within sixty days from the date of such notice such claim shall not have been filed, then the proper officers of the government may proceed to the survey or sale of such lands as public lands, without prejudice, however, to the legal rights of the possessor or claimant, if any he have.

SEC. 9. *And be it further enacted*, That before the boards of commissioners shall be required to receive for record any notice, paper, evidence of title, or testimony, in support of any claim, the claimant shall pay to said board the sum of twenty-five cents for every hundred words required to be recorded, which shall be in full consideration for the recording and the transcript required to be forwarded to the Commissioner of the General Land Office.

SEC. 10. *And be it further enacted*, That at the commencement of each regular session of Congress, it shall be the duty of the Commissioner of the General Land Office to make report of all that has been done under the provisions of this act by the several officers charged with its execution.

SEC. 11. *And be it further enacted*, That in any case of such a claim to lands as is hereinbefore in the first section of this act mentioned, where the lands claimed have not been in possession of, and cultivated by the original claimants, or those holding title under him or them, for the period of twenty years aforesaid, and where such lands are claimed by complete grant or concession, or order of survey duly executed, or by other mode of investiture of title thereto in the original claimant or claimants, by separation thereof from the mass of the public domain, either by actual survey or definition of fixed natural and ascertainable boundaries or initial points, courses and distances, by the competent authority, prior to the cession to the United States of the territory in which said lands were included, or where such title was created and perfected during the period while the foreign governments from which it emanated claimed sovereignty over, or had the actual possession of such territory, the person or persons, his, her, or their heirs, devises, legal representatives or grantees, so claiming such lands, may, at their option, instead of submitting their claim to the officer or officers hereinbefore mentioned, proceed by petition in any district court of the United States, within whose jurisdiction the lands, or any part of the lands, claimed may lie, unless such claim comes within the purview of the third section of this act; to which petition the United States shall be made defendant, and it shall be verified by the oath of the party or parties, and conform to the provisions of section one of this act, and to the practice of such court in chancery, and the attorney of the United States for such district shall defend against the same for the United States; and the court shall decide the claim valid or invalid according to the principles established in this act, and decree accordingly. If the decree be against the United States, an appeal shall be entered to the Supreme Court of the United States; and if it be against the claimant or claimants, he or they may take an appeal directly to that court, as of right and course, without affidavit or security other than for costs; and the same shall be adjudged *de novo* in the Supreme Court as in other cases of appeals thereto in chancery, and as equity, and justice, and the principles aforesaid may require; which decision shall be final, and patent shall thereupon issue, if the claim be adjudged valid, for so much of the lands claimed as remain unsold; and for so much as may have been sold, the provisions of section six of this act shall apply and be in force.

SEC. 12. *And be it further enacted,* That this act shall be and remain in force during the term of five years, unless sooner repealed by Congress; and all claims presented or sued upon, according to the provisions of this act, within the said term of five years, may be prosecuted to final determination and decision, notwithstanding the said term of five years may have expired before such final determination and decision.

Approved, June 22, 1860.

No. 21 B.—An Act in relation to mission claims at Sault Ste Marie, Michigan.

Be it enacted by the Senate and House of Representatives of the United States of America in Congress assembled, That the missionary claims referred to in the fourth section of the act of twenty-sixth September, eighteen hundred and fifty, entitled "An act providing for the examination and settlement of claims for land at the Sault Ste Marie, Michigan," and reported upon by the Register and Receiver at Sault Ste Marie, pursuant to said act, shall be entitled to recognition and confirmation in the same manner and on the same terms as claims of individuals therein provided for; and upon the final approval of the said claims, as provided for in the eighth section of the act aforesaid, patents shall be issued therefor.

Approved, June 22, 1860.

No. 22 B.—An Act to authorize the location of certain warrants for bounty lands heretofore issued.

Be it enacted by the Senate and House of Representatives of the United States of America in Congress assembled, That warrants for bounty lands heretofore issued under the authority of the act entitled "An act to provide for satisfying claims for bounty lands for military services in the late war with Great Britain, and for other purposes," approved the twenty-seventh day of July, in the year eighteen hundred and forty-two,* and of the several acts revising the same, approved the twenty-sixth day of June, in the year eighteen hundred and forty-eight, and the eighth day of February, in the year eighteen hundred and fifty-four, may be located, in conformity with the general laws in force at any time within three years from the date of this act; and that all entries and locations made with such warrants since the twenty-sixth day of June, in the year eighteen hundred and fifty-eight, shall be as valid and effectual as if the several acts aforesaid had not then expired.

Approved, June 23, 1860.

No. 23 B.—An Act to authorize the reissue of land warrants in certain cases, and for other purposes.

Be it enacted by the Senate and House of Representatives of the United States of America in Congress assembled, That whenever it shall appear that any certificate or warrant, issued in pursuance of any law of the United States granting bounty lands, has been lost or destroyed, whether the same had been sold and assigned by the warrantee or not, the Secretary of the Interior shall be, and he is hereby authorized and required to cause a new certificate or warrant of like tenor to be issued in lieu thereof; which new certificate or warrant may be assigned, located, and patented in like manner as other certificates or warrants for bounty land are now authorized by law to be assigned, located, and patented; and in all cases where warrants have been, or may be reissued, the original warrant, in whoseever hands it may be, shall be deemed and held to be null and void, and the assignment thereof, if any there be, fraudulent; and no patent shall ever issue for any land located therewith, unless such presumption of fraud in the assignment be removed by due proof that the same was executed by the warrantee in good faith and for a valuable consideration.

SEC. 2. *And be it further enacted,* That the said Secretary of the Interior shall be, and he is hereby authorized and required to prescribe such rules and regulations for carrying this act into effect as he may deem necessary and proper in order to protect the Government against imposition and fraud by persons claiming the benefit of this act; *and;* and all laws and parts of laws for the punishment of false swearing and frauds against the United States are hereby made applicable to false swearing and fraud under this act.

Approved, June 23, 1860.

No. 24 B.—An Act to grant to the Parish of Point Coupee, Louisiana, certain tracts of land in said parish.

Be it enacted by the Senate and House of Representatives of the United States of America in Congress assembled, That the tracts of land in the

* Vol. I. No. 55.

Parish of Point Coupee, Louisiana, which have been in ancient occupancy as the site of a church and court-house, and which are designated on the plats of the public surveys as sections twenty-three and twenty-four, in township four, south, of range ten, east, in the southeastern district, Louisiana, be, and the same are hereby, granted to the said Parish of Point Coupee, on the condition that the aforesaid section twenty-four, or the church site, shall be held by said parish, for the use of the Catholic congregation now occupying it for public worship and as a burying ground, but not to the prejudice of a valid adverse right, if such exist.

Approved, June 25, 1860.

No. 25 B.—An Act to amend the fourth section of the act for the admission of Oregon into the Union, so as to extend the time for selecting salt springs and contiguous lands in Oregon.

Be it enacted by the Senate and House of Representatives of the United States of America in Congress assembled, That the time for selecting the salt springs and contiguous lands, according to the provisions of the fourth section of the act entitled "An act for the admission of Oregon into the Union," approved February fourteenth, eighteen hundred and fifty-nine, be extended to any time within three years from the passage of this act, anything in said section to the contrary notwithstanding.*

Approved, December 17, 1860.

No. 26 B.—An Act to authorize the institution of a suit against the United States to test the title to lots numbers five and six, in the Hospital Square in San Francisco.

Be it enacted by the Senate and House of Representatives of the United States of America in Congress assembled, That J. G. Ames, S. W. Holladay, and James Blair, and their heirs, assigns, and legal representatives be, and they are hereby, authorized to institute a suit against the United States, in the Circuit Court of the United States for the State of California, for the purpose of recovering from the United States two lots of ground, numbers five and six, in the square in the city of San Francisco on which a hospital has been erected by the United States; which lots are claimed to have been acquired by the said Ames, Holladay, and Blair, by deeds executed in their favor by the sheriff of the county of San Francisco on the twenty-third day of October, eighteen hundred and fifty-one. The said suit to be commenced by citation served on the district attorney of the United States for the northern district of California: *Provided,* That the United States shall have the right in any suit so brought to defend their claim to the title and possession of said property, or any part thereof, on any legal or equitable grounds.

SEC. 2. *And be it further enacted,* That it shall be the duty of the said district attorney, under the direction and advice of the Attorney-General of the United States, to defend any suit brought under the authority of

* Vol. I. No. 351.

the first section of this act, and to take all necessary measures at law or in equity for the protection and defence of the title to the said lots.

SEC. 3. *And be it further enacted*, That either party may appeal or prosecute a writ of error to the Supreme Court of the United States from any final decision rendered by said Circuit Court in any suit instituted as aforesaid.

SEC. 4. *And be it further enacted*, That no suit shall be brought by virtue of the provisions of this act, unless the same be instituted within two years from passage thereof.

SEC. 5. *And be it further enacted*, That, in the event of a final judgment against the United States in any suit instituted as aforesaid, it shall be the duty of the proper officers of the United States, who may be in charge and possession of said lots in behalf of the Government, to deliver up to the claimants said lots, or such parts thereof as may, by said final judgment, be decreed to belong to them; and the said Circuit Court is hereby authorized to issue the process necessary and proper for carrying out the provisions of this act.

Approved, January 26, 1861.

No. 27 B.—An Act for the admission of Kansas into the Union.

Whereas the people of the Territory of Kansas, by their representatives in Convention assembled, at Wyandott, in said Territory, on the twenty-ninth day of July, one thousand eight hundred and fifty-nine, did form for themselves a constitution and State government, republican in form, which was ratified and adopted by the people at an election held for that purpose on Tuesday, the fourth day of October, one thousand eight hundred and fifty-nine, and the said Convention has, in their name and behalf, asked the Congress of the United States to admit the said Territory into the Union as a State, on an equal footing with the other States: Therefore—

Be it enacted by the Senate and House of Representatives of the United States of America in Congress assembled, That the State of Kansas shall be, and is hereby declared to be, one of the United States of America, and admitted into the Union on an equal footing with the original States in all respects whatever. And the said State shall consist of all the territory included within the following boundaries, to wit: Beginning at a point on the western boundary of the State of Missouri, where the thirty-seventh parallel of north latitude crosses the same; thence west on said parallel to the twenty-fifth meridian of longitude west from Washington; thence north on said meridian to the fortieth parallel of latitude; thence east on said parallel to the western boundary of the State of Missouri; thence south with the western boundary of said State to the place of beginning: *Provided*, That nothing contained in the said constitution respecting the boundary of said State shall be construed to impair the rights of person or property now pertaining to the Indians in said Territory, so long as such rights shall remain unextinguished by treaty between the United States and such Indians, or to include any territory which, by treaty with such Indian tribe, is not, without the consent of said tribe, to be included within the territorial limits or jurisdiction of any State or Territory; but all such territory shall be excepted out of the boundaries, and constitute no part of the State of Kansas, until said tribe shall signify their assent to the President of the United States to be included within said State, or to affect the authority of the Government of the United States to make any regulation respecting such Indians, their lands, property, or other rights, by treaty, law, or otherwise, which it would have been competent to make if this act had never passed.

SEC. 2. *And be it further enacted,* That until the next general apportionment of representatives the State of Kansas shall be entitled to one representative in the House of Representatives of the United States.

SEC. 3. *And be it further enacted,* That nothing in this act shall be construed as an assent by Congress to all or to any of the propositions or claims contained in the ordinance of said constitution of the people of Kansas, or in the resolutions thereto attached; but the following propositions are hereby offered to the said people of Kansas for their free acceptance or rejection, which, if accepted, shall be obligatory on the United States and upon the said State of Kansas, to wit: First, That sections numbered sixteen and thirty-six in every township of public lands in said State, and where either of said sections or any part thereof has been sold or otherwise been disposed of, other lands, equivalent thereto and as contiguous as may be, shall be granted to said State for the use of schools. Second, That seventy-two sections of land shall be set apart and reserved for the use and support of a State University, to be selected by the Governor of said State, subject to the approval of the Commissioner of the General Land Office, and to be appropriated and applied in such manner as the Legislature of said State may prescribe for the purpose aforesaid, but for no other purpose. Third, That ten entire sections of land, to be selected by the Governor of said State, in legal subdivisions, shall be granted to said State for the purpose of completing the public buildings, or for the erection of others at the seat of government, under the direction of the Legislature thereof. Fourth, That all salt springs within said State, not exceeding twelve in number, with six sections of land adjoining or as contiguous as may be to each, shall be granted to said State for its use, the same to be selected by the Governor thereof within one year after the admission of said State, and when so selected to be used or disposed of on such terms, conditions, and regulations as the Legislature shall direct: *Provided,* That no salt spring or land, the right whereof is now vested in any individual or individuals, or which may be hereafter confirmed or adjudged to any individual or individuals, shall by this article be granted to said State. Fifth, That five per centum of the net proceeds of sales of all public lands lying within said State which shall be sold by Congress after the admission of said State into the Union, after deducting all the expenses incident to the same, shall be paid to said State for the purpose of making public roads and internal improvements, or for other purposes, as the Legislature shall direct: *Provided,* That the foregoing propositions hereinbefore offered are on the condition that the people of Kansas shall provide by an ordinance, irrevocable without the consent of the United States, that said State shall never interfere with the primary disposal of the soil within the same by the United States, or with any regulations Congress may find necessary for securing the title in said soil to bona fide purchasers thereof. Sixth, And that the said State shall never tax the lands or the property of the United States in said State: *Provided, however,* That in case any of the lands herein granted to the State of Kansas have heretofore been confirmed to the Territory of Kansas for the purposes specified in this act, the amount so confirmed shall be deducted from the quantity specified in this act.

SEC. 4. *And be it further enacted,* That from and after the admission of the State of Kansas, as hereinbefore provided, all the laws of the United States, which are not locally inapplicable, shall have the same force and effect within that State as in other States of the Union.

* * * * * * * * *

Approved, January 29, 1861.

No. 28 B.—An Act making further provision in relation to consolidated land offices.

Be it enacted by the Senate and House of Representatives of the United States of America in Congress assembled, That from and after the passage of this act the register for the consolidated land districts at Boonville, in the State of Missouri, in consequence of additional duties imposed upon him, and in addition to the fees now allowed by law, shall be entitled to charge and receive for making transcript for individuals, or furnishing any other record information respecting public lands or land titles in his consolidated land district, such fees as are properly authorized by the tariff existing in the local courts in said district: *Provided,* The whole amount of the register's compensation, including all fees and commissions to which he is entitled under existing laws, shall not exceed three thousand dollars per annum, or pro rata per quarter, the excess, if any, over that amount, shall be paid into the Treasury of the United States; and the receiver shall receive his equal share of such fees, and it shall be his duty to aid the register in the preparation of the transcripts, or giving the record information as aforesaid.

SEC. 2. *And be it further enacted,* That the Secretary of the Interior be, and he is hereby, authorized to make a reasonable allowance for office rent for such consolidated office, and, when satisfied of the necessity therefor, to approve the employment by said register of one or more clerks, at a reasonable per diem compensation, for such time as said clerk or clerks are absolutely required to keep up the current public business, and who shall be paid out of the surplus fees above authorized to be charged if any, and if no surplus exists, then out of the appropriation for incidental expenses of district land offices; but no clerk shall be so paid unless his employment has been first sanctioned by the Secretary of the Interior.

SEC. 3. *And be it further enacted,* That the provisions of this act be, and they are hereby, extended to all other consolidated land offices: *Provided,* That this act shall be construed to extend to and provide for all expenses heretofore incurred by any register or receiver of any such consolidated land office for additional clerical aid or office room; *Provided further,* That the amount of such indemnity be first approved by the Secretary of the Interior.

SEC. 4. *And be it further enacted,* That it shall be the duty of the Secretary of the Interior to make a reasonable allowance to former registers of consolidated land offices for room rent and clerk hire, made necessary by such consolidation, to be paid out of the appropriation for incidental expenses of district land offices, upon satisfactory vouchers actually filed, or to be filed.

Approved, February 18, 1861.

No. 29 B.—An Act to provide a temporary government for the Territory of Colorado.

Be it enacted by the Senate and House of Representatives of the United States of America in Congress assembled, That all that part of the territory of the United States included within the following limits, viz: commencing on the thirty-seventh parallel of north latitude, where the twenty-fifth meridian of longitude west from Washington crosses the same; thence north on said meridian to the forty-first parallel of north latitude; thence along said parallel west to the thirty-second meridian of longitude west from Washington; thence south on said meridian to the northern line of New Mexico; thence along the thirty-seventh parallel of north latitude to the place of beginning, be and the same is hereby erected into a temporary government by the name of the Territory of Colorado: *Provided,* That nothing in this act contained shall be construed to impair the rights of person or property now pertaining to the Indians in said Territory, so long as such rights shall remain unextinguished by treaty between the United States and such Indians, or to include any territory which, by treaty with any Indian tribe, is not, without the consent of said tribe, to be included within the territorial limits or jurisdiction of any State or Territory; but all such territory shall be excepted out of the boundaries and constitute no part of the Territory of Colorado until said tribe shall signify their assent to the President of the United States to be included within the said Territory, or to affect the authority of the Government of the United States to make any regulations respecting such Indians, their lands, property, or other rights, by treaty, law, or otherwise, which it would have been competent for the Government to make if this act had never passed: *Provided further,* That nothing in this act contained shall be construed to inhibit the Government of the United States from dividing said Territory into two or more Territories, in such manner and at such times as Congress shall deem convenient and proper, or from attaching any portion thereof to any other Territory or State.

* * * * * * * * *

SEC. 6. *And be it further enacted,* That the legislative power of the Territory shall extend to all rightful subjects of legislation consistent with the Constitution of the United States and the provisions of the act; but no law shall be passed interfering with the primary disposal of the soil; no tax shall be imposed upon the property of the United States; nor shall the lands or other property of non residents be taxed higher than the lands or other property of residents; nor shall any law be passed impairing the rights of private property; nor shall any discrimination be made in taxing different kinds of property; but all property subject to taxation shall be in proportion to the value of the property taxed.

* * * * * * * * *

SEC. 14. *And be it further enacted,* That when the land in the said Territory shall be surveyed, under the direction of [the] Government of the United States, preparatory to bringing the same into market, sections numbered sixteen and thirty-six in each township in said Territory shall be, and the same are hereby, reserved for the purpose of being applied to schools in the States hereafter to be erected out of the same.

* * * * * * * * *

SEC. 17. *And be it further enacted,* That the President of the United States, by and with the advice and consent of the Senate, shall be, and he is hereby, authorized to appoint a surveyor-general for Colorado, who shall locate his office at such place as the Secretary of the Interior shall from time to time direct, and whose duties, powers, obligations, responsibilities, compensation, and allowances for clerk hire, office rent, fuel, and incidental expenses, shall be the same as those of the Surveyor-General of New Mexico, under the direction of the Secretary of the Interior, and such instructions as he may, from time to time, deem it advisable to give him.

Approved, February 28, 1861.

No. 30 B.—An Act to provide for bringing up the arrearages of work of the land office at Olympia, Washington Territory.

Be it enacted by the Senate and House of Representatives of the United States of America in Congress assembled, That the Secretary of the Interior be authorized to make such allowances for clerical services in bringing up the arrearages of business at the land office at Olympia, Washington Territory, including payment of clerical services already necessarily incurred, as, on the production of the proper evidence, he may deem equitable and just, the amount not to exceed the sum of three thousand dollars, and to be paid out of the appropriation for incidental expenses of district land offices.

Approved, March 2, 1861.

No. 31 B.—An Act donating to the States of Minnesota and Oregon certain lands reserved by Congress for the Territories of Minnesota and Oregon for university purposes.

Be it enacted by the Senate and House of Representatives of the United States of America in Congress assembled, That the lands reserved for the use of a university in the Territories of Minnesota and Oregon under section second of an act of Congress passed February nineteenth, one thousand eight hundred and fifty-one, entitled "An act to authorize the legislative assemblies of the Territories of Oregon and Minnesota to take charge of the school lands in said Territories, and for other purposes," be hereby donated to the States of Minnesota and Oregon for the use of said university.*

Approved, March 2, 1861.

No. 32 B.—An Act legalizing certain entries of lands on Leavenworth Island, in the State of Missouri.

Be it enacted by the Senate and House of Representatives of the United States of America in Congress assembled, That all pre-emption entries

* Vol I. No. 186.

heretofore made in good faith at the land office at Kickapoo, in the Delaware land district, Kansas Territory, of lands embraced within the island opposite Leavenworth City, known as Leavenworth Island, in the State of Missouri, be, and the same are hereby, declared valid, in the same manner as if made in the proper land district of the State of Missouri: *Provided,* Such entries shall be found by the Secretary of the Interior, in all other respects, to be in accordance with the pre-emption law.

Approved, March 2, 1861.

No. 33 B.—An Act to organize the Territory of Nevada.

Be it enacted by the Senate and House of Representatives of the United States of America in Congress assembled, That all that part of the territory of the United States, included within the following limits, to wit: Beginning at the point of intersection of the forty-second degree of north latitude with the thirty-ninth degree of longitude west from Washington; thence, running south on the line of said thirty-ninth degree of west longitude until it intersects the northern boundary line of the Territory of New Mexico; thence due west to the dividing ridge separating the waters of Carson Valley from those that flow into the Pacific; thence on said dividing ridge northwardly to the forty-first degree of north latitude;* thence due north to the southern boundary line of the State of Oregon; thence due east to the place of beginning, be, and the same is hereby, erected into a temporary government by the name of the Territory of Nevada: *Provided,* That so much of the Territory within the present limits of the State of California shall not be included within this Territory until the State of California shall assent to the same by an act irrevocable without the consent of the United States: *Provided further,* That nothing in this act contained shall be construed to impair the rights of person or property now pertaining to the Indians in said Territory, so long as such rights shall remain unextinguished by treaty between the United States and such Indians, or to include any territory which, by treaty with any Indian tribe, is not, without the consent of said tribe, to be included within the territorial limits or jurisdiction of any State or Territory; but all such territory shall be excepted out of the boundaries and constitute no part of the Territory of Nevada, until said tribe shall signify their assent to the President of the United States to be included within the said Territory, or to affect the authority of the Government of the United States to make any regulations respecting such Indians, their lands, property, or other rights, by treaty, law, or otherwise, which it would have been competent for the Government to make if this act had never passed: *Provided further,* That nothing in this act contained shall be construed to inhibit the Government of the United States from dividing said Territory into two or more Territories, in such manner and at such times as Congress shall deem convenient and proper, or from attaching any portion thereof to any other Territory or State.†

* * * * * * * * *

SEC. 14. *And be it further enacted,* That when the land in said Terri-

* See No. 55 B.; also No. 74 B., No. 156 B., and No. 208 B.

† Sec. 6 provides that no law shall be passed by the Territorial legislature interfering with the primary disposal of the soil.

tory shall be surveyed, under the direction of the Government of the United States, preparatory to bringing the same into market, sections numbered sixteen and thirty-six in each township in said Territory shall be, and the same *is* hereby, reserved for the purpose of being applied to schools in the States hereafter to be erected out of the same.

* * * * * * * * *

Approved, March 2, 1861.

No. 34 B.—An Act to provide a temporary government for the Territory of Dakota, and to create the office of Surveyor-General therein.

Be it enacted by the Senate and House of Representatives of the United States of America in Congress assembled, That all that part of the territory of the United States included within the following limits, namely: commencing at a point in the main channel of the Red River of the North, where the forty-ninth degree of north latitude crosses the same; thence up the main channel of the same, and along the boundary of the State of Minnesota, to Big Stone Lake; thence along the boundary line of the said State of Minnesota to the Iowa line; thence along the boundary line of the State of Iowa to the point of intersection between the Big Sioux and Missouri Rivers; thence up the Missouri River, and along the boundary line of the Territory of Nebraska, to the mouth of the Niobrara or Running Water River; thence following up the same, in the middle of the main channel thereof, to the mouth of the Keha Paha or Turtle Hill River; thence up said river to the forty-third parallel of north latitude; thence due west to the present boundary of the Territory of Washington; thence along the boundary line of Washington Territory, to the forty-ninth degree of north latitude; thence east, along said forty-ninth degree of north latitude, to the place of beginning, be, and the same is hereby, organized into a temporary government, by the name of the Territory of Dakota: *Provided,* That nothing in this act contained shall be construed to impair the rights of person or property now pertaining to the Indians in said Territory, so long as such rights shall remain unextinguished by treaty between the United States and such Indians, or to include any territory which, by treaty with any Indian tribe, is not, without the consent of said tribe, to be included within the territorial limits or jurisdiction of any State or Territory; but all such territory shall be excepted out of the boundaries and constitute no part of the Territory of Dakota, until said tribe shall signify their assent to the President of the United States to be included within the said Territory, or to affect the authority of the Government of the United States to make any regulations respecting such Indians, their lands, property, or other rights, by treaty, law, or otherwise, which it would have been competent for the Government to make if this act had never passed: *Provided further,* That nothing in this act contained shall be construed to inhibit the Government of the United States from dividing said Territory into two or more Territories, in such manner and at such times as Congress shall deem convenient and proper, or from attaching any portion thereof to any other Territory or State.*

* * * * * * * * *

SEC. 14. *And be it further enacted,* That when the land in said Terri-

* SEC. 6. Provides that no law shall be passed by the Territorial Legislature interfering with the primary disposal of the soil.

tory shall be surveyed under the direction of the Government of the United States, preparatory to bringing the same into market, sections numbered sixteen and thirty-six in each township in said Territory shall be, and the same are hereby, reserved for the purpose of being applied to schools in the States hereafter to be erected out of the same.

* * * * * * * * *

SEC. 16. *And be it further enacted,* That the Constitution and all laws of the United States which are not locally inapplicable shall have the same force and effect within the said Territory of Dakota as elsewhere within the United States.

SEC. 17. *And be it further enacted,* That the President of the United States, by and with the advice and consent of the Senate, shall be, and he is hereby, authorized to appoint a Surveyor-General for Dakota, who shall locate his office at such place as the Secretary of the Interior shall from time to time direct, and whose duties, powers, obligations, responsibilities, compensation, and allowances for clerk hire, office rent, fuel and incidental expenses, shall be the same as those of the Surveyor-General of Nebraska and Kansas, under the direction of the Secretary of the Interior, and such instructions as he may from time to time deem it advisable to give him.

SEC. 18. *And be it further enacted,* That so much of the public lands of the United States in the Territory of Dakota, west of its eastern boundary and east and north of the Niobrara, or Running Water River, be formed into a land district, to be called the Yancton district, at such time as the President may direct, the land office for which shall he located at such point as the President may direct, and shall be removed from time to time to other points within said district whenever, in his opinion, it may be expedient.

SEC. 19. *And be it further enacted,* That the President be, and he is hereby, authorized to appoint, by and with the advice and consent of the Senate, a register and receiver for said district, who shall respectively be required to reside at the site of said office, and who shall have the same powers, perform the same duties, and be entitled to the same compensation, as are or may be prescribed by law in relation to other land offices of the United States.

SEC. 20. *And be it further enacted,* That the river in said Territory heretofore known as the "River aux Jacques," or "James River," shall hereafter be called the Dakota River.

SEC. 21. *And be it further enacted,* That, until Congress shall otherwise direct, that portion of the Territories of Utah and Washington between the forty-first and forty-third degrees of north latitude, and east of the thirty-third meridian of longitude west from Washington, shall be, and is hereby, incorporated into and made a part of the Territory of Nebraska.

Approved, March 2, 1861.

No. 35 B.—Joint Resolutions to qui[e]t title to lands in the State of Iowa.

Resolved by the Senate and House of Representatives of the United States of America in Congress assembled, That all the title which the United States still retain in the tracts of land along the Des Moines River, and above the mouth of the Raccoon fork thereof, in the State of Iowa, which have been certified to said State improperly by the Department of the Interior, as part of the grant by act of Congress approved August eight, eighteen hundred and forty-six,* and which is now held by bona fide purchasers under the State of Iowa, be, and the same is hereby, relinquished to the State of Iowa.

Approved, March 2, 1861.

No. 36 B.—An Act making appropriations for the Legislative, Executive, and Judicial expenses of the Government for the year ending thirtieth of June, eighteen hundred and sixty-three, and additional appropriations for the year ending thirtieth of June, eighteen hundred and sixty-two.

* * * * * * * * *

SEC. 4. *And be it further enacted,* That from and after the first day of July next, and until otherwise ordered by the President, the Territories of Utah and Colorado shall constitute one surveying district; and the duties of surveyor-general in said district shall be performed by the Surveyor-General of Colorado; and the surveying district of Nevada shall be united to that of California, the duties of the surveyor-general of the former shall be performed by the Surveyor-General of California; and the transfer of the effects and archives of the said offices shall be made under the instruction of the Commissioner of the General Land Office.

* * * * * * * * *

Approved, March 14, 1862.

No. 37 B.—An Act authorizing floats to issue in satisfaction of claims against the United States for lands sold by them within the Las Ormigas and La Nana grants, in the State of Louisiana.†

Be it enacted by the Senate and House of Representatives of the United States of America in Congress assembled, That it shall be the duty of the Commissioner of the General Land Office to issue and deliver to the respective owner or owners of the Las Ormigas and La Nana tracts of land, formerly situated in the parish of Natchitoches, now parishes of Sabine and De Soto, in the State of Louisiana, or to his or their assigns or other legal representatives, certificates or floats, in the usual form, for so much land as may have been at any time heretofore sold, donated, granted, or reserved by the United States within said tracts of land or either of them; and which certificates or floats may be located by the owner or holder thereof on any lands belonging to the United States, and subject to private entry at a price not exceeding one dollar and twenty-five cents per acre, and which certificates or floats shall be in full satisfaction of all claims against the United States for lands so sold, donated, granted, or reserved: *Provided,* That as a condition precedent to the issuing of the floats hereinbefore authorized, the claimant, or claimants, shall present to the Commissioner of the General Land Office satisfactory

* Vol. I. No. 117.—See also 53 B.

† Amended, No. 102 B.

evidence of title thereto, and that such claimants have been and continue to be loyal to the Government of the United States: *And provided further*, That such certificates and floats shall not exceed in gross seventeen thousand four hundred and seventy-seven and sixty-two hundredths acres.

SEC. 2. *And be it further enacted*, That this act shall take effect immediately.

Approved, March 17, 1862.

No. 38 B.—An Act to secure homesteads to actual settlers on the public domain.

Be it enacted by the Senate and House of Representatives of the United States of America in Congress assembled, That any person who is the head of a family, or who has arrived at the age of twenty-one years, and is a citizen of the United States, or who shall have filed his declaration of intention to become such, as required by the naturalization laws of the United States, and who has never borne arms against the United States Government or given aid and comfort to its enemies, shall, from and after the first of January, eighteen hundred and sixty-three, be entitled to enter one quarter section or a less quantity of unappropriated public lands, upon which said person may have filed a pre-emption claim, or which may, at the time the application is made, be subject to pre-emption at one dollar and twenty-five cents, or less, per acre; or eighty acres or less of such unappropriated lands, at two dollars and fifty cents per acre, to be located in a body, in conformity to the legal subdivisions of the public lands, and after the same shall have been surveyed: *Provided*, That any person owning and residing on land may, under the provisions of this act, enter other land lying contiguous to his or her said land, which shall not, with the land so already owned and occupied, exceed in the aggregate one hundred and sixty acres.

SEC. 2. *And be it further enacted*, That the person applying for the benefit of this act shall, upon application to the register of the land office in which he or she is about to make such entry, make affidavit before the said register or receiver that he or she is the head of a family, or is twenty-one years or more of age, or shall have performed service in the army or navy of the United States, and that he has never borne arms against the Government of the United States or given aid and comfort to its enemies, and that such application is made for his or her exclusive use and benefit, and that said entry is made for the purpose of actual settlement and cultivation, and not either directly or indirectly for the use or benefit of any other person or persons whomsoever; and upon filing the said affidavit with the register or receiver, and on payment of ten dollars, he or she shall thereupon be permitted to enter the quantity of land specified: *Provided, however*, That no certificate shall be given or patent issued therefor until the expiration of five years from the date of such entry; and if, at the expiration of such time, or at any time within two years thereafter, the person making such entry; or, if he be dead, his widow; or in case of her death, her heirs or devisee; or in case of a widow making such entry, her heirs or devisee, in case of her death; shall prove by two credible witnesses that he, she, or they have resided upon or cultivated the same for the term of five years immediately succeeding the time of filing the affidavit aforesaid, and shall make affidavit that no part of said land has been alienated, and that he has borne true allegiance to the Government of the United States; then in such case, he, she, or they, if at that time a citizen of the United States, shall be entitled to a patent, as in other cases provided for by law: *And provided further*, That in case of the death of both father and mother, leaving an infant child, or children, under twenty-one years of age, the right and fee shall enure to the benefit of said infant child or children; and the executor, administrator, or guardian may, at any time within two years after the death of the surviving parent, and in accordance with the laws of the State in which such children for the time being have their domicil, sell said land for the benefit of said infants, but for no other purpose; and the purchaser shall acquire the absolute title by the purchase, and be entitled to a patent from the United States, on payment of the office fees and sum of money herein specified.

SEC. 3. *And be it further enacted*, That the register of the land office shall note all such applications on the tract books and plats of his office, and keep a register of all such entries, and make return thereof to the General Land Office, together with the proof upon which they have been founded.

SEC. 4. *And be it further enacted*, That no lands acquired under the provisions of this act shall in any event become liable to the satisfaction of any debt or debts contracted prior to the issuing of the patent therefor.

SEC. 5. *And be it further enacted*, That if, at any time after the filing of the affidavit, as required in the second section of this act, and before the expiration of the five years aforesaid, it shall be proven, after due notice to the settler, to the satisfaction of the register of the land office, that the person having filed such affidavit shall have actually changed his or her residence, or abandoned the said land for more than six months at any time, then and in that event the land so entered shall revert to the Government.

SEC. 6. *And be it further enacted*, That no individual shall be permitted to acquire title to more than one quarter section under the provisions of this act; and that the Commissioner of the General Land Office is hereby required to prepare and issue such rules and regulations, consistent with this act, as shall be necessary and proper to carry its provisions into effect; and that the registers and receivers of the several land offices shall be entitled to receive the same compensation for any lands entered under the provisions of this act that they are now entitled to receive when the same quantity of land is entered with money, one-half to be paid by the person making the application at the time of so doing, and the other half on the issue of the certificate by the person to whom it may be issued; but this shall not be construed to enlarge the maximum of compensation now prescribed by law for any register or receiver: *Provided*, That nothing contained in this act shall be so construed as to impair or interfere in any manner whatever with existing pre-emption rights: *And provided further*, That all persons who may have filed their applications for a pre-emption right prior to the passage of this act, shall be entitled to all privileges of this act: *Provided further*, That no person who has served, or may hereafter serve, for a period of not less than fourteen days in the army or navy of the United States, either regular or volunteer, under the laws thereof, during the existence of an actual war, domestic or foreign, shall be deprived of the benefits of this act on account of not having attained the age of twenty-one years.

SEC. 7. *And be it further enacted,* That the fifth section of the act entitled "An act in addition to an act more effectually to provide for the punishment of certain crimes against the United States, and for other purposes," approved the third of March, in the year eighteen hundred and fifty-seven, shall extend to all oaths, affirmations, and affidavits required or authorized by this act.*

SEC. 8. *And be it further enacted,* That nothing in this act shall be so construed as to prevent any person who has availed him or herself of the benefits of the first section of this act, from paying the minimum price, or the price to which the same may have graduated, for the quantity of land so entered at any time before the expiration of the five years, and obtaining a patent therefor from the Government, as in other cases provided by law, on making proof of settlement and cultivation as provided by existing laws granting pre-emption rights.†

Approved, May 20, 1862.

No. 39 B.—An Act to reduce the expenses of the survey and sale of the public lands in the United States.

Be it enacted by the Senate and House of Representatives of the United States of America in Congress assembled, That contracts for the survey of the public lands shall not become binding upon the United States until approved by the Commissioner of the General Land Office, except in such cases as said commissioner shall otherwise specially order.

SEC. 2. *And be it further enacted,* That, the printed manual of instructions relating to the public surveys, prepared at the General Land Office, and bearing the date February twenty-second, eighteen hundred and fifty-five, the instructions of the Commissioner of the General Land Office, and the special instructions of the surveyor-general, when not in conflict with said printed manual, or the instructions of said Commissioner, shall be taken and deemed to be a part of every contract for surveying the public lands of the United States.‡

SEC. 3. *And be it further enacted,* That the Commissioner of the General Land Office shall have power, and it shall be his duty, to fix the prices per mile for public surveys, which shall in no case exceed the maximum established by law; and that, under instructions to be prepared by said commissioner, an accurate account shall be kept by each surveyor-general of the cost of surveying and platting private land claims, to be reported to the General Land Office, with the map of such claim, and that patents shall not issue for any such private claim until the cost of survey and platting shall have been paid into the Treasury of the United States by the claimant.

SEC. 4. *And be it further enacted,* That from and after the first day of July next, and upon the recommendation of the Commissioner of the General Land Office, approved by the Secretary of the Interior, the President may order that the Territories of Utah and Colorado shall constitute one surveying district, the duties of surveyor-general in said district to be performed by the Surveyor-General of Colorado; and the surveying

* Vol. I.—page 733—No. 332½.
† Amended, No. 76 B, and No. 146 B.
‡ Vol. I. No. 702.

district of Nevada shall be united to that of California, the duties of the Surveyor-General of the former to be transferred to the Surveyor-General of California; and the transfer of the effects and archives of the offices to be made under the instructions of the Commissioner of the General Land Office.

SEC. 5. *And be it further enacted,* That upon the recommendation of the Commissioner of the General Land Office, approved by the Secretary of the Interior, the President may order the discontinuance of any land office, and the transfer of its business and archives to any other land office within the same State or Territory.

SEC. 6. *And be it further enacted,* That from and after the first day of July next, the compensation of registers and receivers in all the land offices in the United States shall be an annual salary of five hundred dollars to each, with the fees and commissions now prescribed by law, and to be paid by claimants, an additional fee in donation cases of five dollars for each final certificate for one hundred and sixty acres, ten dollars for three hundred and twenty acres, and fifteen dollars for six hundred and forty acres; to be accounted for in the same manner as fees and commissions in warrant and pre-emption locations, with limitations as to maximum of salary prescribed by existing laws, and in accordance with such instructions as shall be given by the Commissioner of the General [Land] Office.

SEC. 7. *And be it further enacted,* That in regard to settlements which by existing laws are authorized in certain States and Territories upon unsurveyed lands, which privilege is hereby extended to California, the pre-emption claimant shall be, and is hereby, in all cases, required, from and after the first day of September, eighteen hundred and sixty-two, to file his declaratory statement within three months from the date of the receipt at the district land office of the approved plat of the township embracing such pre-emption settlement: *Provided,* The provisions of this section shall not be held to authorize pre-emption and settlement of mineral lands, which are hereby exempted from the provisions of this act.

SEC. 8. *And be it further enacted,* That from and after the first day of July next, and until otherwise ordered by the President, the duties of the register and receiver of New Mexico shall be transferred to and devolve upon the Surveyor-General of that Territory, and it shall and may be lawful for the President, in like manner, to transfer the duties of register and receiver in any district to the Surveyor-General where the public interest may require such transfer.

SEC. 9. *And be it further enacted,* That from and after the first day of July next, the salary of the Surveyor-General of California shall not exceed three thousand dollars per annum, and [the] salaries of the Surveyor-General of Oregon and Washington shall not exceed two thousand five hundred dollars each per annum, and should the surveying districts of Utah and Nevada be hereafter established by order of the President, each as an independent district, the salaries of the surveyor-general shall not exceed three thousand dollars each for said districts.

SEC. 10. *And be it further enacted,* That when the settlers in any township or townships, not mineral or reserved by Government, shall desire a survey made of the same, under the authority of the Surveyor-General of the United States, and shall file an application therefor in writing, and deposit in a proper United States depository, to the credit of the United States, a sum sufficient to pay for such survey, together with all expenses incident thereto, without cost or claim for indemnity on the United States, it shall and may be lawful for said Surveyor-General, under such instructions as may be given him by the Commissioner of the

General Land Office, and in accordance with existing laws and instructions, to survey such township or townships, and make return thereof to the general and proper local land office: *Provided*, The townships so proposed to be surveyed are within the range of the regular progress of the public surveys embraced by existing standard lines or bases for the township and sub-divisional surveys.*

Approved, May 30, 1862.

No. 40 B.—An Act for the survey of grants or claims of land.

Be it enacted by the Senate and House of Representatives of the United States of America in Congress assembled, That all claims or grants of land in any of the States or Territories of the United States, derived from any foreign country or government, shall be surveyed under the direction of the proper officers of the Government of the United States upon the application of the parties claiming or owning the same, and at their expense, which shall be paid or secured to the satisfaction of the Secretary of the Interior before the work shall be performed; but nothing in the law requiring the executive officers to survey land claimed or granted under any laws of the United States shall be construed either to authorize such officers to pass upon the validity of the titles granted by or under such laws, or to give any greater effect to the surveys made by them than to make such surveys *primâ facie* evidence of the true location of the land claimed or granted, nor shall any such grant be deemed incomplete for the want of a survey or patent when the land granted may be ascertained without a survey or patent.

Approved, June 2, 1862.

No. 41 B.—An Act to establish a land office in Colorado Territory, and for other purposes.

Be it enacted by the Senate and House of Representatives of the United States of America in Congress assembled, That all the lands belonging to the United States to which the Indian title has been or shall be extinguished shall be subject to the operations of the pre-emption act of the fourth of September, eighteen hundred and forty-one, and under the conditions, restrictions, and stipulations therein mentioned: *Provided, however*, That when unsurveyed lands are claimed by pre-emption, notice of the specific tracts claimed shall be filed within six months after the survey has been made in the field; and on failure to file such notice, or to pay for the tract claimed within twelve months from the filing of such notice, the parties claiming such lands shall forfeit all right thereto, provided said notices may be filed with the Surveyor-General, and to be noted by him on the township plats, until other arrangements have been made by law for that purpose.

SEC. 2. *And be it further enacted*, That the public lands within the Territory of Colorado to which the Indian title is or shall be extinguished

* See No. 121 B.

shall constitute a new land district, to be called the Colorado district; and the President is hereby authorized to appoint, by and with the advice and consent of the Senate, a register and receiver of public moneys for said district, who shall be required to reside at the place at which said office shall be located, and they shall have the same powers, perform the same duties, and be entitled to the same compensation as are or may be prescribed by law in relation to land offices of the United States in the State of Kansas.

SEC. 3. *And be it further enacted,* That an act entitled "An act to graduate [and reduce] the price of the public lands to actual settlers and cultivators," be and the same is hereby repealed.*

Approved, June 2, 1862.

No. 42 B.—An Act supplemental to "An Act granting the right of way to the State of Missouri, and a portion of the public lands to aid in the construction of certain railroads in said State," approved June tenth, eighteen hundred and fifty-two.†

Be it enacted by the Senate and House of Representatives of the United States of America in Congress assembled, That the time required by the act to which this is supplemental, for the completion of the road therein described, "from the city of Saint Louis to such point on the western boundary of said State as may be designated by the authority of said State," as well as the time of reversion to the United States of the lands thereby granted to the State of Missouri for the use of said road, is hereby extended for ten years from the tenth day of June, eighteen hundred and sixty-two: *Provided,* That in case said company fail to complete said road within the time as thus extended, the said lands shall then revert to the United States.

Approved, June 5, 1862.

No. 43 B.—An Act for the collection of direct taxes in insurrectionary districts within the United States, and for other purposes.

* * * * * * * * *

SEC. 11. *And be it further enacted,* That the said board of commissioners, under the direction of the President, may be authorized, instead of leasing the said lands vested in the United States, as above provided, to cause the same, or any portion thereof, to be subdivided and sold in parcels not to exceed three hundred and twenty acres to any one purchaser, at public sale, after giving due notice thereof, as upon the sale of other public lands of the United States, for sixty days, and to issue a certificate therefor; and that, at any such sale, any loyal citizen of the United States, or any person who shall have declared on oath his intention to become such, or any person who shall have faithfully served as an officer, musician, or private soldier or sailor in the army or navy or marine service of the United States, as a regular or volunteer, for the term of three

* Vol. I. No. 251.

† Vol. I. No. 196.

months, may become the purchaser; and if upon such sale any person serving in the army or navy or marine corps shall pay one-fourth part of the purchase money, a certificate shall be given him, and he shall have the term of three years in which to pay the remainder, either in money or in certificates of indebtedness from the United States; and any citizen of the United States, or any person who shall have declared his intention to become such, being the head of a family, and residing in the State or district where said lands are situate, and not the owner of any other lands, may, under such rules as may be established by said board of commissioners, have the right to enter upon and acquire the rights of pre-emption in such lands as may be unimproved and vested in the United States, and as may be selected by said board of commissioners, under the direction of the President, from time to time, for such purpose.

* * * * * * * * *

Approved, June 10, 1862.

No. 44 B.—An Act to protect the property of Indians who have adopted the habits of civilized life.

Be it enacted by the Senate and House of Representatives of the United States of America in Congress assembled, That whenever any Indian, being a member of any band or tribe with whom the Government has or shall have entered into treaty stipulations, being desirous to adopt the habits of civilized life, shall have had a portion of the lands belonging to his tribe allotted to him in severalty, in pursuance of such treaty stipulations, it shall be the duty of the agent and superintendent of such tribe to provide that such Indian shall be protected in the peaceful and quiet occupation and enjoyment of the lands so allotted to him.

SEC. 2. *And be it further enacted,* That whenever any person of Indian blood belonging to a band or tribe who receive, or are entitled to receive, annuities from the Government of the United States, and who has not adopted the habits and customs of civilized life, and received his lands in severalty by allotment, as mentioned in the foregoing section of this act, shall commit any trespass upon the lands or premises of any Indian who has received his lands by allotment, as aforesaid, it shall be the duty of the superintendent and agent of such band or tribe to ascertain the damages resulting from such trespass; and the sum so ascertained shall be withheld from the payment next thereafter to be made, either to the band or tribe to which the party committing such trespass shall belong, as in the discretion of the superintendent he shall deem proper, and the sum so retained shall be paid over by the said agent or superintendent to the party injured, with the approval of the Secretary of the Interior.

SEC. 3. *And be it further enacted,* That in case the trespasser shall be the chief or headman of a band or tribe, in addition to the penalties above provided for, it shall be the duty of the superintendent of Indian affairs in his district to suspend the said trespasser from his office for three months, and during that time to deprive him of all the benefits and emoluments connected therewith: *Provided,* That the said chief or headman may be sooner restored to his former standing if the superintendent shall so direct.

Approved, June 14, 1862.

No. 45 B.—An Act to aid in the construction of a railroad and telegraph line from the Missouri River to the Pacific Ocean, and to secure to the Government the use of the same for postal, military, and other purposes.*

[*The first section of this act provides for incorporation of the company —officers, organization, stock, powers, and fundamental regulations of the Union Pacific Railroad Company.*]

SEC. 2. *And be it further enacted,* That the right of way through the public lands be, and the same is hereby, granted to said company for the construction of said railroad and telegraph line; and the right, power, and authority is hereby given to said company to take from the public lands adjacent to the line of said road, earth, stone, timber, and other materials for the construction thereof: said right of way is granted to said railroad to the extent of two hundred feet in width on each side of said railroad where it may pass over the public lands, including all necessary grounds for stations, buildings, workshops, and depots, machine shops, switches, side tracks, turntables, and water stations. The United States shall extinguish as rapidly as may be the Indian titles to all lands falling under the operation of this act and required for the said right of way and grants hereinafter made.

SEC. 3. *And be it further enacted,* That there be, and is hereby, granted to said company, for the purpose of aiding in the construction of said railroad and telegraph line, and to secure the safe and speedy transportation of the mails, troops, munitions of war, and public stores thereon, every alternate section of public land designated by odd numbers, to the amount of five alternate sections per mile on each side of said railroad, on the line thereof, and within the limits of ten miles on each side of said road, not sold, reserved, or otherwise disposed of by the United States, and to which a pre-emption or homestead claim may not have attached, at the time the line of said road is definitely fixed: *Provided,* That all mineral lands shall be excepted from the operation of this act; but where the same shall contain timber, the timber thereon is hereby granted to said company. And all such lands, so granted by this section, which shall not be sold or disposed of by said company within three years after the entire road shall have been completed, shall be subject to settlement and pre-emption, like other lands, at a price not exceeding one dollar and twenty-five cents per acre, to be paid to said company.

SEC. 4. *And be it further enacted,* That whenever said company shall have completed forty consecutive miles of any portion of said railroad and telegraph line, ready for the service contemplated by this act, and supplied with all necessary drains, culverts, viaducts, crossings, sidings, bridges, turnouts, watering places, depots, equipments, furniture, and all other appurtenances of a first-class railroad, the rails and all the other iron used in the construction and equipment of said road to be American manufacture of the best quality, the President of the United States shall appoint three commissioners to examine the same and report to him in relation thereto; and if it shall appear to him that forty consecutive miles of said railroad and telegraph line have been completed and equipped in all respects as required by this act, then, upon certificate of said commissioner to that effect, patents shall issue conveying the right and title to said lands to said company, on each side of the road as far as the

* Amended, No. 111 B, and No. 126 B. As to pre-emptions and homesteads on even numbered sections, see No. 204 B.

same is completed, to the amount aforesaid; and patents shall in like manner issue as each forty miles of said railroad and telegraph line are completed, upon certificate of said commissioners. Any vacancies occurring in said board of commissioners by death, resignation, or otherwise, shall be filled by the President of the United States: *Provided, however*, That no such commissioners shall be appointed by the President of the United States unless there shall be presented to him a statement, verified on oath by the president of said company, that such forty miles have been completed, in the manner required by this act, and setting forth with certainty the points where such forty miles begin and where the same end; which oath shall be taken before a judge of a court of record.

[SEC. 5. *Provides for issuance of bonds of the United States.*]

SEC. 6. *And be it further enacted*, That the grants aforesaid are made upon condition that said company shall pay said bonds at maturity, and shall keep said railroad and telegraph line in repair and use, and shall at all times transmit despatches over said telegraph line, and transport mails, troops, and munitions of war, supplies, and public stores upon said railroad for the Government, whenever required to do so by any department thereof, and that the Government shall at all times have the preference in the use of the same for all the purposes aforesaid (at fair and reasonable rates of compensation, not to exceed the amounts paid by private parties for the same kind of service); and all compensation for services rendered for the Government shall be applied to the payment of said bonds and interest until the whole amount is fully paid. Said company may also pay the United States, wholly or in part, in the same or other bonds, treasury notes, or other evidences of debt against the United States, to be allowed at par; and after said road is completed, until said bonds and interest are paid, at least five per centum of the net earnings of said road shall also be annually applied to the payment thereof.

SEC. 7. *And be it further enacted*, That said company shall file their assent to this act, under the seal of said company, in the Department of the Interior, within one year after the passage of this act, and shall complete said railroad and telegraph from the point of beginning as herein provided, to the western boundary of Nevada Territory before the first day of July, one thousand eight hundred and seventy-four: *Provided*, That within two years after the passage of this act said company shall designate the general route of said road, as near as may be, and shall file a map of the same in the Department of the Interior, whereupon the Secretary of the Interior shall cause the lands within fifteen miles of said designated route or routes to be withdrawn from pre-emption, private entry, and sale; and when any portion of said route shall be finally located, the Secretary of the Interior shall cause the said lands hereinbefore granted to be surveyed and set off as fast as may be necessary for the purposes herein named: *Provided*, That in fixing the point of connection of the main trunk with the eastern connections, it shall be fixed at the most practicable point for the construction of the Iowa and Missouri branches, as hereinafter provided.

SEC. 8. *And be it further enacted*, That the line of said railroad and telegraph shall commence at a point on the one hundredth meridian of longitude west from Greenwich, between the south margin of the valley of the Republican River and the north margin of the valley of the Platte River, in the Territorry of Nebraska, at a point to be fixed by the President of the United States, after actual surveys; thence running westerly upon the most direct, central, and practicable route through the territories of the United States, to the western boundary of the Territory of Nevada, there to meet and connect with the line of the Central Pacific Railroad Company of California.

SEC. 9. *And be it further enacted*, That the Leavenworth, Pawnee, and Western Railroad Company of Kansas are hereby authorized to construct a railroad and telegraph line, from the Missouri River, at the mouth of the Kansas River, on the south side thereof, so as to connect with the Pacific railroad of Missouri, to the aforesaid point, on the one hundredth meridian of longitude west from Greenwich, as herein provided, upon the same terms and conditions in all respects as are provided in this act for the construction of the railroad and telegraph line first mentioned, and to meet and connect with the same at the meridian of longitude aforesaid; and in case the general route or line of road from the Missouri River to the Rocky Mountains should be so located as to require a departure northwardly from the proposed line of said Kansas railroad before it reaches the meridian of longitude aforesaid, the location of said Kansas road shall be made so as to conform thereto; and said railroad through Kansas shall be so located between the mouth of the Kansas River, as aforesaid, and the aforesaid point, on the one hundredth meridian of longitude, that the several railroads from Missouri and Iowa, herein authorized to connect with the same, can make connection within the limits prescribed in this act, provided the same can be done without deviating from the general direction of the whole line to the Pacific coast. The route in Kansas, west of the meridian of Fort Riley, to the aforesaid point, on the one hundredth meridian of longitude, to be subject to the approval of the President of the United States, and to be determined by him on actual survey. And said Kansas company may proceed to build said railroad to the aforesaid point, on the one hundredth meridian of longitude west from Greenwich, in the Territory of Nebraska. The Central Pacific Railroad Company of California, a corporation existing under the laws of the State of California, are hereby authorized to construct a railroad and telegraph line from the Pacific coast, at or near San Francisco, or the navigable waters of the Sacramento River, to the eastern boundary of California, upon the same terms and conditions, in all respects, as are contained in this act for the construction of said railroad and telegraph line first mentioned, and to meet and connect with the first mentioned railroad and telegraph line on the eastern boundary of California. Each of said companies shall file their acceptance of the conditions of this act in the Department of the Interior within six months after the passage of this act.

SEC. 10. *And be it further enacted*, That the said company chartered by the State of Kansas shall complete one hundred miles of their said road, commencing at the mouth of the Kansas River as aforesaid, within two years after filing their assent to the conditions of this act, as herein provided, and one hundred miles per year thereafter until the whole is completed; and the said Central Pacific Railroad Company of California shall complete fifty miles of their said road within two years after filing their assent to the provisions of this act, as herein provided, and fifty miles per year thereafter until the whole is completed; and after completing their roads, respectively, said companies, or either of them, may unite upon equal terms with the first-named company in constructing so much of said railroad and telegraph line and branch railroads and telegraph lines in this act hereinafter mentioned, through the Territories from the State of California to the Missouri River, as shall then remain to be constructed, on the same terms and conditions as provided in this act in relation to the said Union Pacific Railroad Company. And the

Hannibal and St. Joseph Railroad, the Pacific Railroad Company of Missouri, and the first-named company, or either of them, on filing their assent to this act, as aforesaid, may unite upon equal terms, under this act, with the said Kansas company, in constructing said railroad and telegraph, to said meridian of longitude, with the consent of the said State of Kansas; and in case said first-named company shall complete their line to the eastern boundary of California before it is completed across said State by the Central Pacific Railroad Company of California, said first-named company is hereby authorized to continue in constructing the same through California, with the consent of said State, upon the terms mentioned in this act, until said roads shall meet and connect, and the whole line of said railroad and telegraph is completed; and the Central Pacific Railroad Company of California, after completing its road across said State, is authorized to continue the construction of said railroad and telegraph through the Territories of the United States to the Missouri River, including the branch roads specified in this act, upon the routes hereinbefore and hereinafter indicated, on the terms and conditions provided in this act in relation to the said Union Pacific Railroad Company, until said roads shall meet and connect, and the whole line of said railroad and branches and telegraph is completed.

SEC. 11. *And be it further enacted*, That for three hundred miles of said road most mountainous and difficult of construction, to wit: one hundred and fifty miles westwardly from the eastern base of the Rocky Mountains, and one hundred and fifty miles eastwardly from the western base of the Sierra Nevada mountains, said points to be fixed by the President of the United States, the bonds to be issued to aid in the construction thereof shall be treble the number per mile hereinbefore provided, and the same shall be issued, and the lands herein granted be set apart, upon the construction of every twenty miles thereof, upon the certificate of the commissioners as aforesaid that twenty consecutive miles of the same are completed; and between the sections last named of one hundred and fifty miles each, the bonds to be issued to aid in the construction thereof shall be double the number per mile first mentioned, and the same shall be issued, and the lands herein granted be set apart, upon the construction of every twenty-miles thereof, upon the certificate of the commissioners as aforesaid that twenty consecutive miles of the same are completed: *Provided*, That no more than fifty thousand of said bonds shall be issued under this act to aid in constructing the main line of said railroad and telegraph.

SEC. 12. *And be it further enacted*, That whenever the route of said railroad shall cross the boundary of any State or Territory, or said meridian of longitude, the two companies meeting or uniting there shall agree upon its location at that point, with reference to the most direct and practicable through route, and in case of difference between them as to said location, the President of the United States shall determine the said location; the companies named in each State and Territory to locate the road across the same between the points so agreed upon, except as herein provided. The track upon the entire line of railroad and branches shall be of uniform width, to be determined by the President of the United States, so that, when completed, cars can be run from the Missouri River to the Pacific coast; the grades and curves shall not exceed the maximum grades and curves of the Baltimore and Ohio Railroad; the whole line of said railroad and branches and telegraph shall be operated and used for all purposes of communication, travel, and transportation, so far as the public and government are concerned, as one connected, continuous line; and the companies herein named in Missouri, Kansas, and California, filing their assent to the provisions of this act, shall receive and transport all iron rails, chairs, spikes, ties, timber, and all materials required for constructing and furnishing said first-mentioned line between the aforesaid point, on the one hundredth meridian of longitude and western boundary of Nevada Territory, whenever the same is required by said first-named company, at cost, over that portion of the roads of said companies constructed under the provisions of this act.

SEC. 13. *And be it further enacted,* That the Hannibal and St. Joseph Railroad Company of Missouri may extend its roads from St. Joseph, via Atchison, to connect and unite with the road through Kansas, upon filing its assent to the provisions of this act, upon the same terms and conditions, in all respects, for one hundred miles in length next to the Missouri River, as are provided in this act for the construction of the railroad and telegraph line first mentioned, and may, for this purpose, use any railroad charter which has been or may be granted by the legislature of Kansas: *Provided,* That if actual survey shall render it desirable, the said company may construct their road, with the consent of the Kansas legislature, on the most direct and practicable route west from St. Joseph, Missouri, so as to connect and unite with the road leading from the western boundary of Iowa at any point east of the one hundredth meridian of west longitude, or with the main trunk road at said point; but in no event shall lands or bonds be given to said company, as herein directed, to aid in the construction of their said road for a greater distance than one hundred miles. And the Leavenworth, Pawnee, and Western Railroad Company of Kansas may construct their road from Leavenworth to unite with the road through Kansas.

SEC. 14. *And be it further enacted,* That the said Union Pacific Railroad Company is hereby authorized and required to construct a single line of railroad and telegraph from a point on the western boundary of the State of Iowa, to be fixed by the President of the United States, upon the most direct and practicable route, to be subject to his approval, so as to form a connection with the lines of said company at some point on the one hundredth meridian of longitude aforesaid, from the point of commencement on the western boundary of the State of Iowa, upon the same terms and conditions, in all respects, as are contained in this act for the construction of the said railroad and telegraph first mentioned; and the said Union Pacific Railroad Company shall complete one hundred miles of the road and telegraph, in this section provided for, in two years after filing their assent to the conditions of this act, as by the terms of this act required, and at the rate of one hundred miles per year thereafter, until the whole is completed: *Provided,* That a failure upon the part of said company to make said connection in the time aforesaid, and to perform the obligations imposed on said company by this section, and to operate said road in the same manner as the main line shall be operated, shall forfeit to the Government of the United States all the rights, privileges, and franchises granted to and conferred upon said company by this act. And whenever there shall be a line of railroad completed through Minnesota or Iowa to Sioux City, then the said Pacific Railroad Company is hereby authorized and required to construct a railroad and telegraph from said Sioux City upon the most direct and practicable route to a point on, and so as to connect with, the branch railroad and telegraph in this section hereinbefore mentioned, or with the said Union Pacific Railroad, said point of junction to be fixed by the President of the United States, not further west than the one hundredth meridian of longitude aforesaid, and on the same terms and conditions as provided in this act for the construction of the Union Pacific Railroad as aforesaid, and to complete the same at the rate of one hundred miles per year; and should said company fail to comply with the requirements of this act in relation to the said Sioux City Railroad and telegraph, the said company shall suffer the same forfeitures prescribed in relation to the Iowa branch railroad and telegraph hereinbefore mentioned.

SEC. 15. *And be it further enacted*, That any other railroad company now incorporated, or hereafter to be incorporated, shall have the right to connect their road with the road and branches provided for by this act, at such places and upon such just and equitable terms as the President of the United States may prescribe. Wherever the word company is used in this act it shall be construed to embrace the words their associates, successors, and assigns, the same as if the words had been properly added thereto.

SEC. 16. *And be it further enacted*, That at any time after the passage of this act all of the railroad companies named herein, and assenting hereto, or any two or more of them, are authorized to form themselves into one consolidated company; notice of such consolidation, in writing, shall be filed in the Department of the Interior, and such consolidated company shall thereafter proceed to construct said railroad and branches and telegraph line upon the terms and conditions provided in this act.

SEC. 17. *And be it further enacted*, That in case said company or companies shall fail to comply with the terms and conditions of this act, by not completing said road and telegraph and branches within a reasonable time, or by not keeping the same in repair and use, but shall permit the same, for an unreasonable time, to remain unfinished, or out of repair, and unfit for use, Congress may pass any act to insure the speedy completion of said road and branches, or put the same in repair and use, and may direct the income of said railroad and telegraph line to be thereafter devoted to the use of the United States, to repay all such expenditures caused by the default and neglect of such company or companies: *Provided*, That if said roads are not completed, so as to form a continuous line of railroad, ready for use, from the Missouri River to the navigable waters of the Sacramento River, in California, by the first day of July, eighteen hundred and seventy-six, the whole of all of said railroads before mentioned and to be constructed under the provisions of this act, together with all their furniture, fixtures, rolling stock, machine shops, lands, tenements, and hereditaments, and property of every kind and character, shall be forfeited to and be taken possession of by the United States: *Provided*, That of the bonds of the United States in this act provided to be delivered for any and all parts of the roads to be constructed east of the one hundredth meridian of west longitude from Greenwich, and for any part of the road west of the west foot of the Sierra Nevada mountain, there shall be reserved of each part and instalment twenty-five per centum, to be and remain in the United States treasury, undelivered, until said road and all parts thereof provided for in this act are entirely completed; and of all the bonds provided to be delivered, for the said road, between the two points aforesaid, there shall be reserved out of each instalment fifteen per centum, to be and remain in the treasury until the whole of the road provided for in this act is fully completed; and if the said road or any part thereof shall fail of completion at the time limited therefor in this act, then and in that case the said part of said bonds so reserved shall be forfeited to the United States.

SEC. 18. *And be it further enacted*, That whenever it appears that the net earnings of the entire road and telegraph, including the amount allowed for services rendered for the United States, after deducting all expenditures, including repairs, and the furnishing, running, and managing of said road, shall exceed ten per centum upon its cost, exclusive of the five per centum to be paid to the United States, Congress may reduce the rates of fare thereon, if unreasonable in amount, and may fix and establish the same by law. And the better to accomplish the object of this act, namely, to promote the public interest and welfare by the construction of said railroad and telegraph line, and keeping the same in working order, and to secure to the Government at all times (but particularly in time of war) the use and benefits of the same for postal, military and other purposes, Congress may, at any time, having due regard for the rights of said companies named herein, add to, alter, amend, or repeal this act.

SEC. 19. *And be it further enacted,* That the several railroad companies herein named are authorized to enter into an arrangement with the Pacific Telegraph Company, the Overland Telegraph Company, and the California State Telegraph Company, so that the present line of telegraph between the Missouri River and San Francisco may be moved upon or along the line of said railroad and branches as fast as said roads and branches are built; and if said arrangement be entered into, and the transfer of said telegraph line be made in accordance therewith to the line of said railroad and branches, such transfer shall, for all purposes of this act, be held and considered a fulfilment on the part of said railroad companies of the provisions of this act in regard to the construction of said line of telegraph. And, in case of disagreement, said telegraph companies are authorized to remove their line of telegraph along and upon the line of railroad herein contemplated without prejudice to the rights of said railroad companies named herein.

SEC. 20. *And be it further enacted,* That the corporation hereby created and the roads connected therewith, under the provisions of this act, shall make to the Secretary of the Treasury an annual report wherein shall be set forth—

First. The names of the stockholders and their places of residence, so far as the same can be ascertained;

Second. The names and residences of the directors, and all other officers of the company;

Third. The amount of stock subscribed, and the amount thereof actually paid in;

Fourth. A description of the lines of road surveyed, of the lines thereof fixed upon for the construction of the road, and the cost of such surveys;

Fifth. The amount received from passengers on the road;

Sixth. The amount received for freight thereon;

Seventh. A statement of the expense of said road and its fixtures;

Eighth. A statement of the indebtedness of said company, setting forth the various kinds thereof. Which report shall be sworn to by the president of the said company, and shall be presented to the Secretary of the Treasury on or before the first day of July in each year.

Approved, July 1, 1862.

No. 46 B.—An Act to establish a land district in the Territory of Nevada, and for other purposes.

Be it enacted by the Senate and House of Representatives of the United States of America in Congress assembled, That the public lands of the United States in the Territory of Nevada shall constitute a land district, to be called the District of Nevada, the office for which shall be established at such place within said district as the President of the United States may from time to time direct, and the pre-emption laws are hereby extended to said Territory.

SEC. 2. *And be it further enacted,* That the President be, and he is hereby, authorized to appoint, by and with the advice and consent of the Senate, a register and receiver for said district, who shall be required to reside at the site of said office, and who shall have the same powers and perform the same duties as are now or may hereafter be prescribed by law for other land officers, and whose compensation shall be the same as allowed to such officers by the act approved April twenty, eighteen hundred and eighteen, entitled "An act for changing the compensation of receivers and registers of the land offices."*

SEC. 3. *And be it further enacted,* That when the settlers in any township or townships, not mineral or reserved by Government, shall desire a survey made of the same under the authority of the Surveyor-General of the United States, and shall file an application therefor in writing, and deposit in a proper United States depository to the credit of the United States a sum sufficient to pay for such survey, together with all expenses incident thereto, without cost or claim for indemnity on the United States, it shall and may be lawful for said Surveyor-General, under such instructions as may be given him by the Commissioner of the General Land Office, and in accordance with existing laws and instructions, to survey such township or townships, and make return thereof to the general and proper local land office: *Provided,* That the townships so proposed to be surveyed are within the range of the regular progress of the public surveys embraced by existing standard lines or bases for the township and sub-divisional surveys.

Approved, July 2, 1862.

No. 47 B.—An Act donating public lands to the several States and Territories which may provide colleges for the benefit of agriculture and the mechanic arts.†

Be it enacted by the Senate and House of Representatives of the United States of America in Congress assembled, That there be granted to the several States for the purposes hereinafter mentioned, an amount of public land, to be apportioned to each State, a quantity equal to thirty thousand acres for each senator and representative in Congress to which the States are respectively entitled by the apportionment under the census of eighteen hundred and sixty: *Provided,* That no mineral lands shall be selected or purchased under the provisions of this act.

SEC. 2. *And be it further enacted,* That the land aforesaid, after being surveyed, shall be apportioned to the several States in sections or subdivisions of sections, not less than one quarter of a section; and whenever

* Vol. I. No. 10.

† See No. 78 B. Amended, No. 165 B.

there are public lands in a State subject to sale at private entry at one dollar and twenty-five cents per acre, the quantity to which said State shall be entitled shall be selected from such lands within the limits of such State, and the Secretary of the Interior is hereby directed to issue to each of the States in which there is not the quantity of public lands subject to sale at private entry at one dollar and twenty-five cents per acre, to which said State may be entitled under the provisions of this act, land scrip to the amount in acres for the deficiency of its distributive share: said scrip to be sold by said States and the proceeds thereof applied to the uses and purposes prescribed in this act, and for no other use or purpose whatsoever: *Provided*, That in no case shall any State to which land scrip may thus be issued be allowed to locate the same within the limits of any other State, or of any Territory of the United States, but their assignees may thus locate said land scrip upon any of the unappropriated lands of the United States subject to sale at private entry at one dollar and twenty-five cents, or less, per acre: *And provided further*, That not more than one million acres shall be located by such assignees in any one of the States: *And provided further*, That no such location shall be made before one year from the passage of this act.

SEC. 3. *And be it further enacted*, That all the expenses of management, superintendence, and taxes from date of selection of said lands, previous to their sales, and all expenses incurred in the management and disbursement of the moneys which may be received therefrom, shall be paid by the States to which they may belong, out of the treasury of said States, so that the entire proceeds of the sale of said lands shall be applied without any diminution whatever to the purposes hereinafter mentioned.

SEC. 4. *And be it further enacted*, That all moneys derived from the sale of the lands aforesaid by the States to which the lands are apportioned, and from the sales of land scrip hereinbefore provided for, shall be invested in stocks of the United States, or of the States, or some other safe stocks, yielding not less than five per centum upon the par value of said stocks; and that the moneys so invested shall constitute a perpetual fund, the capital of which shall remain forever undiminished (except so far as may be provided in section fifth of this act), and the interest of which shall be inviolably appropriated, by each State which may take and claim the benefit of this act, to the endowment, support, and maintenance of at least one college where the leading object shall be, without excluding other scientific and classical studies, and including military tactics, to teach such branches of learning as are related to agriculture and the mechanic arts, in such manner as the legislatures of the States may respectively prescribe, in order to promote the liberal and practical education of the industrial classes in the several pursuits and professions in life.

SEC. 5. *And be it further enacted*, That the grant of land and land scrip hereby authorized shall be made on the following conditions, to which, as well as to the provisions hereinbefore contained, the previous assent of the several States shall be signified by legislative acts:—

First. If any portion of the fund invested, as provided by the foregoing section, or any portion of the interest thereon, shall, by any action or contingency, be diminished or lost, it shall be replaced by the State to which it belongs, so that the capital of the fund shall remain forever undiminished; and the annual interest shall be regularly applied, without diminution, to the purposes mentioned in the fourth section of this act, except that a sum, not exceeding ten per centum upon the amount received by any State under the provisions of this act, may be expended for the purchase of lands for sites or experimental farms, whenever authorized by the respective legislatures of said States.

Second. No portion of said fund, nor the interest thereon, shall be applied, directly or indirectly, under any pretence whatever, to the purchase, erection, preservation, or repair of any building or buildings.

Third. Any State which may take and claim the benefit of the provisions of this act shall provide, within five years, at least not less than one college, as described in the fourth section of this act, or the grant to such State shall cease; and said State shall be bound to pay the United States the amount received of any lands previously sold, and that the title to purchasers under the State shall be valid.

Fourth. An annual report shall be made regarding the progress of each college, recording any improvements and experiments made, with their cost and results, and such other matters, including State industrial and economical statistics, as may be supposed useful; one copy of which shall be transmitted by mail free, by each, to all the other colleges which may be endowed under the provisions of this act, and also one copy to the Secretary of the Interior.

Fifth. When lands shall be selected from those which have been raised to double the minimum price, in consequence of railroad grants, they shall be computed to the States at the maximum price, and the number of acres proportionally diminished.

Sixth. No State while in a condition of rebellion or insurrection against the Government of the United States shall be entitled to the benefit of this act.

Seventh. No State shall be entitled to the benefits of this act unless it shall express its acceptance thereof by its legislature within two years from the date of its approval by the President.

SEC. 6. *And be it further enacted*, That land scrip issued under the provisions of this act shall not be subject to location until after the first day of January, one thousand eight hundred and sixty-three.

SEC. 7. *And be it further enacted*, That the land officers shall receive the same fees for locating land scrip issued under the provisions of this act as is now allowed for the location of military bounty land warrants under existing laws: *Provided*, Their maximum compensation shall not be thereby increased.

SEC. 8. *And be it further enacted*, That the Governors of the several States to which scrip shall be issued under this act shall be required to report annually to Congress all sales made of such scrip until the whole shall be disposed of, the amount received for the same, and what appropriation has been made of the proceeds.

Approved, July 2, 1862.

No. 48 B.—An Act making appropriations for the current and contingent expenses of the Indian Department, and for fulfilling treaty stipulations with various Indian tribes, for the year ending June thirtieth, eighteen hundred and sixty-three.

* * * * * * * * *

Provided, That the Secretary of the Interior is hereby authorized and directed to inquire into the expediency of reducing the Indian reservations in California to two in number; the proper places for the same; the probable expense thereof; the propriety of disposing of any of the reservations, and the value thereof, and of the property thereon; of the manner and terms of such disposal; and in what manner, in his judgment, the expense of the Indian Department in that State can be reduced and its system simplified without injury to the same, and report thereon to the next regular session of Congress.

Approved, July 5, 1862.

No. 49 B.—An Act to grant the right of pre-emption to settlers on certain lots in Wisconsin.

Be it enacted by the Senate and House of Representatives of the United States of America in Congress assembled, That the Commissioner of the General Land Office be, and he is hereby, directed to cause survey to be made of that portion of lots numbered ten and eleven, lying east of the River au Diable, in township twenty-three north, of range twenty-one east, in the State of Wisconsin, and which portion was not embraced by the confirmatory provisions of the act of Congress approved February twenty-one, eighteen hundred and twenty-three, entitled "An act to revive and continue in force certain acts for the adjustment of land claims in the Territory of Michigan."

Approved, July 11, 1862.

No. 50 B.—An Act concerning certain lands heretofore granted to the State of Iowa.

Be it enacted by the Senate and House of Representatives of the United States of America in Congress assembled, That the five sections of land granted to the State of Iowa, by the third subdivision of section six of an act entitled "An act supplemental to the act for the admission of the States of Iowa and Florida into the Union," approved March third, eighteen hundred and forty-five,* be, and the same are hereby, released and discharged from the limitation contained in said section; and the General Assembly of the State of Iowa may make such disposition of said land as may be deemed best for the interests of said State.

Approved, July 11, 1862.

No. 51 B.—An Act for the relief of the Register of the Land Office at Vincennes, Indiana, and for other purposes.

Be it enacted by the Senate and House of Representatives of the United States of America in Congress assembled, That the Secretary of the Interior be, and he is hereby, authorized to make such allowance for office rent during the temporary continuance of the land office at Vincennes, Indiana, as may, in his opinion, be just and proper.

SEC. 2. *And be it further enacted,* That the said Secretary be author-

* Vol. I. No. 101.

ized to adjust the account of John Moore, postmaster at Vincennes, Indiana, and allow him at the usual rate for such services, compensation for the custody of the books, papers, and so forth, of the land office at Vincennes, Indiana, during the time the same were in his charge, under instructions from the Commissioner of the General Land Office, dated September third, eighteen hundred and fifty-eight; these allowances to be paid out of the appropriation for incidental expenses of district land offices: *Provided*, That the total sum paid under this act shall not exceed five hundred dollars.

Approved, July 12, 1862.

No. 52 B.—An Act for relief in the land claim in California, known as the claim of Francisco Soberanes to a tract of land known as "Saujon de Santa Rita."

Whereas, in the District Court of the United States for the Southern District of California, in the case of Francisco Soberanes *vs.* The United States, for the rancho lying in the State of California known by the name of Saujon de Santa Rita, a decree filed on the ninth day of February, eighteen hundred and fifty-eight, was entered, confirming to the said Soberanes the said tract of land known by the name of Saujon de Santa Rita; and whereas, on the presentation of the mandate of the Supreme Court of the United States, dismissing the appeal to the said Supreme Court of the United States in said cause, the said decree was made final by a decree of said District Court, rendered on the first day of November, eighteen hundred and sixty; and whereas the land confirmed as aforesaid lies in the northern district of California, as ascertained by a final survey of the same: Therefore—

Be it enacted by the Senate and House of Representatives of the United States of America in Congress assembled, That the said decrees of the District Court of the United States for the Southern District of California shall be, and they are hereby declared to be, as valid and effectual as if the same had been rendered by the District Court of the United States for the Northern District of California.

Approved, July 12, 1862.

No. 53 B.—An Act confirming a land claim in the State of Iowa, and for other purposes.

Be it enacted by the Senate and House of Representatives of the United States of America in Congress assembled, That the grant of lands to the then Territory of Iowa for the improvement of the Des Moines River, made by the act of August eight, eighteen hundred and forty-six,* is hereby extended so as to include the alternate sections (designated by odd numbers) lying within five miles of said river, between the Raccoon fork and the northern boundary of said State; such lands are to be held and applied in accordance with the provisions of the original grant, except that the consent of Congress is hereby given to the application of a portion thereof, to aid in the construction of the Keokuk, Fort Des Moines,

* Vol. I. No. 117. See also 35 B.

and Minnesota railroad, in accordance with the provisions of the act of the general assembly of the State of Iowa, approved March twenty-two, eighteen hundred and fifty-eight. And if any of said lands shall have been sold or otherwise disposed of by the United States before the passage of this act, excepting those released by the United States to the grantees of the State of Iowa under the joint resolution of March second, eighteen hundred and sixty-two, the Secretary of the Interior is hereby directed to set apart an equal amount of lands within said State to be certified in lieu thereof: *Provided*, That if the said State shall have sold and conveyed any portion of the lands lying within the limits of this grant the title of which has proved invalid, any lands which shall be certified to said State in lieu thereof by virtue of the provisions of this act shall inure to, and be held as a trust fund for the benefit of, the person or persons respectively whose titles shall have failed as aforesaid.

Approved, July 12, 1862.

No. 54 B.—An Act for the relief of pre-emptors on the home reservation of the Winnebagoes, in the Blue-earth region, in the State of Minnesota.*

Whereas certain individuals have memorialized Congress, setting forth that they were bona fide actual settlers, under the pre-emption laws of the United States, in the tract of country known as the eighteen-mile-square home reservation of the Winnebagoes, in the Blue-earth region, Minnesota, at a period of time when the Indian title had been extinguished, and prior to the setting apart by legal divisions of the said Indian home reservation, under the second article of the treaty of the twenty-seventh of February, eighteen hundred and fifty-five, and that by reason of the setting apart of said home reservation they were forced from their settlements and subjected to loss and damage by the destruction of their improvements: Therefore:—

Be it enacted by the Senate and House of Representatives of the United States of America in Congress assembled, That it shall and may be lawful for each of such settlers, within three months from and after the passage of this act, to file his declaratory statement with the proper register and receiver, descriptive of the tract so settled upon and improved; and under such regulations as may be prescribed by the Secretary of the Interior, said settler shall be permitted to establish his claim by the production of testimony showing compliance with all the requirements of the pre-emption law up to the period when said settler was ousted by reason of the premises falling within the aforesaid Indian home reservation; that the testimony required under this act shall be the affidavit of the claimant himself, taken before the register and receiver, and shall show the date of the commencement and the period of continuance of his improvements, the extent of the same, size of his habitation, the time and labor required in its construction, extent of other improvements, and the cost to him and value of the same, and value of crop derived from the same. The affidavit to be corroborated by disinterested testimony.

SEC. 2. *And be it further enacted*, That upon the return of such testimony to the department, it shall be the duty of the Secretary of the Interior finally to adjudge the validity or invalidity of each claim; and in

* No. 135 B.—See also No. 63 B.

regard to those shown to be bona fide under the pre-emption law, to report a list of the same, with all the testimony, to Congress, stipulating such award as should be paid as damages growing out of the loss and destruction of such improvements, by reason of the appropriation of such settlements to the Indian reservation, as aforesaid: *Provided,* That the land officers of the local land office herein mentioned shall not receive any additional pay or fees for the services hereby required of them.

Approved, July 14, 1862.

No. 55 B.—An Act to extend the territorial limits of the Territory of Nevada.

Be it enacted by the Senate and House of Representatives of the United States of America in Congress assembled, That all that part of the territory of the United States included within the following limits, namely: beginning at the point of intersection of the forty-second degree of north latitude with the thirty-eighth degree of longitude west from Washington; thence running south on the said thirty-eighth degree of west longitude until it intersects the northern boundary line of New Mexico; thence due west to the thirty-ninth degree of longitude west from Washington; thence with said thirty-ninth degree north to the intersection of said forty-second degree of north latitude; thence east with said forty-second degree of north latitude to the place of beginning, be, and the same is hereby attached to and made a part of the Territory of Nevada, subject to the limitations, restrictions, and provisions of the act organizing the Territory of Nevada.*

Approved, July 14, 1862.

No. 56 B.—An Act to extend the provisions of the act of August four, eighteen hundred and fifty-two, entitled "An act to grant the right of way to all rail and plank roads," &c., for the term of five years, and to amend the same.

Be it enacted by the Senate and House of Representatives of the United States of America in Congress assembled, That the provisions of the act entitled "An act to grant the right of way to all rail and plank roads, and macadamized turnpikes passing through the public lands belonging to the United States," approved August four, eighteen hundred and fifty-two,† and of the act extending the same to all of the public lands of the United States, approved March three, eighteen hundred and fifty-five, be, and the same are hereby extended for the term of five years from the fourth day of August, eighteen hundred and sixty-two.

SEC. 2. *And be it further enacted,* That the right of way for a railroad through the public lands of the United States lying in Wasco County, in the State of Oregon, be, and the same is hereby granted to the Oregon Steam Navigation Company.

Approved, July 15, 1862.

* No. 33 B.

† Vol. I. No. 206. See also No. 59 B.

No. 57 B.—An Act to enlarge the Lake Superior land district, in the State of Michigan.

Be it enacted by the Senate and House of Representatives of the United States of America in Congress assembled, That all that portion of the present "Cheboygan District," in the State of Michigan, lying west of Lake Michigan and south of the line dividing townships forty-one and forty-two north, including Saint Martin's and the adjacent islands near the entrance to "Big Bay De Noc," now forming a part of the present Cheboygan District, and subject to sale at Traverse City, in said State, be, and the same is hereby, attached to the "Lake Superior District," and the lands therein be subject to sale and entry at the site of the land office for said district.

SEC. 2. *And be it further enacted,* That this act shall not take effect until three months after the date of its approval.

Approved, July 16, 1862.

No. 58 B.—A Resolution explanatory of and in addition to the act of June third, eighteen hundred and fifty-six, granting public lands to the State of Wisconsin to aid in the constructing of railroads in said State.*

Resolved by the Senate and House of Representatives of the United States of America in Congress assembled, That the word "northerly," in the first section of the act entitled "An act granting public lands to the State of Wisconsin to aid in the construction of railroads in said State," approved June third, eighteen hundred and fifty-six, shall, without forfeiture to said State or its assigns of any rights or benefits under said act, or exemption from any of the conditions or obligations imposed thereby, be construed to authorize the location of the line of railroad in said first section provided for, upon any eligible route within ranges sixteen to twenty-three, inclusive, east of the fourth principal meridian. And the line of railroad as now located according to the records of the General Land Office in pursuance of said act is hereby authorized to be changed to within the above specified limits : *Provided, however,* That upon the construction of said railroad upon the new line, or of a sufficient part thereof, according to the terms of said act, the State of Wisconsin, its grantees or assigns shall receive upon the route originally located, and in the manner prescribed by the act, the same quantity of lands, and no more or other, except as hereinafter provided for, as it or they would have received if such railroad had been constructed upon the line originally located.

SEC. 2. *And be it further resolved,* That there be and is hereby granted to the State of Wisconsin, for the purpose of aiding in the construction of a railroad from the town of Appleton, in said State, to some point on Green Bay, at or near the mouth of Fox River, in said State, so much of the public lands of the United States lying at or near the mouth of said river, in the county of Brown and State of Wisconsin, known as the Fort Howard Military Reserve, as may be required for right of way, tracks, turnouts, depots, workshops, warehouses, wharves, and other railroad uses, not exceeding eighty acres, to be so selected by the State of Wisconsin or her assigns as to exclude the fort therefrom : *Provided, however,*

* Vol. I. No. 292. See also, No. 66 B. & No. 230 B.

That if no railroad be constructed and in running order between the termini in this section mentioned within three years from the passage of this joint resolution, then this grant shall be void.

SEC. 3. *And be it further resolved,* That the Secretary of the Interior be, and he is hereby, authorized to cause all even sections or parts of even sections of public land that may be brought within six miles of the new line of railroad, as herein provided for, to be sold at the same price and in the same manner as those have been upon the originally located route of railroad. And all purchasers, or their heirs or assigns, within the six-mile limits of the said originally located route, who shall be more than six miles from the new line of route herein authorized, and who have paid the sum of two dollars and fifty cents an acre, shall have the right either to exchange their locations upon the line as first established to the new line, upon the same terms, in like quantities, and in the same manner, as on the line first established as aforesaid, or, at their option, to enter without further payment, anywhere within the Menasha land district, in the State of Wisconsin, an additional quantity of public lands subject to private entry at one dollar and twenty-five cents an acre equal to the quantity entered by them at two dollars and fifty cents an acre, so that the lands originally entered by them shall thus be reduced to the rate of one dollar and twenty-five cents an acre.

SEC. 4. *And be it further resolved,* That the even sections of public lands reserved to the United States by the aforesaid act of June third, eighteen hundred and fifty-six, along the originally located route of railroad north of the said town of Appleton, and along which no railroad has been constructed, shall hereafter be sold at one dollar and twenty-five cents an acre.

Approved, April 25, 1862.

No. 59 B.—Joint Resolution relative to a certain grant of land for railroad purposes made to the State of Michigan in eighteen hundred and fifty-six.*

Resolved by the Senate and House of Representatives of the United States of America in Congress assembled, That the words "Wisconsin State line," in the first section of an act entitled "An act making a grant of lands to the State of Michigan, in alternate sections, to aid in the construction of railroads in said State," approved June third, eighteen hundred and fifty-six, shall, without forfeiture to said State or its assigns of any rights or benefits under said act, or exemption from any of the conditions or obligations imposed thereby, be construed to authorize the location of the line of railroad provided for in said act from Marquette, on Lake Superior, to the Wisconsin State line, upon any eligible route from the township of Marquette aforesaid, to a point on the Wisconsin State line, near the mouth of the Menomonee River, and touching at favorable points on Green Bay, with a view of securing a railroad available for military purposes from Green Bay to the waters of Lake Superior. And the line of railroad as now located in pursuance of said act from Marquette to the Wisconsin State line, according to the records of the General Land Office, is hereby authorized to be changed so as to conform to the route above indicated; which line, when surveyed and

* Vol. 1. No. 293.

the maps and plans thereof filed in the proper office, as required under said act of June third, eighteen hundred and fifty-six, shall confer the same rights upon and benefits to the State of Michigan and its assigns in said new line, as though the same had been originally located under said act.

SEC. 2. *And be it further resolved*, That the provisions of an act of Congress, approved August fourth, eighteen hundred and fifty-two,* entitled "An act to grant the right of way to all rail and plank roads and McAdamized turnpikes passing through the public lands belonging to the United States," be, and the same are hereby, extended so as to be applicable to the new line of railroad so as above to be located: *Provided*, The same shall be commenced within two years from the fourth day of August, eighteen hundred and sixty-two, and shall be completed within five years thereafter.

SEC. 3. *And be it further resolved*, That the Secretary of the Interior be, and he is hereby, authorized to cause all even sections or parts of even sections of public lands that may be brought within six miles of the new line of railroad, as herein provided for, to be sold at the same price and in the same manner those have or might have been, according to the said act of June third, eighteen hundred and fifty-six, upon the originally located route of railroad. And all purchasers, or their heirs or assigns, within the six mile limits of said originally located route, who shall be more than six miles from the new line of route hereby authorized, and who have paid the sum of two dollars and fifty cents an acre, shall have the right either to exchange their locations upon the line as first established to the new line upon the same terms, in like quantities, and in the same manner, as on the line first established, as aforesaid, or at their option to enter, without further payment, anywhere within the Marquette land district, in the State of Michigan, or that of the Grand Traverse land district, in said State, lying north or west of Lake Michigan, an additional quantity of public lands subject to private entry, at one dollar and twenty-five cents an acre, equal to the quantity entered by them at two dollars and fifty cents per acre, so that the lands originally entered by them shall be thus reduced to the rate of one dollar and twenty-five cents an acre.

SEC. 4. *And be it further resolved*, That the even sections of public lands reserved to the United States by the aforesaid act of June third, eighteen hundred and fifty-six, along the originally located route of the Marquette and Wisconsin State Line Railroad Company, except where such sections shall fall within six miles of the new line of road so as aforesaid proposed to be located, and along which no railroad has been constructed, shall hereafter be subject to sale at one dollar and twenty-five cents per acre.

SEC. 5. *And be it further resolved*, That upon the filing in the General Land Office of the lists of said railroad lands, in whole or in part, as now selected and certified in the General Land Office, with the certificate of the Governor of the State of Michigan, under the seal of the State, that said State and its assigns surrender all claim to the lands, as aforesaid, set forth and described in the lists thereof thus certified, and that the same have never been pledged or sold or in anywise encumbered, then the State of Michigan or its assigns shall be entitled to receive a like quantity of land, selected in like manner, upon the new line of road as thus surrendered upon the first line, and to the extent of six sections per

* Vol. I. No. 206. See also No. 56 B.

mile in the aggregate for every mile of the new line, according to the general provisions of the act of June third, eighteen hundred and fifty six. And it shall be the duty of the Commissioner of the General Land Office to re-offer for public sale, in the usual manner, the land embraced in the lists of surrendered lands aforesaid, when duly filed in his office as herein directed.

Approved, July 5, 1862.

No. 60 B.—A Joint Resolution authorizing the State of Minnesota to change the line of certain branch-railroads in said State, and for other purposes.

Whereas, by an act of Congress, approved March third, eighteen hundred and fifty-seven,* there was granted to the Territory of Minnesota lands to aid in the construction of a railroad from Stillwater, via St. Paul and St. Anthony, to a point between the foot of Big Stone Lake and the mouth of Sioux Wood River, with a branch, via St. Cloud and Crow Wing, to the navigable waters of the Red River of the North, the northern terminus of which was fixed by the legislature of said Territory at St. Vincent; and whereas it is now believed that the public interests require a change of location of a part of said branch road: *Therefore*—

Be it resolved by the Senate and House of Representatives of the United States of America in Congress assembled, That in lieu of that part of the railroad grant to Minnesota Territory by act of Congress, approved third March, eighteen hundred and fifty-seven, which extends northwesterly from the intersection of the tenth standard parallel with the fourth guide meridian, there shall be granted to the State of Minnesota the alternate sections within six mile limits of such new branch line of route as the authorities of the State may designate, having its southwestern terminus at any point on the existing line, between the Falls of Saint Anthony and Crow Wing, and extending in a northeasterly direction to the waters of Lake Superior, with a right of indemnity between the fifteen mile limits thereof, provided this resolution shall take effect from the filing in the General Land Office of the acceptance by the authorities aforesaid of such substitution; whereupon the land north of the intersection aforesaid in the grant as authorized by the said act of third March, eighteen hundred and fifty-seven, being by said acceptance disencumbered of the railroad grant, shall be dealt with as other public lands of the United States.

Approved, July 12, 1862.

No. 61 B.—A Resolution to repeal and modify sections two and three of an act entitled "An Act to settle the titles to certain lands set apart for the use of certain half-breed Kansas Indians in Kansas Territory," approved May twenty-six, eighteen hundred and sixty, and to repeal part of section one of said act.†

Resolved by the Senate and House of Representatives of the United States of America in Congress assembled, That sections two and three of an act entitled "An act to settle the titles to certain lands set apart for the use of certain half-breed Kansas Indians in Kansas Territory," approved

* Vol. I. No. 312.

† No. 4 B.

May twenty-six, one thousand eight hundred and sixty, and so much of the first section as authorizes the Secretary of the Interior to decide what persons are heirs to deceased reservees as mentioned therein be, and the same are hereby, repealed.

Approved, July 17, 1862.

No. 62 B.—An Act for the relief of persons for damages sustained by reasons of depredations and injuries by certain bands of Sioux Indians.

* * * * * * * * *

SEC. 9. *And be it further enacted,* That the Secretary of the Interior is hereby authorized to set apart of the public lands, not otherwise appropriated, eighty acres in severalty to each individual of the before-named bands who exerted himself in rescuing the whites from the late massacre of said Indians. The land so set apart shall not be subject to any tax, forfeiture, or sale, by process of law, and shall not be aliened or devised, except by the consent of the President of the United States, but shall be an inheritance to said Indians and their heirs forever.

* * * * * * * * *

Approved, February 16, 1863.

No. 63 B.—An Act for the removal of the Winnebago Indians and for the sale of their reservation in Minnesota for their benefit.*

Be it enacted by the Senate and House of Representatives of the United States of America in Congress assembled, That the President of the United States is authorized to assign to and set apart for the Winnebago Indians a tract of unoccupied land beyond the limits of any State, in extent at least equal to their diminished reservation, the same to be well adapted for agricultural purposes. And it shall be lawful for the President to take such steps as he may deem proper to effect the peaceful and quiet removal of the said Indians from the State of Minnesota, and to settle them upon the lands which may be assigned to them under the provisions of this act.

SEC. 2. *And be it further enacted,* That, upon the removal of the said Indians from the reservation where they now reside, it shall be the duty of the Secretary of the Interior to cause each legal subdivision of the said lands to be appraised by discreet persons to be appointed by him for that purpose. And in each instance where there are improvements upon any legal subdivision of said lands, the improvements shall be separately appraised. But no portion of the said lands shall be subject to pre-emption, settlement, entry, or location under any act of Congress, unless the party pre-empting, settling upon, or locating any portion of said lands shall pay therefor the full appraised value thereof, including the value of the said improvements, under such regulations as hereinafter provided.

SEC. 3. *And be it further enacted,* That after the appraisal of the said reservation the same shall be opened to pre-emption, entry, and settlement, in the same manner as other public lands: *Provided,* That before any

* See No. 54 B.

person shall be entitled to enter any portion of the said lands, by pre-emption or otherwise, previous to their exposure to sale to the highest bidder, at public outcry, he shall become an actual bona fide settler thereon, and shall conform to all the regulations now provided by law in cases of pre-emption, and shall pay, within the term of one year from the date of his settlement, the full appraised value of the land, and the improvements thereon, to the land officers of the district where the said lands are situated. And the portion of the said reservation which may not be settled upon, as aforesaid, may be sold at public auction, as other public lands are sold, after which they shall be subject to sale at private entry, as other public lands of the United States, but no portion thereof shall be sold for a sum less than their appraised value before the first of January, Anno Domini eighteen hundred and sixty-five, nor for a less price than one dollar and twenty-five cents per acre, unless otherwise provided by law: *Provided*, That where improvements have been made upon said lands by persons authorized by law to trade with said Indians, the value of such improvements, or the price for which the same may be sold, shall be paid to the parties making the same; and in case the land upon which such improvements shall have been made shall be purchased by the parties making the same, at the appraised value as aforesaid, the value of the improvements so made by him shall form no part of the purchase price to be paid for said land.

SEC. 4. *And be it further enacted*, That the lands of said Indians which have been set apart for the payment of the debts of the said Indians, shall be sold on sealed bids for the best price the same will bring; but no bids shall be received for said lands until the first day of January, Anno Domini eighteen hundred and sixty-five, for less than two dollars and fifty cents per acre. Bids shall be received for tracts of quarter sections; and for such tracts conforming to the Government surveys less than one hundred and sixty acres as will secure the largest price for said lands, the Secretary is authorized to receive, in payments of said lands, certificates of indebtedness of said Indians, issued by the Commissioner of Indian Affairs for the debts of said Indians, secured to be paid out of the sale of said lands by the third article of the treaty of the said Indians with the United States, concluded at Washington on the fifteenth day of April, eighteen hundred and fifty-nine. The money arising from the sale of their said lands, after paying the indebtedness required by said treaty to be paid, shall be paid into the treasury of the United States, and shall be expended as the same is received, under the direction of the Secretary of the Interior, in necessary improvements upon their new reservation; and it shall be the duty of the Secretary of the Interior to allot to said Indians in severalty lands which they may respectively cultivate and improve, not exceeding eighty acres to each head of a family other than to the chiefs, to whom larger allotments may be made, which lands, when so allotted, shall be vested in said Indian and his heirs, without the right of alienation, and shall be evidenced by patent.

* * * * * * * * *

Approved, February 21, 1863.

No. 64 B.—An Act to provide a temporary government for the Territory of Arizona, and for other purposes.

Be it enacted by the Senate and House of Representatives of the United States of America in Congress assembled, That all that part of the present Territory of New Mexico situate west of a line running due south from the point where the southwest corner of the Territory of Colorado joins the northern boundary of the Territory of New Mexico to the southern boundary line of said Territory of New Mexico be, and the same is hereby, erected into a temporary government by the name of the Territory of Arizona: *Provided,* That nothing contained in the provisions of this act shall be construed to prohibit the Congress of the United States from dividing said Territory or changing its boundaries in such manner and at such time as it may deem proper: *Provided further,* That said government shall be maintained and continued until such time as the people residing in said Territory shall, with the consent of Congress, form a State government, republican in form, as prescribed in the Constitution of the United States, and apply for and obtain admission into the Union as a State, on an equal footing with the original States.

* * * * * * * * *

[SEC. 2. *Provides for the appointment of a Surveyor-General, continues in force the act organizing the Territory of New Mexico, and extends the same to Arizona.*]

Approved, February 24, 1863.

No. 65 B.—An Act for increasing the revenue by reservation and sale of town sites on public lands.

Be it enacted by the Senate and House of Representatives of the United States of America in Congress assembled, That it shall be the duty of the President of the United States to reserve from the public lands, whether surveyed or unsurveyed, town sites on the shores of harbors, at the junction of rivers, important portages, or any natural or prospective centres of population.

SEC. 2. *And be it further enacted,* That when, in the opinion of the President, the public interests require it, it shall be the duty of the Secretary of the Interior to cause any of said reservations, or part thereof, to be surveyed into urban or suburban lots of suitable size, and to fix by appraisement of disinterested persons their cash value, and to offer the same for sale at public outcry to the highest bidder, and thence afterward to be held subject to sale at private entry according to such regulations as the Secretary of the Interior may prescribe: *Provided,* That no lot shall be disposed of at public sale or private entry for less than the appraised value thereof: *And provided further,* That said sales shall be conducted by the register and receiver of the land office in the district in which said reservations may be situated, in accordance with the laws and rules and instructions of the department regulating the sales of public lands.

Approved, March 3, 1863.

No. 66 B.—An Act to provide for the disposal of certain lands therein named

Be it enacted by the Senate and House of Representatives of the United States of America in Congress assembled, That the Commissioner of the General Land Office shall, as soon as may be, cause that portion of the public domain known as the Fort Howard Military Reserve, including the site of the fort, containing three acres and four-hundredths of an acre, which is situated in the county of Brown and State of Wisconsin, between Fox River and Beaver Dam Run, and which is not included in the confirmations to Talbot C. Dousman and Daniel Whitney, nor in the grant to the State of Wisconsin under the resolution of Congress approved April twenty-fifth, eighteen hundred and sixty-two, entitled "A resolution explanatory of, and in addition to, the act of June third, eighteen hundred and fifty-six, granting public lands to the State of Wisconsin to aid in the construction of railroads in said State,"* as heretofore surveyed under the direction of the Surveyor-General of Wisconsin and Iowa, to be surveyed and subdivided into lots of such form and of such size, not less than one-fourth of an acre, and not more than forty acres, as he may deem expedient, dedicating such portions of the same to the use of the public for streets and highways as he may think the public interest and convenience may require; and shall cause a plat thereof to be duly and properly certified by such Surveyor-General, and recorded in the office of the register of deeds for said county of Brown; and when so surveyed, platted, and recorded, he shall cause each and all said lots to be sold separately at public auction, giving not less than two months' notice of the time and place of such sale by advertising the same in such newspapers and for such period of time as he may deem best. Every such lot shall be sold to the highest bidder for cash, and when not paid for within twenty-four hours from the time of purchase, it shall be liable to be resold under the order of the Commissioner of the General Land Office aforesaid, but no sale shall be binding until approved by the Secretary of the Interior.

SEC. 2. *And be it further enacted,* That it shall be the duty of the President to cause patents to be issued in due form of law for each and every such lot as soon as may be after the purchase of and payment for the same.

SEC. 3. *And be it further enacted,* That it shall also be the duty of the Commissioner of the Land Office to cause so much of the public domain adjacent to said reserve as lies between said Beaver Dam Run and Duck Creek to be re-surveyed into lots, the lines of which shall conform as near as may be to the lines of the survey formerly made by Albert G. Ellis, and shall cause certified plats thereof to be returned, as is provided by law in the case of other surveys of the public domain; and he shall thereupon proceed to dispose of the same as other public lands are disposed of, saving to every person who, upon the passage of this act, may be in possession of any part of said lands, and shall have made improvements thereon, as provided under the pre-emption laws of the United States, the right to purchase any lots so improved, lying contiguous to each other, and not exceeding in the aggregate eighty acres, upon making proof of such possession and improvements, and paying for such lots the sum of one dollar and twenty-five cents per acre, within six months after public notice shall be given of the time and place for making such proof and payment.

* See No. 58 B.

SEC. 4. *And be it further enacted,* That the Commissioner of the General Land Office shall cause the military reserve of Fort Crawford, in the County of Crawford, in the same State, to be surveyed and disposed of in the manner prescribed in the first and second sections of this act, for the disposition of the Fort Howard Reserve.

Approved, March 3, 1863.

No. 67 B.—An Act for a grant of lands to the State of Kansas, in alternate sections, to aid in the construction of certain railroads and telegraphs in said State.*

Be it enacted by the Senate and House of Representatives of the United States of America in Congress assembled, That there be, and is hereby, granted to the State of Kansas, for the purpose of aiding in the construction: First. Of a railroad and telegraph from the city of Leavenworth, by the way of the town of Lawrence, and via the Ohio City crossing of the Osage River, to the southern line of the State, in the direction of Galveston Bay, in Texas, with a branch from Lawrence by the valley of the Wakarusa River, to the point on the Atchison, Topeka, and Santa Fé Railroad where said road intersects the Neosho River. Second. Of a railroad from the city of Atchison, via Topeka, the capital of said State, to the western line of the State, in the direction of Fort Union and Santa Fé, New Mexico, with a branch from where this last-named road crosses the Neosho, down said Neosho Valley to the point where the said first-named road enters the said Neosho Valley; every alternate section of land, designated by odd numbers, for ten sections in width on each side of said road and each of its branches. But in case it shall appear that the United States have, when the lines or routes of said road and branches are definitely fixed, sold any section, or any part thereof, granted as aforesaid, or that the right of pre-emption or homestead settlement has attached to the same, or that the same has been reserved by the United States for any purpose whatever, then it shall be the duty of the Secretary of the Interior to cause to be selected, for the purposes aforesaid, from the public lands of the United States nearest to tiers of sections above specified, so much land, in alternate sections, or parts of sections, designated by odd numbers, as shall be equal to such lands as the United States have sold, reserved, or otherwise appropriated, or to which the rights of pre-emption or homestead settlements have attached as aforesaid; which lands, thus indicated by odd numbers and selected by direction of the Secretary of the Interior, as aforesaid, shall be held by the State of Kansas for the use and purpose aforesaid: *Provided,* That the land to be so selected shall, in no case, be located further than twenty miles from the lines of said road and branches: *Provided further,* That the lands hereby granted for and on account of said roads and branches severally, shall be exclusively applied in the construction of the same, and for no other purpose whatever, and shall be disposed of only as the work progresses through the same, as in this act hereinafter provided: *Provided, also,* That no part of the land granted by this act shall be applied to aid in the construction of any railroad, or part thereof, for the construction of which any previous grant of land or bonds may have

* See No. 106 B.

been made by Congress: *And provided further*, That any and all lands heretofore reserved to the United States, by any act of Congress, or in any other manner by competent authority, for the purpose of aiding in any object of internal improvement, or for any other purpose whatsoever, be, and the same are hereby, reserved to the United States from the operations of this act, except so far as it may be found necessary to locate the routes of said road and branches through such reserved lands; in which case the right of way only shall be granted, subject to the approval of the President of the United States.

SEC. 2. *And be it further enacted*, That the sections and parts of sections of land which, by such grant, shall remain to the United States, within ten miles on each side of said road and branches, shall not be sold for less than double the minimum price of the public lands when sold; nor shall any of said lands become subject to sale at private entry until the same shall have been first offered at public sale to the highest bidder, at or above the increased minimum price, as aforesaid: *Provided*, That actual and bona fide settlers, under the provisions of the pre-emption and homestead laws of the United States, may, after due proof of settlement, improvement, cultivation, and occupation, as now provided by law, purchase the same, at the increased minimum price aforesaid: *And provided, also*, That settlers on any of said reserved sections, under the provisions of the homestead law, who improve, occupy, and cultivate the same for a period of five years, and comply with the several conditions and requirements of said act, shall be entitled to patents for an amount not exceeding eighty acres each, anything in this act to the contrary notwithstanding.

SEC. 3. *And be it further enacted*, That the said lands hereby granted to said State shall be subject to the disposal of the legislature thereof, for the purposes aforesaid, and no other; and the said railroads and branches shall be and remain public highways, for the use of the Government of the United States, free from all toil or other charge upon the transportation of any property or troops of the United States.

SEC. 4. *And be it further enacted*, That the lands hereby granted to said State shall be disposed of by said State only in manner following, that is to say: when the Governor of said State shall certify to the Secretary of the Interior that any twenty consecutive miles of either of said roads or branches is completed in a good, substantial, and workmanlike manner, as a first-class railroad, and the said Secretary shall be satisfied that said State has complied in good faith with this requirement, the said State may cause to be sold all the lands granted as aforesaid situated opposite to and within a limit of ten miles of the line of said section of road thus completed, extending along the whole length of said completed section of twenty miles of road, and no further. And when the Governor of said State shall certify to the Secretary of the Interior, and the Secretary shall be satisfied, that another section of said roads or branches, twenty consecutive miles in extent, connecting with the preceding section, is completed as aforesaid, the said State may cause to be sold all the lands granted and situated opposite to and within the limit of ten miles of the line of said completed section of road, and extending the length of said section, and so, from time to time, until said roads and branches are completed. And when the Governor of said State shall so certify, and the Secretary of the Interior shall be satisfied, that the whole of said roads and branches and telegraph are completed in a good, substantial, and workmanlike manner, as first-class railroads and telegraph, the said State may cause to be sold all the remaining lands granted and selected for the purposes indicated in this act situated within the said limits of twenty miles from the line thereof throughout the entire length of said road and branches: *Provided*, That if any part of said roads and branches is not completed within ten years from the passage of this act, no further sale shall be made, and the lands unsold shall revert to the United States.

SEC. 5. *And be it further enacted*, That the United States mail shall be transported over said roads and branches, under the direction of the Post-Office Department, at such price as Congress may by law direct; *Provided*, That until such price is fixed by law the Postmaster-General shall have the power to determine the same.

Approved, March 3, 1863.

No. 68 B.—An Act making appropriations for the current and contingent expenses of the Indian Department, and for fulfilling treaty stipulations with various Indian Tribes, for the year ending June thirtieth, eighteen hundred and sixty-four.

* * * * * * * * *

SEC. 4. *And be it further enacted*, That the President of the United States be, and is hereby, authorized to enter into treaties with the several tribes of Indians, respectively, now residing in the State of Kansas, providing for the extinction of their titles to lands held in common within said State, and for the removal of such Indians of said tribes as hold their lands in common to suitable localities, elsewhere within the territoral limits of the United States, and outside the limits of any State.

SEC. 5. *And be it further enacted*, That the President of the United States be, and is hereby, authorized to enter into negotiations, by treaty or otherwise, with such loyal tribes, or the loyal portions of such tribes, now residing in the country south of Kansas and west of Arkansas, commonly known as the "Indian Country" as may be necessary in order to secure for the Indians of Kansas who shall be removed to said Indian country under the provisions of the preceding section of this act, the title to the lands to which they may be so removed.

* * * * * * * * *

Approved, March 3, 1863.

No. 69 B.—An Act granting lands to the States of Michigan and Wisconsin to aid in the construction of a "military road" from Fort Wilkins, Copper Harbor, Kewenaw County, in the State of Michigan, to Fort Howard, Green Bay, in the State of Wisconsin.*

Be it enacted by the Senate and House of Representatives of the United States of America in Congress assembled, That there be, and is hereby, granted to the State of Michigan, to aid in the construction of a military wagon-road from Fort Wilkins, Copper Harbor, to Houghton, Portage Lake, and thence, in a southerly direction, to the State line of Wisconsin, every alternate section of public land, designated by even numbers, for three sections in width, on each side of said road, and also a like quantity, to be taken and designated in same manner, to the State of Wisconsin, to aid in the construction of a like road from the last-mentioned place

* Amended, No. 207 B.

on the State line of Wisconsin to Fort Howard, Green Bay, in the said State of Wisconsin. But in case it shall appear that the United States have, when the line or route of said road is definitely fixed, sold any section, or any part thereof, granted as aforesaid, or that the right of pre-emption or homestead settlement has attached to the same, then it shall be the duty of the Secretary of the Interior to set apart from the public lands of the United States, as near to said even sections aforesaid as may be, so much land as shall be equal to such lands as the United States have sold, or otherwise appropriated, or to which the right of pre-emption or homestead settlement has attached; which lands (thus selected in lieu of those sold, and to which the right of pre-emption or homestead settlement has attached as aforesaid), together with the sections and parts of sections designated by even numbers as aforesaid, and approved as aforesaid, shall be held by the States of Michigan and Wisconsin for the use and purposes aforesaid: *Provided,* That the lands to be selected for and on account thereof shall in no case be further than fifteen miles from said road: *Provided further,* That the lands hereby granted shall be exclusively applied in the construction of that road for and on account of which such lands are hereby granted, and shall be disposed of only as the work progresses, and the same shall be applied to no other purposes whatever: *And provided further,* That any and all lands heretofore reserved to the United States by any act of Congress, or in any other manner by competent authority, for the purpose of aiding in any object of internal improvement, or for any other purposes whatsoever, be, and the same are hereby, reserved to the United States from the operation of this act, except so far as it may be found necessary to locate the route of said road through such reserved lands; in which case the right of way only shall be granted.

SEC. 2. *And be it further enacted,* That the said lands hereby granted to the said States shall be subject to the disposal of the legislature thereof, for the purposes aforesaid, and no other; and the said road shall be and remain [a] public highway for the use of the Government of the United States, free from tolls or other charge upon the transportation of any property, troops, or mails of the United States.

SEC. 3. *And be it further enacted,* That the lands hereby granted to said States shall be disposed of only in the following manner, that is to say: That a quantity of land, not exceeding thirty sections, for said road, may be sold; and when the Governors of said States shall certify to the Secretary of the Interior that any ten continuous miles of said road are completed, then another quantity of land, hereby granted, not to exceed thirty sections for said road, having ten continuous miles completed as aforesaid, may be sold, and so, from time to time, until the said road is completed; and if said road is not completed within five years, no further sales shall be made, and the lands unsold shall revert to the United States.

SEC. 4 *And be it further enacted,* That said military road shall be constructed with sufficient drains and ditches, and not less than forty feet in width, with a grade not less than sixteen feet wide, with such graduation and bridges as shall permit of its regular use as a wagon road in all seasons of the year, and in such other special manner as the States of Michigan and Wisconsin may prescribe.

Approved, March 3, 1863.

No. 70 B.—An Act to grant the right of pre-emption to certain purchasers on the "Soscol Ranch," in the State of California.

Be it enacted by the Senate and House of Representatives of the United States of America in Congress assembled, That it may and shall be lawful for the Commissioner of the General Land Office to cause the lines of the public surveys to be extended over the tract of country known as the "Soscol Ranch," in California, the claim to which by Don Mariana Ga*u*dalupe Vallejo has been adju*gd*ed invalid by the Supreme Court of the United States, and to have approved plats thereof duly returned to the proper district land office: *Provided,* That the actual cost of such survey and platting shall first be paid into the surveying fund by settlers, according to the requirements of the tenth section of the act of Congress, approved thirtieth of May, eighteen hundred and sixty-two, "to reduce the expenses of the survey and sale of the public lands in the United States."

SEC. 2. *And be it further enacted,* That after the return of such approved plats to the district office, it may and shall be lawful for individuals, bona fide purchasers from said Vallejo, or his assigns, to enter, according to the lines of the public surveys, at one dollar and twenty-five cents per acre, the land so purchased, to the extent to which the same had been reduced to possession at the time of said adjudication of said Supreme Court, joint entries being admissible by coterminous proprietors to such an extent as will enable them to adjust their respective boundaries.

SEC. 3. *And be it further enacted,* That municipal claims within the limits of the said "Soscol Ranch" may be entered under the terms, limitations, and conditions of the town-site act of twenty-third of May, eighteen hundred and forty-four.

SEC. 4. *And be it further enacted,* That all claims within the purview of this act shall be presented to the register and receiver within twelve months after the return of such surveys to the district land office, accompanied by proof of bona fide purchase under Vallejo, of settlement, and the extent to which the tracts claimed had been reduced into possession at the time of said adjudication; and thereupon each case shall be adjudged by the register and receiver under such instructions as shall be given by the Commissioner of the General Land Office, to whom the proof and adjudication shall be returned by the local land office, and no adjudication shall be final until confirmed by the said commissioner.

SEC. 5. *And be it further enacted,* That any claim not brought before the register and receiver within twelve months, as aforesaid, shall be barred, and the lands covered thereby, with any other tracts within the limits of said "Soscol Ranch," the titles to which are not established under this act, shall be dealt with as other public lands: *Provided,* That no entry shall be made of lands reserved and occupied for military, naval, or other public uses, or which may be designated for such purposes by the President, nor shall any claim under this act extend to mineral lands.

Approved, March 3, 1863.

No. 71 B.—An Act to provide a temporary government for the Territory of Idaho.

Be it enacted by the Senate and House of Representatives of the United States of America in Congress assembled, That all that part of the territory of the United States included within the following limits, to wit: Beginning at a point in the middle channel of the Snake River where northern boundary of Oregen intersects the same; then follow down said channel of Snake River to a point opposite the mouth of the Kooskooskia, or Clear Water River; thence due north to the forty-ninth parallel of latitude; thence east along said parallel to the twenty-seventh degree of longitude west of Washington; thence south along said degree of longitude to the northern boundary of Colorado Territory; thence west along said boundary to the thirty-third degree of longitude west of Washington; thence north along said degree to the forty-second parallel of latitude; thence west along said parallel to the eastern boundary of the State of Oregon; thence north along said boundary to place of beginning. And the same is hereby created into a temporary government, by the name of the Territory of Idaho: *Provided,* That nothing in this act contained shall be construed to inhibit the Government of the United States from dividing said territory or changing its boundaries in such manner and at such time as Congress shall deem convenient and proper, or from attaching any portion of said territory to any other State or territory of the United States: *Provided, further,* That nothing in this act contained shall be construed to impair the rights of person or property now pertaining to the Indians in said territory, so long as such rights shall remain unextinguished by treaty between the United States and such Indians, or to include any territory which, by treaty with any Indian tribes, is not, without the consent of said tribe, to be included within the territorial limits or jurisdiction of any State or territory; but all such territory shall be excepted out of the boundaries, and constitute no part of the Territory of Idaho, until said tribe shall signify their assent to the President of the United States to be included within said territory, or to affect the authority of the Government of the United States to make any regulations respecting such Indians, their lands, property, or other rights, by treaty, law, or otherwise, which it would have been competent for the Government to make if this act had never passed.

* * * * * * * * *

SEC. 14. *And be it further enacted,* That when the lands in the said territory shall be surveyed, under the direction of the Government of the United States, preparatory to bringing the same into market, sections numbered sixteen and thirty-six in each township in said territory shall be, and the same are hereby, reserved for the purpose of being applied to schools in said territory, and in the States and territories hereafter to be erected out of the same.

* * * * * * * * *

Approved, March 3, 1863.

No. 72 B.—An Act for the removal of the Sisseton, Wahpaton, Medawakanton, and Wahpakoota Bands of Sioux or Dakota Indians, and for the disposition of their lands in Minnesota and Dakota.*

Be it enacted by the Senate and House of Representatives of the United States of America in Congress assembled, That the President is authorized and hereby directed to assign to and set apart for the Sisseton, Wahpaton,

* No. 205 B.

Medawakanton, and Wahpakoota bands of Sioux Indians a tract of unoccupied land outside of the limits of any State, sufficient in extent to enable him to assign to each member of said bands (who are willing to adopt the pursuit of agriculture) eighty acres of good agricultural lands, the same to be well adapted to agricultural purposes.

SEC. 2. *And be it further enacted,* That the several tracts of land within the reservations of the said Indians, shall be surveyed, under the direction of the Commissioner of the General Land Office, into legal subdivisions to conform to the surveys of the other public lands. And the Secretary of the Interior shall cause each legal subdivision of the said lands to be appraised by discreet persons to be appointed by him for that purpose. And in each instance where there are improvements upon any legal subdivision of said lands, the improvements shall be separately appraised. But no portion of the said lands shall be subject to pre-emption, settlement, entry, or location, under any act of Congress, unless the party pre-empting, settling upon, or locating any portion of said lands shall pay therefor the full appraised value thereof, including the value of the said improvements, under such regulations as hereinafter provided.

SEC. 3. *And be it further enacted,* That after the survey of the said reservations the same shall be open to pre-emption, entry, and settlement in the same manner as other public lands : *Provided,* That before any person shall be entitled to enter any portion of the said lands by pre-emption or otherwise, previous to their exposure to sale to the highest bidder, at public outcry, he shall become an actual bona fide settler thereon, and shall conform to all the regulatious now provided by law in cases of pre-emption ; and shall pay within the term of one year from the date of his settlement, the full appraised value of the land, and the improvements thereon, to the land officers of the district where the said lands are situated. And the portions of the said reservations which may not be settled upon, as aforesaid, may be sold at public auction, as other public lands are sold, after which they shall be subject to sale at private entry, as other public lands of the United States, but no portion thereof shall be sold for a sum less than their appraised value, before the first of January, Anno Domini eighteen hundred and sixty-five, nor for a less price than one dollar and twenty-five cents per acre, until otherwise provided for by law.

SEC. 4. *And be it further enacted,* That the money arising from said sale shall be invested by the Secretary of the Interior for the benefit of said Indians in their new homes, in the establishing them in agricultural pursuits : *Provided,* That it shall be lawful for said Secretary to locate any meritorious individual Indian of said bands, who exerted himself to save the lives of the whites in the late massacre upon said lands on which the improvements are situated, assigning the same to him to the extent of eighty acres, to be held by such tenure as is or may be provided by law : *And provided, further,* That no more than eighty acres shall be awarded to any one Indian, under this or any other act.

* * * * * * * * *

Approved, March 3, 1863.

No. 73 B.—An Act in relation to University lands in Washington Territory.

Whereas it is declared in the fourth section of the act of Congress approved July seventeenth, eighteen hundred and fifty-four, amendatory of the act approved September twenty-seventh, eighteen hundred and fifty,* creating the office of Surveyor-General of the public lands in Oregon, etc., "that in lieu of the two townships of land granted to the Territory of Oregon, by the tenth section of the act of eighteen hundred and fifty, for Universities, there shall be reserved to each of the Territories of Washington and Oregon, two townships of land of thirty-six sections each, to be selected in legal subdivisions, for University purposes, under the direction of the legislatures of said Territories respectively;" and whereas it is represented that sales have been made by territorial authorities of lands selected in virtue of the terms of said act of seventeenth of July, eighteen hundred and fifty-four, authorizing selections to be "reserved," merely under the conviction that they had the power to dispose of the same as a fee-simple grant: Therefore—

Be it enacted by the Senate and House of Representatives of the United States of America in Congress assembled, That in all cases of sales made to individuals by the territorial authorities prior to the passage of this act, in which it may be shown to the satisfaction of the Secretary of the Interior, that such sales were bona fide and of the class hereinbefore mentioned, and that the tracts so sold are selections in all other respects regular and proper, it shall and may be lawful for the said Secretary to approve such selection as a grant in fee-simple, and a transcript, certified under the seal of the General Land Office by the Commissioner thereof, of such approval, shall vest the title in the Territory and in its *bona fide* vendees.

Approved, March 14, 1864.

No. 74 B.—An Act to enable the people of Nevada to form a Constitution and State Government, and for the admission of such State into the Union on equal footing with the original States.†

Be it enacted by the Senate and House of Representatives of the United States of America in Congress assembled, That the inhabitants of that portion of the Territory of Nevada included in the boundaries hereinafter designated be, and they are hereby, authorized to form for themselves, out of said Territory, a State Government, with the name aforesaid, which said State, when formed, shall be admitted into the Union upon an equal footing with the original States, in all respects whatsoever.

SEC. 2. *And be it further enacted,* That the said State of Nevada shall consist of all the territory included within the following boundaries, to wit: Commencing at a point formed by the intersection of the thirty-eighth degree of longitude west from Washington with the thirty-seventh degree of north latitude; thence due west along said thirty-seventh degree of north latitude to the eastern boundary line of the State of California; thence in a northwesterly direction along the said eastern boundary line of the State of California to the forty-third degree of longitude west from Washington; thence north along said forty-third degree of west longitude and said eastern boundary line of the State of California to the forty-second degree of north latitude; thence due east along the said forty-second degree of north latitude to a point formed by its intersection with the aforesaid thirty-eighth degree of longitude west from

* Vol. I. No. 181.

† See Nos. 55 B. No. 74 B. No. 208 B.

Washington; thence due south down said thirty-eighth degree of west longitude to the place of beginning.

* * * * * * * * *

SEC. 3. * * * *And provided further*, That said convention shall provide, by an ordinance irrevocable, without the consent of the United States and the people of said State:—

* * * * * * * * *

Third. That the people inhabiting said Territory do agree and declare that they forever disclaim all right and title to appropriated public lands lying within said Territory, and that the same shall be and remain at the sole and entire disposition of the United States; and that the lands belonging to citizens of the United States residing without the said State shall never be taxed higher than the land belonging to the residents thereof, and that no taxes shall be imposed by said State on lands or property therein belonging to, or which may hereafter be purchased by, the United States.

* * * * * * * * *

SEC. 7. *And be it further enacted*, That sections numbered sixteen and thirty-six, in every township, and where such sections have been sold or otherwise disposed of by any act of Congress, other lands equivalent thereto in legal subdivisions of not less than one quarter-section, and as contiguous as may be, shall be, and are hereby, granted to said State for the support of common schools.

SEC. 8. *And be it further enacted*, That provided the State of Nevada shall be admitted into the Union, in accordance with the foregoing provisions of this act, *that* twenty entire sections of the unappropriated public lands within said State, to be selected and located by direction of the legislature thereof, on or before the first day of January, Anno Domini eighteen hundred and sixty-eight, shall be, and they are hereby, granted, in legal subdivisions of not less than one hundred and sixty acres, to said State, for the purpose of erecting public buildings at the capital of said State, for legislative and judicial purposes, in such manner as the legislature shall prescribe.

SEC. 9. *And be it further enacted*, That twenty other entire sections of land, as aforesaid, to be selected and located as aforesaid, in legal subdivisions, as aforesaid, shall be, and they are hereby, granted to said State for the purpose of erecting a suitable building for a penitentiary or State prison in the manner aforesaid.

SEC. 10. *And be it further enacted*, That five per centum of the proceeds of the sales of all public lands lying within said State, which shall be sold by the United States subsequent to the admission of said State into the Union, after deducting all the expenses incident to the same, shall be paid to the said State for the purpose of making and improving public roads, constructing ditches or canals, to effect a general system of irrigation of the agricultural land in the State, as the legislature shall direct.

SEC. 11. *And be it further enacted*, That from and after the admission of the said State of Nevada into the Union, in pursuance of this act, the laws of the United States, not locally inapplicable, shall have the same force and effect within the said State as elsewhere within the United States, and said State shall constitute one judicial district, and be called the District of Nevada.

Approved, March 21, 1864.

No. 75 B.—An Act to enable the people of Colorado to form a Constitution and State Government, and for the admission of such State into the Union on an equal footing with the original States.

Be it enacted by the Senate and House of Representatives of the United States of America in Congress assembled, That the inhabitants of that portion of the territory of Colorado included in the boundaries hereinafter designated be, and they are hereby, authorized to form for themselves, out of said territory, a State government, with the name aforesaid; which said State, when formed, shall be admitted into the Union upon an equal footing with the original States, in all respects whatsoever.

SEC. 2. *And be it further enacted,* That the said State of Colorado shall consist of all the territory included within the following boundaries, to wit: Commencing at a point formed by the intersection of the thirty-seventh degree of north latitude with the twenty-fifth degree of longitude west from Washington; extending thence due west along said thirty-seventh degree of north latitude to a point formed by its intersection with the thirty-second degree of longitude west from Washington; thence due north along said thirty-second degree of west longitude to a point formed by its intersection with the forty-first degree of north latitude; thence due east along said forty-first degree of north latitude to a point formed by its intersection with the twenty-fifth degree of longitude west from Washington; thence due south along said twenty-fifth degree of west longitude.

* * * * * * * * *

SEC. 3. * * * *And provided, further,* That said convention shall provide, by an ordinance, irrevocable without the consent of the United States and the people of said State:—

* * * * * * * * *

Third. That the people inhabiting said territory do agree and declare that they forever disclaim all right and title to the unappropriated public lands lying within said territory, and that the same shall be and remain at the sole and entire disposition of the United States, and that the lands belonging to citizens of the United States, residing without the said State, shall never be taxed higher than the land belonging to residents thereof, and that no taxes shall be imposed by said State on lands or property therein belonging to, or which may hereafter be purchased by the United States.

* * * * * * * * *

SEC. 7. *And be it further enacted,* That sections numbered sixteen and thirty-six, in every township, and where such sections have been sold, or otherwise disposed of by any act of Congress, other lands equivalent thereto in legal subdivisions of not less than one quarter-section, and as contiguous as may be, shall be, and are hereby, granted to said state for the support of common schools.

SEC. 8. *And be it further enacted,* That provided the State of Colorado shall be admitted into the Union, in accordance with the foregoing provisions of this act, *that* twenty entire sections of the unappropriated public lands within said State, to be selected and located by direction of the legislature thereof on or before the first day of January, Anno Domini eighteen hundred and sixty-eight, shall be, and they are hereby, granted in legal subdivisions of not less than one hundred and sixty acres to said State, for the purpose of erecting public buildings at the capital of said State for legislative and judicial purposes, in such manner as the legislature shall prescribe.

SEC. 9. *And be it further enacted,* That twenty other entire sections of land, as aforesaid, to be selected and located as aforesaid, in legal subdivisions as aforesaid, shall be, and they are hereby, granted to said State for the purpose of erecting a suitable building for a penitentiary or State prison in the manner aforesaid.

SEC. 10. *And be it further enacted,* That five per centum of the proceeds of the sales of all public lands lying within said State, which shall be sold by the United States subsequent to the admission of said State into the Union, after deducting all the expenses incident to the same, shall be paid to the said State, for the purpose of making and improving public roads, constructing ditches or canals, to effect a general system of irrigation of the agricultural land in the State, as the legislature shall direct.

SEC. 11. *And be it further enacted,* That from and after the admission of the said State of Colorado into the Union, in pursuance of this act, the laws of the United States not locally inapplicable shall have the same force and effect within the said State as elsewhere within the United States, and said State shall constitute one judicial district, and be called the District of Colorado.

Approved, March 21, 1864.

No. 76 B.—An Act amendatory of the homestead law, and for other purposes.

Be it enacted by the Senate and House of Representatives of the United States of America in Congress assembled, That in case of any person desirous of availing himself of the benefits of the homestead act of twentieth of May, eighteen hundred and sixty-two,* but who, by reason of actual service in the military or naval service of the United States, is unable to do the personal preliminary acts at the district land office which the said act of twentieth May, eighteen hundred and sixty-two, requires, and whose family, or some member thereof, is residing on the land which he desires to enter, and upon which a bona fide improvement and settlement have been made, it shall and may be lawful for such person to make the affidavit required by said act before the officer commanding in the branch of the service in which the party may be engaged, which affidavit shall be as binding in law, and with like penalties, as if taken before the register or receiver; and upon such affidavit being filed with the register by the wife or other representative of the party, the same shall become effective from the date of such filing, provided the said application and affidavit are accompanied by the fee and commissions, as required by law.

SEC. 2. *And be it further enacted,* That besides the ten-dollar fee exacted by the said act, the homestead applicant shall hereafter pay to the register and receiver each, as commissions, at the time of entry, one per centum upon the cash price as fixed by law, of the land applied for, and like commissions when the claim is finally established and the certificate therefor issued as the basis of a patent.

SEC. 3. *And be it further enacted,* That in any case hereafter in which the applicant for the benefit of the homestead, and whose family, or some member thereof, is residing on the land which he desires to enter, and

* See No. 38 B. and No. 146 B.

upon which a bona fide improvement and settlement have been made, is prevented, by reason of distance, bodily infirmity, or other good cause, from personal attendance at the district land office, it shall and may be lawful for him to make the affidavit required by the original statute before the clerk of the court for the county in which the applicant is an actual resident, and to transmit the same, with the fee and commissions, to the register and receiver.

SEC. 4. *And be it further enacted*, That in lieu of the fee allowed by the twelfth section of the pre-emption act of fourth September, eighteen hundred and forty-one, the register and receiver shall each be entitled to one dollar for their services in acting upon pre-emption claims, and shall be allowed, jointly, at the rate of fifteen cents per hundred words for the testimony which may be reduced by them to writing for claimants, in establishing pre-emption or homestead rights, the regulations for giving proper effect to the provisions of this act to be prescribed by the Commissioner of the General Land Office.

SEC. 5. *And be it further enacted*, That where a pre-emptor has taken the initiatory steps required by existing laws in regard to actual settlement, and is called away from such settlement by being actually engaged in the military or naval service of the United States, and by reason of such absence is unable to appear at the district land office, to make, before the register or receiver, the affidavits required by the thirteenth section of the pre-emption act of fourth of September, eighteen hundred and forty-one, the time for filing such affidavit and making final proof and entry or location, shall be extended six months after the expiration of his term of service, upon satisfactory proof by affidavit, or the testimony of witnesses, that the said pre-emptor is so in the service, being filed with the register of the land office for the district in which his settlement is made.

SEC. 6. *And be it further enacted*, That the registers and receivers in the State of California, in the State of Oregon, and in the Territories of Washington, Nevada, Colorado, Idaho, New Mexico, and Arizona, shall be entitled to collect and receive, in addition to the fees and allowances provided by this act, fifty per centum of said fees and allowances as compensation for their services: *Provided*, That the salary and fees allowed any register or receiver shall not exceed in the aggregate the sum of three thousand dollars per annum.

Approved, March 21, 1864.

No. 77 B.—An Act to provide for the better organization of Indian affairs in California.*

Be it enacted by the Senate and House of Representatives of the United States of America in Congress assembled, That, from and after the first day of April, Anno Domini eighteen hundred and sixty-four, the State of California shall, for Indian purposes, constitute one superintendency, for which there shall be appointed by the President of the United States, by and with the advice and consent of the Senate, a superintendent of Indian affairs for said superintendency, at a salary of three thousand six hundred dollars per annum, who shall reside at a point within said State, to be selected by the Secretary of the Interior, and who, upon executing a bond,

* Amended No. 134 B.

upon such terms and such sum as may be prescribed by the Secretary of the Interior, and taking the usual oath of office, shall have under his control and management, in like manner and subject to like rules and regulations as are prescribed for superintendents of other superintendencies, the Indians and Indian reservations that are or may hereafter be established in said State: *Provided*, That the superintendent shall be authorized to appoint a clerk, at a compensation not to exceed eighteen hundred dollars per annum.

SEC. 2. *And be it further enacted*, That there shall be set apart by the President, and at his discretion, not exceeding four tracts of land, within the limits of said State to be retained by the United States for the purposes of Indian reservations, which shall be of suitable extent for the accommodation of the Indians of said State, and shall be located as remote from white settlements as may be found practicable, having due regard to their adaptation to the purposes for which they are intended: *Provided*, That at least one of said tracts shall be located in what has heretofore been known as the northern district: *And provided further*, That if it shall be found impracticable to establish the reservations herein contemplated without embracing improvements made within their limits by white persons lawfully there, the Secretary of the Interior is hereby authorized and empowered to contract for the purchase of such improvements, at a price not exceeding a fair valuation thereof, to be made under his direction. But no such contract shall be valid, nor any money paid thereon, until, upon a report of said contract and of said valuation to Congress, the same shall be approved and the money appropriated by law for that purpose: *And provided further*, That said tracts to be set apart as aforesaid may, or may not, as in the discretion of the President may be deemed for the best interests of the Indians to be provided for, include any of the Indian reservations heretofore set apart in said State, and that in case any such reservation is so included, the same may be enlarged to such an extent as in the opinion of the President may be necessary, in order to its complete adaptation to the purposes for which it is intended.

SEC. 3. *And be it further enacted*, That the several Indian reservations in California which shall not be retained for the purposes of Indian reservations under the provisions of the preceding section of this act, shall, by the Commissioner of the General Land Office, under the direction of the Secretary of the Interior, be surveyed into lots or parcels of suitable size, and as far as practicable in conformity to the surveys of the public lands, which said lots shall, under his direction, be appraised by disinterested persons at their cash value, and shall thereupon, after due advertisement, as now provided by law in case of other public lands, be offered for sale at public outcry, and thence afterward shall be held subject to sale at private entry, according to such regulations as the Secretary of the Interior may prescribe: *Provided*, That no lot shall be disposed of at less than the appraised value, nor at less than one dollar and twenty-five cents per acre: *And provided further*, That said sale shall be conducted by the register and receiver of the land office in the district in which such reservation or reservations may be situated, in accordance with the instructions of the department regulating the sale of public land.

SEC. 4. *And be it further enacted*, That the President of the United States be, and he is hereby, authorized, by and with the advice and consent of the Senate, to appoint an Indian agent for each of the reservations which shall be established under the provisions of this act, which said agent shall reside upon the reservation for which he shall be appointed, and shall discharge all the duties now or hereafter to be required of

Indian agents by law, or by rules and regulations adopted, or to be adopted for the regulation of the Indian service, so far as the same may be applicable. Each of the agents appointed as aforesaid shall, before entering upon the duties of his office, give bond in such penalties and with such conditions and such security as the President or Secretary of the Interior may require, and shall hold his office for the term of four years, unless sooner removed by the President, and shall receive an annnal salary at the rate of eighteen hundred dollars.

SEC. 5. *And be it further enacted*, That there may be appointed, in the manner prescribed by law, for each of said reservations, if in the opinion of the Secretary of the Interior the welfare of said Indians shall require it, one physician, one blacksmith, one assistant blacksmith, one farmer, and one carpenter, who shall each receive compensation at rates to be determined by the Secretary of the Interior, not exceeding fifty dollars per month.

SEC. 6. *And be it further enacted*, That hereafter, when it shall become necessary to survey any Indian or other reservations, or any lands, the same shall be surveyed under the direction and control of the General Land Office, and as nearly as may be in conformity to the rules and regulations under which other public lands are surveyed.

SEC. 7. *And be it further enacted*, That all Indian agents shall reside at their respective agencies, and shall in no case be permitted to visit the city of Washington except when ordered to do so by the Commissioner of Indian affairs. And it is hereby made the duty of the said Commissioner to report all cases of the violation of this section to the President, with the request that the agents disregarding the provisions herein contained be at once removed from office.

SEC. 8. *And be it further enacted*, That all acts or parts of acts in conflict with the provisions of this act, be, and the same are hereby, repealed; and all offices and employments connected with Indian affairs in California not provided for in this act be, and the same are hereby, abolished.

Approved, April 8, 1864.

No. 78 B.—An Act extending the time within which the States and Territories may accept the grant of lands made by the act entitled "An Act donating public lands to the several States and Territories which may provide colleges for the benefit of agriculture and the mechanic arts," approved July second, eighteen hundred and sixty-two.*

Be it enacted by the Senate and House of Representatives of the United States of America in Congress assembled, That any State or Territory may accept and shall be entitled to the benefits of the act entitled "An act donating public lands to the several States and Territories which may provide colleges for the benefit of agriculture and the mechanic arts," approved July second, eighteen hundred and sixty-two, by expressing its acceptance thereof as provided in said act, within two years from the date of the approval of this act, subject, however, to the conditions in said act contained.

SEC. 2. *And be it further enacted*, That the benefit of the provisions of

* No. 47 B.

this act, and of the said act approved July second, eighteen hundred and sixty-two, be, and the same are hereby, extended to the State of West Virginia.

Approved, April 14, 1864.

No. 79 B.—An Act to enable the people of Nebraska to form a Constitution and State Government, and for the admission of such State into the Union on an equal footing with the original States.

Be it enacted by the Senate and House of Representatives of the United States of America in Congress assembled, That the inhabitants of that portion of the Territory of Nebraska included in the boundaries hereinafter designated be, and they are hereby, authorized to form for themselves a constitution and State government, with the name aforesaid, which State, when so formed, shall be admitted into the Union as hereinafter provided.

SEC. 2. *And be it further enacted,* That the said State of Nebraska shall consist of all the territory included within the following boundaries, to wit: Commencing at a point formed by the intersection of the western boundary of the State of Missouri with the fortieth degree of north latitude; extending thence due west along said fortieth degree of north latitude to a point formed by its intersection with the twenty-fifth degree of longitude west from Washington; thence north along said twenty-fifth degree of longitude to a point formed by its intersection with the forty-first degree of north latitude; thence west along said forty-first degree of north latitude to a point formed by its intersection with the twenty-seventh degree of longitude west from Washington; thence north along said twenty-seventh degree of west longitude to a point formed by its intersection with the forty-third degree of north latitude; thence east along said forty-third degree of north latitude to the Reya Paha River; thence down the middle of the channel of said river, with its meanderings, to its junction with the Niobrara River; thence down the middle of the channel of said Niobrara River, and following the meanderings thereof, to its junction with the Missouri River; thence down the middle of the channel of said Missouri River, and following the meanderings thereof, to the place of beginning.

* * * * * * * * *

SEC. 4. * * * *And provided further,* That said constitution shall provide, by an article forever irrevocable, without the consent of the Congress of the United States:

* * * * * * * * *

Third. That the people inhabiting said Territory do agree and declare that they forever disclaim all right and title to the unappropriated public lands lying within said Territory, and that the same shall be and remain at the sole and entire disposition of the United States, and that the lands belonging to citizens of the United States residing without the said State shall never be taxed higher than the land belonging to residents thereof; and that no taxes shall be imposed by said State on lands or property therein belonging to or which may hereafter be purchased by the United States.

* * * * * * * * *

SEC. 7. *And be it further enacted,* That sections numbered sixteen and thirty-six in every township, and when such sections have been sold or otherwise disposed of by any act of Congress, other lands equivalent thereto, in legal subdivisions of not less than one quarter section, and as contiguous as may be, shall be, and are hereby, granted to said State for the support of common schools.

SEC. 8. *And be it further enacted,* That provided the State of Nebraska shall be admitted into the Union in accordance with the foregoing provisions of this act, that twenty entire sections of the unappropriated public lands within said State, to be selected and located by direction of the legislature thereof, on or before the first day of January, Anno Domini eighteen hundred and sixty-eight, shall be and they are hereby granted, in legal subdivisions of not less than one hundred and sixty acres, to said State for the purpose of erecting public buildings at the capital of said State for legislative and judicial purposes, in such manner as the legislature shall prescribe.

SEC. 9. *And be it further enacted,* That fifty other entire sections of land, as aforesaid, to be selected and located as aforesaid, in legal subdivisions as aforesaid, shall be, and they are hereby, granted to said State for the purpose of erecting a suitable building for a penitentiary or State prison in the manner aforesaid.

SEC. 10. *And be it further enacted,* That seventy-two other sections of land shall be set apart and reserved for the use and support of a State university, to be selected in manner as aforesaid, and to be appropriated and applied as the legislature of said State may prescribe for the purpose named, and for no other purpose.

SEC. 11. *And be it further enacted,* That all salt springs within said State, not exceeding twelve in number, with six sections of land adjoining, or as contiguous as may be to each, shall be granted to said State for its use, the said land to be selected by the Governor thereof, within one year after the admission of the State, and when so selected to be used or disposed of on such terms, conditions, and regulations as the legislature shall direct: *Provided,* That no salt spring or lands, the right whereof is now vested in any individual or individuals, or which hereafter shall be confirmed or adjudged to any individual or individuals, shall, by this act, be granted to said State.

SEC. 12. *And be it further enacted,* That five per centum of the proceeds of the sales of all public lands lying within said State, which have been or shall be sold by the United States prior or subsequent to the admission of said State into the Union, after deducting all expenses incident to the same, shall be paid to the said State for the support of common schools.

SEC. 13. *And be it further enacted,* That from and after the admission of the said State of Nebraska into the Union in pursuance of this act, the laws of the United States, not locally inapplicable, shall have the same force aud effect within the said State as elsewhere within the United States; and said State shall constitute one judicial district, and be called the District of Nebraska.

* * * * * * * * *

Approved, April 19, 1864.

No. 80 B.—An Act in reference to donation claims in Oregon and Washington.

Be it enacted by the Senate and House of Representatives of the United States of America in Congress assembled, That whenever it shall appear that two donation settlers in the State of Oregon or Washington Territory shall hold their conterminous improvements in such a manner as may require a half quarter section to be divided into two eqnal parts by a line north and south or east and west, it shall and may be lawful for the Commissioner of the General Land Office to issue patents recognizing for each claimant such subdivisions; this enactment to include cases existing at the date of this act, where the claim may be proved and established according to law.*

Approved, April 29, 1864.

No. 81 B.—An Act to vacate and sell the present Indian reservations in Utah Territory, and to settle the Indians of said Territory in the Uinta Valley.

Be it enacted by the Senate and House of Representatives of the United States of America in Congress assembled, That the Secretary of the Interior be, and he is hereby, authorized and required to cause the several Indian reservations heretofore made, or occupied as such, in the Territory of Utah, excepting Uinta Valley, to be surveyed into tracts or lots, not exceeding eighty acres each, under the direction of the Commissioner of the General Land Office, and upon the completion of such surveys shall cause said tracts or lots to be sold, upon sealed bids, to be duly invited by public advertisement, for a period not less than three months, in a newspaper of general circulation published in the Territory of Utah, and also a newspaper published in Washington, to the highest and best bidder; said bids may be filed with the Governor of said Territory at the seat of government thereof, and with the Secretary of the Interior in Washington; such bids as may be received by said Governor shall, without opening the same, be forwarded to the Secretary of the Interior, when the same, with the bids filed with him, shall be opened in the presence of the Secretary of the Interior, the Commissioner of Public Lands, and the Commissioner of Indian Affairs, and any bidders who may choose to be present at the opening thereof; and the Secretary of the Interior shall apply the proceeds of such sales to the construction of improvements upon the reservations which may be established under the provisions of this act, or by other lawful authority, or to the purchase of stock, agricultural implements, or such other useful articles as to him may seem best adapted to the wants and requirements of the Indians: *Provided,* That no tract of land shall be sold under the provisions of this section for less than its appraised value in cash, to be duly ascertained by commissioners appointed by the Secretary of the Interior for that purpose.

SEC. 2. *And be it further enacted,* That the Superintendent of Indian Affairs for the Territory of Utah be, and he is hereby, authorized and required to collect and settle all or so many of the Indians of said Territory as may be found practicable in the Uinta Valley, in said Territory, which is hereby set apart for the permanent settlement and exclusive occupation of such of the different tribes of Indians of said Territory as may be induced to inhabit the same.

* * * * * * * * *

Approved, May 5, 1864.

* See Vol. I. No. 181. See also No. 98 B.

No. 82 B.—An Act making a grant of lands to the State of Minnesota, to aid in the construction of the railroad from St. Paul to Lake Superior.*

Be it enacted by the Senate and House of Representatives of the United States of America in Congress assembled, That there be, and there is hereby, granted to the State of Minnesota, for the purpose of aiding in the construction of a railroad in said State from the city of St. Paul to the head of Lake Superior, every alternate section of public land of the United States, not mineral, designated by odd numbers, to the amount of five alternate sections per mile on each side of the said railroad on the line thereof, within the State of Minnesota; but in case it shall appear that the United States have, when the line or route of said road is definitely fixed, sold, appropriated, reserved, or otherwise disposed of any sections, or any part thereof, granted as aforesaid, or that the right of pre-emption or homestead settlement has attached to the same, then it shall be the duty of the Secretary of the Interior to select from the lands of the United States nearest to the lines of sections above specified, in alternate sections, or parts thereof, so much public land of the United States, not mineral, as shall be equal in amount to such lands as the United States have sold or otherwise appropriated, or to which the rights of pre-emption or homestead settlement may have attached, as aforesaid; which lands thus selected in lieu of those sold, reserved, or otherwise appropriated or disposed of, or to which the rights of pre-emption or homestead settlement may have attached, as aforesaid, together with the sections and parts of sections designated as aforesaid, and appropriated as aforesaid, shall be held and disposed of by the said State for the use and purpose aforesaid: *Provided,* That the land to be so selected shall in no case be located farther than twenty miles from the lines of said road: *And provided further,* That the lands hereby granted for and on account of said road shall be exclusively applied in the construction of the same, and for no other purpose whatever, and shall be disposed of only as the work progresses through the same, as in this act hereinafter provided: *Provided also,* That no part of the land granted by this act shall be applied to aid in the construction of any railroad, or part thereof, for the construction of which any previous grant of land may have been made by Congress: *And provided further,* That any and all lands heretofore reserved to the United States by any act of Congress, or in any other manner by competent authority, for the purpose of aiding in any object of internal improvement, or for any other purpose whatsoever, be, and the same are hereby, reserved to the United States, from the operations of this act, except so far as it may be found necessary to locate the route of the said road through such reserved lands; in which case the right of way only shall be granted, subject to the approval of the President of the United States: *Provided further,* That the minimum price of the even sections and parts of sections of the public lands of the United States, within the limits of ten miles on each side of the line of said road, shall be two dollars and fifty cents per acre.

SEC. 2. *And be it further enacted,* That whenever said State shall cause to be completed twenty consecutive miles of any portion of said railroad, supplied with all necessary drains, culverts, viaducts, crossings, sidings, bridges, turn-outs, watering-places, depots, equipments, furniture, and all other appurtenances of a first-class railroad, patents shall issue convey-

* Amended, No. 161 B. No. 163 B.

ing the right and title to said lands to said State, on each side of the road, as far as the same is completed, and coterminous with said completed section, not exceeding the amount aforesaid, and patents shall in like manner issue as each twenty miles of said road is completed: *Provided, however,* That no patents shall issue for any of said lands unless there shall be presented to the Secretary of the Interior a statement, certified by the Governor of the State of Minnesota, that such twenty miles have been completed in the manner required by this act, and setting forth with certainty the points where such twenty miles begin and where the same end.

SEC. 3. *And be it further enacted,* That when the said road shall be definitely located, and a plat thereof filed with the Secretary of the Interior, the lands hereby granted shall not thereafter be subject to settlement, pre-emption, or private entry adverse to this grant.

SEC. 4. *And be it further enacted,* That the said State, in addition to the grant heretofore mentioned, is hereby authorized to locate the said road over any public lands of the United States, not otherwise appropriated, reserved, or disposed of, and that the right of way over said lands of the United States, for the purpose aforesaid, is hereby granted to said State to the width of one hundred feet on each side of said road as located.

SEC. 5. *And be it further enacted,* That the said lands hereby granted, when patented to said State, shall be subject to the disposal of said State for the purposes aforesaid, and for no other; and the said railroad shall be and remain a public highway for the use of the Government of the United States, free from all toll or other charge, for the transportation of any property or troops of the United States.

SEC. 6. *And be it further enacted,* That if said road is not completed within eight years from the time of the passage of this act, as provided herein, no further patents shall be issued for said lands, and no further sale shall be made, and the lands unsold shall revert to the United States.

SEC. 7. *And be it further enacted,* That the United States mail shall be transported over said road, under the direction of the Post-Office Department, at such price as Congress may by law direct: *Provided,* That until such price is fixed by law the Postmaster-General shall have the power to determine the same.

SEC. 8. *And be it further enacted,* That any railroad which may hereafter be constructed from any point on the Bay of Superior, in the State of Wisconsin, shall be permitted to connect with the said railroad, for the construction of which the said lands are hereby granted, at any point which may be selected by the president and directors of said railroad company so permitted to connect their said road, and the said railroad company so permitted to connect shall have the right and privilege to transport, or have transported, over the track of said railroad, for the construction of which the said lands are hereby granted, all or any of its cars, passengers, or freights, and the said railroad company controlling the said road, for the construction of which the said lands are hereby granted, shall have the same right and privilege to transport or have transported all or any of its cars, freights, or passengers over the track of the said railroad of the company so permitted to connect, and said transportation shall be paid by the railroad company using, to the railroad company according the same, at the usual rates or charges which may be imposed by the said company upon all other cars, freights, or passengers.

Approved, May 5, 1864.

No. 83 B.—An Act granting lands to aid in the construction of certain railroads in the State of Wisconsin.*

Be it enacted by the Senate and House of Representatives of the United States of America in Congress assembled, That there be, and is hereby, granted to the State of Wisconsin, for the purpose of aiding in the construction of a railroad from a point on the Saint Croix River or Lake, between townships twenty-five and thirty-one, to the west end of Lake Superior, and from some point on the line of said railroad, to be selected by said State, to Bayfield, every alternate section of public land designated by odd numbers, for ten sections in width on each side of said road, deducting any and all lands that may have been granted to the State of Wisconsin for the same purpose, by the act of Congress of June three, eighteen hundred and fifty-six, upon the same terms and conditions as are contained in the act granting lands to the State of Wisconsin, to aid in the construction of railroads in said State, approved June three, eighteen hundred and fifty-six.† But in case it shall appear that the United States have, when the line or route of said road is definitely fixed, sold, reserved, or otherwise disposed of, any sections or parts thereof, granted as aforesaid, or that the right of pre-emption or homestead has attached to the same, then it shall be lawful for any agent or agents, to be appointed by said company, to select, subject to the approval of the Secretary of the Interior, from the public lands of the United States nearest to the tier of sections above specified, as much land in alternate sections or parts of sections, as shall be equal to such lands as the United States have sold or otherwise appropriated, or to which the right of pre-emption or homestead has attached as aforesaid, which lands (thus selected in lieu of those sold, and to which pre-emption or homestead right has attached as aforesaid, together with sections and parts of sections designated by odd numbers as aforesaid, and appropriated as aforesaid) shall be held by said State for the use and purpose aforesaid : *Provided,* That the lands to be so located shall in no case be further than twenty miles from the line of the said roads, nor shall such selection or location be made in lieu of lands received under the said grant of June three, eighteen hundred and fifty-six, but such selection and location may be made for the benefit of said State, and for the purpose aforesaid, to supply any deficiency under the said grant of June third, eighteen hundred and fifty-six, should any such deficiency exist.

SEC. 2. *And be it further enacted,* That there be, and is hereby, granted to the State of Wisconsin, for the purpose of aiding in the construction of a railroad from the town of Tomah, in the county of Monroe, in said State, to the Saint Croix River or Lake, between townships twenty-five and thirty-one, every alternate section of public land designated by odd numbers for ten sections in width on each side of said road, deducting any and all lands that may have been granted to the State of Wisconsin for the same purpose, by the act of Congress granting lands to said State to aid in the construction of certain railroads, approved June three, eighteen hundred and fifty-six, upon the same terms and conditions as are contained in the said act of June three, eighteen hundred and fifty-six. But in case it shall appear that the United States have, when the line or route of said road is definitely fixed, sold, reserved, or otherwise disposed of any sections, or parts of sections, granted as aforesaid, or that the right of pre-emption or

* Vol. I. No. 292.

† Extended, No. 225 B.

homestead has attached to the same, then it shall be lawful for any agent or agents to be appointed by said State to select, subject to the approval of the Secretary of the Interior, from the public lands of the United States nearest to the tier of sections above specified, as much land, in alternate sections, or parts of sections, as shall be equal to such lands as the United States have sold, or otherwise appropriated, or to which the right of pre-emption or homestead has attached, as aforesaid, which lands (thus selected in lieu of those sold, and to which pre-emption or homestead right has attached as aforesaid, together with sections and parts of sections, designated by odd numbers as aforesaid, and appropriated as aforesaid) shall be held by said State for the use and purpose aforesaid: *Provided*, That the lands to be so located shall in no case be further than twenty miles from the line of the said road, nor shall such selection or location be made in lieu of lands received under the said grant of June three, eighteen hundred and fifty-six, but such selections and locations may be made for the benefit of said State, and for the purpose aforesaid, to supply any deficiency under the said grant of June three, eighteen hundred and fifty-six, should any such deficiency exist.

SEC. 3. *And be it further enacted*, That there be, and is hereby, granted to the State of Wisconsin, for the purpose of aiding in the construction of a railroad from Portage city, Berlin, Doty's Island, or Fon du Lac, as said State may determine, in a northwestern direction, to Bayfield, and thence to Superior, on Lake Superior, every alternate section of public land, designated by odd numbers, for ten sections in width on each side of said road, upon the same terms and conditions as are contained in the act granting lands to said State to aid in the construction of railroads in said State, approved June three eighteen hundred and fifty-six. But in case it shall appear that the United States have, when the line or route of said road is definitely fixed, sold, reserved or otherwise disposed of any sections or parts thereof, granted as aforesaid, or that the right of pre-emption or homestead has attached to the same, that it shall be lawful for any agent or agents of said State, appointed by the Governor thereof, to select, subject to the approval of the Secretary of the Interior, from the lands of the United States nearest to the tier of sections above specified, as much public land in alternate sections, or parts of sections, as shall be equal to such lands as the United States have sold or otherwise appropriated, or to which the right of pre-emption or homestead has attached as aforesaid, which lands (thus selected in lieu of those sold and to which the right of pre-emption or homestead has attached as aforesaid, together with sections and parts of sections designated by odd numbers as aforesaid, and appropriated as aforesaid) shall be held by said State, or by the company to which she may transfer the same, for the use and purpose aforesaid: *Provided*, That the lands to be so located shall in no case be further than twenty miles from the line of said road.*

SEC. 4. *And be it further enacted*, That the sections and parts of sections of lands which shall remain to the United States within ten miles on each side of said roads shall not be sold for less than double the minimum price of the public lands when sold; nor shall any of the said reserved lands become subject to private entry until the same have been first offered at public sale at the increased price.

SEC. 5. *And be it further enacted*, That the time fixed and limited for the completion of said roads in the act aforesaid of June three, eighteen

* See No. 184 B.

hundred and fifty-six, be and the same is hereby extended to a period of five years from and after the passage of this act.

SEC. 6. *And be it further enacted*, That any and all lands reserved to the United States by any act of Congress for the purpose of aiding in any object of internal improvement, or in any manner for any purpose whatsoever, and all mineral lands be and the same are hereby reserved and excluded from the operation of this act, except so far as it may be found necessary to locate the route of such railroads through such reserved lands, in which case the right of way only shall be granted, subject to the approval of the President of the United States.

SEC. 7. *And be it further enacted*, That whenever the companies to which this grant is made, or to which the same may be transferred, shall have completed twenty consecutive miles of any portion of said railroads, supplied with all necessary drains, culverts, viaducts, crossings, sidings, bridges, turn-outs, watering-places, depots, equipments, furniture, and all other appurtenances of a first-class railroad, patents shall issue conveying the right and title to said lands to the said company entitled thereto, on each side of the road, so far as the same is completed, and coterminous with said completed section, not exceeding the amount aforesaid, and patents shall in like manner issue as each twenty miles of said road is completed: *Provided, however*, That no patents shall issue for any of said lands unless there shall be presented to the Secretary of the Interior a statement, verified on oath or affirmation by the president of said company, and certified by the Governor of the State of Wisconsin, that such twenty miles have been completed in the manner required by this act, and setting forth with certainty the points where such twenty miles begin and where the same end; which oath shall be taken before a judge of a court of record of the United States.

SEC. 8. *And be it further enacted*, That the said lands hereby granted shall, when patented as provided in section seven of this act, be subject to the disposal of the companies respectively entitled thereto, for the purposes aforesaid, and no other, and the said railroads be, and shall remain, public highways for the use of the Government of the United States, free from all toll or other charge, for the transportation of any property or troops of the United States.

SEC. 9. *And be it further enacted*, That if said road mentioned in the third section aforesaid is not completed within ten years from the time of the passage of this act, as provided herein, no further patents shall be issued to said company for said lands, and no further sale shall be made, and the lands unsold shall revert to the United States.

Approved, May 5, 1864.

No. 84 B.—An Act for the relief of the settlers upon certain lands in California.

Be it enacted by the Senate and House of Representatives of the United States of America in Congress assembled, That any and all persons claiming, whether as pre-emptors or settlers, or under any grant or title, any of the lands included within the exterior boundaries of a certain grant for the rancho San Ramon, situate in the county of Contra Costa, in California, made to Bartolo Pacheco and Mariana Castro by Don José Figuerea, Governor of Upper California, on or about the tenth day of June, eighteen hundred and thirty-three, and which claim, or two leagues thereof, has been confirmed by the District Court of the United States in separate moieties, one in the name of Horace W. Carpenter, and the other in the name of Rafael Soto de Pacheco and others, by a decree of said court made and entered on or about the fourth day of June, eighteen hundred and sixty-two, shall have the right in all courts to contest the correctness of the location of the lands so confirmed, within the said exterior boundaries, notwithstanding any official or approved survey thereof now made, or hereafter to be made, under the said decree of confirmation, and notwithstanding any stipulation or consent given by the District Attorney of the United States authorizing such locations.

SEC. 2. *And be it further enacted*, That in case it shall be found that the United States have title to any of said lands within said exterior boundaries, which have been settled upon and improved by any person, in good faith, under a bona fide claim of title, such occupant, and each settler upon said lands so situated, shall be entitled to enter and receive a patent for one hundred and sixty acres of land, including his improvements, upon payment, at the proper land office, of the Government price of one dollar and twenty-five cents per acre, and proving that he was one of the actual and bona fide settlers on said lands, and had made improvements thereon before the passage of this act.

SEC. 3. *And be it further enacted*, That this act shall take effect immediately.

Approved, May 5, 1864.

No. 85 B.—An Act for a grant of lands to the State of Iowa, in alternate sections, to aid in the construction of a railroad in said State.

Be it enacted by the Senate and House of Representatives of the United States of America in Congress assembled, That there be, and is hereby, granted to the State of Iowa, for the purpose of aiding in the construction of a railroad from Sioux City, in said State, to the south line of the State of Minnesota, at such point as the said State of Iowa may select between the Big Sioux and the west fork of the Des Moines River; also, to said State, for the use and benefit of the McGregor Western Railroad Company, for the purpose of aiding in the construction of a railroad from a point at or near the foot of Main Street, South McGregor, in said State, in a westerly direction, by the most practicable route, on or near the forty-third parallel of north latitude, until it shall intersect the said road running from Sioux City to the Minnesota State line, in the county of O'Brien, in said State, every alternate section of land designated by odd numbers for ten sections in width on each side of rail roads; but, in case it shall appear that the United States have, when the lines or routes of said roads are definitely located, sold any section, or any part thereof, granted as aforesaid, or that the right of pre-emption or homestead settlement has attached to the same, or that the same has been reserved by the United States for any purpose whatever, then it shall be the duty of the Secretary of the Interior to cause to be selected, for the purposes aforesaid, from the public lands of the United States nearest to the tiers of sections above specified, so much land in alternate sections, or parts of sections, designated by odd numbers, as shall be equal to such lands as the United States have sold, reserved, or otherwise appropriated, or to which the right of homestead settlement or pre-emption has attached, as aforesaid, which lands thus indicated by odd numbers and sections, by the direction of the Secretary of the Interior, shall be held by the State of Iowa for the uses and purposes aforesaid: *Provided*, That the lands so selected shall in no case be located more than twenty miles from the lines of said roads: *Provided further*, That any and all lands heretofore reserved to the United States by any act of Congress, or in any other manner by competent authority, for the purpose of aiding in any object of internal improvement, or other purpose whatever, be, and the same are hereby, reserved and excepted from the operation of this act, except so far as it may be found necessary to locate the routes of said roads through such reserved lands, in which case the right of way shall be granted, subject to the approval of the President of the United States.

SEC. 2. *And be it further enacted*, That the sections and parts of sections of land which by such grant shall remain to the United States, within ten miles on each side of said roads, shall not be sold for less than double the minimum price of public lands when sold, nor shall any of said lands become subject to sale at private entry until the same shall have been first offered at public sale to the highest bidder at or above the minimum price as aforesaid: *Provided*, That actual bona fide settlers under the pre-emption laws of the United States may, after due proof of settlement, improvement, and occupation, as now provided by law, purchase the same at the increased minimum price: *And provided, also*, That settlers under the provisions of the homestead law, who comply with the terms and requirements of said act, shall be entitled to patents for an amount not exceeding eighty acres each, anything in this act to the contrary notwithstanding.

SEC. 3. *And be it further enacted*, That the lands hereby granted shall be subject to the disposal of the legislature of Iowa, for the purposes aforesaid and no other. And the said railroads shall be, and remain, public highways for the use of the Government of the United States, free of all toll or other charges upon the transportation of any property or troops of the United States.

SEC. 4. *And be it further enacted*, That the lands hereby granted shall be disposed of by said State, for the purposes aforesaid only, and in manner following, namely: When the Governor of said State shall certify to the Secretary of the Interior that any section of ten consecutive miles of either of said roads is completed in a good, substantial, and workmanlike manner as a first-class railroad, then the Secretary of the Interior shall issue to the State, patents for one hundred sections of land for the benefit of the road having completed the ten consecutive miles as aforesaid. When the Governor of said State shall certify that another section of ten consecutive miles shall have been completed as aforesaid, then the Secretary of the Interior shall issue patents to said State in like manner, for a like number; and when certificates of the completion of additional sections of ten consecutive miles of either of said roads are, from time to time, made as aforesaid, additional sections of lands shall be patented as aforesaid, until said roads, or either of them, are completed, when the whole of the lands hereby granted shall be patented to the State for the uses aforesaid and none other: *Provided*, That if the said McGregor Western Railroad Company, or assigns, shall fail to complete at least twenty miles of its said road during each and every year from the date of its acceptance of the grant provided for in this act, then the State may resume said grant, and so dispose of the same as to secure the completion of a road on said line and upon such terms, within such time as the State shall determine: *Provided further*, That if the said roads are not completed within ten years from their several acceptance of this grant, the said lands hereby granted and not patented shall revert to the State of Iowa for the purpose of securing the completion of the said roads within such time, not to exceed five years, and upon such terms as the State shall determine: *And provided further*, That said lands shall not in any manner be disposed of or encumbered, except as the same are patented under the provisions of this act; and should the State fail to complete said roads within five years after the ten years aforesaid, then the said lands undisposed of as aforesaid shall revert to the United States.

SEC. 5. *And be it further enacted*, That as soon as the Governor of said State of Iowa shall file or caused to be filed with the Secretary of the Interior maps designating the routes of said roads, then it shall be the duty of the Secretary of the Interior to withdraw from market the lands embraced within the provisions of this act.

SEC. 6. *And be it further enacted*, That the United States mail shall be transported on said roads and branch, under the direction of the post-office department, at such price as Congress may by law provide: *Provided*, That until such price is fixed by law the Postmaster-General shall have power to fix the rate of compensation.

SEC. 7. *And be it further enacted*, That there be, and is hereby, granted to the State of Minnesota for the purpose of aiding in the construction of a railroad from St. Paul and St. Anthony, via Minneapolis, to a convenient point of junction west of the Mississippi, to the southern boundary of the State, in the direction of the mouth of the Big Sioux River, four additional alternate sections of land per mile, to be selected upon the same conditions, restrictions, and limitations as are contained in the act of Congress entitled "An act making a grant of land to the Territory of Minnesota, in alternate sections, to aid in the construction of certain railroads in said Territory, and granting public lands, in alternate sections, to the State of Alabama, to aid in the construction of a certain railroad in said State," approved March third, eighteen hundred and fifty-seven: *Provided*, That the land be so located by virtue of this section may be selected within twenty miles of the line of said road, but in no case at a greater distance therefrom.

Approved, May 12, 1864.

No. 86 B.—An Act to provide a temporary government for the Territory of Montana.

Be it enacted by the Senate and House of Representatives of the United States of America in Congress assembled, That all that part of the territory of the United States included within the limits, to wit: Commencing at a point formed by the intersection of the twenty-seventh degree of longitude west from Washington with the forty-fifth degree of north latitude; thence due west on said forty-fifth degree of latitude to a point formed by its intersection with the thirty-fourth degree of longitude west from Washington; thence due south along said thirty-fourth degree of longitude to its intersection with the forty-fourth degree and thirty minutes of north latitude; thence due west along said forty-fourth degree and thirty minutes of north latitude to a point formed by its intersection with the crest of the Rocky Mountains; thence following the crest of the Rocky Mountains northward till its intersection with the Bitter Root Mountains; thence northward along the crest of said Bitter Root Mountains to its intersection with the thirty-ninth degree of longitude west from Washington; thence along said thirty-ninth degree of longitude northward to the boundary line of the British possessions; thence eastward along said boundary line to the twenty-seventh degree of longitude west from Washington; thence southward along said twenty-seventh degree of longitude to the place of beginning, be, and the same is hereby, created into a temporary government by the name of the Territory of Montana: *Provided*, That nothing in this act contained shall be construed to inhibit the Government of the United States from dividing said Territory or changing its boundaries in such manner and at such time as Congress shall deem convenient and proper, or from attaching any portion of said Territory to any other State or Territory of the United States: *Provided further*, That nothing in this act contained shall be construed to impair the rights of person or property now pertaining to the Indians in said Territory so long as such rights shall remain unextinguished by treaty between the United States and such Indians, or to include any Territory which, by treaty with any Indian tribes, is not, without the consent of said tribe, to be included within the territorial limits or jurisdiction of any State or Territory; but all such Territory shall be excepted out of the boundaries, and constitute no part of the Territory of Montana, until said tribe shall signify their assent to the President of the United States to be included within said Territory, or to affect the authority of the Government of the United States to make any regulations respecting such Indians, their lands, property, or other rights, by treaty, law, or otherwise, which it would have been competent for the Government to make if this act had never passed.

* * * * * * * * *

SEC. 10. * * * There shall also be appointed by the President of the United States, by and with the advice and consent of the Senate, a Surveyor-General for said Territory, who shall locate his office at such place as the Secretary of the Interior shall from time to time direct, and whose duties, powers, obligations, responsibilities, compensation, and allowances for clerk-hire, office-rent, fuel, and incidental expenses, shall be the same as those of the Surveyor-General of New Mexico, under the direction of the Secretary of the Interior, and such instructions as he may from time to time deem it advisable to give.

* * * * * * * * *

SEC. 14. *And be it further enacted*, That when the lands in the said Territory shall be surveyed under the direction of the Government of the United States, preparatory to bringing the same into market, sections numbered sixteen and thirty-six in each township in said Territory shall be, and the same are hereby, reserved for the purpose of being applied to schools in said Territory and in the States and Territories hereafter to be erected out of the same.

SEC. 15. *And be it further enacted*, That until otherwise provided by law, the Governor of said Territory may define the judicial districts of said Territory, and assign the judges who may be appointed for said Territory to the several districts, and also appoint the times and places for holding courts in the several counties or subdivisions in each of said judicial districts, by proclamation to be issued by him; but the legislative assembly, at their first or any subsequent session, may organize, alter, or modify such judicial districts, and assign the judges, and alter the times and places of holding the courts, as to them shall seem proper and convenient.

SEC. 16. *And be it further enacted*, That all officers to be appointed by the President of the United States, by and with the advice and consent of the Senate, for the Territory of Montana, who, by virtue of the provisions of any law now existing, or which may be enacted by Congress, are required to give security for moneys that may be intrusted with them for disbursement, shall give such security at such time and in such manner as the Secretary of the Treasury may prescribe.

SEC. 17. *And be it further enacted,* That all treaties, laws, and other engagements made by the Government of the United States with the Indian tribes inhabiting the territory embraced within the provisions of this act, shall be faithfully and rigidly observed, anything contained in this act to the contrary notwithstanding; and that the existing agencies and superintendencies of said Indians be continued, with the same powers and duties which are now prescribed by law, except that the President of the United States may, at his discretion, change the location of the office of said agencies or superintendents.

SEC. 18. *And be it further enacted,* That, until Congress shall otherwise direct, all that part of the Territory of Idaho included within the following boundaries, to wit: Commencing at a point formed by the intersection of the thirty-third degree of longitude west from Washington with the forty-first degree of north latitude; thence along said thirty-third degree of longitude to the crest of the Rocky Mountains; thence northward along the said crest of the Rocky Mountains to its intersection with the forty-fourth degree and thirty minutes of north latitude; thence eastward along said forty-fourth degree thirty minutes north latitude to the thirty-fourth degree of longitude west from Washington; thence northward along said thirty-fourth degree of longitude to its intersection with the forty-fifth degree north latitude; thence eastward along said forty-fifth degree of north latitude to its intersection with the twenty-seventh degree of longitude west from Washington; thence south along said twenty-seventh degree of longitude west from Washington to the forty-first degree north latitude; thence west along said forty-first degree of latitude to the place of beginning, shall be, and is hereby, incorporated temporarily into and made part of the Territory of Dakota.

Approved, May 26, 1864.

No. 87 B.—An Act for the relief of the citizens of Denver, in the Territory of Colorado.

Be it enacted by the Senate and House of Representatives of the United States of America in Congress assembled, That the provisions of an act of Congress entitled "An act for the relief of the citizens of towns upon the lands of the United States, under certain circumstances," approved May twenty-third, eighteen hundred and forty-four,* be so extended as to authorize the Probate Judge of Arapahoe County, in the Territory of Colorado, to enter, at the minimum price, in trust for the several use and benefit of the rightful occupants of said land and the bona fide owners of the improvements thereon, according to their respective interests, the following legal subdivisions of land, or such portions thereof as are settled and actually occupied for town purposes by the town of Denver aforesaid, to wit: Section number thirty-three, and the west half of section number

* Vol. I. No. 79.

thirty-four, in township number three south of range number sixty-eight west of the sixth principal meridian: *Provided, however*, That there shall be reserved from such sale and entry such blocks or lots in the town of Denver as may be necessary for government purposes, to be designated by the Commissioner of the General Land Office.

SEC. 2. *And be it further enacted*, That in all respects, except as herein modified, the execution of the foregoing provisions shall be controlled by the provisions of said act of twenty-third May, eighteen hundred and forty-four, and the rules and regulations of the Commissioner of the General Land Office.

Approved, May 28, 1864.

No. 88 B.—An Act to amend an act entitled "An act making a grant of Land[s] to the State of Iowa, in alternate sections, to aid in the construction of certain railroads in said State," approved May fifteen, eighteen hundred and fifty-six.*

Be it enacted by the Senate and House of Representatives of the United States of America in Congress assembled, That the Mississippi and Missouri Railroad Company, a corporation established by the laws of the State of Iowa, and to which the said State granted a portion of the land-grant mentioned in the title of this act, to aid in the construction of a railroad from Davenport to Council Bluffs in said State, may modify or change the location of the uncompleted portion of its line, as shown by the map thereof now on file in the General Land Office of the United States, so as to secure a better and more expeditious line for connection with the Iowa branch of the Union Pacific Railroad: *Provided, nevertheless*, That said new line, if located, shall in every case pass through the corporate limits of the cities of Des Moines and Council Bluffs; and the right of way over the public lands of the United States is hereby granted to said railroad company for that purpose: *Provided*, That said line shall pass through the town of Newton, in Jasper County or as near said town as may be found practicable, and not further north of said town than the north line of section twenty-two, township eighty north, of range nineteen, according to the United States surveys, if the citizens of the county of Jasper shall first pay to said company the difference in cost, if any, between the line proposed by the company and the one contemplated by this proviso, including extra cost of right of way, if any, said difference in cost to be estimated by competent engineers to be selected by the parties.

SEC. 2. *And be it further enacted*, That whenever such new location shall have been established, the said railroad company shall file in the General Land Office at Washington a map, definitely showing such new location; and the Secretary of the Interior shall cause to be certified and conveyed to said company from time to time, as the road progresses, out of any public lands now belonging to the United States not sold, reserved, or otherwise disposed of, or to which a pre-emption claim or right of homestead settlement has not attached, and on which a bona fide settlement and improvement has not been made under color of title derived from the United States or from the State of Iowa, within six miles of such newly located line, an amount of land per mile equal to that origi-

* Vol. I. No. 288. See also No. 181 B.

nally authorized to be granted to aid in the construction of said road by the act to which this is an amendment; and if the amount of land granted by the original act to aid in the construction of said railroad shall not be found within the limit of six miles from such line, then such selections may be made along such line within twenty miles thereof: *Provided*, That the said company shall not be entitled to, and shall not receive, any land under this grant which is situate within fifteen miles of the line of the Burlington and Missouri River Railroad, as indicated by the map of said road, now on file in the General Land Office.

SEC. 3. *And be it further enacted*, That the Burlington and Missouri River Railroad Company, a corporation organized under the laws of the State of Iowa, and to which said State granted a portion of the land-grant mentioned in the title of this act to aid in the construction of a railroad from Burlington in said State to the Missouri River, shall be entitled to receive, and the Secretary of the Interior shall cause to be certified and conveyed to said company from time to time, as the road progresses, out of any public lands now belonging to the United States not sold, reserved, or otherwise disposed of, or to which a pre-emption claim or right of homestead settlement has not attached, and on which a bona fide settlement and improvement has not been made under color of title derived from the United States or from the State of Iowa, within six miles of said road, as now located, an amount of land per mile equal to that mentioned in the act to which this act is an amendment, as intended to aid in the construction of said road; and if the amount of land granted by the original act to aid in the construction of said road shall not be found within the limit of six miles from the line of said road, then such selections may be made along such line within twenty miles thereof.

SEC. 4. *And be it further enacted*, That the Cedar Rapids and Missouri River Railroad Company, a corporation established under the laws of the State of Iowa, and to which the said State granted a portion of the land mentioned in the title to this act, may modify or change the location of the uncompleted portion of its line, as shown by the map thereof now on file in the General Land Office of the United States, so as to secure a better and more expeditious line to the Missouri River, and to a connection with the Iowa branch of the Union Pacific Railroad; and for the purpose of facilitating the more immediate construction of a line of railroads across the State of Iowa, to connect with the Iowa branch of the Union Pacific Railroad Company, aforesaid, the said Cedar Rapids and Missouri River Railroad Company is hereby authorized to connect its line by a branch with the line of the Mississippi and Missouri Railroad Company; and the said Cedar Rapids and Missouri River Railroad Company shall be entitled for such modified line to the same lands and to the same amount of lands per mile, and for such connecting branch the same amount of land per mile, as originally granted to aid in the construction of its main line, subject to the conditions and forfeitures mentioned in the original grant, and, for the said purpose, right of way through the public lands of the United States is hereby granted to said company. *And it is further provided*, That whenever said modified main line shall have been established or such connecting line located, the said Cedar Rapids and Missouri River Railroad Company shall file in the General Land Office of the United States a map definitely showing such modified line and such connecting branch aforesaid; and the Secretary of the Interior shall reserve and cause to be certified and conveyed to said company, from time to time, as the work progresses on the main line, out of any public lands now belonging to the United States, not sold, reserved, or otherwise disposed of, or to which a pre-emption right or right of homestead settlement has not attached, and on which a bona fide settlement and improvement has not been made under color of title derived from the United States or from the State of Iowa, within fifteen miles of the original main line, an amount of land equal to that originally authorized to be granted to aid in the construction of the said road by the act to which this is an amendment. And if the amount of lands per mile granted, or intended to be granted, by the original act to aid in the construction of said railroad shall not be found within the limits of the fifteen miles therein prescribed, then such selections may be made along said modified line and connecting branch within twenty miles thereof: *Provided, however,* That such new located or modified line shall pass through or near Boonsboro', in Boon County, and intersect the Boyer River not further south than a point at or near Dennison, in Crawford County: *And provided further,* That in case the main line shall be so changed or modified as not to reach the Missouri River at or near the forty-second parallel north latitude, it shall be the duty of said company, within a reasonable time after the completion of its road to the Missouri River, to construct a branch road to some point in Monona County, in or at Onawa City; and to aid in the construction of such branch, the same amount of lands per mile are hereby granted as for the main line, and the same shall be reserved and certified in the same manner; said lands to be selected from any of the unappropriated lands, as hereinbefore described, within twenty miles of said main line and branch; and said company shall file with the Secretary of the Interior a map of the location of the said branch: *And provided further,* That the lands hereby granted to aid in the construction of the connecting branch aforesaid shall not vest in said company, nor be encumbered or disposed of except in the following manner: When the Governor of the State of Iowa shall certify to the Secretary of the Interior that said company has completed, in good running order, a section of twenty consecutive miles of the main line of said road west of Nevada, then the Secretary shall convey to said company one-third, and no more, of the lands granted for said connecting branch. And when said company shall complete an additional section of twenty consecutive miles, and furnish the Secretary of the Interior with proof as aforesaid, then the said Secretary may convey to the said company another third of the lands granted for said connecting branch; and when said company shall complete an additional section of twenty miles, making in all sixty miles west of Nevada, the Secretary, upon proof furnished as aforesaid, may convey to the said company the remainder of said lands to aid in the construction of said connecting branch: *Provided, however,* That no lands shall be conveyed to said company on account of said connecting branch road until the Governor of the State of Iowa shall certify to the Secretary of the Interior that the same shall have been completed as a first-class railroad. And no land shall be conveyed to said company situate and lying within fifteen miles of the original line of the Mississippi and Missouri Railroad, as laid down on a map on file in the General Land Office: *Provided further,* That it shall be the duty of the Secretary of the Interior, and he is hereby required, to reserve a quantity of land embraced in the grant described in this section, sufficient, in the opinion of the Governor of Iowa, to secure the construction of a branch railroad from the town of Lyons, in the State of Iowa, so as to connect with the main line in or west of the town of Clinton in said State, until the Governor of said State shall certify that said branch railroad is completed according to the requirements of the laws of said State: *Provided further*, That nothing herein contained shall be so construed as to release said company from its obligation to complete the said main line within the time mentioned in the original grant: *Provided further*, That nothing in this act shall be construed to interfere with, or in any manner impair, any rights acquired by any railroad company named in the act to which this is an amendment, or the rights of any corporation, person or persons, acquired through any such company; nor shall it be construed to impair any vested right of property; but such rights are hereby reserved and confirmed: *Provided, however*, That no lands shall be conveyed to any company or party whatsoever, under the provisions of this act and the act amended by this act, which have been settled upon and improved in good faith by a bona fide inhabitant, under color of title derived from the United States, or from the State of Iowa, adverse to the grant made by this act, or the act to which this act is an amendment. But each of said companies may select an equal quantity of public lands, as described in this act, within the distance of twenty miles of the line of each of said roads, in lieu of lands thus settled upon and improved by bona fide inhabitants, in good faith, under color of title as aforesaid.

SEC. 5. *And be it further enacted*, That the Mississippi and Missouri Railroad Company shall have the right to transfer and assign all or any part of the grant hereby made to said company to any other company, or person or persons, if, in the opinion of said company, the construction of the said railroad across the State of Iowa will be thereby sooner and more satisfactorily completed; but such assignee shall not in any case be released from the liabilities and conditions accompanying this grant, nor acquire perfect title in any other manner than the same would have been acquired by the grantee herein named: *Provided*, That said transfer and assignment shall first be authorized by the Governor of the State of Iowa.

SEC. 6. *And be it further enacted*, That the Dubuque and Sioux City Railroad Company may so far change their line between Fort Dodge and Sioux City as to secure the best route between those points; said change shall not impair the right to, nor change the location of, their present land grant. A map of the change shall be filed with the Commissioner of the General Land Office within one year after the passage of this act.

SEC. 7. *And be it further enacted*, That all of the conditions and limitations contained in the act to which this act is an amendment, and not expressly changed by this act, shall attach to and run with the grants made by this act, except as the said conditions and limitations have been modified, and may hereafter be modified, by the General Assembly of the State of Iowa.

SEC. 8. *And be it further enacted*, That no lands hereby granted shall be certified to either of said companies until the Governor of the State of Iowa shall certify to the Secretary of the Interior that the said company has completed, ready for the rolling stock, within one year from the first day of July next, a section of not less than twenty miles from the present terminus of the completed portion of said railroad, and in each year thereafter an additional section of twenty miles; but the number of sections per mile originally authorized shall be certified to each company, upon proof as aforesaid of the completion of the additional sections of the road as aforesaid: and upon the failure of either company to complete either section as aforesaid, to be annually built, the portion of the land remaining uncertified shall become subject to the control and disposition of the legislature of the State of Iowa, to aid in the completion of such road.

SEC. 9. *And be it further enacted*, That all lands hereafter certified to either of the land-grant railroads in said State, and lying opposite any completed section of such road, shall be offered for sale by the company to which they shall be certified within three years from the completion of such section, if then certified; and if not, then within three years from the date of such certificate at reasonable prices; and if not all sold within that period then during the fourth year all such lands remaining unsold shall be exposed to public sale, after previous notice posted at the county seat of the county in which such lands shall be situated, to the highest bidder, and in tracts not exceeding one hundred and sixty acres each.

Approved, June 2, 1864.

No. 89 B.—An Act to amend an act entitled "An act making a grant of alternate sections of [the] public lands to the State of Michigan to aid in the construction of certain railroads in said State, and for other purposes."*

Be it enacted by the Senate and House of Representatives of the United States of America in Congress assembled, That the act entitled "An act making a grant of alternate sections of [the] public lands to the State of Michigan to aid in the construction of certain railroads in said State, and for other purposes," be, and the same is hereby, amended as follows, namely: Substitute for the words "and from Grand Rapids to some point on or near Traverse Bay," contained in the first section of said act, these words: And from Fort Wayne, in the State of Indiana, to a point on the southern boundary line of the State of Michigan, in the township of Sturgis, thence, by way of Grand Rapids, to some point on or near Traverse Bay. And the said act shall be, and is hereby, so amended as to substitute for the first clause of the first proviso in the first section thereof, so far as the same shall be applicable to the grant of lands made to aid in the construction of the railroad described by the foregoing amendment, these words: *Provided,* That the lands so to be selected shall in no case be further than twenty miles from the line of said road: *Provided further,* That the time specified in the 4th section of the act hereby amended for the completion of said road shall not be extended.

SEC. 2. *And be it further enacted,* That the lands granted by the act amended by this act, and also by the provisions of this act, to aid in the construction of the railroad described in the foregoing section, shall be disposed of only in the following manner, that is to say, when the Governor of the State of Michigan shall certify to the Secretary of the Interior that ten consecutive miles of said road have been completed in a good and substantial manner as a first-class railroad, indicating definitely where said completed section commences and where the same terminates, the said Secretary shall cause patents to issue to said State for so much of said lands as are located opposite to, and coterminous with, said completed section of said road, and so from time to time for each completed section of ten miles of said road until the whole shall be completed.

Approved, June 7, 1864.

* Vol. I. No. 293. Amended, No. 131 B. and No. 231 B.

No. 90 B.—An Act to amend an act entitled "An act to confirm certain private land claims in the Territory of New Mexico."*

Be it enacted by the Senate and House of Representatives of the United States of America in Congress assembled, That the sixth section of the act entitled "An act to confirm certain private land claims in the Territory of New Mexico," approved June twenty-first, eighteen hundred and sixty, be, and the same is hereby, so amended as to enable the heirs of Luis Maria Baca to raise and withdraw the selection and location of one of the square bodies of land confirmed to them by said act, heretofore located by said heirs on the Pecos River, adjoining the Fort Sumner reservation, and to select and re-locate the same, in the manner provided by said act, at any time before the twenty-first day of June, in the year eighteen hundred and sixty-five, upon any of the public lands, unoccupied and not mineral, within the limits of the Territory of New Mexico, as said limits were known and defined by law on the twenty-first day of June, in the year eighteen hundred and sixty; and upon such selection and re-location, the title to said square body of land, the same being the one fifth part of the private claim confirmed to said heirs as aforesaid, so selected and re-located, shall be, and is hereby, confirmed to the said heirs of the said Luis Maria Baca as fully and perfectly as if the same had been selected and located within three years from and after the approval of the act aforesaid.

SEC. 2. *And be it further enacted,* That upon such selection and re-location all right, title, and interest of the said heirs of Luis Maria Baca, of, in, and to the square body of land heretofore selected and located by them on the Pecos River, adjoining the Fort Sumner reservation in New Mexico, is hereby divested and declared null and void, and the same shall revest in the Government of the United States.

Approved, June 11, 1864.

No. 91 B.—An Act concerning certain school lands in township forty-five north, range seven east, in the State of Missouri.

Be it enacted by the Senate and House of Representatives of the United States of America in Congress assembled, That all of the right, title, and interest of the United States in and to all of the lots, tracts, pieces, and parcels of land within the Grand Prairie common field, in township forty-five north of the base line, in range seven east of the fifth principal meridian line in the State of Missouri, which have not heretofore been disposed of by the United States, shall be, and the same are hereby, granted, relinquished, and conveyed by the United States, in fee simple and in full property, to the State of Missouri, for the support of schools in said township: *Provided,* That nothing in this act shall in any manner abridge, divest, impair, injure, or prejudice any adverse right, title, or interest of any person or persons in or to any portion or part of the aforesaid lots, tracts, pieces, or parcels of land which are granted, relinquished, or conveyed by this act.

Approved, June 15, 1864.

* Amended, No. 16 B.

No. 92 B.—An Act to grant the right of pre-emption to certain settlers on the Rancho Bolsa de Tomales, in the State of California.

Be it enacted by the Senate and House of Representatives of the United States of America in Congress assembled, That it may and shall be lawful for the Commissioner of the General Land Office to cause the lines of the public surveys to be extended over the tract of country known as the Rancho Bolsa de Tomales, in Marin County, California, the claim to which, by James D. Galbraith, has been adjudged invalid by the Supreme Court of the United States, and to have approved plats thereof duly returned to the proper district land office: *Provided,* That the actual cost of such survey and platting shall first be paid into the surveying fund by settlers, according to the requirements of the tenth section of the act of Congress approved thirtieth of May, eighteen hundred and sixty-two, "to reduce the expenses of the survey and sale of the public lands in the United States."*

SEC. 2. *And be it further enacted,* That after the return of such approved plats to the district office, it may and shall be lawful for individuals, settlers upon the said Rancho Bolsa de Tomales, to enter, according to the lines of the public surveys, at one dollar and twenty-five cents per acre, the land settled upon by them to the extent to which the same had been reduced to possession at the time of said adjudication of said Supreme Court, joint entries being admissible by coterminous proprietors, in order that their respective boundaries may be adjusted in accordance with their several possessions.

SEC. 3. *And be it further enacted,* That all claims within the purview of this act shall be presented to the register and receiver within twelve months after the return of such surveys to the district land office, accompanied by proof of settlement, and the extent to which the tracts claimed had been reduced into possession at the time of said adjudication; and thereupon each case shall be adjudged by the register and receiver, under such instructions as shall be given by the Commissioner of the General Land Office, to whom the proof and adjudication shall be returned by the local land office, and no adjudication shall be final until confirmed by the said commissioner: *Provided,* That the confirmation by said commissioner shall be conclusive and final between coterminous proprietors, and the correctness thereof shall not be open to contestation in any action at law or suit in equity between them or between parties claiming under them by title subsequent: *And provided further,* That any claim not brought before the register and receiver within twelve months, as aforesaid, shall be barred, and the lands covered thereby, with any other tracts within the limits of said rancho, the titles to which are not established under this act, shall be dealt with as other public lands, but subject to the adjudicated boundaries of the claims which are presented within the limit of the time prescribed as aforesaid: *Provided,* That no person under the provisions of this act shall be allowed to enter a greater quantity of land than three hundred and twenty acres.

Approved, June 17, 1864.

* See No. 39 B.

No. 93 B.—An Act extending the time for the completion of the Marquette and Ontonagon Railroad, of the State of Michigan.

Be it enacted by the Senate and House of Representatives of the United States of America in Congress assembled, That the time limited for the completion of the Marquette and Ontonagon Railroad, of the State of Michigan, be, and the same is hereby, extended for the term of five years beyond the time fixed for its completion by the act of Congress of June third, A. D. eighteen hundred and fifty-six,* entitled "An act making a grant of alternate sections of the public lands to the State of Michigan to aid in the construction of certain railroads in said State, and for other purposes:" *Provided,* That the State of Michigan shall have the same control over the said grant of lands hereby extended for five years, for the benefit of said railroad, which was given to said State under said original act of Congress; and said State may prescribe the time within which the several sections of said road shall be completed.†

Approved, June 18, 1864.

No. 94 B.—An Act granting lands to the State of Michigan for the construction of certain wagon roads for military and postal purposes.

Be it enacted by the Senate and House of Representatives of the United States of America in Congress assembled, That there be, and hereby is, granted to the State of Michigan, for the construction of a wagon-road for military and postal purposes, from Saginaw City, in said State, by the shortest and most feasible route to the Straits of Mackinaw, every alternate or odd section of public land not mineral, for three miles in width on each side of said road to the extent of three sections to the mile. Also for a road from Grand Rapids, in said State, through Newaygo, Traverse City, and Little Traverse, to the Straits of Mackinaw, every alternate or odd section of public land, not mineral, for three sections in width on each side of said road to the extent of three sections to the mile. And it is hereby provided that in case it shall appear that the United States shall have (when the lines or routes of said roads are definitely established) sold or reserved any sections or parts of sections, granted as aforesaid, or that the rights of pre-emption or homestead have attached to the same, so as to leave a deficiency in the amount to be selected within the limits designated, then it shall be the duty of the Secretary of the Interior to select such lands from the odd sections, or parts of sections, nearest to the three-mile limits aforesaid, such quantity as shall be necessary to make up the deficiency thus created: *Provided further,* That the lands hereby granted shall be exclusively reserved, held, and applied in the construction of said roads, and shall be appropriated and disposed of only as the work progresses, in quantities and under such regulations and restrictions as the State shall provide; and in no event shall they be appropriated or disposed of for any other purpose whatsoever.

SEC. 2. *And be it further enacted,* That any and all lands heretofore reserved to the United States by any act of Congress, or in any other manner by competent authority, for any public work, or for any other purpose whatsoever, be, and the same are hereby, reserved to the United

* Vol. I. No. 293.

† See No. 119 B.

States from the operation of this act, except so far as it may be necessary to locate the routes of said roads through such reserved lands; in which case the rights of way shall be, and are hereby, granted, subject to the approval of the President of the United States.

SEC. 3. *And be it further enacted,* That said roads shall be located, surveyed, and constructed, under the direction of such agents or commissioners as the Governor may appoint, and shall be chopped out a uniform width of at least six rods. The road-bed proper to be not less than thirty-two feet wide, and constructed with ample ditches on both sides, so as to afford sufficient drains, with good and substantial bridges and proper culverts and sluices when necessary. All stumps and roots to be thoroughly grubbed out between the ditches the entire length of said road, the central portion of which to be sufficiently raised to afford a dry road-bed by means of drainage from the centre to the side ditches; the hills to be levelled and valleys raised so as to make as easy a grade as practicable.

SEC. 4. *And be it further enacted,* That when the Governor of the State of Michigan shall furnish the Secretary of the Interior with maps and charts showing the definite location of the line of each of said roads, it shall be his duty to have the land granted to each of said roads withheld from market, and reserved exclusively for the purposes aforesaid. And when the said Governor shall certify to the Secretary of the Interior that any ten consecutive miles of either of said roads have been completed under the provisions of this act, and in accordance with the third section thereof, stating definitely where said completed section of road commences and where it terminates, it shall be the duty of the said Secretary to cause patents to issue to said State for three sections of land for each mile of road thus completed, as aforesaid, and so on until the whole of said roads is completed: *Provided,* That no patents shall be given for any of the aforesaid lands before the completion of ten consecutive miles of road, or for any road, or for any part of any road, made before the passage of this act, or for any greater quantity than thirty sections for each ten miles completed according to the provisions of this act. Nothing in this proviso, however, shall be construed so as to prevent the application of so much of the said three sections per mile as may be necessary to finish any part of said roads partly made before the passage of this act.

SEC. 5. *And be it further enacted,* That this grant is made upon the express conditions that the roads shall be and remain public highways, free from all toll and other charges; and that if any portion of said roads shall remain uncompleted for a period of more than five years from the approval of this act by the President, the lands granted for such portion shall revert to the United States.

Approved, June 20, 1864.

No. 95 B.—An Act to confirm certain entries of land in the State of Missouri.

Be it enacted by the Senate and House of Representatives of the United States of America in Congress assembled, That all entries heretofore made under the graduation act of August fourth, eighteen hundred and fifty-four,* in township forty-five north, of range nine west, south of Mis-

* Vol. I. No. 251.

souri River, in the district of land subject to sale at St. Louis, Missouri, shall be and are hereby confirmed: *Provided, however*, That this act shall not extend to any entry of land aforesaid upon which there was an actual settler other than the purchaser at the date of such entry, and that it shall first be shown to the satisfaction of the Secretary of the Interior that the entry has been made in good faith, and is founded upon actual settlement and cultivation, or is for the use of an adjoining farm: *Provided further*, That the lands shall be paid for in money, or in land warrants, to the amount of one dollar and twenty-five cents per acre.

Approved, June 20, 1864.

No. 96 B.—An Act concerning certain lands in the State of California.

Be it enacted by the Senate and House of Representatives of the United States of America in Congress assembled, That, under the patent of the United States, issued on the 28th day of February, 1861, to Joseph S. Alemany, as the Bishop of Monterey, and his successors, for the tract of land or rancho known as Canada de los Pinos, or College Rancho, situate in the county of Santa Barbara, State of California, as described in such patent, to have and to hold the same to him and them "in trust for the religious purposes and uses" therein mentioned, it shall be lawful for the said Joseph S. Alemany, and his successors, as the grantees of said patent, to sell the said tract or rancho, or any part thereof, and all proper conveyances in that behalf to make and deliver, and the proceeds thereof to apply, under the direction of the Roman Catholic Archbishop of San Francisco, in the State of California, and his successors in office, or other proper authority of the Roman Catholic Church in said State, for the purposes of education anywhere within said State, not inconsistent with the laws thereof; anything in such patent, or in the original grant or concession of said tract or rancho, or other title whereby the same was acquired from and under the authorities of Spain or Mexico, to the contrary notwithstanding; and all trusts, conditions, provisions, or covenants, precedent or subsequent, expressed or implied, in said patent, grant, concession, or title, to the contrary hereof, and all breaches of the same, are hereby wholly waived, abrogated, discharged, dispensed with, and released on the part of the United States, for the purposes of this act; and any conveyance or disposition made in pursuance thereof shall operate to pass all the right and interest of the United States in said lands to the grantee.

Approved, June 20, 1864.

No. 97 B.—An Act granting lands to the State of Wisconsin to build a military road to Lake Superior.

feasible and direct route, to a point on the State line between the States of Wisconsin and Michigan, in a direction leading to Ontonagon, on Lake Superior, every alternate section of public land, not mineral, designated odd numbers, for three sections in width on each side of said road. But in case it shall appear that the United States have, when the line or route of said road is definitely fixed, sold, reserved, or otherwise disposed of any section, or any part thereof, granted as aforesaid, or that the right of pre-emption or homestead settlement has attached to the same, then it shall be the duty of the Secretary of the Interior to set apart from the public lands of the United States, as hereinbefore described, designated by odd numbers, as near to said even section aforesaid as may be, and the same shall be located within six miles of said road, so much land as shall be equal to such lands as the United States have sold or otherwise appropriated, or to which the right of pre-emption or homestead settlement has attached; which lands (thus selected in lieu of those sold, reserved, or otherwise appropriated, and to which the right of pre-emption or homestead settlement has attached as aforesaid), together with the sections and parts of sections designated by odd numbers as aforesaid, and approved as aforesaid, shall be held by the State of Wisconsin for the use and purpose aforesaid: *Provided*, That the lands hereby granted shall be exclusively applied in the construction of that road for and on account of which such lands are hereby granted, and shall be disposed of only as the work progresses, and the same shall be applied to no other purpose whatever: *Provided further*, That any and all lands heretofore reserved to the United States, or granted by any act of Congress, or in any other manner by competent authority, for the purpose of aiding in any object of internal improvement, or for any other purpose whatsoever, be, and the same are hereby, reserved and excluded from the operation of this act, except so far as it may be found necessary to locate the route of said road through such reserved lands, in which case the right of way only shall be granted.

SEC. 2. *And be it further enacted*, That, the said lands hereby granted to the said State shall be subject to the disposal of the legislature thereof, for the purposes aforesaid and no other; and the said road shall be, and remain, a public highway for the use of the Government of the United States, free from tolls or other charge upon the transportation of any property, troops, or mails of the United States.

SEC. 3. *And be it further enacted*, That the lands hereby granted to said State shall be disposed of only in the following manner—that is to say, when the said Governor shall certify to the Secretary of the Interior that any ten consecutive miles of said road has been completed under the provisions of this act, and in accordance with the fourth section of this act, stating definitely where said completed section of road commences and where it terminates, it shall be the duty of the said Secretary to cause patents to issue to said State for three sections of land for each mile of road thus completed as aforesaid, and so on until the whole of said road is completed: *Provided further*, That no patent shall be given for any of the aforesaid lands before the completion of ten consecutive miles of road, or for any road, or for any part of any road, made before the passage of this act, or for any greater quantity than thirty sections for each ten miles completed according to the provisions of this act; and if said road is not completed within five years, no further sales shall be made, and the lands unsold shall revert to the United States.

SEC. 4. *And be it further enacted*, That said military road shall be constructed under the direction of such agents or commissioners as the

Governor of said State may appoint, and where it passes through timbered lands shall be chopped out at uniform width of at least six rods. The road-bed proper to be not less than thirty-two feet wide, and constructed with ample ditches on both sides, so as to afford sufficient drains, with good and substantial bridges and proper culverts and sluices where necessary. All stumps and roots to be thoroughly grubbed out between the ditches the entire length of said road; the central portion of which to be sufficiently raised to afford a dry road-bed by means of drainage from the centre to the side ditches: the hills to be levelled and valleys raised so as to make as easy a grade as practicable.

Approved, June 25, 1864.

No. 98 B.—An Act to amend the act of Congress making donations to the settlers on the public lands in Oregon, approved September twenty-seven, eighteen hundred and fifty, and the acts amendatory thereto.*

Be it enacted by the Senate and House of Representatives of the United States of America in Congress assembled, That in all cases under the act of Congress approved September twenty-seventh, eighteen hundred and fifty,* entitled "An act to create the office of Surveyor-General of the public lands in Oregon, and to provide for the survey, and to make donations to settlers of said public lands," and the several acts amendatory and supplemental thereto, in which the actual settlement may be shown to be bona fide, and the claim in all respects to be fully within the requirements of existing laws, except as to the failure of the party to file notice within the time fixed by statute, such failure shall not work forfeiture when no adverse rights intervene before the filing of the required notification by the claimant.

Approved, June 25, 1864.

No. 99 B.—An Act to grant to the State of California certain lands for State prison purposes.

Be it enacted by the Senate and House of Representatives of the United States of America in Congress assembled, That the right of the United States to the lands comprising that portion of the promontory or point known as "Punta de Quintin," or "Point San Quintin," lying east of the north and south line, dividing sections number three and ten from number two and eleven in township number one north, range number six west, of Mount Diablo meridian, embracing portions numbers eleven, twelve, thirteen, and fourteen of the said township number one north, range number six west, upon which the State prison of the State of California is now located, not exceeding in quantity four hundred and fifty acres, be, and the same is hereby, ceded, granted, and confirmed to the said State of California, without prejudice to the rights or claims of any other parties.

Approved, June 25, 1864.

* Vol. I. No. 181. See, also, No. 73 B. and 80 B.

No. 100 B.—An Act to aid in the settlement, subsistence, and support of the Navajoe Indian captives upon a reservation in the Territory of New Mexico.

Be it enacted by the Senate and House of Representatives of the United States of America in Congress assembled, That there be, and hereby is, appropriated, out of any moneys in the treasury not otherwise appropriated, to be expended under the direction of the Secretary of the Interior, for the purpose of settling the Navajoe Indians, now captives in New Mexico, upon a reservation upon the Pecos River, in New Mexico, for the purchase of agricultural implements, seeds, and other articles necessary for such purpose, for breaking the ground, and for subsistence of said Indians to the end of the next fiscal year, the sum of one hundred thousand dollars.

SEC. 2. *And be it further enacted,* That the said reservation may, under the direction of the Secretary of the Interior, be so extended and enlarged on the south, as to include the entire valley of the Pecos River, known as the Bosqué Grandé, and that the whole of said reservation, so enlarged, shall be designated and known as the Navajoe and Apache Reservation, and as such shall, until otherwise ordered by law, be exempt from sale, and free from all occupancy except by the said Indians for the purposes herein mentioned; excepting such portion of the said land as is now occupied by Fort Sumner, or as may be needed for the use of said post.

SEC. 3. *And be it further enacted,* That the southern Apache agency of New Mexico is hereby abolished, and that an agent for the Kioway, Apache, and Camanche Indians be appointed, at a salary of fifteen hundred dollars per annum.

Approved, June 30, 1864.

No. 101 B.—An Act authorizing a grant to the State of California of the "Yo-Semite Valley," and of the land embracing the "Mariposa Big Tree Grove."

Be it enacted by the Senate and House of Representatives of the United States of America in Congress assembled, That there shall be, and is hereby, granted to the State of California the "Cleft" or "Gorge" in the granite peak of the Sierra Nevada Mountains, situated in the county of Mariposa, in the State aforesaid, and the headwaters of the Merced River, and known as the Yo-Semite Valley, with its branches or spurs, in estimated length fifteen miles, and in average width one mile back from the main edge of the precipice, on each side of the valley, with the stipulation, nevertheless, that the said State shall accept this grant upon the express conditions that the premises shall be held for public use, resort and recreation; shall be inalienable for all time; but leases not exceeding ten years may be granted for portions of said premises. All incomes derived from leases of privileges to be expended in the preservation and improvement of the property, or the roads leading thereto; the boundaries to be established at the cost of said State by the United States Surveyor-General of California, whose official plat, when affirmed by the Commissioner of the General Land Office, shall constitute the evidence of the locus, extent, and limits of the said Cleft or Gorge; the premises to be managed by the Governor of the State with eight other commissioners, to be appointed by the executive of California, and who shall receive no compensation for their services.

SEC. 2. *And be it further enacted*, That there shall likewise be, and there is hereby, granted to the said State of California the tracts embracing what is known as the "Mariposa Big Tree Grove," not to exceed the area of four sections, and to be taken in legal subdivisions of one quarter section each, with the like stipulation as expressed in the first section of this act as to the State's acceptance, with like conditions as in the first section of this act as to inalienability, yet with same lease privilege; the income to be expended in preservation, improvement, and protection of the property; the premises to be managed by commissioners as stipulated in the first section of this act, and to be taken in legal subdivisions as aforesaid; and the official plat of the United States Surveyor-General, when affirmed by the Commissioner of the General Land Office, to be the evidence of the locus of the said Mariposa Big Tree Grove.

Approved, June 30, 1864.

No. 102 B.—An Act authorizing the issue of patents for locations made with certificates granted under authority of the act of Congress approved March seventeenth, eighteen hundred and sixty-two, allowing floats in satisfaction of lands sold by the United States within the limits of the Las Ormegas and La Nana grants in Louisiana.

Be it enacted by the Senate and House of Representatives of the United States of America in Congress assembled, That in the case of all locations made with certificates issued under the act of Congress approved seventeenth March, eighteen hundred and sixty-two,* "authorizing floats to issue in satisfaction of claims against the United States for lands sold by them within the Las Ormegas and La Nana grants, in the State of Louisiana," it shall and may be lawful for the Commissioner of the General Land Office to cause patents to issue for such locations, where the same may be found bona fide and satisfactory to the said commissioner.

Approved, June 30, 1864.

No. 103 B.—An Act to expedite the settlement of titles to lands in the State of California.

Be it enacted by the Senate and House of Representatives of the United States of America in Congress assembled, That whenever the Surveyor-General of California shall, in compliance with the thirteenth section of an act entitled "An act to ascertain and settle the private land claims in the State of California," approved March third, eighteen hundred and fifty-one,† have caused any private land claim to be surveyed and a plat to be made thereof, he shall give notice that the same has been done by a publication, once a week for four consecutive weeks, in two newspapers, one published in the city of San Francisco, and one published near the land surveyed; and shall retain in his office, for public inspection, the survey and plat until ninety days from the date of the first publication in

* No. 37 B. † See Vol. I. No. 189. No. 169 B.

San Francisco shall have expired; and if no objections are made to said survey, he shall approve the same, and transmit a copy of the survey and plat thereof to the Commissioner of the General Land Office at Washington, for his examination and approval; but if objections are made to said survey within the said ninety days, by any party claiming to have an interest in the tract embraced by the survey, or in any part thereof, such objections shall be reduced to writing, stating distinctly the interest of the objector, and signed by him or his attorney, and filed with the Surveyor-General, together with such affidavits or other proofs as he may produce in support of the objections. At the expiration of said ninety days the Surveyor-General shall transmit to the Commissioner of the General Land Office at Washington a copy of the survey and plat, and objections, and proofs filed with him in support of the objections, and also of any proofs produced by the claimant and filed with him in support of the survey, together with his opinion thereon; and if the survey and plat are approved by the said commissioner, he shall indorse thereon a certificate of his approval. If disapproved by him, or if, in his opinion, the ends of justice would be subserved thereby, he may require a further report from the Surveyor-General of California, touching the matters indicated by him, or proofs to be taken thereon, or may direct a new survey and plat to be made. Whenever the objections are disposed of, or the survey and plat are corrected, or a new survey and plat are made in conformity with his directions, he shall indorse upon the survey and plat adopted his certificate of approval. After the survey and plat have been, as hereinbefore provided, approved by the Commissioner of the General Land Office, it shall be the duty of the said commissioner to cause a patent to issue to the claimant as soon as practicable after such approval.

SEC. 2. *And be it further enacted*, That the provisions of the preceding section shall apply to all surveys and plats by the Surveyor-General of California heretofore made, which have not already been approved by one of the district courts of the United States for California, or by the Commissioner of the General Land Office: *Provided*, That where proceedings for the correction or confirmation of a survey are pending on the passage of this act in one of the said district courts, it shall be lawful for such District Court to proceed and complete its examination and determination of the matter, and its decree thereon shall be subject to appeal to the Circuit Court of the United States for the district in like manner, and with like effect, as hereafter provided for appeals in other cases to the Circuit Court; and such appeals may be in like manner disposed of by said Circuit Court.

SEC. 3. *And be it further enacted*, That where a plat and survey have already been approved or corrected by one of the district courts of the United States for California, and an appeal from the decree of approval or correction has already been taken to the Supreme Court of the United States, the said Supreme Court shall have jurisdiction to hear and determine the appeal. But where from such decree of approval or correction no appeal has been taken to the Supreme Court, no appeal to that court shall be allowed, but an appeal may be taken, within twelve months after this act shall take effect, to the Circuit Court of the United States for California, and said Circuit Court shall proceed to fully determine the matter. The said Circuit Court shall have power to affirm or reverse or modify the action of the District Court, or order the case back to the Surveyor-General for a new survey. When the case is ordered back for a new survey, the subsequent survey of the Surveyor-General shall be under the supervision of the Commissioner of the General Land Office, and not of the District or Circuit Court of the United States.

SEC. 4. *And be it further enacted*, That whenever the district judge of any one of the District Courts of the United States for California is interested in any land, the claim to which, under the said act of March third, eighteen hundred and fifty-one, is pending before him, on appeal from the Board of Commissioners created by said act, the said District Court shall order the case to be transferred to the Circuit Court of the United States for California, which court shall thereupon take jurisdiction and determine the same. The said District Courts may also order a transfer to the said Circuit Court of any other cases arising under said act, pending before them, affecting the title to lands within the corporate limits of any city or town, and in such cases both the District and Circuit Judges may sit.

SEC. 5. *And be it further enacted*, That all the right and title of the United States to the lands within the corporate limits of the city of San Francisco, as defined in the act incorporating said city, passed by the legislature of the State of California, on the fifteenth of April, one thousand eight hundred and fifty-one, are hereby relinquished and granted to the said city and its successors, for the uses and purposes specified in the ordinances of said city, ratified by an act of the legislature of the said State, approved on the eleventh of March, eighteen hundred and fifty-eight, entitled "An act concerning the city of San Francisco, and to ratify and confirm certain ordinances of the common council of said city," there being excepted from this relinquishment and grant all sites or other parcels of land which have been, or now are, occupied by the United States for military, naval, or other public uses, or such other sites or parcels as may hereafter be designated by the President of the United States, within one year after the rendition to the General Land Office, by the Surveyor-General, of an approved plat of the exterior limits of San Francisco, as recognized in this section, in connection with the lines of the public surveys: *And provided*, That the relinquishment and grant by this act shall in no manner interfere with or prejudice any bona fide claims of others, whether asserted adversely under rights derived from Spain, Mexico, or the laws of the United States, nor preclude a judicial examination and adjustment thereof.

SEC. 6. *And be it further enacted*, That it shall be the duty of the Surveyor-General of California to cause all the private land claims finally confirmed to be accurately surveyed and plats thereof to be made, whenever requested by the claimants: *Provided*, That each claimant requesting a survey and plat shall first deposit in the District Court of the district within which the land is situated a sufficient sum of money to pay the expenses of such survey and plat, and of the publication required by the first section of this act. Whenever the survey and plat requested shall have been completed and forwarded to the Commissioner of the General Land Office, as required by this act, the District Court may direct the application of the money deposited, or so much thereof as may be necessary, to the payment of the expenses of said survey and publication.

SEC. 7. *And be it further enacted*, That it shall be the duty of the Surveyor-General of California, in making surveys of the private land claims finally confirmed, to follow the decree of confirmation as closely as practicable whenever such decree designates the specific boundaries of the claim. But when such decree designates only the out-boundaries, within which the quantity confirmed is to be taken, the location of such quantity shall be made, as near as practicable, in one tract and in a compact form. And if the character of the land, or intervening grants, be such as to render the location impracticable in one tract, then each separate location shall be made, as near as practicable, in a compact form. And it shall be the duty of the Commissioner of the General Land Office to require a substantial compliance with the directions of this section before approving any survey and plat forwarded to him.

SEC. 8. *And be it further enacted,* That the act entitled "An act to amend an act entitled 'An act to define and regulate the jurisdiction of the District Courts of the United States in California, in regard to the survey and location of confirmed private land claims,'" approved June fourteen, eighteen hundred and sixty, and all provisions of law inconsistent with this act are hereby repealed.*

Approved, July 1, 1864.

No. 104 B.—An Act for the sale of a lot of land in Iowa, in the Fort Crawford Reservation.

Be it enacted by the Senate and House of Representatives of the United States of America in Congress assembled, That it shall and may be lawful for the Commissioner of the General Land Office to cause to be sold, after public notice, the tract described as lot numbered one, in township ninety-five north, of range three west of the fifth principal meridian, in the State of Iowa, situated in what is known as the Fort Crawford military reservation, subject to such minimum price per acre as the said Commissioner may establish as fair and reasonable, not less than two dollars and fifty cents per acre; and in the event of said lot not being disposed of at public sale, the Commissioner is hereby authorized to reoffer the same at public sale; or after the second offering to dispose of said lot at such minimum as he may establish, and for the sale so made a patent shall issue as in ordinary cases.

SEC. 2. *And be it further enacted,* That if it shall appear that there are any other lots in said reserve not disposed of by the United States, it shall and may be lawful for the said commissioner to dispose of the same in the manner provided in the foregoing section.

Approved, July 1, 1864.

No. 105 B.—An Act to regulate the compensation of registers and receivers of the land offices in the several States and Territories, in the location of lands by States and corporations under grants from Congress.

Be it enacted by the Senate and House of Representatives of the United States of America in Congress assembled, That from and after the passage of this act, in the location of lands by States and corporations under grants from Congress for railroads and other purposes (except for agricultural colleges), the registers and receivers of the land offices of the several States and Territories, in the districts where such lands may be located, for their services therein shall be entitled to receive a fee of one dollar for each final location of one hundred and sixty acres, to be paid by the State or corporation making such location, the same to be accounted for in the same manner as fees and commissions on warrants and pre-emption locations, with limitations as to maximums of salary prescribed by existing laws, in accordance with such instructions as shall be given by the Commissioner of the General Land Office.

SEC. 2. *And be it further enacted*, That the Burlington and Missouri River Railroad Company may so far change or modify the location of the uncompleted portion of its line, as shown by the map thereof now on file in the General Land Office of the United States, so as to secure a better and more expeditious route to the terminus of said line on the Missouri River, said new line to be located within the limits of the land grant made by the United States to aid in its construction; and said change shall not impair the right to, nor change the location of, their present land grant. A map of the change shall be filed with the Commissioner of the General Land Office within one year after the passage of this act.*

Approved, July 1, 1864.

No. 106 B.—An Act making an additional grant of lands to the State of Kansas to aid in the construction of railroad and telegraph lines.

Be it enacted by the Senate and House of Representatives of the United States of America in Congress assembled, That there be, and hereby is, granted to the State of Kansas, to aid in the construction of a railroad and telegraph line from Emporia, via Council Grove, to a point near Fort Riley, on the branch Union Pacific Railroad, in said State, every alternate section of land designated by odd numbers for ten sections in width on each side of said road: *Provided*, That this grant shall be subject to all the provisions, restrictions, limitations, and conditions, in regard to selection and location of lands and otherwise, of an act of Congress approved March three, eighteen hundred and sixty-three,† entitled "An act for a grant of lands to the State of Kansas, in alternate sections, to aid in the construction of certain railroads and telegraphs in said State": *Provided*, That said railroad shall be a public highway and shall transport troops and munitions of war of the United States free of charge.

SEC. 2. *And be it further, enacted*, That the branch railroad and telegraph from "Lawrence, by the valley of the Wakarusa River, to a point on the Atchison, Topeka, and Santa Fee Railroad, where said road intersects the Neosho River," to aid in the construction of which a grant of lands was made by the said act of third of March, eighteen hundred and sixty-three, shall be so changed as to run from Lawrence to Emporia, and have and receive the grant of lands made by said act: *Provided*, That the line of railroad and telegraph from Leavenworth, by way of Lawrence and the Ohio City crossing of the Osage River, to the southern line of the State in the direction of Galveston Bay, shall run via Baldwin City.

Approved, July 1, 1864.

* No. 138 B. Amended, No. 129 B.

† No. 67 B.

No. 107 B.—An Act to encourage and facilitate telegraph communication between the Eastern and Western Continents.

Whereas the Governments of Russia and Great Britain have granted to Perry MacDonough Collins, a citizen of the United States, the right to construct and maintain a line of electric telegraph through their respective territories, from the mouth of the Amoor River, in Asiatic Russia, by way of Behring's Strait and along the Pacific coast to the northern boundary of the United States, with a view of thereby uniting the telegraphic systems of both continents, and of promoting international and commercial intercourse; and whereas, the Government of Russia, in furtherance of that object, is now constructing a line of telegraph through its Asiatic territory to unite at the mouth of the Amoor River with the line projected by said Collins; and whereas the Government of the United States desires cordially to co-operate with Russia and Great Britain in the establishment and maintenance of such a line of communication; now, therefore—

Be it enacted by the Senate and House of Representatives of the United States of America in Congress assembled, That Perry MacDonough Collins, of California, his associates and assignees, shall have the right to construct and maintain a line or lines of telegraph from any point or points on the line of the Pacific telegraph, constructed in pursuance of the act of Congress, approved June sixteen, eighteen hundred and sixty, northerly, through any of the Territories of the United States, to the boundaries of British America, with such branch lines as may be needed to open communication with the various mining districts and other settlements in said Territories. And for the purposes aforesaid, the said Collins, his associates and assignees, shall have a permanent right of way over any unappropriated public lands of the United States, together with the right to take any timber and stone for construction purposes; and for the purpose of establishing and maintaining said lines and the stations necessary for the repair and working thereof, there is hereby granted to said parties the use of so much unappropriated public lands not sold, granted, reserved, pre-empted, nor occupied by homestead settlers, as may be necessary for stations, not exceeding forty acres for each fifteen miles of line constructed across the public lands of the United States, so long as the same may be used for said purpose: *Provided, however,* That so much of section one of this act as authorizes the construction of telegraph lines to open communications with the various mining districts and other settlements in said Territories, shall be null and void, unless said branch-lines shall be completed within five years from the approval hereof.

* * * * * * * * *

Approved, July 1, 1864.

No. 108 B.—An Act for the disposal of coal lands and of town property in the public domain.*

Be it enacted by the Senate and House of Representatives of the United States of America in Congress assembled, That where any tracts embracing coal-beds or coal-fields, constituting portions of the public domain, and which as " mines," are excluded from the pre-emption act of eighteen hundred and forty-one, and which under past legislation are not liable to ordinary private entry, it shall and may be lawful for the President to cause such tracts, in suitable legal subdivisions, to be offered at public sale to the highest bidder, after public notice of not less than three months, at a minimum price of twenty dollars per acre; and any lands not thus disposed of shall thereafter be liable to private entry at said minimum.

SEC. 2. *And be it further enacted,* That in any case in which parties have already founded, or may hereafter desire to found, a city or town on the public lands, it shall and may be lawful for them to cause to be filed with the recorder for the county in which the same is situated, a plat thereof, for not exceeding six hundred and forty acres, describing its exterior boundaries according to the lines of the public surveys, where such surveys have been executed; also giving the name of such city or town, and exhibiting the streets, squares, blocks, lots, and alleys, the size of the same, with measurements and area of each municipal subdivision, the lots in which shall each not exceed four thousand two hundred square feet, with a statement of the extent and general character of the improvements; the said map and statement to be verified under oath by the party acting for, and in behalf, of the persons proposing to establish such city or town; and within one month after such filing there shall be transmitted to the General Land Office a verified transcript of such map and statement, accompanied by the testimony of two witnesses that such city or town has been established in good faith, and when the premises are within the limits of an organized land district, a similar map and statement shall be filed with the register and receiver, and at any time after the filing of such map, statement, and testimony in the General Land Office, it shall and may be lawful for the President to cause the lots embraced within the limits of such city or town to be offered at public sale to the highest bidder, subject to a minimum of ten dollars for each lot; and such lots as may not be disposed of at public sale, shall thereafter be liable to private entry at said minimum, or at such reasonable increase or diminution thereafter as the Secretary of the Interior may order from time to time, after at least three months' notice, in view of the increase or decrease in the value of the municipal property: *Provided,* That any actual settler upon any one lot, as aforesaid, and upon any additional lot in which he may have substantial improvements, shall be entitled to prove up and purchase the same as a pre-emption, at said minimum, at any time before the day fixed for the public sale.

SEC. 3. *And be it further enacted,* That when such cities or towns are established upon unsurveyed lands, it shall and may be lawful, after the extension thereto of the public surveys, to adjust the extension limits of the premises according to those lines, where it can be done without interference with rights which may be vested by sale; and patents for all lots so disposed of at public or private sale shall issue as in ordinary cases.

SEC. 4. *And be it further enacted,* That if within twelve months from the establishment of a city or town, as aforesaid in the public domain, the parties interested shall refuse or fail to file in the General Land Office transcript map with the statement and testimony called for by the provisions of the second section of this act, it shall and may be lawful for the Secretary of the Interior to cause a survey and plat to be made of such city or town, and thereafter the lots in the same shall be disposed of as required by said provisions, with this exception, that they shall each be at an increase of fifty per centum on the aforesaid minimum of ten dollars per lot.

SEC. 5. *And be it further enacted*, That effect shall be given to the foregoing act, according to such regulations as may be prescribed by the Secretary of the Interior. The act entitled "An act for the relief of the citizens of towns upon the lands of the United States, under certain circumstances," approved May twenty-three, Anno Domini eighteen hundred and forty-four,* and all other acts and parts of acts inconsistent with this act, be, and the same are hereby, repealed.

Approved, July 1, 1864.

No. 109 B.—An Act making appropriations for sundry civil expenses of the Government for the year ending the thirtieth of June, eighteen hundred and sixty-five, and for other purposes.

* * * * * * * * *

SEC. 8. *And be it further enacted*, That until otherwise directed by law, the Territory of New Mexico, and the Territory of Arizona shall constitute one Surveyor-General's district; That the Territory of Idaho and Nevada shall constitute, and be a part of, the Surveyor-General's district of Colorado; That the Territory of Dakota and Montana shall constitute one Surveyor-General's district, and that there shall be but one office of Surveyor-General for each Surveyor-General's district; That the provisions of this section shall be executed under such rules and regulations as may be prescribed by the Commissioner of the General Land Office; and that all acts and parts of acts in conflict with the provisions of this section are hereby repealed.

* * * * * * * * *

Approved, July 2, 1864.

No. 110 B.—An Act granting lands to the State of Oregon, to aid in the construction of a military road from Eugene City to the eastern boundary of said State.†

Be it enacted by the Senate and House of Representatives of the United States of America in Congress assembled, That there be, and hereby is, granted to the State of Oregon, to aid in the construction of a military wagon-road from Eugene City, by way of Middle Fork of Willamette River, and the most feasible pass in Cascade range of mountains, near Diamond Peak, to the eastern boundary of the State, alternate sections of public lands, designated by odd numbers, for three sections in width on each side of said road: *Provided*, That the lands hereby granted shall be exclusively applied in the construction of said road, and shall be disposed of only as the work progresses; and the same shall be applied to no other purpose whatever; *and provided further*, That any and all lands heretofore reserved to the United States by act of Congress, or other competent authority, be, and the same are, reserved from the operation of this act, except so far as it may be necessary to locate the route of said road through the same, in which case the right of way is granted.

* Vol. I. No. 179.

† Amended, No. 186 B.—No. 234 B.

SEC. 2. *And be it further enacted,* That the said lands hereby granted to said State shall be disposed of by the legislature thereof for the purpose aforesaid, and for no other; and the said road shall be and remain a public highway for the use of the Government of the United States, free from tolls or other charge upon the transportation of any property, troops, or mails of the United States.

SEC. 3. *And be it further enacted,* That said road shall be constructed with such width, graduation, and bridges, as to permit of its regular use as a wagon-road, and in such other special manner as the State of Oregon may prescribe.

SEC. 4. *And be it further enacted,* That the lands hereby granted to said State shall be disposed of only in the following manner, that is to say: that a quantity of land not exceeding thirty sections for said road may be sold; and when the Governor of said State shall certify to the Secretary of the Interior that any ten continuous miles of said road are completed, then another quantity of land hereby granted, not to exceed thirty sections, may be sold, and so from time to time until said road is completed; and if said road is not completed within five years, no further sales shall be made, and the land remaining unsold shall revert to the United States.

Approved, July 2, 1864.

No. 111 B.—An Act to amend an act entitled "An act to aid in the construction of a railroad and telegraph line from the Missouri River to the Pacific Ocean, and to secure the Government the use of the same for postal, military, and other purposes," approved July first, eighteen hundred and sixty-two.*

Be it enacted by the Senate and House of Representatives of the United States of America in Congress assembled, That the capital stock of the company entitled the Union Pacific Railroad Company, authorized by the act of which this act is amendatory, shall be in shares of one hundred dollars, instead of one thousand dollars, each; that the number of shares shall be one million, instead of one hundred thousand; and that the number of shares which any person shall hold to entitle him to serve as a director in said company (except the five directors to be appointed by Government) shall be fifty shares, instead of five shares; and that every subscriber to said capital stock for each share of one thousand dollars, heretofore subscribed, shall be entitled to a certificate for ten shares of one hundred dollars each; and that the following words in section first of said act: "which shall be subscribed for and held in not more than two hundred shares by any one person," be, and the same are hereby, repealed.

[SEC. 2. *Provides that books of subscription shall be kept open in certain cities—and for subscription to stock assessment, &c.*]

[SEC. 3. *Provides that railroads may purchase and hold lands necessary for road, for appraisement, damages to absent land-owners, &c.*]

SEC. 4. *And be it further enacted,* That section three of said act be hereby amended by striking out the word "five," where the same occurs in said section, and by inserting in lieu thereof the word "ten;" and by striking out the word "ten," where the same occurs in said section, and by inserting in lieu thereof the word "twenty." And section seven of

* No. 45 B.—No. 182 B.—No. 150 B.

said act is hereby amended by striking out the word "fifteen," where the same occurs in said section, and inserting in lieu thereof the word "twenty-five." And the term "mineral land," wherever the same occurs in this act, and the act to which this is an amendment, shall not be construed to include coal and iron land. And any lands granted by this act, or the act to which this is an amendment, shall not defeat or impair any pre-emption, homestead, swamp land, or other lawful claim, nor include any Government reservation or mineral lands, or the improvements of any bona fide settler or* [on] any lands returned and denominated as mineral lands, and the timber necessary to support his said improvements as a miner, or agriculturalist, to be ascertained under such rules as have been or may be established by the Commissioner of the General Land Office, in conformity with the provisions of the pre-emption laws: *Provided*, That the quantity thus exempted by the operation of this act, and the act to which this act is an amendment, shall not exceed one hundred and sixty acres for each settler who claims as an agriculturalist, and such quantity for each settler who claims as a miner, as the said commissioner may establish by general regulation: *Provided, also,* That the phrase "but where the same shall contain timber, the timber thereon is hereby granted to said company," in the proviso to said section three, shall not apply to the timber growing or being on any land farther than ten miles from the centre line of any one of said roads or branches mentioned in said act, or in this act. And all lands shall be excluded from the operation of this act, and of the act to which this act is an amendment, which were located, or selected to be located, under the provisions of an act entitled "An act donating lands to the several States and territories which may provide colleges for the benefit of agriculture and the mechanic arts," approved July second, eighteen hundred and sixty-two, and notice thereof given at the proper land office.

SEC. 5. *And be it further enacted*, That the time for designating the general route of said railroad, and of filing the map of the same, and the time for the completion of that part of the railroads required by the terms of said act of each company, be, and the same is hereby, extended one year from the time in said act designated; and that the Central Pacific Railroad Company of California shall be required to complete twenty-five miles of their said road in each year thereafter, and the whole to the State line within four years, and that only one-half of the compensation for services rendered for the Government by said companies shall be required to be applied to the payment of the bonds issued by the Government in aid of the construction of said roads.

SEC. 6. *And be it further enacted*, That the proviso to section four of said act is hereby modified as follows, viz: And the President of the United States is hereby authorized, at any time after the passage of this act, to appoint for each and every of said roads three commissioners, as provided for in the act to which this is amendatory; and the verified statement of the President of the California Company, required by said section four, shall be filed in the office of the United States Surveyor-General for the State of California, instead of being presented to the President of the United States; and the said Surveyor-General shall thereupon notify the said commissioners of the filing of such statement, and the said commissioners shall thereupon proceed to examine the portion of said railroad and telegraph line so completed, and make their

* The word *on* should here be substituted for *or*, the latter being an error in the Statutes at Large, as certified by the State Department.

report thereon to the President of the United States, as provided by the act of which this is amendatory. And such statement may be filed, and such railroad and telegraph line be examined and reported on, by the said commissioners, and the requisite amount of bonds may be issued, and the lands appertaining thereto may be set apart, located, entered, and patented, as provided in this act and the act to which this is amendatory, upon the construction by said railroad company of California of any portion of not less than twenty consecutive miles of their said railroad and telegraph line, upon the certificate of said commissioners that such portion is completed as required by the act to which this is amendatory. And section ten of the act of which this is amendatory is hereby amended by inserting, after the words "United States," in the last clause, the words "and States intervening."

SEC. 7. *And be it further enacted*, That so much of section seventeen of said act as provides for a reservation by the Government of a portion of the bonds to be issued to aid in the construction of the said railroads is hereby repealed. And the failure of any one company to comply fully with the conditions and requirements of this act, and the act to which this is amendatory, shall not work a forfeiture of the rights, privileges, or franchise of any other company or companies that shall have complied with the same.

[SEC. 8. *Provides that a portion of the bonds may be issued when engineer certifies that part of the work is done.*]

SEC. 9. *And be it further enacted*, That to enable any one of said corporations to make convenient and necessary connections with other roads, it is hereby authorized to establish and maintain all necessary ferries upon and across the Missouri River and other rivers which its road may pass in its course; and authority is hereby given said corporation to construct bridges over said Missouri River, and all other rivers for the convenience of said road: *Provided*, That any bridge or bridges it may construct over the Missouri River, or any other navigable river on the line of said road shall be constructed with suitable and proper draws for the passage of steamboats, and shall be built, kept, and maintained, at the expense of said company in such manner as not to impair the usefulness of said rivers for navigation to any greater extent than such structures of the most approved character necessarily do: *And provided further*, That any company authorized by this act to construct its road and telegraph line from the Missouri River to the initial point aforesaid, may construct its road and telegraph line so as to connect with the Union Pacific Railroad at any point westwardly of such initial point, in case such company shall deem such westward connection more practicable or desirable; and in aid of the construction of so much of its road and telegraph line as shall be a departure from the route hereinbefore provided for its road, such company shall be entitled to all the benefits, and be subject to all the conditions and restrictions, of this act: *Provided further, however*, That the bonds of the United States shall not be issued to such company for a greater amount than is hereinbefore provided, if the same had united with the Union Pacific Railroad on the 100th degree of longitude; nor shall such company be entitled to receive any greater amount of alternate sections of public lands than are also herein provided.

SEC. 10. *And be it further enacted*, That section five of said act be so modified and amended that the Union Pacific Railroad Company, the Central Pacific Railroad Company, and any other company authorized to participate in the construction of said road, may, on the completion of each section of said road, as provided in this act and the act to which this act is an amendment, issue their first mortgage bonds on their respective railroad and telegraph lines to an amount not exceeding the amount of the bonds of the United States, and of even tenor and date, time of maturity, rate and character of interest with the bonds authorized to be issued to said railroad companies respectively. And the lien of the United States bonds shall be subordinate to that of the bonds of any or either of said companies hereby authorized to be issued on their respective roads, property, and equipments, except as to the provisions of the sixth section of the act to which this act is an amendment, relating to the transmission of dispatches and the transportation of mails, troops, munitions of war, supplies and public stores for the Government of the United States. And said section is further amended by striking out the word "forty," and inserting in lieu thereof the words "on each and every section of not less than twenty."

SEC. 11. *And be it further enacted*, That if any of the railroad companies entitled to bonds of the United States, or to issue their first mortgage bonds herein provided for, has, at the time of the approval of this act, issued, or shall thereafter issue, any of its own bonds or securities in such form or manner as in law or equity to entitle the same to priority or preference of payment to the said guaranteed bonds, or said first mortgage bonds, the amount of such corporate bonds outstanding and unsatisfied, or uncancelled, shall be deducted from the amount of such Government and first mortgage bonds which the company may be entitled to receive and issue; and such an amount only of such Government bonds and such first mortgage bonds shall be granted or permitted, as added to such outstanding, unsatisfied, or uncancelled bonds of the company shall make up the whole amount per mile to which the company would otherwise have been entitled: *And provided further*, That before any bonds shall be so given by the United States, the company claiming them shall present to the Secretary of the Treasury an affidavit of the President and Secretary of the company, to be sworn to before the judge of a court of record, setting forth whether said company has issued any such bonds or securities, and if so, particularly describing the same, and such other evidence as the Secretary may require, so as to enable him to make the deduction herein required; and such affidavit shall then be filed and deposited in the office of the Secretary of the Interior. And any person swearing falsely to any such affidavit, shall be deemed guilty of perjury, and on conviction thereof, shall be punished as aforesaid: *Provided, also*, That no land granted by this act shall be conveyed to any party or parties, and no bonds shall be issued to any company or companies, party or parties, on account of any road or part thereof, made prior to the passage of the act to which this act is an amendment, or made subsequent thereto under the provisions of any act or acts other than this act, and the act amended by this act.

SEC. 12. *And be it further enacted*, That the Leavenworth, Pawnee, and Western Railroad Company, now known as the Union Pacific Railroad Company, eastern division, shall build the railroad from the mouth of Kansas River, by the way of Leavenworth, or, if that be not deemed the best route, then the said company shall, within two years, build a railroad from the city of Leavenworth to unite with the main stem at or near the city of Lawrence; but to aid in the construction of said branch the said company shall not be entitled to any bonds. And if the Union Pacific Railroad Company shall not be proceeding in good faith to build the said railroad through the territories when the Leavenworth, Pawnee, and Western Railroad Company, now known as the Union Pacific Railroad Company eastern division, shall have completed their road to the hundredth degree of longitude, then the last-named company may proceed to make said road westward until it meets and connects with the Central Pacific Railroad Company on the same line. And the said railroad from the mouth of Kansas River to the one hundredth meridian of longitude shall be made by the way of Lawrence and Topeka, or on the bank of the Kansas River opposite said towns: *Provided*, That no bonds shall be issued or land certified by the United States to any person or company, for the construction of any part of the main trunk-line of said railroad west of the one hundredth meridian of longitude and east of the Rocky Mountains, until said road shall be completed from or near Omaha, on the Missouri River, to the said one hundredth meridian of longitude.

SEC. 13. *And be it further enacted*, That at and after the next election of directors, the number of directors to be elected by the stockholders shall be fifteen; and the number of directors to be appointed by the President shall be five; and the President shall appoint three additional directors to serve until the next regular election, and thereafter five directors. At least one of said government directors shall be placed on each of the standing committees of said company, and at least one on every special committee that may be appointed. The government directors shall, from time to time, report to the Secretary of the Interior, in answer to any inquiries he may make of them, touching the condition, management, and progress of the work, and shall communicate to the Secretary of the Interior, at any time, such information as should be in the possession of the department. They shall, as often as may be necessary to a full knowledge of the condition and management of the line, visit all portions of the line of road, whether built or surveyed; and while absent from home, attending to their duties as directors, shall be paid their actual travelling expenses, and be allowed and paid such reasonable compensation for their time actually employed as the board of directors may decide.

SEC. 14. *And be it further enacted*, That the next election for directors of said railroad shall be held on the first Wednesday of October next, at the office of said company in the city of New York, between the hours of ten o'clock A. M. and 4 o'clock P. M. of said day; and all subsequent regular elections shall be held annually thereafter at the same place; and the directors shall hold their offices for one year, and until their successors are qualified.

SEC. 15. *And be it further enacted*, That the several companies authorized to construct the aforesaid roads are hereby required to operate and use said roads and telegraph for all purposes of communication, travel, and transportation, so far as the public and the government are concerned, as one continuous line; and, in such operation and use, to afford and secure to each equal advantages and facilities as to rates, time, and transportation, without any discrimination of any kind in favor of the road or business of any or either of said companies, or adverse to the road or business of any or either of the others, and it shall not be lawful for the proprietors of any line of telegraph, authorized by this act, or the act amended by this act, to refuse, or fail to convey for all persons requiring the transmission of news and messages of like character, on pain of forfeiting to the person injured for each offence, the sum of one hundred dollars, and such other damage as he may have suffered on account of said refusal or failure, to be sued for and recovered in any court of the United States, or of any State or territory of competent jurisdiction.

SEC. 16. *And be it further enacted*, That any two or more of the companies authorized to participate in the benefits of this act, are hereby authorized at any time to unite and consolidate their organizations, as the same may or shall be, upon such terms and conditions, and in such manner as they may agree upon, and as shall not be incompatible with this act, or the laws of the State or States in which the roads of such companies may be, and to assume and adopt such corporate name and style as they may agree upon, with a capital stock not to exceed the actual cost of the roads so to be consolidated, and shall file a copy of such consolidation in the Department of the Interior; and thereupon such organization, so formed and consolidated, shall succeed to, possess, and be entitled to receive from the Government of the United States, all and singular the grants, benefits, immunities, guarantees, acts, and things to be done and performed, and be subject to the same terms, conditions, restrictions, and requirements which said companies respectively, at the time of such consolidation, are or may be entitled or subject to under this act, in place and substitution of said companies so consolidated respectively. And all other provisions of this act, so far as applicable, relating or in any manner appertaining to the companies so consolidated, or either thereof, shall apply and be of force as to such consolidated organization. And in case upon the completion by such consolidated organization of the roads, or either of them, of the companies so consolidated, any other of the road or roads of either of the other companies authorized as aforesaid (and forming, or intended or necessary to form, a portion of a continuous line from each of the several points on the Missouri River, hereinbefore designated, to the Pacific coast), shall not have constructed the number of miles of its said road within the time herein required, such consolidated organization is hereby authorized to continue the construction of its road and telegraph in the general direction and route upon which such incomplete or unconstructed road is hereinbefore authorized to be built, until such continuation of the road of such consolidated organization shall reach the constructed road and telegraph of said other company, and at such point to connect and unite therewith; and for and in aid thereof the said consolidated organization may do and perform, in reference to such portion of road and telegraph as shall so be in continuation of its constructed road and telegraph, and to the construction and equipment thereof, all and singular, the several acts and things hereinbefore provided, authorized, or granted to be done by the company hereinbefore authorized to construct and equip the same, and shall be entitled to similar and like grants, benefits immunities, guarantees, acts, and things to be done and performed by the Government of the United States, by the President of the United States, by the Secretaries of the Treasury and Interior, and by commissioners in reference to such company, and to such portion of the road hereinbefore authorized to be constructed by it, and upon the like and similar terms and conditions, so far as the same are applicable thereto. And said consolidated company shall pay to said defaulting company the value to be estimated by competent engineers of all the work done and material furnished by said defaulting company, which may be adopted and used by said consolidated company in the progress of the work under the provisions of this section: *Provided, nevertheless,* That said defaulting company may at any time, before receiving pay for its said work and material, as hereinbefore provided, on its own election, pay said consolidated company the value of the work done and material furnished by said consolidated company, to be estimated by competent engineers, necessary for, and used in, the construction of the road of said defaulting company, and resume the control of its said road; and all the rights, benefits, and privileges which shall be acquired, possessed or exercised, pursuant to this section, shall be to that extent an abatement of the rights, benefits, and privileges hereinbefore granted to such other company. And in case any company authorized thereto, shall not enter into such consolidated organization, such company, upon the completion of its road as hereinbefore provided, shall be entitled to, and is hereby authorized to, continue and extend the same under the circumstances, and in accordance with the provisions of this section, and to have all the benefits thereof, as fully and completely as are herein provided, touching such consolidated organization. And in case more than one such consolidated organization shall be made, pursuant to this act, the terms and conditions of this act, hereinbefore recited as to one, shall apply in like manner, force, and effect to the other: *Provided, however,* That rights and interests at any time acquired by one such consolidated organization, shall not be impaired by another thereof. It is further provided that, should the Central Pacific Railroad Company of California complete their line to the eastern line of the State of California, before the line of the Union Pacific Railroad Company shall have been extended westward so as to meet the line of said first-named company, said first named company may extend their lines of road eastward one hundred and fifty miles on the established route, so as to meet and connect with the line of the Union Pacific Road, complying in all respects with the provisions and restrictions of this act as to said Union Pacific Road, and upon doing so, shall enjoy all the rights, privileges, and benefits conferred by this act on said Union Pacific Railroad Company.

SEC. 17. *And be it further enacted,* That so much of section fourteen of said act as relates to a branch from Sioux City be, and the same is hereby, amended so as to read as follows: That whenever a line of railroad shall be completed through the States of Iowa, or Minnesota, to Sioux City, such company, now organized or may hereafter be organized under the laws of Iowa, Minnesota, Dakota, or Nebraska, as the President of the United States, by its request, may designate or approve for that purpose, shall construct and operate a line of railroad and telegraph from Sioux City, upon the most direct and practicable route, to such a point on, and so as to connect with, the Iowa branch of the Union Pacific Railroad from Omaha, or the Union Pacific Railroad, as such company may select, and on the same terms and conditions as are provided in this act and the act to which this is an amendment, for the construction of the said Union Pacific Railroad and telegraph line and branches; and said company shall complete the same at the rate of fifty miles per year: *Provided,* That said Union Pacific Railroad Company shall be, and is hereby, released from the construction of said branch. And said company constructing such branch shall not be entitled to receive in bonds an amount larger than the said Union Pacific Railroad Company would be entitled to receive if it had constructed the branch under this act and the act to which this is an amendment; but said company shall be entitled to receive alternate sections of land for ten miles in width on each side of the same along the whole length of said branch: *And provided further,* That if a railroad should not be completed to Sioux City, across Iowa or Minnesota, within eighteen months from the date of this act, then said company designated by the President, as aforesaid, may commence, continue, and complete the construction of said branch as contemplated by the provisions of this act: *Provided, however,* That if the said company so designated by the President as aforesaid shall not complete the said branch from Sioux City to the Pacific Railroad within ten years from the passage of this act, then, and in that case, all of the railroad which shall have been constructed by said company shall be forfeited to, and become the property of, the United States.

SEC. 18. *And be it further enacted,* That the Burlington and Missouri River Railroad Company, a corporation organized under and by virtue of the laws of the State of Iowa, be, and hereby is, authorized to extend i[t]s road through the Territory of Nebraska from the point where it strikes the Missouri River, south of the mouth of the Platte River, to some point not further west than the one hundredth meridian of west longitude, so as to connect, by the most practicable route, with the main trunk of the Union Pacific Railroad, or that part of it which runs from Omaha to the said one hundredth meridian of west longitude. And for the purpose of enableing said Burlington and Missouri River Railroad Company to construct that portion of their road herein authorized, the right of way through the public lands is hereby granted to said company for the construction of said road. And the right, power, and authority is hereby given to said company to take from the public lands adjacent to the line of said road, earth, stone, timber, and other materials for the construction thereof. Said right of way is granted to said company to the extent of two hundred feet where it may pass over the public lands, including all necessary grounds for stations, buildings, workshops, depots, machine shops, switches, side-tracks, turn-tables, and water-stations. And the United States shall extinguish, as rapidly as may be consistent with public policy and the welfare of the said Indians, the Indian titles to all lands falling under the operation of this section and required for the said right of way and grant of land herein made.

SEC. 19. *And be it further enacted,* That for the purpose of aiding in the construction of said road, there be, and hereby is, granted to the said Burlington and Missouri River Railroad Company, every alternate section of public land (excepting mineral lands as provided in this act) designated by odd numbers, to the amount of ten alternate sections per mile on each side of said road, on the line thereof, and not sold, reserved, or otherwise disposed of by the United States, and to which a pre-emption or homestead claim may not have attached at the time the line of said road is definitely fixed: *Provided,* That said company shall accept this grant within one year from the passage of this act, by filing such acceptance with the Secretary of the Interior, and shall also establish the line of said road, and file a map thereof with the Secretary of the Interior within one year of the date of said acceptance, when the said Secretary shall withdraw the lands embraced in this grant from market.

SEC. 20. *And be it further enacted,* That whenever said Burlington and Missouri River Railroad Company shall have completed twenty consecutive miles of the road mentioned in the foregoing section, in the manner provided for other roads mentioned in this act, and the act to which this is an amendment, the President of the United States shall appoint three commissioners to examine and report to him in relation thereto; and if it shall appear to him that twenty miles of said road have been completed as required by this act, then, upon certificate of said commissioner[s] to that effect, patents shall issue conveying the right and title to said lands to said company on each side of said road, as far as the same is completed, to the amount aforesaid; and such examination, report, and conveyance, by patents, shall continue from time to time, in like manner, until said road shall have been completed. And the President shall appoint said commissioners, fill vacancies in said commission, as provided in relation to other roads mentioned in the act to which this is an amendment. And the said company shall be entitled to all the privileges and immunities granted to the Hannibal and Saint Joseph's Railroad Company by the said last-mentioned act, so far as the same may be applicable: *Provided,* That no Government bonds shall be issued to the said Burlington and Missouri River Railroad Company to aid in the construction of said extension of its road: *And provided further,* That said extension shall be completed within the period of ten years from the passage of this act.

SEC. 21. *And be it further enacted,* That before any land granted by this act shall be conveyed to any company or party entitled thereto under this act, there shall first be paid into the treasury of the United States, the cost of surveying, selecting, and conveying the same, by the said company or party in interest, as the titles shall be required by said company, which amount shall, without any further appropriation, stand to the credit of the proper account, to be used by the Commissioner of the General Land Office for the prosecution of the survey of the public lands along the line of said road, and so from year to year until the whole shall be completed, as provided under the provisions of this act.

SEC. 22. *And be it further enacted,* That Congress may, at any time, alter, amend, or repeal this act.

Approved, July 2, 1864.

No. 112 B.—An Act granting lands to aid in the construction of a railroad and telegraph line from Lake Superior to Puget's Sound, on the Pacific coast, by the northern route.

Be it enacted by the Senate and House of Representatives of the United States of America in Congress assembled, That Richard D. Rice * * * (and others), * * * and all such persons who shall or may be associated with them, and their successors, are hereby created and erected into a body corporate and politic, in deed and in law, by the name, style, and title of the "Northern Pacific Railroad Company," and by that name shall have perpetual succession, and shall be able to sue and to be sued, plead and be impleaded, defend and be defended, in all courts of law and equity within the United States, and may make and have a common seal. And said corporation is hereby authorized and empowered to lay out, locate, construct, furnish, maintain, and enjoy a continuous railroad and telegraph line, with the appurtenances, namely, beginning at a point on Lake Superior, in the State of Minnesota or Wisconsin; thence westerly by the most eligible railroad route, as shall be determined by said company, within the territory of the United States, on a line north of the forty-fifth degree of latitude to some point on Puget's Sound, with a branch, via the valley of the Columbia River, to a point at or near Portland, in the State of Oregon, leaving the main trunk-line at the most suitable place, not more than three hundred miles from its western terminus; and is hereby vested with all the powers, privileges, and immunities necessary to carry into effect the purposes of this act as herein set forth. The capital stock of said company shall consist of one million shares of one hundred dollars each, which shall in all respects be deemed personal property, and shall be transferable in such manner as the by-laws of said corporation shall provide. The persons hereinbefore named are hereby appointed commissioners, and shall be called the Board of Commissioners of the "Northern Pacific Railroad Company," and fifteen shall constitu[t]e a quorum for the transaction of business.

* * * * * * * * *

SEC. 2. *And be it further enacted*, That the right of way through the public lands be, and the same is hereby, granted to said "Northern Pacific Railroad Company," its successors and assigns, for the construction of a railroad and telegraph as proposed; and the right, power, and authority is hereby given to said corporation to take from the public lands, adjacent to the line of said road, material of earth, stone, timber, and so forth, for the construction thereof. Said way is granted to said railroad to the extent of two hundred feet in width on each side of said railroad where it may pass through the public domain, including all necessary ground for station buildings, workshops, depots, machine shops, switches, side tracks, turn-tables, and water-stations; and the right of way shall be exempt from taxation within the territories of the United States. The United States shall extinguish, as rapidly as may be consistent with public policy and the welfare of the said Indians, the Indian titles to all lands falling under the operation of this act, and acquired in the donation to the [road] named in this bill.

SEC. 3. *And be it further enacted*, That there be, and hereby is, granted to the "Northern Pacific Railroad Company," its successors and assigns, for the purpose of aiding in the construction of said railroad and telegraph line to the Pacific coast, and to secure the safe and speedy transportation of the mails, troops, munitions of war, and public stores, over the route of said line of railway, every alternate section of public land, not mineral, designated by odd numbers, to the amount of twenty alternate sections per mile, on each side of said railroad line, as said company may adopt, through the territories of the United States, and ten alternate sections of land per mile on each side of said railroad whenever it passes through any State, and whenever on the line thereof, the United States have full title, not reserved, sold, granted, or otherwise appropriated, and free from pre-emption, or other claims or rights, at the time the line of said road is definitely fixed, and a plat thereof filed in the office of the Commissioner of the General Land Office; and whenever prior to said time, any of said sections or parts of sections shall have been granted, sold, reserved, occupied by homestead settlers, or pre-empted, or otherwise disposed of, other lands shall be selected by said company in lieu thereof, under the direction of the Secretary of the Interior, in alternate sections, and designated by odd numbers, not more than ten miles beyond the limits of said alternate sections: *Provided*, That if said route shall be found upon the line of any other railroad route to aid in the construction of which lands have been heretofore granted by the United States, as far as the routes are upon the same general line, the amount of land heretofore granted shall be deducted from the amount granted by this act: *Provided further*, That the railroad company receiving the previous grant of land may assign their interest to said "Northern Pacific Railroad Company," or may consolidate, confederate, and associate with said company upon the terms named in the first section of this act: *Provided further*, That all mineral lands be, and the same are hereby, excluded from the operations of this act, and in lieu thereof a like quantity of unoccupied and unappropriated agricultural lands, in odd numbered sections, nearest to the line of said road may be selected as above provided: *And provided further*, That the word "mineral," when it occurs in this act, shall not be held to include iron or coal: *And provided further*, That no money shall be drawn from the treasury of the United States to aid in the construction of the said "Northern Pacific Railroad."

SEC. 4. *And be it further enacted*, That whenever said "Northern Pacific Railroad Company" shall have twenty-five consecutive miles of any portion of said railroad and telegraph line ready for the service contemplated, the President of the United States shall appoint three commissioners to examine the same, and if it shall appear that twenty-five consecutive miles of said road and telegraph line have been completed in a good, substantial, and workmanlike manner, as in all other respects required by this act, the commissioners shall so report to the President of the United States, and patents of lands, as aforesaid, shall be issued to said company, confirming to said company the right and title to said lands, situated opposite to, and coterminous with, said completed section of said road; and, from time to time, whenever twenty-five additional consecutive miles shall have been constructed, completed, and in readiness as aforesaid, and verified by said commissioners to the President of the United States, then patents shall be issued to said company conveying the additional sections of land as aforesaid, and so on as fast as every twenty-five miles of said road is completed as aforesaid: *Provided*, That not more than ten sections of land per mile, as said road shall be completed, shall be conveyed to said company for all that part of said railroad lying east of the western boundary of the State of Minnesota, until the whole of said railroad shall be finished and in good running order, as a first-class railroad, from the place of beginning on Lake Superior to the western boundary of Minnesota: *Provided, also*, That lands shall not be granted under the provisions of this act on account of any railroad, or part thereof, constructed at the date of the passage of this act.

* * * * * * * * *

SEC. 6. *And be it further enacted*, That the President of the United States shall cause the lands to be surveyed for forty miles in width on both sides of the entire line of said road, after the general route shall be fixed, and as fast as may be required by the construction of said railroad; and the odd sections of land hereby granted shall not be liable to sale, or entry, or pre-emption before or after they are surveyed, except by said company, as provided in this act; but the provisions of the act of September [fourth], eighteen hundred and forty-one,* granting pre-emption rights, and the acts amendatory thereof, and of the act entitled "An act to secure homesteads to actual settlers on the public domain," approved May twenty, eighteen hundred and sixty-two, shall be, and the same are hereby, extended to all other lands on the line of said road, when surveyed, excepting those hereby granted to said company. And the reserved alternate sections shall not be sold by the Government at a price less than two dollars and fifty cents per acre, when offered for sale.

SEC. 7. *And be it further enacted*, That the said "Northern Pacific Railroad Company" be, and is hereby, authorized and empowered to enter upon, purchase, take, and hold any lands or premises that may be necessary and proper for the construction and working of said road, not exceeding in width two hundred feet on each side of the line of its railroad, unless a greater width be required for the purpose of excavation or embankment; and also any lands or premises that may be necessary and proper for turnouts, standing places for cars, depots, station-houses, or any other structures required in the construction and working of said road. And the said company shall have the right to cut and remove trees and

* Vol. I. No. 48.

other material that might, by falling, encumber its road-bed, though standing or being more than two hundred feet from the line of said road.

* * * * * * * * *

SEC. 8. *And be it further enacted,* That each and every grant, right, and privilege herein are so made and given to, and accepted by, said Northern Pacific Railroad Company, upon and subject to the following conditions, namely: That the said company shall commence the work on said road within two years from the approval of this act by the President, and shall complete not less than fifty miles per year after the second year, and shall construct, equip, furnish, and complete the whole road by the fourth day of July, anno Domini eighteen hundred and seventy-six.*

* * * * * * * * *

SEC. 17. *And be it further enacted,* That the said company is authorized to accept to its own use any grant, donation, loan, power, franchise, aid, or assistance which may be granted to, or conferred upon, said company by the Congress of the United States, by the Legislature of any State, or by any corporation, person, or persons; and said corporation is authorized to hold and enjoy any such grant, donation, loan, power, franchise, aid, or assistance, to its own use for the purpose aforesaid.

* * * * * * * * *

Approved, July 2, 1864.

No. 113 B.—An Act to quiet the titles to lands within the Rancho Laguna de Santos Callé, in the State of California.

Be it enacted by the Senate and House of Representatives of the United States of America in Congress assembled, That it may and shall be lawful for all purchasers from the grantees or their assigns of lands within the Rancho Laguna de Santos Callé, in the State of California, to file, within twelve months from the passage of this act, with the register of the land office at Marysville, applications describing the lands so purchased by them respectively, with proofs of bona fide purchase from the said grantees or their assigns; and upon such proofs being found satisfactory, the said purchasers shall be permitted to enter, according to the lines of the public surveys, at one dollar and twenty-five cents per acre, the lands so purchased within the limits of said rancho, as described in the petition presented to the Board of Commissioners under the act of March 3, 1851, entitled "An act to ascertain and settle the private land claims in the State of California," to the extent to which the lands so purchased have been reduced to possession, and are now held by said purchasers: *Provided,* That any person who shall avail himself of the provisions of this act shall be thereafter debarred any further claim under the grantee in the event of a final confirmation of the grant.

SEC. 2. *And be it further enacted,* That where any additional surveys may be found necessary to give full effect to this act, the Commissioner of the General Land Office shall cause such surveys to be made at the cost of the purchasers, as provided by the 10th section of the act of May 30th, 1862,† entitled "An act to reduce the expenses of the survey and sale of the public lands of the United States:" *Provided,* That no entry of mineral lands or lands reserved for military or other public uses, shall be

* Extended—182 B. No. 224 B.

† No. 39 B.

permitted under this act, nor shall any rights acquired under the pre-emption laws of the United States be affected hereby.

SEC. 3. *And be it further enacted*, That it shall be the duty of the register and receiver of the proper land office to receive all applications in cases presented under this act, pursuant to such instructions as may be prescribed by the Commissioner of the General Land office, and to adjudge all such cases as preliminary to a final decision in due course of law.

Approved, July 2, 1864.

No. 114 B.—An Act for increased facilities of telegraph communication between the Atlantic and Pacific States and the Territory of Idaho.

Be it enacted by the Senate and House of Representatives of the United States of America in Congress assembled, That the United States Telegraph Company, and their associates, are hereby authorized to erect a line or lines of magnetic telegraph between the Missouri River and the city of San Francisco, in the State of California, on such route as they may select, to connect with the lines of the said United States Telegraph Company, now constructed, and being constructed through the States of the Union. The said company shall have the use of such unoccupied lands of the United States as may be necessary for the right of way, and materials, and for the establishing of stations along said line for repairs, not exceeding at any station one quarter section of land; and such stations not to exceed one in fifteen miles on the average of the whole line, unless said lands shall be required by the Government of the United States for railroad or other purposes: *And provided*, That no right to pre-empt any of said lands under the laws of the United States shall enure to said company or their agents, or any other person or persons whatsoever.

* * * * * * * * *

Approved, July 2, 1864.

No. 115 B.—An Act in relation to the sale of reservations of the public lands.

Be it enacted by the Senate and House of Representatives of the United States of America in Congress assembled, That whenever any reservation of public lands shall be brought into market under existing laws, it shall be lawful for the Commissioner of the General Land Office to fix a minimum price, not less than one dollar and twenty-five cents per acre, below which such lands shall not be disposed of.

Approved, July 2, 1864.

No. 116 B.—An Act prescribing the terms on which exemplifications shall be furnished by the General Land Office.

Be it enacted by the Senate and House of Representatives of the United States of America in Congress assembled, That from and after the first day of July next, all exemplifications of patents, or papers on file, or of record in the General Land Office, which may be required by parties interested, shall be furnished by the commissioner of said office upon the payment by such parties at the rate of fifteen cents per hundred words, and two dollars for copies of township plat[e]s or diagrams, with an additional sum of one dollar for the commissioner's certificate of verification with the General Land Office seal; and one of the employees of said office shall be designated by the said commissioner as the receiving clerk, and the amounts so received shall, under the direction of said commissioner, be paid into the Treasury of the United States; effect to be given to this act according to such regulations as may be prescribed by the Secretary of the Interior not inconsistent with the laws of the United States: *Provided*, That the fees stipulated in the foregoing provisions shall not apply to such authenticated copies as may be required by the officers of any branch of the Government, nor to such unverified copies as the commissioner in his discretion may deem proper to furnish.

Approved, July 2, 1860.

No. 117 B.—An Act providing for satisfying claims for bounty lands, and for other purposes.

Be it enacted by the Senate and House of Representatives of the United States of America in Congress assembled, That the act entitled "An act to provide for satisfying claims for bounty lands for military services in the late war with Great Britain, and for other purposes," approved July twenty-seventh, in the year one thousand eight hundred and forty-two,* and the two acts approved January twenty-seventh, in the year one thousand eight hundred and thirty-five, therein and thereby revived, and also the two acts to the same intent and purpose, respectively approved the twenty-sixth day of June, in the year eighteen hundred and forty-eight, and the eighth day of February, in the year eighteen hundred and fifty-four, be, and the same are hereby, renewed and continued in force and effect, without restriction or limitation as to the time of location of said warrants issued in virtue thereof.

SEC. 2. *And be it further enacted*, That all warrants for bounty lands heretofore issued in virtue of any of the several acts hereinbefore named, may be located at any time subsequent to the passage of this act, in conformity with the general laws in force at the time of such location; and that all entries and locations heretofore made with such warrants shall be as valid and effectual as if the several acts aforesaid had not expired at the time of such entry and location, any law to the contrary notwithstanding.

SEC. 3. *And be it further enacted*, That all acts and parts of acts inconsistent with the provisions of this act, be, and the same are hereby, repealed.

Approved, July 2, 1864.

* Vol. I. No. 55.

No. 118 B.—Joint Resolution granting certain privileges to the City of Des Moines, in the State of Iowa.

Be it resolved by the Senate and House of Representatives of the United States of America in Congress assembled, That the United States hereby relinquish to the City of Des Moines, in the State of Iowa, a municipal corporation established under the laws of said State, all their right and interest in the coal-beds underlying the River Des Moines, within the limits of said city: *Provided,* That no disposition or use thereof shall be made which shall obstruct the free navigation of said river; nor shall any one grant of the privilege of mining the same extend for a longer period than ten years.

Approved, June 15, 1864.

No. 119 B.—A Resolution explanatory of an act entitled "An act extending the time for the completion of the Marquette and Ontonagon Railroad of the State of Michigan."*

Resolved by the Senate and House of Representatives of the United States of America in Congress assembled, That the provisions of the act entitled "An act extending the time for the completion of the Marquette and Ontonagon Railroad of the State of Michigan," shall be so construed as to extend the time for completing only so much of said road as lies between Marquette and Ontonagon.

Approved, June 18, 1864.

No. 120 B.—A Resolution for the relief of the State of Wisconsin.

Resolved by the Senate and House of Representatives of the United States of America in Congress assembled, That the Secretary of the Department of the Interior shall, in adjusting the amount due the State of Wisconsin, under existing laws, as five per centum of the net proceeds of sales of the public lands within her limits, estimate and charge against her the value of the one hundred and twenty-five thousand four hundred and thirty-one and eighty-two one-hundredths acres of land granted to the Territory of Wisconsin, to aid in the construction of the Milwaukee and Rock River Canal which have been sold by said Territory or said State, at one dollar and twenty-five cents per acre, and as much more as the Territory and State received upon the same upon sales of any part thereof at a higher price, and shall credit said State with the amount that has been legally and properly applied by said State or Territory towards the cost of selling said land and towards the construction of said canal. And the said secretary shall also settle and allow to the Milwaukee and Rock River Canal Company such sums of money as have been properly expended by said company in the survey and location of said canal, in the construction thereof, as far as the same has been constructed, together

* No. 93 B.

with dams, locks, and slack-water navigation, and in the management and keeping the same in repair; and the same shall be paid to the said canal company out of any money in the treasury not otherwise appropriated, not exceeding in amount, however, the balance charged against the State of Wisconsin upon the sales of said canal lands, as above required, after deducting the sum allowed said State for money paid by her out of the same fund. The same to be received by said canal company in full payment and satisfaction of all claims of said company against the State of Wisconsin and of the United States on account of said canal land grant, or on account of any action of the Territory or State of Wisconsin, or of the United States, in relation thereto.

SEC. 2. *And be it further resolved*, That the Commissioner of the General Land Office be, and he is hereby, appointed commissioner to adjust the accounts herein provided for, under the supervision of the Secretary of the Interior, and to determine what sum shall be charged to said State of Wisconsin for the lands granted for the construction of said canal; and what sums shall be credited, respectively, to said State and said company for the moneys expended by them in the construction of said locks and canal as herein provided.

Approved, July 1, 1864.

No. 121 B.—A Resolution explanatory of the tenth section of "An act to reduce the expenses of the survey and sale of the public lands in the United States," approved, May 30, 1862.*

Resolved by the Senate and House of Representatives of the United States of America in Congress assembled, That the tenth section of an act entitled "An act to reduce the expenses of the survey and sale of the public lands in the United States," approved the thirtieth day of May, eighteen hundred and sixty-two, providing for the deposit of money in a proper United States depository to pay for the survey of public lands, shall be construed to be an appropriation of the sums so deposited for the objects contemplated in the said tenth section, and the Secretary of the Treasury is authorized to cause the sums deposited under the said section to be placed to the credit of the proper appropriations for the surveying service: *Provided*, That any excesses in the sums so deposited, over and above the actual cost of the surveys, comprising all expenses incident thereto, for which they were severally deposited, shall be repaid to the depositors respectively.

Approved, July 1, 1864.

No. 122 B.—An Act to extinguish the Indian title to lands in the Territory of Utah suitable for agricultural and mineral purposes.

Be it enacted by the Senate and House of Representatives of the United States of America in Congress assembled, That the President of the United States be, and he is hereby, authorized, by and with the advice and consent of the Senate, to enter into treaties with the various tribes

* No. 39 B.

of Indians of Utah Territory, upon such terms as may be deemed just to said Indians and beneficial to the Government of the United States: *Provided*, That such treaties shall provide for the absolute surrender to the United States, by said Indians, of their possessory right to all the agricultural and mineral lands in said territory, except such agricultural lands as by said treaties may be set apart for reservations for said Indians: *And provided further*, That all such reservations shall be selected at points as remote as may be practicable from the present settlements in Utah Territory.

SEC. 2. *And be it further enacted*, That in agreeing with said Indians upon the amounts to be paid to them under the provisions of the treaties to be negotiated in pursuance of this act, care shall be taken to obtain from the Indians, to the greatest possible extent, their consent to receive for such payments agricultural implements, stock, and other useful articles, rather than money.

SEC. 3. *And be it further enacted*, That for the purpose of negotiating said treaties and carrying out the provisions of this act, making presents to said Indians, and defraying the necessary expenses incident to such negotiation, there is hereby appropriated, out of any money in the treasury of the United States not otherwise appropriated, the sum of twenty-five thousand dollars.

Approved, February 23, 1865.

No. 123 B.—An Act to provide for the payment of the value of certain lands and improvements of private citizens, appropriated by the United States for Indian reservations, in the Territory of Washington.

Be it enacted by the Senate and House of Representatives of the United States of America in Congress assembled, That the sum of eighteen thousand six hundred and eleven dollars and sixty-two cents, or so much thereof as may be necessary, is hereby appropriated out of any money in the treasury not otherwise appropriated, for the purpose of paying for the lands and improvements of private citizens, taken and appropriated, by order of the Department of the Interior, for Indian reservations and uses in the Territory of Washington; and the claims herein provided to be paid shall be allowed and paid in such manner and upon such proofs of the value of the property as shall be prescribed by the Secretary of the Interior.

Approved, February 23, 1865.

No. 124 B.—An Act providing for a District and a Circuit Court of the United States for the District of Nevada, and for other purposes.

* * * * * * * * *

SEC. 9. *And be it further enacted*, That no possessory action between individuals in any of the courts of the United States for the recovery of any mining title, or for damages to any such title, shall be affected by the fact that the paramount title to the land on which such mines are, is in the United States, but each case shall be adjudged by the law of possession.

Approved, February 27, 1865.

No. 125 B.—An Act making appropriations for the legislative, executive, and judicial expenses of the Government for the year ending June thirtieth, eighteen hundred and sixty-six, and additional appropriations for the current fiscal year.*

* * * * * * * * *

SEC. 3. *And be it further enacted,* That from and after the passage of this act, the public lands in the State of Nevada shall, for surveying purposes, be attached to and included in the surveying district of California.

Approved, March 2, 1865.

No. 126 B.—An Act to amend an act entitled "An act to aid in the construction of a railroad and telegraph line from the Missouri River to the Pacific Ocean, and to secure to the Government the use of the same for postal, military, and other purposes," approved July first, eighteen hundred and sixty-two, and to amend an act amendatory thereof, approved July second, eighteen hundred and sixty-four.†

* * * * * * * * *

SEC. 2. *And be it further enacted,* That the assignment made by the Central Pacific Railroad Company of California to the Western Pacific Railroad Company of said State, of the right to construct all that portion of said railroad and telegraph from the City of San José to the City of Sacramento is hereby ratified and confirmed to the said Western Pacific Railroad Company, with all the privileges and benefits of the several acts of Congress relating thereto, and subject to all the conditions thereof: *Provided,* That the time within which the said Western Pacific Railroad Company shall be required to construct the first twenty miles of their said road, shall be one year from the first day of July, eighteen hundred and sixty-five, and that the entire road shall be completed from San José to Sacramento, connecting at the latter point with the said Central Pacific Railroad, within four years thereafter.

Approved, March 3, 1865.

No. 127 B.—An Act granting land to the State of Michigan, to aid in building a harbor and ship canal at Portage Lake, Kewenaw Point, Lake Superior.‡

Be it enacted by the Senate and House of Representatives of the United States of America in Congress assembled, That there be, and is hereby, granted to the State of Michigan the right of locating and constructing a breakwater and harbor and ship canal through any public lands at or upon the neck of land on Lake Superior known as "The Portage:" *Provided,* That not more than one thousand feet in width on the bank of Lake Superior shall be occupied by said breakwater and harbor, and that a strip of land not more than four hundred feet in width on said neck of land shall be occupied by said canal: *And provided further,* That said ship canal shall be at least one hundred feet in width, with a depth of water not less than thirteen feet.

* See No. 36 B. and No. 39 B.

† No. 45 B. No. 111 B.

‡ See No. 152 B.

SEC. 2. *And be it further enacted*, That there be, and hereby is, granted to the State of Michigan, for the purpose of aiding said State in constructing and completing a harbor and ship canal to connect the waters of Lake Superior with the waters of Portage Lake, two hundred thousand acres of public lands, to be selected in subdivisions agreeably to the United States survey, by an agent or agents appointed by the Governor of said State, subject to the approval of the Secretary of the Interior, from any lands in the upper peninsula of said State subject to private entry: *Provided*, That said selections shall be made from alternate and odd numbered sections of land nearest the location of said canal in said upper peninsula, not otherwise appropriated, and not from lands designated by the United States as "mineral" before the passage of this act, nor from lands to which the rights of pre-emption or homestead have attached.

SEC. 3. *And be it further enacted*, That the said lands hereby granted shall be subject to the disposal of the legislature of said State, or, if the legislature thereof shall not be in session, or shall adjourn within ten days after the passage and approval of this act, then said lands shall be subject to the disposal of the Governor and board of control of said State, for the purpose aforesaid and for no other; and the said canal shall be and remain a public highway for the use of the Government of the United States, free from toll or charge upon the vessels of said Government, or upon vessels employed by said Government in the transportation of any property or troops of the United States.

SEC. 4. *And be it further enacted*, That before it shall be competent for said State to dispose of any of said lands, to be selected as aforesaid, the plan of said breakwater and harbor, and the route of said canal shall be established as aforesaid, and a plat or plats thereof shall be filed in the office of the War Department, and a duplicate thereof in the office of the Commissioner of the General Land Office.

SEC. 5. *And be it further enacted*, That if the said breakwater, harbor, and ship canal shall not be completed within two years from the passage of this act, the lands hereby granted shall revert to the United States.

SEC. 6. *And be it further enacted*, That the Legislature of said State shall cause to be kept an accurate account of the sales and net proceeds of the lands hereby granted, and of all expenditures in the construction, repairs, and operating of said canal, and of the earnings thereof, and shall return a statement of the same annually to the Secretary of the Interior; and whenever said State shall be fully reimbursed for all advances made for the construction, repairs, and operating of said canal, with legal interest on all advances, until the reimbursement of the same, or upon payment by the United States of any balance of such advances over such receipts from said lands and canal, with such interest, the said State shall be allowed to tax for the use of said canal only such tolls as shall be sufficient to pay all necessary expenses for the care, charge, and repair of the same.

Approved, March 3, 1865.

No. 128 B.—An Act to extend the time for the completion of certain railroads to which land grants have been made in the States of Michigan and Wisconsin.*

Be it enacted by the Senate and House of Representatives of the United States of America in Congress assembled, That there be, and hereby is, granted to the State of Michigan, for the purpose of aiding in the construction of a railroad from Marquette, on Lake Superior, to the Wisconsin State line, at or near the mouth of the Menomonee River, for the benefit and use of the Chicago and Northwestern Railway Company, a corporation of the States of Michigan, Illinois, Wisconsin, and from Marquette to Ontonagon, for the use and benefit of the Marquette and Ontonagon Railroad Company, a corporation of the State of Michigan, and for twenty miles westerly from Marquette *of* the Bay de Noquet and Marquette Railroad, for the benefit and use of the Bay de Noquet and Marquette Railroad Company, four additional alternate sections of land, per mile, to that already granted by act of Congress approved June third, A. D. eighteen hundred and fifty-six, and joint resolution supplementary thereto, to be selected upon the same conditions, restrictions, and limitations as are contained in the act of Congress entitled "An act making a grant of lands to the State of Michigan, in alternate sections, to aid in the construction of railroads in said State," approved June third, eighteen hundred and fifty-six: *Provided,* That the land to be so located by either of said roads shall be selected from the alternate sections, designated by odd numbers, within twenty miles of the line of said road.

SEC. 2. *And be it further enacted,* That the lands granted by said act of Congress and by this act shall be disposed of only in the following manner, that is to say: When the Governor of the State of Michigan shall certify to the Secretary of the Interior that any ten consecutive miles, upon the route of either of said roads, is completed in a good and substantial manner, as a first-class railroad, then the Secretary of the Interior shall cause a certificate or certificates to issue to said State for one hundred sections of land, for the benefit and use of such company, and so from time to time for each completed section of ten miles of either of said roads, one hundred sections of land, until the whole shall be completed: *Provided,* That none of the additional lands granted by this act for that portion of the Marquette and Ontonagon Railroad now completed shall be certified to the State of Michigan, by the terms hereof, until the said railroad shall be completed from a point twenty miles west of Marquette to Ontonagon; and that none of the additional lands granted by this act for that portion of the railroad from Marquette to the Wisconsin State line at or near the mouth of the Menomonee River, now completed, shall be so certified until the said railroad shall be completed from Bay de Noquet to the said Wisconsin State line, at or near the mouth of the Menomonee River aforesaid.

SEC. 3. *And be it further enacted,* That the time limited for the completion of the road from Marquette to the Wisconsin State line, at or near the mouth of the Menomonee River, be, and the same is hereby, extended for the term of five years, from and after the third day of June, A. D. eighteen hundred and sixty-six.

SEC. 4. *And be it further enacted,* That no lands to be set apart for

* See Vol. I. Nos. 292 and 293, and also 223 B.

the road from Marquette to Bay de Noquet, and from Marquette to Ontonagon, shall be selected and certified east of that portion of the range line dividing ranges twenty-six and twenty-seven, that is, south of the township line between townships forty-seven and forty-eight, nor south of that portion of the township line dividing townships forty-seven and forty-eight, that lies east of the dividing range line above named; and that no lands to be set apart for the road from Marquette, on Lake Superior, to the Wisconsin State line, at or near the mouth of the Menomonee River, shall be selected and certified west of that portion of the range line dividing ranges twenty-six and twenty-seven, that is, north of the township line dividing townships forty-two and forty-three, nor north of the township line dividing townships forty-seven and forty-eight; and that for the purpose of making up any deficiency of lands to which the line of road from Marquette to Bay de Noquet may be entitled to make its grant equal to ten sections to the mile, the same shall be certified on the route from Marquette to Ontonagon, within twenty miles of the line of said road, and east of the range line dividing ranges thirty-one and thirty-two, and in accordance with the provisions hereinbefore contained. And that, whenever the Governor of the State of Michigan shall certify to the Secretary of the Interior that twenty consecutive miles of the line of road from Marquette to Bay de Noquet has been completed in a good and substantial manner, as a first-class railroad, the Secretary of the Interior shall cause to be issued to said State of Michigan, for the use and benefit of the Bay de Noquet and Marquette Railroad Company, assignee of the State of Michigan, a certificate or certificates for two hundred sections of land, to be selected and located from the sections designated by odd numbers, on the line from Marquette to Ontonagon, and within twenty miles of said line.

SEC. 5. *And be it further enacted*, That the time for the completion of the railroad from Fond du Lac, on Lake Winnebago, to the Wisconsin State line, at or near the mouth of the Menomonee River, shall be, and hereby is, extended for the period of five years from and after the third day of June, one thousand eight hundred and sixty-six; and that any and all grants of land to said road shall continue and remain in full force and effect.

SEC. 6. *And be it further enacted*, That each of said companies shall grade, in a good and substantial manner, ready for the ties, twenty miles of its road within two years, and twenty miles additional thereof, in each year thereafter: *Provided*, That if said companies, or either of them, shall neglect or fail to do so, or to complete its road within the time herein specified, the land granted to such company shall revert to the United States.

Approved, March 3, 1865.

No. 129 B.—An Act extending the time for the completion of certain land-grant railroads in the States of Minnesota and Iowa, and for other purposes.*

Be it enacted by the Senate and House of Representatives of the United States of America in Congress assembled, That the quantity of lands granted to the State of Minnesota, to aid in the construction of certain

* See Vol. I. Nos. 312 and 313.

railroads in said State, as indicated in the first section of an [act] entitled "An act making a grant of land to the Territory of Minnesota, in alternate sections, to aid in the construction of certain railroads in said Territory, and granting public lands, in alternate sections, to the State of Alabama, to aid in the construction of a certain railroad in said State," approved March third, eighteen hundred and fifty-seven, shall be increased to ten sections per mile for each of said railroads and branches, subject to any and all limitations contained in said act and subsequent acts, and as hereinafter provided.

SEC. 2. *And be it further enacted*, That the first proviso in the first section of the act aforesaid shall be so amended as to read as follows, to wit: *Provided*, That the land to be so located shall in no case be further than twenty miles from the lines of said roads and branches, to aid in the construction of each of which said grant is made; and said lands granted shall, in all cases, be indicated by the Secretary of the Interior.

SEC. 3. *And be it further enacted*, That any and all lands heretofore reserved to the United States by any act of Congress, or in any other manner by competent authority, for the purpose of aiding in any object of internal improvement or other purpose whatever, be, and the same are hereby, reserved and excepted from the operations of this act, except so far as may be found necessary to locate the route of said road through such reserved lands, in which case the right of way shall be granted, subject to the approval of the President of the United States: *Provided further*, That any lands which may have been granted to the Territory or State of Minnesota for the purpose of aiding in the construction of any railroad, which lands may be located within the limits of this extension of said grant or grants, shall be deducted from the full quantity of lands hereby granted, and that any lands which may have been so granted shall be strictly applied in accordance with the terms and conditions of said act or acts, unless subsequently modified by law.

SEC. 4. *And be it further enacted*, That the sections and parts of sections of land, which by said acts and this grant shall remain to the United States, within ten miles on each side of said roads and branches, shall not be sold for less than double the minimum price of public lands when sold, nor shall any of said lands become subject to sale at private entry until the same shall have been first offered at public sale to the highest bidder at or above the minimum price as aforesaid: *Provided*, That actual bona fide settlers under the pre-emption laws of the United States may, after the proof of settlement, improvement, and occupation, as now provided by law, purchase the same at the increased minimum price: *And provided, also*, That settlers under the provisions of the homestead law, who comply with the terms and requirements of said act, shall be entitled to patents for an amount not exceeding eighty acres each, anything in this act to the contrary notwithstanding.

SEC. 5. *And be it further enacted*, That the lands hereby granted shall be subject to the disposal of the Legislature of the State of Minnesota, for the purposes aforesaid, and no other. And the said railroads and branches shall be and remain public highways for the use of the Government of the United States, free of all toll or other charges upon the transportation of any property or troops of the United States.

SEC. 6. *And be it further enacted*, That the lands hereby and heretofore granted to said Territory or State of Minnesota shall be disposed of by said State for the purposes aforesaid only, and in manner following, namely: When the Governor of said State shall certify to the Secretary of the Interior that any section of ten consecutive miles of said road is completed in a good, substantial, and workmanlike manner, as a first-class railroad, and the said Secretary shall be satisfied that said State has complied in good faith with this requirement, the said Secretary of the Interior shall issue to the said State patents for all the lands granted and selected as aforesaid, not exceeding ten sections per mile, situated opposite to and within a limit of twenty miles of the line of said section of road thus completed, extending along the whole length of said completed section of ten miles of road, and no further. And when the Governor of said State shall certify to the Secretary of the Interior, and the Secretary shall be satisfied that another section of said road, ten consecutive miles in extent, connecting with the preceding section, or with some other first-class railroad, which may be at the time in successful operation, is completed as aforesaid, the said Secretary of the Interior shall issue to the said State patents for all the lands granted and situated opposite to and within the limit of twenty miles of the line of said completed section of road or roads, and extending the length of said section, and no further, not exceeding ten sections of land per mile for all that part of said road thus completed under the provisions of this act and the act to which this is an amendment, and so, from time to time, until said roads and branches are completed. And when the Governor of said State shall so certify, and the Secretary of the Interior shall be satisfied that the whole of any one of said roads and branches is completed in a good, substantial, and workmanlike manner, as a first-class railroad, the said Secretary of the Interior shall issue to the said State patents to all the remaining lands granted for and on account of said completed road and branches in this act, situated within the said limits of twenty miles from the line thereof, throughout the entire length of said road and branches: *Provided*, That no land shall be granted or conveyed to said State under the provisions of this act on account of the construction of any railroad or part thereof that has been constructed under the provisions of any other act at the date of the passage of this act, and adopted as a part of the line of railroad provided for in this act: *And provided*, That nothing herein contained shall interfere with any existing rights acquired under any law of Congress heretofore enacted making grants of land to the State of Minnesota to aid in the construction of railroads: *And provided further*, That said lands, granted by this or prior acts, shall not in any manner be disposed of, except as the same are patented under the provisions of this act; and should the State fail to complete any one of said roads or branches within eight years after the passage of this act, then the said lands undisposed of as aforesaid, granted on account of said road or branches, shall revert to the United States.

SEC. 7. *And be it further enacted*, That as soon as the Governor of the said State of Minnesota shall file or cause to be filed with the Secretary of the Interior maps designating the routes of said road and branches, then it shall be the duty of the Secretary of the Interior to withdraw from market the lands embraced within the provisions of this act.

SEC. 8. *And be it further enacted*, That the United States mail shall be transported on said road, under the direction of the Post-Office Department, at such price as Congress may by law provide: *Provided*, That until such price is fixed by law the Postmaster-General shall have power to fix the rate of compensation.

SEC. 9. *And be it further enacted*, That the provisions of this act shall also be construed so as to apply and extend to that portion of the line authorized to be vacated by the joint resolution approved July twelfth, eighteen hundred and sixty-two, entitled a joint resolution authorizing the State of Minnesota to change the line of certain branch railroads in said State, and for other purposes, notwithstanding the vacation thereof by said State, as though said joint resolution had not passed, and also to the line adopted by said State, in lieu of the portion of the line so vacated.

SEC. 10. *And be it further enacted,* That the time mentioned in an act entitled "An act making a grant of lands to the State of Iowa, in alternate sections, to aid in the construction of certain railroads in said State," for the completion of the railroads named in said act, be, and the same is hereby, extended two years.

SEC. 11. *And be it further enacted,* That the last clause of the second section of an act entitled "An act to regulate the compensation of registers and receivers of the land offices in the several States and Territories in the location of lands by States and corporations under general grants from Congress, and for other purposes," be, and the same is hereby, so amended as to read: "A map of the change shall be filed with the Commissioner of the General Land Office within three months after the said change of location shall be made."*

Approved, March 3, 1865.

No. 130 B.—An Act supplemental to the act approved first July, eighteen hundred and sixty-four, "for the disposal of coal lands and of town property in the public domain."†

Be it enacted by the Senate and House of Representatives of the United States of America in Congress assembled, That in the case of any citizen of the United States who, at the passage of this act, may be in the business of bona fide actual coal mining on the public lands, except on lands reserved by the President of the United States for public uses, for purposes of commerce, such citizen, upon making proof satisfactory to the register and receiver to that effect, shall have the right to enter, according to legal subdivisions, a quantity of land not exceeding one hundred and sixty acres, to embrace his improvements and mining premises at the minimum price of twenty dollars per acre, fixed in the coal and town property act of first July, eighteen hundred and sixty-four: *Provided,* That where the mining improvements and premises are on land surveyed at the passage of this act, a sworn declaratory statement descriptive of the tract and premises, showing also the extent and character of the improvements, shall be filed within six months from the date of this act; and proof and payment shall be made within one year from the date of such filing; but where such mining premises may be on lands hereafter to be surveyed, such declaratory statement shall be filed within three months from the return to the district land office of the official township plat; and proof and payment shall be made within one year from the date of such filing.

SEC. 2. *And be it further enacted,* That in the case of any city or town which, at the passage of this act, may be existing on the public lands, in which the lots therein may be variant as to size from the limitation fixed in the said act of first July, eighteen hundred and sixty-four, and in which the lots and buildings as municipal improvements shall cover an area

* No. 105 B.

† No. 108 B.

greater than six hundred and forty acres, such variance as to size of lots or excess in area shall prove no bar to such city or town claim, under said act of first July, eighteen hundred and sixty-four, effect to be given to this act according to such regulations as may be prescribed by the Secretary of the Interior: *Provided*, That the minimum price of each said lots in any such town or city, which may contain a greater number of square feet that the maximum named in the act to which this is an amendment, shall be increased to such reasonable amount as the Secretary of the Interior may by rule establish: *Provided further*, That where mineral veins are possessed, which possession is recognized by local authority, and to the extent so possessed and recognized, the title to town lots to be acquired shall be subject to such recognized possession and the necessary use thereof: *Provided, however*, That nothing contained herein shall be so construed as to recognize any color of title in possessors for mining purposes as against the Government of the United States.

Approved, March 3, 1865.

No. 131 B.—An Act to amend an act entitled "An act to amend an act entitled 'An act making a grant of alternate sections of public lands to the State of Michigan, to aid in the construction of certain railroads in said State, and for other purposes.' "*

Be it enacted by the Senate and House of Representatives of the United States of America in Congress assembled, That section one of an act entitled "An act to amend an act entitled 'An act making a grant of alternate sections of public lands to the State of Michigan, to aid in the construction of certain railroads in said State, and for other purposes,' " which said amendatory act was approved June seventh, eighteen hundred and sixty-four, be, and the same is hereby, amended so as to make the last proviso in said section to read as follows, to wit: *Provided further*, That the time specified in the fourth section of the act hereby amended, for the completion of said road, shall be, and the same is hereby, extended eight years.

Approved, March 3, 1865.

No. 132 B.—An Act to authorize the issuing of patents for certain lands in the town of Stockbridge, State of Wisconsin, and for other purposes.

Be it enacted by the Senate and House of Representatives of the United States of America in Congress assembled, That, upon satisfactory proof being made that any occupant[s] of unpatented land in the town of Stockbridge, Calumet County, in the State of Wisconsin, which has, by treaty or otherwise, been allotted to any individual members of the Stockbridge or Munsee tribe of Indians, are the purchasers, grantees, or assignees of such members of said tribes, the President of the United States be authorized to issue patents for the land so occupied to such purchasers, grantees, or assignees, respectively: *Provided*, That in case of conflicting claims to any of the lots of land the Commissioner of the

* No. 89 B.

General Land Office is authorized to hear the proofs of the respective claimants, and to decide which of such claimants are justly entitled to said land, and patents shall be issued in accordance with such decision.

SEC. 2. *And be it further enacted*, That patents issued according to this act shall vest in the patentee title to the land described in such patent, in fee simple, subject to any valid lien or incumbrance thereon created by said patentee or those under whom he claims.

SEC. 3. *And be it further enacted*, That the lots of land in said town of Stockbridge belonging to the United States, not hereinbefore directed to be patented, shall be attached to and form a part of the Menasha land district, and if, in the opinion of the Commissioner of the General Land Office, it shall be for the public interest, the same may be sold at the minimum price of three dollars per acre for lots fronting on Lake Winnebago, five dollars per acre for the two tiers of lots fronting on the military road, one tier of lots on each side thereof, and two dollars and fifty cents per acre for the residue of said land to actual settlers thereon possessing the qualifications requisite to acquire pre-emption rights, who shall prove to the satisfaction of the register of the land office at Menasha, Wisconsin, that he or she has made improvements to the value of not less than fifty dollars, and is actually residing upon the land; the time of paying the purchase price may be extended for a period not exceeding one year from the passage of this act: *Provided*, That no such actual settler shall be permitted to pre-empt more than two contiguous lots on which he or she has made improvements of the value of not less than one hundred dollars. The lands not sold within one year as hereinbefore provided, shall be brought into market and sold at not less than the minimum prices fixed by this act.

Approved, March 3, 1865.

No. 133 B.—An Act for the relief of the occupants of the lands of the ex-mission of San José, in the State of California.

Be it enacted by the Senate and House of Representatives of the United States of America in Congress assembled, That every person who has the possession rightfully as against all others except the United States, or, being out of possession, is, as against all others except as aforesaid, entitled to the possession of any portion of the tract of land situate in the county of Almeda, State of California, known as the lands of the ex-mission of San José, as included in the map and survey thereof, made October, eighteen hundred and sixty-four, by E. H. Dyer, Deputy United States Surveyor, shall have the right, and the right is hereby granted to each and every such person, to enter and purchase of the United States, at the sum or price of one dollar and twenty-five cents per acre, such portion of said tract so rightfully possessed by him, her, or them, or to which he, she, or they may so have such right of possession, whether such person claim the same by conveyance from or under Andres Pico and Juan B. Alvarado, or either of them, or by possession only: *Provided, however*, That any person entitled under this act to a parcel of less than eight acres shall in all such cases pay ten dollars for the same.

SEC. 2. *And be it further enacted*, That every person claiming any benefit under this act shall, within one year from the passage thereof, present to the register and receiver of the United States Land Office at

San Francisco a survey or plat of the portion of said tract claimed by him, her, or them, and which shall exhibit the quarter section or sections, or parts thereof, included in said plat, made by or under the direction of the United States Surveyor-General for California, and therewith a written statement setting forth the right of such claimant to enter and purchase such portion under the provisions of this act, and whether the said claimant has acquired the alleged title of said Pico and Alvarado, or either of them thereto, or holds by possession only; and thereupon such register and receiver shall, under such rules as may be prescribed by the Commissioner of the General Land Office, proceed and take, hear, and examine the evidence which may be offered in support of or against such claim, and, upon the proofs being closed, shall determine upon and decide the same: *Provided*, That no decision of said register and receiver shall be final until approved by the Commissioner of the General Land Office.

SEC. 3. *And be it further enacted*, That the claimant in whose favor final decision has been made, upon paying to the receiver of the land office at San Francisco for the land embraced in such final decision the sum therefor prescribed in the first section of this act, shall be entitled to a patent for such land from the United States, conveying all the interest of the United States therein to such claimant.

SEC. 4. *And be it further enacted*, That upon all proceedings under this act being closed, and upon the appeal, taken to the Supreme Court of the United States by E. L. Beard and others, claimants of said lands against the United States, being dismissed, or the decree appealed from affirmed, the Surveyor-General of the United States for California shall cause the lines of the public surveys to be extended over all portions of said land which shall not have been disposed of under the provisions hereof, and thereafter the same shall be disposed of as in the case of other public lands.

Approved, March 3, 1865.

No. 134 B.—An Act to amend an act entitled "An act to provide for the better organization of Indian affairs in California."*

Be it enacted by the Senate and House of Representatives of the United States of America in Congress assembled, That the sum of sixty thousand dollars, or so much thereof as may be necessary, be, and the same is hereby, appropriated, out of any money in the treasury not otherwise appropriated, for the purpose of enabling the Secretary of the Interior to pay the settlers in Hoopa Valley, California, for their improvements on the Indian reservation therein: *Provided*, That before the same or any part of the money hereby appropriated shall be paid, the said improvements shall be appraised by the superintendent of Indian affairs, the Indian agent at said reservation, and the Surveyor-General of California; and if, in the opinion of the Secretary of the Interior, their appraisement shall be reasonable, and shall not in the aggregate exceed the sum herein appropriated, the said Secretary is hereby authorized to apply the same, or so much thereof as may be necessary, in payment for the said improvements, taking the proper releases therefor: *And provided further*, That the moneys hereby appropriated be reimbursed from the

* No. 77 B.

proceeds of the sales of Indian reservations in said State under the provisions of the act to provide for the better organization of Indian affairs in California, approved April eight, eighteen hundred and sixty-four.

Approved, March 3, 1865.

No. 135 B.—An Act making appropriations for the current and contingent expenses of the Indian Department, and for fulfilling treaty stipulations with various Indian tribes for the year ending thirtieth June, eighteen hundred and sixty-six, and for other purposes.

* * * * * * * * *

For the payment of awards made by the Secretary of the Interior, to be paid as damages growing out of the loss and destruction of improvements made upon the lands known as the Winnebago Reservation, in Blue Earth County, Minnesota, by the bona fide actual settlers thereon, under the pre-emption laws of the United States, before the same was selected and set apart as an Indian reservation, and which award was made pursuant to an act of Congress entitled "An act for the relief of pre-emptors on the home reservation of the Winnebagoes, in the Blue Earth region in the State of Minnesota," approved July fourteenth, eighteen hundred and sixty-two,* and to be paid to the several parties named in the said award, seven thousand three hundred and two dollars and six cents.

* * * * * * * * *

SEC. 4. *And be it further enacted,* That each of the chiefs, warriors, and heads of families of the Stockbridge Munsee tribes of Indians residing in the County of Shawana and State of Wisconsin, may, under the direction of the Secretary of the Interior, enter a homestead and become entitled to all the benefits of an act entitled "An act to secure homesteads to acutal settlers on the public domain," approved May twenty, eighteen hundred and sixty-two, free from any fee or charge whatever, and any part of the lands being a part of their present reservation, which may be abandoned under the foregoing provisions, may be sold under the direction of the Secretary of the Interior, and the proceeds applied for the benefit of such Indians as may settle on said homesteads, to aid them in improving the same. The said homestead thus secured shall not be subject to any tax, levy, or sale whatever, nor shall the same be sold, conveyed, mortgaged, or in any manner encumbered except upon the decree of the District Court of the United States, as hereinafter provided. Whenever any of said chiefs, warriors, or heads of families of said tribes, having filed with the clerk of the District Court of the United States a declaration of his intention to become a citizen of the United States, and to dissolve all relations with any Indian tribe, two years previous thereto, shall appear in said court, and prove to the satisfaction thereof, by the testimony of two citizens of the United States, that for five years last past he has adopted the habits of civilized life, that he has maintained himself and family by his own industry, that he reads and speaks the English language, that he is well disposed to become a peaceable and orderly citizen; and that he has sufficient capacity to manage his own affairs; the court may enter a decree admitting him to all the rights of a citizen of the United States, and thenceforth he shall be no longer held or treated as a member of any Indian tribe, but shall be entitled to all the rights

* No. 54 B.

and privileges, and be subject to all the duties and liabilities to taxation of other citizens of the United States. But nothing herein contained shall be construed to deprive them of annuities to which they are or may be entitled.

* * * * * * * * *

Approved, March 3, 1865.

No. 136 B.—Joint Resolution reserving mineral lands from the operation of all acts, passed at the first session of the thirty-eighth Congress, granting lands, or extending the time of former grants.

Be it resolved by the Senate and House of Representatives of the United States of America in Congress assembled, That no act passed at the first session of the thirty-eighth Congress, granting lands to States or corporations, to aid in the construction of roads or for other purposes, or to extend the time of grants heretofore made, shall be so construed as to embrace mineral lands, which in all cases shall be, and are, reserved exclusively to the United States, unless otherwise specially provided in the act or acts making the grant.

Approved, January 30, 1865.

No. 137 B.—A Resolution to extend the time for the reversion to the United States of the lands granted by Congress to aid in the construction of a railroad from Pere Marquette to Flint, and for the completion of said road.

Resolved by the Senate and House of Representatives of the United States of America in Congress assembled, That the time specified in the fourth section of the act of Congress approved June three, eighteen hundred and fifty-six,* entitled "An act making a grant of alternate sections of the public lands to the State of Michigan to aid in the construction of certain railroads in said State, and for other purposes," for the reversion to the United States of the lands granted by said act to aid in the construction of a railroad from Pere Marquette to Flint, and for the completion of said road, be, and the same is hereby, extended for the term of five years.

Approved, February 17, 1865.

No. 138 B.—A resolution to extend the time for constructing the Burlington and Missouri River Railroad, in Iowa, and filing a map of re-location.

Resolved by the Senate and House of Representatives of the United States of America in Congress assembled, That the time allowed by the eighth section of the act entitled "An act to amend an act entitled 'An act making a grant of lands to the State of Iowa, in alternate sections,

* Vol. I. No. 293. No. 149 B

to aid in the construction of certain railroads in said State,' approved May fifteenth, eighteen hundred and fifty-six,"* for the construction annually of sections of twenty miles each of the Burlington and Missouri River Railroad, be, and the same is hereby, extended one year, and that the provision of the second section of the act approved first of July, eighteen hundred and sixty-four, entitled "An act to regulate the compensation of registers and receivers of the land offices in the several States and Territories in the location of lands by the States and corporations under grants by Congress," which requires that a map of the change of location shall be filed with the Commissioner of the General Land Office within one year, be, and the same is hereby, repealed.†

Approved, March 3, 1865.

No. 139 B.—An Act to quiet the title to certain lands within the corporate limits of the city of San Francisco.

Be it enacted by the Senate and House of Representatives of the United States of America in Congress assembled, That all the right and title of the United States to the land situated within the corporate limits of the city of San Francisco, in the State of California, confirmed to the city of San Francisco by the decree of the Circuit Court of the United States for the Northern District of California, entered on the eighteenth day of May, one thousand eight hundred and sixty-five, be, and the same are hereby, relinquished and granted to the said city of San Francisco and its successors, and the claim of the said city to said land is hereby confirmed, subject, however, to the reservations and exceptions designated in said decree, and upon the following trusts, namely, that all the said land, not heretofore granted to said city, shall be disposed of and conveyed by said city to parties in the bona fide actual possession thereof, by themselves or tenants, on the passage of this act, in such quantities and upon such terms and conditions as the Legislature of the State of California may prescribe, except such parcels thereof as may be reserved and set apart by ordinance of said city for public uses: *Provided, however,* That the relinquishment and grant by this act shall not interfere with or prejudice any valid adverse right or claim, if such exist, to said land, or any part thereof, whether derived from Spain, Mexico, or the United States, or preclude a judicial examination and adjustment thereof.

Approved, March 8, 1866.

No. 140 B.—An Act quieting doubts in relation to the validity of certain locations of lands in the State of Missouri, made by virtue of certificates issued under the act of Congress of February the seventeenth, eighteen hundred and fifteen.

Be it enacted by the Senate and House of Representatives of the United States of America in Congress assembled, That all locations of lands in the State of Missouri, purporting to have been made by virtue of certificates issued under the act of Congress, approved February the seven-

* Vol. I. No. 288. † No. 105 B.

teenth, eighteen hundred and fifteen, entitled "An act for the relief of the inhabitants of the late County of New Madrid, in the Missouri Territory, who suffered by earthquakes," which are invalid in consequence of having been made or located after the expiration of the time specified by law for making said locations, shall be, and the same are hereby declared to be, as valid, and as binding, as if the said locations had been made and fully completed within the time prescribed by law, provided said locations shall be according to law in all other respects; but the foregoing provisions of this section shall not apply to, comprehend, include, or extend to any land within township forty-five, north of the base line, in range seven, east of the fifth principal meridian line in said State of Missouri.

SEC. 2. *And be it further enacted*, That the United States do hereby grant, relinquish, and convey, in fee simple, and in full property, to James Y. O'Carroll, or his legal representatives, all of the right, title, and interest of the United States in and to all of the land within survey number two thousand four hundred and ninety-eight, in township forty-five, north of the base line in range seven, east of the fifth principal meridian line, in the State of Missouri, being the same land that was located by virtue of certificate number one hundred and fifty, issued to the said James Y. O'Carroll, or his legal representatives, under the act of Congress approved February the seventeenth, eighteen hundred and fifteen, entitled "An act for the relief of the inhabitants of the late County of New Madrid, in the Missouri Territory, who suffered by earthquakes:" *Provided, however*, That nothing in this section shall grant, relinquish, or convey the whole, or any part of any lot, tract, piece, or parcel of land in said township, which has been heretofore confirmed by the United States to any person or persons, or to the legal representatives of any person or persons: *And provided, further*, That nothing in this act shall be so construed as to invalidate or impair any patent heretofore issued by the United States, or shall in any manner abridge, divest, impair, injure, or prejudice any valid adverse right, title, or interest of any person or persons in or to any portion or part of the aforesaid land which is granted, relinquished, and conveyed by this act.

Approved, March 21, 1866.

No. 141 B.—An Act granting to the State of Wisconsin a donation of public lands to aid in the construction of a breakwater and harbor and ship canal at the head of Sturgeon Bay, in the County of Door, in said State, to connect the waters of Green Bay with Lake Michigan, in said State.

Be it enacted by the Senate and House of Representatives of the United States of America in Congress assembled, That there be, and hereby is, granted to the State of Wisconsin for the purpose of aiding said State in constructing and completing a breakwater and harbor and ship canal to connect the waters of Green Bay with the waters of Lake Michigan, two hundred thousand acres of public lands, to be selected in subdivisions agreeably to the United States survey, by an agent or agents appointed by the Governor of said State, subject to the approval of the Secretary of the Interior, from lands subject to private entry: *Provided*, That said selections shall be made from alternate and odd numbered sections of land nearest the location of said harbor and canal in said State not otherwise appropriated, and not from lands designated by the United States as "mineral" before the passage of this act, nor from lands to which the rights of pre-emption or homestead have attached.

SEC. 2. *And be it further enacted*, That the said lands hereby granted shall be subject to the disposal of the Legislature of said State, or, if the Legislature thereof shall not be in session, or shall adjourn within ten days after the passage and approval of this act, then said lands shall be subject to the disposal of the Governor and board of commissioners of school, university, and swamp lands of said State, for the purposes aforesaid, and for no other; and the said canal shall be and remain a public highway for the use of the Government of the United States, free from toll or charge upon the vessels of said Government, or upon vessels employed by said Government in the transportation of any property or troops of the United States.

SEC. 3. *And be it further enacted*, That before it shall be competent for said State to dispose of any of said lands, to be selected as aforesaid, the plan of said breakwater and harbor and the route of said canal shall be established, and a plat or plats thereof shall be filed in the office of the War Department, and a duplicate thereof filed in the office of the Commissioner of the General Land Office.

SEC. 4. *And be it further enacted*, That if the said breakwater, harbor, and canal, shall not be completed within three years from the passage of this act, the lands hereby granted and remaining unsold shall revert to the United States.

SEC. 5. *And be it further enacted*, That the Legislature of said State shall cause to be kept an accurate account of the sales and net proceeds of the lands hereby granted, and of all expenditures in the construction, repairs, and operating of said canal, and of the earnings thereof, and shall return a *a* statement of the same annually to the Secretary of the Interior. And whenever said State shall be fully reimbursed for all advances made for the construction, repairs, and operating of said canal, with legal interest on all advances until the reimbursement of the same, or upon payment by the United States of any balance of such advances over such receipts from said lands and canal, with such interest, the said State shall be allowed to tax for the use of said canal only such tolls as shall be sufficient to pay all necessary expenses for the care, charge, and repair of the same.

SEC. 6. *And be it further enacted*, That said ship canal shall be at least one hundred feet in width, with a depth of water not less than thirteen feet.

Approved, April 10, 1866.

No. 142 B.—An Act to grant the right of way to the "Cascade Railroad Company" through a military reserve in Washington Territory.

Whereas the Cascade Railroad Company, a corporation duly created and organized under the laws of Washington Territory, has constructed and put in operation a railroad on the Cascade Portage of the Columbia River, in said Territory, a portion of which said road is constructed through a military reserve of the United States; and whereas doubts have arisen as to the right to construct such road through said reserve and the validity of the charter of said company: Therefore,

Be it enacted by the Senate and House of Representatives of the United States of America in Congress assembled, That there shall be, and is hereby, granted to the said Cascade Railroad Company a right of way of sixty feet in width along the line of said road as at present constructed and along the changes of location hereafter made to straighten and render said road safe, through the public lands of the United States, the military reserve, and the lands of private persons agreeing thereto, including all necessary grounds for stations, buildings, workshops, depots, machine shops, switches, side tracks, and wharves. And the charter of said company is hereby adopted and declared to be valid: *Provided*, That nothing in this act shall be so construed as to give said company the right to occupy for any purpose whatever more than sixty feet in width on the line of said road at any point or points where the space or pass between the river and bluff or mountain is so narrow as not to admit of the construction of another parallel railroad, turnpike, road, canal, or other public work for transportation of freight or passengers.

Approved, April 10, 1866.

No. 143 B.—An Act concerning the boundaries of the State of Nevada.

Be it enacted by the Senate and House of Representatives of the United States of America in Congress assembled, That, as provided for and consented to in the constitution of the State of Nevada, all that territory and tract of land adjoining the present eastern boundary of the State of Nevada, and lying between the thirty-seventh and the forty-second degrees of north latitude and west of the thirty-seventh degree of longitude west of Washington, is hereby added to and made a part of the State of Nevada.

SEC. 2. *And be it further enacted*, That there is hereby added to and made a part of the State of Nevada all that extent of territory lying within the following boundaries, to wit: Commencing on the thirty-seventh degree of north latitude, at the thirty-seventh degree of longitude west from Washington; and running thence south on said degree of longitude to the middle of the river Colorado of the West; thence down the middle of said river to the eastern boundary of the State of California; thence northwesterly along said boundary of California to the thirty-seventh degree of north latitude; and thence east along said degree of latitude to the point of beginning: *Provided*, That the territory mentioned in this section shall not become a part of the State of Nevada until said State shall, through its Legislature, consent thereto: *And provided further*, That all possessory rights acquired by citizens of the United States to mining claims discovered, located, and originally recorded in compliance with the rules and regulations adopted by miners in the Pah-Ranagat and other mining districts in the Territory incorporated by the provisions of this act into the State of Nevada shall remain as valid subsisting mining claims; but nothing herein contained shall be so construed as granting a title in fee to any mineral lands held by possessory titles in the mining States and Territories.

Approved, May 5, 1866.

No. 144 B.—An Act authorizing documentary evidence of titles to be furnished to the owners of certain lands in the city of St. Louis.

Whereas, within the city of St. Louis, in the State of Missouri, there are many lots, tracts, pieces, and parcels of land which were confirmed by the act of Congress of June the thirteenth, eighteen hundred and twelve, on the ground of inhabitation, possession, or cultivation of the same prior to December the twentieth, eighteen hundred and three, and in some cases there is no adequate documentary evidence of said confirmations; and in consequence of the death of the ancient witnesses, who knew the facts of said inhabitation, possession, or cultivation, the owners of said lands, in said cases where there is no adequate documentary evidence of said confirmations, are without complete evidence of title to the same, as against the United States; and whereas persons holding grants and confirmations of lands in said city of St. Louis, under other acts of Congress heretofore passed, may, in some cases, be without perfect documentary evidence of said grants or confirmations by the United States, and difficulties may hereafter arise therefrom, to the great injury of such persons: Therefore—

Be it enacted by the Senate and House of Representatives of the United States of America in Congress assembled, That the District Court of the United States for the Eastern District of Missouri is hereby authorized, by proper decree, to declare released, granted, relinquished, and conveyed by the United States, in fee simple and in full property, all of the right, title, and interest of the United States in and to any lot, tract, piece, or parcel of land within the city of St. Louis, in the State of Missouri, to the person or persons having the best claim or claims to the same; but nothing in this act shall authorize said court to declare released, granted, relinquished, and conveyed, as aforesaid, any land within any wharf, street, lane, avenue, alley, or other public thoroughfare, or within the boundaries of any land which has been heretofore granted or assigned by the United States for the use or support of schools, or within the boundaries of any land heretofore lawfully confirmed or lawfully granted by the United States, where full, sufficient, and complete documentary evidence of such confirmation or grant now exists of record.

SEC. 2. *And be it further enacted,* That every person desiring a decree in his or her favor, under this act, shall file a petition in said District Court, asking for such decree, and describing the land for which said decree is desired; and the United States and all persons claiming such land adversely to said petitioner (if there be any such adverse claimants), shall be made defendants in said cause; and if any party to any such cause shall be a minor under the age of twenty-one years, a guardian ad litem shall be appointed by said court for said minor; and said District Court shall have full and complete power, jurisdiction, and authority to hear, try, and determine all questions arising in said cause relating to the claim of the petitioner, the extent, locality, and boundaries of said claim, and all other matters connected therewith or concerning the same; and said District Court shall also have power to make, prescribe, and enforce such rules and regulations as may be necessary and proper to carry this act into full and complete execution.

SEC. 3. *And be it further enacted,* That a copy of every petition which shall be filed under this act, and a copy of the writ or process thereto attached, shall be delivered to the District Attorney of the United States for said eastern district of Missouri, by the United States Marshal for said district, which said delivery shall make the United States a party to the cause specified in such petition, without any other or further proceedings, notice, service, writ or process whatever; and said District Attorney shall make such defence therein for the United States, as in his opinion the public interest may require; but no answer or other pleadings filed by said Attorney in such cause shall be required to be verified by oath or affirmation.

SEC. 4. *And be it further enacted*, That for the purpose of more completely describing, identifying, and defining the boundaries, situation, and locality of any lot, tract, piece or parcel of land sought to be released, granted, relinquished and conveyed under this act, the said District Court shall have power to cause an accurate survey, plat, and description thereof to be made by a competent person at the expense of the petitioner; and all of the expenses and costs of all suits and other proceedings under this act shall be paid by the respective petitioners, and the payment thereof may be enforced by execution or otherwise.

SEC. 5. *And be it further enacted*, That every decree which shall be rendered under this act in favor of any petitioner shall be deemed a full, sufficient, and complete release, grant, relinquishment, and conveyance, in fee simple and in full property, to such petitioner, and to his or her heirs and assigns, forever, of all the right, title, and interest of the United States in and to the land described in such decree.

SEC. 6. *And be it further enacted*, That whenever said District Court or the Circuit Court shall render a final decree under this act, concerning any lot, tract, piece or parcel of land, such court shall cause to be transmitted to the Commissioner of the General Land Office a full, true and complete transcript of said final decree, and of the description or survey of said land.

SEC. 7. *And be it further enacted*, That any party to any final decree rendered by said District Court in any suit or cause commenced under this act may appeal from said final decree of said District Court to the Circuit Court of the United States for the district of Missouri, at any time within one year from the time of the rendition of said final decree, and not after that time; and on the granting of said appeal, a full, true, and complete transcript of said final decree, and of the petition, and all other pleadings and proceedings in said cause, and of the evidence therein, shall be transmitted to said Circuit Court. And when said appeal shall have been completed, said Circuit Court shall have full and complete jurisdiction over said cause, and may allow the pleadings to be amended if necessary, and may admit new parties if necessary, and shall hear, try, and determine said cause de novo, without regarding any error, defect, or other imperfection in the proceedings of said District Court, and shall render such final decree therein as the facts and the justice of said cause may require.

SEC. 8. *And be it further enacted*, That in case of any difference of opinion between the judges of the said Circuit Court upon any question arising in any such cause, the same may be certified to the Supreme Court of the United States, for its decision thereon as in other cases.

SEC. 9. *And be it further enacted*, That all of the right, title, and interest of the United States in and to all of the wharves, streets, lanes, avenues, alleys, and other public thoroughfares which are situate, lying, and being within the corporate limits of the City of St. Louis, in the State of Missouri, shall be, and the same are hereby, granted, relinquished and conveyed by the United States, in fee simple and in full property, to the said city of St. Louis, and to the successors and assigns forever of said city : *Provided, however,* That no individual rights or titles acquired previously hereto shall be in any manner impaired or prejudiced hereby.

Approved, June 12, 1866.

No. 145 B.—An Act to grant the right of way to the "Humboldt Canal Company" through the public lands of the United States.

Be it enacted by the Senate and House of Representatives of the Untied States of America in Congress assembled, That the right of way for a canal through the public lands of the United States lying in Humboldt County, State of Nevada, and the use of the land for tow-paths, cuttings, and embankments, to the extent of fifty feet on each side of the centre of the canal, shall be, and is hereby, granted to the Humboldt Canal Company: *Provided,* That in cases where deep excavation or heavy embankment is required, such greater width, not exceeding two hundred feet, may be taken by said company as may be necessary.

SEC. 2. *And be it further enacted,* That, in order to create a reservoir for said company sufficient to feed said canal in all seasons, said company shall be, and is hereby, authorized, by a dam across the Humboldt River, at such a point at or near the gap in the Fremont range of Mountains through which said river passes, to flow so much of the public lands above said dam as may be required for the purpose of said reservoir.

SEC. 3. *And be it further enacted,* That there shall be, and is hereby, granted to said company the necessary sites along said canal for waste-gates, mill-sites, depots, and other uses of said canal, so far as places convenient for the same fall upon the public lands, and also the privilege of discharging the waste waters of said canal over any public lands into the said Humboldt River, at such places as may be suitable for that purpose: *Provided,* That the proper officers of said company shall transmit to the Commissioner of the General Land Office a correct plat of the survey and location of said canal, and of the sites needed for mills, depots, waste-gates, and other uses of said canal, before the appropriation thereof for said uses shall become operative: *And provided further,* That unless thirty miles of said canal shall be excavated within one year, [and] the whole within three years, from the date hereof, the grants hereby made shall cease and determine: *And provided further,* That if said canal shall at any time after its completion be discontinued or abandoned by said company, the grants hereby made shall cease and determine, and the lands hereby granted shall revert to the United States: *And provided further,* That nothing in this act shall be so construed as to interfere with any grant of the right of way and of public lands heretofore made to any railroad company.

Approved, June 12, 1866.

No. 146 B.—An Act for the disposal of the public lands for homestead actual settlement in the States of Alabama, Mississippi, Louisiana, Arkansas, and Florida.

Be it enacted by the Senate and House of Representatives of the United States of America in Congress assembled, That from and after the passage of this act all the public lands in the States of Alabama, Mississippi, Louisiana, Arkansas, and Florida shall be disposed of according to the stipulations of the homestead law of twentieth May, eighteen hundred and sixty-two, entitled "An act to secure homesteads to actual settlers on the public domain," and the act supplemental thereto, approved twenty-first of March, eighteen hundred and sixty-four,* but with this restriction, that until the expiration of two years from and after the passage of this act, no entry shall be made for more than a half-quarter section, or eighty acres, and in lieu of the sum of ten dollars required to be paid by the second section of said act, there shall be paid the sum of five dollars at the time of the issue of each patent; and that the public lands in said States shall be disposed of in no other manner after the passage of this act: *Provided*, That no distinction or discrimination shall be made in the construction or execution of this act on account of race or color: *And provided further*, That no mineral lands shall be liable to entry and settlement under its provisions.

SEC. 2. *And be it further enacted*, That section second of the above-cited homestead law, entitled "An act to secure homesteads to actual settlers on the public domain," approved May twentieth, eighteen hundred and sixty-two, be so amended as to read as follows: That the person applying for the benefit of this act shall, upon application to the register of the land office in which he or she is about to make such entry, make affidavit before the said register or receiver that he or she is the head of a family, or is twenty-one years or more of age, or shall have performed service in the army or navy of the United States, and that such application is made for his or her exclusive use and benefit, and that said entry is made for the purpose of actual settlement and cultivation, and not either directly or indirectly for the use or benefit of any other person or persons whomsoever; and upon filing the said affidavit with the register or receiver, and on payment of five dollars, when the entry is of not more than eighty acres, he or she shall thereupon be permitted to enter the amount of land specified: *Provided, however*, That no certificate shall be given, or patent issued therefor, until the expiration of five years from the date of such entry; and if, at the expiration of such time, or at any time within two years thereafter, the person making such entry, or, if he be dead, his widow; or in case of her death, his heirs or devisee; or in case of a widow making such entry, her heirs or devisee, in case of her death, shall prove by two credible witnesses that he, she, or they have resided upon or cultivated the same for the term of five years immediately succeeding the time of filing the affidavit aforesaid, and shall make affidavit that no part of said land has been alienated, and that he will bear true allegiance to the Government of the United States; then, in such case, he, she, or they, if at that time a citizen of the United States, shall be entitled to a patent, as in other cases provided by law: *And provided further*, That in case of the death of both father and mother, leaving an infant child or children under twenty-one years of age, the right and fee shall enure to the benefit of said infant child or children; and the executor, administrator, or guardian may, at any time within two years after the death of the surviving parent, and in accordance with the laws of the State in which such children, for the time being, have their domicile, sell said land for the benefit of said infants, but for no other purpose; and the purchaser shall acquire the absolute title by the purchase, and be entitled to a patent from the

* No. 38 B. and No. 76 B.

United States on the payment of the office fees and sum of money herein specified: *Provided*, That until the first day of January, eighteen hundred and sixty-seven, any person applying for the benefit of this act shall, in addition to the oath hereinbefore required, also make oath that he has not borne arms against the United States, or given aid and comfort to its enemies.

SEC. 3. *And be it further enacted*, That all the provisions of the said homestead law, and the act amendatory thereof, approved March twenty-first, eighteen hundred and sixty-four, so far as the same may be applicable, except so far as the same are modified by the preceding sections of this act, are applied to and made part of this act as fully as if herein enacted and set forth.

Approved, June 21, 1866.

No. 147 B.—An Act to establish a land office in the Territory of Idaho.

Be it enacted by the Senate and House of Representatives of the United States of America in Congress assembled, That the public lands within the Territory of Idaho, to which the Indian title is or shall be extinguished, shall constitute a new land district, to be called the Idaho District, to be located at Boise City, Ada County; and the President is hereby authorized to appoint, by and with the advice and consent of the Senate, a register and receiver of public moneys for said district, who shall be required to reside at the place at which said office shall be located, and they shall have the same powers, perform the same duties, and be entitled to the same compensation as are or may be prescribed by law in relation to land offices of the United States in other Territories.

Approved, June 27, 1866.

No. 148 B.—An Act to create the office of Surveyor-General in Idaho Territory.

Be it enacted by the Senate and House of Representatives of the United States of America in Congress assembled, That the President, by and with the advice and consent of the Senate, shall be, and he is hereby, authorized to appoint a Surveyor-General for Idaho, whose annual salary shall be three thousand dollars, and whose power, authority, and duties shall be the same as those provided by law for the Surveyor-General of Oregon. He shall have proper allowances for clerk hire, office rent, and fuel, not exceeding what is now allowed by law to the Surveyor-General of Oregon, and he shall locate his office at Boise City, in said Territory of Idaho.

Approved, June 29, 1866.

No. 149 B.—An Act to extend the time for the reversion to the United States of the lands granted by Congress to aid in the construction of a railroad from Amboy, by Hillsdale and Lansing, to some point on or near Traverse Bay, in the State of Michigan, and for the completion of said road.

Be it enacted by the Senate and House of Representatives of the United States of America in Congress assembled, That the time limited by the fourth section of an act entitled "An act making a grant of alternate sections of the public lands to the State of Michigan, to aid in the construction of certain railroads in said State, and for other purposes, approved June three, eighteen hundred and fifty-six,* for the completion of the railroad from Amboy, by Hillsdale and Lansing, to some point on or near Traverse Bay, shall be, and hereby is, revived and extended for the period of seven years, from and after the third day of June, one thousand eight hundred and sixty-six ; and that said grants shall continue and remain in full force and effect for and during that period, as if it had been so provided in said fourth section of said act of June three, eighteen hundred and fifty-six : *Provided*, That the Amboy, Lansing, and Traverse Bay Railroad Company, a corporation organized under the laws of the State of Michigan, shall forfeit all right to said grant, or any part thereof which it may now have, or which may hereafter be conferred upon it, by the Legislature of the State of Michigan, if and whenever the said company shall fail, in whole or in part fully and completely to perform any of the following conditions, that is to say : First, to clear, grub, and grade twenty consecutive miles of the road-bed of said road between Owasso and Saginaw City, so that the same shall be in readiness for the ties and iron by the first day of February, eighteen hundred and sixty-seven ; Second, to fully complete said road from Owasso to Saginaw City, so that the same shall be in readiness for the running of trains by the first day of November, eighteen hundred and sixty-seven : Third, to fully complete in like manner twenty miles of said road in each and every year after the said first day of November, eighteen hundred and sixty-seven, and to fully complete the entire road by the time limited by this act : *And provided further*, That in case of failure of said Amboy, Lansing, and Traverse Bay Rail Company to perform any of the above conditions by the respective times limited therefor, the Legislature of the State of Michigan may at its first session after any such failure, confer the said grant upon some other railroad corporation, or corporations, upon such terms and conditions as the Legislature may see fit to carry out the purposes of the said act of June three, eighteen hundred and fifty-six, and when so conferred, such corporation or corporations shall be entitled to have and enjoy all of the said grant, which shall not then have been lawfully disposed of, to the same extent and in the same manner and for the same purposes, as if the same had been originally confered upon such corporation or corporations. And any such railroad corporation or corporations, whether now organized or hereafter to be organized, upon which said grant may be so conferred in whole or in part, may receive the same without prejudice to any land grant, or other rights or franchises previously acquired. But in no case shall such corporation or corporations be entitled to receive more than ten sections of land to the mile, for that portion of said road which may be consolidated in accordance with the provisions of this act: *And provided further*, That if the Legislature shall, in any such case of

* Vol. I. No. 293. No. 190 B.

failure, so confer said grant as above provided, then the said lands, or so much thereof as shall then remain not lawfully disposed of, shall be subject to the disposal and future control of said Legislature, as provided in section three of said act of June three, eighteen hundred and fifty-six, until the expiration of the time limited by this act. But in case the said Legislature shall in such case fail to so confer said grant, then the said lands shall revert to the United States.

SEC. 2. *And be it further enacted*, That the Flint and Pere Marquette* Railroad Company may change the western terminus of its road to some point on Lake Michigan, at or south of Grand Traverse Bay; and any railroad corporations having a right to the respective land grants specified in the said act of June three, eighteen hundred and fifty-six, located in the lower peninsula of the State of Michigan, may unite and contract with each other, or with any other railroad corporation or corporations, for the construction and operation of a single line of road for any portion of their routes, without prejudice to any land grants, or other rights or franchises previously acquired. And any and all such corporations are hereby authorized to change the location of their lines of road, so far as may be necessary, for the purpose of such consolidation, but not so as to change their respective termini otherwise than is authorized by this act. And whenever any change of terminus or location of line is made, as provided for in this act, the corporation or corporations making such change, shall file in the General Land Office new maps definitely showing such change and the new line of road adopted: *Provided*, That the road mentioned in the first section of this act shall run on the west side of Saginaw River, and that the principal depot shall be located in the northern portion of the plat of Saginaw City, so as best to accommodate the cities of Saginaw and East Saginaw.

SEC. 3. *And be it further enacted*, That the lands granted by the said act of June three, eighteen hundred and fifty-six, to aid in the construction of the railroad described in the first section of this act, shall be disposed of only in the following manner, that is to say: when the Governor of the State of Michigan shall certify to the Secretary of the Interior that ten or more consecutive miles of said road have been completed in a good and substantial manner, as a first-class railroad, stating definitely the commencement and termination of each completed portion of said road and the corporation or corporations so entitled to lands on account thereof, the Secretary of the Interior shall cause patents for lands for such completed portion of said road to be issued to said corporation or corporations: *Provided*, That none of said lands shall be acquired or so patented for any portion of said road so completed south of the intersection of said road with the Detroit and Milwaukee Railway, until the whole of said road north of said intersection shall have been completed and the lands therefor patented as aforesaid: *And provided further*, That the road mentioned in the first section of this act shall be and remain a public highway for the use of the Government of the United States, and shall transport, free from toll or other charges, all property, troops, and munitions of war belonging to the same.

SEC. 4. *And be it further enacted*, That all laws and parts of laws inconsistent with the provisions of this act are hereby repealed.

Approved, July 3, 1866.

* No. 137 B.

No. 150 B.—An Act to amend an act entitled "An act to amend an act entitled 'An act to aid in the construction of a railroad and telegraph line from the Missouri River to the Pacific Ocean, and to secure to the Government the use of the same for postal, military, and other purposes,' approved July 1, 1862," approved July 2, 1864.*

Be it enacted by the Senate and House of Representatives of the United States of America in Congress assembled, That the Union Pacific Railway Company, eastern division, is hereby authorized to designate the general route of their said road and to file a map thereof, as now required by law, at any time before the first day of December, eighteen hundred and sixty-six; and upon the filing of the said map, showing the general route of said road, the lands along the entire line thereof, so far as the same may be designated, shall be reserved from sale by order of the Secretary of the Interior: *Provided,* That said company shall be entitled to only the same amount of the bonds of the United States to aid in the construction of their line of railroad and telegraph as they would have been entitled to if they had connected their said line with the Union Pacific Railroad on the one hundredth degree of longitude, as now required by law: *And provided further,* That said company shall connect their line of railroad and telegraph with the Union Pacific Railroad, but not at a point more than fifty miles westwardly from the meridian of Denver, in Colorado.

SEC. 2. *And be it further enacted,* That the Union Pacific Railroad Company, with the consent and approval of the Secretary of the Interior, are hereby authorized to locate, construct, and continue their road from Omaha, in Nebraska Territory, westward, according to the best and most practicable route, and without reference to the initial point on the one hundredth meridian of west longitude, as now provided by law, in a continuous completed line, until they shall meet and connect with the Central Pacific Railroad Company of California; and the Central Pacific Railroad Company of California, with the consent and approval of the Secretary of the Interior, are hereby authorized to locate, construct, and continue their road eastward, in a continuous completed line, until they shall meet and connect with the Union Pacific Railroad: *Provided,* That each of the above-named companies shall have the right, when the nature of the work to be done, by reason of deep cuts and tunnels, shall for the expeditious construction of the Pacific Railroad require it, to work for an extent of not to exceed three hundred miles in advance of their continuous completed lines.

Approved, July 3, 1866.

No. 151 B.—An Act granting certain lands to the State of Michigan to aid in the construction of a ship canal to connect the waters of Lake Superior with the lake known as Lac La Belle, in said State.

Be it enacted by the Senate and House of Representatives of the United States of America in Congress assembled, That there be, and is hereby, granted to the State of Michigan, for the use and benefit of the "Lac La Belle Harbor Improvement Company," a company organized under

* No. 111 B. and No. 231 B.

and by virtue of the laws of the State of Michigan, for the purpose of aiding in the construction of a ship canal to connect the waters of Lake Superior with the lake known as Lac La Belle, in said State, one hundred thousand acres of the public lands of the United States in the upper peninsula of Michigan, to be selected from the odd-numbered sections of land nearest the location of the said canal, not otherwise reserved or appropriated, nor designated by the United States as "mineral lands" prior to the passage of this act, nor to which the rights of pre-emption or homestead have attached: *Provided*, That the said canal shall be at least one hundred feet wide at the top, seventy-five feet wide at the bottom, and shall have, when completed, a depth of water through its entire length of at least twelve feet, running from sixteen feet of water in Lake Superior to fourteen feet of water in Lac La Belle: *And provided further*, That said canal shall be and remain a public highway for the use of the Government of the United States, free from toll or charge upon the vessels of said Government, or upon vessels employed by said Government in the transportation of any property or troops of the United States.

SEC. 2. *And be it further enacted*, That the lands hereby granted shall be subject to the disposal of the Legislature of the State of Michigan for the purposes aforesaid, and no other; that as soon as the Governor of the said State shall file, or cause to be filed, with the Secretary of the Interior, a map or plan showing the location of the said canal, then it shall be the duty of the Secretary of the Interior to withdraw from market the lands applicable and subject to the provisions of this act; and whenever the Governor of the State of Michigan shall certify to the Secretary of the Interior that the said ship canal has been completed, in a good, substantial, and workmanlike manner, in all respects in conformity with the provisions of this act, and to his satisfaction, then it shall be the duty of the Secretary of the Interior to issue patents to the said State of Michigan for the lands hereby granted.

SEC. 3. *And be it further enacted*, That if the said ship canal shall not be completed within two years from and after the passage of this act, the lands hereby granted shall revert to the United States.

Approved, July 3, 1866.

No. 152 B.—An Act granting lands to the State of Michigan to aid in the construction of a harbor and ship canal at Portage Lake, Keewenaw Point, Lake Superior, in said State.

Be it enacted by the Senate and House of Representatives of the United States of America in Congress assembled, That there be, and hereby is, granted to the State of Michigan, to aid in the building of a harbor and ship canal at Portage Lake, Keewenaw Point, Lake Superior, in addition to a former grant for that purpose, approved March the third, eighteen hundred and sixty-five, two hundred thousand acres of land in the upper peninsula of the State of Michigan, and from land to which the right of homestead or pre-emption has not attached: *Provided*, That one hundred and fifty thousand acres of said lands shall be selected from alternate odd-numbered sections, and fifty thousand acres from even-numbered sections of the lands of the United States. Said grant of lands shall inure to the use and benefit of the Portage Lake and Lake Superior Ship Canal Company, in accordance with an act of the legislature of the State of Michigan, conferring the land granted to the said State, by the act herein referred to, on said company: *And provided further*, That the time allowed for the completion of said work and the right of reversion to the United States, under the said act of Congress, approved March the third, eighteen hundred and sixty-five, be extended three additional years: *And provided further*, That no lands designated by the United States as "mineral" before the passage of this act* shall be included within this grant.

Approved, July 3, 1866.

No. 154 B.—An Act to create an additional land district in the State of Oregon.

Be it enacted by the Senate and House of Representatives of the United States of America in Congress assembled, That the President of the United States be, and he is hereby, authorized to establish an additional land district in the State of Oregon, and to fix from time to time the boundaries thereof, which district shall be named after the place at which the office shall first be established; and the President shall be authorized hereafter, from time to time, as circumstances may require, to adjust the boundaries of any and all of the land districts in said State, and change the location of the land office from time to time when the same shall be expedient.

SEC. 2. *And be it further enacted*, That the President is hereby authorized to appoint, by and with the advice and consent of the Senate, or during the recess thereof, and until the end of the next ensuing session, a register and receiver for said land district, who shall be required to reside at the site of the office, shall be subject to the same laws and responsibilities, and whose compensation and fees shall be respectively the same per annum, as are now allowed by law to other land officers in said State.

Approved, July 3, 1866.

No. 155 B.—An Act making a grant of lands in alternate sections to aid in the construction and extension of the Iron Mountain Railroad, from Pilot Knob, in the State of Missouri, to Helena, in Arkansas.

Be it enacted by the Senate and House of Representatives of the United States of America in Congress assembled, That there be, and is hereby, granted to the State of Missouri, for the purpose of aiding in the construction and extension of the Iron Mountain Railroad, from its present terminus at Pilot Knob to a point on the southern boundary line of the State of Missouri, every alternate section of land, designated by odd numbers, for ten sections in width on each side of said road; but in case it shall appear when the route of said road is definitely fixed that the United States have sold any sections or parts thereof, granted as aforesaid, or that the right of pre-emption has attached to the same, then it shall be lawful for any agent or agents to be appointed by the Governor

* See No. 127 B.

of said State to select, subject to the approval of the Secretary of the Interior, from the lands of the United States nearest to the tiers of sections above specified so much land in sections or parts of sections, to be selected as aforesaid, as shall be equal to such lands as the United States have sold or otherwise appropriated or to which the rights of pre-emption have attached, which lands thus selected shall be held by the State of Missouri for the use and purposes aforesaid, and for none other: *Provided*, That the lands so located shall be within the Ironton land district as now established and not more than twenty miles from the line of said road: *And provided further*, That all mineral lands except those containing coal and iron, and any lands heretofore reserved to the United States by any act of Congress or in any other manner by competent authority for the purpose of aiding in any object of internal improvement, or for any other purpose whatever, be, and the same are reserved to the United States from the operation of this act, except so far as it may be found necessary to locate the routes of said railroad through the same, in which case the right of way only shall be granted, subject to the approval of the President of the United States.

SEC. 2. *And be it further enacted*, That there be, and is hereby, granted to the State of Arkansas for the purpose of aiding in the construction and extension of a railroad from the point where the Iron Mountain Railroad intersects the southern boundary line of Missouri, by the nearest and most practicable route, to a point at or near the town of Helena, on the Mississippi River, every alternate section of land, designated by odd numbers for ten sections in width on each side of said road; but in case it shall appear, when the line of said road is definitely fixed, that the United States have sold any sections or parts thereof, granted as aforesaid, or that the right of pre-emption has attached to the same, then it shall be lawful for any agent or agents to be appointed by the Governor of said State, to select, subject to the approval of the Secretary of the Interior, from the lands of the United States nearest to the tiers of sections above specified so much land, in alternate sections, designated as aforesaid, as shall be equal to such lands as the United States have sold or otherwise appropriated, or to which the rights of pre-emption have attached, which lands thus selected shall be held by the State of Arkansas for the use and purposes aforesaid, and for none other: *Provided*, That the land so selected and located shall in no case be further than twenty miles from the line of road when the same shall be located: *And provided further*, That all mineral lands, except those containing coal and iron, and any lands heretofore reserved to the United States by any act of Congress, or in any other manner by competent authority, for the purpose of aiding in any object of internal improvement, or for any other purpose whatever, be, and the same are, reserved to the United States from the operation of this act, except so far as it may be found necessary to locate the routes of said railway through the same, in which case the right of way only shall be granted, subject to the approval of the President of the United States.

SEC. 3. *And be it further enacted*, That the sections and parts of sections of land which shall remain to the United States within ten miles on either side of said road, and the even sections and parts of sections corresponding to the odd ones selected within twenty miles of the same, shall not be sold for less than double the minimum price of the public lands when sold, nor shall any of the said lands become subject to private entry until the same shall have been first offered at public sale to the highest bidder at or above the minimum price as aforesaid: *Provided*, That actual bona fide settlers under the pre-emption laws of the United States may, after the proof of settlement, improvement, and occupation, as now provided by law, purchase the same at the increased minimum price : *And provided also*, That settlers under the provisions of the homestead law, who comply with the terms and requirements of *this* [said] act, shall be entitled to patents for an amount not exceeding eighty acres each, anything in this act to the contrary notwithstanding.

SEC. 4. *And be it further enacted*, That the said railroads shall be, and remain, public highways, so far as the same may be constructed under this act for the use of the Government of the United States, free of all toll or other charges upon the transportation of any property or troops of the United States, and at the costs in all respects of said railroad companies; and the said roads are hereby required to be constructed within the term of five years from and after the first day of July, Anno Domini eighteen hundred and sixty-six.

SEC. 5. *And be it further enacted*, That the lands hereby granted to said States of Missouri and Arkansas shall be disposed of by said States for the purposes aforesaid only, and in manner following, namely : Whenever the Governor of either of said States shall certify to the Secretary of the Interior, that any section of ten consecutive miles of either of said roads is completed in a good, substantial, and workmanlike manner, as a first-class railroad, and the said Secretary shall be satisfied that said State has complied in good faith with this requirement, the said Secretary of the Interior shall issue to the said State patents for all the lands granted and selected as aforesaid, not exceeding ten sections per mile, situated opposite to and within a limit of twenty miles of the line of said section of road thus completed, extending along the whole length of said completed section of ten miles of road, and no further. And when the Governor of said State shall certify to the Secretary of the Interior, and the Secretary shall be satisfied that another section of said road, ten consecutive miles in extent, connecting with the preceding section or with some other first-class railroad which may be at the time in successful operation, is completed as aforesaid, the said Secretary of the Interior shall issue to the said State patents for all the lands granted and situated opposite to and within the limits of twenty miles of the line of said completed section of road or roads, and extending the length of said section, and no further, and not exceeding ten sections of land per mile for all that part of said road thus completed under the provisions of this act and the act to which this is an amendment, and so, from time to time, until said roads and branches are completed. And when the Governor of said State shall so certify, and the Secretary of the Interior shall be satisfied that the whole of any one of said roads and branches is completed in a good, substantial, and workmanlike manner, as a first-class railroad, the said Secretary of the Interior shall issue to the said State patents to all the remaining lands granted for and on account of said completed road and branches in this act, situated within the said limits of twenty miles from the line thereof, throughout the entire length of said road and branches: *Provided*, That no land shall be granted or conveyed to said State under the provisions of this act on account of the construction of any railroad or part thereof that has been constructed under the provisions of any other act at the date of the passage of this act, and adopted as a part of the line of railroad provided for in this act: *And provided*, That nothing herein contained shall interfere with any existing rights acquired under any law of Congress heretofore enacted, making grants of land to the said States of Missouri and Arkansas to aid in the construction of railroads: *And pro-*

vided further, That should said States, or either of them, fail to complete the roads herein recited within the time prescribed by this act, then the lands undisposed of, as aforesaid, within the States so failing shall revert to the United States.

SEC. 6. *And be it further enacted*, That so soon as the Governor of either of said States shall file or cause to be filed with the Secretary of the Interior maps designating the routes of said roads herein mentioned, then it shall be the duty of the Secretary of the Interior to withdraw from market the lands embraced within the provisions of this act.

SEC. 7. *And be it further enacted*, That nothing contained in this act shall be held as vesting in the State of Arkansas title to the lands herein recited for the trust purpose aforesaid, or authorizing said State to make any disposition of the same, until said State shall be restored in all respects to its former relation to the national government and be represented in the Congress of the United States.

Approved, July 4, 1866.

No. 156 B.—An Act concerning certain lands granted to the State of Nevada.

Be it enacted by the Senate and House of Representatives of the United States of America in Congress assembled, That the appropriation by the constitution of the State of Nevada to educational purposes of the five hundred thousand acres of land granted to said State by the law of September fourth, eighteen hundred and forty-one, for purposes of internal improvement, is hereby approved and confirmed.

SEC. 2. *And be it further enacted*, That land equal in amount to seventy-two entire sections, for the establishment and maintenance of a university in said State, is hereby granted to the State of Nevada.

SEC. 3. *And be it further enacted*, That the grant made by law of the second day of July, eighteen hundred and sixty-two, to each State, of land equal to thirty thousand acres for each of its Senators and Representatives in Congress, is extended to the State of Nevada; and the diversion of the proceeds of these lands in Nevada from the teaching of agriculture and mechanic arts to that of the theory and practice of mining is allowed and authorized without causing a forfeiture of said grant.*

SEC. 4. *And be it further enacted*, That the President of the United States, by and with the advice and consent of the Senate, shall be, and he is hereby, authorized to appoint a Surveyor-General for Nevada, who shall locate his office at such place as the Secretary of the Interior shall from time to time direct, whose compensation shall be three thousand dollars per annum, and whose duties, powers, obligations, responsibilities, and allowances for clerk hire, office rent, fuel, and incidental expenses shall be the same as those of the Surveyor-General of Oregon, under the direction of the Secretary of the Interior, and such instructions as he may from time to time deem it advisable to give him.

SEC. 5. *And be it further enacted*, That in extending the surveys of the public lands in the State of Nevada, the Secretary of the Interior may, in his discretion, vary the lines of the subdivisions from a rectangular form, to suit the circumstances of the country; but in all cases lands

* No. 47 B. See also No. 33 B., No. 55 B., No. 74 B., No. 208 B.

valuable for mines of gold, silver, quicksilver, or copper, shall be reserved from sale.

SEC. 6. *And be it further enacted,* That until the State of Nevada shall have received her full quota of lands named in the first, second, and third sections of this act, the public lands in that State shall not be subject to entry, sale, or location under any law of the United States, or any scrip or warrants issued in pursuance of any such law except the homestead act of May twentieth, eighteen hundred and sixty-two, and acts amendatory thereto, and the acts granting and regulating pre-emptions, but shall be reserved exclusively for entry by the said State for the period of two years after such survey shall have been made: *Provided,* That said State shall select said lands in her own name and right, in tracts of not less than forty acres, and dispose of the same in tracts not exceeding three hundred and twenty acres, only to actual settlers and bona fide occupants: *And provided further,* That city and town property shall not be subject to selection under this act: *And provided further,* That this section shall not be construed to interfere with or impair rights heretofore acquired under any law of Congress.

Approved, July 4, 1866.

No. 157 B.—An Act granting lands to the State of Oregon, to aid in the construction of a military road from Corvallis to the Acquinna Bay.

Be it enacted by the Senate and House of Representatives of the United States of America in Congress assembled, That there be, and is hereby, granted to the State of Oregon, to aid in the construction of a military wagon road from the town of Corvallis to the Acquinna Bay, three alternate sections per mile from the unoccupied public lands, designated by odd numbers, and not more than six miles from said road: *Provided,* That the lands hereby granted shall be exclusively applied in the construction of said road, and shall be disposed of only as the work progresses; and the same shall be applied to no other purposes whatever: *And provided further,* That any and all lands heretofore reserved to the United States by act of Congress, or other competent authority, be, and the same are, reserved from the operation of this act, except so far as it may be necessary to locate the route of said road through the same, in which case the right of way is granted.

SEC. 2. *And be it further enacted,* That the said lands hereby granted to said State shall be disposed of by the Legislature thereof for the purpose aforesaid, and for no other; and the said road shall be and remain a public highway for the use of the Government of the United States, free from tolls or other charges upon the transportation of any property, troops, or mails of the United States.

SEC. 3. *And be it further enacted,* That the said road shall be constructed with such graduation and bridges as to permit of its regular use as a wagon road, and in such other special manner as the State of Oregon may prescribe.

SEC. 4. *And be it further enacted,* That the lands hereby granted to said State shall be disposed of only in the following manner, that is to say: when the Governor of said State shall certify to the Secretary of the Interior that any ten continuous miles of said road are completed, then a quantity of land hereby granted coterminous to said completed portion of said road, not to exceed thirty sections, may be sold, and so from time to time until said road is completed; and if said road is not completed within five years, no further sales shall be made, and the land remaining unsold shall revert to the United States.

Approved, July 4, 1866.

No. 158 B.—An Act making an additional grant of lands in the State of Minnesota, in alternate sections, to aid in the construction of railroads in said State.

Be it enacted by the Senate and House of Representatives of the United States of America in Congress assembled, That there be, and is hereby, granted to the State of Minnesota, for the purpose of aiding in the construction of a railroad from Houston, in the County of Houston, through the Counties of Fillmore, Mower, Freeborn, and Faribault, to the western boundary of the State; and also for a railroad from Hastings, through the Counties of Dakota, Scott, Carver, and McLeod, to such point on the western boundary of the State as the Legislature of the State may determine, every alternate section of land designated by odd numbers to the amount of five alternate sections per mile on each side of said road; but in case it shall appear that the United States have, when the lines or route of said roads are definitely located, sold any section, or part thereof, granted as aforesaid, or that the right of pre-emption or homestead settlement has attached to the same, or that the same has been reserved by the United States for any purpose whatever, then it shall be the duty of the Secretary of the Interior to cause to be selected for the purposes aforesaid, from the public lands of the United States nearest to the tiers of sections above specified, so much land in alternate sections or parts of sections, designated by odd numbers, as shall be equal to such lands as the United States have sold, reserved, or otherwise appropriated, or to which the right of homestead settlement or pre-emption has attached as aforesaid, which lands, thus indicated by odd numbers and sections, by the direction of the Secretary of the Interior, shall be held by said State of Minnesota for the purposes and uses aforesaid: *Provided,* That the land so selected shall in no case be located more than twenty miles from the lines of said road: *And provided further,* That no land shall be granted or transferred by the provisions of this act not included within the jurisdiction of the State of Minnesota: *And provided further,* That any and all lands heretofore reserved to the United States by any act of Congress, or in any other manner by competent authority, for the purpose of aiding in any object of internal improvement, or other purpose whatever, be, and the same are hereby, reserved and excepted from the operations of this act, except so far as it may be found necessary to locate the route of said road through such reserved lands, in which case the right of way shall be granted, provided the United States has yet in possession the title thereto.

SEC. 2. *And be it further enacted,* That the sections and parts of sections of land which by such grant shall remain to the United States within ten miles on each side of said road shall not be sold for less than double the minimum price of public lands when sold, nor shall any of said lands become subject to sale at private entry until the same shall have been first offered at public sale to the highest bidder at or above the minimum price as aforesaid: *Provided,* That actual bona fide settlers under the pre-emption laws of the United States may, after due proof of settlement, improvement, and occupation as now provided by law, purchase the same at the increased minimum price: *And provided also,* That settlers under the provisions of the homestead law who shall make entries after the passage of this act, upon the sections numbered by even numbers, and who comply with the terms and requirements of said act shall be entitled to patents for an amount not exceeding eighty acres each, anything in this act to the contrary notwithstanding.

SEC. 3. *And be it further enacted,* That the lands hereby granted shall be subject to the disposal of the Legislature of Minnesota for the purposes aforesaid and no other; and the said railroad shall be and remain public highways for the use of the Government of the United States, free of all toll or other charges upon the transportation of any property or troops of the United States, and the same shall at all times be transported at the cost, charge, and expense in all respects of the company or corporation, or their successors or assigns, having or receiving the benefit of the land grants herein made.

SEC. 4. *And be it further enacted,* That the lands hereby granted shall be disposed of by said State for the purposes aforesaid only, and in manner following, namely: When the Governor of said State shall certify to the Secretary of the Interior that any section of ten consecutive miles of said road is completed, in a good, substantial, and workmanlike manner, as a first-class railroad, then the Secretary of the Interior shall issue to the State patents for all the lands in alternate sections, or parts of sections, designated by odd numbers, situated within twenty miles of the road so completed and lying coterminous to said completed section of ten miles, and not exceeding one hundred sections, for the benefit of the road having completed the ten consecutive miles as aforesaid: *Provided, however,* That the coterminous principle hereby applied shall not extend to such lands as are taken by the said railroad companies to make up deficiencies, provided that no land to make up such deficiencies shall be taken at any point within ten miles upon each side of the line of said roads. When the Governor of said State shall certify that another section of ten consecutive miles shall have been completed as aforesaid, then the Secretary of the Interior shall issue patents to said State in like manner for a like number; and when certificates of the completion of additional sections of ten consecutive miles of said roads are from time to time made as aforesaid, until said roads are completed, when the whole of the lands hereby granted shall be patented to the State for the uses aforesaid, and none other: *Provided,* That if said roads are not completed within ten years from the acceptance of this grant, the said lands hereby granted and not patented shall revert to the United States.

SEC. 5. *And be it further enacted,* That as soon as the Governor of said State shall file or cause to be filed with the Secretary of the Interior maps designating the routes of said roads, then it shall be the duty of the Secretary of the Interior to withdraw from market the lands embraced within the provisions of this act.

SEC. 6. *And be it further enacted,* That the United States mail shall be transported on said road, under the direction of the Post Office Department, at such price as Congress may by law provide: *Provided,* That until such price is fixed by law, the Postmaster-General shall have power to fix the rate of compensation.

Approved, July 4, 1866.

No. 159 B.—An Act to provide for the disposal of certain lands therein named.

Be it enacted by the Senate and House of Representatives of the United States of America in Congress assembled, That the Commissioner of the General Land Office be, and he is hereby, authorized to cause to be offered at public auction all the unsold lots of that portion of the public domain known as the Fort Howard Military Reserve, which is situated in the County of Brown, and State of Wisconsin, giving not less than two months' notice of the time and place of such sale, by advertising the same in such newspapers and for such period of time as he may deem best. Every such lot shall be sold separately to the highest bidder for cash, and when not paid for within twenty-four hours from the time of purchase, it shall be liable to be resold under the order of the Commissioner of the General Land Office aforesaid, at such reasonable minimum as may be fixed by the Secretary of the Interior, and no sale shall be binding until approved by that officer.

SEC. 2. *And be it further enacted,* That it shall be the duty of the President to cause patents to be issued in due form of law for each and every such lot, as soon as may be after the purchase of and payment for the same.

Approved, July 4, 1866.

No. 160 B.—An Act granting lands to the State of Oregon, to aid in the construction of a military road from Albany, Oregon, to the eastern boundary of said State.

Be it enacted by the Senate and House of Representatives of the United States of America in Congress assembled, That there be, and hereby is, granted to the State of Oregon, to aid in the construction of a military wagon road from Albany, Oregon, by way of Canyon City, and the most feasible pass in Cascade range of mountains, to the eastern boundary of the State alternate sections of public lands, designated by odd numbers, three sections per mile, to be selected within six miles of said road: *Provided,* That the lands hereby granted shall be exclusively applied in the construction of said road, and shall be disposed of only as the work progresses; and the same shall be applied to no other purpose whatever: *And provided further,* That any and all lands heretofore reserved to the United States by act of Congress or other competent authority be, and the same are, reserved from the operation of this act, except so far as it may be necessary to locate the route of said road through the same, in which case the right of way is granted, subject to the approval of the President of the United States.

SEC. 2. *And be it further enacted,* That the said lands hereby granted to said State shall be disposed of by the Legislature thereof for the purpose aforesaid, and for no other; and the said road shall be and remain a public highway for the use of the Government of the United States, free from tolls or other charge upon the transportation of any property, troops, or mails of the United States.

SEC. 3. *And be it further enacted,* That said road shall be constructed with such width, graduation, and bridges, as to permit of its regular use as a wagon road, and in such other special manner as the State of Oregon may prescribe.

SEC. 4. *And be it further enacted,* That the lands hereby granted to said State shall be disposed of only in the following manner, that is to say: that when ten miles of said road shall be completed, a quantity of land not exceeding thirty sections for said road may be sold coterminous to said completed portion of said road; and when the Governor of said State shall certify to the Secretary of the Interior that any ten continuous miles of said road are completed, then another quantity of land hereby granted, not to exceed thirty sections, may be sold, coterminous to said completed portion of said road, and so from time to time until said road is completed: and if said road is not completed within five years, no further sales shall be made, and the land remaining unsold shall revert to the United States.

Approved, July 5, 1866

No. 161 B.—An act to amend "An act making a grant of lands to the State of Minnesota to aid in the construction of the railroad from St. Paul to Lake Superior," approved May fifth, eighteen hundred and sixty-four.*

Be it enacted by the Senate and House of Representatives of the United States of America in Congress assembled, That section one of the act entitled "An act making a grant of lands to the State of Minnesota to aid in the construction of the railroad from Saint Paul to Lake Superior," approved May fifth, eighteen hundred and sixty-four, be amended by adding thereto the following: *Provided further,* That in case it shall appear, when the line of the Lake Superior and Mississippi Railroad is definitely located, that the quantity of land intended to be granted by the said act in aid of the construction of the said road shall be deficient by reason of the line thereof running near the boundary line of the said State of Minnesota, the said company shall be entitled to take from other public lands of the United States within thirty miles of the west line of said road such an amount of lands as shall make up such deficiency: *Provided,* That the same shall be taken in alternate odd sections as provided for in said act.

Approved, July 13, 1866.

No. 162 B.—An Act granting aid in the construction of a railroad and telegraph line from the town of Folsom to the town of Placerville, in the State of California.

Be it enacted by the Senate and House of Representatives of the United States of America in Congress assembled, That the right of way through the public lands be, and the same is hereby, granted to the Placerville and Sacramento Valley Railroad Company, a corporation existing under the laws of the State of California, and designated by the Legislature thereof, to construct the road hereinafter named, and to its successors and assigns, for the construction of a railroad and telegraph line from the town of Folsom to the town of Placerville, in said State; and the right

* No. 82 B.

is hereby given to said corporation to take from the public lands adjacent to the line of said road material for the construction thereof; said right of way is granted to said railroad to the extent of one hundred feet in width on each side of said road, where it may pass over the public lands; also, all necessary ground for station buildings, workshops, depots, machine shops, switches, side tracks, turn-tables, and water stations.

SEC. 2. *And be it further enacted*, That there be, and is hereby, granted to the Placerville and Sacramento Valley Railroad Company, its successors and assigns, for the purpose of aiding in the construction of said railroad and telegraph line, and to secure the safe and speedy transportation of the mails, troops, munitions of war, and public stores over the route of said line of railway, every alternate section of public land, not containing gold or silver, designated by odd numbers, to the amount of ten alternate sections per mile, on each side of said railroad line, as said company may adopt, whenever, on the line thereof, the United States have full title, not reserved, sold, granted, or otherwise appropriated, and free from pre-emption or other claims or rights at the time the line of said road is definitely fixed, and a plat thereof filed in the office of the Commissioner of the General Land Office: *Provided*, That the word "mineral," when it occurs in this act, shall not be held to include iron or coal.

SEC. 3. *And be it further enacted*, That whenever said Placerville and Sacramento Valley Railroad Company shall have ten consecutive miles of any portion of said railroad and telegraph line ready for the service contemplated, the President of the United States shall appoint three commissioners to examine the same, and if it shall appear that ten miles of said railroad and telegraph line have been completed in a good and substantial manner, and in all respects as required by this act, the commissioners shall so report to the President of the United States, and patents of lands, as aforesaid, shall be issued to said company, confirming to said company the right and title to said lands, situated opposite to and coterminous with said completed section of said road, unless said lands are covered by the exceptions of this act. And from time to time, whenever ten additional miles shall have been constructed, completed, and in readiness, as aforesaid, and verified by the commissioners to the President of the United States, then patents shall be issued to said company, conveying the additional sections of land, as aforesaid; and so on as fast as every ten miles of said road is completed, as aforesaid: *Provided*, That said commissioners named in this section shall be paid by the company ten dollars per day for the time actually employed, and ten cents per mile for the distance actually and necessarily travelled each way.

* * * * * * * * *

SEC. 5. *And be it further enacted*, That the President of the United States shall cause such lands to be surveyed for twenty miles in width on both sides of the entire line of said road, after the general route shall be fixed, and as fast as may be required by the construction of said railroad; and the odd sections of land hereby granted shall not be liable to sale, or entry, or pre-emption, before or after they are surveyed, except by said company, as provided in this act; but the provisions of the act of September, eighteen hundred and forty-one, granting pre-emption rights, and the acts amendatory thereof and of the act entitled "An act to secure homesteads to actual settlers on the public domain," approved May twenty, eighteen hundred and sixty-two, shall be, and the same are hereby, extended to all other lands on the line of said road when surveyed, excepting those hereby granted to said company: and the sections and parts of sections of land which by the aforesaid grant shall remain in the United States within ten miles on each side of said road, shall not be sold for less than double the minimum price of public lands when sold.

SEC. 6. *And be it further enacted*, That each and every grant, right, and privilege herein are so made and given to and accepted by said Placerville and Sacramento Valley Railroad Company, upon and subject to the following conditions, namely: That the said company shall commence the work on said road within one year from the approval of this act by the President, and shall complete the whole road by the fourth day of July, eighteen hundred and sixty-nine.

SEC. 7. *And be it further enacted*, That the United States make the several conditioned grants herein, and that the said Placerville and Sacramento Valley Railroad Company accept the same, upon the further condition that if the said company make any breach of the conditions hereof, and allow the same to continue for upwards of one year, then in such case the title to the public lands herein reserved for the construction of said road shall revert to the United States.

SEC. 8. *And be it further enacted*, That all people of the United States shall have the right to subscribe to the stock of the said Placerville and Sacramento Valley Railroad Company until the whole capital is taken up, by complying with the terms of subscription.

SEC. 9. *And be it further enacted*, That the acceptance of the terms, conditions, and impositions of this act by the said Placerville and Sacramento Valley Railroad Company shall be signified in writing, under the corporate seal of the said company, duly executed, pursuant to the direction of its board of directors first had and obtained, which acceptance shall be made within one year after the passage of this act, and not afterwards, and shall be deposited with the Secretary of the Interior.

SEC. 10. *And be it further enacted*, That the said company is authorized to accept to its own use any grant, donation, or loan, power, franchise, aid or assistance which may be granted to or conferred upon said company by the Congress of the United States, by the legislature of any State, county, or municipal corporation, or by any corporation, person or persons, and said corporation is authorized to hold and enjoy any such grant, donation, loan, or power, franchise, aid, or assistance, to its own use, for the purpose aforesaid.

SEC. 11. *And be it further enacted*, That unless the said Placerville and Sacramento Valley Railroad Company shall obtain bona fide subscription to the stock of said company to the amount of four hundred thousand dollars, with five per centum paid within one year after the passage and approval of this act, it shall be null and void.

SEC. 12. *And be it further enacted*, That Congress may at any time, having due regard for the rights of said Placerville and Sacramento Valley Railroad Company, add to, alter, amend, or repeal this act.

SEC. 13. *And be it further enacted*, That all lots in villages, towns, and cities shall be exempted from, and not subject to, the operations of this act.

Approved, July 13, 1866.

No. 163 B.—An Act relating to lands granted to the State of Minnesota to aid in constructing railroads.

Be it enacted by the Senate and House of Representatives of the United States of America in Congress assembled, That whenever it shall appear that the United States have sold or disposed of any lands granted to the Territory or State of Minnesota for the purpose of aiding in the construction of railroads, after the definite location of the line of road, and before the withdrawal of said lands from sale at the proper local land office, said State may by its agent select, in lieu of the lands so sold or disposed of, from any of the lands of the United States subject to sale, being odd numbered sections, within twenty miles of the line of the proper road, a quantity of land equal to that so sold or disposed of; and the lands so selected shall be substituted for those so sold or disposed of by the United States, and may be disposed of by said State in all respects as if said substituted lands had been parcel of the original grant to the State. *Provided, however,* That nothing herein contained shall be so construed as to diminish the quantity of land granted by act of May fifth, eighteen hundred and sixty-four, to the State of Minnesota to aid in the construction of a railroad from St. Paul to Lake Superior.*

SEC. 2. *And be it further enacted,* That the time named in the act granting lands to the Territory of Minnesota to aid in the construction of a certain railroad, "from Saint Paul and from Saint Anthony, by the way of Minneapolis, to a convenient point of junction west of the Mississippi River, to the southern boundary of the Territory," approved March third, eighteen hundred and fifty-seven, for the construction and completion of said road, is hereby extended for seven years from the passage of this act.†

SEC. 3. *And be it further enacted,* That all the lands heretofore granted to the Territory and State of Minnesota to aid in the construction of railroads, shall be certified to said State by the Secretary of the Interior, from time to time, whenever any of said roads shall be definitely located, and shall be disposed of by said State in the manner and upon the conditions provided in the particular act granting the same, as modified by the provisions of this act: *Provided,* That when the original quantity granted to aid in the construction of any road has been increased, the quantity authorized to be sold from time to time shall be increased correspondingly: *And provided further,* That on the completion of any ten miles of road, the State may sell one half the quantity of lands which said State is authorized to dispose of on the completion of twenty miles.

SEC. 4. *And be it further enacted,* That the lands granted by any act of Congress to the State of Minnesota, to aid in the construction of railroads in said State, specifically, lying in place, on any division of ten miles of road, shall not be disposed of until the road shall be completed through and conterminous with the same: *Provided, however,* That this provision shall not extend to any lands authorized to be taken to make up deficiencies.

SEC. 5. *And be it further enacted,* That so much of any act as conflicts with the provisions of this act is hereby repealed.

Approved, July 13, 1866.

* No. 82 B. No. 161 B.

† Vol. I. No. 312.

No. 164 B.—An Act making appropriations for the Legislative, Executive, and Judicial expenses of the Government for the year ending the thirtieth of June, eighteen hundred and sixty-seven, and for other purposes.

* * * * * * * * *

Surveyors-General and their Clerks.—For compensation of the Surveyor-General of Wisconsin and Iowa, and clerks for completing and winding up the business in his office, four thousand eight hundred dollars: *Provided,* That when this appropriation shall have been exhausted, the said office shall be abolished.

* * * * * * * * *

Approved, July 23, 1866.

No. 165 B.—An act to amend the fifth section of an act entitled "An act donating public lands to the several States and Territories which may provide colleges for the benefit of agriculture and the mechanic arts," approved July 2, 1862, so as to extend the time within which the provisions of said act shall be accepted and such colleges established.*

Be it enacted by the Senate and House of Representatives of the United States of America in Congress assembled, That the time in which the several States may comply with the provisions of the act of July two, eighteen hundred and sixty-two, entitled "An act donating public lands to the several States and Territories which may provide colleges for the benefit of agriculture and the mechanic arts," is hereby extended so that the acceptance of the benefits of the said act may be expressed within three years from the passage of this act, and the colleges required by the said act may be provided within five years from the date of the filing of such acceptance with the Commissioner of the General Land Office: *Provided,* That when any Territory shall become a State and be admitted into the Union, such new State shall be entitled to the benefits of the said act of July two, eighteen hundred and sixty-two, by expressing the acceptance therein required within three years from the date of its admission into the Union, and providing the college or colleges within five years after such acceptance, as prescribed in this act: *Provided further,* That any State which has heretofore expressed its acceptance of the act herein referred to shall have the period of five years within which to provide at least one college, as described in the fourth section of said act, after the time for providing said college, according to the act of July second, eighteen hundred and sixty-two, shall have expired.

Approved, July 23, 1866.

No. 166 B.—An Act to quiet the title to certain lands within the corporate limits of the City of Benicia and the town of Santa Cruz in the State of California.

Be it enacted by the Senate and House of Representatives of the United States of America in Congress assembled, That all the right and title of the United States to the land situated within the corporate limits of the

*No. 47 B., No. 78 B.

City of Benicia, in the County of Solano, State of California, as defined in the act incorporating said city, passed by the Legislature of the State of California, April twenty-four, eighteen hundred and fifty-one, be, and the same are hereby relinquished and granted to the said city and its successors, upon trust, however, that so much of said lands as is in the bona fide occupancy of parties upon the passage of this act, by themselves or tenants, shall be conveyed by said city to such parties : *Provided, however*, That the relinquishment and grant by this act shall not extend to any lands within said corporate limits occupied as a military depot of the United States, or heretofore reserved by the United States for public purposes ; nor shall they interfere with or prejudice any valid adverse right or claim, if such exist to said land or any part thereof, or preclude a judicial examination and adjustment thereof.

SEC. 2. *And be it further enacted*, That all the right and title of the United States to the land within the corporate limits of the town of Santa Crux in the State of California, as defined in the act of the Legislature of that State incorporating said town, be, and the same are hereby, relinquished and granted to the corporate authorities of said town and their successors, in trust for and with authority to convey so much of said lands as are in the bona fide occupancy of parties upon the passage of this act by themselves or tenants, to such parties : *Provided*, That this grant shall not extend to any reservation of the United States, nor prejudice any valid adverse right or claim, if such exist, to said land or any part thereof, nor preclude a judicial examination and adjustment thereof.

Approved, July 23, 1866.

No. 167 B.—An Act for a grant of lands to the State of Kansas to aid in the construction of the Northern Kansas Railroad and Telegraph.

Be it enacted by the Senate and House of Representatives of the United States of America in Congress assembled, That there is hereby granted to the State of Kansas, for the use and benefit of the Saint Joseph and Denver City Railroad Company, the same being a corporation organized under the laws of the State of Kansas, to construct and operate a railroad from Elwood, in Kansas, westwardly, via Maryville, in the same State, so as to effect a junction with the Union Pacific Railroad, or any branch thereof not farther west than the one hundredth meridian of west longitude, every alternate section of land designated by odd numbers, for ten sections in width on each side of said road, to the point of intersection. But in case it shall appear that the United States have, when the line or route of said road is definitely fixed, sold any section or any part thereof, granted as aforesaid, or that the right of pre-emption or homestead settlement has attached to the same, or that the same has been reserved by the United States for any purpose whatever, then it shall be the duty of the Secretary of the Interior to cause to be selected for the purposes aforesaid, from the public lands of the United States nearest to tiers of sections above specified, so much land, in alternate sections or parts of sections designated by odd numbers, as shall be equal to such lands as the United States have sold, reserved, or otherwise appropriated, or to which the rights of pre-emption or homestead settlements have attached as aforesaid; which lands, thus indicated by odd numbers, and selected by direction of the Secretary of the Interior as aforesaid, shall be held by the State of

Kansas for the use and purpose aforesaid: *Provided*, That the land to be so selected shall in no case be located farther than twenty miles from the line of said road: *Provided further*, That the lands hereby granted for and on account of said road shall be exclusively applied in the construction of the same and for no other purpose whatever, and shall be disposed of only as in this act hereinafter provided: *Provided, also*, That no part of the land granted by this act shall be applied to aid in the construction of any railroad or part thereof for the construction of which any previous grant of land or bonds has been made by Congress: *And provided further*, That any and all lands heretofore reserved to the United States by any act of Congress, or in any other manner by competent authority, for the purpose of aiding in any object of internal improvement, or for any other purpose whatsoever, be, and the same are hereby, reserved to the United States from the operations of this act, except so far as may be found necessary to locate the route of said road through said lands; in which case the right of way for one hundred feet on each side of said road only shall be granted, subject to the approval of the President of the United States.

SEC. 2. *And be it further enacted*, That the sections and parts of sections of land which by such grant shall remain to the United States, within ten miles on each side of said road, shall not be sold for less than double the minimum price of the public lands when sold; nor shall any of said lands become subject to sale at private entry until the same shall have been first offered at public sale to the highest bidder, at or above the increased minimum price, as aforesaid: *Provided*, That actual and bona fide settlers, under the provisions of the pre-emption and homestead laws of the United States, may, after due proof of settlement, improvement, cultivation, and occupation, as now provided by law, purchase the same, at the increased minimum price aforesaid: *And provided also*, That settlers on any of said reserved sections, under the provisions of the homestead law, who improve, occupy, and cultivate the same for a period of five years, and comply with the several conditions and requirements of said act, shall be entitled to patents for an amount not exceeding eighty acres each, anything in this act to the contrary notwithstanding.

SEC. 3. *And be it further enacted*, That the grant of the lands hereby made is upon condition that said company, after the construction of its road, shall keep it in repair and use, and shall at all times be in readiness to transport troops, munitions of war, supplies, and public stores upon its roads for the Government when required to do so by any department thereof, the Government at all times having the preference in the use of the road for all the purposes aforesaid at fair and reasonable rates of compensation, not exceeding that paid by private individuals or the average paid for like services on other roads. And the lands hereby granted, held, and reserved as aforesaid shall inure to the benefit of said company, as follows: When the Governor of the State of Kansas shall certify that any section of ten consecutive miles of said road is completed in a good, substantial, and workmanlike manner as a first-class railroad, then the said Secretary of the Interior shall issue to the said company patents for so many sections of the land hereinbefore granted as lie opposite to and coterminous with the said completed sections. And when certificates of the Governor, aforesaid, shall be presented to said Secretary, of the completion, as aforesaid, of each successive section of ten consecutive miles of said road, the said Secretary shall in like manner issue to said company patents for the said sections of said land as aforesaid for each of said sections of road until said road shall be completed: *Provided*, That if said railroad company or its assigns shall fail to complete at least one section of said road each year from the date of its acceptance of the grant provided for in this act, then its right to the lands for said section so failing of completion shall revert to the Government of the United States: *Provided, further,* That if said road is not completed within ten years from the date of the acceptance of the grant hereinbefore made, the lands remaining unpatented shall revert to the United States.

SEC. 4. *And be it further enacted,* That as soon as the said company shall file with the Secretary of the Interior maps of its lines, designating the route hereof, it shall be the duty of the said Secretary to withdraw from the market the lands granted by this act, in such manner as may be best calculated to effect the purposes of this act and subserve the public interest.

SEC. 5. *And be it further enacted,* That the United States mail shall be transported on said road and its extension, under the direction of the Post Office Department, at such price as Congress may by law provide: *Provided,* That until such price is fixed by law the Postmaster-General shall have power to fix the compensation.

SEC. 6. *And be it further enacted,* That the right of way through the public lands be, and the same is hereby, granted to said Saint Joseph and Denver City Railroad Company, its successors and assigns, for the construction of a railroad as proposed; and the right is hereby given to said corporation to take from the public lands adjacent to the line of said road material for the construction thereof. Said way is granted to said railroad to the extent of one hundred feet in width on each side of said road where it may pass through the public domain; also all necessary ground for station buildings, workshops, depots, machine shops, switches, side-tracks, turn-tables, and water-stations.

SEC. 7. *And be it further enacted,* That the acceptance of the terms, conditions, and impositions of this act by the said Saint Joseph and Denver City Railroad Company shall be signified in writing, under the corporate seal of the said company, duly executed pursuant to the direction of its board of directors first had and obtained, which acceptance shall be made within six months after the passage of this act, and not afterwards, and shall be deposited with the Secretary of the Interior.

Approved, July 23, 1866.

No. 168 B.—An Act to authorize the construction of a railroad through certain land of the United States in Kansas.

Be it enacted by the Senate and House of Representatives of the United States of America in Congress assembled, That the Leavenworth City Railroad Company be, and are hereby, authorized to construct a horse railway, with one or two tracks, through the military reservation from Fort Leavenworth to the city of Leavenworth, Kansas, and take for the accommodation of the said road, or the business thereof, a strip of land over said reservation not exceeding twenty feet in width: *Provided,* That the location of said railroad through said reservation shall be on and along the west side of the wagon road leading from the said city to the said fort, and that the said company shall erect their own bridges and crossings, and not be permitted to use those of the wagon road: *And provided also,* That whenever said strip of land shall cease to be used for the purposes of said railroad company or the accommodation of the business thereof, the same shall revert to the United States; that this privilege shall be allowed as long as the Secretary of War shall, in his discretion, determine, and no longer.

Approved, July 23, 1866.

No. 169 B.—*An Act to quiet land titles in California.*

Be it enacted by the Senate and House of Representatives of the United States of America in Congress assembled, That in all cases where the State of California has heretofore made selections of any portion of the public domain in part satisfaction of any grant made to said State by any act of Congress, and has disposed of the same to purchasers in good faith under her laws, the lands so selected shall be, and hereby are, confirmed to said State: *Provided,* That no selection made by said State contrary to existing laws shall be confirmed by this act for lands to which any adverse pre-emption, homestead, or other right has, at the date of the passage of this act, been acquired by any settler under the laws of the United States, or to any lands which have been reserved for naval, military, or Indian purposes by the United States, or to any mineral land, or to any land held or claimed under any valid Mexican or Spanish grant, or to any land which, at the time of the passage of this act, was included within the limits of any city, town, or village, or within the county of San Francisco: *And provided further,* That the State of California shall not receive under this act a greater quantity of land for school or improvement purposes than she is entitled to by law.

SEC. 2. *And be it further enacted,* That where the selections named in section one of this act have been made upon land which has been surveyed by authority of the United States, it shall be the duty of the proper authorities of the State, where the same has not already been done, to notify the register of the United States land office for the district in which the land is located of such selection, which notice shall be regarded as the date of the State selection, and the Commissioner of the General Land Office shall, immediately after the passage of this act, instruct the several local registers to forward to the General Land Office, after investigation and decision, all such selections, which if found to be in accordance with section one of this act, the commissioner shall certify over to the State in the usual manner.

SEC. 3. *And be it further enacted,* That where the selections named in section one of this act have been made from lands which have not been surveyed by authority of the United States, but which selections have been surveyed by authority of and under the laws of said State, and the land sold to purchasers in good faith under the laws of the State, such selections shall, from the date of the passage of this act, when marked off and designated in the field, have the same force and effect as the pre-emption rights of a settler upon unsurveyed public land; and if, upon survey of such lands by the United States, the lines of the two surveys shall be found not to agree, the selection shall be so changed as to include those legal subdivisions which nearest conform to the identical land included in the State survey and selection. Upon the filing with the register of the proper United States land office of the township plat in which any such selection of unsurveyed land is located, the holder of the

State title shall be allowed the same time to present and prove up his purchase and claim under this act as is allowed pre-emptors under existing laws; and if found in accordance with section one of this act, the land embraced therein shall be certified over to the State by the Commissioner of the General Land Office.

SEC. 4. *And be it further enacted*, That in all cases where township surveys have been, or shall hereafter be, made under authority of the United States, and the plats thereof approved, it shall be the duty of the Commissioner of the General Land Office to certify over to the State of California, as swamp and overflowed, all the lands represented as such, upon such approved plats, within one year from the passage of this act, or within one year from the return and approval of such township plats. The commissioner shall direct the United States Surveyor-General for the State of California to examine the segregation maps and surveys of the swamp and overflowed lands made by said State; and where he shall find them to conform to the system of surveys adopted by the United States, he shall construct and approve township plats accordingly, and forward to the General Land Office for approval: *Provided*, That in segregating large bodies of land, notoriously and obviously swamp and overflowed, it shall not be necessary to subdivide the same, but to run the exterior lines of such body of land. In case such State surveys are found not to be in accordance with the system of United States surveys, and in such other townships as no survey has been made by the United States, the commissioner shall direct the Surveyor-General to make segregation surveys, upon application to said Surveyor-General by the Governor of said State within one year of such application, of all the swamp and overflowed land in such townships, and to report the same to the General Land Office, representing and describing what land was swamp and overflowed under the grant, according to the best evidence he can obtain. If the authorities of said State shall claim as swamp and overflowed any land not represented as such upon the map or in the returns of the surveyors, the character of such land at the date of the grant, September twenty-eight, eighteen hundred and fifty, and the right to the same, shall be determined by testimony to be taken before the Surveyor-General, who shall decide the same, subject to the approval of the Commissioner of the General Land Office.

SEC. 5. *And be it further enacted*, That it shall be the duty of the Commissioner of the General Land Office to instruct the officers of the local land offices and the Surveyor-General, immediately after the passage of this act, to forward lists of all selections made by the State referred to in section one of this act, and lists and maps of all swamp and overflowed lands claimed by said State, or surveyed as provided in this act, for final disposition and determination, which final disposition shall be made by the Commissioner of the General Land Office without delay.

SEC. 6. *And be it further enacted*, That an act entitled "An act to provide for the survey of the public lands in California, the granting of pre-emption rights therein, and for other purposes,"* approved March third, one thousand eight hundred and fifty-three, shall be construed as giving the State of California the right to select for school purposes other lands in lieu of such sixteenth and thirty-sixth sections as were settled upon prior to survey, reserved for public uses, covered by grants made under Spanish or Mexican authority, or by other private claims, or where such sections would be so covered if the lines of the public surveys were

* Vol. I. No. 224.

extended over such lands, which shall be determined whenever township lines shall have been extended over such land, and in case of Spanish or Mexican grants, when the final survey of such grants shall have been made. The Surveyor-General for the State of California shall furnish the State authorities with lists of all such sections so covered, as a basis of selection, such selections to be made from surveyed lands, and within the same land district as the section for which the selection is made.

SEC. 7. *And be it further enacted*, That where persons in good faith and for a valuable consideration, have purchased lands of Mexican grantees or assigns, which grants have subsequently been rejected, or where the lands so purchased have been excluded from the final survey of any Mexican grant, and have used, improved, and continued in the actual possession of the same as according to the lines of their original purchase, and where no valid adverse right or title (except of the United States) exists, such purchasers may purchase the same, after having such lands surveyed under existing laws, at the minimum price established by law, upon first making proof of the facts as required in this section, under regulations to be provided by the Commissioner of the General Land Office, joint entries being admissible by coterminous proprietors to such an extent as will enable them to adjust their respective boundaries: *Provided*, That the provisions of this section shall not be applicable to the city and county of San Francisco: *Provided*, That the right to purchase herein given shall not extend to lands containing mines of gold, silver, copper, or cinnabar: *Provided*, That whenever it shall be made to appear by petition from the occupants of such land that injury to permanent improvements would result from running the lines of the public surveys through such permanent improvements, the Commissioner of the General Land Office may recognize existing lines of subdivisions.

SEC. 8. *And be it further enacted*, That in all cases where a claim to land by virtue of a right or title derived from the Spanish or Mexican authorities has been finally confirmed, and a survey and plat thereof shall not have been requested within ten months from the passage of this act, as provided by sections six and seven of the act of July first, eighteen hundred and sixty-four,* "To expedite the settlement of titles to lands in the State of California," and in all cases where a like claim shall hereafter be finally confirmed, and a survey and plat thereof shall not be requested, as provided by said sections within ten months after the passage of this act, or any final confirmation hereafter made, it shall be the duty of the Surveyor-General of the United States for California, as soon as practicable after the expiration of ten months from the passage of this act, or such final confirmation hereafter made, to cause the lines of the public surveys to be extended over such land, and he shall set off, in full satisfaction of such grant, and according to the lines of the public surveys, the quantity of land confirmed in such final decree, and as nearly as can be done in accordance with such decree; and all the land not included in such grant as so set off shall be subject to the general land laws of the United States: *Provided*, That nothing in this act shall be construed so as in any manner to interfere with the rights of bona fide pre-emption claimants.

SEC. 9. *And be it further enacted*, That from the decrees of the District Courts of the United States for the district of California, approving or correcting the surveys of private land claims under Spanish or Mexican grants, rendered after the first day of July, one thousand eight hun-

* No. 103 B. See also No. 37 B and Vol. I. No. 189.

dred and sixty-five, an appeal shall be allowed for the period of one year after the entry of such decrees to the Circuit Court of the United States for California, as provided by section three of the act of July first, one thousand eight hundred and sixty-four, to expedite the settlement of titles to land in the State of California, and the decision of the Circuit Court shall be final: *Provided, however,* That from decrees of the District Courts, as aforesaid, made after July one, eighteen hundred and sixty-five, and prior to the passage of this act, an appeal may be taken to the United States Circuit Court for the State of California within one year from the approval of this act.

Approved, July 23, 1866.

No. 170 B.—An Act to aid in the construction of telegraph lines, and to secure to the Government the use of the same for postal, military, and other purposes.

Be it enacted by the Senate and House of Representatives of the United States of America in Congress assembled, That any telegraph company now organized, or which may hereafter be organized under the laws of any State in this Union, shall have the right to construct, maintain, and operate lines of telegraph through and over any portion of the public domain of the United States, over and along any of the military or post roads of the United States which have been or may hereafter be declared such by act of Congress, and over, under, or across the navigable streams or waters of the United States: *Provided,* That such lines of telegraph shall be so constructed and maintained as not to obstruct the navigation of such streams and waters, or interfere with the ordinary travel on such military or post roads. And any of said companies shall have the right to take and use from such public lands the necessary stone, timber, and other materials for its posts, piers, stations, and other needful uses in the construction, maintenance, and operation of said lines of telegraph, and may pre-empt and use such portion of the unoccupied public lands subject to pre-emption, through which its said lines of telegraph may be located, as may be necessary for its stations, not exceeding forty acres for each station; but such stations shall not be within fifteen miles of each other.

SEC. 2. *And be it further enacted,* That telegraphic communications between the several departments of the Government of the United States and their officers and agents shall, in their transmission over the lines of any of said companies, have priority over all other business, and shall be sent at rates to be annually fixed by the Postmaster-General.

SEC. 3. *And be it further enacted,* That the rights and privileges hereby granted shall not be transferred by any company, acting under this act, to any other corporation, association, or person: *Provided, however,* That the United States may, at any time after the expiration of five years from the date of the passage of this act, for postal, military, or other purposes, purchase all the telegraph lines, property, and effects of any or all of said companies at an appraised value, to be ascertained by five competent, disinterested persons, two of whom shall be selected by the Postmaster-General of the United States, two by the company interested, and one by the four so previously selected.

SEC. 4. *And be it further enacted,* That before any telegraph company shall exercise any of the powers or privileges conferred by this act, such company shall file their written acceptance with the Postmaster-General of the restrictions and obligations required by this act.

Approved, July 24, 1866.

No. 171 B.—An Act granting lands to the State of Kansas to aid in the construction of the Kansas, and Neosho Valley Railroad and its extension to Red River.

Be it enacted by the Senate and House of Representatives of the United States of America in Congress assembled, That for the purpose of aiding the Kansas and Neosho Valley Railroad Company, the same being a corporation organized under the laws of the State of Kansas, to construct and operate a railroad from the eastern terminus of the Union Pacific Railroad, eastern division, at the line between Kansas and Missouri, at or near the mouth of the Kansas River, on the south side thereof, southwardly, through the eastern tier of counties in Kansas, with a view of its extension, so as to effect a junction at Red River with a railroad now being constructed from Galveston to Red River at or near Preston, in Texas, there is hereby granted to the State of Kansas, for the use and benefit of said railroad company, every alternate section of land or parts thereof, designated by odd numbers, to the extent of ten sections per mile on each side of said road, to be selected within twenty miles *ofrom* [of] the line of said road; but in case it shall appear that the United States have, when the line of said road is definitely located, sold any section, or any part thereof, granted as aforesaid, or that the right of pre-emption or homestead settlement has attached to the same, or that the same has been reserved by the United States for any purpose whatever, then it shall be the duty of the Secretary of the Interior to cause to be selected for the purposes aforesaid, from the public lands of the United States nearest to the sections above specified, so much land as shall be equal to the amount of such lands as the United States have sold, reserved, or otherwise appropriated, or to which the right of homestead settlement or pre-emption has attached as aforesaid, which lands, thus indicated by the direction of the Secretary of the Interior, shall be reserved and held for the State of Kansas for the use of said company by the said Secretary for the purpose of the construction and operation of said railroad, as provided by this act: *Provided*, That any and all lands heretofore reserved to the United States by any act of Congress, or in any other manner by competent authority, for the purpose of aiding in any object of internal improvement or other purpose whatever, be, and the same are hereby, reserved and excepted from the operation of this act, except so far as it may be found necessary to locate the route of said road through such reserved lands, in which case the right of way two hundred feet in width is hereby granted subject to the approval of the President of the United States: *And provided further*, That none of the lands hereby granted shall be selected beyond twenty miles from the said road.

SEC. 2. *And be it further enacted*, That the sections and parts of sections of land which by the aforesaid grant shall remain in the United States, within ten miles on each side of said road, shall not be sold for less than double the minimum price of public lands when sold, nor shall any of said lands become subject to sale at private entry until the same shall have been first offered at public sale to the highest bidder, at or above the minimum price aforesaid : *Provided*, That actual bona fide settlers under the pre-emption laws of the United States may, after due proof of settlement, improvement, and occupation, as now provided by law, purchase the same at the price fixed for said lands at the date of such settlement, improvement, and occupation : *And provided also*, That settlers under the provisions of the homestead act, who make their settlement after the passage of this act, and comply with the terms and requirements of said act, shall be entitled, within the said limits of ten miles, to patents for an amount not exceeding eighty acres each.

SEC. 3. *And be it further enacted*, That the grant of lands hereby made is upon condition that said company, after the construction of its road, shall keep it in repair and use, and that [it will] at all times be in readiness to transport troops, munitions of war, supplies, and public stores upon its road for the Government, when required to do so by any department thereof, at the cost, charge, and expense of said company. And the lands hereby granted, held, and reserved as aforesaid shall inure to the benefit of said company, as follows: When the Governor of the State of Kansas shall certify that any section of ten consecutive miles of said road is completed in a good, substantial, and workmanlike manner as a first-class railroad, then the said Secretary of the Interior shall issue to the said company patents for so many sections of the land within the limits above named as are coterminous with said completed section hereinbefore granted ; and when certificates of the Governor aforesaid shall be presented to said Secretary, of the completion, as aforesaid, of each successive section of ten consecutive miles of said road, the said Secretary shall in like manner issue to said company patents for the land for each of said sections of road as in the first instance, until said road shall be completed : *Provided*, That if said road is not completed within ten years from the date of the acceptance of the grant hereinbefore made, the lands remaining unpatented shall revert to the United States : *And provided further*, That the said lands shall not, in any manner, be disposed of or incumbered by said company or its assigns, except as the same are patented under the provisions of this act.

SEC. 4. *And be it further enacted*, That as soon as said company shall file with the Secretary of the Interior maps of its line, designating the route thereof, it shall be the duty of the said Secretary to withdraw from the market the lands granted by this act, in such manner as may be best calculated to effect the purposes of this act and subserve the public interest.

SEC. 5. *And be it further enacted*, That the United States mail shall be transported on said road and its extension, under the direction of the Post Office Department, at such price as Congress may by law provide : *Provided*, That until such price is fixed by law the Postmaster-General shall have power to fix the compensation.

SEC. 6. *And be it further enacted*, That the right of way through the public lands be, and the same is hereby, granted to said Kansas and Neosho Valley Railroad Company, its successors and assigns, for the construction of a railroad as proposed ; and the right is hereby given to said corporation to take from the public lands adjacent to the line of said road material for the construction thereof. Said way is granted to said railroad to the extent of one hundred feet in width on each side of said road where it may pass through the public domain ; also all necessary ground for station buildings, workshops, depots, machine-shops, switches, sidetracks, turn-tables, and water-stations.

SEC. 7. *And be it further enacted,* That the acceptance of the terms, conditions, and impositions of this act by the said Kansas and Neosho Valley Railroad Company shall be signified in writing, under the corporate seal of the said company, duly executed pursuant to the direction of its board of directors first had and obtained, which acceptance shall be made within one year after the passage of this act, and not afterwards, and shall be deposited with the Secretary of the Interior.

SEC. 8. *And be it further enacted,* That said Kansas and Neosho Valley Railroad Company, its successors and assigns, is hereby authorized and empowered to extend and construct its railroad from the southern boundary of Kansas south, through the Indian Territory, to Red River, at or near Preston, in the State of Texas, so as to connect with the railway now being constructed from Galveston to a point at or near Preston, in said State; and the right of way through the Indian Territory, wherever such right is now reserved or may hereafter be reserved to the United States by treaty with the Indian tribes, is hereby granted to said company, to the same extent as granted by the sixth section of this act through the public lands; and in all cases where the right of way, as aforesaid, through the Indian lands, shall not be reserved to the Government, the said company shall, before constructing its road, procure the consent of the tribe or tribes interested, which consent, with all its terms and conditions, shall be previously approved and indorsed by the President and filed with the Secretary of the Interior.

SEC. 9. *And be it further enacted,* That the same grants of lands through said Indian Territory are hereby made as provided in the first section of this act, whenever the Indian title shall be extinguished by treaty or otherwise, not to exceed the ratio per mile granted in the first section of this act: *Provided,* That said lands become a part of the public lands of the United States.

SEC. 10. *And be it further enacted,* That said Kansas and Neosho Valley Railroad Company, its successors and assigns, shall have the right to negotiate with, and acquire from any Indian nation or tribe, authorized by the United States to dispose of lands for railroad purposes, and from any other nation or tribe of Indians through whose lands said railroad may pass, subject to the approval of the President of the United States, or from any company or parties incorporated or authorized for such purposes, by such nation or tribe, or which such parties may have acquired under the laws of the United States.

SEC. 11. *And be it further enacted,* That any railroad company chartered under any law of the United States, or of the State of Kansas, which may have been heretofore or shall hereafter be recognized and subsidized by any act of the Congress of the United States, may connect, unite, and consolidate with this railroad company, after the same shall be located to the valley of the Neosho River, upon just, fair, and equitable terms, to be agreed upon between the parties, and shall not be against the public interest or the interest of the United States; nor shall any road authorized to connect as aforesaid charge the road so connecting a greater tariff per mile for freight or passengers than is charged for the same per mile by its own road: *And provided further,* That should the Leavenworth, Lawrence, and Fort Gibson Railroad Company, or the Union Pacific Railroad Company, southern branch, construct and complete its road to that point on the southern boundary of the State of Kansas where the line of said Kansas and Neosho Valley Railroad shall cross the same, before the said Kansas and Neosho Valley Railroad Company shall have constructed and completed its said road to said point, then and in that event the company so first reaching in completion the said point on the southern boundary of the State of Kansas shall be authorized, upon obtaining the written approval of the President of the United States, to construct and operate its line of railroad from said point to a point at or near Preston, in the State of Texas, with grants of land according to the provisions of this act, but upon the further special condition, nevertheless, that said railroad company shall have commenced in good faith the construction thereof before the said Kansas and Neosho Valley Railroad Company shall have completed its said railroad to said point: *And provided further*, That said other railroad company, so having commenced said work in good faith, shall continue to prosecute the same with sufficient energy to insure the completion of the same within a reasonable time, subject to the approval of the President of the United States: *And provided further*, That the right of way through private property when not otherwise provided for in this act, or by the law of any State through which the road may pass, shall be obtained by said Kansas and Neosho Valley Railroad Company, or either of the other companies named in this act, in accordance with the provisions of section three of an act to amend an act entitled "An act to aid in the construction of a railroad and telegraph line from the Missouri River to the Pacific Ocean, and to secure to the Government the use of the same for postal, military, and other purposes," approved July first, eighteen hundred and sixty-two.

Approved, July 25, 1866.

No. 172 B.—An Act granting lands to aid in the construction of a railroad and telegraph line from the Central Pacific Railroad, in California, to Portland, in Oregon.*

Be it enacted by the Senate and House of Representatives of the United States of America in Congress assembled, That the "California and Oregon Railroad Company," organized under an act of the State of California, to protect certain parties in and to a railroad survey, "to connect Portland, in Oregon, with Marysville, in California," approved April sixth, eighteen hundred and sixty-three, and such company organized under the laws of Oregon as the legislature of said State shall hereafter designate, be, and they are hereby, authorized and empowered to lay out, locate, construct, finish, and maintain a railroad and telegraph line between the city of Portland, in Oregon, and the Central Pacific Railroad, in California, in the manner following, to wit: The said California and Oregon Railroad Company to construct that part of the said railroad and telegraph within the State of California, beginning at some point (to be selected by said company) on the Central Pacific Railroad in the Sacramento valley, in the State of California, and running thence northerly, through the Sacramento and Shasta valleys, to the northern boundary of the State of California; and the said Oregon company to construct that part of the said railroad and telegraph line within the State of Oregon, beginning at the city of Portland, in Oregon, and running thence southerly through the Willamette, Umpqua, and Rogue River valleys to the southern boundary of Oregon, where the same shall connect with the

* Amended, No. 209 B.

part aforesaid to be made by the first-named company: *Provided*, That the company completing its respective part of the said railroad and telegraph from either of the termini herein named to the line between California and Oregon before the other company shall have likewise arrived at the same line, shall have the right, and the said company is hereby authorized, to continue in constructing the same beyond the line aforesaid, with the consent of the State in which the unfinished part may lie, upon the terms mentioned in this act, until the said parts shall meet and connect, and the whole line of said railroad and telegraph shall be completed.

SEC. 2. *And be it further enacted*, That there be, and hereby is, granted to the said companies, their successors and assigns, for the purpose of aiding in the construction of said railroad and telegraph line, and to secure the safe and speedy transportation of the mails, troops, munitions of war, and public stores over the line of said railroad, every alternate section of public land, not mineral, designated by odd numbers, to the amount of twenty alternate sections per mile (ten on each side) of said railroad line; and when any of said alternate sections or parts of sections shall be found to have been granted, sold, reserved, occupied by homestead settlers, pre-empted, or otherwise disposed of, other lands, designated as aforesaid, shall be selected by said companies in lieu thereof, under the direction of the Secretary of the Interior, in alternate sections designated by odd numbers as aforesaid, nearest to and not more than ten miles beyond the limits of said first-named alternate sections; and as soon as the said companies, or either of them, shall file in the office of the Secretary of the Interior a map of the survey of said railroad, or any portion thereof, not less than sixty continuous miles from either terminus, the Secretary of the Interior shall withdraw from sale public lands herein granted on each side of said railroad, so far as located and within the limits before specified. The lands herein granted shall be applied to the building of said road within the States, respectively, wherein they are situated. And the sections and parts of sections of land which shall remain in the United States within the limits of the aforesaid grant shall not be sold for less than double the minimum price of public lands when sold: *Provided*, That bona fide and actual settlers under the pre-emption laws of the United States may, after due proof of settlement, improvement, and occupation, as now provided by law, purchase the same at the price fixed for said lands at the date of such settlement, improvement, and occupation: *And provided also*, That, settlers under the provisions of the homestead act, who comply with the terms and requirements of said act, shall be entitled, within the limits of said grant, to patents for an amount not exceeding eighty acres of the land so reserved by the United States, anything in this act to the contrary notwithstanding.

SEC. 3. *And be it further enacted*, That the right of way through the public lands be, and the same is hereby, granted to said companies for the construction of said railroad and telegraph line; and the right, power, and authority are hereby given to said companies to take from the public lands adjacent to the line of said road, earth, stone, timber, water, and other materials for the construction thereof. Said right of way is granted to said railroad to the extent of one hundred feet in width on each side of said railroad where it may pass over the public lands, including all necessary grounds for stations, buildings, workshops, depots, machine-shops, switches, side-tracks, turn-tables, water stations, or any other structures required in the construction and operating of said road.

SEC. 4. *And be it further enacted*, That whenever the said companies, or either of them, shall have twenty or more consecutive miles of any portion of said railroad and telegraph line ready for the service contemplated by this act, the President of the United States shall appoint three commissioners, whose compensation shall be paid by said company, to examine the same, and if it shall appear that twenty consecutive miles of railroad and telegraph shall have been completed and equipped in all respects as required by this act, the said commissioners shall so report under oath to the President of the United States, and thereupon patents shall issue to said companies, or either of them, as the case may be, for the lands hereinbefore granted to the extent of and conterminous with the completed section of said railroad and telegraph line as aforesaid; and from time to time, whenever twenty or more consecutive miles of the said road and telegraph shall be completed and equipped as aforesaid, patents shall in like manner issue upon the report of the said commissioners, and so on until the entire railroad and telegraph authorized by this act shall have been constructed, and the patents of the lands herein granted shall have been issued.

SEC. 5. *And be it further enacted*, That the grants aforesaid are made upon the condition that the said companies shall keep said railroad and telegraph in repair and use, and shall at all times transport the mails upon said railroad, and transmit despatches by said telegraph line for the Government of the United States, when required so to do by any department thereof, and that the Government shall at all times have the preference in the use of said railroad and telegraph therefor at fair and reasonable rates of compensation, not to exceed the rates paid by private parties for the same kind of service. And said railroad shall be and remain a public highway for the use of the Government of the United States free of all toll or other charges upon the transportation of the property or troops of the United States; and the same shall be transported over said road at the cost, charge, and expense of the corporations or companies owning or operating the same, when so required by the Government of the United States.

SEC. 6. *And be it further enacted*, That the said companies shall file their assent to this act in the Department of the Interior within one year after the passage hereof, and shall complete the first section of twenty miles of said railroad and telegraph within two years, and at least twenty miles in each year thereafter, and the whole on or before the first day of July, one thousand eight hundred and seventy-five; and the said railroad shall be of the same gauge as the "Central Pacific Railroad" of California, and be connected therewith.

SEC. 7. *And be it further enacted*, That the said companies named in this act are hereby required to operate and use the portions or parts of said railroad and telegraph mentioned in section one of this act for all purposes of transportation, travel, and communication, so far as the Government and public are concerned, as one connected and continuous line; and in such operation and use to afford and secure to each other equal advantages and facilities as to rates, time, and transportation, without any discrimination whatever, on pain of forfeiting the full amount of damage sustained on account of such discrimination, to be sued for and recovered in any court of the United States, or of any State of competent jurisdiction.

SEC. 8. *And be it further enacted*, That in case the said companies shall fail to comply with the terms and conditions required, namely, by not filing their assent thereto as provided in section six of this act, or by not completing the same as provided in said section, this act shall be null and void, and all the lands not conveyed by patent to said company or companies, as the case may be, at the date of any such failure, shall revert to the United States. And in case the said road and telegraph line shall not be kept in repair and fit for use, after the same shall have been completed, Congress may pass an act to put the same in repair and use, and may direct the income of said railroad and telegraph line to be thereafter devoted to the United States, to repay all expenditures caused by the default and neglect of said companies or either of them, as the case may be, or may fix pecuniary responsibility, not exceeding the value of the lands granted by this act.

SEC. 9. *And be it further enacted*, That the said "California and Oregon Railroad Company" and the said "Oregon Company" shall be governed by the provisions of the general railroad and telegraph laws of their respective States, as to the construction and management of the said railroad and telegraph line hereinbefore authorized, in all matters not provided for in this act. Wherever the word "company" or "companies" is used in this act it shall be construed to embrace the words "their associates, successors, and assigns," the same as if the words had been inserted, or thereto annexed.

SEC. 10. *And be it further enacted*, That all mineral lands shall be excepted from the operation of this act; but where the same shall contain timber, so much of the timber thereon as shall be required to construct said road over such mineral land is hereby granted to said companies: *Provided*, That the term "mineral lands" shall not include lands containing coal and iron.

SEC. 11. *And be it further enacted*, That the said companies named in this act shall obtain the consent of the Legislatures of their respective States, and be governed by the statutory regulations thereof in all matters pertaining to the right of way, wherever the said road and telegraph line shall not pass over or through the public lands of the United States.

SEC. 12. *And be it further enacted*, That Congress may at any time, having due regard for the rights of said California and Oregon Railroad Companies, add to, alter, amend, or repeal this act.

Approved, July 25, 1866.

No. 173 B.—An Act granting to A. Sutro the right of way, and granting other privileges to aid in the construction of a draining and exploring tunnel to the Comstock Lode, in the State of Nevada.

Be it enacted by the Senate and House of Representatives of the United States of America in Congress assembled, That, for the purpose of the construction of a deep draining and exploring tunnel to and beyond the "Comstock Lode," so called, in the State of Nevada, the right of way is hereby granted to A. Sutro, his heirs and assigns, to run, construct, and excavate a mining, draining, and exploring tunnel; also to sink mining, working, or air shafts along the line or course of said tunnel, and connecting with the same at any point which may hereafter be selected by the grantee herein, his heirs or assigns. The said tunnel shall be at least eight feet high and eight feet wide, and shall commence at some point to be selected by the grantee herein, his heirs or assigns, at the hills near Carson River, and within the boundaries of Lyon County, and extending from said initial point in a westerly direction seven miles, more or less, to and beyond said Comstock Lode; and the same right of way shall extend northerly and southerly on the course of said lode, either within the same, or east or west of the same; and also on or along any other lode which may be discovered or developed by the said tunnel.

SEC. 2. *And be it further enacted*, That the right is hereby granted to the said A. Sutro, his heirs and assigns, to purchase, at one dollar and twenty-five cents per acre, a sufficient amount of public land near the mouth of said tunnel for the use of the same, not exceeding two sections, and such land shall not be mineral land or in the bona fide possession of other persons who claim under any law of Congress at the time of the passage of this act, and all minerals existing or which shall be discovered therein are excepted from this grant; that upon filing a plat of said land the Secretary of the Interior shall withdraw the same from sale, and upon payment for the same a patent shall issue. And the said A. Sutro, his heirs and assigns, are hereby granted the right to purchase, at five dollars per acre, such mineral veins and lodes within two thousand feet on each side of said tunnel as shall be cut, discovered, or developed by running and constructing the same, through its entire extent, with all the dips, spurs, and angles of such lodes, subject, however, to the provisions of this act, and to such legislation as Congress may hereafter provide: *Provided*, That the Comstock Lode with its dips, spurs, and angles, is excepted from this grant, and all other lodes, with their dips, spurs, and angles, located within the said two thousand feet, and which are or may be, at the passage of this act, in the actual bona fide possession of other persons, are hereby excepted from such grant. And the lodes herein excepted, other than the Comstock Lode, shall be withheld from sale by the United States; and if such lodes shall be abandoned or not worked, possessed, and held in conformity to existing mining rules, or such regulations as have been or may be prescribed by the Legislature of Nevada, they shall become subject to such right of purchase by the grantee herein, his heirs or assigns.

SEC. 3. *And be it further enacted*, That all persons, companies, or corporations owning claims or mines on said Comstock Lode or any other lode drained, benefited, or developed by said tunnel, shall hold their claims subject to the condition (which shall be expressed in any grant they may hereafter obtain from the United States) that they shall contribute and pay to the owners of said tunnel the same rate of charges for drainage or other benefits derived from said tunnel or its branches, as have been, or may hereafter be, named in agreement between such owners and the companies representing a majority of the estimated value of said Comstock Lode at the time of the passage of this act.

Approved, *July* 25, 1866.

No. 174 B.—An Act granting the right of way to ditch and canal owners over the public lands, and for other purposes.

Be it enacted by the Senate and House of Representatives of the United States of America in Congress assembled, That the mineral lands of the public domain, both surveyed and unsurveyed, are hereby declared to be free and open to exploration and occupation by all citizens of the United States, and those who have declared their intention to become citizens, subject to such regulations as may be prescribed by law, and subject also to the local customs or rules of miners in the several mining districts, so far as the same may not be in conflict with the laws of the United States.

SEC. 2. *And be it further enacted,* That whenever any person or association of persons claim a vein or lode of quartz, or other rock in place, bearing gold, silver, cinnabar, or copper, having previously occupied and improved the same according to the local custom or rules of miners in the district where the same is situated, and having expended in actual labor and improvements thereon an amount of not less than one thousand dollars, and in regard to whose possession there is no controversy or opposing claim, it shall and may be lawful for said claimant, or association of claimants, to file in the local land office a diagram of the same, so extended laterally or otherwise as to conform to the local laws, customs, and rules of miners, and to enter such tract and receive a patent therefor, granting such mine, together with the right to follow such vein or lode with its dips, angles, and variations, to any depth, although it may enter the land adjoining, which land adjoining shall be sold subject to this condition.

SEC. 3. *And be it further enacted,* That upon the filing of the diagram as provided in the second section of this act, and posting the same in a conspicuous place on the claim, together with a notice of intention to apply for a patent, the register of the land office shall publish a notice of the same in a newspaper published nearest to the location of said claim, and shall also post such notice in his office for the period of ninety days; and after the expiration of said period, if no adverse claim shall have been filed, it shall be the duty of the Surveyor-General, upon application of the party, to survey the premises and make a plat thereof, indorsed with his approval, designating the number and description of the location, the value of the labor and improvements, and the character of the vein exposed; and upon the payment to the proper officer of five dollars per acre, together with the cost of such survey, plat, and notice, and giving satisfactory evidence that said diagram and notice have been posted on the claim during said period of ninety days, the register of the land office shall transmit to the general land office said plat, survey, and description; and a patent shall issue for the same thereupon. But said plat, survey, or description shall in no case cover more than one vein or lode, and no patent shall issue for more than one vein or lode, which shall be expressed in the patent issued.

SEC. 4. *And be it further enacted,* That when such location and entry of a mine shall be upon unsurveyed lands, it shall and may be lawful, after the extension thereto of the public surveys, to adjust the surveys to the limits of the premises according to the location and possession and plat aforesaid, and the Surveyor-General may, in extending the surveys, vary the same from a rectangular form to suit the circumstances of the country, and the local rules, laws, and customs of miners: *Provided,* That no location hereafter made shall exceed two hundred feet in length along the vein for each locator, with an additional claim for discovery to the discoverer of the lode, with the right to follow such vein to any depth, with all its dips, variations, and angles, together with a reasonable quantity of surface for the convenient working of the same, as fixed by local rules: *And provided further,* That no person may make more than one location on the same lode, and not more than three thousand feet shall be taken in any one claim by any association of persons.

SEC. 5. *And be it further enacted,* That as a further condition of sale, in the absence of necessary legislation by Congress, the local legislature of any State or Territory may provide rules for working mines involving easements, drainage, and other necessary means to their complete development; and those conditions shall be fully expressed in the patent.

SEC. 6. *And be it further enacted*, That whenever any adverse claimants to any mine located and claimed as aforesaid shall appear before the approval of the survey, as provided in the third section of this act, all proceedings shall be stayed until a final settlement and adjudication in the courts of competent jurisdiction of the rights of possession to such claim, when a patent may issue as in other cases.

SEC. 7. *And be it further enacted*, That the President of the United States be, and is hereby, authorized to establish additional land districts and to appoint the necessary officers under existing laws, wherever he may deem the same necessary for the public convenience in executing the provisions of this act.

SEC. 8. *And be it further enacted*, That the right of way for the construction of highways over public lands, not reserved for public uses, is hereby granted.

SEC. 9. *And be it further enacted*, That whenever, by priority of possession, rights to the use of water for mining, agricultural, manufacturing, or other purposes, have vested and accrued, and the same are recognized and acknowledged by the local customs, laws, and the decisions of courts, the possessors and owners of such vested rights shall be maintained and protected in the same; and the right of way for the construction of ditches and canals for the purposes aforesaid is hereby acknowledged and confirmed: *Provided, however*, That whenever, after the passage of this act, any person or persons shall, in the construction of any ditch or canal, injure or damage the possession of any settler on the public domain, the party committing such injury or damage shall be liable to the party injured for such injury or damage.

SEC. 10. *And be it further enacted*, That wherever, prior to the passage of this act, upon the lands heretofore designated as mineral lands, which have been excluded from survey and sale, there have been homesteads made by citizens of the United States, or persons who have declared their intention to become citizens, which homesteads have been made, improved, and used for agricultural purposes, and upon which there have been no valuable mines of gold, silver, cinnabar, or copper discovered, and which are properly agricultural lands, the said settlers or owners of such homesteads shall have a right of pre-emption thereto, and shall be entitled to purchase the same at the price of one dollar and twenty-five cents per acre, and in quantity not to exceed one hundred and sixty acres; or said parties may avail themselves of the provisions of the act of Congress approved May twenty, eighteen hundred and sixty-two, entitled "An act to secure homesteads to actual settlers on the public domain," and acts amendatory thereof.

SEC. 11. *And be it further enacted*, That upon the survey of the lands aforesaid, the Secretary of the Interior may designate and set apart such portions of the said lands as are clearly agricultural lands, which lands shall thereafter be subject to pre-emption and sale as other public lands of the United States, and subject to all the laws and regulations applicable to the same.

Approved, July 26, 1866.

No. 175 B.—An Act granting lands to the State of Kansas to aid in the construction of a southern branch of the Union Pacific Railway and Telegraph, from Fort Riley, Kansas, to Fort Smith, Arkansas.

Be it enacted by the Senate and House of Representatives of the United States of America in Congress assembled, That for the purpose of aiding the Union Pacific Railroad Company, southern branch, the same being a corporation organized under the laws of the State of Kansas to construct and operate a railroad from Fort Riley, Kansas, or near said military reservation, thence down the valley of the Neosho River to the southern line of the State of Kansas, with a view to an extension of the same through a portion of the Indian Territory to Fort Smith, Arkansas, there is hereby granted to the State of Kansas, for the use and benefit of said railroad company, every alternate section of land or parts thereof designated by odd numbers, to the extent of five alternate sections per mile on each side of said road and not exceeding in all ten sections per mile; but in case it shall appear that the United States have, when the line of said road is definitely located, sold any section, or any part thereof, granted as aforesaid, or that the right of pre-emption or homestead settlement has attached to the same, or that the same has been reserved by the United States for any purpose whatever, then it shall be the duty of the Secretary of the Interior to cause to be selected for the purposes aforesaid, from the public lands of the United States nearest to the sections above specified, so much land as shall be equal to the amount of such lands as the United States have sold, reserved, or otherwise appropriated, or to which the right of homestead settlement or pre-emption has attached as aforesaid, which lands, thus indicated by the direction of the Secretary of the Interior, shall be reserved and held for the State of Kansas for the use of said company by the said Secretary for the purpose of the construction and operation of said railroad, as provided by this act: *Provided,* That any and all lands heretofore reserved to the United States by any act of Congress, or in any other manner by competent authority, for the purpose of aiding in any object of internal improvement or other purpose whatever, be, and the same are hereby, reserved and excepted from the operation of this act, except so far as it may be found necessary to locate the route of said road through such reserved lands, in which case the right of way, two hundred feet in width, is hereby granted, subject to the approval of the President of the United States: *And provided further,* That said lands hereby granted shall not be selected beyond twenty miles from the line of said road.

SEC. 2. *And be it further enacted,* That the sections and parts of sections of land which by the aforesaid grant shall remain in the United States, within ten miles on each side of said road, shall not be sold for less than double the minimum price of public lands when sold: *Provided,* That actual bona fide settlers under the pre-emption laws of the United States may, after due proof of settlement, improvement, and occupation, as now provided by law, purchase the same at the price fixed for said lands at the date of such settlement, improvement, and occupation: *Provided also,* That settlers under provisions of the homestead act, who make their settlement after the passage of this act and comply with the terms and requirements of said act, shall be entitled, within the said limits of ten miles, to patents for an amount not exceeding eighty acres each.

SEC. 3. *And be it further enacted,* That the grant of lands hereby made is upon condition that said company, after the construction of its road, shall keep it in repair and use, and shall at all times transport troops, munitions of war, supplies, and public stores upon its road for the Government of the United States, free from all cost or charge therefor to the Government, when required to do so by any department thereof. And the lands hereby granted shall inure to the benefit of said company, as follows: When the Governor of the State of Kansas shall certify that any section of ten consecutive miles of said road is completed in a good, substantial, and workmanlike manner as a first-class railroad, then the said Secretary of the Interior shall issue to said company patents for so many sections of the land herein granted within the limits above named, and coterminous with said completed section hereinbefore granted; and when certificates of the Governor aforesaid shall be presented to said Secretary of the completion, as aforesaid, of each successive section of ten consecutive miles of said road, the said Secretary shall in like manner issue to said company patents for the land for each of said sections of road as in the first instance, until said road shall be completed: *Provided*, That if said road is not completed within ten years from the date of the acceptance of the grant hereinbefore made, the lands remaining unpatented shall revert to the United States.

SEC. 4. *And be it further enacted*, That as soon as said company shall file with the Secretary of the Interior maps of its line, designating the route thereof, it shall be the duty of *of* said Secretary to withdraw from the market the lands granted by this act, in such manner as may be best calculated to effect the purposes of this act and subserve the public interest.

SEC. 5. *And be it further enacted*, That the United States mail shall be transported on said road, and under the direction of the Post Office Department, at such price as Congress may by law provide: *Provided*, That until such price is fixed by law the Postmaster-General shall have power to fix the compensation.

SEC. 6. *And be it further enacted*, That the right of way through the public lands be, and the same is hereby, granted to said Pacific Railroad Company, southern branch, its successors and assigns, for the construction of a railroad as proposed: and the right is hereby given to said corporation to take from the public lands adjacent to the line of said road material for the construction thereof. Said way is granted to said railroad to the extent of one hundred feet in width on each side of said road where it may pass through the public domain; also all necessary ground for station buildings, work-shops, depots, machine-shops, switches, side-tracks, turn-tables, and water-stations.

SEC. 7. *And be it further enacted*, That the acceptance of the terms, conditions, and impositions of this act by the said Pacific Railroad Company, southern branch, shall be signified in writing, under the corporate seal of the said company, duly executed pursuant to the direction of its board of directors first had and obtained, which acceptance shall be made within one year after the passage of this act, and not afterwards, and shall be deposited with the Secretary of the Interior.

SEC. 8. *And be it further enacted*, That said Pacific Railroad Company, southern branch, its successors and assigns, is hereby authorized and empowered to extend and construct its railroad from the southern boundary of Kansas, south through the Indian Territory, with the consent of the Indians, and not otherwise, along the valley of Grand and Arkansas Rivers, to Fort Smith, in the State of Arkansas; and the right of way through said Indian Territory is hereby granted to said company, its successors and assigns, to the extent of one hundred feet on each side of said road or roads, and all necessary grounds for stations, buildings, workshops, machine-shops, switches, side-tracks, turn-tables, and water-stations.

SEC. 9. *And be it further enacted*, That the same grant[s] of lands through said Indian Territory are hereby made as provided in the first section of this act, whenever the Indian title shall be extinguished by treaty or otherwise, not to exceed the ratio per mile granted in the first section of this act: *Provided*, That said lands become a part of the public lands of the United States.

SEC. 10. *And be it further enacted*, That said Pacific Railroad Company, southern branch, its successors and assigns, shall have the right to negotiate with, and acquire title to land for railroad purposes from, any Indian nation or tribe authorized by the United States to dispose of lands, and from any other nation or tribe of Indians through whose lands said railroad may pass, subject to the approval of the [President of the] United States, or from any company or parties incorporated or authorized for such purposes, by such nation or tribe, or which such parties may have acquired under the laws of the United States.

SEC. 11. *And be it further enacted*, That any railroad company chartered under any law of the United States, or of any State which may have been heretofore or shall hereafter be organized by any act of the Congress of the United States, may connect, unite, and consolidate with this railroad company, after the same shall be located to the valley of the Neosho or Grand River, upon just, fair, and equitable terms, to be agreed upon between the parties, as shall not be against the public interest, or the interest of the United States.

Approved, July 26, 1866.

No. 176 B.—An Act granting lands to aid in the construction of a railroad and telegraph line from the States of Missouri and Arkansas to the Pacific coast.

Be it enacted by the Senate and House of Representatives of the United States of America in Congress assembled, That John B. Brown, * * * (and others) * * * and all such other persons who shall or may be associated with them, and their successors, are hereby created and erected into a body corporate and politic, in deed and in law, by the name, style, and title of the "Atlantic and Pacific Railroad Company," and by that name shall have perpetual succession, and shall be able to sue and be sued, plead and be impleaded, defend and be defended, in all courts of law and equity within the United States, and may make and have a common seal. And said corporation is hereby authorized and empowered to lay out, locate, and construct, furnish, maintain, and enjoy, a continuous railroad and telegraph line, with the appurtenances, namely: Beginning at or near the town of Springfield, in the State of Missouri, thence to the western boundary line of said State, and thence by the most eligible railroad route as shall be determined by said company to a point on the Canadian River, thence to the town of Albuquerque, on the River Del Norte, and thence, by way of the Agua Frio, or other suitable pass, to the head-waters of the Colorado Chiquito, and thence, along the thirty-fifth parallel of latitude, as near as may be found most suitable for a railway route, to the Colorado River, at such point as may be *be* selected by said company for crossing; thence by the most practicable and eligible route, to the Pacific.

The said company shall have the right to construct a branch from the point at which the road strikes the Canadian River eastwardly, along the most suitable route as selected, to a point in the western boundary line of Arkansas, at or near the town of Van Buren. And the said company is hereby vested with all the powers, privileges, and immunities necessary to carry into effect the purposes of this act, as herein set forth. The capital stock of said company shall consist of one million shares of one hundred dollars each, which shall in all respects be deemed personal property, and shall be transferable in such manner as the laws of said corporation shall provide. The persons hereinbefore named are hereby appointed commissioners, and shall be called the board of commissioners of the "Atlantic and Pacific Railroad Company," and fifteen shall constitute a quorum for the transaction of business.

* * * * * * * * *

SEC. 2. *And be it further enacted,* That the right of way through the public lands be, and the same is hereby, granted to the said Atlantic and Pacific Railroad Company, its successors and assigns, for the construction of a railroad and telegraph as proposed; and the right, power, and authority is hereby given to said corporation to take from the public lands adjacent to the line of said road material of earth, stone, timber, and so forth, for the construction thereof. Said way is granted to said railroad to the extent of one hundred feet in width on each side of said railroad where it may pass through the public domain, including all necessary grounds for station-buildings, workshops, depots, machine-shops, switches, side-tracks, turn-tables, and water-stations; and the right of way shall be exempt from taxation within the Territories of the United States. The United States shall extinguish, as rapidly as may be consistent with public policy and the welfare of the Indians, and only by their voluntary cession the Indian title to all lands falling under the operation of this act and acquired in the donation to the road named in the act.

SEC. 3. *And be it further enacted,* That there be, and hereby is, granted to the Atlantic and Pacific Railroad Company, its successors and assigns, for the purpose of aiding in the construction of said railroad and telegraph line to the Pacific coast, and to secure the safe and speedy transportation of the mails, troops, munitions of war, and public stores, over the route of said line of railway and its branches, every alternate section of public land, not mineral, designated by odd numbers, to the amount of twenty alternate sections per mile, on each side of said railroad line, as said company may adopt, through the Territories of the United States; and ten alternate sections of land per mile on each side of said railroad whenever it passes through any State, and whenever, on the line thereof, the United States have full title, not reserved, sold, granted, or otherwise appropriated, and free from pre-emption or other claims or rights, of any Territory or State in which the same may be situated, to form running connections with it, on fair and equitable terms.

SEC. 6. *And be it further enacted,* That the President of the United States shall cause the lands to be surveyed for forty miles in width on both sides of the entire line of said road after the general route shall be fixed, and as fast as may be required by the construction of said railroad; and the odd sections of land hereby granted shall not be liable to sale or entry, or pre-emption, before or after they are surveyed, except by said company, as provided in this act; but the provisions of the act of September, eighteen hundred and forty-one, granting pre-emption rights, and the acts amendatory thereof, and of the act entitled "An act to secure homesteads to actual settlers on the public domain," approved May twenty, eighteen hundred and sixty-two, shall be, and the same are hereby, extended to all other lands on the line of said road when surveyed, excepting those hereby granted to said company.

* * * * * * * * *

SEC. 8. *And be it further enacted,* That each and every grant, right, and privilege herein are so made and given to and accepted by said Atlantic and Pacific Railroad Company, upon and subject to the following conditions, namely: That the said company shall commence the work on said road within two years from the approval of this act by the President, and shall complete not less than fifty miles per year after the second year, and shall construct, equip, furnish, and complete the main line of the whole road by the fourth day of July, Anno Domini eighteen hundred and seventy-eight.

SEC. 9. *And be it further enacted,* That the United States make the several conditional grants herein, and that the said Atlantic and Pacific Railroad Company accept the same, upon the further condition that if the said company make any breach of the conditions hereof, and allow the same to continue for upwards of one year, then, in such case, at any time hereafter, the United States may do any and all acts and things which may be needful and necessary to insure a speedy completion of the said road.

* * * * * * * * *

SEC. 17. *And be it further enacted,* That the said company is authorized to accept to its own use any grant, donation, loan, power, franchise, aid, or assistance which may be granted to or conferred on said company by the Congress of the United States, by the Legislature of any State, or by any corporation, person, or persons, or by any Indian tribe or nation through whose reservation the road herein provided for may pass; and said corporation is authorized to hold and enjoy any such grant, donation, loan, power, franchise, aid, or assistance, to its own use, for the purpose aforesaid: *Provided,* That any such grant or donation, power, aid, or assistance from any Indian tribe or nation shall be subject to the approval of the President of the United States.

SEC. 18. *And be it further enacted,* That the Southern Pacific Railroad, a company incorporated under the laws of the State of California, is hereby authorized to connect with the said Atlantic and Pacific Railroad, formed under this act, at such point, near the boundary line of the State of California, as they shall deem most suitable for a railroad line to San Francisco, and shall have a uniform gauge and rate of freight or fare with said road; and in consideration thereof, to aid in its construction, shall have similar grants of land, subject to all the conditions and limitations herein provided, and shall be required to construct its road on the like regulations, as to time and manner, with the Atlantic and Pacific Railroad herein provided for.*

SEC. 19. *And be it further enacted,* That unless the said Atlantic and Pacific Railroad Company shall obtain bona fide subscriptions to the stock of said company to the amount of one million of dollars, with ten per centum paid, within two years after the passage of and approval of this act, it shall be null and void.

SEC. 20. *And be it further enacted,* That the better to accomplish the object of this act, namely, to promote the public interest and welfare by the construction of said railroad and telegraph line, and keeping the same in working order, and to secure to the Government at all times, but par-

* Time extended, No. 217 B.

ticularly in time of war, the use and benefits of the same for postal, military, and other purposes, Congress may, at any time, having due regard for the rights of said Atlantic and Pacific Railroad Company, add to, alter, amend, or repeal this act.

SEC. 21. *And be it further enacted*, That whenever in any grant of land or other subsidies, made or hereafter to be made, to railroads or other corporations, the United States has reserved the right, or shall reserve it, to appoint directors, engineers, commissioners, or other agents to examine said roads, or act in conjunction with other officers of said company or companies, all the costs, charges, and pay of said directors, engineers, commissioners, or agents, shall be paid by the respective companies. Said directors, engineers, commissioners, or agents shall be paid for said services the sum of ten dollars per day, for each and every day actually and necessarily employed, and ten cents per mile for each and every mile actually and necessarily travelled, in discharging the duties required of them, which per diem and mileage shall be in full compensation for said services. And in case any company shall refuse or neglect to make such payments, no more patents for lands or other subsidies shall be issued to said company until these requirements are complied with.

Approved, July 27, 1866.

No. 177 B.—An Act to supply deficiencies in the appropriations for the service of the fiscal year ending June thirty, eighteen hundred and sixty-six, and for other purposes.

* * * * * * * * *

SEC. 3. *And be it further enacted*, That the sum of thirty-two thousand dollars be, and is hereby, appropriated to enable the Secretary of the Interior to quiet the title of the occupants of the following lands, conveyed by the United States to Joseph Richardville, senior, and Joseph Richardville, junior, by treaty at Saint Mary's, October sixth, eighteen hundred and eighteen, to wit: The west half of section number twenty-six (26), the east half of section number twenty-eight (28), and section number twenty-seven (27), of township five south, range four east, lying in the county of Auglaize and State of Ohio.

* * * * * * * * *

Approved, July 28, 1866.

No. 178 B.—An Act to revive and extend the provisions of "An act granting the right of way and making a grant of land to the States of Arkansas and Missouri, to aid in the construction of a railroad from a point upon the Mississippi opposite the mouth of the Ohio River, via Little Rock, to the Texas boundary, near Fulton, in Arkansas, with branches to Fort Smith and the Mississippi River," approved February nine, eighteen hundred and fifty-three, and for other purposes.*

Be it enacted by the Senate and House of Representatives of the United States of America in Congress assembled, That the "Act granting the right of way and making a grant of land to the States of Arkansas and

* Vol. I. No. 216.

Missouri to aid in the construction of a railroad from a point upon the Mississippi opposite the mouth of the Ohio River, via Little Rock, to the Texas boundary, near Fulton, in Arkansas, with branches to Fort Smith and the Mississippi River," approved February nine, eighteen hundred and fifty-three, with all the provisions therein made, be, and the same is hereby, revived and extended for the term of ten years from the passage of this act; and all the lands therein granted, which reverted to the United States under the provisions of said act, be, and the same are hereby, restored to the same custody, control, and condition, and made subject to the uses and trusts in all respects as they were before and at the time such reversion took effect: *Provided,* That all mineral lands within the limits of this grant and the grant made in section two of this act are hereby reserved to the United States: *And provided further,* That all property and troops of the United States shall at all times be transported over said railroad and branches at the cost, charge, and expense of the company or corporation owning or operating said road and branches respectively, when so required by the Government of the United States.

SEC. 2. *And be it further enacted,* That there *is* hereby granted, added to, and made part of the donation of lands hereby renewed and made, subject to the same uses and trusts, and under the same custody, control, and conditions, and to be held and disposed of in the same manner as if included in the original grant, all the alternate sections and parts of sections, designated by odd numbers, lying along the outer line of lands heretofore granted, and within five miles on each side thereof, excepting lands reserved or otherwise appropriated by law, or to which the right of pre-emption or homestead settlement has attached: *Provided,* That the additional quantity of lands hereby granted, when added to the lands specified in section one hereof, shall not exceed, in the aggregate quantity of lands by this act granted, sufficient to amount to ten sections for each mile of railroad: *And provided further,* That the lands embraced in this grant and the grant revived by section one of this act shall be disposed of only as follows: Whenever proof shall be furnished, satisfactory to the Secretary of the Interior, that any section of ten consecutive miles of said road and branches is completed in a good, substantial, and workmanlike manner as a first-class railroad, the said Secretary of the Interior shall issue patents for all the lands granted as aforesaid, not exceeding ten sections per mile situate opposite to and within the limits of twenty miles of the section of said road and branches thus completed, and when like proof shall be furnished that another section of ten miles of said road in said State or on the said branches respectively connecting with the preceding section is completed as aforesaid, the Secretary of the Interior shall issue patents in like manner as *as* in case of the first completed sections, and so on from time to time until the whole is completed as herein provided, when the Secretary of the Interior shall issue patents for all the remaining lands herein granted, not exceeding the aggregate amount provided for and located as required by sections one and two of this act: *And provided further,* That if one section of twenty miles of each of said railroads and branches shall not be fully constructed and completed as a first class railroad within three years from the time this act becomes a law, and at least one section of twenty miles of each of said roads and branches in each year thereafter, and the whole of said roads and branches within ten years from the time this act shall take effect, then and in either of said cases all the lands granted or the grant of which is revived or extended by this act, and which at the time shall be unpatented to or for the benefit of the road or company making or suffering such failure, shall revert to the United States.

SEC. 3. *And be it further enacted,* That all the lands mentioned in this act, and hereby granted, are hereby reserved from entry, pre-emption, or appropriation to any other purpose than herein contemplated, for the said term of ten years, from the passage of this act: *Provided,* That all lands heretofore given to the State of Missouri for the construction of the Cairo and Fulton Railroad, or for the use of said road lying in the State of Missouri, and all lands proposed to be granted by this act for the use or in aid of the road herein named, and lying in said State of Missouri, shall be granted and patented to the said State whenever the road shall be completed through said State, which lands may be held by said State and used toward paying the State the amount of bonds heretofore issued by it to aid said company, and all interest accrued or to accrue thereon: *Provided further,* That the provisions of this act, so far as the same relate to the Memphis and Little Rock and the Little Rock and Fort Smith branches of said road, shall not take effect until the Secretary of the Interior shall make and file a certificate in his office and the office of the Secretary of State of Arkansas, stating that the companies or corporations claiming the benefit of this act in behalf of said branches have reorganized their boards of directors in a lawful manner, and, after such reorganization, that they have respectively rescinded all acts, resolutions, or other proceedings, transferring the lands, rights, or privileges of such corporations or companies to any convention, State, or authority recognizing or acting in concert with, or under the authority of the late so-called Confederate States of America.

Approved, July 28, 1866.

No. 179 B.—An Act to remove the office of Surveyor-General of the States of Iowa and Wisconsin to Plattsmouth, Nebraska.

Be it enacted by the Senate and House of Representatives of the United States of America in Congress assembled, That it shall be the duty of the Secretary of the Interior, as soon after the passage of this act as may be, to cause the office of Surveyor-General of Iowa and Wisconsin to be removed to Plattsmouth, in the Territory of Nebraska, and to make the necessary provisions for immediate and effective operations; and when so removed the duties and jurisdiction of said Surveyor-General shall be co-extensive with the limits of the Territory of Nebraska, and include the State of Iowa, and the same shall constitute a surveying district.

SEC. 2. *And be it further enacted,* That all acts and parts of acts inconsistent with the provisions of this act, be, and the same are hereby, repealed.

Approved, July 28, 1866.

No. 180 B.—Joint Resolution authorizing the Secretary of War to grant the use of a portion of military reserve on St. Clair River, in the State of Michigan, for railroad purposes.

Be it resolved by the Senate and House of Representatives of the United States of America in Congress assembled, That the Secretary of War be and he is hereby, authorized to grant to Guerdon O. Williams, of the city of Detroit, in the State of Michigan, and his associates, the use of so much of the military reserve on the St. Clair River, in the State of Michigan, known as the site of Fort Gratiot, as is necessary for extending a horse railroad from Port Huron city to the depot of the Port Huron and Detroit Railroad, at such rental and upon such terms and conditions as to him may seem proper, reserving to the United States, however, the right of removing the rails, ties, and other parts of said road whenever the Secretary of War shall direct, without any claim or right for damages on the part of the said Williams and associates, or their legal representatives.

Approved, January 31, 1866.

No. 181 B.—A Resolution extending the time for the completion of the Burlington and Missouri River Railroad.

Resolved by the Senate and House of Representatives of the United States of America in Congress assembled, That in case the Burlington and Missouri River Railroad Company shall complete the section of twenty miles from the present terminus of its road by the first day of December, Anno Domini eighteen hundred and sixty-six, and the certificate of the Governor shall be filed with the Secretary of the Interior of such completion, then the said company shall be entitled to its lands, due by reason of the completion of said section of twenty miles, as provided in section eight of the act entitled "An act to amend an act entitled 'An act making a grant of land to the State of Iowa, in alternate sections, to aid in the construction of certain railroads in said State,'" and its rights shall be in all respects the same as if the same section should have been completed on the first day of July next.*

Approved, February 10, 1866.

No. 182 B.—A Resolution extending the time for the completion of the Union Pacific Railway, Eastern Division.

Resolved by the Senate and House of Representatives of the United States of America in Congress assembled, That the time for the completion of the first one hundred miles of railroad and telegraph line by the Leavenworth, Pawnee, and Western Railroad Company (since called the "Union Pacific Railway Company, eastern division"), mentioned in the tenth section of the charter of the Union Pacific Railroad Company, of July first, one thousand eight hundred and sixty-two, and in the fifth section of the amendment thereof, of July second, one thousand eight hundred and sixty-four,† be, and the same is hereby, extended until the twenty-seventh day of June, one thousand eight hundred and sixty-six; and that the time for completing each succeeding section of one hundred miles shall be reckoned from the said twenty-seventh day of June in said year.

* No. 88 B.

† No. 45 B. and No. 111 B.

SEC. 2. *And be it further enacted*, That the time for commencing and completing the Northern Pacific Railroad, and all its several sections, is extended for the term of two years.*

Approved, May 7, 1866.

No. 183 B.—A Resolution to extend the time for the construction of the first section of the Western Pacific Railroad.

Resolved by the Senate and House of Representatives of the United States of America in Congress assembled, That the time for the construction of the first twenty miles of the "Western Pacific Railroad" be extended to the first day of January, eighteen hundred and sixty-seven ; but this extension is upon the condition to be accepted by said company, and notice of such acceptance to be given by them to the Secretary of the Interior, that the lands known as the lands of the ex-mission of San Jose as included in the map and survey thereof made October, eighteen hundred and sixty-four, by E. H. Dyer, Deputy United States Surveyor, shall not be included in the grant heretofore made to the said Western Pacific Railroad Company.†

Approved May 21, 1866.

No. 184 B.—A Resolution explanatory of, and in addition to, the act of May fifth, eighteen hundred and sixty-four, entitled "An act granting lands to aid in the construction of certain railroads in Wisconsin."‡

Resolved by the Senate and House of Representatives of the United States of America in Congress assembled, That the words "in a northwestern direction," in the third section of the act entitled "An act granting lands to aid in the construction of certain railroads in the State of Wisconsin," approved May fifth, eighteen hundred and sixty-four, shall, without forfeiture to said State, or its assigns, of any rights or benefits under said act, or exemption from any of the conditions or obligations imposed thereby, be construed to authorize the location of the line of said road, in said third section provided for, along and upon the following route, that is to say : from the city of Portage, by the way of the city of Ripon, in the county of Fond du Lac, and the city of Berlin, in the county of Green Lake, to Steven's Point, and thence to Bayfield, and thence to Superior, on Lake Superior. And the Legislature of the said State of Wisconsin, having, in and by an act entitled "An act to incorporate the Portage and Superior Railroad Company, and to execute the trust created by section three of the act of Congress entitled 'An [act] granting lands to aid in the construction of certain railroads in the State of Wisconsin,' approved May fifth, eighteen hundred and sixty-four," approved April —, eighteen hundred and sixty-six, authorized and required the said Portage and Superior Railroad Company to construct the line of road in the said third section of the said act of Congress provided for, upon and along the route hereinbefore set forth and described, the Con-

* No. 112 B. Extended 224 B.
† No. 45 B, and No. 126 B. ‡ No. 83 B.

gress of the United States hereby gives its assent to the route of the said railroad, as the same is hereinbefore described and set forth, and consents to the selection and application of the lands granted to the State of Wisconsin by the third section of the said act of Congress hereinbefore mentioned, for and to the line of the said railroad, as the same is hereinbefore defined and described, in the same manner and with the same effect as if the said railroad was located and constructed in strict conformity with and upon the route prescribed in the said third section of the said act of Congress. It being the intention of this resolution to give the assent of the United States to the disposition made by the Legislature of the State of Wisconsin of the land grant herein referred to, and the change of route for the railroad in aid of which the same is granted, and not to make any other disposition, change, or alteration of the grant aforesaid.

Approved, June 21, 1866.

No. 185 B.—A Resolution granting the right of way through military reserves to the Union Pacific Railroad Company and its branches.

Resolved by the Senate and House of Representatives of the United States of America in Congress assembled, That, subject to approval by the President, the right of way, one hundred feet in width, is hereby granted to the Union Pacific Railroad Company and the companies constructing the branch roads connecting therewith, for the construction and operation of their roads over and upon all military reserves through which the same may pass; and the President is hereby authorized to set apart to the Union Pacific Railway Company, eastern division, twenty acres of the Fort Riley military reservation, for depot and other purposes, in the bottom opposite "Riley City;" also fractional section "one" on the west side of said reservation, near Junction City, for the same purposes; and also to restore from time to time, to the public domain, any portion of said military reserve over which the Union Pacific Railroad, or any of its branches may pass, and which shall not be required for military purposes: *Provided,* That the President shall not permit the location of any such railroad or the diminution of any such reserve in any manner so as to impair its usefulness for military purposes, so long as it shall be required therefor.

Approved, July 26, 1866.

No. 186 B.—An Act to amend an act entitled "An act granting lands to the State of Oregon to aid in the construction of a military road from Eugene City to the eastern boundary of said State."*

Be it enacted by the Senate and House of Representatives of the United States of America in Congress assembled, That an act entitled "An act granting lands to the State of Oregon, to aid in the construction of a military road from Eugene City to the eastern boundary of said State" be amended as follows: That there be, and is hereby, granted to said State, for the purposes aforesaid, such odd sections or parts of odd sections not

*No. 110 B. No. 234 B.

reserved or otherwise legally appropriated, within six miles on each side of said road, to be selected by the Surveyor-General of said State, as shall be sufficient to supply any deficiency in the quantity of said grant as described, occasioned by any lands sold or reserved, or to which the rights of pre-emption or homestead have attached, or which for any reason were not subject to said grant within the limits designated in said act.

Approved, December 26, 1866.

No. 187 B.—An Act granting lands to the State of Oregon to aid in the construction of a military wagon road from Dalles City, on the Columbia River, to Fort Boise, on the Snake River.

Be it enacted by the Senate and House of Representatives of the United States of America in Congress assembled, That there be, and hereby is, granted to the State of Oregon, to aid in the construction of a military wagon road from Dalles City, on the Columbia River, by way of Camp Watson, Canon City, and Mormon or Humboldt Basin, to a point on Snake River opposite Fort Boise, in Idaho Territory, alternate sections of public lands, designated by odd numbers, to the extent of three sections in width on each side of said road: *Provided,* That the lands hereby granted shall be exclusively applied to the construction of said road, and to no other purpose; and shall be disposed of only as the work progresses: *And provided further,* That any and all lands heretofore reserved to the United States, or otherwise appropriated by act of Congress or other competent authority, be, and the same are hereby, reserved from the operation of this act, except so far as it may be necessary to locate the route of said road through the same, in which case the right of way to the width of one hundred feet is granted: *And provided further,* That the grant hereby made shall not embrace any mineral lands of the United States.

SEC. 2. *And be it further enacted,* That the lands hereby granted to said State shall be disposed of by the Legislature thereof for the purpose aforesaid, and for no other; and the said road shall be and remain a public highway for the use of the Government of the United States, free from tolls or other charges upon the transportation of any property, troops, or mails of the United States.

SEC. 3. *And be it further enacted,* That said road shall be constructed with such width, gradation, and bridges as to permit of its regular use as a wagon road, and in such other special manner as the State of Oregon may prescribe.

SEC. 4. *And be it further enacted,* That the State of Oregon is authorized to locate and use in the construction of said road an additional amount of public lands, not previously reserved to the United States nor otherwise disposed of, and not exceeding ten miles in distance from it, equal to the amount reserved from the operation of this act in the first section of the same, to be selected in alternate odd sections as provided in section first of this act.

SEC. 5. *And be it further enacted,* That lands hereby granted to said State shall be disposed of only in the following manner, that is to say: when the Governor of said State shall certify to the Secretary of the Interior that ten continuous miles of said road are completed, then a quantity of the land hereby granted, not to exceed thirty sections, may be sold, and so on from time to time until said road shall be completed; and if said road is not completed within five years, no further sales shall be made, and the lands remaining unsold shall revert to the United States.

SEC. 6. *And be it further enacted*, That the United States Surveyor-General for the district of Oregon shall cause said lands so granted to be surveyed at the earliest practicable period after said State shall have enacted the necessary legislation to carry this act into effect.

Approved, February 25, 1867.

No. 188 B.—An Act to amend an act granting the right of way over the military reserve at Fort Gratiot, Michigan.

Be it enacted by the Senate and House of Representatives of the United States of America in Congress assembled, That the act entitled "An act granting the right of way over, and depot grounds upon, the military reserve of Fort Gratiot in the State of Michigan," passed February the eighth, eighteen hundred and fifty-nine, be, and the same is hereby, amended by inserting in the last proviso, after the word "wood," the words "or fire-proof," so that the same shall read, "that all buildings to be erected upon said reservation shall be of wood or fire-proof."*

Approved, February 25, 1867.

No. 189 B.—An Act to quiet title to land in the towns of Santa Clara and Petaluma, in the State of California.

Be it enacted by the Senate and House of Representatives of the United States of America in Congress assembled, That all the right and title of the United States to the land situated within the corporate limits of the towns of Santa Clara and Petaluma, in the State of California, as defined in the acts of the Legislature of that State incorporating said towns, be, and the same are hereby, relinquished and granted to the corporate authorities of said towns and their successors, in trust, for and with authority to convey so much of said land as is in the bona fide occupancy of parties upon the passage of this act, by themselves or tenants, to such parties: *Provided*, That this grant shall not extend to any reservation of the United States, nor prejudice any valid adverse right or claim, if such exist, to said land or any part thereof, nor preclude a judicial examination and adjustment thereof.

Approved, March 1, 1867.

* See Vol. I. No. 350.

No. 190 B.—An Act to amend an act entitled "An act to extend the time for the reversion to the United States of the lands granted by Congress to aid in the construction of a railroad from Amboy, by Hillsdale and Lansing, to some point on or near Traverse Bay, in the State of Michigan, and for the completion of said road," approved July three, eighteen hundred and sixty-six.*

Be it enacted by the Senate and House of Representatives of the United States of America in Congress assembled, That the first section of the act entitled "An act to extend the time for the reversion to the United States of the lands granted by Congress to aid in the construction of a railroad from Amboy, by Hillsdale and Lansing, to some point on or near Traverse Bay, in the State of Michigan, and for the completion of said road," approved July three, eighteen hundred and sixty-six, be and the same is hereby amended by striking out the word "February" where it occurs in said section, and inserting the word "July" in lieu thereof.

Approved, March 2, 1867.

No. 191 B.—An Act making appropriations and to supply deficiencies in the appropriations for the service of the Government for the fiscal year ending June thirtieth, eighteen hundred and sixty-seven, and for other purposes.

* * * * * * * * *

SEC. 2. *And be it further enacted,* That the unexpended balance of the appropriations heretofore made for defraying the expenses of the Legislative Assembly of the Territory of Nebraska is hereby diverted and set aside for the purpose of procuring a geological survey of Nebraska, said survey to be prosecuted under the direction of the Commissioner of the General Land Office.

* * * * * * * * *

Approved, March 2, 1867.

No. 192 B.—An Act for the relief of the inhabitants of cities and towns upon the public lands.†

Be it enacted by the Senate and House of Representatives of the United States of America in Congress assembled, That whenever any portion of the public lands of the United States have been or shall be settled upon and occupied as a town site, and therefore not subject to entry under the agricultural pre-emption laws, it shall be lawful, in case such town shall be incorporated, for the corporate authorities thereof, and if not incorporated, for the judge of the county court for the county in which such town may be situated, to enter at the proper land office, and at the minimum price, the land so settled and occupied, in trust for the several use and benefit of the occupants thereof, according to their respective interests; the execution of which trust, as to the disposal of the lots in such town, and the proceeds of the sales thereof, to be conducted under such rules and regulations as may be prescribed by the legislative authority of the

* No. 149 B.

† Amended, No. 206 B.

State or Territory in which the same may be situated: *Provided*, That the entry of the land intended by this act to be made shall be made, or a declaratory statement of the purpose of the inhabitants to enter it as a town site under this act shall be filed with the register of the proper land office, prior to the commencement of the public sale of the body of land in which it is included, and that the entry or declaratory statement shall include only such lands as is actually occupied by the town and the title to which is in the United States. If upon surveyed lands the entry shall in its exterior limit be made in conformity to the legal subdivisions of the public lands authorized by the act of twenty-fourth April, one thousand eight hundred and twenty; and where the inhabitants are in number one hundred and less than two hundred, shall embrace not exceeding three hundred and twenty acres; and in cases where the inhabitants of such town are more than two hundred and less than one thousand, shall embrace not exceeding six hundred and forty acres; and where the number of inhabitants is one thousand and over one thousand, shall embrace not exceeding twelve hundred and eighty acres: *Provided*, That for each additional one thousand inhabitants, not exceeding five thousand in all, a further grant of three hundred and twenty acres shall be allowed: *And provided further*, That in any Territory in which a land office may not havebeen established, declaratory statements as herein before provided may be filed with the Surveyor-General of the surveying district in which the lands are situate, who shall transmit said declaratory statement to the General Land Office: *And provided further*, That any act of said trustees not made in conformity to the rules and regulations herein alluded to shall be void; effect to be given to the foregoing provisions according to such regulations as may be prescribed by the Secretary of the Interior: *And provided further*, That the provisions of this act shall not apply to military or other reservations heretofore made by the United States, nor to reservations for lighthouses, custom-houses, mints, or such other public purposes as the interests of the United States may require, whether held under reservations through the land office by title derived from the Crown of Spain, or otherwise: *And provided further*, That no title shall be acquired, under the provisions of this act, to any mine of gold, silver, cinnabar, or copper.

Approved, March 2, 1867.

No. 193 B.—An Act to create the office of Surveyor-General in the Territories of Utah and Montana, and establish a land office in the Territories of Utah, Montana, and Arizona.

Be it enacted by the Senate and House of Representatives of the United States of America in Congress assembled, That the President, by and with the advice and consent of the Senate, shall be, and he is hereby, authorized to appoint a Surveyor-General for each of the Territories of Utah and Montana, whose annual salary shall be three thousand dollars, and whose power, authority, and duties shall be the same as those provided by law for the Surveyor-General of Oregon. He shall have proper allowances for clerk-hire, office rent, and fuel, what is now allowed by law to the Surveyor-General of Oregon.

SEC. 2. *And be it further enacted*, That the public lands within the Territories of Montana, Utah, and Arizona, to which the Indian title is or shall be extinguished, shall each respectively constitute a new land district, to be called the Montana district, the Utah district, and the Arizona district, respectively, and the President is hereby authorized to appoint, by and with the advice and consent of the Senate, a register and receiver of public moneys for each of said districts, respectively, who shall be required to reside at the places at which said offices shall be located, and they shall have the same powers, perform the same duties, and be entitled to the same compensation as are or may be prescribed by law in relation to land offices of the United States in other Territories.

SEC. 3. *And be it further enacted,* That the Secretary of the Interior is hereby authorized to locate said offices of Surveyor-General and registers and receivers of public moneys.

SEC. 4. *And be it further enacted,* That the Territory of Arizona is hereby attached to the surveying district of California.

Approved, March 2, 1867.

No. 194 B.—An Act to extend the provisions of an act entitled "An act for the final adjustment of private land claims in the States of Florida, Louisiana, and Missouri, and for other purposes."*

Be it enacted by the Senate and House of Representatives of the United States of America in Congress assembled, That the provisions of the act entitled "An act for the final adjustment of private land claims in the States of Florida, Louisiana, and Missouri, and for other purposes," approved June twenty-second, eighteen hundred and sixty, be, and the same are hereby, extended, and the same shall continue in force for a period of three years from and after the passage of this act.

Approved, March 2, 1867.

No. 195 B.—An Act granting lands to aid in the construction of a railroad from the city of Stockton to the town of Copperopolis, in the State of California.

Be it enacted by the Senate and House of Representatives of the United States of America in Congress assembled, That the right of way through the public lands be, and the same is hereby, granted to the Stockton and Copperopolis Railroad Company, a corporation organized under the laws of the State of California, its successors and assigns, for the construction of a railroad from the city of Stockton to the town of Copperopolis, in the State of California, by the most feasible route, to be selected by said company; and the right is hereby given to said company to take from the public lands adjacent to the line of said road material for the construction thereof. Said right of way is granted to said company to the extent of one hundred feet in width on each side of said road where it may pass through the public domain; also all necessary ground for station buildings, workshops, depots, machine-shops, switches, side-tracks, turn-tables, and water-stations: *Provided,* That all the rights conferred upon said

* No. 20 B.

railroad company by this act are made upon the express condition that said company shall first be designated by the Legislature of the State of California as the company to be vested with the rights, privileges, franchises, and grants created or conferred by this act.

SEC. 2. *And be it further enacted,* That there be, and is hereby, granted to the State of California, for the construction of the said Stockton and Copperopolis Railroad, its successors and assigns, for the purpose of aiding in the construction of the said railroad, upon the condition prescribed in section one of this act, and to secure the safe and speedy transportation of the mails, troops, munitions of war, and public stores over the route of said line of railway, every alternate section of public land designated by odd numbers to the extent of five alternate sections on each side of said railroad line as said company may adopt, whenever on the line thereof the United States have full title, not reserved, sold, granted, or otherwise appropriated, and free from pre-emption or other claims or rights at the time the line of said road is definitely fixed and a plot thereof filed in the office of the Commissioner of the General Land Office. And whenever, prior to said time, any of said sections or parts of sections shall have been granted, sold, reserved, or covered by private land grants, or occupied by homestead settlers, or pre-empted, or otherwise disposed of, other lands shall be selected by said company, in lieu thereof, on the line of said road, within twenty miles of the same, under the direction of the Secretary of the Interior, in alternate sections, and designated by odd numbers: *Provided,* That all lands containing gold or silver, or copper, be, and the same are hereby, excluded from the operations of this act, and in lieu thereof a like quantity of unoccupied and unappropriated lands, in odd-numbered sections, within the said twenty miles of the line of said road, may be selected as above provided: *And provided further,* That the word "mineral," when it occurs in this act, shall not be held to include iron or coal.

SEC. 3. *And be it further enacted,* That whenever said railroad company shall have ten consecutive miles of any portion of said railroad ready for the service contemplated, the Pacific railroad commissioners shall examine the same; and if it shall appear that ten miles of said road have been completed in a good and substantial manner, and in all respects as required by this act, the commissioners shall so report to the President of the United States, and patents of lands, as aforesaid, shall be issued to said company, confirming to said company the right and title to said lands hereinbefore granted, situated opposite to and coterminous with said completed section of said road, within twenty miles thereof. And from time to time, whenever ten additional miles shall have been constructed, completed, and in readiness as aforesaid, and verified by the commissioners to the President of the United States, then patents shall be issued to said company, conveying the additional sections of land as aforesaid, and so on as fast as every ten miles of said road is completed. The services of said commissioners under this act shall be paid by said company.

SEC. 4. *And be it further enacted,* That said railroad shall be constructed in a substantial and workmanlike manner, with all the necessary draws, culverts, bridges, viaducts, crossings, turnouts, stations, and watering places, and all other appurtenances, including furniture and rolling stock, equal in all respects to railroads of the first-class when prepared for business, with rails of the best quality; and a uniform gauge with the Pacific Railroad shall be established the entire length of the road.

SEC. 5. *And be it further enacted,* That the President of the United States shall cause the lands to be surveyed for twenty miles in width on both sides of the entire line of the said road, after the general route shall be fixed, and as fast as may be required by the construction of said railroad; and the odd sections of land hereby granted shall not be liable to sale or entry, or pre-emption, before or after they are surveyed, except by said company, as provided in this act; but the provisions of the act of September, eighteen hundred and forty-one, granting pre-emption rights, and the acts amendatory thereof, and of the act entitled "An act to secure homesteads to actual settlers on the public domain," approved May twenty, eighteen hundred and sixty-two, shall be, and the same are hereby, extended to all other lands on the line of said road when surveyed, excepting those hereby granted to said company; and the sections and parts of sections which shall remain in the United States within ten miles of said railroad on each side thereof shall not be sold for less than two dollars and fifty cents per acre.

SEC. 6. *And be it further enacted,* That each and every grant, right, and privilege are so made and given to and accepted by said Stockton and Copperopolis Railroad Company upon and subject to the following conditions, namely: That the said company shall commence the work on said road within two years from the approval of this act by the President, and shall complete not less than ten miles per year after the second year, and shall construct, furnish, equip, and complete the whole road by the fourth day of July, eighteen hundred and seventy-two; and upon a failure of said company to comply with either of said conditions, the lands then unpatented to said company shall revert to the United States.

SEC. 7. *And be it further enacted,* That the United States make the several conditioned grants herein, and that the said Stockton and Copperopolis Railroad Company accept the same, upon the further condition that if the said company make any breach of the conditions thereof, and allow the same to continue for upwards of one year, then, in such case, at any time hereafter, Congress may do any and all acts and things which may be needful and necessary to insure a speedy completion of said road.

SEC. 8. *And be it further enacted,* That said Stockton and Copperopolis Railroad, or any part thereof, shall be a post-route and military railroad, subject to the use of the United States for postal, military, naval, and all other Government service, and also subject to such regulations as Congress may impose restricting the charges for such Government transportation, and all troops and munitions of war of the United States shall be transported over the said railroad free of all expense or charge to the Government therefor, whenever the same shall be required by the Government of the United States.

SEC. 9. *And be it further enacted,* That the acceptance of the terms, conditions, and impositions of this act, by the said Stockton and Copperopolis Railroad Company, shall be signified in writing, under the corporate seal of the said company, duly executed pursuant to the direction of its board of directors first had and obtained, which acceptance shall be made within two years after the passage of this act, and not afterward, and shall be served on the President of the United States, and filed in the office of the Secretary of the Interior.

SEC. 10. *And be it further enacted,* That unless the said Stockton and Copperopolis Railroad Company shall obtain bona fide subscription to the stock of said company to the amount of two hundred thousand dollars, with five per centum paid within two years after the passage and approval of this act, it shall be null and void.

SEC. 11. *And be it further enacted,* That Congress may, at any time, having due regard for the rights of said railroad company, add to, alter, amend, or repeal this act.

SEC. 12. *And be it further enacted*, That lots in towns and villages shall be exempt from the provisions of this act.

Approved, March 2, 1867.

No. 196 B.—Joint Resolution to extend the provisions of the act in regard to agricultural colleges, to the State of Tennessee.

Be it resolved by the Senate and House of Representatives of the United States of America in Congress assembled, That the provisions of the act of July two, eighteen hundred and sixty-two, entitled "An act donating public lands to the several States and Territories which may provide colleges for the benefit of agriculture and the mechanic arts," and of the "act to amend the fifth section" thereof, approved July twenty-third, eighteen hundred and sixty-six, are hereby extended and made applicable to the State of Tennessee.*

Approved, February 28, 1867.

No. 197 B.—Joint Resolution for the reduction of the military reservation of Fort Riley, and to grant land for bridge purposes to the State of Kansas.

Be it resolved by the Senate and House of Representatives of the United States of America in Congress assembled, That the southwestern boundary of the military reservation of Fort Riley, in the State of Kansas, be, and the same is hereby, declared to be hereafter the channel of the Republican River, from its mouth to the point where said river intersects the present western line of said reservation, and the land released from said reservation and lying between the Smoky Hill and Republican Rivers, is hereby granted to the State of Kansas to aid in the construction of a bridge over the Republican River, on the public highway leading through the present reservation; but upon the express condition that this grant shall be accepted by the State of Kansas with a guaranty given by said State, by an act of the legislature thereof, that said bridge shall be kept up and maintained in good condition, and shall be free to the use of the Government of the United States, for all transit purposes forever, without tolls or charges, and on such acceptance and guaranty being filed in the office of the Secretary of the Interior, together with the certificate of the Governor of Kansas that a good and permanent bridge has been constructed over the said Republican River, it shall be the duty of said Secretary to issue patent, for the land hereby granted, to the State of Kansas, or to such company as may be authorized, by act of the legislature of said State, to construct said bridge: *Provided, however*, That nothing herein contained shall be construed to interfere with any grant of any part of said land heretofore made by the United States.

Approved, March 2, 1867.

* No. 47 B. and No. 165 B.

No. 198 B.—An Act in relation to a certain tract of land in Burlington, Iowa.

Be it enacted by the Senate and House of Representatives of the United States of America in Congress assembled, That a certain ordinance, adopted by the City Council of the city of Burlington, in the State of Iowa, of date of December tenth, Anno Domini eighteen hundred and sixty-six, entitled "An ordinance devoting Market Square to certain public purposes, and providing for the location of certain railroad tracks upon certain streets, and for other purposes," is hereby ratified, approved, and made legal and valid, so far as relates to said public square; and that said ordinance shall operate to convey to the Burlington and Missouri River Railroad Company all right and interest of the United States in the premises known as Market Square, in the said city of Burlington, upon the terms and conditions and for the purposes and uses therein designated, and shall have the same force, operation, and effect as if the fee simple title to said Market Square and streets were owned by said city at the date of said ordinance.

Approved, March 22, 1867.

No. 199 B.—An Act extending to the State of Nebraska the provisions of an act relating to agricultural colleges.

Be it enacted by the Senate and House of Representatives of the United States of America in Congress assembled, That the grant made by law of the second day of July, eighteen hundred and sixty-two, to each State, of land equal to thirty thousand acres for each of its Senators and Representatives in Congress, for the purpose of establishing agricultural colleges, is extended to the State of Nebraska in the same manner as if Nebraska had been a State of the Union at the date of the passage of said law.*

Approved, March 30, 1867.

No. 200 B.—A Resolution extending the time for the completion of the improvement of the Fox and Wisconsin Rivers.†

Resolved by the Senate and House of Representatives of the United States of America in Congress assembled, That the time provided for the completion of the improvement of the Fox and Wisconsin Rivers, and a canal connecting the same, by section three of an act of Congress, approved August eighth, eighteen hundred and forty-six, entitled "An act to grant a certain quantity of land to aid in the improvement of the Fox and Wisconsin Rivers, and to connect the same by a canal in the Territory of Wisconsin," be, and the same hereby is, extended for the term of five years from and after the approval of this resolution, with all the rights and privileges conferred by said act.

Approved, March 12, 1867.

* No. 47 B. † Vol. I. No. 120.

No. 201 B.—Joint Resolution relating to the issue of agricultural college scrip to the States lately in rebellion.

Whereas, on the third day of April, eighteen hundred and sixty-six, by the authority and direction of the President of the United States, agricultural college scrip, covering nearly two hundred and seventy thousand acres, was issued and delivered to the State of North Carolina, under the act of Congress of July fifth, (second),* eighteen hundred and sixty-two, providing for agricultural colleges; and whereas, by the same authority, the General Land Office is now preparing to issue scrip in like manner to the States of Virginia, Georgia, and Mississippi; and whereas, said action of the President takes for granted that said States are restored to their proper constitutional relation to the Union, and are to be recognized in all respects as entitled to the rights of the other States of the Union, which questions Congress alone can rightfully determine, therefore :—

Be it resolved by the Senate and House of Representatives of the United States of America in Congress assembled, That the further issue or delivery of such scrip to any of the States lately in rebellion against the United States, except the State of Tennessee, or the acceptance of such scrip or of any heretofore issued by the registers or receivers of any of the land offices of said States be, and the same is hereby, prohibited until they shall be fully restored to their rights as States by Congress.

Approved, March 29, 1867.

No. 202 B.—An Act extending the time for the completion of the Dubuque and Sioux City Railroad.

Be it enacted by the Senate and House of Representatives of the United States of America in Congress assembled, That the time for completing a line of railroad from Dubuque to Sioux City, in the State of Iowa, for the construction of which lands were granted in alternate sections to said State by act entitled "An act making a grant of lands to the State of Iowa in alternate sections to aid in the construction of railroads in said State," approved May fifteenth, eighteen hundred and fifty-six,† be, and the same is, extended until the first day of January, eighteen hundred and seventy-two, subject to the reverter mentioned in said act at the expiration of the time herein limited: *Provided,* [That] said road shall be constructed on the most practical route by way of Webster City and Fort Dodge to Sioux City, which route shall be at all points within the limits of said land grant, and the same shall be completed to Fort Dodge on or before the first day of July, eighteen hundred and sixty-nine, and thereafter at the rate of not less than forty miles each year; and the said road shall be constructed, operated, and maintained as one continuous and unbroken line of road from Dubuque to Sioux City; and no lands shall be disposed of, or patented, or certified for said purposes more than forty miles in advance of the point to which said road may be constructed from time to time.

Approved, March 2, 1868.

* No. 47 B.

† Vol. I. No. 288.

No. 203 B.—An Act in relation to islands in the Great Miami River.

Be it enacted by the Senate and House of Representatives of the United States of America in Congress assembled, That in the case of such islands in the Great Miami River, in the State of Ohio, as are undisposed of, or any vacant public lands adjacent thereto, which are in the actual and exclusive occupancy of any persons who have made improvements thereon, or of their heirs or assigns, such occupants thereof shall have the preference right to enter the same at two dollars and fifty cents per acre, on making proof of the facts to the satisfaction of the Commissioner of the General Land Office, and paying for the land within twelve months from the passage of this act, and patents shall issue for the tracts so entered as usual in entries of public lands.

Approved, March 2, 1868.

No. 204 B.—An Act restoring lands to market along the line of the Pacific Railroads and branches.*

Be it enacted by the Senate and House of Representatives of the United States of America in Congress assembled, That nothing in the act approved July first, eighteen hundred and sixty-two, entitled "An act to aid in the construction of a railroad and telegraph line from the Missouri River to the Pacific Ocean, and to secure to the Government the use of the same for postal, military, and other purposes," and the acts amendatory thereof, shall be held to authorize the withdrawal or exclusion from settlement and entry, under the provisions of the pre-emption or homestead laws, the even-numbered sections along the routes of the several roads therein mentioned which have been or may be hereafter located: *Provided,* That such sections shall be rated at two dollars and fifty cents per acre, and subject only to entry under those laws; and the Secretary of the Interior be, and is hereby, authorized and directed to restore to homestead settlement, pre-emption, or entry, according to existing laws, all the even-numbered sections of land belonging to the Government, and now withdrawn from market, on both sides of the Pacific Railroad and branches, wherever said road and branches have been definitely located.

Approved, March 6, 1868.

No. 205 B.—An Act for the relief of settlers on the late Sioux Indian reservation in the State of Minnesota.

Be it enacted by the Senate and House of Representatives of the United States of America in Congress assembled, That all actual settlers, who have duly filed their declaratory statements under the pre-emption laws with the register of the proper local land office, upon the unsold lands now included within the limits of the late Sioux Indian reservation, in the State of Minnesota, shall be allowed two years from and after the passage of this act within which to make proof and payment for their

* No. 45 B.

claims, in accordance with the provisions of the second and third sections of the act approved March third, eighteen hundred and sixty-three, providing for the disposal of said reservation.*

Approved, March 6, 1868.

No. 206 B.—An Act to amend an act entitled "An act for the relief of the inhabitants of cities and towns upon the public lands," approved March two, eighteen hundred and sixty-seven.†

Be it enacted by the Senate and House of Representatives of the United States of America in Congress assembled, That, the inhabitants of any town located on the public land of the United States may avail themselves, if the town authorities elect so to do, of the provisions of the act of March two, eighteen hundred and sixty-seven, entitled "An act for the relief of the inhabitants of cities and towns upon the public lands: *Provided,* This act shall not prevent the issuance of patents to persons who have made, or may make, entries and elect to proceed under existing laws: *And provided further,* That no title under said act of March two, eighteeen hundred and sixty-seven, shall be acquired to any valid mining claim or possession held under the existing laws of Congress: *Provided also,* That in addition to the minimum price of the lands included in any town site entered under the provisions of this act and "An act for the relief of the inhabitants of cities and towns upon the public lands," approved March two, eighteen hundred and sixty-seven, there shall be paid by the parties availing themselves of the provisions of said acts all costs of surveying and platting any such town site, and expenses incident thereto, incurred by the United States, before any patent shall issue therefor.

Approved, June 8, 1868.

No. 207 B.—An Act to extend the time for completing the military road authorized by an act entitled "An act granting lands to the States of Michigan and Wisconsin to aid in the construction of a military road from Fort Wilkins, Copper Harbor, Kewenaw County, in the State of Michigan, to Fort Howard, Green Bay, in the State of Wisconsin."‡

Be it enacted by the Senate and House of Representatives of the United States of America in Congress assembled, That the time for completing the military road, and for the sales of lands, authorized by an act entitled "An act granting lands to the States of Michigan and Wisconsin to aid in the construction of a military road from Fort Wilkins, Copper Harbor, Kewenaw County, in the State of Michigan, to Fort Howard, Green Bay, in the State of Wisconsin," approved March third, eighteen hundred and sixty-three, be, and the same is hereby, extended to March first, eighteen hundred and seventy.

Approved, June 8, 1868.

* No. 72 B. † No. 192 B. ‡ No. 69 B.

No. 208 B.—An act to further provide for giving effect to the various grants of public lands to the State of Nevada.

Be it enacted by the Senate and House of Representatives of the United States of America in Congress assembled, That the State of Nevada is authorized to select the alternate even-numbered sections within the limits of any railroad grant in said State, in satisfaction, in whole or in part, of the several grants made in the following acts of Congress, to wit: the act organizing the Territory of Nevada,* passed March second, eighteen hundred and sixty-one; the act admitting the State of Nevada into the Union, passed March twenty-one, eighteen hundred and sixty-four: and the act concerning certain lands granted to Nevada, passed July fourth, eighteen hundred and sixty-six: *Provided,* That this privilege shall not extend to lands upon which there may be rightful claims under the pre-emption and homestead laws: *And provided,* That if lands be selected, the minimum price of which is two dollars and fifty cents per acre, each acre so selected shall be taken by the State in satisfaction of two acres, the minimnm price of which is one dollar and twenty-five cents per acre: *And provided further,* That the lands granted in the eighth and ninth sections of the said act admitting Nevada into the Union shall be selected within four years from the passage of this act, and the period for the selection of said lands is hereby so extended.

SEC. 2. *And be it further enacted,* That the lands known and designated for the establishment of an agricultural college by the act of July second, eighteen hundred and sixty-two, and the acts amendatory thereto, shall be selected in the same manner and of the same character of lands as may be selected in satisfaction of any other grants referred to in the first section of this act. But this act shall not authorize the selection of lands valuable for mines of gold, silver, quicksilver, or copper.†

SEC. 3. *And be it further enacted,* That the county of Esmeralda, in the State of Nevada, and the counties of Mono and Inyo, in the State of California, are hereby created a land district; and the land office for such district shall be located at Aurora, in Esmeralda County; and the President shall be authorized hereafter, from time to time, as circumstances may require, to adjust the boundaries of any and all of the land districts in said State, and change the location of the land office from time to time, when the same shall be expedient.

SEC. 4. *And be it further enacted,* That the lands granted to the State of California for the establishment of an agricultural college by the act of July second, eighteen hundred and sixty-two, and acts amendatory thereto, may be selected by said State from any lands within said State subject to pre-emption and sale: *Provided,* That this privilege shall not extend to lands upon which there may be rightful claims under the pre-emption and homestead laws, nor to mineral lands: *And provided further,* That if lands be selected as aforesaid, the minimum price of which is two dollars and fifty cents per acre, each acre so selected shall be taken by the State in satisfaction of two acres, the minimum price of which is one dollar and twenty-five cents per acre: *And provided further,* That such selections shall be made in every other respect subject to the conditions, restrictions, and limitations contained in the acts hereby modified.

Approved, June 8, 1868.

* No. 33 B. No. 74 B. No. 166 B. No. 55 B.

† No. 47 B.

No. 209 B.—An Act to amend an act entitled "An act granting lands to aid in the construction of a railroad and telegraph line from the Central Pacific Railroad, in California, to Portland, in Oregon."*

Be it enacted by the Senate and House of Representatives of the United States of America in Congress assembled, That section six of an act entitled "An act granting lands to aid in the construction of a railroad and telegraph line from the Central Pacific Railroad, in California, to Portland, in Oregon," approved July twenty-fifth, eighteen hundred and sixty-six, be so amended as to provide that instead of the times now fixed in said section, the first section of twenty miles of said railroad and telegraph shall be completed within eighteen months from the passage of this act, and at least twenty miles in each two years thereafter, and the whole on or before the first day of July, Anno Domini eighteen hundred and eighty.

Approved, June 25, 1868.

No. 210 B.—An Act confirming the title to a tract of land in Burlington, Iowa.

Be it enacted by the Senate and House of Representatives of the United States of America in Congress assembled, That all of the title of the United States in and to a certain tract of land in the city of Burlington, Des Moines County, in the State of Iowa, described as being west of lot number nine hundred and seventy-eight, in said city, south of Valley Street, west of Boundary Street, and north of Market Street, and which was originally reserved from sale by the United States and dedicated to public burial purposes, be, and the same is hereby, confirmed to and vested in the "Independent School District" of said city, to be forever dedicated to and used by said school district for public school purposes, and for no other use or purpose whatever.

Approved, July 4, 1868.

No. 211 B.—An Act to create the office of Surveyor-General in the Territory of Utah, and establish a land office in said Territory, and extend the homestead and pre-emption laws over the same.

Be it enacted by the Senate and House of Representatives of the United States of America in Congress assembled, That the President, by and with the advice [and consent] of the Senate, shall be, and he is hereby, authorized to appoint a Surveyor-General for the Territory of Utah, whose annual salary shall be three thousand dollars, and whose power, authority, and duties shall be the same as those provided by law for the Surveyor-General of Oregon. He shall have proper allowances for clerk hire, office rent, and fuel, not exceeding what is now allowed by law to the Surveyor-General of Oregon.

SEC. 2. *And be it further enacted,* That the public lands of the United States, within said Territory of Utah, shall constitute a new land district,

* 172 B.

to be called the Utah District; and the President is hereby authorized to appoint, by and with the advice and consent of the Senate, a register and receiver of public money for said district, who shall be required to reside at the places at which said offices shall be located, and they shall have the same powers, perform the same duties, and be entitled to the same compensation as are or may be prescribed by law in relation to land offices of the United States in other Territories.

SEC. 3. *And be it further enacted,* That the Secretary of the Interior is hereby authorized to locate said offices of Surveyor-General and register and receiver of public moneys at some suitable place or places in said Territory.

SEC. 4. *And be it further enacted,* That the pre-emption, homestead, and other laws of the United States applicable to the disposal of the public lands, are hereby extended over said district.

Approved, July 16, 1868.

No. 212 B.—An Act making appropriations for sundry civil expenses of the Government for the year ending June thirty, eighteen hundred and sixty-nine, and for other purposes.

SEC. 6. *And be it further enacted,* That the Commissioner of the General Land Office is hereby authorized to continue the extension of the geological explorations as begun in Nebraska under the provisions of the second section of the deficiency act of Congress, approved March two, eighteen hundred and sixty-seven, United States Statutes, eighteen hundred and sixty-six, and eighteen hundred and sixty-seven, page four hundred and seventy, to other portions of the public lands; and for that purpose the sum of five thousand dollars is hereby appropriated, out of any money in the treasury not otherwise appropriated.*

Approved, July 20, 1868.

No. 213 B.—An Act providing for the sale of a portion of the Fort Gratiot military reservation in St. Clair County, in the State of Michigan.

Be it enacted by the Senate and House of Representatives of the United States of America in Congress assembled, That the Secretary of War be, and he is hereby, authorized to sell, at such times as he may deem most advantageous to the interests of the Government, and in such manner as hereinafter provided, all that portion of the military reservation known as Fort Gratiot, in St. Clair County, in the State of Michigan, which lies south of a line running due west from the south end of the Grand Trunk railroad wharf, on the St. Clair River, until it intersects the road known as the Lexington road, and all that portion which lies west of said Lexington road.

SEC. 2. *And be it further enacted,* That all that portion of the above-described lands which lies east of a line running due south from the point of intersection with the Lexington road, mentioned in the foregoing section of this act, shall be divided into blocks and lots of convenient size

* See No. 191 B.

for building purposes, with public streets conforming as near as may be, without detriment to the interests of the Government or the State, to the public streets of the city of Port Huron, adjoining such ground, and sold by lots at public auction, at the city of Port Huron, to the highest bidder, public notice of such sale having first been given for thirty days by advertisement in all the papers published in the city of Port Huron, and in at least two papers published in the city of Detroit, Michigan. A plat of this division, made in accordance with the laws of the State of Michigan, shall be filed with the register of deeds of the county of St. Clair, State of Michigan. The remaining portion of said military reservation, for the sale of which provision is made in the first section of this act, shall be sold at public auction at the city of Port Huron, after due notice, as prescribed in the foregoing paragraph, at such times and in such parcels as may be deemed most advantageous to the interests of the Government, by the Secretary of War.

SEC. 3. *And be it further enacted,* That the proceeds arising from the sale herein provided for, shall be paid into the treasury of the United States in the same manner as the proceeds from the sale of other public lands.

Approved, July 20, 1868.

No. 214 B.—An Act making a grant of land to the State of Minnesota to aid in the improvement of the navigation of the Mississippi River.

Be it enacted by the Senate and House of Representatives of the United States of America in Congress assembled, That there be, and hereby is, granted to the State of Minnesota, for the purpose of aiding said State in constructing and completing a lock and dam at Meeker's island (so called), in the Mississippi River, in said State, and thereby facilitating the navigation of the Mississippi River between the falls of St. Anthony and the mouth of the Minnesota River, two hundred thousand acres of public lands, to be selected in alternate odd-numbered sections by an agent to be appointed by the Governor of said State, subject to the approval of the Secretary of the Interior: *Provided,* That said lands shall be selected from the public lands lying within the limits of the said State of Minnesota, and that not more than one section thereof shall be selected in any one township: *Provided further,* That said selections shall not be made from any lands containing mines of gold, silver, cinnabar, or copper, nor from any lands to which rights of pre-emption or homestead have attached.

SEC. 2. *And be it further enacted,* That said lands so granted shall be subject to the disposal of the Legislature of said State for the purposes mentioned in the first section of this act, and no other; and the said lock and dam shall be and remain forever a public highway, free from any toll or charge of any kind whatever; and the said legislature shall have power to pass all needful rules and regulations that may be necessary to fully carry out the purposes of this act.

SEC. 3. *And be it further enacted,* That the work shall be done under the direction of the engineer department of the United States, according to the plan and estimate submitted by Major-General Warren, and that if said lock and dam are not constructed within two years from and after the date of the acceptance and disposition of this grant by the legislature of the said State, the lands hereby granted shall revert to the United States.

SEC. 4. *And be it further enacted*, That at any time after the selection of the said lands, and subsequent to the completion of said lock and dam, the lands hereby granted shall be open for settlement by actual settlers upon paying to the State of Minnesota a price not exceeding one dollar and twenty-five cents per acre for the same, which shall be paid by the State to the company who may construct said lock and dam.

SEC. 5. *And be it further enacted*, That if at any time prior to the completion of the said lock and dam the Government of the United States shall make an appropriation in money sufficient to construct said lock and dam, then the grant of lands herein made shall revert to the United States: *Provided*, That this act shall have no effect on lands already granted for railroad purposes.

Approved, July 23, 1868.

No. 215 B.—An Act to provide a temporary government for the Territory of Wyoming.

Be it enacted by the Senate and House of Representatives of the United States of America in Congress assembled, That all that part of the United States described as follows: Commencing at the intersection of the twenty-seventh meridian of longitude west from Washington with the forty-fifth degree of north latitude, and running thence west to the thirty-fourth meridian of west longitude, thence south to the forty-first degree of north latitude, thence east to the twenty-seventh meridian of west longitude, and thence north to the place of beginning, be and the same is hereby, organized into a temporary government by the name of the Territory of Wyoming: *Provided*, That nothing in this act shall be construed to impair the rights of person or property now pertaining to the Indians in said Territory, so long as such rights shall remain unextinguished by treaty between the United States and such Indians: *Provided further*, That nothing in this act contained shall be construed to inhibit the Government of the United States from dividing said Territory into two or more Territories, in such manner and at such time as Congress shall deem convenient and proper, or from attaching any portion thereof to any other Territory or State.

* * * * * * * * *

SEC. 6. *And be it further enacted*, [That] the legislative power of the Territory shall extend to all rightful subjects of legislation consistent with the Constitution of the United States and the provisions of this act; but no law shall be passed interfering with the primary disposal of the soil; no tax shall be imposed upon the property of the United States. * *

* * * * * * * * *

SEC. 14. *And be it further enacted*, That sections numbered sixteen and thirty-six in each township in said Territory shall be, and the same are hereby, reserved for the purpose of being applied to public shools in the State or States hereafter to be erected out of the same.

* * * * * * * * *

Approved, July 25, 1868.

No. 216 B.—An Act to create an additional land district in the State of Minnesota.*

Be it enacted by the Senate and House of Representatives of the United States of America in Congress assembled, That the President of the United States be, and he is hereby, authorized to establish an additional land district in the State of Minnesota, embracing all that part of the present northwestern land district which lies north of township number one hundred and twenty-four north, and west of range number thirty-five, west of the fifth principal meridian, and to fix, from time to time, the boundaries thereof, which district shall be named after the place at which the office shall first be established; and the President shall have power to fix, from time to time, the location of the office for such district.

SEC. 2. *And be it further enacted,* That the President is hereby authorized to appoint, by and with the advice and consent of the Senate, a register and receiver for said land district, who shall be required to reside at the site of the land office for said district, who shall be subject to the same laws and responsibilities, and whose compensation respectively shall be the same as that now allowed by law to other land officers in said State.

Approved, July 25, 1868.

No. 216½ B.—An Act to confirm the title to certain lands in the State of Nebraska.

Be it enacted by the Senate and House of Representatives of the United States of America in Congress assembled, That in alll cases in which the Commissioner of the General Land Office, or the Secretary of the Interior, has finally decided in favor of pre-emption settlers or the locators of Indian or half-breed scrip, and issued patents to them for lands within the corporate limits of the city of Omaha, in the State of Nebraska, the right and the title of the patentee or patentees shall not be defeated or impaired because such land was within the said corporate limits, but if good in every other respect the title shall be good and valid notwithstanding such lands may have been within the said corporate limits, and notwithstanding the entry thereof, by any pre-emptor, or locator of Indian or half-breed scrip, was forbidden by the tenth section of the act of September fourth, eighteen hundred and forty-one,† because so within said limits: *Provided,* That the following tracts of lands, to wit: the north half of the northwest quarter of section fifteen; the west half of the southwest quarter of section ten; the east half of the southeast quarter, and the northwest quarter of the southeast quarter of section nine; township fifteen north of range thirteen, east of the sixth principal meridian, are hereby excepted from the operation of this act.

Approved, July 25, 1868.

* Vol. I. No 48. See also No. 226 B.

† Amended, No. 237 B.

No. 217 B.—An Act to extend the time for the construction of the Southern Pacific Railroad in the State of California.*

Be it enacted by the Senate and House of Representatives of the United States of America in Congress assembled, That the Southern Pacific Railroad Company of the State of California shall, instead of the times now fixed by law for the construction of the first section of its road and telegraph line, have until the first day of July, eighteen hundred and seventy, for the construction of the first thirty miles, and they shall be required to construct at least twenty miles every year thereafter, and the whole line of their road within the time now provided by law.

Approved, July 25, 1868.

No. 218 B.—An Act making appropriations for the current and contingent expenses of the Indian Department, and for fulfilling treaty stipulations with various Indian tribes for the year ending thirtieth June, eighteen hundred and sixty-nine, and for other purposes.

* * * * * * * * *

SEC. 6. *And be it further enacted,* That the Mendocino Indian reservation in California be restored to the public lands of the United States, and the Secretary of the Interior shall cause the same to be surveyed and offered for sale in legal subdivisions, at not less than one dollar and twenty-five cents per acre: *Provided,* That any improvement of the United States on said reservation shall be appraised by the register and receiver of the land office of the district, and be paid for by the purchaser of the land on which they are located: *Provided further,* That all improvements made by any persons on said reservation before the passage of this act shall be the sole property of the person making them, who shall have priority of purchase of six hundred and forty acres of land covering and adjoining said improvements, and all said lands shall be sold and disposed of for money only.

Approved, July 27, 1868.

No. 219 B.—An Act to establish a new land district in the State of Nebraska.

Be it enacted by the Senate and House of Representatives of the United States of America in Congress assembled, That all that portion of the Omaha land district in the State of Nebraska included within the following limits, to wit: On the east by the line dividing ranges six and seven east; on the north by the line dividing townships twenty and twenty-one north; on the south by the south bank of the Platte River; and on the west by the west boundary of the State, shall constitute an additional land district, to be called the "Grand Island" District, the location of the office for which shall be designated by the President of the United States, and shall by him, from time to time, be changed as the public interest may seem to require.

* See No. 176 B. Section 18.

SEC. 2. *And be it further enacted,* That the President be, and is hereby, authorized to appoint, by and with the advice and consent of the Senate, a register and a receiver for said land district, who shall be required to reside at the site of their office, have the same powers, responsibilities, and emoluments, and be subject to the same acts and penalties which are or may be prescribed by law in relation to other land officers in said State.

SEC. 3. *And be it further enacted,* That the President is hereby authorized to cause the public lands in said district, with the exception of such as may have been or may be reserved for other purposes, to be exposed to sale in the same manner and upon the same terms and conditions as other public lands of the United States: *Provided,* That all sales and locations made at the office of the old district of lands situated within the limits of the new district which shall be valid and right in other respects, up to the day on which the new office shall go into operation, be, and the same are hereby, confirmed.

Approved, July 27, 1868.

No. 220 B.—An Act to protect the rights of actual settlers upon the public lands of the United States.

Be it enacted by the Senate and House of Representatives of the United States of America in Congress assembled, That in no case shall more than three sections of public lands of the United States be entered in any one township by scrip issued to any State under the act approved July second, eighteen hundred and sixty-two, for the establishment of an agricultural college therein.*

Approved, July 27, 1868.

No. 221 B.—An Act amendatory of an Act entitled "An act granting public lands to the State of Wisconsin, to aid in the construction of railroads in said State," approved June 3, 1856.†

Be it enacted by the Senate and House of Representatives of the United States of America in Congress assembled, That it shall and may be lawful for the Legislature of the State of Wisconsin to dispose of the lands granted and which may have enured and been certified to the State of Wisconsin under the act of Congress approved June third, eighteen hundred and fifty-six, to aid in the construction of a railroad "from Madison or Columbus, by way of Portage City to the Saint Croix River or lake, between township twenty-five and thirty-one," and commonly known as La Crosse and Milwaukee Railroad, for the benefit of the Wisconsin Railroad Farm Mortgage Land Company, existing under and by virtue of the laws of Wisconsin: *Provided, however,* That this act shall apply only to such lands as may be due the State of Wisconsin for the portion of said road already completed.

Approved, July 27, 1868.

* No. 47 B. † Vol. I. No. 292.

No. 221½ B.—An Act granting the right of way to certain railway companies over the military reservation at Fort Leavenworth.

Be it enacted by the Senate and House of Representatives of the United States of America in Congress assembled, That the right of way, not exceeding one hundred feet in width, is hereby granted to the Leavenworth and Des Moines Railway Company, a corporation created under the laws of the State of Missouri, to construct and operate a railway across the military reservation at Fort Leavenworth, on the east side of the Missouri River, upon a line to be designated and fixed by the Secretary of War.

SEC. 2. *And be it further enacted,* That the right of way, not exceeding one hundred feet in width, is hereby granted to the Leavenworth, Atchison and Northwestern Railway Company, a corporation created under the laws of the State of Kansas, to construct and operate a railroad across and over the military reservation at Fort Leavenworth, in the State of Kansas, upon such line as shall be designated and fixed by the Secretary of War: *Provided,* That if the said company shall not construct, within one year from the passage of this act, a railway from the city of Leavenworth to the city of Atchison, then, and in that case, a like privilege is hereby conferred upon any other company that shall construct a railway between said cities.

Approved, July 27, 1868.

No. 222 B.—An Act donating a portion of the Fort Leavenworth military reservation for the exclusive use of a public road.

Be it enacted by the Senate and House of Representatives of the United States of America in Congress assembled, That a strip of land one hundred feet in width along *along* the southern boundary of the Fort Leavenworth military reservation, in the State of Kansas, extending from the Missouri River to the western boundary thereof, be set apart for the perpetual and exclusive use of a public road; and the said road shall be and remain a public highway for the use of the Government of the United States, free from tolls or other charges upon the transportation of any property, troops, or mails of the United States.

SEC. 2. *And be it further enacted,* That Congress may at any time amend or repeal this act.

Approved, July 27, 1868.

No. 223 B.—Joint Resolution concerning certain lands granted to railroad companies in the States of Michigan and Wisconsin.

Be it resolved by the Senate and House of Representatives of the United States of America in Congress assembled, That a failure to grade twenty miles of the roads within two years from the passage of the act entitled "An act to extend the time for the completion of certain railroads to which land grants have been made in the States of Michigan and Wisconsin," approved on the third day of March, Anno Domini eighteen hundred and sixty-five,* and twenty miles additional thereof in each year thereafter, as required by said act, shall not cause any forfeiture or reversion to the United States of any lands granted to the said States, or either of them, to aid in the construction of the railroads described: *Provided*, That said companies, or either of them, shall fully complete their said railroads in the manner required by law on or before the thirty-first December, Anno Domini eighteen hundred and seventy-two, at which time a failure shall forfeit the lands to the United States: *Provided*, [That] the provisions of this section shall apply only to the chartered and projected line of railway from the city of Fond du Lac in the State of Wisconsin, northerly to Esconaba, in the State of Michigan, and the chartered and projected line of railway from Marquette, in the State of Michigan, westerly to Ontonagon, in the same State: *And provided further*, That if the said Marquette and Ontonagon Railroad Company, in the State of Michigan, shall not have completed according to law ten additional miles of their railroad, on or before the first day of January, A. D. eighteen hundred and sixty-nine, and shall not in like manner complete ten miles of said railroad in each and every year thereafter, then it shall be lawful for the Legislature of the said State of Michigan to declare the grant of lands to said company to be forfeited and to confer the said grant of lands upon some other company in the same manner as if the said grant was now for the first time made to the said State of Michigan.

SEC. 2. *And be it further resolved*, That the Commissioner of the General Land Office be, and he hereby is, authorized and directed to cause a patent in due form of law, to be issued to the Chicago and Northwestern Railway Company, in pursuance of a resolution passed by Congress granting the same to the State of Wisconsin, approved April twenty-five, Anno Domini eighteen hundred and sixty-two, and an act of the Legislature of Wisconsin, approved June sixteen, Anno Domini eighteen hundred and sixty-two, granting the same to said company for eighty acres of land of the Fort Howard military reserve, as the same was surveyed and approved by said commissioner on the eleventh June, Anno Domini eighteen hundred and sixty-four.

Approved, May 20, 1868.

No. 224 B.—Joint Resolution extending the time for the completion of the Northern Pacific Railroad.†

Be it resolved by the Senate and House of Representatives of the United States of America in Congress assembled, That section eight of an act entitled "An act granting lands to aid in the construction of a railroad and telegraph line from Lake Superior to Puget Sound, on the Pacific coast," is hereby so amended as to read as follows: That each and every grant, right, and privilege herein, are so made and given to and accepted by said Northern Pacific Railroad Company upon and subject to the following conditions, namely: That the said company shall commence the work on said road within two years from and after the second day of July, eighteen hundred and sixty-eight, and shall complete not less than

* No. 128 B.

† See No. 112 B, and 182 B.

one hundred miles per year after the second year thereafter, and shall construct, equip, furnish, and complete the whole road by the fourth day of July, Anno Domini eighteen hundred and seventy-seven.

Approved, July 1, 1868.

No. 225 B.—Joint Resolution to extend the time for the completion of the West Wisconsin Railroad.

Be it resolved by the Senate and House of Representatives of the United States of America in Congress assembled, That the time fixed and limited by an act entitled "An act granting lands to aid in the construction of certain railroads in the State of Wisconsin," approved May five, eighteen hundred and sixty-four;* for the completion of the railroad from Tomah, in the county of Monroe, to Saint Croix River or lake, between townships twenty-five and thirty-one, be, and the same is hereby, further extended for a period of three years to the West Wisconsin Railroad Company, a corporation established by the laws of the State of Wisconsin, and which, by the law of said State, is entitled to the land grant made in the second section of said act: *Provided,* That if said railway company shall not have completed said railroad from Tomah to Black River Falls on or before the expiration of one year from the passage of this resolution, this act shall be null and void.

Approved, July 13, 1868.

No. 226 B.—An Act supplementary to an act entitled "An act to confirm the titles to certain lands in the State of Nebraska."†

Be it enacted by the Senate and House of Representatives of the United States of America in Congress assembled, That the provisions and benefits of an act entitled "Act to confirm the titles to certain lands in the State of Nebraska," approved the twenty-fifth day of July, anno Domini eighteen hundred and sixty-eight, be, and the same are hereby, extended to the east half and northwest quarter of the southeast quarter of section nine, township fifteen, range thirteen east, sixth principal meridian, in Douglas County, Nebraska, and that the title to the same is hereby confirmed to the parties holding by deed from the patentee.

Approved, February 2, 1869.

No. 227 B.—An Act to amend "An act to confirm certain private land claims in the Territory of New Mexico."‡

Be it enacted by the Senate and House of Representatives of the United States of America in Congress assembled, That the exterior lines of the Cornelio Vigil and Cram St. Vrain claims of eleven leagues each, subject to claims derived from said parties as confirmed by the act of

* See No. 83 B. † No. 216 B. ‡ No. 16 B.

Congress approved twenty-first June, eighteen hundred and sixty, United States Statutes, volume twelve, page seventy-one, shall be adjusted according to the lines of public surveys, as nearly as practicable, with the limits of said claims, yet in as compact a form as possible; and the claims of all actual settlers upon the tracts heretofore claimed by the said Vigil and St. Vrain, holding possession under titles or promises to settle, which have been made by said Vigil and St. Vrain or their legal representatives prior to the passage of this act, who may establish their claims within one year from the passage of this act, to the satisfaction of the register and receiver of the proper land district, shall in like manner be adjusted according to the subdivisional lines of survey, so as to include the lands so settled upon or purchased, and the areas of the same shall be deducted and excluded from the adjusted limits of the claims of said Vigil and St. Vrain respectively; and the claims of all other actual settlers falling within the limits of the located claims of Vigil and St. Vrain shall be adjusted to the extent which shall embrace their several settlements upon their several claims being established either as pre-emption or homesteads, according to law; and for the aggregate of the areas of the latter class of claims the said Vigil and St. Vrain, or their legal representatives, shall be entitled to locate a like quantity of public lands, not mineral, according to the lines of the public surveys, and not to exceed one hundred and sixty acres in one section.

SEC. 2. *And be it further enacted,* That it shall be the duty of the General Land Office to cause the lines of the public surveys to be run in the regions where a proper location would place the said Vigil and St. Vrain claims, and that the expense of the same shall be paid out of any moneys in the treasury not otherwise appropriated; yet, before the confirmation of the said act of June twenty-first, eighteen hundred and sixty, shall become legally effective, the said Vigil and St. Vrain, or their legal representatives, shall pay the cost of so much of said surveys as enures to their benefit respectively, and that all settlers of the said third-class, whose claims may be adjusted as valid, shall have the right to enter their improvements by a strict compliance with the pre-emption or homestead laws.

SEC. 3. *And be it further enacted,* That upon the adjustment of the Vigil and St. Vrain claims according to the provisions of this act, it shall be the duty of the Surveyor-General of the district to furnish proper approved plats to said claimants, or their legal representatives, and so in like manner to said derivative claimants, which shall be evidence of title, the same to be done according to such instructions as may be given by the Commissioner of the General Land Office.

SEC. 4. *And be it further enacted,* That immediately upon running the lines as provided in section second of this act, the Surveyor-General of said district shall notify the said Vigil and St. Vrain, or their agents or legal representatives, of the fact of such survey being made, and said claimants shall, within three months after notice of such survey, select and locate their said claims in accordance with such survey and the provisions of this act and of the act to which this is amendatory, so far as the same is not changed by this act, and shall within the said time furnish the Surveyor-General with the description of such location, specifying the lines of the same. And the party failing to make such selection and location, in such manner and within such time, shall be deemed and held to have abandoned their claim, and their rights and equities under this act, and the act to which this is amendatory, shall cease and terminate.

SEC. 5. *And be it further enacted,* That in case of the neglect or refusal of the said Vigil and St. Vrain, or either of them, to accept of the provisions of this act, and the act to which this is amendatory, and to locate their said claims, as provided therein, no suit shall be brought or proceedings instituted in any of the courts of the United States, by such party or by any one claiming through or under them, to establish or enforce said claims, or for any cause of action founded upon the same, after six months from the passage of this act.

Approved, February 25, 1869.

No. 228 B.—An Act granting a portion of the military reservation of Sault Ste. Marie, Michigan, to the American Baptist Home Mission Society.

Be it enacted by the Senate and House of Representatives of the United States of America in Congress assembled, That the Secretary of War is hereby authorized to convey to the American Baptist Home Mission Society, by good and sufficient title, a portion of the military reservation at Sault Ste. Marie, in the State of Michigan, not to exceed one acre, now occupied by a mission building owned by said society.

Approved, March 1, 1869.

No. 229 B.—An Act to authorize the county commissioners of Ada County, Idaho, to select a site for a territorial prison.

Be it enacted by the Senate and House of Representatives of the United States of America in Congress assembled, That the county commissioners of the county of Ada, in the Territory of Idaho, be, and they are hereby, authorized, under direction of the Secretary of the Interior, to select a site upon which to erect a territorial prison for said Territory.

Approved, March 1, 1869.

No. 230 B.—An Act making appropriations for sundry civil expenses of the Government for the year ending June thirtieth, eighteen hundred and seventy, and for other purposes.*

* * * * * * * * *

For surveying the public lands in Minnesota, at rates not exceeding ten dollars per lineal mile for standard lines, seven dollars for township, and six dollars for section lines, twenty thousand dollars; and such construction shall be given to the joint resolution number thirty, approved twenty-fifth April, eighteen hundred and sixty-two, as shall not abridge the grant under the act of June third, eighteen hundred and fifty-six, for a railroad from Fon du Lac northerly to the State line, and the Chicago and Northwestern Railroad Company may select their lands along the full extent of the original route of said road as filed under the said act.

* * * * * * * * *

* See Vol. I. No. 292, and No. 58 B.; also No. 66 B.

For surveying the public lands in Oregon, at rates not exceeding fifteen dollars per lineal mile for standard lines, twelve dollars for township, and ten dollars for section lines, forty thousand dollars: *Provided*, That the Commissioner of the General Land Office, in his discretion, may authorize public lands in said State densely covered with forests or thick undergrowth to be surveyed at augmented rates, not exceeding eighteen dollars per mile for standard parallels, fifteen dollars for township, and twelve dollars for section lines.

* * * * * * * * *

Approved, March 3, 1869.

No. 231 B.—An Act to authorize the transfer of lands granted to the Union Pacific Railway Company, eastern division, between Denver and the point of its connection with the Union Pacific Railroad, to the Denver Pacific Railway and Telegraph Company, and to expedite the completion of railroads to Denver, in the Territory of Colorado.*

Be it enacted by the Senate and House of Representatives of the United States of America in Congress assembled, That the Union Pacific Railway Company, eastern division, be, and it hereby is, authorized to contract with the Denver Pacific Railway and Telegraph Company, a corporation existing under the laws of the Territory of Colorado, for the construction, operation, and maintenance of that part of its line of railroad and telegraph between Denver City and its point of connection with the Union Pacific Railroad, which point shall be at Cheyenne, and to adopt the road bed already graded by said Denver Pacific Railway and Telegraph Company as said line, and to grant to said Denver Pacific Railway and Telegraph Company the perpetual use of its right of way and depot grounds, and to transfer to it all the rights and privileges, subject to all the obligations pertaining to said part of its line.

SEC. 2. *And be it further enacted,* That the said Union Pacific Railway Company, eastern division, shall extend its railroad and telegraph to a connection at the city of Denver, so as to form with that part of its line herein authorized to be constructed, operated, and maintained by the Denver Pacific Railway and Telegraph Company, a continuous line of railroad and telegraph from Kansas City, by way of Denver, to Cheyenne. And all the provisions of law for the operation of the Union Pacific Railroad, its branches and connections, as a continuous line, without discrimination, shall apply the same as if the road from Denver to Cheyenne had been constructed by the said Union Pacific Railway Company, eastern division; but nothing herein shall authorize the said eastern division company to operate the road or fix the rates of tariff for the Denver Pacific Railway and Telegraph Company.

SEC. 3. *And be it further enacted,* That said companies are hereby authorized to mortgage their respective portions of said road, as herein defined, for an amount not exceeding thirty-two thousand dollars per mile, to enable them respectively to borrow money to construct the same; and that each of said companies shall receive patents to the alternate sections of land along their respective lines of road, as herein defined, in like manner and within the same limits as is provided by law in the case

* See No. 89 B. and No. 150 B.

of lands granted to the Union Pacific Railway Company, eastern division: *Provided*, That neither of the companies hereinbefore mentioned shall be entitled to subsidy in United States bonds under the provisions of this act.

Approved, March 3, 1869.

No. 232 B.—An Act granting the right of way to the Walla-Walla and Columbia River Railroad Company, and for other purposes.

Be it enacted by the Senate and House of Representatives of the United States of America in Congress assembled, That the right of way through the public lands be, and the same is hereby, granted to the Walla-Walla and Columbia River Railroad Company, a corporation existing under the laws of the Territory of Washington, and duly incorporated for the purpose of constructing a railroad from said town of Walla-Walla to some eligible point on the navigable waters of said Columbia River, in said Territory; said right of way hereby granted to said railroad is to the extent of one hundred feet in width on each side of said road, where it may pass over the public lands; also, all necessary ground, not to exceed five acres at each station, for station buildings, workshops, depots, machine-shops, switches, side-tracks, turn-tables, and water-stations.

SEC. 2. *And be it further enacted*, That the county commissioners of the county of Walla-Walla, in the Territory of Washington, be, and they are hereby, authorized and empowered to aid in the construction of the Walla-Walla and Columbia River Railroad by subscribing to the capital stock of said Walla-Walla and Columbia River Railroad Company in the name and on behalf of said county of Walla-Walla, and by issuing bonds of said county, payable at such time as said commissioners shall think proper, and bearing interest of not more than eight per cent. per annum, in payment for said stock so by them taken in said railroad company, or by issuing bonds, bearing interest as aforesaid, as a loan to said company, to be used in the construction of said road, or to aid said company in the construction of said road by the credit of said county in any other manner the said commissioners may think proper: *Provided*, That the said subscription, loan, or other aid so given by said commissioners to said company shall in no case exceed the sum of three hundred thousand dollars: *And provided further*, That the said subscription, loan, or other aid, shall have been submitted to the people of said county and been voted for by three-fourths of the legal vote cast at an election held for that purpose: *And provided further*, That if said vote be taken at a special election, the notice shall be the same as provided by the laws of said Territory for general elections.

SEC. 3. *And be it further enacted*, That the county commissioners of the county of Walla-Walla, in the Territory of Washington, be, and they are hereby, authorized and empowered to hold a special election, at such times as they may designate, after twenty days' public notice, which said election shall be governed by the general laws of the Territory upon the subject of elections, at which election the aid to be given by said county to said Walla-Walla and Columbia River Railroad Company, either by subscriptions to stock or otherwise, shall be submitted to and be voted upon by the legal voters of said county in such manner as said commissioners may designate: *Provided*, That this grant is made upon the express condition that any effort by said company hereafter to obtain any land grant, subsidy, or pecuniary aid from the United States Government shall work a forfeiture of this grant.

Approved, March 3, 1869.

No. 233 B.—An Act explanatory of the act entitled "An act declaring the title to land warrants in certain cases."*

Be it enacted by the Senate and House of Representatives of the United States of America in Congress assembled, That the act entitled "An act declaring the title to land warrants in certain cases," approved June third, eighteen hundred and fifty-eight, be so construed and applied as to authorize the legal representatives of deceased claimants whose claims were filed prior to their decease to file the proof necessary to perfect the same.

Approved, March 3, 1869.

No. 234 B.—An Act to amend an act entitled "An act granting lands to the State of Oregon to aid in the construction of a military road from Eugene City to the eastern boundary of said State."†

Whereas by an act granting lands to the State of Oregon to aid in the construction of a military road from Eugene City to the eastern boundary of said State, approved July second, eighteen hundred and sixty-four, *and whereas* the time designated for the completion of said road expires on the second day of July, eighteen hundred and sixty-nine: Therefore,

Be it enacted by the Senate and House of Representatives of the United States of America in Congress assembled, That the time for the completion of said road be, and hereby is, extended to the second day of July, eighteen hundred and seventy-two.

Approved, March 3, 1869.

No. 235 B.—An Act granting lands to the State of Oregon to aid in the construction of a military wagon road from the navigable waters of Coos Bay to Roseburg in said State.

Be it enacted by the Senate and House of Representatives of the United States of America in Congress assembled, That there be, and hereby is, granted to the State of Oregon, to aid in the construction of a military wagon road from the navigable waters of Coos Bay to Roseburg, alternate sections of public lands, designated by odd numbers, to the extent of three sections in width on each side of said road: *Provided*, That the lands hereby granted shall be exclusively applied to the construction of said road and to no other purpose, and shall be disposed of only as the

* Vol. I. No. 335.

† No. 110 B. See also No. 186 B.

work progresses: *Provided further*, That the grant of lands hereby made shall be upon the condition that the lands shall be sold to any one person only in quantities not greater than one quarter section, and for a price not exceeding two dollars and fifty cents per acre: *And provided further*, That any and all lands heretofore reserved to the United States, or otherwise appropriated by act of Congress or other competent authority, be, and the same are hereby, reserved from the operation of this act, except so far as it may be necessary to locate the route of said road through the same, in which case the right of way to the width of one hundred feet is granted: *And provided further*, That the grant hereby made shall not embrace any mineral lands of the United States, or any lands to which homestead or pre-emption rights have attached.

SEC. 2. *And be it further enacted*, That the lands hereby granted to said State shall be disposed of by the legislature thereof for the purpose aforesaid, and for no other; and the said road shall be and remain a public highway for the use of the Government of the United States, free from tolls or other charges upon the transportation of any property, troops, or mails of the United States.

SEC. 3. *And be it further enacted*, That said road shall be constructed with such width, graduation, and bridge as to permit of its regular use as a wagon road, and in such other special manner as the State of Oregon may prescribe.

SEC. 4. *And be it further enacted*, That the State of Oregon is authorized to locate and use in the construction of said road an additional amount of public lands, not previously reserved to the United States nor otherwise disposed of, and not exceeding six miles in distance from it, equal to the amount reserved from the operation of this act in the first section of the same, to be selected in alternate odd sections, as provided in section first of this act.

SEC. 5. *And be it further enacted*, That lands hereby granted to said State shall be disposed of only in the following manner, that is to say, when the Governor of said State shall certify to the Secretary of the Interior that ten continuous miles of said road are completed, then a quantity of the land hereby granted, not to exceed thirty sections, may be sold, and so on from time to time, until said road shall be completed; and if said road is not completed within five years no further sales shall be made, and the lands remaining unsold shall revert to the United States: *Provided, however*, That the entire amount of public land granted by this act shall not exceed three sections per mile for each mile actually constructed.

SEC. 6. *And be it further enacted*, That the United States Surveyor-General for the district of Oregon, shall cause said lands, so granted, to be surveyed at the earliest practicable period after said State shall have enacted the necessary legislation to carry this act into effect.

Approved, March 3, 1869.

No. 236 B.—An Act to confirm certain private land claims in the Territory of New Mexico.

Be it enacted by the Senate and House of Representatives of the United States of America in Congress assembled, That private land claims numbered forty-one, forty-two, forty-four, forty-six, and forty-seven, Territory of New Mexico, as known and designated by the numbers aforesaid in the reports of the Surveyor-General of the said Territory and on the books of the Commissioner of the General Land Office, be, and the same are hereby, confirmed: *Provided,* That such confirmation shall only be construed as a quit-claim or relinquishment of all title or claim on the part of the United States to any of the lands not improved by or on behalf of the United States, and not including any military or other reservation embraced in either of the said claims, and shall not affect the adverse rights of any person or persons to the same, or any part or parcel thereof.

SEC. 2. *And be it further enacted,* That the Commissioner of the General Land Office shall, without unreasonable delay, cause the lands embraced in said several claims to be surveyed and platted, at the proper expense of the claimants thereof, and upon the filing of said surveys and plats in his office he shall issue patents for said lands in said Territory which have heretofore been confirmed by acts of Congress and surveyed, and plats of such survey filed in his office as aforesaid, but for which no patents have heretofore been issued.

SEC. 3. *And be it further enacted,* That all surveys authorized by this act shall conform to and be connected with the public surveys of the United States in said Territories, so far as the same can be done consistently with the landmarks and boundaries specified in the several grants upon which said claims are founded: *Provided, however,* That when said lands are so confirmed, surveyed, and patented, they shall in each case be held and taken to be in full satisfaction of all further claims or demands against the United States.

Approved, March 3, 1869.

No. 237 B.—Joint Resolution explanatory of the act to create an additional land office in the State of Minnesota, approved July twenty-fifth, eighteen hundred and sixty-eight.*

Be it resolved by the Senate and House of Representatives of the United States of America in Congress assembled, That the limits of the land district as designated in the act entitled "An act to create an additional land district in the State of Minnesota," approved July twenty-fifth, eighteen hundred and sixty-eight, to wit: "all that part of the northwestern land district which lies north of township number one hundred and twenty-four north and west of range number thirty-five west of the fifth principal meridian," shall be construed to embrace all the lands north of township one hundred and twenty-four and west of said range thirty-five.

Approved, January 14, 1869.

No. 238 B.—A Resolution requiring the Commissioner of the General Land Office to transfer certain money.

Resolved by the Senate and House of Representatives of the United States of America in Congress assembled, That the Commissioner of the General Land Office be, and he is hereby, authorized to transfer to the Treasury

* No. 216 B.

Department the twenty-five hundred dollars appropriated "for collecting statistics of mines and mining," by act of Congress approved July twenty, eighteen hundred and sixty-eight, and that the Secretary of the Treasury be required to disburse the same as provided for in said act.

Approved, March 3, 1869.

No. 239 B.—A Resolution extending the time for the completion of the first twenty miles of the Cairo and Fulton Railroad.

Resolved by the Senate and House of Representatives of the United States of America in Congress assembled, That in case the Cairo and Fulton Railroad Company shall complete the first section of twenty miles of said road by the twenty-eighth day of April, eighteen hundred and seventy, and the Secretary of the Interior shall be satisfied of such completion, then the said company shall be entitled to its lands in all respects and to the same extent as it would have been had said twenty miles been completed by the twenty-eighth of July, eighteen hundred and sixty-nine, as provided by law relating to said railroad company approved July twenty-eighth, eighteen hundred and sixty-six.

Approved, March 3, 1869.

PART FOURTH.

TITLE I.

Disposal of Public Lands.

No. 240 B.

Circular No. 26.

From the General Land Office, showing the manner of proceeding to obtain title to public lands, by purchase, by location with warrants or agricultural college scrip, by pre-emption and homestead, issued March 10, 1869.

DEPARTMENT OF THE INTERIOR,
GENERAL LAND OFFICE,
Washington, D. C., March 10, 1869.

The following is communicated in reference to the manner of acquiring title to the public lands under different laws of Congress.

There are two classes of public lands, the one class at $1.25 per acre, which is designated as *minimum*, and the other at $2.50 per acre, or *double minimum*.

Grants of public lands.

The provision in the acts of Congress establishing territorial governments respectively for Oregon and Washington Territories, confirmed the title of the St. James Mission to the lands occupied by it in those territories, at the date of either of the acts.—(Opinion of Attorney-General, vol. 9, p. 339.)

The subsequent declaration of a military reserve, embracing the buildings and enclosed grounds of the mission, could not divest the right thus perfected.—*Ibid.*

When the United States, by a legislative grant, gives land for public purposes, all the title which the United States had at the time of the grant, or may afterwards acquire, vests in the grantee, unless the grantee has done something in the mean time which estops him from claiming.—(Opinion of Attorney-General, vol. 9, p. 346.)

A State to which land is granted by act of Congress cannot accept the benefits of the grant and repudiate its restrictions.—*Ibid.*

Where there is a conflict between the titles derived from the same source, either of which would be good if the other were out of the way, the elder must prevail.—(Opinion of Attorney-General, vol. 9, p. 253.)

A grant by Congress does of itself, *proprio vigore*, pass to the grantee all the estate of the United States except what is expressly excepted.—*Ibid.*

Under the act of 28th September, 1850, granting to the State of Arkansas all the swamp lands within her limits, the title vested in the State before a patent issued.—*Ibid.*

Title may be acquired by purchase at public sale, or by ordinary "private entry," and in virtue of the pre-emption and homestead laws.

1. At public sale where lands are "offered" at public auction to the highest bidder, either pursuant to proclamation by the President, or public notice given in accordance with directions from the General Land Office.

BY "PRIVATE ENTRY" OR LOCATION.

2. The lands of this class liable to disposal are those which have been offered at public sale, and thereafter remain unsold, and which have not

---

The general description of all swamp lands within the limits of the State, was certain and definite enough for purposes of notice.—*Ibid.*

Where Congress after the grant of September 28, 1850, made another grant to the State of Arkansas, to aid in the construction of a railroad, under which a part of the lands previously granted under the denomination of swamp lands was included, it was *held* that the State took the lands under the first grant.—*Ibid.*

A grant of public land by statute is the highest and strongest form of title known to our law. It is stronger than a patent, which may be annulled by the judiciary upon a proper case shown; whereas even Congress cannot repeal a statutory grant. —(Opinion of Attorney-General, vol. 11, p. 47.)

The government, like an individual has no power to withdraw or annul its grant of land. The first lawful grant must stand; and the second cannot operate as a conveyance, for the reason that the grantor, when he made it, had no estate to convey.—*Ibid.*

The State of Iowa is entitled to the purchase money of swamp lands within her limits, which were entered with cash, prior to the act of 3d March, 1857, and to indemnity in land for such swamp lands as were located with warrant or scrip prior to the passage of that act.—(Opinion of the Attorney-General, vol. 11, p. 467.)

Supervisory powers of the Commissioner and Secretary.

Surveys under confirmations of Spanish titles in the upper Louisiana country are, in regard to their correctness, within the jurisdiction of the Commissioner of the General Land Office, and that officer has power to adjudge the question of accuracy preliminary to the issuing of a patent.—*Maguire* v. *Tyler et al.*, 1 Black, p. 195.

The Secretary of the Interior has the power of supervision and appeal in all matters relating to the General Land Office, and that power is co-extensive with the authority of the commissioner to adjudge.—*Ibid.*

The act of the Secretary of the Interior, and Commissioner of the Land Office, in cancelling an entry for land, is not a ministerial duty, but is a matter resting in the judgment and discretion of those officers as representing the Executive Department. Accordingly, the Supreme Court will not interfere by injunction, more than by mandamus to control it.—*Gaines* v. *Thompson*, 7 Wallace, p. 347.

Land entries, and decisions of registers and receivers thereon.

A fraudulent entry of public land allowed by a register and receiver, upon false proof of settlement, occupancy and housekeeping, may be set aside and vacated by the Commissioner of the General Land Office.—*Harkness and Wife* v. *Underhill*, 1 Black, p. 316.

A contract between two persons, neither of them being settlers or housekeepers, that one of them shall enter land for the benefit of both under the pre-emption laws, is a combination to defraud the government, contrary to public policy, illegal, and void.—*Ibid.*

Such a contract will not operate by way of estoppel to prevent one of the parties from setting up a good legal title subsequently acquired, against the fraudulent title obtained by the other in accordance with the contract.—*Ibid.*

In the State Courts of Missouri, when a suit at law is brought by a patentee, the defendant may set up his prior equitable title as a bar.—*O'Brien* v. *Perry*, 1 Black, p. 132.

been subsequently reserved or otherwise withdrawn from market. In this class of offered and unreserved public lands the following steps may be taken to acquire title.

CASH PURCHASES.

3. The applicant must present a written application to the register for the district in which the land desired is situated, describing the tract he wishes to purchase, giving its area. Thereupon the register, if the tract is vacant, will so certify to the receiver, stating the price, and the applicant must then pay the amount of the purchase money.

The receiver will then issue to the purchaser a duplicate receipt, and

---

The decisions of the register and receiver of lands for the Territory of Minnesota, are not of conclusive efficacy. They may be inquired into and declared inoperative by the courts.—*State of Minnesota* v. *Bachelder*, 1 Wallace, p. 109.

The court will inquire into the facts of a disputed entry of public land, and set aside or correct the decision of a register or receiver, or the Commissioner of the General Land Office, as equity may require.—*Lindsey* v. *Haines*, 2 Black, p. 554.

Where a party takes up and resides upon a tract of land within a quarter section, whose limits have been fixed by an authorized government survey, pays for it, and receives his patent certificate from the proper officers, and by a subsequent survey it is found that the house of the pre-emption is not within the tract for which he has paid, the Commissioner of the Land Office cannot, for this reason, set aside the sale. —*Ibid.*

In such a case the government is bound by the original survey.—*Ibid.*

Where the house of a pre-emptor is built on the line dividing two quarter sections, his residence in it avails as the foundation of a pre-emption right in either.—*Ibid.*

Receivers of public moneys.
A receiver of public moneys is not entitled to an allowance for extra clerk hire, under the act of August 18, 1856, in the absence of an appropriation from which it can be paid.—(Opinion of Attorney-General, vol. 10, p. 456.)

A receiver is entitled to mileage for transporting money to a place of deposit, even. if the journey be made by his agent and not by himself.—*Ibid.*

Fees of registers.
The register of a land office is not entitled to retain a larger sum than three thousand dollars, as commissions for locating military bounty land warrants, under the acts of February 11, 1847, September 25, 1850, March 22, 1852, and March 3, 1855. —*United States* v. *Babbit*, 1 Black, U. S. Reports, p. 55.

All fees received by a register, whether for locating military bounty land warrants, or for other services, in excess of the maximum fixed by law, must be paid into the treasury.—*Ibid.*

Land patents, &c.
The right to a patent once vested is equivalent, as respects the government dealing with the public lands, to a patent issued; and when issued, it relates so far as may be necessary to cut off intervening claimants, to the inception of the right of the patentee.—*Stark* v. *Starrs*, 6 Wallace, p. 402.

Patents by the United States for lands which it has previously granted, reserved from sale, or appropriated, are void.—*Reichart* v. *Phelps*, 6 Wallace, p. 160.

A patent or instrument of confirmation, by an officer authorized by Congress to make it, followed by a survey of the land described in the instrument, is conclusive evidence that the land described and surveyed was reserved from sale.—*Ibid.*

The fourth section of the act of Congress of 27th September, 1850, donating lands in Oregon, embraced within the term *single man* an unmarried woman.—*Silver* v. *Ladd*, 7 Wallace, p. 219.

Residence in a house, divided by a quarter section line, enables the occupant to claim either quarter in which he may have made the necessary cultivation.—*Ibid.*

at the close of the month the register and receiver will make returns of the sale to the General Land Office, from whence, when the proceedings are found regular, a patent or complete title will be issued ; and on surrender of the duplicate receipt such patent will be delivered, at the option of the patentee, either by the commissioner at Washington, or by the register at the district land office.

LOCATIONS WITH WARRANTS.

4. Application must be made as in cash cases, but must be accompanied by a warrant duly assigned as the consideration for the land ; yet where the tract is $2.50 per acre, the party, in addition to the surrendered warrant, must pay in *cash* $1.25 per acre, as the warrant is in satisfaction of only so many acres at $1.25 per acre as are contained in the tract located.

A duplicate certificate of location will then be furnished the party, to be held until the patent is delivered, as in cases of cash sales.

The following fees are chargeable by the land officers, and the several amounts must be *paid at the time of location* :—

Military reservations.
The reservation of Rock Island for military purposes, derives its validity not alone from the act of selection performed by the President, but primarily from the statute of June 14, 1809.—(Opinion of Attorney-General, vol. 10, p. 359.)

It was not in the power of the President to relinquish that reservation, and thus throw the island back into the general body of the public lands, without the consent of Congress.—*Ibid.*

An act of Congress repealing all laws authorizing the sale of military sites which are or may become useless for military purposes, did not repeal an act granting to a railroad company the right of way over the military reserve at Fort Gratiot.—(Opinion of the Attorney-General, vol. 9, p. 282.)

Bounty lands.
Under the act of 28th September, 1850, the right of the claimant will not be defeated by his or her majority before the case is finally disposed of.—(Opinion of the Attorney General, vol. 9, p. 427.)

The act does not vest the right to the warrant for bounty land in the child of a minor, before his or her claim is filed.—*Ibid.*

Minor children born after the date of the act are included within its provisions.—*Ibid.*

Taxes.
Lands originally public are liable to taxation after they have been entered at the land office, and a certificate of entry has been obtained ; and if the taxes remain unpaid, they may be sold like other lands, even though no patent may, as yet, have issued.—*Witherspoon* v. *Duncan*, 4 Wallace, p. 210.

The right to tax attaches as well to donation entries as to cash entries.—*Ibid.*

School reservations.
Neither the act of Congress of 3d March, 1849—the organic law of the Territory of Minnesota, which declared that when the public lands in that Territory shall be surveyed, certain sections, designated by numbers, shall be and "hereby *are*," "*reserved* for the purpose of being applied to schools"—nor the subsequent act of February 26, 1857, providing for the admission of that Territory into the Union—and making the same reservation for the same object—amounts so completely to a "dedication," in the stricter legal sense of that word, of these sections, to school purposes, that Congress, with the assent of the Territorial Legislature, could not bring them within the terms of the pre-emption act of 1841, and give them to settlers who, on the faith of that act, which had been extended in 1854 to this Territory, had settled on and improved them.—*State of Minnesota* v. *Bachelder*, 1 Wallace, p. 109.

For a 40-acre warrant,	50 cents each	to the	Register and	Receiver—	Total,	$1.00.
For a 60-acre warrant,	75 cents	" "	"	"	"	$1.50.
For an 80-acre warrant,	$1.00	" "	"	"	"	$2.00.
For a 120-acre warrant,	$1.50	" "	"	"	"	$3.00.
For a 160-acre warrant,	$2.00	" "	"	"	"	$4.00.

AGRICULTURAL COLLEGE SCRIP.

5. This scrip is applicable to lands *not mineral*, which may be subject to private entry at $1.25 per acre, yet is restricted to a technical "*quarter section*;" that is, lands embraced by the quarter section lines indicated on the official plats of survey, or it may be located on a *part* of a "quarter-section," where such part is taken as in full for a quarter, but it cannot be applied to different subdivisions to make an area equivalent to a quarter section. The manner of proceeding to acquire title with this class of paper is the same as in cash and warrant cases, the fees to be paid being the same as on warrants. The location of this scrip is restricted to three sections in each township of land.

PRE-EMPTIONS TO THE EXTENT OF ONE QUARTER SECTION, OR ONE HUNDRED AND SIXTY ACRES.

6. These may be made under the general pre-emption laws of 4th September, 1841 [U. S. Statutes, vol. 5, page 455], (see vol. 1, No. 48), 3d March, 1843 [vol. 5, page 610] (see vol. 1, No. 72), upon "offered" and "unoffered" land, and in certain States and Territories west of the Mississippi, including that part of Minnesota east of the river, may have legal inception by actual settlement upon *unsurveyed* land, although in such cases no definitive proceedings can be had as to the completion of title until after the surveys are officially returned to the district land office.

7. The act of 3d March, 1853 (vol. 1, No 222), extends the pre-emption for one quarter, or 160 acres, at $2.50 per acre to every "*alternate*" United States or *reserved* section along the line of railroads.

8. The act of 27th March, 1854 (vol. 1, No. 264), protects the right of settlers on sections along the line of railroads, where settlement existed prior to withdrawal, and in such cases allows the tract to be taken by pre-emptors at $1.25 per acre. Copies of these laws, marked A, B, C, and D, will be found herewith.

9. Where the tract is "*offered*," the party must file with the district land office his declaratory statement as to the fact of his settlement within thirty days from the date of said sttlement, and, within one year from that date, must appear before the Register and Receiver and make proof of his actual residence on and cultivation of the tract, and secure the same by paying *cash*, or by filing warrant duly assigned to the pre-emptor.

10. Where the tract has been surveyed and *not* offered at public sale, the claimant must file within three months from the date of settlement, and make proof and payment before the day designated in President's proclamation for offering the lands at public sale.

11. Should the settler in either of the aforesaid cases die before establishing his claim within the period limited by law, the title may be perfected by the executor, administrator, or one of the heirs, by making the requisite proof of settlement and paying for the land; the entry to be made in the name of "the heirs" of the deceased settler, and the patent will be issued accordingly.

12. In those States and Territories in which settlements are authorized by law on *unsurveyed* land, the claimant must file notice of settlement within three months after the receipt of the township plat of survey at the

district land office, and make proof and payment as required under 10th head in the foregoing.

The act of June 2, 1862, vol. 12, page 413, in relation to *Colorado*, contains special provisions in this respect. (See No. 41 B.)

LAWS EXTENDING THE HOMESTEAD PRIVILEGE.

13. The original homestead act of May 20, 1862 (No. 38 B), gives to every citizen, and to those who had declared their intentions to become such, the right to a homestead on *surveyed* lands. This is conceded to the extent of one quarter section, or 160 acres, at $1.25 per acre, or 80 acres of double minimum in any *organized district* embracing *surveyed* public lands.

14. To obtain homesteads the party must, in connection with his application, make an affidavit before the Register or Receiver that he is over the age of twenty-one, or the head of a family; that he is a citizen of the United States, or has declared his intention to become such, and that the entry is made for his exclusive use and benefit and for actual settlement and cultivation.

15. Where the applicant is prevented by reason of bodily infirmity, distance, or other good cause, from personal attendance at the district land office, the affidavit may be made before the clerk of the court for the county within which the party is an actual resident.

16. The amendatory act of 21st March, 1864 (No. 76 B), U. S. Statutes, Vol. 13, page 35, relaxes the requirements of personal attendance at the district office to persons in the military or naval service, where the party's family, or some member, *is residing on the land* that it is desired to enter, and upon which a bona fide improvement and cultivation had been made. In such cases the said act of 1864 allows the beneficiary to make the affidavit before the officer commanding in the branch of service in which he may be engaged, and the same may be filed, by the wife or other representative of the absentee, with the register, together with the homestead application.

His claim in that case will become effective from the date of filing, provided the required fee and commissions accompany the same; but immediately upon his discharge he must enter upon the land and make it his bona fide home, as required by the original act of 20th May, 1862.

17. For homestead entries on *surveyed* lands in Michigan, Wisconsin, Iowa, Missouri, Minnesota, Kansas, Nebraska, Dakota, Alabama, Mississippi, Louisiana, Arkansas, and Florida, fees are to be paid according to the following table :—

Acres.	Price per Acre.	Commissions.		Fees.	Total Fees and Commissions.
		Payable *when entry is made.*	Payable when *certificate* issues.	Payable when entry is made.	
160	$1.25	$4.00	$4.00	$10.00	$18.00
80	1.25	2.00	2.00	5.00	9.00
40	1.25	1.00	1.00	5.00	7.00
80	2.50	4.00	4.00	10.00	18.00
40	2.50	2.00	2.00	5.00	9.00

These rates will also apply to Ohio, Indiana, and Illinois, if any vacant tracts can be found liable to homestead in those three States, where but very few isolated tracts of public land remain undisposed of.

18. In the Pacific *and other* political divisions, viz: On *surveyed* lands in California, Nevada, Oregon, Colorado, New Mexico, and Washington, and in Arizona, Idaho, and Montana, where subdivisional surveys shall have been made in the three last-mentioned Territories, the commissions and fees are to be paid according to the following table:—

Acres.	Price per acre.	Commissions.		Fees.	Total Fees and Commissions.
		Payable *when entry is made.*	Payable on issue of *certificate.*	Payable when entry is made.	
160	$1.25	$6.00	$6.00	$10.00	$22 00
80	1.25	3.00	3.00	5.00	11.00
40	1.25	1.50	1.50	5.00	8.00
80	2.50	6.00	6.00	10.00	22.00
40	2.50	3.00	3.00	5.00	11.00

19. By the act of 21st June, 1866 (No. 146 B.), U. S. Statutes, vol. 14, page 66, the public lands of Alabama, Mississippi, Louisiana, Arkansas, and Florida are subject to disposal under the provisions of the homestead laws only.

20. Upon payment of the fee and commissions in accordance with the above tables, the Receiver will issue his receipt therefor and furnish a duplicate to the claimant.

The matter will then be entered on their records and reported to the General Land Office.

21. An inceptive right is vested in the settler by such proceedings, and upon faithful observance of the law in regard to settlement and cultivation for the continuous term of five years, and at the expiration of that time, or within two years thereafter, upon proper proof to the satisfaction of the land officers, and payment to the Receiver, the Register will issue his certificate, and make proper returns to this office as the basis of a patent or complete title for the homestead.

In making final proof, it is indispensable, under the statute, that the homestead party shall appear in person at the district land office and there make the affidavit required of him by law in support of his claim. Where, from physical disability, distance, or other good cause, the witnesses of said party cannot attend in person at the district office, their testimony in support of the claim may be taken where they reside before an officer authorized by law to administer oaths.

Their testimony must state satisfactorily the reason of their inability to attend at the district office; and the credibility and responsibility of the witnesses must be certified by the officiating magistrate, whose official character must be certified under seal.

The corroborating testimony thus prepared must be deposited with the Register and Receiver and filed with the affidavit of the homestead party, and the decision of the Register and Receiver endorsed thereon as preliminary to the transmission of the same to the General Land Office.

22. Where a homestead settler dies before the consummation of his claim, the heirs may continue the settlement and cultivation, and obtain title upon requisite proof at the proper time.

Where both parents die, leaving infant heirs, the homestead may be sold for cash for the benefit of such heirs, and the purchaser will receive title from the United States.

23. The sale of a homestead claim by the settler to another party be-

fore completion of title is not recognized by this office, and not only vests no title or equities in the purchaser, but would be *prima facie* evidence of abandonment, and give cause for cancellation of the claim.

A party may relinquish his claim, but only to the Government; and in such cases should surrender his duplicate receipt, with a relinquishment endorsed thereon; or if the duplicate has been lost, that fact should be stated in the relinquishment, duly signed and acknowledged.

Where application is made for the cancellation of a homestead entry on the ground of abandonment, the party must file his affidavit with the local land officers, setting forth the facts on which his allegations are founded, describing the tract and giving the name of the settler. Upon this the officers will set apart a day for a hearing, giving all the parties in interest due notice of the time and place of trial.

After the trial the land officers will transmit the testimony, with their joint report, for the action of this office.

The expenses incident to such contest must be defrayed by the contestant, and no entry of the land can be made until the local officers have received notice from this office of the cancellation of the entry covering the same.

24. As the law allows but one homestead privilege, a settler relinquishing or abandoning his claim cannot thereafter make a second entry. Where an individual has made settlement on a surveyed tract and filed his pre-emption declaration therefor, he may change his filing into homestead; yet such change is inadmissible where an adverse right has intervened; but in such cases the settler has the privilege of perfecting his title under the pre-emption laws.

25. If the homestead settler does not wish to remain five years on his tract, the law permits him to pay for it with cash or warrants, upon making proof of settlement and cultivation from the date of entry to the time of payment.

This proof of actual settlement and cultivation must be the affidavit of the party made before the local officers, corroborated by the testimony of two credible witnesses.

26. There is another class of homesteads, designated as "adjoining farm homesteads." In these cases the law allows an applicant *owning* and *residing* on an original farm, to enter other land lying contiguous thereto, which shall not, with such farm, exceed in the aggregate 160 acres. Thus, for example, a party owning or occupying 80 *acres*, may enter 80 additional of $1.25, or 40 acres of $2.50 land. Or suppose the applicant to own 40 *acres*, then he may enter 120 acres at $1.25, or 40 at $1.25, and 40 at $2.50, if both classes of land should be found contiguous to his original farm. In entries of "adjoining farms" the settler must describe, in his affidavit, the tract he owns and is settled upon as his original farm. Actual residence on the tract entered as an adjoining farm is not required, but *bona fide* improvement and cultivation of it must be shown for the period required by the statute.

27. Lands obtained under the homestead laws are exempted from liability for debts contracted prior to the issuing of a patent therefor.

Copies of the homestead laws are hereto annexed, marked E, F, and G, as also forms of affidavits and applications, numbered from one to four, required upon initiation of claim. (These laws are to be found in the order of their date, Part 3.)

REGISTERS' AND RECEIVERS' RETURNS.

28. Within three days from the close of each month the district land officers are required to make out and transmit to the General Office a statement of the business of their respective offices for the preceding month.

These reports are in form of abstracts of declarations of settlements filed, lands sold, homesteads entered, military warrants and agricultural college scrip located, accompanied by the certificates of purchase, Receivers' receipts, homestead applications and affidavits, warrants and agricultural college scrip, and certificates of location.

The abstracts are all to be duly certified to as correct and agreeing with the local records and the papers, and that all agree with each other.

The Receiver is required also to render a monthly *account of the moneys received* and, in the character of disbursing agent, of moneys paid out, showing the balance due the Government at the close of each month.

At the end of every quarter he also transmits a quarterly account; upon the several accounts a statement is made up and submitted to the Treasury Department of the Government for final settlement.

The Receiver is required to deposit the moneys received by him at some depository designated by the Secretary of the Treasury when the amount on hand shall have reached the sum of *two thousand dollars;* and in no case is he authorized, without special instructions, to hold a larger amount in his hands.

29. It is the duty of the registers and receivers to be in attendance at their offices, and give proper facilities and information to persons applying for lands.

30. A list of all the land offices in the United States is hereto annexed.

JOS. S. WILSON,
Commissioner of the General Land Office.

1. HOMESTEAD.

APPLICATION No. —— } LAND OFFICE at ——, 18—

I, ——, of ——, do hereby apply to enter, under the provisions of the act of Congress approved May 20, 1862, entitled "An act to secure homesteads to actual settlers on the public domain," the —— of section ——, in township —— of range ——, containing —— acres.

LAND OFFICE at ——, 18—

I, ——, Register of the Land Office, do hereby certify that the above application is for surveyed lands of the class which the applicant is legally entitled to enter under the homestead act of May 20, 1862, and that there is no prior, valid, adverse right to the same.

——, Register.

2. HOMESTEAD.

LAND OFFICE at ——,
Affidavit. Date ——

I, ——, of ——, having filed my *Application No.* ——, for an entry under the provisions of the act of Congress, approved May 20, 1862, entitled "An act to secure homesteads to actual settlers on the public domain," do solemnly swear, that [*Here state whether the applicant is the head of a family, or over twenty-one years of age; whether a citizen of the United States, or has filed his declaration of intention of becoming such; or, if under twenty-one years of age, that he has served not less than fourteen days in the army or navy of the United States during actual war; that said Application No. —— is made for his or her exclusive benefit; and that said entry is made for the purpose of actual settlement and cultivation, and not, directly or indirectly, for the use or benefit of any other person or persons whomsoever*], and that the applicant has not heretofore had the benefit of this act.

Sworn to and subscribed, this —— day of ——, before —— [Register or Receiver] of the Land Office.

3. MILITARY OR NAVAL HOMESTEAD.

APPLICATION No. ——

LAND OFFICE at ——, 18—

I, ——, of ——, being in the service of the United States, do hereby apply to enter, under the provisions of the act approved March 21, 1864, amendatory of the homestead act of May 20, 1862, and for other purposes, a certain tract of land, which —— is hereby authorized to designate, at the foot of this application, as my homestead, and which I agree to hold as my own selection.

Attest: ——, Commanding officer at ——.

———

I, ——, as named in the foregoing Application No. ——, do designate the tract selected for his homestead as the —— of Section —— in Township —— of Range ——, containing —— acres, and on which there is BONA FIDE improvement and settlement, and on which I am residing and in charge for said applicant.

WITNESS my hand, this —— day of ——, 18—

———

Attest: ——, Register.

LAND OFFICE at ——, 18—

I, ——, Register of the Land Office, do hereby certify that the above application is for surveyed lands of the class which the applicant is legally entitled to enter under the homestead act of May 20, 1862, and that there is no prior, valid, adverse right to the same.

——, Register.

4. MILITARY OR NAVAL HOMESTEAD.

Amendatory Homestead Act of March 21, 1864.

STATE OF —— COUNTY OF ——,

Affidavit.

Date ——

I, ——, of——, being now in the [*military or naval service*] of the United States, and proposing to file my application, No. ——, for an entry under the provisions of the act of Congress approved March 21, 1864, amendatory of the original homestead act of May 20, 1862, and for other purposes, do solemnly swear that [*Here state whether applicant is the head of a family, or over twenty-one years of age; whether a citizen of the United States, or has filed his declaration of intention of becoming such; or, if under twenty-one years of age, that he has served not less than fourteen days in the army or navy of the United States during actual war; that said Application No. —— is made for his or her exclusive benefit; and that said entry is made for the purpose of actual settlement and cultivation, and not directly or indirectly, for the use or benefit of any other person or persons whomsoever*], and that the applicant has not heretofore had the benefit of this act.

I further swear that I have made bona fine settlement and improvement upon the tract which [*here give name of representative*] is authorized to designate as my homestead.

———

Sworn to and subscribed, this ——— day of ———, before ——— U. S. Commanding Officer of ——— at ———.

[Rank and Service].

United States Land Offices, December, 1869.

OHIO.
Chillicothe.
INDIANA.
Indianapolis.
ILLINOIS.
Springfield.
MISSOURI.
Booneville,
Ironton,
Springfield.
ALABAMA.
Mobile,
Huntsville,
Montgomery.
MISSISSIPPI.
Jackson.
LOUISIANA.
New Orleans,
Monroe,
Natchitoches.
MICHIGAN.
Detroit,
East Saginaw,
Ionia,
Marquette,
Traverse City.
ARKANSAS.
Little Rock,
Washington,
Clarksville.
FLORIDA.
Tallahassee.

IOWA.
Fort Des Moines,
Council Bluffs,
Fort Dodge,
Sioux City.
WISCONSIN.
Menasha,
Falls at St. Croix,
Stephens' Point,
La Crosse,
Bayfield,
Eau Claire.
CALIFORNIA.
San Francisco,
Marysville,
Humboldt,
Stockton,
Visalia,
Sacramento,
Los Angeles.
NEVADA.
Carson City,
Austin,
Belmont,
Aurora.
WASHINGTON T.
Olympia,
Vancouver.
OREGON.
Oregon City,
Roseburg,
Le Grand.

MINNESOTA.
Taylor's Falls,
St. Cloud,
Winnebago City,
St. Peter,
Greenleaf,
Du Luth,
Alexandria.
KANSAS.
Topeka,
Junction City,
Humboldt,
NEBRASKA.
Omaha City,
Beatrice,
Lincoln,
Dakota City.
NEW MEXICO T.
Santa Fé.
DAKOTA T.
Vermillion.
COLORADO T.
Denver City,
Fair Play,
Central City.
IDAHO T.
Boise City,
Lewiston.
MONTANA T.
Helena.
ARIZONA T.
Prescott.
UTAH T.
Salt Lake City.

TITLE II.

Homesteads.

[See also Title III. PRE-EMPTION CLAIMS.]

No. 241 B.

Circular.—Homestead Law.

GENERAL LAND OFFICE,
October 30, 1862.

Gentlemen :—Annexed is a copy of the act of Congress approved May 20, 1862,* entitled "An act to secure homesteads to actual settlers on the public domain." The privileges of this law are extended to every person who is the head of a family, or who has arrived at the age of twenty-one years, and is a citizen of the United States, or has declared his intention of becoming such, and who has done no disloyal act, direct or indirect. An exception, however, to the foregoing requirement as to *age* is made in the 6th section of the act, in favor of any person who has served not less than fourteen days in the army or navy of the United States, either regular or volunteer, during actual war, domestic or foreign. Any person coming within the foregoing requirements will, from and after January 1, 1863, have the right to enter one quarter section, or a less quantity, of unappropriated public land, upon which said person may have filed a pre-emption claim, or which, at time of application, is subject to pre-emption, at $1.25 per acre ; or eighty acres, or less, of such unappropriated lands, at $2.50 per acre.

The law requires the land "to be located in one body, in conformity to the legal subdivisions of the public lands, and after the same shall have been surveyed."

Any person owning and residing on land may enter contiguous land, which, with that already owned and occupied, shall not exceed in the aggregate one hundred and sixty acres.

The applicant for the benefit of the law is required by the 2d section to file with the Register his "application," which should designate the tract desired to be entered. He must also file his "affidavit," to be taken before the Register or Receiver, setting forth the facts which bring him within the requirements of the law, and adding that the "application is made for his or her exclusive use and benefit, and that the said entry is made for the purpose of actual settlement and cultivation, and not, either directly or indirectly, for the use or benefit of any other person or persons whomsoever."

The said 2d section of the act further provides for the issue of patent to the applicant after five years' settlement; also for the succession in case of his death, and for the *sale* of the land for the benefit of infant heirs, but for no other purpose.

* No. 38 B.

The 3d section requires the Register to enter all applications on the tract books and plats of his office; to keep a register of entries, and make returns to this office with the proof.

The 4th section declares lands acquired under this act not liable for debts contracted prior to the issuing of the patent.

The 5th section makes abandonment of the land for more than six months, at any time within the five years, cause of forfeiture.

The 6th section forbids the acquirement of more than one quarter section, by any individual, under this act; protects existing pre-emptions, repeating the provision of section 1 in regard to pre-emptions, giving them all the privileges of the act; allowing the Registers and Receivers the same compensation for lands entered under this act which they are entitled to when the same quantity is entered with money; one-half to be paid by the person making the application, at the time of so doing, and the other half on the issue of the certificate, to be paid by the person to whom it may be issued, but not to enlarge the maximum compensation now allowed by law.

The 7th section stipulates the penalty for false swearing.

The 8th section permits claimants to pay for their entries at any time before the expiration of five years, and obtain patents, upon making proof of settlement and cultivation as required by the pre-emption laws.

You will accordingly be prepared, on the first day of January next, to receive applications and affidavits (forms A and B herewith). The Register should test the correctness of the "application" by his records, being careful that the tract applied for shall be of the class and quantity stipulated by the first section of the act, lying in one body, and comprising legal subdivisions; and will then append thereto his certificate of its regularity.

1. The applicant will then be allowed to enter the tract applied for, by paying to the Receiver the $10 fee stipulated in the act; and the further payment, as *commissions* of Register and Receiver, of *one-half of one per cent.* to each upon the cash value of the quantity of land applied for; the other half of the one per cent., as *commissions* to said officers, not to be paid until the certificate is issued, when the party obtaining such certificate is to make that payment.

2. The Receiver will issue homestead duplicate receipts for each entry (form C herewith); one to be delivered to the applicant, the other returned to this office. A new and independent series of numbers to be adopted for such receipts.

3. No certificate is to be issued at the time of entry, nor until the expiration of five years therefrom (see first proviso, sec. 2), except in the case of a sale for the benefit of infant heirs (second proviso, sec. 2), or where payment in full is made, as provided by sec. 8, in which cases certificates must be issued.

4. In the case of a sale for the benefit of infant heirs, the certificate (form D herewith) will issue in the name of the purchaser, upon evidence of sale, made in obedience to a decree or order of a court having jurisdiction in such matters.

5. In a case where full payment is proposed to be made by a party under the 8th section, he must first make proof of settlement and cultivation, as required by existing pre-emption laws and instructions; whereupon you will require his homestead duplicate receipt to be surrendered, and will admit the pre-emption as a new and original entry, and issue pre-emption certificate and receipt, as in ordinary pre-emption cases, returning the same with the monthly abstracts. The Register will take

care, however, to make a note on the face of the certificate, and the Receiver on the receipt, showing the change of the entry from homestead donation to pre-emption purchase under said 8th section.

6. Each entry will be registered in the tract books in *red* ink, noting opposite the entry, on the left-hand margin, "H. Act of May 20, 1862," also in red.

7. In reference to the requirement of the 3d section of the act, the Register will procure a suitable bound volume, to be denominated "Register of Entries—Homestead Act of May 20, 1862," having ruled columns, showing number of application, date of same, description of tract, with area; name of applicant. The ruled columns of the "register" should occupy the left-hand page only, reserving the opposite page for "remarks," and allowing four lines space for each entry, on which will be noted all particulars in regard to subsequent action, especially in cases of sale for the benefit of infant heirs, and of pre-emption proof and full payment, under section 8.

8. Let the entries in the "register" be summed up monthly, to correspond with a monthly abstract, which must be returned by the Receiver and certified by the Register as correct, and as agreeing with the original applications and with his "register of entries." Such returns, of course, to be separate and distinct from ordinary returns of sales and locations.

9. In reference to the *compensation*—being the commissions of the Register and Receiver for services under this act, as regulated by the 6th section—the same allowance is to be made as at present on cash entries; that is, each entry is to be estimated as a sale of so much land at $1.25 or $2.50 per acre, and payment made thereon as indicated under the first head in the foregoing.

In order that proper effect may be given to the beneficent provisions of the law, I request your careful observance of those provisions, and the instructions contained in the foregoing.

Very respectfully, your obedient servant,

J. M. EDMUNDS, Commissioner.

To the Registers and Receivers of the United States Land Offices.

FORM A. HOMESTEAD.

APPLICATION No. —— } LAND OFFICE at ——
Date ——

I, ——, of ——, do hereby apply to enter, under the provisions of the act of Congress approved May 20, 1862, entitled "An act to secure homesteads to actual settlers on the public domain," the —— of section —— in township —— of range ——, containing —— acres.

[*In pre-emption cases let the following be added: "Having filed my pre-emption declaration thereto on the —— day of ——."*]

LAND OFFICE at——
——, 18—

I, ——, Register of the Land Office, do hereby certify that the above application is for surveyed lands of the class which the applicant is legally entitled to enter under the homestead act of May 20, 1862, and that there is no prior, valid, adverse right to the same.

——, Register.

FORM B. HOMESTEAD.

LAND OFFICE at———
Date ———

Affidavit.

I, ———, of ———, having filed my *Application No.* ——, for an entry under the provisions of the act of Congress, approved May 20, 1862, entitled "An act to secure homesteads to actual settlers on the public domain," do solemnly swear, that [*Here state whether applicant is the head of a family, or over twenty-one years of age; whether a citizen of the United States, or has filed his declaration of intention of becoming such; or, if under twenty-one years of age, that he has served not less than fourteen days in the army or navy of the United States during actual war; that he has never borne arms against the Government, or given aid and comfort to its enemies; that said Application No.* —— *is made for his or her exclusive benefit; and that said entry is made for the purpose of actual settlement and cultivation, and not, directly or indirectly, for the use or benefit of any other person or persons whomsoever.*]

Sworn to and subscribed, this ——— day of ———, before ———.
[Register or Receiver] of the Land Office.

FORM C. HOMESTEAD.

RECEIVER'S OFFICE, ———
Date ———

RECEIVER'S RECEIPT, No. —— } { APPLICATION, No. ——

Received of ——— the sum of ——— dollars ——— cents, being the amount of fee and one-half the compensation of register and receiver, for the entry of ——— of section ——— in township ——— of range ———, under the act of Congress approved May 20, 1862, entitled "An act to secure homesteads to actual settlers on the public domain."

———, Receiver.

$———

FORM D. HOMESTEAD.

LAND OFFICE at ———
Date ———

CERTIFICATE, No. —— } { APPLICATION, No. ——

IT IS HEREBY CERTIFIED, That pursuant to the provisions of the act of Congress, approved May 20, 1862, entitled "An act to secure homesteads to actual settlers on the public domain," ——— has made payment in full for ——— of section ——— in township ——— of range ——— containing ——— acres.

NOW, THEREFORE, BE IT KNOWN, That on presentation of this certificate to the Commissioner of the General Land Office, the said ——— shall be entitled to a patent for the tract of land above described.

———, Register.

No. 242 B.

Circular.—Homestead Law.

GENERAL LAND OFFICE,
February 26, 1863.

Gentlemen :—Since the circular of October 30th, 1862,* several questions have arisen requiring further instructions in regard to the returns required under the homestead act of May 20, 1862 :—

1st. The Register will transmit at the close of the month an abstract of his "Register of entries," the Receiver's receipts, with the affidavits and applications. The affidavits and applications to be filed within the appropriate receipt, to be properly numbered and endorsed on the back.

2d. The Receiver will transmit a transcript of his "Register of receipts" with his other monthly returns.

3d. The Register and Receiver will use the blank cash abstracts and Register of receipts (until other blanks shall have been received, with the required alteration of heading) in reporting to this office homestead entries, giving therein the date of entry (or application), number, name, place of residence, tract, section, township, range, acres, price per acre, and fee and commissions in separate columns. A recapitulation must be stated in both the Register of entries and transcript of Register of receipts, showing the amount of land taken at $1.25 and $2.50 per acre.

4th. Where there is an excess over the maximum area (that is, 80 acres at $2.50, or 160 acres at $1.25 per acre), you will require payment for such excess at those rates respectively. Such payments are to be reported in the Register's and Receiver's cash returns, and accounted for in the Receiver's monthly and quarterly accounts.

5th. You will give the number of excess receipts in the Register of entries; also, in the transcript of Register of receipts at the end of the entry; also, give the number of excess receipt in red ink, on the back of homestead receipt.

6th. The Receiver will give in his monthly fee statements (of warrant locations) the number of acres at $2.50 per acre, and the commissions received thereon; also, separately, the number of acres at $1.25, and the commissions received thereon.

7th. The $10 stipulated in the homestead act belong to the United States, and will be credited by the Receiver in his monthly and quarterly accounts as revenue from public lands under said act. The commissions allowed will also be credited by the Receiver in like manner, and disbursed at the close of the quarter to himself and the Register, and charged in his disbursing account.

8th. Where applications are made under this act for an adjoining farm, you will require that fact to be stated in the affidavit, giving therein a description of the land owned; also, write across the face of the receipt the words (in red ink) "adjoining farm."

The Register will annex the following certificate to his Register of entries, before transmitting it to this office:

REGISTER'S OFFICE at ———,
———, 18—

I hereby certify that the foregoing abstract of homestead entries for the month of ————, 18—, has been carefully examined and compared with the applications, register of entries, entries on the plats; also, with

* No. 38 B.

the Receiver's receipts and Register of receipts; and all of these with each other, under the superintendence of Receiver and myself; and that they are found to agree, and are correct.

———, Register.

The following is the form of certificate required to be annexed to the Receiver's transcript of Register of receipts.

RECEIVER'S OFFICE at ———,
———, 18—

I hereby certify that the foregoing transcript of Register of receipts of homestead entries, issued at this office during the month ending ———, 18—, has been carefully examined and compared with the applications, receipts, register of entries, and entries on the plats; and all of these with each other, under the superintendence of the Register and myself; and that they all agree with each other, and are correct.

———, Receiver.

You are requested to acknowledge the receipt of this communication, and enjoined strictly to observe its requirements; otherwise, confusion and unnecessary labor and delay must inevitably follow.

J. M. EDMUNDS, Commissioner.

To the Registers and Receivers of the United States Land Offices.

No. 243 B.

Circular.—Homestead Amendment and Fees.

Respecting the act of Congress approved March 21, 1864, amendatory of the homestead law, and for other purposes.

DEPARTMENT OF THE INTERIOR,
GENERAL LAND OFFICE, April 18, 1864.

Gentlemen:—Annexed is the act of Congress, approved March 21, 1864, amendatory of the original homestead law of May 28, 1862, and for other purposes:—*

1st. The 1st section of this act is designed to enable persons in the United States military or naval service to take preliminary steps, whilst absent on duty, to secure for themselves homesteads on the public lands. To this end—

The *affidavit* herewith, No. 1, corresponding, as near as the case will admit, with B, on 6th page of circular dated October 30, 1862, may be made by the party before his commanding officer, who may be any *commissioned* officer immediately commanding by *land* or *sea*, and who, in certifying to the fact that the oath has been duly administered, should add that, at its date, he *was* commanding, giving his rank and particular service.

The affidavit thus taken should be accompanied by *the application* of the party (also to be attested by the said commanding officer, according to Form No. 2), which, for *this* class of cases, takes the place of Form A, on page 5 of said circular of October 30, 1862. As the absent military or naval homestead party would not be likely to know the exact official designation of the land selected, the Form of Application No. 1 requires this to be done by the wife or other representative of the party;

* No. 76 B.

which designation must be attested by the Register, and his certificate of verification must also be appended according to said form.

Upon the affidavit and application being filed by the wife or representative of the absent party, the same will take effect from *the date of filing;* and if regular in all respects, the entry will have legal inception from that date, provided the fee and commissions are paid as hereinafter specified, viz :—

Section 2.—This section of the said act of 1864 requires, besides the $10 fee to be paid at the time of entry, that there shall likewise be paid to the Register and Receiver each *one* per centum on the cash value of the land as fixed by law, with like commissions when the claim is finally established and certificate issued as basis of the patent, thereby increasing the fees over the tariff fixed by act 1682.

3d. The effect of the 3d section of this law is merely to relieve parties from personal attendance at the district land office, in making homestead entries, who are prevented from such attendance by reason of distance, bodily infirmity, or other good cause. This class of persons the law allows to make the affidavit required by the original statute "before the clerk of the court for the county in which the applicant is an actual resident.

Form B of affidavit in circular of October 30, 1862, may be used in this class of cases by adding, in the body of the affidavit, the averment, under oath, stating explicitly the cause of disability. Then the clerk of the county administering the oath must certify under seal as to the making of the affidavit, and also as to the actual residence of the party in the county.

4th. The 4th section increases the fee to *one* dollar *each* to Register and Receiver for services in acting upon each pre-emption case ; but as in many instances the parties do nothing more than file the "notice" required by law, this office has long since determined that there is no objection to the *Register* receiving his fee (now $1) at the time of filing such notice, making subsequently no further charge ; but that as the Receiver has no labor in the case until the proof is filed and submitted for his action, the latter officer has no right to the fee until he shall be called upon to perform the duty for which payment is to be provided.

As the *proviso* in the last section of said act was passed in this connection, it will hereafter be necessary for the Register and Receiver to account in *all* cases for pre-emption fees received as *revenue*, using the form of fee statement already provided.

There is another service, however, contemplated in said 4th section, which involves personal labor and perhaps occasional clerical assistance, which is not to be accounted for as fees constituting a source of revenue ; and that is the authority the said section gives to the Register and Receiver for receiving, "jointly, at the rate of fifteen cents per hundred words, for the testimony which may be reduced by them to writing for claimants in establishing pre-emption or homestead rights."

The Register and Receiver, however, will be careful in this service to have the record *condensed* as far as consistent with the presentation of all the facts, so that claimants may not be unnecessarily taxed with cost in the matter.

5th. The 5th section of this statute deals with cases in which the preliminary steps have been taken by a pre-emptor to give legal inception to his claim, but who is called away from his settlement by being in the military or naval service. To such pre-emptors this law allows the claimant a period of six months after expiration of his military or naval service in which to file his affidavit as called for by the 13th section of the pre-emption act of 1841. This extension, however, can only be secured by compliance with the legal requirement that the pre-emptor shall cause to be filed with the Register "satisfactory proof, by affidavit or the testimony of witnesses, that" he "is so in the service." The affidavit must be filed *before* the expiration of the period stipulated in the pre-emption act of 1841 for proving up and payment, and must explicitly state the date of expiration of such term of military or naval service.

6th. By the 6th section of this enactment, the Registers and Receivers in California, Oregon, Washington, Nevada, Colorado, Idaho, New Mexico, and Arizona, are allowed, "in addition to the fees and allowances provided by this act, fifty per centum of said fees and allowances as compensation for their services."

The said States and Territories have all been organized into land districts, except Idaho and Arizona. In those now organized, and in the two last mentioned when they shall be so organized, the Registers and Receivers will each be entitled as follows:—

1st. For services to *each* officer in acting upon pre-emptions, $1.50.

2d. For homestead commissions to the Register and Receiver, *each*, $3 on 160 acres of $1.25 lands at *time* of entry, and also a like sum *when finally established.* Like sums on 80 acres of $2.50 lands, and in same ratio on the different classes of lands in lesser subdivisions.

3d. For taken down testimony *jointly* as contemplated by 4th section, the sum of 22½ cents per hundred words.

It will be observed, however, that the proviso in the said section as hereinbefore alluded to expressly restricts the salary and fees to an aggregate not exceeding $3000 per annum, or in that *ratio* for any part of an official year.

The receipt of this you are requested to acknowledge.

Very respectfully,

J. M. EDMUNDS, Commissioner.

Register and Receiver.

FORM No. 1.

Amendatory Homestead Act of March 21, 1864.

STATE OF —— COUNTY OF ——,

Affidavit. Date ——

I, ——, of ——, being now in the [*military or naval service*] of the United States, and proposing to file my application, No. ——, for an entry under the provisions of the act of Congress approved March 21, 1864, amendatory of the original homestead act of May 20, 1862, and for other purposes, do solemnly swear that [*Here state whether applicant is the head of a family, or over twenty-one years of age; whether a citizen of the United States, or has filed his declaration of intention of becoming such; or, if under twenty-one years of age, that he has served not less than fourteen days in the army or navy of the United States during actual war; that he has never borne arms against the Government, or given aid and comfort to its enemies; that said Application, No. ——, is made for his or her exclusive benefit; and that said entry is made for the purpose of actual settlement and cultivation, and not, directly or indirectly, for the use or benefit of any other person or persons whomsoever*].

Sworn to and subscribed, this —— day of ——, before ——, U. S. Commanding Officer of ——, at ——.

[Rank and Service.]

FORM No. 2.

Amendatory Homestead Act of March 21, 1864.

APPLICATION, No. —— STATE OF ——, COUNTY OF ——,
Date ——

I, ——, of ——, being in the [*military or naval*] service of the United States, do hereby apply to enter, under the provisions of the act approved May 21, 1864, amendatory of the homestead act approved May 20, 1862, and for other purposes, a certain tract of land which [*A. B.*] [*my wife or duly authorized representative*] is hereby authorized to designate, at the foot of this application, as my homestead, and which I hereby agree to hold as my own selection.

Attest: ——, Commanding Officer at ——,
[Rank and service.]

I, —— [*wife or duly authorized representative*], as named in the foregoing application, No. ——, do hereby designate the tract selected for his homestead as the —— section, township ——, range ——, containing —— acres, and on which there is *bona fide* improvement and settlement, and on which I am residing and in charge for said applicant.

Witness my hand, this —— day of ——, 18—

——

Attest: ——, Register.

LAND OFFICE at ——,
——, 18—

I, ——, Register of the Land Office, do hereby certify that the above application is for surveyed lands of the class which the applicant is legally entitled to enter under the homestead act of May 20, 1862, and that there is no prior valid adverse right to the same.

——, Register.

Note in reference to 3d section of amendatory homestead act of March 21, 1864.

Where affidavits are taken before clerks of courts, Form B, page 6, of original circular of October 30, 1862, may be adopted with the addition and modification suggested under 3d head in this circular.

Further: the same forms, C and D, which are presented on pages 7 and 8 for receivers' homestead receipts and for registers' patent certificates, may be used for similar instruments required in view of the said amendatory homestead act of March 21, 1864.

No. 244 B.

Homestead Circular.

DEPARTMENT OF THE INTERIOR,
GENERAL LAND OFFICE, March 1, 1865.

Gentlemen:—In connection with the act of Congress approved March 21, 1864,* extending the homestead law to persons on actual duty in the military or naval service of the United States, and the official circular dated April 18, 1864,† on the subject, many inquiries have been received bearing upon the principles which should govern in the practical operations of the statute.

* No. 76 B. † No. 243 B.

With a view to meet such inquiries, and for the information of all concerned, you are advised as follows :—

This office has given the most liberal construction with a view to realize the purposes of the statute. Hence, where the military or naval applicant has an actual settlement on a parcel of land, through his family or some member thereof, the way is open for the consummation of his right; provided that immediately after his discharge from actual military or naval service he enters in good faith upon the land and keeps up his homestead as his *bona fide* residence with cultivation; the liberal construction of this office even going so far as this, that where the tract is not in possession of a party held for the principal, the right of the latter will be held good if the requisite affidavit and application have been filed, through an agent or otherwise, tract designated, and register's certificate obtained; provided that immediately upon his discharge from actual military or naval service he enters upon the land and makes it emphatically his home, by residence and cultivation, in good faith, for the full term of five years, and the time he is necessarily absent in the actual service, military or naval, of his country shall not be counted against him, but treated as a part of his five years' residence and cultivation.

I am, very respectfully, your obedient servant,

J. M. EDMUNDS, Commissioner.

To ——, Register and Receiver at ——.

No. 245 B.

Circular (No. 1, New Series).

In relation to the purchase of public lands, or the entry of the same under the pre-emption and homestead laws.

DEPARTMENT OF THE INTERIOR,
GENERAL LAND OFFICE, July 19, 1865.

Numerous questions having arisen as to the mode of proceeding to purchase public lands, or acquire title to the same by bounty land locations, by pre-emptions, or by homestead, this circular is communicated for the information of all concerned.

In order to acquire title to public lands the following steps must be taken :—

1st. Application must be made to the *Register* of the district land office in which the land desired may be situated.

A list of all the land offices in the United States is hereto appended (see p. 247), with the seat of the different offices, where it is the duty of the Register and Receiver to be in attendance, and give proper facilities and information to persons desirous of obtaining lands.

The minimum price of ordinary public lands is $1.25 per acre. The *even* or *reserved* sections falling within railroad grants are increased to double the minimum price, being $2.50 per acre.

Lands *once offered at public sale*, and not afterwards kept out of market by reservation, or otherwise, so as to prevent free competition, may be entered or located.

2d. By the applicant filing with the Register his *written* application, describing the tract, with its area, the Register will then certify to the Receiver whether the land is vacant, with its price; and when found to be so, the applicant must pay that price per acre, or may locate the same with land warrant, and thereafter the Receiver will give him a "duplicate receipt," which he is required to surrender prior to the delivery to him of the patent, which may be had either by application for it to the Register or to the General Land Office.

3d. If the tract has not been offered at public sale, it is not liable to ordinary private entry, but may be secured by a party legally qualified, upon his compliance with the requirements of the pre-emption laws of 4th September, 1841,* and 3d March, 1843;† and after such party shall have made actual settlement for such a length of time as will show he designs it for his permanent home, and is acting in good faith, building a house and residing therein, he may proceed to the district land office, establish his pre-emption claim according to law by proving his actual residence and cultivation, and showing that he is otherwise within the purview of these acts. Then he can enter the land at $1.25, either with cash or with bounty land warrant, unless the premises should be $2.50 acre lands. In that case the whole purchase-money can be paid in *cash*, or one-half in *cash*, the residue with a bounty land warrant.

4th. But if parties legally qualified desire to obtain title under the homestead act of 20th May, 1862, they can do so on complying with the enclosed circular, dated 30th October, 1862.

The circular herewith, dated April 18, 1864, shows how parties in the military or naval service may, whilst in actual duty, acquire the inceptive title without going to the district office. After entry the soldier or sailor stands excused from actual residence during the period after entry in which he may be in actual service; but when discharged must immediately go on the tract, reside there, and cultivate for the residue of the full period of five years from date of entry. The five-year settlement is an absolute, unconditional requirement in regard to all persons, except as stated, as to soldiers or sailors in actual service, who only for the period in which after entry they are in such service are relieved, but with the positive requirement that after discharge they must go on the land and reside upon and cultivate it as their home until the expiration of the five years.

5th. The law confines homestead entries to surveyed lands, and although in certain States and Territories noted in the subjoined list pre-emptors may go on land *before survey*, yet they can only establish their claim after return of survey, but must file their pre-emption declaration within three months after receipt of official plat at the local land office where the settlement was made *before* survey. Where, however, it was made *after* survey, the claimant must file within three months after date of settlement; and where actual residence and cultivation have been long enough to show that the claimant has made the land his permanent home, he can establish his claim and pay for the same at any time before the date of the public sale of lands within the range of which his settlement may fall.

6th. All unoffered surveyed lands not acquired under pre-emption, homestead, or otherwise, under express legal sanction, must be offered at public sale under the President's proclamation, and struck off to the highest bidder, as required by the act of 24th April, 1820.

J. M. EDMUNDS,
Commissioner General Land Office.

* Vol. I. No. 48. † Vol. I. No. 72.

No. 246 B.

Circular. New Series. Relinquishment of Homesteads.

DEPARTMENT OF THE INTERIOR,
GENERAL LAND OFFICE, December 14, 1865.

Gentlemen:—In order to secure a regular system and facilitate the business of the department, you are hereby instructed to observe the following regulations respecting all cases of abandoned and relinquished homesteads:—

1. A settler desiring to relinquish to the United States his homestead claim, must surrender his duplicate receipt, his relinquishment being endorsed thereon. If, however, he has lost his duplicate receipt, that fact must be stated in his relinquishment, to be signed by the settler, acknowledged before the Register or Receiver, or notary public using a seal, and attested by two witnesses.

2. When a homestead entry is contested and application is made for cancellation, the party so applying must file an affidavit setting forth the facts on which his allegations are grounded, describing the tract and giving the name of the settler. You will then set apart a day for a hearing, giving all the parties in interest notice of the time and place of trial.

On the day of hearing you will distinctly show at the caption of the papers in the proceedings the name of the settler, description of the tract, number and date of entry. You will then proceed with the examination of the witnesses. Each deposition must be signed by the witness and acknowledged before either the Register or Receiver; and at the conclusion of the trial you will briefly review the testimony, and thereafter will transmit to this office all the papers, with your joint decision thereon annexed thereto, for final determination.

3. The notice to a settler that his claim is contested must be served by a disinterested party, and a copy must be filed, with an affidavit that the notice has been served upon the homestead party, or brought home to him so as to be a legal notice, such copy of notice and affidavit to accompany the papers.

The expenses incident to such contest must be defrayed by the contestant.

4. Application for the cancellation of entries for the reason that the settler is dead, must be dealt with as per instructions in 2d paragraph of this circular, taking care that the settler's death is fully established.

5. You will not permit another entry of the land to be made, whether the tract has been voluntarily relinquished or under consideration, on the ground of non-compliance with the homestead law, until you have received notice from this office of the cancellation of the entry covering the same.

6. The land covered by cancelled homestead entries having been thereby withdrawn from market, you will embrace it in a docket which you will keep of tracts in that condition; and when a sufficient number have accumulated to justify the expense of advertising, you will report them to this office; and, until restored to market by advertisement under instructions, they will only be subject to entry under the pre-emption or homestead laws, except where the same, upon such cancellations being made, may fall within railroad limits. In such cases the odd sections must be withheld from further entry, and the even ones treated at their proper ratability.

7. The evidence of two witnesses is required to establish the facts of abandonment.

All cases of the above character must be reported to this office with special communications. You are requested to acknowledge the receipt of this circular and enjoined *strictly* to observe its requirements.

J. M. EDMUNDS, Commissioner.

To the Registers and Receivers of the United States Land Offices.

No. 247 B.

Homestead Circular. New Series, No. 5.

DEPARTMENT OF THE INTERIOR,
GENERAL LAND OFFICE, January 19, 1866.

Gentlemen :—Under the recent ruling, bearing date 15th inst., of the Secretary of the Interior, a pre-emptor filing after the date of the homestead act of 20th of May, 1862,* has a right to change said pre-emption into a homestead, except where the settlement is shown to have been made upon UNSURVEYED land, in which case he must perform his engagements under the pre-emption laws, and cannot change to a homestead.

Therefore, where a party seeks to commute his pre-emption claim into a homestead, you are directed to "ascertain whether his settlement commenced PRIOR TO THE SURVEY of the land, and if it did, you will disallow the entry.

Be pleased to acknowledge the receipt of this circular.

Very respectfully,
J. M. EDMUNDS, Commissioner.

To ——— Register and Receiver at ———.

No. 248 B.

Circular.—Homestead.—New Series No. 7.

DEPARTMENT OF THE INTERIOR,
GENERAL LAND OFFICE, April 20, 1866.

Gentlemen :—In taking the proof, when homesteads are transmuted to *cash entries* and warrant locations under the 8th section of the homestead act, we notice that the blanks furnished for pre-emption cases have been used, upon the supposition, no doubt, that when a homestead is paid for under the 8th section it is thereby transmuted to a pre-emption.

The payment, under the 8th section of the act, is simply a consummation of the homestead as allowed by law, upon the party making proof of settlement and cultivation, as required of parties purchasing under the pre-emption laws.

For your future guidance, in dealing with this class of cases, I have to communicate the following directions :—

1st. You will require the affidavit of the party setting forth the facts as to his settlement and improvement to date of payment.

2d. The corroborating testimony of two disinterested witnesses.

3d. That the homestead duplicate receipt be surrendered and transmitted with the other papers in the case to this office.

4th. You will note on your abstracts and on the papers in the case, the following : "Commuted from homestead entry No.   , under 8th

* No. 33 B.

section of homestead act ;" and on your records, against the homestead entry, you will note, "Commuted under 8th section by wt., , act , or cash entry No. ," as the case may be, and against the wt., or cash entry, make a reference to the homestead.

Proper blanks for affidavit and proof of settlement and cultivation will be prepared and furnished you as soon as possible.

Be pleased to acknowledge receipt of this circular.

Very respectfully,
J. M. EDMUNDS, Commissioner.

To Register and Receiver ———.

No. 249 B.

Circular Letter.

DEPARTMENT OF THE INTERIOR,
GENERAL LAND OFFICE, August, 25, 1866.

Gentlemen:—The Secretary of the Interior, under date of June 22, 1866, decided that a pre-emption settler who had made his filing on an odd numbered section within railroad limits could not change to a homestead, the following being an extract from said decision:—

"The homestead settler's right attaches only from the date of entry, the pre-emptor's from the date of his actual personal settlement. The title in either case is consummated by a full compliance with the terms and conditions imposed by law. The grant to said company does not embrace lands to which a valid right arising either under the homestead or pre-emption laws had previously attached, but if such right be abandoned or forfeited the grant would immediately thereafter take effect. A pre-emptor cannot abandon his claim as such, or transmute it to a homestead entry so as to defeat the right of the company, which enured before such entry be made. If a pre-emption settlement had been commenced upon surveyed land the latter might be entered as a homestead before the right of the company attached, but not at subsequent date."

Therefore settlers on such lands will be required to establish and pay for their claims under the pre-emptlon laws.

2d. In case any such settlers have made entries under the homestead act, the same will be suspended and they will be required to conform to this ruling of the head of the Department, and furnish proof and pay for their claims under the pre-emption act.

You will please acknowledge the receipt hereof.

Very respectfully, your obedient servant,
JOS. S. WILSON, Acting Commissioner.

No. 250 B.

Circular.—Homestead Law of 1866.

DEPARTMENT OF THE INTERIOR,
GENERAL LAND OFFICE, September 25, 1866.

Gentlemen:—Annexed is the act of Congress "approved June 21, 1866,"* providing for the disposal of the public lands for homestead actual settlement in the States of Alabama, Mississippi, Louisiana, Arkansas, and Florida.

* No. 166 B.

The 1st section of this act, in providing for the disposal of the public lands in the States above mentioned, according to the provisions of the homestead act of May 20, 1862, and the amendatory act of March 21, 1864, restricts entries to not more than a half-quarter section or 80 acres when held at $1.25 per acre. Should the tract selected, however, be $2.50 per acre land, only half that quantity, or 40 acres, can be entered according to the principle fixed in the original statute of 1862, the law imposing this restriction as to quantity in said States for two years from its passage. After the expiration of that time, however, entries as to quantity of acres, should no other legislation be had, will be governed by the provisions of the 1st section of the act of the 20th May, 1862.

This section of the act of 1866 provides further that the benefits of the law shall be extended to citizens of the United States without distinction or discrimination as to race or color, and that no *mineral lands* shall be liable to homestead entry for settlement under its provisions. In lieu of the $10 fee required by act of May 20, 1862, to be paid at the time of entry, the sum of $5 is to be paid *at the time of the issue of patent* in each case. The commissions of the Register and Receiver will be the same as provided for in acts of May 20, 1862, and March 21, 1864, viz: One per cent. on the cash value of the land to each officer, with additional 50 per centum provided for in the 6th section of the act of March 21, 1864, to the officers in the several regions of country therein named.

The foregoing provisions are mainly of *special* application to the States first above mentioned. The 2d section of the act is of *general* application to *all* the States and Territories, and re-enacts the 2d section of the act of May 20, 1862, with the following modifications, viz:—

Until the 1st of January, 1867, the applicant is required to make affidavit, in addition to the oath required by said section, that he has not borne arms against the United States or given aid and comfort to its enemies. This requirement is already inserted in the form B of affidavit adopted in the administration of the original act, and forms part of the instructions in circular of October 30, 1862. The effect, then, of this legal stipulation is to limit that particular requirement to the 1st of January, 1867.

The law in question is further of general application in this, that the fee is reduced to $5 when the entry shall not embrace more than *eighty* acres held at $1.25 per acre; but when the entry is in excess of that quantity, the usual fee ($10) must be paid. The 3d section of the act stipulates that all the provisions of the homestead law of May 20, 1862, and the amendatory act of 1864, so far as the same may be applicable, except as modified by act of June 21, 1866, are to be held and regarded a part of said act of 1866 as fully as if therein enacted and set forth.

Very respectfully, your obedient servant,

JOS. S. WILSON, Commissioner.

To the Registers and Receivers of the United States Land Offices.

No. 251 B.

DEPARTMENT OF THE INTERIOR,
GENERAL LAND OFFICE, May 15, 1868.

Gentlemen:—There appears to be an uncertainty existing among some of the local land officers as to the proper course to adopt in the adjustment of final homestead entries; therefore, whilst it is, of course, impossible to give special instructions applicable to all cases that may be presented, yet, by a classification and the application of general rules to each class, the difficulties may be overcome, and harmonious administration of the law secured.

These cases then may be divided into three classes:—

1st. Those who have fully met the requirements of the law.

2d. Those partially failing, yet within equitable rulings.

3d. Those where the claimants are clearly without the protection of the statute.

Of the *first class* it is unnecessary to treat (the proof, of course, sustaining the claim), further than to direct that you promptly return the cases with your decision thereon.

In the *second class*, where equity strongly points to recognition of the claim, yet where, in view of the statute, you do not feel authorized to allow the same, you will transmit the proof, with your joint decision thereon, for the consideration and determination of this office, and hold the entry subject to our ruling, of which you will be advised without unnecessary delay.

With regard to the *third class*, wherein the testimony is not satisfactory, and you are convinced that the party has made no proper effort to comply with the law, you will reject the claim, and transmit the proof, with your decision, to this office, so that your action may be reviewed, and, if sustained, that the original entry may be cancelled; but in all cases notify the party that, if he so desires, an appeal may be taken from your decision.

This appeal should be in writing, with the grounds stated, and should be filed with you within thirty days from date of your notice to the party of the rejection of the claim. In case of appeal, transmit the same to this office.

Action will then be here taken, and the result made known to you.

In the case of "adjoining farm" entries you will require the following proof:—

1st. That the party is the owner of and settled upon an "original farm"—particularly describing the same by subdivision of section, township, and range—at the date of his homestead entry, and that said farm is contiguous to and adjoining the lands embraced in such homestead.

2d. That he has continued to reside upon and improve said original farm during the five years.

3d. That he has, during said five years, also cultivated and improved the adjoining farm tract, in conjunction with the original farm, satisfactorily showing the value and extent of such improvement.

You will please acknowledge receipt of this.

Respectfully,

Register and Receiver. JOS. S. WILSON, Commissioner.

No. 252 B.

Settlement on abandoned homestead prior to withdrawal for railroad purposes does not give right of pre-emption, etc.

GENERAL LAND OFFICE,
July 17, 1869.

Gentlemen:—A party settling on an abandoned homestead entry, and purchasing the homestead settler's improvements, the homestead entry

* No. 146 B.

not being cancelled until after withdrawal for railroad purposes, does not acquire the right of a pre-emptor; the land is not and has not been vacant and unappropriated public land at any time since the date of homestead entry of 1864, and withdrawal in 1866, and is not subject to pre-emption entry.

Respectfully, etc.,

Jos. S. WILSON, Commissioner.

Register and Receiver, Denver, Colorado.

No. 253 B.

HOMESTEAD RULINGS.

Extracted from the able and comprehensive Annual Reports of the Hon. Joseph S. Wilson, Commissioner of the General Land Office, for the years 1868, 1867, and 1866.

Where different parties hold an undivided interest as tenants in common in an original farm, it has been decided that until a decision is made so as to fix the description of the tract taken by each, there cannot be a separate entry made as an adjoining farm by any one holding such individual interest, because the law contemplates a fee simple ownership in a particular tract as an essential preliminary to making an entry of other land as a farm adjoining.

Inquiry has been made as to the proof requisite where the parties apply to make payment under the 8th section of the homestead act of 20th May, 1862.

It has been ruled that proof must be made of settlement and cultivation up to the time of payment, so as to show a *bona fide* purpose on the part of the settler to make the land his permanent homestead. Wherever the proof may show an honest effort by the claimant to meet the requirements of the statute, the Register and Receiver are directed to deal with the matter in no narrow, but in a liberal spirit, yet in subordination to the requirement of the statute. In cases where the settler is deceased, and his legal representatives thereafter discover that the homestead papers describe other land than the tract embraced by his actual settlement, it has been ruled that the widow or representatives may prove and thereafter certify on the application to the correct description of the tract upon which the deceased party actually settled, and when satisfactory, the error in description may be corrected.

Applications have been made to relinquish a homestead claim, in order to a subsequent filing on the same tract under the pre-emption laws. If the party relinquishing is entitled to the pre-emption, and sees fit to avail himself of it on the tract he had relinquished under the homestead, he has a right to do so, as it is not in any view a consummation, but a separate, distinct transaction, initiated and perfected under another law.

Cases have arisen where persons have made homestead entry on tracts previously offered, and complaint has been entered that settlers had failed to meet the requirements of the homestead law. Where such parties have made considerable improvements, but failed in residence, their rights as homestead claimants have been forfeited; but in view of the improvements existing, they have been allowed to purchase the land at private entry, because it was liable to such entry, having been duly offered.

When a settler upon an "offered tract" dies before the expiration of the five years, and his heirs, living at a distance from the premises, have failed to continue the settlement to the end of the five years, or to prove up under the 8th section of the act of 20th May, 1862, within the six months' limitation, we have allowed the heirs to take the tract at private entry.

* * * * * * * * *

Cases of abandonment have been presented wherein it has been shown that, by reason of sickness, want of means or other good causes, the parties although they had cultivated had failed to meet the requirements of the law as to residence within the prescribed time. Where the intention was *bona fide* we have refused to cancel entries, but have allowed the five years' residence to take date from the day of actual settlement by residence on the tract, provided that the party file his affidavit within a reasonable period that he has permanently renewed settlement on the claim.

Where the widow of a deceased settler marries again, before the expiration of five years, it is held that if she continues the settlement and improvement of the claim to the expiration of the period fixed by the statute, the fee inures to the heirs, and final proof may be made in the name of the said heirs.

The amendatory act of 21st March, 1864, authorizes parties in the military or naval service, whose families, or some member thereof, are residing upon lands desired to be entered, to make the affidavit required by the homestead law of May 20, 1862, before the officer commanding in the branch of the service in which the applicant may be engaged; the affidavit, accompanied by the application, to be filed with the Register and Receiver of the Land Office, by the wife or other representative of the party and become effective from the date of such filing.

Persons in both the army and navy have made application through agents, under the impression that no settlement is required until the expiration of their term of service, and that should their service absorb five years, such service will be accepted in lieu of settlement and cultivation.

The law recognizes no such arrangement, and means have been taken properly to explain the scope and meaning of the statute, in order to counteract the evil, which has been so extensive as to induce this officer to dispatch to the several district officers a circular letter, directing them to receive no applications except such as may be accompanied by evidence of pre-existing settlement, as the law requires, on the part of the wife or representatives of the parties.

Since our last annual report the two years' restrictive clause in the act of 21st June, 1866, applicable to Southern States, as to the quantity of an entry, has expired, and the question has arisen whether the fee required under the act was increased with the quantity allowed to be taken.

It has been determined that the fee is the same as under the original act of 20th May, 1862, which was amended by the second section of the act of 1866; namely, five dollars for eighty acres or less, and ten dollars for a greater quantity, payable at date of entry.

The officers at Huntsville, Alabama, had erroneously made sale for cash of tracts formerly in the Cherokee Indian reservation.

The Commissioner has apprised them that by treaty stipulations, the lands had been quit-claimed to the United States and restored to the public domain, hence subject to disposal only in conformity with the provisions of the act of 21st of June, 1866, and that to sell for cash any tract would be in violation of law, and consequently the Register and Receiver are without authority for the sale of the premises.

(Report of 1868, page 98).

HOMESTEAD RULINGS.

A case was before the Commissioner, upon an application to cancel homestead entry, in which the testimony showed it to have been made while the claimant was serving in the army of the United States; that he was mustered out of the service in May, 1866; soon thereafter built a small shanty and commenced work upon the homestead, continuing to occupy the same, with frequent absences, though not at distant intervals.

It was held that the claimant had not abandoned his tract; yet the character of his improvement and manner of residence were not such as the law contemplates. The cancellation of this entry was declined on the evidence adduced, while a more complete compliance was called for under the law. It was insisted that the settler must put upon the land such a house as may answer for permanent residence—not merely a place of temporary resort in order to show his intention to comply with the law—and make the land what the statute intends—his actual homestead. A period of sixty days from the date of notice was allowed within which to complete his house and move therein, it being required at the expiration of that time that he should appear before the Register and Receiver and show by affidavit, supported by corroborative testimony, compliance with such requirements.

An entry has been presented in which the homestead was made and commuted before the expiration of five years from its date, and the point submitted was whether the settler could make another like entry. The sixth section of the homestead act of 1862 is specific in its declaration "that no individual shall be permitted to acquire title to more than one quarter section under the provisions of this act." Therefore it is held that when a party acquires title under any of the provisions of this act, his privilege is thereby exhausted.

Inquiry has been made whether persons employed in the military or naval service of the Government may take homesteads under the amendatory act of 21st March, 1864, and obtain title to the land, supposing their time of service to absorb all of the five-year period for settlement and cultivation.

The ruling is that actual settlement and cultivation of the land are required by law; hence title cannot be acquired unless the party, immediately upon discharge from service, enters upon the land, makes it his home, and cultivates the same, as required by the original act of 20th May, 1862; actual settlement upon and cultivation being required in all cases.

In the second section of the law of 20th May, 1862, it is stipulated in regard to settlers that in the case of the death of both father and mother, leaving an infant child, or children under twenty-one years of age, the right and fee shall enure to the benefit of the infant child or children; and that the executor, administrator, or guardian may sell the premises for the benefit of the infant heirs at any time within two years after death of the surviving parent, and in accordance with the law of the domicil.

The question has been made as to whether it is imperative the land shall thus be sold under the statute for the benefit of the heirs, or whether they can retain title under the original settlement.

The Commissioner rules that there is no objection under the general provisions of the law to the maintenance of settlement and cultivation on the part of the heirs, and the issue of the patent in their names at the expiration of the required time; yet in such case the minor heirs must continue to reside upon the homestead, and the settlement and cultivation of the same must be continued for their benefit.

In the case of a homestead settler who died unmarried, and whose father applied for preference right to take by ordinary purchase at $1.25 per acre, it is held that although privilege could not be granted, yet on satisfactory showing of the death of the settler, with proof of his previous settlement and cultivation, the land could be paid for at $1.25 per acre by the heirs of the deceased settler, under the eighth section of the act of 20th May, 1862, and entry made under that section in favor of the heirs of the decedent, following in this respect the rule prescribed by the second section of the act of 3d March, 1843, in regard to deceased pre-emptors. (Report of 1867, p. 82.)

HOMESTEAD COMMUTATIONS WITHIN RAILROAD LIMITS.

In the Secretary's decision of 22d June, 1866, as communicated in our circular of 25th August, 1866, the question discussed was the rights of pre-emption settlers to commute their filings on odd sections after the railroad withdrawal had been made. The Secretary then decided "the homestead settler's right attaches only from the date of entry," the pre-emptor from the date of his actual personal settlement; hence, if the commutation is not made prior to withdrawal, it cannot be made afterwards, the railroad grant taking effect immediately upon the abandonment of the pre-emption for the homestead.

By parity of reasoning this principle will apply to the *even sections* within the granted limits, in the matter of price; hence, if a party fail to commute prior to the increase from minimum to double minimum, he cannot commute afterwards at the rate of $1.25 per acre, because upon the relinquishment of the pre-emption claim, the double minimum immediately attaches, and he will be required either to prove up as an original pre-emptor at $1.25 per acre, or in commuting to restrict the homestead claim to eight acres.

Inquiries have been presented as to what is required of heirs at law desirous of making payment under the eighth section of the act.

The requirements are the production of evidence of heirship, with proof that the deceased settler had fully met the requirements of the statute by residing upon and cultivating the tract up to the date of decease; and further that the improvements had been continued and residence maintained by the heirs upon the homestead after the death of the settler; or, in case residence and cultivation had not been continued, proof that at the date of the application sufficient time had not elapsed since the decease to work a forfeiture of the claim. Instances have occurred in which a widow has made a homestead settlement and thereafter marries a person who, likewise had made a similar settlement on another tract. It is ruled that the parties may elect which tract they will retain for permanent residence, and that on proving up settlement under the eighth section of May 23, 1862, the title to the remaining entry may be perfected by the original settler. (Report of 1867, p. 83.)

HOMESTEADS.

The question has been raised in behalf of settlers whether a person who has availed himself of the benefits of the homestead, and pays for his claim under the eighth section of the act, can thereafter enter other land under pre-emption, provided he has never had the benefit of the latter statute.

On this point it has been ruled that where a party legally entitled makes an entry under the homestead law of May 20, 1862, and thereafter, at any time before the expiration of five years, shall come forward, make satisfactory proof of his actual settlement and cultivation to a given day, and then pay for the tract, the proceedings merely consummate his homestead right as the act allows; the payment being a legal substitution for the continuous labor the law would otherwise exact at his hands.

A claim of this character is not a pre-emption, but a homestead, and, as such, will be no bar to the same party acquiring a pre-emption right, provided he can legally show his right in virtue of actual settlement and cultivation on another tract at a period subsequent to the consummation of his homestead.

Cases have arisen where persons have made homestead settlements on unsurveyed tracts, and who, after the lines are established, find the premises falling in two different land districts.

The law restricts such settlements to *surveyed* lands, and hence, prior to survey, no rights attach under the statute. Then, as the law authorizes only *one* entry to be made by the same person, it is necessary for the party seeking the benefit of the statute to make the selection of his whole farm within one and the same land district. To entitle an applicant to enter an adjoining tract for the use of a farm, he must both *own* and occupy the *original* farm tract.

In regard to certain classes of contests which have arisen for entries under the homestead [act], it has been ruled, that where two persons apply at the same time for a tract on which neither has settlement and improvements, it must be awarded to the highest bidder—that is, to the party who will pay the highest price for the privilege of entering.

If two parties apply at the same time for a tract on which one of them has actual settlement and improvements, and the other has not, it must be awarded to the former, because it is not the policy of the system to allow one man to appropriate to himself the improvements resulting from the labor of another.

If a tract is simultaneously applied for by two persons, each having settlement and improvements on the same, an investigation is ordered, and if it is found that one has precedence by reason of prior actual settlement and substantial improvements, so as to be notice on the ground to any competitor, the award of entry will be made accordingly; but if neither has such substantial interests, the tract must be conceded to the highest bidder.

In reference to settlements on odd-numbered sections within the limits of withdrawals under railroad grants, the department in June last ruled that the homestead settler's right attaches only from the date of entry, the pre-emptor's from the date of his actual personal settlement. The title in either case is to be consummated by a full compliance with the terms and conditions imposed by law. The grant in aid of the railroad does not embrace lands to which a valid right arising either under the homestead or pre-emption had previously attached; but if such right be abandoned or forfeited, the grant would immediately thereafter take effect; that a pre-emptor cannot change his claim to a homestead entry so as to defeat the right which may have inured to the railroad company before the individual entry was made. If a pre-emption settlement had been commenced upon surveyed lands, it might be entered as a homestead before the right of the company attached, but not at a subsequent date. This ruling has been duly communicated for the government of the district land officers. (Report of 1866, p. 19.)

TITLE III.

Pre-emption Claims.

[See also Title II. HOMESTEADS.]

I. PRE-EMPTION GENERALLY.

No. 254 B.

The location of Louisiana internal improvement scrip on more than 320 *acres of other land, disqualifies the locator thereof, as a pre-emptor.*

ATTORNEY-GENERAL'S OFFICE,
November 15, 1860.

Sir :—The papers which you have sent me relative to the contest between Albert Rust and James M. Faust, have been examined. Faust has a pre-emption right to the land in dispute, unless his title be defeated by the showing of his adversary, that he was the owner or proprietor of three hundred and twenty acres of other land at the time he made his entry. In point of fact, he had located Louisiana internal improvement scrip on more than that quantity, and the sole question submitted is, whether that made him an owner or proprietor of such land within the meaning of the law. I am of opinion that it did, for although it did not make his legal title complete, it gave him an equitable estate, which carried, to all intents and purposes, the exclusive use and dominion over it. The conveyance which Faust made to his son is dated subsequently to the entry, and therefore is a fact of no importance in the case.

The affidavit of a party claiming a pre-emption right, denying the ownership of other land, is only one means of ascertaining the fact. It is not conclusive ; you are not required by the law to close your eyes upon other evidence which clearly shows the contrary.

Very respectfully yours, &c.
J. S. BLACK, Attorney-General.

Where a settler made a mistake in his declaratory statement, as to the particular tract intended to be claimed, but failed for three years to make the necessary proof and payment, and during his lifetime the land was granted away by Congress, it was held that a pre-emption entry of his heirs was not confirmable by the Commissioner of the Land Office. Opns. vol. 9, p. 515.

No. 255 B.

The pre-emption act of May 29th, 1830, did not vest any right in a settler to the land occupied and improved by him. The Government had the right at any time before proof and payment were made, to reserve the land from sale.

The decision of the Register and Receiver that a claimant had settled upon and occupied the land in accordance with said act is not, of necessity final and conclusive.

In cases of obvious conflict between the provisions of the constitution and those of a statute, every department of the Government required to act upon the matter, must determine what the law is, and obey the constitution.

ATTORNEY GENERAL'S OFFICE,
June 12, 1861.

SIR:—Your letter of the 2d ultimo relative to the claim of Belding's heirs for a patent for the Hot Springs Tract in Arkansas, has received my consideration.

1. The first question presented is, whether an entry upon lands of the United States, made in 1829, and a continued occupancy and improvement of the same from that time until the passage of the act of May 20, 1830, give such occupier a vested interest in the land.

A mere entry upon land with continued occupancy and improvement thereof, gives no vested interest in it. It may, however, give under our national land system, a privilege of pre-emption. But this is only a privilege conferred on settlers to purchase the land in preference to others (2 Bouv. L. Dic., 351). Of course it amounts to nothing until the land is actually open to sale, and until the settler takes the steps necessary to procure the Government title. His settlement protects him from intrusion or purchase by others, but confers no right against the Government. Until he makes an entry in the land office, and pays the purchase money, he is on the land only by sufferance, and may be turned off at the pleasure of the Government. To obtain a right to the land he must comply with the conditions of an act of Congress, which give the privilege of pre-emption; and it is in compliance with those conditions, and not the settlement, which vests in him an interest in the land.

The act of May 29th, 1830 (4 Stats. at L., 420), authorized the settler or occupant of the public lands who was then in possession, and had cultivated any part thereof in the year 1829, to enter with the Register of the land office for the proper district, any number of acres not more than a quarter section, to include his improvements, upon paying to the United States the then minimum price. This act gives to the occupant an inchoate right of entry, and if he had taken the steps directed by the act to enforce that right, before the passage of the act of 20th April, 1832, it would have become vested. But failing to do that, the land was left open to the operation of the act last named, and was by its force exempted from entry, location, or appropriation.

When the act of 1832 became a law, the tract in question was yet the property of the United States, and the occupant's possession and cultivation of it conferred simply a privilege to acquire the title in preference to others, if he chose to do so. But he had taken no step to avail himself of that privilege, and therefore the act of 1832 withdrew the land from entry, exactly as if no one had ever occupied it. Being thus withdrawn, it seems clear that the claimant cannot, by any subsequent proceedings, recover the foothold of which the act deprived him.

2. Your second question is: "If, after such occupation and improvement, the entry was not made before the land officers until the year 1838, because the land was not surveyed until that year, did the occupier lose his right of entry in consequence of such delay in proving it?"

We have seen that the occupant acquired no right until he complied with the conditions of the act of 29th May, 1830. One of these conditions was (sec. 3) that, prior to any entry being made under the privileges given by the act, proof of settlement or improvement should be made, to the satisfaction of the Register and Receiver of the district, agreeably to the rules to be prescribed by the Commissioner of the General Land Office for that purpose. This proof must have preceded the entry in the land office, and if not made until the year 1838, I am of the opinion that the occupier has lost his right of entry. The act of 20th April, 1832, as I have said, intervened, and deprived the occupant of the privilege of which he might have availed himself before its passage.

If the fact was that he could not make the entry because the land was not surveyed until the year 1838, I do not see that it makes any difference. It may have been his misfortune that Congress took away a privilege that he might have reduced to a right, if the land had been surveyed; but the power of Congress to do so was unquestionable, and as there is no evidence that he did anything to procure a title before the act of 1832 was passed, it left him in no worse condition than he was in before the act of 1830 was passed. But I do not think it was necessary for him to wait until the land was surveyed before doing any thing to secure his right. If he had, before the act of 1832 was passed, made the proof of settlement or improvement required by the act of 1830, and taken all the steps in his power to designate and assert his claim, it would present a grave question whether he had not removed the land from the operation of the act of 1832, or, in other words, whether the failure of the Government officers to do their duty would have deprived him of his land. However this may be, it is clear that, having waited until long after the act of 1832 had exempted this land from entry, location, or appropriation, his entry was made too late.

That the occupant's right to the land sprung, not from the settlement, but from the proof thereof, and the subsequent proceedings in the land office, is apparent from the fact that the fourth section of the act of 1830 declares that its provisions shall not be available to any persons who shall fail to make the proof and payment required before the day appointed for the commencement of the sales of lands including the tract on which the right of pre-emption is claimed. The fifth section limits the operation of the act to one year after its passage. If the right to the land grew out of the settlement, and not out of the proceedings before the land office, this limitation was useless, for the right being once created by the act, the lapse of a year would not destroy it. The obvious purpose of the limitation was to compel those who were settlers prior to the passage of the act to make proof and payment within the year, failing which, the privilege of pre-emption was at an end. None of the acts which were passed afterwards, extending and renewing the provisions of the act of 1830, applied to the tract of land in question, as they were passed after the act of 20th April, 1832, which withdrew four sections, including Hot Springs, from entry or appropriation.

3. Was the decision of the land officers, that the claimant had settled upon and occupied the land in accordance with the act of 29th May, 1830, final and conclusive upon that point?

I answer that, even if their decision was final and conclusive, that he had settled on and occupied the land, it does not follow that he thereby acquired a right to the title to this land. It is not the want of a settlement or occupancy that stands in the way, but the failure to take the steps necessary to make the settlement available under the act of 1830, before the act of 1832 was passed.

By the "land officers" referred to in this question, I understand you to mean the Register and Receiver of the land office of the district in which the land was situated, who reported that Belding had settled upon and occupied the land. It is true that the third section of the act of 1830, makes the Register and Receiver the tribunal to whose "satisfaction" proof of the requisite facts must be made, agreeably to the rules prescribed by the Commissioner of the General Land Office. By the first section of the act of 4th July, 1836 (5 Stats. at Large, 107)* it is provided that the executive duties prescribed by law, appertaining to the surveying and sale of the public lands of the United States, or in any wise respecting such lands, and also such as relate to private claims of land, and the issuing of patents for all grants of land under the authority of the Government of the United States, shall be subject to the supervision and control of the General Land Office, under the direction of the President of the United States.

And in Barnard *v.* Ashley (18 How. 44) it is held that the powers of Registers and Receivers under the acts of 29th May, 1830, and 19th June, 1834, are modified by this act of 1836, so as to be under the supervision of the commissioner. I am of the opinion that the decision of the land officers, that the claimants had settled upon and occupied the land in accordance with the act of 29th May, 1830, was not of necessity final and conclusive.

4. The fourth question concerns the power of an executive department to examine and decide upon the validity of an act of Congress, and to disregard its provisions.

There may possibly arise cases of plain and obvious conflict between the provisions of the constitution, and the provisions of a statute. In such cases there is no room for construction, no ground for argument; and in all such cases, not only the judiciary department but every department, and indeed every private man who is required to act upon the subject matter, must determine for himself what the law of the land, as applicable to the case in hand, really is. He must obey the law, the whole law; and if the conflict between the constitution and the act of Congress —the higher and the lower law—be plain and unquestionable, he must, of necessity, disregard the one or the other. He cannot disregard the constitution, for that is the supreme law; and therefore he must obey the constitution, even though, in doing so, he must disregard a statute. The constitution is the highest and strongest law of all, and therefore the lower and weaker law must yield to it in every case, before every tribunal, high or low, judicial or executive. This is predicated of cases where the conflict of law is plain and obvious. But in cases in which the conflict of law is doubtful, and its existence has to be made out by argument, I think it far more prudent for the administrative officer to follow the statute and leave the party who may be dissatisfied with his decision to seek his remedy in the courts. But in this case, I see no conflict at all. The form of the question leaves me to infer—for it is not plainly stated—that the supposed conflict arises out of the two acts of Congress of 1830 and 1832. The first gives the right of pre-emption, the second reserves the land from sale; and it seems to be supposed that the first gave to the pre-emptor a vested right to the land, and that the second in reserving

* Vol. i. No. 32.

the land from sale, assumed to take away that vested right; and so, that there is a conflict between the act of 1832 and the constitution.

I do not think so. The act of 1830 did not vest in the claimant any right to the land; it gave him only a contingent right (not binding on him, but to be used or waived at his pleasure) to become the first purchaser of the land, without competition, when the government should think fit to bring the lands into general market. This is not a vested right, it is not any present title to the land, but only a personal privilege, gratuitous, prospective, and contingent; and the general proprietor (the Government) had perfect right to reserve the land from sale. And, therefore, there is no good reason for supposing that the act of 1832 is unconstitutional.

5. Is it within the power of the head of an executive department to examine and allow a claim which has before been examined and rejected by one of his predecessors, without new evidence?

I know of no statute which prohibits the head of a department from examining and allowing a claim which has been before rejected by his predecessor; even where no new evidence is adduced, and without a statutory prohibition, I presume that he would have the power to do so. I do not think that the decision of the head of a department upon a claim before him has, upon the rights of claimants, the final and irrevocable effect of the judgment of a court of justice. Before giving them such effect it would be necessary to introduce the care and precision in commencing and conducting proceedings, strictness in the admission of evidence, fulness of argument, and facility of appeal to the tribunal of last resort, with which, in courts of justice, the law surrounds suitors. In the administration of the executive departments, as a general rule, these forms are neither appropriate nor possible, since the duties are ministerial rather than judicial.

But whilst these decisions are not, therefore, of final effect, they are certainly entitled to great respect, and should not be lightly overthrown. The Supreme Court, in the case of the United States *v.* The Bank of the Metropolis (15 Pet. 400–1) have gone so far as to say that, where the rights of a third party had intervened, upon the decision of the Postmaster-General allowing a credit, the succeeding Postmaster-General had no power to reverse the decision of his predecessor, but resort could only be had to the judicial tribunals of the country to correct the illegal allowance. And in 5 Opin. 187, Mr. Attorney-General Johnson treated the practice of the treasury department in cases analogous to the one before him, as conclusive upon the head of the department. Whilst I cannot accord to the decisions, or even the practice of a department, an effect so binding, I concur fully in the propriety of giving to them full weight and authority. Legal certainty is always desirable, and it can only be attained by respecting carefully considered precedents. And it is quite impossible to establish any departmental system of practice, if the opinions of each secretary are to furnish, for the time, the only rule of action. The convenience and interests of the Government and the rights of claimants require uniformity and certainty; and the well-considered decision of the head of a department ought only to be revised upon clear evidence of mistake or wrong.

Very respectfully,

EDWARD BATES, Attorney-General.

HON. Caleb B. Smith, Secretary of the Interior.

No. 256 B.

A legal pre-emption settlement cannot be made by a homestead claimant in case stated.

Homestead entries on tracts covered by pre-emption filings, cannot be allowed on affidavit that there are no improvements, &c.

Hearings in cases of conflict between homestead and pre-emption claimants —how conducted.

DEPARTMENT OF THE INTERIOR,
GENERAL LAND OFFICE, July 20, 1869.

Gentlemen :—This office has considered Register's letter of the 3d ult., in which instructions are asked on several points relative to the pre-emption laws.

1. It is stated that A. J. Botterf entered certain tracts March 2, 1866, as a homestead entry, and on the 2d Dec. 1868, commuted said entry under the 8th sec., act of May 20, 1862, and on the same day filed a D. S. for other tracts as a pre-emption.

To initiate a pre-emption claim actual personal settlement must be made on the tracts claimed prior to the filing of a D. S. therefor; Mr. Botterf could not have made a legal pre-emption settlement on any public land prior to his consummation by commutation on the 2d Dec. 1868, of his homestead entry.

The 10th sec., act of Sept. 4, 1841, provides that "no person who shall quit or abandon his residence on his own land to reside on the public land in the same State or Territory shall acquire any right of pre-emption under this act." In view of this inhibition, and the fact that no settlement preceded his filing, the D. S. is invalid, and Mr. Botterf has not acquired any pre-emption right to the tracts embraced therein, viz: W. ½ of SE. ¼, and E. ½ of SW. ¼, sec. 13, T. 23, R. 1 east.

2. Where offered lands are embraced in the declaratory statements, and such filings are formally abandoned or are forfeited for want of compliance with the requirements of law, the tracts covered thereby are subject to private entry without being advertised and offered for sale. Where such lands are embraced in homestead or other entries which have been subsequently cancelled by direction of this office, they *are not* subject to private entry until properly restored by being advertised and offered for sale.

3. You have *no* authority to allow homestead entries on tracts covered by pre-emption filings upon affidavits that there are no improvements on such tracts. In the case of filings on *offered* lands, where proof and payment are not made within the 12 months allowed by law, the filings are forfeited, and the tracts are subject to entry. In all other cases where allegations are made of non-compliance with the requirements of law, by persons claiming under declaratory statements, you will, on the application of parties for their cancellation, require such allegations to be made under oath, and if satisfactory cause is shown appoint a day of hearing, giving the parties in interest at least 30 days' notice thereof by personal service, if practicable, otherwise by such publication in a newspaper nearest the tracts claimed, at the expense of the applicant, as prescribed by the laws of the State, or by the rules of practice in the courts thereof in similar cases.

Conduct the hearings as in other contested cases, requiring the applicant's affirmative testimony in corroboration of his allegations of non-compliance with requirements of law, and when closed, report the testimony, with your opinion thereon, for our adjudication, awaiting instructions in each case before cancellation of filing or permitting entries of such tracts.

5. The Register states that there are many cases where single men have taken land under the pre-emption and homestead laws, who go on their claims, break a few acres or hire it done, build a small shanty, and live there a few days or weeks, and then go away, being absent four or five months, return for a short time, taking care not to be absent at any one time for the full period of six months. Also that in many cases pre-emptors work at a trade twelve or fifteen miles from their claims, hire some person to make improvements for them, and occasionally go to their claims themselves, sleep on the land once in a while, and when proof and payment are made, never go near their claims again.

The object of the pre-emption and homestead statutes is to secure the development of the public lands by actual and permanent settlement thereon and cultivation thereof, as a means of increasing the national wealth and resources.

Our practice requires that claimants under said statutes shall show actual and continuous personal residence upon the tracts claimed from the inception of such claim to its consummation, with such amount of improvements and extent of actual cultivation as will clearly identify the claimant with the tracts claimed as a permanent and *bona fide* settler.

Also, that no entries should be permitted under the pre-emption statutes unless at least *six* months of actual and continuous personal residence is shown by the pre-emptor and *his family*, if he have one, prior to the date of entry, except in cases where the extent of cultivation and value of improvements clearly identify the claimant with the claim as a permanent settler.

The same rule is applicable in cases of applications to commute homestead entries under the 8th sec., act of May 20, 1862.

You will thoroughly investigate all cases of the character referred to where absence is shown, or where you have grounds for belief that the claimant is not a *bona fide* settler, and require the testimony of two witnesses in each case, which must be satisfactory to you before you are authorized to permit an entry.

In case where the testimony *is not* satisfactory to you, and the claimant insists upon the right of entry under the pre-emption laws, without further proof, render your decision and notify him thereof, in order that an appeal may be taken to this office, if he desires; and if taken, forward the testimony, with your decision thereon, for our adjudication.

Respectfully, &c.,

JOS. S. WILSON, Commissioner.

Register and Receiver, West Point, Nebraska.

No. 257 B.

Pre-emption claim by a party who has made a homestead entry, invalid, in the case stated.

GENERAL LAND OFFICE,
July 24, 1869.

Sir :—Referring to our letter of the 23d ult., relative to the pre-emption claim of John Brabeck, of Big Blue, Saline County, Nebraska, per his letter of 30th of May last to you, referred to this office, I have the honor now to advise you that our records and the report of the Register of the land office at Lincoln, Nebraska, of the 15th instant, show that under the date of June 22, 1867, John Brabeck made an entry, No. 1,376, of S ½ of NW. ¼ of sec. 8, T. 7 N., R. 4 E., under the homestead statutes of May 20, 1862.

Also that under date of October 10, 1868, said John Brabeck filed a D. S., No. 2,611, for the N. ½ of NW. ¼ of sec. 8, T. 7 N., R. 4 E., claiming the same under the pre-emption statutes of sec. 4, 1841.

The homestead entry of Mr. Brabeck does not appear to have been consummated by commutation to a cash entry under the 8th sec. of the act of May 20, 1862, and the five years allowed him before he can make his final homestead proof will not expire until June 22, 1872; therefore he cannot initiate a valid claim under the pre-emption statutes, which, as well as the homestead statutes, require that the claimant shall have an actual continuous personal residence on the tract claimed thereunder from the inception to the commutation of such claim.

Mr. Brabeck cannot have such actual residence on two different tracts of land at the same time, and cannot carry out the requirements of the homestead and pre-emption statutes *pari passu.*

The claim thus sought to be initiated under the pre-emption statutes by said Brabeck is invalid in view of his prior homestead entry; therefore the action of the district officers in admitting the claim of Anthony Santin to said tract under the pre-emption statutes is correct and proper.

With great respect, &c.,

JOS. S. WILSON, Commissioner.

General W. T. Sherman.

No. 258 B.

A settler on an odd section withdrawn for railroad purposes cannot acquire a pre-emption right thereto.

GENERAL LAND OFFICE,
June 4, 1869.

A person settling on an odd section homestead covered by an entry not cancelled until after withdrawal for railroad purposes cannot acquire any pre-emption rights thereto, the land not being subject to settlement.

Respectfully, &c.,

JOS. S. WILSON, Commissioner.

W. C. Brown, Esq., St. Peters, Minnesota.

No. 259 B.

Fees of Registers and Receivers under the mining act of July 26, 1866.

GENERAL LAND OFFICE,
December 10, 1869.

This office has received a communication making inquiries as to the fees allowed by law to Registers and Receivers for services under the mining act of July 26, 1866.

In reply to similar inquiries heretofore made, the Commissioner of the General Land Office has decided that as the act referred to makes no specific provision on the subject of fees, the question must be determined by a well-known rule constantly applied in similar cases, and that the fees chargeable under the law must be the same as are specifically provided for like services under other acts of Congress; that the mining act is substantially a pre-emption law, and as the 4th and 6th sections of the act of March 21, 1864, amendatory of the homestead law, and for other purposes, provides that the Register and Receiver shall each be entitled to receive one dollar and fifty cents for their services in acting upon pre-emption claims in Montana and the other localities named, and shall be allowed jointly, at the rate of twenty-two and one-half cents per hundred words, for the testimony which may be reduced to writing by them, the same act will furnish a rule regulating the fees allowed under the act of July 26, 1866. The charge of twenty-two and one-half cents per hundred words need not be limited to what is technically called "testimony" in courts, but may very properly apply to all written matter necessary to prepare the case for administrative action in this office, whether the same be in the form of affidavits, certificates, or other appropriate and necessary writing, providing the same are prepared by the Register and Receiver, or according to their direction and under their supervision.

Respectfully, &c.,

JOS. S. WILSON, Commissioner.

No. 260 B.

PRE-EMPTION RULING.

The question has been raised whether "an unmarried woman, over the age of twenty-one years, not the head of a family," has the right to pre-empt, on making proof of settlement, and cultivation, as required by the pre-emption act of 1841.

The law extends the privilege to three classes, each having the qualification of citizenship, or having filed a declaration to that end:—

1. "Every person being the head of a family."
2. "A widow."
3. "A single man over the age of twenty-one years."

The case presented not coming within the first or second class, the question arises whether it does fall within the third class, according to the spirit and intent of the statute.

In the opinion of all etymologists, the name designating our race is derived from the power or faculties of body and mind, with which man has been furnished by nature above all other animals. * * *

Understanding the terms of the law in their wider sense, this office has decided that an unmarried or single woman over the age of twenty-one years, not the head of a family, but able to meet all the requirements of the pre-emption law, has a right to claim its benefits, and that while *man* is the general term including each sex, the specific name in the Anglo-Saxon of wif-man having been given to the female from her in-door employment at the *woof*, shows that in the ordinary doings of society the sphere of woman is generally in household, rather than in the duties requiring labor in the field essential to the establishment of a farm.

Therefore district officers have been charged in administering the law, under this construction, that it must be borne in mind the relations to agricultural labor of single women are generally different from those of single men; the former possessing more delicate organization are not usually separated from their parents or natural protectors, and hence that care must be taken this ruling shall not lead to abuse; that the claims of unmarried daughters are not to be recognized when their parents are householders, and where the purpose of the applicants in separating from their families may be merely to secure several different tracts of land, so that the title may eventually centre in a common head.

All the facts of individuality of interest, of residing on and cultivating the tract for a period long enough to show good faith, are required to be fully proven, so that, while abuse of the privilege is avoided, the right to the meritorious may be secured. (Annual report of Hon. Jos. S. Wilson, Commissioner for 1867, p. 80.)

No. 260½ B.

Pre-emption and Homestead Rulings from the Report of the Commissioner of the General Land Office for the year 1869.

PRE-EMPTION AND HOMESTEAD RULINGS.

In the administration of the settlement statutes, cases have arisen of the following character:—

A party who had made an entry under the homestead law commuted his title under the eighth section of the homestead act of May 20, 1862. Upon the same day that he perfected his homestead title he filed a declaratory statement for other tracts as a pre-emption.

It was held, that to initiate a pre-emption claim, actual personal settlement must be made on the tracts claimed prior to the filing of a declaratory statement, and consequently that the homestead settler could not have made a legal *pre-emption* settlement on any public land *prior* to his consummation of his homestead.

The tenth section, act of September 4, 1841, granting the right of pre-emption, provides that "no person who shall quit or abandon his residence on his own land to reside on the public land in the same State or Territory shall acquire any right of pre-emption under this act."

In view of this inhibition, and the fact that no settlement preceded the filing of the pre-emption declaration, such declaration is held to be invalid, and that the party connected with the proceedings acquired no pre-emption right under such circumstances.

In another case, a settler entered certain tracts as a homestead, and within a year and a half filed his pre-emption declaration for other tracts, not having either abandoned or consummated his homestead.

In this case, it was ruled that claims could not be initiated and carried forward by the same parties, *pari passu*, under the pre-emption and homestead statutes, for the reason that continuous personal residence on the tracts claimed, from the inception to the consummation of the claim, was an essential condition under each of said statutes, and that as the homestead party could not have an actual personal residence on two different tracts at the same time, the pre-emption filing made after the initiation of his homestead was unlawful.

Where lands have once been offered at public sale, and are afterwards withdrawn from market for railroad purposes, pre-emption settlements made thereon in good faith, *prior to date of withdrawal*, are subject to consummation within the period fixed by law for proving up and entering offered lands, to wit: in twelve months from the date of settlement at the ordinary minimum of $1.25 per acre.

Where *offered* lands are embraced in a declaratory statement and the filing is formally abandoned or forfeited for want of compliance with the legal requirements, the tracts embraced in such statement are subject to private entry without being again advertised and re-offered.

Where lands of this class are embraced in homestead or other entries, subsequently cancelled, they *are not* subject to ordinary private entry until properly restored by advertisement and re-offering.

It is ruled that the Register and Receiver have no authority to allow homesteads on tracts covered by pre-emption filings, upon *ex parte* affidavit that there are no pre-emption improvements thereon.

In the case of filings on *offered* lands, where proof and payment are not made within the twelve months allowed by law, the filings are forfeited and the tracts are subject to homestead.

In other cases, where allegations are made of non-compliance with the requirements of the statutes by parties claiming under pre-emption, the Register and Receiver, on application for cancellation, require such allegations to be made under oath; and if satisfactory cause is shown, the land officers are required to appoint a day of hearing, giving the parties in interest at least thirty days' notice; and thereafter they are required to make a report for final decision of the department.

It has been represented by the district officers that there are many cases where single men have taken land under the pre-emption and homestead statutes, who go on their claims and plow a few acres, or have such work done, build a shanty, and live there a few days or weeks, and then, after absence of four or five months, return for a short period, taking care not to be absent for the full period of six months. And further, that cases have occurred where pre-emptors work at a trade, or practise a profession some miles from their claims, hire persons to make improvements for them, and occasionally go to the premises, the claimants making slight improvements at or prior to the time of filing their declaratory statements.

The object of the pre-emption and homestead statutes is to secure the development of the public lands by actual and permanent settlement thereon, and cultivation, as a means of increasing the national wealth and resources. Our general practice requires claimants under these statutes to show actual and continuous personal residence upon the land from the inception of claim to its consummation, with such extent of improvements and of actual cultivation as will clearly identify the claimant with the premises as a permanent and *bona fide* settler. Further, that no entries should be permitted under the pre-emption statutes unless the fact is shown that at least six months of actual and continuous residence is made by the pre-emptor prior to date of entry, except in cases where the extent of cultivation and value of improvements clearly identify the claimant as a permanent settler.

The same rule is applicable, in cases of commutations of homestead, under the homestead act of May 20, 1862.

It has been enjoined upon the Registers and Receivers, in all cases of the character referred to, where absence is shown, or where they have grounds for belief that the claimant is not a *bona fide* settler, to require satisfactory testimony by two witnesses in each case, before they are authorized to permit an entry.

Where the testimony is not satisfactory to the district land officers and the claimant insists upon the right of pre-emption entry without further proof, the Register and Receiver are required to render their decision and notify the party thereof, in order that an appeal may be submitted to the department for final decision.

Cases have arisen where settlers have found it necessary, temporarily, to leave their tracts in view of Indian incursions. In such cases the department will treat the temporary absence as caused by duress, and as of no prejudice to the settler where all other requirements of the statute have been complied with, and where the parties return to their claims as early as may be consistent with personal safety to themselves and their families.

II. CALIFORNIA PRE-EMPTION LAND CLAIMS.

No. 261 B.

Settlement on the public lands confers no right as against the Government. Congress had power to dispose of lands claimed by settlers upon the Soscol Ranch, in California, under the pre-emption laws, at any time before proof and payment by claimants.

OPINION OF THE ATTORNEY-GENERAL IN THE CASE OF THE SOSCOL RANCHO.

ATTORNEY-GENERAL'S OFFICE,
May 26, 1866.

To Hon. James Harlan, Secretary of the Interior:—

SIR:—According to the view I take of the case of the "Soscol Rancho," stated in your letter of the 21st inst., it is entirely unimportant to determine at what time that tract became open to settlement under the general pre-emption laws, since, in my opinion, Congress had full power to dispose of the lands claimed by settlers under the pre-emption laws at any time before the proof and payment required by those laws were made. The purpose and effect of the act of March 3, 1863, were to remove from entry at the land office, by persons claiming to be settlers under the pre-emption laws, all the land within the limits of the "Soscol

---

California Lands and Land Claims.

Congress had power to dispose of lands claimed by settlers upon the Soscol Ranch, in California, under the pre-emption laws, at any time before the proof and payment required by those laws were made.—(Opinions of Attorney-General, vol. ii. p. 490.)

Settlement on the public lands of the United States confers of itself no right against the Government. It gives the settler, under the pre-emption laws, a right to enter the lands occupied and improved, when they are open to sale and he has complied with the laws in respect to proof of settlement and payment of the prescribed consideration.—*Ibid.*

Congress had power, as against persons who, before the passage of the act of March 3, 1863, had settled upon the lands in that ranch, but who had not perfected their right of entry, to confer upon claimants, under the Vallejo title, an absolute title to all the land purchased from Vallejo or his heirs.—*Ibid.*

It was the intention of Congress to enable any bona fide purchaser from Vallejo, whether resident or not of California, who settled either by himself or tenant part of the tract claimed by him, to acquire title thereto from the United States.—*Ibid.*

When the boundaries designated in a decree of the District Court, confirming a

Rancho," in California, until the expiration of twelve months after the return of the public surveys authorized by the statute to be extended over the tract of country embraced by that rancho. During that period each purchaser from Vallejo, or his assigns, was authorized to enter according to the lines of the public survey, at a dollar and a quarter per acre, so much of the land purchased from Vallejo, or those claiming under him, as he had reduced into possession at the date of the adjudication of the Supreme Court, which determined the invalidity of Vallejo's title. It was not until the expiration of the time limited for the establishment of the claims of the purchasers from Vallejo that any part of the land in "Soscol Rancho" was liable, after the passage of the act of 1863, to be dealt with as other public land, and then only such lands as remained unclaimed by purchasers from Vallejo or his assigns, or were embraced by claims of those purchasers which had been rejected by the Register and Receiver, were thrown open to entry under the general pre-emption laws. In this view of the purpose and effect of the statute of 1863, I have no difficulty in saying, in reply to your second inquiry, that a party who, prior to the passage of the act of March 3, 1863, commenced or continued a settlement in person upon a parcel of land within the "Soscol Rancho," and so complied with the terms and conditions of the pre-emption laws as to be entitled by virtue thereof, on making the proof and payment thereby required, to enter such parcel and obtain a patent therefor, is precluded from making such entry and obtaining such patent if the parcel claimed forms a part of a tract of land which at the time of the adjudication referred to had been reduced to possession by a bona fide purchaser from Vallejo or his assigns, who, within the period and in the mode prescribed by the statute of 1863, made claim to such tract, accompanied by the required proof showing his bona fide purchase, settlement, and reduction into possession of such tract.

It is not to be doubted that settlement on public lands of the United States, no matter how long continued, confers no right against the Government. It only gives the settler under the pre-emption laws a right to enter the land occupied and improved when it is open to sale, and when he has complied with the conditions as to proof of settlement and improvement and payment of the consideration prescribed by the statutes. It is compliance with those conditions that alone vests an interest in the land.

Mexican grant in California, embrace a greater tract than the quantity confirmed, the grantees have the right to select the location of this quantity in one body and in a compact form.—(United States *v.* Pacheco, 2 Wallace, p. 587.)

A confirmation of a Mexican land title in a proceeding conducted in the name of the original grantee is binding upon the United States and upon all the assignees of the original grantee.—(United States *v.* Covilland *et al.*, 1 Black. p. 339.)

When a survey is executed conformably to the decree of confirmation, the alienees of the original grantee may intervene to protect their own rights.—*Ibid.*

When the survey is completed and a patent issued to the original grantee, his assignees can assert their rights against him in the ordinary courts of the country.—*Ibid.*

But the extraordinary tribunals, proceeding under the act of 1851, cannot order a second patent to issue for a part of the land previously confirmed to the original grantee.—*Ibid.*

A claim under a Mexican grant cannot be confirmed without record evidence.—(United States *v.* Knight's Administrator, 1 Black. p. 227; United States *v.* Neeleigh, 1 Black. 298.)

The land continues subject to the absolute disposing power of Congress until the settler has made the required proofs of settlement and improvement, and has paid the requisite purchase money. Before those steps are taken for the designation and assertion of his claim, Congress may at any time intervene, and either exempt the land from entry, location, or appropriation, or dispose of it by grant to other parties. Before proof and payment are made, the only right which the settler has is an inchoate right of entry. When proof and payment are duly made, his right of entry becomes choate, and he acquires (perhaps even before entry) a vested interest in the land. The question may be a delicate one, whether Congress can impair a vested right of entry; but there is no doubt that before the settler has taken the steps necessary to convert the privilege of pre-emption into a vested right of entry, by establishing the fact of his settlement and paying the purchase money in the manner prescribed by law, Congress has absolute power to place the land beyond the operation of the statutes under which the settlement was made.

Pending the adjudication of the claim presented by Vallejo to the Board of Land Commissioners under the act of 1851, the lands embraced by his claim were not liable to be dealt with as public lands of the United States. The statute of 1851 declares, that "all lands (in California) the claims to which have been finally rejected by the commissioners * * or which shall be finally decided to be invalid by the District or Supreme Court * * * shall be deemed, held, and considered as a part of the public domain of the United States." When, therefore, the Supreme Court reversed the decree of the District Court affirming the validity of Vallejo's claim to the "Soscol Rancho," the lands embraced thereby became public lands, and liable to be appropriated by Congress, under its general constitutional power over the subject.

It is not necessary to determine whether, immediately on the decision of the Supreme Court, or at any time after, the lands in question, by operation of any statutes, became subject to pre-emption; whether, in other words, there was any law under which persons not claiming under grants from Vallejo or his assigns could have acquired by settlement proof thereof, and payment of purchase money, a right to enter the lands at the land office, if such right had not been defeated by the statute of 1863.

I assume that the lands embraced by the Vallejo claim fell, upon the adjudication of the Supreme Court, under the operation of the general pre-emption laws, as other public lands, or were subject to the operation of special laws of that denomination, applicable to public lands in California. But under those laws settlers could acquire, as I have already stated, no interest, which it was not competent for Congress to direct, until they had taken all the steps necessary to perfect their right to make entries of the lands settled and improved.

They were required not only to file declaratory statements within a time limited after the receipt at the district land office of the plats of the township embracing such settlements, but they were required also to establish their claims in the manner prescribed by law, and to pay the nominated consideration for the lands; and it was not until those proceedings at the land office had all been completed and consummated that any vested right or interest could be acquired which it was incompetent for Congress to disturb or affect by its legislation.

Now, I understand from your statement of the facts of the case under consideration, that although there may have been persons claiming adversely to the Vallejo grantees, who had perfected a right by continued settlement to make proof and payment as required by law, and who would have been entitled to enter the lands at the land office, and to obtain patents if such proof and payment had been actually made, yet that, at the date of the statute of 1863, such persons had not complied with those conditions, on which their right to make entry depended, and was alone capable of being perfected.

On the passage of the act of 1863, the right of such persons to make proof and payment, and of necessity therefor to make entries of the lands claimed by them, was placed in abeyance, and, by the operation of that statute, remained in abeyance until it was ascertained in the manner designated by the act, that the lands claimed had not been, at the date or the adjudication of the Supreme Court, reduced into possession by a *bona fide* purchase from Vallejo or his assigns, either through the neglect of any such purchaser to present his claim to the Register and Receiver, within the time limited by the statute, or through the failure of any such purchaser to establish his title to the tract comprehending the lands claimed under pre-emption laws.

Congress by the act of 1863 made new and different disposition of the property. It was passed in recognition of the high equities of the purchasers from Vallejo, whose claim was rejected on technical grounds by the supreme appellate tribunal, and was intended to afford such relief as not only a beneficent but a just government was bound to extend to persons in their situation.

It declared, without qualification, that every purchaser from Vallejo or his assigns might buy at the minimum price as much of the land as he had reduced into possession under his deed of conveyance when the adjudication occurred, and it gave him twelve months after the return of the survey within which to prove his title under Vallejo, and the extent to which the land claimed was at that date in his possession. If within the time limited for these proceedings any such purchaser duly established his title under Vallejo, he was entitled to enter, and obtain a patent for all the land which he proved had been reduced into his possession at the date of the decree of the Supreme Court, although a part of such tract was claimed by settlers who may have acquired, before the passage of the statute of 1863, a right to enter the land they claimed, on making the proof and payment required by the pre-emption laws.

It would seem to be unnecessary, in view of the foregoing considerations, that I should make extended answer to the second question stated in your letter.

I have already said that a settler under the pre-emption laws, acquires and can acquire no vested interest in the land he occupies by virtue simply of settlement; and that no vested interest is obtained until the settler has taken all the legal steps necessary to perfect an entry in the land office. Before such steps are taken, he has nothing but a contingent, personal privilege to become, without competition, the first purchaser of the property which he may never exercise, or which he may waive or abandon.

During the interval between the institution of the settlement, and the establishment of the claim by proof, and payment of the consideration nominated in the law, Congress has power to dispose of the land at its pleasure. It may recall the privilege previously conferred, or invest any one else with the same privilege, or it may make an absolute grant of the land to other parties, with, or without consideration. There is no constitutional objection to the exercise by Congress of any power over the land after settlement made, but before right of entry has been perfected, that it was competent to exercise before the land was thrown open to pre-emption.

Entertaining these opinions, I cannot doubt that Congress might, as against persons who, before the passage of the act of 1863, had actually settled upon the land in question, but who had not perfected their right of entry in the manner indicated, confer upon claimants under Vallejo an absolute title to all the land which they might prove was purchased from him or his assigns, and was reduced to possession at the date of the decision of the court.

This power, I am of opinion, also, Congress exercised by enacting the statute of 1863. It appearing, therefore, that a claimant under Vallejo was in possession, at the date of the decision, of any part of the land called for by his deed or purchase, his right to enter the tract so possessed, and obtain a patent therefor, is rendered absolute by the statute of 1863, and no supposed equity, based upon simple settlement, set up by a claimant under the pre-emption laws, can prevail against that right, or should be allowed to interfere with the full consummation of it, according to the intent of Congress.

The last point presented for my consideration is, whether a *bona fide* purchaser of a tract of this land from Vallejo or his assigns, is bound, in order to bring himself within the act of 1863, to prove an actual personal settlement on such tract at the date of the adjudication of the case, or whether a settlement at that date on such tract, by another person as the tenant of such purchaser is sufficient, although such purchaser be a non-resident of California.

The Supreme Court, in Hickie *et al. vs.* Starke *et al.* (1 Peters, 98), in giving interpretation to the words "*actual settlers*," in the cession act of Georgia, held that a settlement made on the land claimed by another person who cultivated it for the proprietor, was sufficient to satisfy the requisitions of the act, though the proprietor neither resided in person on the estate, or, indeed, in the territory. Even if there were doubt upon principle as to the legal import of the term "*settlement*," as used in the statute of 1863, I should not hesitate, in view of this high judicial authority on the point, to determine that personal settlement at the date of the adjudication mentioned is in no case necessary to be proved by a claimant under the statute in order to satisfy its requirement. The better opinion I think is, that the two forms of expressions used in the statutes to indicate the particular relation to, or connection with, the land, on the part of the claimant necessary to be established by proof, are, considering their contexts, really convertible, and that the ideas involved in them are not distinguishable. The cardinal idea of the statute was the one conveyed by the expression "*reduced to possession*," the only one employed in section 2, which contains the words of grant on which the rights of the claimants depend. The maxim *qui facet per alium, facet per es*, whether of universal application in cases of claims under the general pre-emption laws or not (and I am inclined to agree with Mr. Attorney-General Butler in the opinion that it is not), expresses, in my opinion, the legal rule for the determination of claims under the special act of 1863. It was not the equity possessed by the claimants under Vallejo, derived from settlement, occupation, or cultivation alone of the lands they had purchased, which induced Congress to give the relief provided by that act. The act was passed in recognition of the view so ably and powerfully enforced by Mr. Justice Grier, in his opinion dissenting from the judgment of the court, that the grant to Vallejo was a genuine grant for a consideration paid, and so universally acknowledged in the country of its origin, which the Mexican government would never have disturbed on any of the grounds on which the invalidity was affirmed by the majority of the judges of the

Supreme Court. That was the superior equity possessed by all *bona fide* purchasers from Vallejo or his assigns, which Congress deemed eminently worthy of protection. If the grant set up by Vallejo had been rejected as fabricated or spurious, there is no reason to believe that Congress would have extended protection to any who deduced title through such a grant, however strongly their claims as mere settlers or occupants of the land might have been commended to its consideration. Congress did not require the claimant to prove any connection with the lands which they had purchased earlier than the date of the adjudication of the case; it was not thought that parties whose relations to the property were of earlier inception had superior rights to those possessed by persons who at that date had reduced the lands they claimed into their possession; nor were the equities of the latter deemed in any sense inferior to the equities of the former. The beneficent provisions of the statute were grounded upon a consideration higher and deeper than the settlement of the lands by the Vallejo claimants; they were suggested and framed in the belief that those claimants possessed an equity as purchasers of a genuine though defective title derived from Mexico, to which this government in good faith was bound liberally to extend protection.

I hold, therefore, that in view of the general policy of the statute, it is the duty of the department charged with its execution to give such construction and effect to its provisions as is most consonant with its reason, and will best promote its objects. I think it was plainly the intention of Congress to enable any *bona fide* purchaser from Vallejo or his assigns, whether resident or not of California, who should prove within the time limited that he had effected, either personally or through a tenant, a settlement of a part of the tract embraced by his claim, to acquire the title thereto from the United States.

I am, sir, most respectfully,

(Signed) JAMES SPEED, Attorney-General.

No. 262 B.

Opinion of Mr. Justice Wylie as to the rights of pre-emptors on the "Soscol Ranch," in California.

SUPREME COURT DISTRICT OF COLUMBIA.

At Chambers, August 16, 1866.

LEVI H. WHITNEY
v.
JOHN B. FRISBIE.

Both parties to this suit are citizens of California, and the land in controversy is in that State also. For these reasons the jurisdiction of this court has been earnestly called in question by the defendant—a question which will be examined presently.

The land consists of a single quarter section, part of a large tract embracing nearly 100,000 acres, known by the name of the Soscol Ranch, and on which are situated the city of Benicia, the town of Vallejo, the United States Navy Yard on Mare Island, and the depot of the Pacific Steamship Company, besides numerous cultivated farms, and a considerable population.

The decision of the questions involved in this controversy, it is said, will affect the interests of many other persons, and a large amount of property in that ranch.

The present motion is to obtain an injunction to restrain the defendant from taking out a patent for the quarter section in controversy, and cannot be disposed of, properly, without deciding upon the claims of the respective parties, as stated by themselves in the bill, the answer, and their respective exhibits.

The Soscol Ranch was sold by Micheltorena, then Governor of California, to Col. Vallejo, in the year 1844, for the sum of about $5000, as alleged.

After the Mexican war had closed, and in the year 1851, Congress passed an act under which commissioners were appointed to investigate, and decide upon the validity of private land claims in California, and giving the right of appeal first to the District Court, and finally to the Supreme Court of the United States.

Both the board of commissioners and the District Court decided in favor of the validity of Vallejo's title to the whole of the Soscol Ranch; but, on appeal to the Supreme Court, that judgment was reversed, and Vallejo's title held to be bad.

In such case, the act of 1851, declared the land should "be deemed, held, and considered as part of the public domain of the United States." But as these lands had not then been officially surveyed, they were not open to settlement and pre-emption, under the laws at that time governing pre-emptions.

The act of 3d March, 1853, which provided a special land system for California, subjected the unsurveyed, as well as the surveyed public lands in that State, to the operation of the act of 4th September, 1841, with certain reservations and exceptions, and on certain terms and conditions therein stated. One of these exceptions was in these words, "and excepting also the lands claimed under any foreign grant or title."

It has been argued that this exception cannot apply to the land in controversy in this case, because the Supreme Court has decided that Vallejo never had any valid grant or title to them from the government of Mexico; that a void grant or title amounts to no title at all, and therefore he claimed under no title whatever; that this ranch, therefore, was not embraced by the exception, and was always open to settlement and pre-emption.

To this, it is sufficient to say, in answer, that unless the exception was meant to apply to this case, it could have no application to any other. For, if Vallejo's title had been good, the land would have been private property, and not subject to the operation of the act which applied only to "the public lands in the State of California." But by the third proviso of the sixth section of this act, the privilege of settlement and pre-emption on the unsurveyed lands, was to continue but for one year from its date. The act of March 1, 1854, extended this privilege till March 1, 1856, when it expired. From this last date, therefore, there existed no right of settlement and pre-emption on any of the unsurveyed lands of the United States, in the State of California, until after the passage of the act of June 2, 1862, ch. 94, which again subjected "all the lands belonging to the United States to which the Indian title has been, or shall be extinguished, whether surveyed or unsurveyed, to the operation of the act of 4th September, 1841.

On the 24th day of March, immediately preceding the date of the act of June 2, 1862, the Supreme Court of the United States pronounced its decision declaring void and null the claim of Vallejo to all the lands within the limits of the Soscol Ranch. (See United States *v.* Vallejo, 1 Black, Rep. 541.)

Both by the special provision which has been referred to in the act of 1851, and by the highest judicial decision, therefore, the lands embraced in the Soscol Ranch became a part of the public domain; and by the act of 2d of June, 1862, although unsurveyed, was thrown open to actual settlement and pre-emption.

The quarter section of land now in controversy, was entered upon by the complainant in the month of October, 1862; and, it appears, he has made the necessary improvements and cultivation, and complied, or tendered himself ready to comply, with all the other terms and conditions required by law to entitle him to obtain a patent for the land from the government.

Thus we see that complainant, from this date, had acquired as good and valid a right to pre-empt this tract of land, as can ever be obtained by any settler prior to the completion of his title by patent. But after he had thus acquired an inchoate equitable title to the land, Congress, by passing the act of 3d March, 1863, interposed in behalf of the *bona fide* purchasers under Vallejo, to take it away from him and sell the land to them.

This act provided first for a survey to be made of the Soscol Ranch, as a portion of the public lands.

Second, that after the plats of survey had been returned to the district land office, "it shall, and may be lawful for individuals, *bona fide* purchasers from said Vallejo or his assigns to enter, according to the lines of the public surveys, at $1.25 per acre, the land so purchased, to the extent to which the same had been reduced to possession at the time of said adjudication of said Supreme Court."

Section fourth provides that all claims within the purview of the act should be presented to the Register and Receiver within twelve months after the return of the surveys, accompanied by proof of *bona fide* purchase under Vallejo, of settlement, and the extent to which the lands claimed had been reduced to possession at the time of the adjudication of the Supreme Court, and said Register and Receiver were to decide upon said claims, under such instructions as should be given them by the Commissioner of the General Land Office, to whom the proof and adjudication were to be returned by the local land office, and no adjudication should be final until confirmed by the commissioner.

This act constitutes the foundation of the defendant's claim in the present case.

Defendant is the son-in-law of Vallejo, and claims to have purchased from him in the year 1855, *bona fide*, a large tract of the Soscol Ranch, including the quarter section here in controversy.

The Register and Receiver, under instructions from the Commissioner of the General Land Office, "took proof" as required, in regard to the claim of the defendant, and decided the case in his favor.

This decision of the Register and Receiver, however, was reversed by the commissioner of the land office, on the ground that the settlers had obtained a valid right of pre-emption to the land in controversy, prior to the passage of the act of March 3, 1863.

The case was then taken on appeal to the Secretary of the Interior, who referred the legal questions involved in the controversy to the Attorney-General of the United States, who advised the secretary "that a settler under the pre-emption laws acquires, and can acquire, no vested interest in the land he occupies by virtue simply of settlement; and that no vested interest is obtained until the settler has taken *all* the legal steps necessary to perfect an entrance in the land office. Before such steps are taken, he has nothing but a contingent, personal privilege to become, without competition, the first purchaser of the property, which he may never exercise, or which he may waive or abandon. During the interval between the institution of the settlement and the establishment of the claim by proof and payment of the consideration nominated in the law, Congress has power to dispose of the land at its pleasure. It may recall the privilege previously conferred, or invest any one else with the same privilege, or it may make an absolute grant of the land to other parties, with or without consideration."

Accepting this opinion of the Attorney-General as his guide, the Secretary of the Interior has reversed the decision of the Commissioner of the Land Office in this case, made in favor of complainant's right of pre-emption, and as a complainant alleges, a patent is about to issue to defendant, for the land in dispute, unless the same should be prevented by the injunction of this court, whereby he might be expelled from his possession, or the title be conveyed by defendant to some purchaser without notice, litigation be multiplied, a cloud be cast over his title, and irreparable injury be done him.

It is with much hesitancy that I find myself compelled to dissent from the doctrines of law laid down by so high an authority. But my own convictions are very strong, and I follow them with the less diffidence since the learned Attorney-General has failed to support his opinion by reference to any decisions or other authority whatever, or by any arguments deduced from general principles.

In the United States *v.* Fitzgerald, 15 Peters, 407, it was decided, that no reservation or appropriation of public land can be made after a citizen has acquired the right of pre-emption.

The doctrine is thus broadly laid down in the opinion of the court in that case. But there the defendant had not only made his settlement and entry, but had paid his money to the Receiver for it. I do not consider that this last fact affects the principle established by that decision, however; for if Congress may disregard and override the rights acquired by actual settlement, and the expenditure of labor and money in erecting improvements upon the land and subduing it by cultivation, it must possess an equal right to refuse its patent to the pre-emptioner after he has added to these considerations the payment also of the purchase money.

In Lytle *v.* The State of Arkansas, 9 Howard, 333, the Court say: "The claim of pre-emption is not that shadowy right which by some it is considered to be. Until sanctioned by law, it has no existence as a substantive right; but when covered by the law it becomes a legal right, subject to be defeated only by a failure to perform the conditions annexed to it."

In Delassus *v.* The United States, 9 Peters, 133, Chief Justice Marshal says that "no principle is better settled in this country than an inchoate title to lands is property," and again he says: "The inquiry then is whether this concession was legally made by the proper authorities, and might have been perfected into a complete title." His inference was that the inchoate right, which might have been perfected into a complete title, was "property."

In Smith *v.* The United States, 10 Peters, 330, Mr. Justice Baldwin, in delivering the opinion of the court, says: "It was never doubted by this court that property of every description in Louisiana was protected by the law of nations, the terms of the treaty, and the act of Congress; nor that in the term 'property' was comprehended every species of title, inchoate, or perfect, embracing those rights which lie in contract, those which are executory, as well as those which are executed." (See also Rice *v.* Railroad Company, 1 Black, 358.)

It seems to me these authorities are conclusive of the question.

But the question is equally clear, also, on general principles. It has been for many years the policy of the Government to invite immigration, to encourage the growth of the new States, and by this means to increase the population, the wealth and prosperity of the whole country, and add to the greatness, strength, and resources of the Government itself.

In pursuance of this policy it has passed laws proclaiming the terms upon which persons possessing the requisite qualifications, may obtain the right to pre-emption of the public lands; namely, to go themselves, in person, and settle upon and improve the lands they may select, and pay for them afterwards, at the rate of a dollar and a quarter an acre.

If an individual were to offer such terms in any case, he would be bound by his offer, and no court in the land would sustain his defence, that he had only offered these terms as a bounty, and could retract them at his pleasure, and sell the land to another.

To be sure the settler has the option, after making his entry and settlement and up to the time of paying the purchase money and getting out his patent, to remove from the land and abandon his claim. But that option allowed him, is part of his contract. The Government has granted him the option in the bargain either to go on and fulfil it until his title is perfected by the patent, or to quit the land at his pleasure. In the latter event the Government can suffer no damage, for it has parted with no value, and retains the title to the land. It is like a contract for the sale of land in which the owner retains the title as security for the purchase money. The purchaser, unless he have given his personal contract to the contrary, may at any time abandon his improvements, and leave the property to its owner without further liability. And yet had he remained and complied with the terms of his agreement, the owner would have been bound to him for the title, and in the mean time, the purchaser had an equitable interest of which no power could deprive him without his own consent, unless taken for public use by the Government on payment of its value.

The notion, that the right of pre-emption of the actual settler is no more than a "bounty" from the Government, which the latter may at any time recall, originated probably in this way, and was undoubtedly correct under the early acts of Congress relating to pre-emption.

In the beginning, all persons entering upon the public lands without title or permission from the Government were regarded as trespassers, and were so spoken of and threatened with penalties, in several acts of Congress. Nevertheless, persons continued to go upon the public lands and make their settlements, in defiance of the laws. In 1830, '32, '33, '38, and '40, however, Congress, instead of providing means for driving these trespassers off the lands, enacted several statutes giving those who were thus settled upon the public domain, at the date of the passage of those acts, the privilege of pre-emption for their respective quarter sections, on certain terms therein specified. This privilege was, in truth, bounty to these trespassers, which they had no right to demand of the Government; for they had gone upon the lands not only without inducement, but in defiance of law. Until after the passage of the act of 4th September, 1841, no one could become a pre-emptioner unless he had first been a trespasser. But the act of the 4th September, 1841, introduced a new system, prospective in operation, and pledged the faith of the Government that it would grant to all future settlers upon the public lands, possessing the qualifications prescribed, and who should make improvements and bring their respective tracts into cultivation, the privilege of pre-emption. The former acts are obsolete, and this act now constitutes the general land system on this subject. Under it the settler who enters upon the public land and complies with its terms, has the right, by law, to demand his title from the Government, by the strict terms of a contract, and not as bounty which the Government is at liberty to grant or to withhold, at its pleasure.

If these views be correct, the complainant, by making his entry and settlement on the land in controversy in this cause, in the month of October, 1862, and erecting his buildings and cultivating the land, acquired a vested interest therein, which the Constitution has placed beyond the reach of even an act of Congress to take from him and grant to another. I am of opinion, therefore, that complainant shows a valid equitable inchoate right to the property in question, which he had acquired anterior to the passage of the act of Congress of March 3, 1863, under which defendant denies his claim to have a title granted to him by the Government; and that the decision of the Commissioner of the Land Office in favor of the settlers, which was reversed by the Secretary of the Interior, on the advice of the Attorney-General, was clearly correct.

But defendant's counsel have, both by the answer in the case, and on the argument of the present motion, most earnestly denied the jurisdiction of the Supreme Court of this district over the subject of this controversy, on the ground that it is a suit to decide the title to land which lies in California, over which, therefore, none but the local court in that State possesses rightful jurisdiction.

If such were, indeed, the nature of this controversy, this court would be without jurisdiction to decide it. (See Massie *v.* Watts, 6 Cranch, 148.) But if I correctly comprehend the nature of this controversy, the object of the complainant is not to recover the possession of the land in question—for he is already in possession of it—but it is to obtain a decree on the ground of fraud and trust, which will prohibit the defendant from obtaining from the Government a patent for the land, which in equity ought to be made to himself; or, in case a patent should be granted to the defendant, he may be declared to be a trustee of the legal title for the complainant.

That is a very different question from a question of simple superiority of titles derived from distinct sources, the decision of which belongs to the court having jurisdiction over the land.

Questions involving trust or fraud are personal matters, of which a court of equity will take jurisdiction wheresoever the defendant may be found and served with process.

In the celebrated case of Penn *v.* Ld. Baltimore (1 Ves. Sr. 444), the Chancellor of England (Ld. Hardwicke) decreed a specific performance of a contract respecting lands lying in North America, because, as said by the Ld. Chancellor, "the conscience of the party was bound by the agreement, and being within the jurisdiction of this court, which acts in *personam*, the court may properly decree it as an agreement, if a foundation for it."

In Massie *v.* Watts, 6 Cranch, 148, a suit was instituted in the Circuit Court of Kentucky to compel a conveyance of the legal title to land in Ohio, by the defendant, on the ground that he had notice, when it was purchased, of the prior equity of the complainant; and the defence taken was that the land lay beyond the jurisdiction of the court and within the State of Ohio. This defence was overruled by the court below, and afterwards by the Supreme Court, who held that as the facts set forth in the bill showed that defendant was equitably bound to convey the land, equity would enforce the fulfilment of this obligation, without regard to the place where the land was situated.

"When the defendant is liable," said Marshall, C. J., "either in consequence of contract, or as trustee, or as the holder of a legal title, acquired by any species of *mala fides* practised on the plaintiff, the principles of equity give a court jurisdiction wherever the person may be found, and the circumstance that a question of title may be involved in the inquiry, and may even constitute the essential point on which the case depends, does not seem to arrest that jurisdiction."

Again he says upon this point: "Upon the authority of these cases and of others which are to be found in the books, as well as upon general principles, this court is of opinion that in a case of fraud, of trust, or of contract, the jurisdiction of a court of chancery is sustainable wherever the person be found, although lands not within the jurisdiction of that court may be affected by the decree."

And on this subject it will make no difference whether the defendant be actually domiciled here, or is here only temporarily. In Archer *v.* Preston, cited by Ld. Nottingham and Ld. Keeper Guilford, in the case of Earl of Arglasse *v.* Muschamp, 1 Vern. 77-135, a decree was made for the specific performance of a contract respecting lands in Ireland, the defendant having been served with process whilst temporarily within the jurisdiction of the court.

In Baker *v.* Dumaresque, 2 Atk. R. 66, Ld. Hardwicke restrained a defendant from leaving the kingdom for the place of his abode until he should give security to abide the decree.

In Atkinson *v.* Leonard, 3 Bro. C. C. 218, the writ of *ne exeat* was granted in favor of an inhabitant of Antigua against another resident of that island who had come to England with his wife for medical advice.

In Shattuck *v.* Cassidy, 3 Edw. Ch. R. 152, and in De Klyn *v.* Watkins, 3 Sandf. Ch. R. 185, it was held that the jurisdiction of the Court of Chancery in a case of fraud, of trust, or of contract, is sustainable wherever the person sought to be affected is found, although lands not within the jurisdiction of the court may be affected by the decree.

In Guarrant *v.* Fowler, 1 Hen. & Munf. 4, it was decided that where the decree would affect the lands directly, as in a suit for partition, the court has not jurisdiction if the land lie in another State, but a person within the commonwealth may be decreed to execute a conveyance of lands in another State, or to cancel a deed for such lands obtained by fraud. Even a bill for the foreclosure of the equity of redemption in lands is transitory, and any court where the defendant is found has jurisdiction. Caufman *v.* Sayre, 2 B. Mon. Rep. 202.

In Buchannan *v.* Lorman, 3 Gill, R. 52, the land in question lay in Virginia, but the defendant was found in Maryland. He had previously obtained a decree in Virginia under which he had purchased the land. The Maryland court decided that it was bound to give full faith and credit to the Virginia decree, but as it would be a fraud on the complainant if defendant were permitted to get the land, the court enjoined him from taking a conveyance under the Virginia decree in his favor.

The only question, then, to be considered is whether, in the language of Chief Justice Marshall, in Massie *v.* Watts, "the defendant is liable, either in consequence of contract, or as trustee, or as the holder of a legal title acquired by any species of *mala fides* practised on the plaintiff;" or, as said by Ld. Hardwicke in Penn. *v.* Baltimore, "the conscience of the party is bound."

Now, it has been shown that the complainant possesses an equitable inchoate title to the land in dispute, in consequence of his entry and actual settlement and improvements made thereon, of all which defendant had notice at the date of the act of 3d March, 1863; and that notwithstanding this, defendant has been endeavoring to procure a patent from the Government with a view to claim the land as his own, and deprive complainant of the rights acquired by his settlement.

If defendant were to succeed in procuring a patent for this land, under these circumstances, a court of equity must hold him to be a trustee of the title for the complainant.

In the United States *v.* Hughes, 11 Howard, 552, it was held that "when a person entering land according to law, but omitted to obtain a patent for it, and another person afterwards obtained a patent from the United States by proceeding as if it were vacant land, knowing at the same time that it was not vacant, the patent thus obtained will be set aside." And this on the ground that the patentee had been guilty of a fraud upon the Government in procuring his patent when he was all the time aware that another person had made an entry of the same land. Here we have decided, what will constitute fraud in the eye of equity.

Story says: "Another class of constructive frauds consists of those where a person purchases with full notice of the legal or equitable title of other persons to the same property. In such cases he will not be permitted to protect himself against such claims, but his own title will be postponed and made subservient to theirs. It would be a gross injustice to allow him to defeat the just rights of others by his own iniquitous bargains. He becomes by such conduct a *particeps criminis* of the fraudulent grantor; and the rule of equity as well as of law is *Dolus et fraus nemini patrocinari debent.*" 1 Com. on Equity, section 395.

Again the same author says: "The same principle applies to cases of contract to sell lands or to grant leases thereof. If a subsequent purchaser has notice of the contract he is liable to the same equity, and stands in the same place, and is bound to do that which the person who contracted, and whom he represents, would be bound to do." Ib., sec. 396.

We have seen in the case before us that the Government had pledged its faith to grant a title to the complainant for the land in question; that complainant, before the passage of the act of 3d March, 1863, had acquired a valid inchoate equitable interest in the land, of which he could not be deprived even by an act of Congress without his own consent, or just compensation, should it be required for public use. We have seen an act of Congress passed for the benefit of this defendant, the effect of which would be to deprive complainant of his property, and sell it to the defendant for a dollar and a quarter an acre. The Supreme Court of the United States have frequently declared that in the measures adopted by the Government to dispose of the public lands, it is bound by the same obligations of right and law which apply to individuals in like circumstances.

Here, then, is the case of a party who has entered into contract to sell a portion of his land, on certain terms and conditions to be complied with by the purchaser. The purchaser has gone on and fully complied, or offered to comply, with those terms and conditions. Subsequently the owner enters into another contract or engagement to sell the same land to a different person, who has full notice of the previous contract with the other.

In the case of individuals this would amount to constructive fraud, at least, on the part of both, and equity would forbid or annul the transaction. It is not, for a moment, to be imagined that the Congress of the United States could have intended to do injustice to any one by the act of 3d March, 1863. We are to presume that Congress was unaware at the time of its passage of the existence of rights to the Soscol property which had sprung up under the pre-emption laws. That was a private act, and in legal presumption was passed on the application and through the representations of those who were to receive benefit from its enactment. "Every bill for the particular benefit of a person, a company, or a locality in which the whole community is not interested is, in a parliamentary sense, a private bill, brought in on the solicitation of parties." Dwarris on St. 354.

Although the British Parliament will not allow a private bill to be reported, unless on previous notice published in the Gazette, and petition of the parties interested, and, in regard to the Crown lands, on certificate of the Crown, that the case is a proper one for Parliamentary relief, yet I think that even in this country, where these wise preliminaries are not required by Congress, it cannot be regarded as a strained presumption that whenever a private act has been passed by Congress conferring privileges, or affording relief, it was done on the petition and representations of those for whose interests it was passed.

If these be fair presumptions, it follows, that the act of 3d March, 1863, was passed in consequence of representations made by parties claiming the Soscol Ranch under Vallejo's title, then recently pronounced by the Supreme Court to be void—that there were no pre-emption rights in existence as to the land in question with which the act could interfere.

Such representations, whether made in good faith or otherwise, were not true, as we have seen, and for that deception the claimants under Vallejo are responsible.

Now, although this court cannot control the acts of the Secretary of the Interior in this matter, by direct interference, yet, after the subject has been properly brought under its judicial cognizance, it is certainly not bound to adopt the construction given to a law by the Secretary, and if it supposes his decision to be wrong, will, of course, so pronounce its judgment. See Decatur *v.* Spalding, 14 Peters, 497.

In this respect, the court proceeds upon the same principles in reference to the acts of the Government, that it does in regard to the judgment of other courts.

If a proper case for relief in equity be made out, a court of chancery will enjoin all proceedings by a plaintiff in his action at law, against the complainant in equity; and the injunction will be granted at any stage of these proceedings, either before or after judgment. In doing so, however, the court of law is not made a party to the bill, nor is the injunction issued against the court; but it is issued against the plaintiff in the action forbidding him to take any benefit from his inequitable judgment, or other proceedings. So in the case of the Government, or one of the Secretaries in his official capacity, this court will not assume to control his acts by direct interference, but it will reach the ends of justice by injunction against the private individual who is attempting to gain an inequitable advantage over his adversary through a decision of the Government's officer.

Complainant's equity is therefore shown to be clear; and it is equally clear that this court has jurisdiction to decree relief. The only question that remains to be considered is whether the circumstances of his case are such as require the protecting power of an injunction, to shield him from danger during the pendency of his suit, and before a final decree can be obtained.

Although an injunction is something extraneous to a cause, and not a proceeding in it, and ought not to be granted except where it is recommended by the dictates of conscience, and the clearest principles of justice yet where it is requested upon principles of equity and justice, it should not be refused. The interference rests on the principle of a clear and certain right to the enjoyment of the subject in question, and a probable injurious interruption of that right, which, on just and equitable grounds, ought to be prevented. See Hillard on Injunctions, section 18.

In Carroll *v.* Safford, 3 How. R. 441, the Supreme Court of the United States held that "in case of controversy, a court of equity is the proper tribunal to *prevent* an injurious act by a public officer, for which the law might give no adequate redress, or to avoid a multiplicity of suits, or to prevent a cloud from being cast over the title."

Equity rejoices more in the exercise of her power to prevent than in that of redressing injuries; and the injunction has been well called the right arm of her authority.

If the defendant in this case were to obtain a patent for the land in question, it would enable him to bring his action at law in California to recover the possession and oust the complainant, notwithstanding the equitable title of the latter. Without the patent, he cannot maintain any such action. Nor is it in the constitutional power of that State to authorize him to recover the land from the defendant, unless he have obtained a patent. Wilcox *v.* Jackson, 13 Peters, 498.

To issue the injunction in this case will prevent that litigation. Complainant is in possession of the land under the pledged faith, and by positive contract with the United States for a valuable consideration. He is entitled in equity, to a patent for this land. This court has obtained jurisdiction over the controversy. Without its intervention, the defendant whose claim is also under a professed grant from the Government, and is void, as we have seen, may obtain the means of turning out of possession the rightful equitable owner, through measures of additional and expensive litigation, to end, possibly, in the defeat of justice, or in its establishment at a ruinous cost, and after protracted delay.

But it has been asked in the argument of the case, why not refuse the injunction, and then dismiss the bill, so that this controversy may be settled by the courts of California? That to assume jurisdiction over this cause in this district, would be an unjust imputation upon the courts of that State.

To this it is enough to say in answer, that I entertain the highest regard for the learning and integrity of those courts, and have not a doubt, that in all cases, the cause of justice may be as safely intrusted to their protection, as to that of any court in the land. But that is not a question which I have a right to consider. Complainant and defendant are both found within our jurisdiction, and this suit has been instituted in this court, and process served upon the defendant. The suit is here and is to be considered judicially. If we have jurisdiction according to established principles of the law, we must decide the questions in the cause, without considering whether some other court might not have been better able to decide them than ours is. Besides, a suit of the character of this one can only be brought and relief obtained against the defendant personally, and how can this court determine whether it is or is not the purpose of the defendant ever to return to California? If it should not, then complainant would have lost his present remedy, without obtaining the other.

An injunction will, therefore, be granted on the present motion, prohibiting the defendant from accepting from the Government of the United States a patent for the land in controversy, to continue in force till the final hearing of the cause.

ANDREW WYLIE.

No. 263 B.

Decision of the Secretary of the Interior in the case of the Soscol Rancho.

DEPARTMENT OF THE INTERIOR,
Washington, D. C., January 4, 1867.

Sir—I have received your report of the 18th of September last, and the papers therewith transmitted, upon the appeal of sundry claimants, under the general pre-emption laws, from the decision of your office, rendered on the 14th day of August last, in cases No. 12, 13, 15, 16, 17, 21, 22, 26, 30, 32, 33, 37, 38, 39, and 40, of what is known as the "Soscol Ranch," in the State of California.

Your decision awards the rights to enter tracts in controversy to the parties claiming under the act entitled "An act to grant the right of pre-emption to certain purchasers on the 'Soscol Ranch,' in the State of California," as they have proved all the facts necessary to bring themselves within its provisions.

This is in conformity with the ruling of my predecessor in previous similar cases. I have been earnestly invited to reconsider the questions involved.

Able and elaborate briefs have been filed by the respective parties; and, after a full and careful examination, I am of the opinion that your decision ought to be affirmed.

The act which I have cited "bears date the third of March, 1863, and directs the lines of the public surveys to be extended over the tract of country known as the 'Soscol Ranch,' and to have approved plats thereof duly returned to the proper district land office."

It then provides "that after the return of such approved plats to the district office, it may and shall be lawful for individuals, *bona fide* purchasers from said Vallejo (who claimed by grant from the Mexican government, and whose claim had been decided against by the Supreme Court of the United States), or his assigns, to enter, according to the lines of said surveys, at one dollar and twenty-five cents per acre, the land so purchased, *to the extent to which the same had been reduced to possession* at the time of said adjudication of said Supreme Court, joint entries being admissible by coterminous proprietors to such an extent as will enable them to adjust their respective boundaries."

All claims within the purview of the act are to be "presented to the Register and Receiver within twelve months after the return of such surveys to the district land office, accompanied by proof of *bona fide* purchase under Vallejo of settlement, and the extent to which the tracts claimed had been reduced into possession at the time of said adjudication."

Municipal claims and lands reserved and occupied for military, naval, and other public uses, or which might thereafter be designated by the

President for such uses, and mineral lands are excepted from the operation of the act. There are no other exceptions.

The fifth and last section of the act then provides "that any claim not brought before the Register and Receiver within twelve months, as aforesaid, shall be barred, and the lands covered thereby, within any other tracts within the limits of said 'Soscol Ranch,' the titles to which are not established under this act, shall be dealt with as other public lands."

The foregoing recital presents all the substantial provisions of the law, and all which are deemed necessary to the proper consideration and decision of this case. A number of persons, not purchasers from Vallejo, or his assigns, at some time after the decision of the case by the Supreme Court, and before the passage of the above-recited law, entered upon the land and made improvements thereon, and they now claim to have acquired rights of pre-emption, under the general pre-emption laws, to the tracts respectively occupied by them, not exceeding in extent one hundred and sixty acres. And it is insisted that, notwithstanding the law above referred to, these parties are entitled, under the general pre-emption laws, to a preference of purchase of the tracts so settled upon and occupied by them. It is insisted that these parties had acquired vested interests in the tracts of land so occupied, of which Congress could not, by subsequent legislation, deprive them, and that this act must receive such a construction by this department as will give effect to the general pre-emption laws in behalf of such settlers. In other words, it is contended that if the act was intended to preclude the class of settlers referred to, and to give the exclusive right of entry, in the first place, to the claimants under Vallejo and his assigns, that then the law is to that extent unconstitutional; that it was not within the constitutional competency of Congress to pass it, and that, notwithstanding the law, the rights of claimants under the general pre-emption laws, should be protected and enforced.

If it was really the intention of the legislative department to give to the purchasers from Vallejo and his assigns an exclusive prior right to the land which they had purchased, and reduced to possession before the decision by the Supreme Court, without respect to quantity, then I am clearly of opinion that the executive department of the Government is bound by that intention, and that it would be transcending the powers of an executive officer to assume that the law was so far in conflict with constitutional provisions as to warrant him in declaring it unconstitutional and void. That is a judicial function which I cannot assume to exercise. I can only inquire what the law is, and am bound to accept as law all acts which have regularly passed the two houses of Congress and received the approval of the President, and am not at liberty to inquire whether, under the Constitution, Congress possessed the authority to enact such a law or not. I am, then, in the decision of this case, simply to construe and execute the law as Congress intended it should be, and that intention I am to derive from the language which they have thought proper to adopt to express it, and from that alone, if it be free from doubt and ambiguity.

If that language be clear and unambiguous, I am not at liberty to resort to any extraneous aids in its construction. It is only when a law is doubtful—when it is susceptible of *two* or more meanings or constructions—that resort may be had to extrinsic facts and circumstances in exploring the will and intention of the legislature. Such resort is never admissible for the purpose of first introducing uncertainty, and then, to remove such uncertainty, giving to the law an interpretation not only not in harmony with, but in direct contravention of, the natural import of the language in which the law is expressed. In this case the language of the law is clear, explicit, and unambiguous, and I have only to give it its natural and obvious meaning, and execute it according to that meaning, and my duty will be performed.

The law distinctly declares that "*bona fide* purchasers from Vallejo or his assigns shall have the right to enter according to the lines of survey, at $1.25 per acre, the lands so purchased to the extent to which the same had been reduced to possession at the time of the adjudication of the Supreme Court." But from this general provision it excepts municipal claims and lands reserved and occupied for military, naval, and other public uses, or which may thereafter be designated by the President for such uses, and mineral land. But it makes no exception of lands claimed by other persons, not being such purchasers, under the general pre-emption laws. It takes no cognizance of them—it recognizes no existing right in them. It clearly intended, if there were such occupants, that their claims should be postponed to the claims of the purchasers from Vallejo and his assigns. Upon a well-known general principle the expression of some exceptions is the exclusion of all others; and the intention to exclude all except the purchasers from Vallejo and his assigns, until their claims were satisfied, is made still more pointed and manifest by the provision of the fifth section of the act, "that any claim not brought before the Register and Receiver within twelve months shall be barred, and the lands covered thereby, with any other tracts within the limits of said 'Soscol ranch,' the titles to which are not established under this act shall be dealt with as other public lands." The intention that they should not be so dealt with, except to the extent that claims were not made or not sustained by such purchasers, could not be more distinctly expressed.

And this view of the law is greatly strengthened by the provision of the fourth section, "that all claims *within the purview of this act* shall be presented to the Register and Receiver within twelve months," &c.

Now what claims are within the purview of this act? Claims derived by *bona fide* purchase from Vallejo or his assigns, which had been reduced to possession at the time of the adjudication by the Supreme Court, and none other. No other claims are mentioned or hinted at. No other could be presented or adjudicated; and if others had been presented the Register and Receiver would have been compelled to reject them, for they were not within the purview of the law, and the law gave no authority to receive and consider them. It was not claims within the purview of some other law—the general pre-emption law, for instance—but of this law, and this law alone, that could be presented and acted upon by the Register and Receiver, and if *they* could not, under this law, hear and decide upon cases arising under the general pre-emption laws, clearly *I* cannot, for my jurisdiction is derivative and appellate only.

But, it is said, the true interpretation of the act of 1863 is, "to give the Vallejo claimants a right to enter their lands, in so far as that right does not conflict with rights previously acquired under prior laws," meaning the pre-existing pre-emption laws.

But this interpretation is directly contradicted by the language of the law. It expressly gives to the purchasers from Vallejo or his assigns a priority of right over all others, except municipal claims and military, naval, and other public reservations and mineral lands, and forbids the "Soscol ranch" from being dealt with as other public lands until said purchasers shall have had their claims adjudicated or have made default in the presentation of them; and it was only the residue, after these claims were satisfied, that was remitted to the condition of other public lands and subjected to the operation of the general pre-emption laws.

I do not inquire whether this was right. I do not ask whether Congress possessed the constitutional power to do this. I am forbidden to enter upon any such inquiry. My duty, and my whole duty, is to ascertain the meaning of the law, taking where, as in this case, the language is unambiguous, its plainest and most obvious sense, and then to execute it in that sense. I have no such judicial function or authority as would justify me in refusing to execute the law, or to execute it in a sense not authorized by its terms, because I may think it in conflict with the constitution or with the fundamental principles of equity and justice. If I may do this in one instance, I may in all.

If *I* may do it, all other executive officers may do the same thing, and the greatest confusion and uncertainty be introduced into the administration of the laws.

Yet this is what I am asked to do.

I am asked to say that, when Congress declared that "*bona fide* purchasers from Vallejo or his assigns should have the right to enter, according to the lines of surveys, the land so purchased to the extent to which the same had been reduced to possession," they did not mean that; but that they meant to say that the pre-emption right was conferred upon such purchasers only "to whom Congress had a *constitutional right* to grant the privilege, and to the *extent* to which Congress might grant it, and to such as brought themselves by purchase, possession, and *settlement* within the provisions of this law, and of the *system of pre-emption laws* already established," &c.

But this would not be to *interpret* and *execute* a law, but to *make* and *substitute* a new law for the one made by Congress; for it is not claimed that any such terms and conditions are found in the law which Congress did actually make. If they get there at all it will be by my interpretation. I would be greatly overstepping the boundaries of my powers and duties so to interpolate.

The argument is that the *settlers*, who were not purchasers, had acquired vested rights under the general pre-emption laws which Congress could not constitutionally divest, and that if the law under consideration intended to divest them and to give the purchasers from Vallejo or his assigns a priority of right over such settlers, then the law is, to that extent, unconstitutional, and that in such case I ought to seek for another meaning in the law, which would avoid such a consequence, although that meaning should be contrary to the plain import of the language of the law.

I agree that it is my duty to construe the law and to execute it according to my understanding of the intention of the legislators who made it; but in seeking that intention there are plain rules by which I must be governed and from which I cannot depart. Even the courts, whose latitude of construction is much larger than mine, are bound by the same rules.

Where the language of a law is clear and unambiguous even a judicial tribunal cannot put upon it a forced construction contrary to the natural and obvious sense of such language. It may deny the authority of the legislature and declare the law unconstitutional, but in construing it the plain import of its language must be accepted as its true interpretation. An executive officer must take the law as it is, and execute it as it is, without questioning the authority of the legislative department which enacted it. We cannot declare it unconstitutional, either in whole or in part, nor supplement it so as to give it a meaning and effect not derivable from its terms.

Now, if the act under consideration be taken just as it is, and construed without reference to or aid from extrinsic circumstances, I do not understand counsel to deny that the natural and obvious meaning to be derived from the language in which it is couched is to give to the purchasers from Vallejo or his assigns a priority of right over the settlers claiming under the general pre-emption laws. Indeed, it is because this is the only meaning to be extracted from the language of the law that I am urged to explore the title of the act, the reports of committees, the general pre-emption laws, &c., in search of another and different construction.

The most enlightened and experienced judges have often lamented that courts of justice have departed from the plain construction of the words of statutes.

Thus, in Edrick's case (5 *Rep.* 118), the judges said "that they ought not to make any construction against the express letter of the statute, for nothing can so express the meaning of the makers of the act as their own direct words."

So Ashurst, justice, said "it is safer to adopt what the legislature have actually said than to suppose what they meant to say." (1 *Tr. Rep.* 51.)

And whenever the intention of the legislature can be indubitably ascertained, courts are bound to give it effect, whatever may be their opinion of its wisdom and policy.

In the case of Fisher *v.* Blight (2 *Cranch*, 389), quoted by the able and distinguished gentleman who has filed a brief on behalf of the claimants under the general pre-emption laws, Chief Justice Marshall said: "That the consequences are to be considered in expounding laws, *where the intent is doubtful*, is a principle not to be controverted, but it is also true that it is a principle *which must be applied with caution*, and which has a degree of influence dependent on the nature of the case to which it is applied."

And again, in the same case: "*Where the intent is plain, nothing is left to construction.* Where the mind labors to discover the design of the legislature, it seizes everything from which it can be derived; and in such case the title claims a degree of notice and will have its due share of consideration."

In the case of Litchfield *v.* Dubuque and Pacific Railroad Company (23 *Howard*, 88), quoted by the same learned counsel, the Supreme Court of the United States said: "If the words admit of *different* meanings it would be right to adopt that which is more favorable to the interests of the public," and that this rule is "intended to prevent parties from inserting ambiguous language for the purpose of taking by ungenerous interpretation that which cannot be obtained by express terms."

Now, these rules clearly forbid me to give to the law the construction which is contended for. I would be doing precisely what the court admonishes us to avoid—"*inserting ambiguous language for the purpose of taking by ungenerous interpretation that which cannot be obtained by the express terms of the law.*"

But it is said that this is a pre-emption law, and to be construed and executed in connection and harmony with the system of pre-emption laws previously existing. I concede it to be a pre-emption law, but it is no part of the general system of pre-emption laws. It is a special law for a special case, limited to the "Soscol Ranch," and having no effect on operation outside of that. When the lands in that ranch, to which it applies, shall have been disposed of, the whole purpose of this law will have been accomplished. It will no longer have an operation anywhere. It will not be a part of the system of pre-emption laws, or of any other system of laws. It will be *functus officio.*

Whilst it remains to be executed it is not subject to the terms and conditions of other pre-emption laws, but to the terms and conditions to be found in its own language. The pre-emptive privileges which it grants are not to be secured by a compliance with the requirements of the general pre-emption laws, but depend upon conditions totally and essentially different.

Settlement upon the land *in person* is not required. The amount of land to be taken is not limited to one hundred and sixty acres, and the acts to be performed by the claimants to secure the benefit of the law are not the same with those required of claimants under the general pre-emption laws.

In construing and executing this law, therefore, I do not inquire, nor do I feel at liberty to inquire, what the requirements of the general pre-emption laws applicable to our vast public domain, and to our people at large, are. They have nothing to do with this case. This case is peculiar and stands alone. It grew out of the circumstances which attended the settlement of this land, and the law was made to apply to this, and to this alone. And, in executing it, its language being clear, unambiguous, and unmistakable, I am only to ask what Congress intended, deriving that intention from the plain and distinct language in which they have expressed it, and then give it effect.

It is further insisted that, even if limited to claimants under Vallejo, the benefits of the act were intended to be conferred only upon such purchasers as were *actual settlers upon the land purchased,* and that purchasers in good faith, who had taken possession of the land purchased, and who maintained that possession at the date of the adjudication of the case by the Supreme Court, but without personal residence thereon, cannot participate in its benefits. I cannot assent to this interpretation of the law. It is not one of its provisions. The language of the law is that they shall have the privilege "to enter, according to the lines of surveys, at one dollar and twenty-five cents per acre, *the land so purchased, to the extent to which the same had been reduced to possession, at the time of said adjudication of said Supreme Court.*"

The law does not require actual personal settlement, and the law not requiring it, I cannot require it.

Taking, then, all the provisions of the act into consideration, I entertain no doubt that the possession spoken of in the law, and meant by the law, is the common law possession, which may exist as well without personal presence upon the land as with it; nor have I any doubt that all the incidents of a common law possession attach to the possession required by this law, and that an actual possession of any part of a tract held by title, or color of title, draws to it the possession of all the land included within the calls of the deed. The only mention made of "settlement" in the act is to be found in the fourth section, after the class of persons to take under the provisions of the land had been designated by the second section. They were "bona fide purchasers from Vallejo, or his assigns, who had reduced the land purchased to possession at the time of the adjudication of the Supreme Court"—not those who had *personally settled upon the land and continued to reside there.* Then, the fourth section provides that the claims, within the purview of the act, shall be presented to the Register and Receiver of the district land office, "accompanied by proof of bona fide purchase, under Vallejo, of settlement, and the extent to which the tracts claimed had been reduced into possession at the time of said adjudication."

The proofs were to be of the purchase of the land, of the settlement of the *lands*, and of the extent to which the lands purchased had been reduced to possession. No proof of the settlement of the purchaser was required.

Now, a settlement may be made of land as well by colonizing it as by going to reside upon it in person.

The purchaser may not *settle* upon it himself, but he makes a *settlement* of it by placing others there; and, taking all the provisions of the law together, as I must do, and so construe it as to give every part of it a reasonable operation, I am of opinion that this kind of settlement, as well as settlement by actual residence, was intended.

And this conclusion is made irresistible by the fact already mentioned, that in describing the persons who are to avail themselves of the privileges of the law, no allusion is made to personal settlement or residence, and to give such a construction to the act, upon the language of the fourth section, would be materially to limit and restrict the natural meaning of the language in the second section.

The construction I give secures to them both a harmonious, just, and reasonable operation.

I have, therefore, reached the conclusion that bona fide purchasers from Vallejo, or his assigns, have a right to enter, according to the lines of the surveys, at one dollar and twenty-five cents per acre, the land so purchased, to the extent to which the same had been reduced to possession, at the time of said adjudication of said Supreme Court, without any reference whatever to the quantity of land embraced in the purchases, or to the question of personal residence or occupation.

I herewith return the papers.

The remaining cases in your office will be disposed of in accordance with the views and principles which I have set forth in this communication.

I am, sir, very respectfully, your obedient servant,

O. H. BROWNING, Secretary of the Interior.

Hon. Jos. S. Wilson, Commissioner General Land Office.

No. 263½ B.

Decision of the Acting Secretary of the Interior in the case, involving the title to a private land claim known as the Santos Calla Rancho, of Davis v. *Lober.*

DEPARTMENT OF THE INTERIOR,
July 10, 1867.

* * * * * * * * *

To a determination of the rights of the respective parties it becomes necessary to ascertain the condition of this land at the date of the passage of the act of July 2d, 1864. The question then arises, Is said act a confirmation of the original grant claim, or did it only give the grant claimants or their assigns the privilege of purchasing such of said lands at $1.25 per acre as the United States had title to, when Congress passed the said act?

It seems to me this statement in itself answers the question. If this act confirms the original claim, why are the claimants required to pay for their land?

The Ranch claim was rejected by the Board of Commissioners January 15, 1856, and on appeal to the District Court it was "decided to be invalid" September 18, 1860. No appeal was taken from this decision.

The Swamp grant was passed September 28, 1850, and was the first disposition made by Congress of lands in California, and by opinion of Attorney-General Black, dated November 10, 1858 (opinions vol. 9 page 254), the grant was in itself a present grant, wanting nothing but a definition of boundaries to make it perfect; and to obtain that object the Secretary of the Interior was directed to make out an accurate list and plot of the lands and cause a patent to issue therefor. It was not necessary that a patent should issue to the State. The patent was merely the evidence of title, nothing more.

Secretary Stewart said, Dec. 23, 1851, that the grant of Swamp and overflowed lands was a grant *in presenti*. That when the selections were made and approved, or the patent issued, the title therefor becomes perfect, *and has relation back to the date of the grant*, and Secretary McClelland, under date of June 21, 1856, decided that land erroneously embraced in a private claim, if swamp, at the date of the act, would be subject to selection. That "in the matter of the reservation or setting apart certain tracts of land for these alleged private claims, is merely a withholding them from sale or other disposition by the land officers, during the continuance of the reservation, with a view of preventing conflicts of interest whilst the investigations were in progress as to the *public* or *private* character of the land, and when the former was settled as its status, it became, on the return thereof to the mass of the public lands, subject to the laws which made a specific grant of all *public* lands for other purposes, according to the provision thereof existing at the time of such return."

Under the treaty with Mexico the United States was to recognize such rights of property as was protected by the treaty. If there were no such rights in this case, or the claim of right was rejected, from that date the land became a part of the public domain of the United States, and the Swamp land passed to the State as of the date when it was granted to her, September 28, 1850.

The 6th Section of the act entitled "An act to provide for the survey of the public lands in California" &c., approved March 3, 1853 (vol. 10, page 246), granted to the State of California, of the public lands, whether surveyed or unsurveyed sections sixteen and thirty-six, for the purposes of public schools in each township. The 13th section of an act entitled "An act to ascertain and settle the private land claims in the State of California" approved March 3, 1851 (vol. 9, page 633), declares what lands in California belong to the public domain of the United States. It says "that all lands the claims to which have been finally rejected by the Commissioners * * * which shall be finally decided to be invalid by the District or Supreme Court * * shall be deemed, held, and considered as part of the public domain of the United States."

The final decision in this Ranch case was made September 18, 1860. These lands were surveyed long prior to July 2, 1864, and the township plats were in the local office before and at that date, consequently the land had been previous to said act, and was at the date of its passage, *public land*, and as such subject to the operation of the laws in force for the disposal of the public domain in California.

It is not probable, therefore, that Congress intended by the said act to give the grantees or their assigns of land within said Ranch, the privilege of purchasing lands to which the United States had previously divested itself of the title, or had granted preference rights therein. The express exemption from purchase by grant claimants of any lands to which pre-emption rights had attached is sufficient evidence of the intention of Congress on this point. If otherwise, which I do not admit, the rule laid down by the Attorney-General in the opinion before referred to, would govern the action of the Department. He said, "When there is a conflict between two titles derived from the same source, either of which would be good if the other were out of the way, the elder one must always prevail, *prior in tempore, portior est in jure.*"

* * * * * * * * *

W. T. OTTO, Acting Secretary.

TITLE IV.

Coal Lands and Town Property.

No. 264 B.

Circular.

Instructions to give effect to the act of Congress approved July 1, 1864, for the disposal of "Coal Lands" and of "Town Property" in the public domain.

INTERIOR DEPARTMENT,
GENERAL LAND OFFICE, August 20, 1864.

Gentlemen :—Annexed is the act of Congress approved July 1, 1864,* for the disposal of "Coal Land" and of "Town Property" on the public domain.

It will be observed that the word "mines," as used in the pre-emption act of 1841, is recognized in the first section of this law as importing any tracts of the public domain embracing "coal beds or coal fields," which are to be treated as *mineral lands*, and not subject to ordinary private entry.

2d. That said tracts are to be disposed of at public sale, on not less than three months' public notice, to the highest bidder, in such "suitable legal subdivisions" as the President may direct, at the minimum price of $20 per acre; all tracts not thus disposed of are thereafter to be liable to private entry at said minimum.

3d. In order that this office may have reliable information as to what lands embrace "coal beds or coal fields," it will be your duty to institute proper inquiries, directed to reliable sources, as to the mineral character of the lands in your district; to ascertain what tracts of land come within the meaning of the terms "coal beds or coal fields," and make a prompt report of all such lands to this office.

4th. In reference to this matter, special orders will be given to the United States Surveyors-General to require their Deputy Surveyors, in executing the public surveys, carefully to designate in their field notes all localities of coal beds or coal fields in the *smallest legal sub-division;* and thereafter to have the same properly delineated on the official township plats returned to the General and District Land Offices.

5th. The second section of this act relates to "Town Property," or the founding of cities or towns on the public domain, and limits the extent of the area of the city or town to 640 acres, to be laid off into lots, and which, after filing in the General Land Office the transcript, statement, and testimony required by the act, are to be offered at public sale, to the highest bidder, at a minimum of ten dollars for each lot. Lots not thus disposed of are made thereafter liable to private entry at said mini-

* No. 108 B.

mum, or at such reasonable price as the Secretary of the Interior may order from time to time, as the municipal property may increase or decrease, after at least three months' notice.

A privilege, however, is granted to any *actual settler* upon any *one* lot, of pre-empting that and any additional lot on which he may have "substantial improvements," at said minimum, at any time before the day fixed for the public sale.

There are, however, certain preliminary conditions to be complied with, in order to the enjoyment of the privileges granted in this section.

Parties who have already founded or may hereafter found a city or town are required :—

6th. To file with the recorder of the county in which the town or city is situate a plat thereof, not exceeding 640 acres, describing its exterior boundaries according to the lines of the public surveys, where such surveys have been executed.

7th. Also, the plat or map of such city or town must exhibit the name of the city or town, the streets, squares, blocks, lots, and alleys; the size of the same, with measurements and area of each municipal subdivision, the lots in which shall each not exceed 4200 square feet, with a statement of the extent and general character of improvements.

8th. Further, the said map and statement to be verified by oath by the party acting for and in the behalf of the founders of the city or town.

9th. Within one month after filing the map or plat with the recorder of the county, a verified copy of said map and statement is to be sent to the General Land Office, accompanied by the testimony of two witnesses that such city or town has been established in good faith.

10th. Where the city or town is within the limits of an organized land district, a similar copy of the map and statement must be filed with the Register and Receiver.

11th. The third section provides for cities or towns founded on *unsurveyed* lands, and directs that it may be lawful to adjust the exterior limits of the premises with the lines of the public surveys, where it can be done without impairing the rights of others.

Patents are to issue for all lots sold under the provisions of this act as in ordinary cases.

12th. Section four authorizes the Secretary of the Interior, in case the parties interested shall fail or refuse, within twelve months of the founding of a city or town on the public domain, to file in the General Land Office a copy of the map, with the statement and testimony called for by the second section, to cause a survey and plat to be made of the said city or town, and thereafter the lots to be sold as provided, at an increase of fifty per cent. on the minimum price of ten dollars per lot.

13th. The fifth section repeals the act for the relief of the citizens of towns on the public lands, approved 23d May, 1844, and all other acts or parts of acts inconsistent with this act.

You are requested to acknowledge the receipt of this circular.

Very respectfully,

JOS. S. WILSON, Acting Commissioner.

Registers and Receivers, United States Land Offices.

No. 265 B.

Circular.

In relation to the Supplemental Act, approved March 3, 1865, for the Disposal of Coal Lands and Town Property on the public domain.

DEPARTMENT OF THE INTERIOR,
GENERAL LAND OFFICE, April 26, 1865.

Gentlemen:—The act of Congress of 3d March, 1865,* copy hereto appended, *supplementary* to the act of July 1, 1864, "for the disposal of coal lands and of town property in the public domain," is to enable citizens of the United States who, at the date of the "act, may be in the business of *bona fide* actual coal mining on the public lands, for the purpose of commerce," to enter 160 acres, or less quantity, in legal subdivisions, including their improvements and mining premises, at the premium price of $20 per acre.

The law, however, expressly *excludes* from its provisions any lands "reserved by the President of the United States for public uses."

The privilege granted is not a general one, but restricted to a single entry by a designated class of individuals, viz: such as are citizens, and who, on the 3*d March*, 1865, the date of the act, were actually engaged, for "*purposes of commerce*," in "the business of *bona fide* actual coal mining." All persons not so occupied at that date are excluded from the enjoyment of the privilege.

1st. Testimony should be produced satisfactory to the Register and Receiver, showing the party to be a citizen of the United States, and that, at the date of the act, he was engaged "in the business of bona fide actual coal mining on the public lands," and "*for the purposes of* commerce."

The facts must be stated in detail, both as to the nature and extent of the coal mining; the period in which the business has been conducted, and in regard to the coal being made by the party an article of commerce, so that a correct judgment may be formed from these facts as to whether the case comes within the purview of the statute. Where the proof is clear and conclusive, the Register and Receiver are authorized to permit the entry, according to "legal subdivisions," in compact form, and so as not to exceed 160 acres.

2d. Where the mining improvements and premises are on land *surveyed* "*at the passage of this act*," it is required that a sworn declaratory statement descriptive of the tract and premises, and also of the extent and character of the improvements, *be filed* within *six months* from the date of the act, and that proof and payment must be made within *one year* from the *date* of such filing.

3d. If the mining premises be on land which may be *surveyed* after the passage of said act, then the declaratory statement shall be filed within three months from the return of the plat to the district land office, and proof and payment must be made within *one year* from the date of such filing.

TOWN LOTS.

4th. The 2d section of the act relates to any city or town *existing* on the public lands at the *date* of the act, and modifies the limitation as to the

* No. 130 B.

extent of the areas of the town claim and town lots imposed by the act of 1st July, 1864.

The act of July 1, 1864, limits the town claim to 640 acres, and the town lots to 4200 feet each; but—

5th. This supplemental act embraces interests "in which the lots and buildings, as municipal improvements, shall cover an area greater than" 640 acres, and removes the limitation in regard to subsisting cases by declaring that any city or town existing on 3*d March*, 1865, shall not be debarred entry because of such excess of area over, or of variance from, the size of the town claim or town lots as limited by the act of 1st July, 1864; that for the excess of square feet contained in said lots beyond the *maximum* named in the act to which this is amendatory, the *minimum* price of each lot shall be increased to such reasonable amount as the Secretary may establish.

6th. In the 2d section of this supplemental act, it is provided that parties having a *possessory* right to *mineral* veins, "which possession *is recognized by local authority*," are to be protected therein; and titles to be acquired to town lots under this act are made subject to "such recognized possession and the necessary use thereof," yet with an *express saving of the paramount title* of the United States.

7th. The act of 1st July, 1864, relating to town property, is only modified as regards the *extent* of the town claim and the *size* of town lots, and by it you will be governed when not in conflict with this supplemental act. Hence it will be necessary for the citizens of the town or city existing at the date of the supplementary act—

First. To file with the Recorder of the county in which the town or city is situate, a plat thereof, describing its exterior boundaries, and according to the lines of the public surveys, where such surveys have been executed.

Second. Also, the plat or map of such city or town must exhibit the name of the city or town, the streets, squares, blocks, lots, and alleys, the *size* of the same, *with actual measurements* and area of each municipal division, and a statement of the extent and general character of improvements.

Third. Further, the said map and statement to be verified by oath of the party acting for and on behalf of the city or town; and—

Fourth. Within one month after filing the map or plat with the Recorder of the county, a verified copy of said map and statement must be sent to the Commissioner of the General Land Office, with the testimony of two witnesses that such a town is a bona fide one, established and existing at the date of this act.

Fifth. Where the city or town is within the limits of an organized land district, a similar copy of the map and statement must be filed with the Register and Receiver thereof.

Sixth. Where the city or town is founded *on unsurveyed* lands, the exterior lines of the same must be distinctly marked and established, so that, when the lines of the public surveys shall hereafter be run, they may be properly closed thereon; and yet it may be lawful to adjust the exterior limits of the premises with the lines of the public surveys, when it can be done without impairing the rights of others.

Seventh. Patents are to issue for all lots sold under the provisions of this act.

Eighth. By the 2d section of the act of 1st July, 1864, after the transcript and statement have been filed in the General Land Office, the lots are to be offered at public sale to the highest bidder at a *minimum* of ten dollars per lot; but, by the supplemental act, where the *area of each lot* exceeds the *maximum* of 4200 *square feet*, the *minimum price* of each lot shall be increased to such reasonable amount as the Secretary of the Interior may establish.

A privilege, however, is granted to any actual settler upon any *one* lot of pre-empting that, and any additional lot on which he may have "substantial improvements," at said *minimum* or increased price, at any time before the day fixed for the *public sale*.

Very respectfully,

J. M. EDMUNDS, Commissioner.

Approved: Jas. Harlan, Secretary of the Interior.

No. 266 B.

Circular.

Instructions, under the direction of the Secretary of the Interior, in reference to the act of Congress, approved March 2, 1867, for the relief of the inhabitants of cities and towns upon the public lands, and the act amendatory thereof, approved June 8, 1868.

DEPARTMENT OF THE INTERIOR,
GENERAL LAND OFFICE, September 21, 1868.

Gentlemen:—The act of Congress, hereto appended, *approved March* 2, 1867—Statutes, vol. 14, page 541 (No. 192 B.)—

1st. Grants to the inhabitants of cities and towns on the public lands the privilege of entering the lands occupied as town sites at the minimum price of one dollar and twenty-five cents per acre, through the corporate authorities of such towns and cities, or the judges of the county courts acting as trustees for the occupants thereof.

This privilege is granted where such mode of obtaining title to town property is preferred to that provided in the act of July 1, 1864, Statutes, vol. 13, page 343, and the amendatory act of March, 3, 1865, vol. 13, page 529, the said statute of 1867 not repealing the enactments of 1864 and 1865. The inhabitants of these towns or cities are limited, however, to one or the other of the modes provided in these statutes, and cannot commence proceedings under both systems.

2d. The act of June 8, 1868 (No. 206 B.), herewith amendatory of the act of March 2, 1867, stipulates that the inhabitants of any town located on the public lands may avail themselves, if the town authorities elect to do so, of the provisions of said last named act: *Provided* the issuing of patents to persons who have made or may make entries, and elect to proceed under existing laws, shall not thereby be prevented.

As proceedings to acquire title to town property cannot be commenced under both systems in force since March 2, 1867, the amendatory act must refer to cases where, previous to March 2, 1867, the inhabitants of any town or city had filed a plat of the same with the County Recorder, pursuant to the act of July 1, 1864, and had partly proved up and paid for the lots claimed by them under the proviso in the 2d section of the said, act, and extends the privileges of the act of March 2, 1867, if the town authorities elect to proceed under it, to such of the inhabitants as have not yet paid for their lots, without interfering with the issuing of patents to those who had made, or might make, entries, and elect to proceed under the acts of July 1, 1864, and March 3, 1865.

3d. Accordingly, where proceedings had been commenced by the inhabitants of any town or city before the passage of the act of March 2, 1867, and a part of them, not having entered and paid for their lots, desire to proceed under said last named act, you will allow the town authorities, if they apply to you for that purpose, to enter or file upon, pursuant to the provisions of said act, such portion of the town site as has not already been entered and paid for, and is not in possession of parties electing to complete their titles under the original proceedings; after which that part of the town site so entered or filed upon, will be disposed of under the statutes of 1867 and 1868, and the remaining portion, if any, under the enactments of 1864 and 1865.

4th. The aforesaid amendatory act of June 8, 1868, further provides that, in addition to the minimum price of the lands included in any town site entered under the statute of March 2, 1867, and said act of June 8, 1868, there shall be paid by the parties availing themselves of the provisions of said acts all costs of surveying and platting any such town site, and expenses incident thereto, incurred by the United States, before any patent therefor shall issue. Hence, when it is desired to enter a town site found upon the *unsurveyed* public lands, a written application should be presented to the Surveyor-General of the proper district for a survey of the same, under the 10th section of the act of May 30, 1862, vol. 12, pages 409 and 410, and the amount estimated by him as sufficient to cover the said costs and expenses deposited with any Assistant U. S. Treasurer, or designated depository in favor of the United States Treasurer, to be passed to the credit of the fund created by "Individual Depositors for the Survey of the Public Lands," the depositor taking a duplicate certificate of deposit, one to be filed with the Surveyor-General to be sent to the General Land Office, and the other retained by the depositor. On receiving such certificate, showing that the requisite sum has been deposited in a proper manner to pay for the work, the Surveyor-General will transmit to the Register and Receiver of the District Land Office his certificate of such payment having been made, and will contract with a competent U. S. Deputy Surveyor, and have the survey made and returned in the same manner as other public surveys, after which the lands embraced within the site may be entered, or filed upon, as in the case of town sites upon surveyed lands.

5th. When town sites are located upon land already surveyed, the entry must be made in conformity to the legal subdivisions of the public lands, and here no costs in regard to past surveys will be exacted. When sites are upon *unsurveyed* land it will be necessary, after the extension thereto of the public surveys, to close those lines upon the exterior limits of the town site.

6th. The aforesaid act of 2d March, 1867, it will be observed, stipulates that there shall be conceded, where the number of inhabitants is one hundred and less than two hundred, not exceeding three hundred and twenty acres where the population is more than two hundred and less than one thousand, not exceeding six hundred and forty acres; and where the inhabitants number one thousand and over, not exceeding twelve hundred and eighty acres; and for each additional one thousand inhabitants, not exceeding five thousand in all, a further grant of three hundred and twenty acres.

All military and other reservations of the United States, private grants, and valid mining claims, are excluded from the operation of these town-site laws.

7th. In any Territory in which a land office may not have been established, the declaratory statements provided for in the foregoing acts may be filed with the Surveyor-General of the proper district.

Very respectfully,

JOS. S. WILSON, Commissioner.

Approved: W. T. OTTO, Acting Secretary.

No. 267 B.

Cities and towns on the public lands, acts July 1, 1864, *and March* 3, 1865.

By the act of July 1, 1864, it is "provided that any actual settler upon any one lot as aforesaid, and upon any additional lot in which he may have substantial improvements, shall be entitled to prove up and purchase the same as a pre-emption, at said minimum, at any time before the day fixed for the public sale."

The Registers and Receivers of the local offices have been instructed that, under this proviso, any actual settler may pre-empt the lot upon which he resides, with *one* additional lot upon which he has substantial improvements; that no more than two lots can be pre-empted by any one settler; and that the persons claiming the benefit of this proviso must be actual residents of the town or city in which the lots claimed may be situated, and must have the personal qualifications required by the general pre-emption laws.

The General Land Office holds that this limitation is clearly to *one* additional lot and no more; that, had the legislative mind intended otherwise, the word *lots* would have been used instead of *lot*, as it now stands in the statute, but that the department will, in cases where expensive municipal or business improvements, as mills, warehouses, furnaces, machine shops, &c., are shown to exist, take care that no such interests shall suffer by the intrusion of an adverse claim, or purpose to purchase to the prejudice of the owner of such interest, such protection of course to be subordinate to the requirements of law in regard to public sales.

The substantial improvements for the purposes contemplated in this statute are understood to mean permanent buildings or works for municipal use; a mere inclosure by temporary fence for gardening or other incidental use not being considered as satisfying this requirement of law.

In some sections of the country cases of hardship have arisen under the provisions of the statute, and particularly on the Pacific slope, where some of the towns the claims of which are pending under the acts of July 1, 1864, and March 3, 1865, have considerable population, and are located upon old Mexican or Spanish grants, but recently declared to be invalid, and where it is represented that many persons own more than two lots each, purchased oftentimes at great expense and containing valuable improvements upon which the claimants have paid taxes and received rents for many years, without any question ever having been raised as to their title.

It is claimed that to limit such persons to a pre-emption of but two lots, and to expose to sale other lots worth oftentimes thousands of dollars, and compel them to purchase the second time at their market value, or even to suffer them to pass into other hands without the consent of those who had held them under a title recognized as valid in many cases for more than fifteen years, would be an act of great injustice.

It is also contended that in most of the new towns of the west, many of the lots and improvements are owned by persons residing elsewhere; that many of the miners in the western Territories purchase lots in the neighboring towns with the view of making their future residences upon them; and that where none but actual *residents* are allowed to pre-empt lots they must necessarily suffer loss, which in mining towns is often considerable, unless provision is made, which is recommended, to relieve this particular class of cases, and also to relieve the class possessing more than two lots, where the excess lot is covered by valuable improvements.

The aforesaid act of 1864 declares that where parties have founded or may desire to found a city or town on the public lands, it shall and may be lawful "for them to cause to be filed with the recorder for the county in which the land is situated a plat thereof for not exceeding 640 acres, describing its exterior boundaries," giving the name of the city or town, and exhibiting the streets, squares, blocks, lots, and alleys, the size of the same, with measurements and area of the municipal subdivision, the statement of the extent and general character of the improvements, the map and statement to be verified under oath by the party acting for and in behalf of the persons proposing to establish the city or town, and within one month after the filing there shall be transmitted to the General Land Office a verified transcript map and statement, accompanied by the testimony of two witnesses, that such city or town has been established in good faith.

It is further required that the exterior lines of the whole city be run and *established* by *actual survey*, to be perpetuated by permanent visible objects, and said actual lines by a scientific surveyor must be shown on the map with the exact measurement of the exterior lines, and also of the municipal subdivisions as specifically designated in the statute.

The verified manuscript map is required to be sent to this office with an authenticated copy of the field-notes of survey. The map of survey must also be accompanied by the sworn statements of the parties as "to the extent and general character of the improvements," and with it should be transmitted a general map of the region, indicating the locality of the town site as near as possible to some prominent place in the geography of the country.

A point has been made as to the hardship of requiring municipal settlers to pay the cost of survey, while non-residents are permitted to purchase within the limits of a town who may not have contributed to the payment of the expense of such survey. This objection is obviated by restricting the survey to the area applied for by the settlers; yet should there be surplus lots not claimed, the sale of them would enhance the value of the settlement, as increase of population is increase of the productive power, thereby offsetting any inconsiderable outlay originally incurred in founding the city. (Annual Report of the Hon. Joseph S. Wilson, Commissioner, for 1866, pp. 20, 21.)

No. 267½ B.

Cities and towns on the public lands.

Rulings contained in the report of the Hon. Joseph S. Wilson, Commissioner, for the year 1869 :—

Various questions have arisen as to the location of towns in the mineral regions, and as to the authority of the mayor of a town to receive a patent *in trust* for persons residing and owning lots outside of corporate limits. Under date of April 21, 1869, the commissioner decided that the town of Nevada City, California, could enter a certain tract which had been once used for mining, the evidence showing the mines were worked out and exhausted, and the premises more valuable for purposes of trade and agriculture than for mining.

In the case of the application of the corporate authorities of Grass Valley, California, it was held, that it was not the intention of the statute in donating lands for town-site purposes, to extend the operation of the grant beyond the limits of an incorporated town; for the reason that the trust must be executed by the mayor or other corporate authorities, in his or their official capacity, for the benefit of the actual residents of the town, and not for those residing outside the corporate limits.

TITLE V.

Mineral Lands and Mining Claims.

No. 268 B.

Circular.

In relation to mining claims under the act of Congress approved July 26, 1866.—United States Statutes, page 251, chapter cclxii.

DEPARTMENT OF THE INTERIOR,
GENERAL LAND OFFICE, January 14, 1867.

Gentlemen:—Herewith will be found the act of Congress approved 26th July, 1866,* "granting the right of way to ditch and canal owners over the public lands, and for other purposes."

By the first section of this act all the mineral lands of the United States, surveyed and unsurveyed, are laid open to "all citizens of the United States, and to those who have declared their intention to become such, subject to statutory regulations," and also "to the local customs or rules of miners in the several mining districts not in conflict with the laws of the United States."

It therefore becomes your duty, *in limine*, to acquaint yourselves with the local mining customs and usages in the district in which you may be called upon to do those official acts which are required by law, whether the same are reduced to authentic written form, or are to be ascertained by the testimony of intelligent miners, which you are to obtain as occasion may require and justify, in acting upon individual claims, a perfect record whereof is to be carefully taken and preserved by the Register and Receiver, and to be accompanied by a diagram or plat fixing the out boundaries of the district in which such customs and usages exist.

The second section of the act declares that "wherever any person or association of persons claim a vein or lode of quartz or other rock in place, bearing gold, silver, cinnabar, or copper, having previously occupied and improved the same according to the local custom or rules of miners in the district where the same is situated, and having expended in actual labor and improvements thereon an amount of not less than one thousand dollars, and in regard to whose possession there is no controversy or opposing claim, it shall and may be lawful for said claimant, or association of claimants, to file in the local land office a diagram of the same, so extended *laterally* or otherwise, as to conform to the local laws, customs and rules of miners, and to enter such tract and receive a patent therefor, granting such mine, together with the right to follow such vein or lode with its dips, angles, and variations, to any depth, although it may enter the land adjoining, which land adjoining shall be sold subject to this condition."

* No. 174 B.

Mining claims may be entered at any district land office in the United States under this law by any person, or association of persons, corporate or incorporate. In making the entry, however, such a description of the tract must be filed as will indicate the vein or lode, or part or portion thereof claimed, together with a diagram representing, by reference to some natural or artificial monument, the position and location of the claim and the boundaries thereof, so far as such boundaries can be ascertained.

First. In all cases the number of feet in length claimed on the vein or lode shall be stated in the application filed as aforesaid, and the lines limiting the length of the claim shall, also, in all cases be exhibited on the diagram, and the course or direction of such end lines, when not fixed by agreement with the adjoining claimants, nor by the local customs or rules of the miners of the district, shall be drawn at right angles to the ascertained or apparent general course of the vein or lode.

Second. Where, by the local laws, customs, or rules of miners of the district, no surface ground is permitted to be occupied for mining purposes except the surface of the vein or lode, and the walls of such vein or lode are unascertained, and the lateral extent of such vein or lode unknown, it shall be sufficient, after giving the description and diagram aforesaid, to state the fact that the extent of such vein or lode cannot be ascertained by actual measurement, but that the said vein or lode is bounded on each side by the wall of the same, and to estimate the amount of ground contained between the given end lines and the unascertained walls of the vein or lode; and in such case the patent will issue for all the land contained between such end lines and side walls, with the right to follow such vein or lode, with all its dips, angles, and variations, to any depth, although it may enter the land adjoining: *Provided*, The estimated quantity shall be equal to a horizontal plane bounded by the given end lines, and the walls on the sides of such vein or lode.

Third. Where, by the local laws, customs, or rules of miners of the district, no surface ground is permitted to be occupied for mining purposes, except the surface of the vein or lode, and the walls of such vein or lode are ascertained and well known, such wall shall be named in the description, and marked in the diagram, in connection with the end lines of such claims.

Fourth. Where, by the laws, customs, or rules of miners of the district, a given quantity of surface ground is fixed for the purpose of mining or milling the ore, the aforesaid diagram and description in the entry shall correspond with and include so much of the surface as shall be allowed by such laws, customs, or rules for the purpose aforesaid.

Fifth. In the absence of uniform rules in any mining district limiting the amount of surface to be used for mining purposes, actual and peaceable use and occupation for mining or milling purposes shall be regarded as evidence of a custom of miners authorizing the same, and the ground so occupied and used in connection with the vein or lode, and being adjacent thereto, may be included within the entry aforesaid, and the diagram shall embrace the same as appurtenant to the mine.

Where the claimant or claimants desire to include within their entry and diagram any surface ground beyond the surface of the vein, it shall be necessary, upon filing the application, to furnish the Register of the land office with proof of the usage, law, or custom under which he or they claim such surface ground, and such evidence may consist either of the written rules of the miners of the district or the testimony of two credible witnesses to the uniform custom or the actual use and occupation as aforesaid, which testimony shall be reduced to writing by the Register and Receiver, and filed in the Register's office, with the application, a record thereof to be made as contemplated under the first head in the foregoing.

By the *third section* of the act it is required that upon the filing of the diagram as provided in the second section, and posting the same in a conspicuous place on the claim, with notice of intention to apply for a patent, the Register shall publish a notice of the same in a newspaper nearest the location of said claim, which notice shall state name of the claimant, name of mine, names of adjoining claimants on each end of the claim, the district and county in which the mine is situated, informing the public that application has been made for a patent for same, the Register also to post such notice in his office for ninety days.

Thereafter, should no adverse claim have been filed, and satisfactory proof should be produced that the diagram and notice have been posted in the manner and for the period stipulated in the statute, it will become the duty of the Surveyor-General, upon application of the party, to survey the premises, and make plat thereof, indorsed with his approval, designating the number and description of the location, the value of the labor and improvements, and the character of the vein exposed. As preliminary to the survey, however, the Surveyor-General must estimate the expense of surveying, platting, and ascertain from the Register the cost of the publication of notice, the amount of all of which must be deposited by the applicant for survey with any assistant U. S. treasurer or designated depositary, in favor of the U. S. Treasurer, to be passed to the credit of the fund created by "individual depositors for the surveys of public lands." Duplicate certificates of such deposits must be filed with the Surveyor-General for transmission to this office, as in the case of deposits for surveys of public lands under the 10th section of the act of Congress approved May 30th, 1862, and joint resolution of July 1st, 1864.

After the survey thus paid for shall have been duly executed and the plat thereof approved by the Surveyor-General, designating the number and the description of the location, accompanied by his official certificate of the value of the labor and improvements and character of the vein exposed, with the testimony of two or more reliable persons cognizant of the facts on which his certificate may be founded as to the value of the labor and improvements, the party claiming shall file the same with the Register and Receiver, and thereupon pay to the said Receiver five dollars per acre for the premises embraced in the survey, and shall file with those officers a triplicate certificate of deposit showing the payment of the cost of survey, plat, and notice, with satisfactory evidence, which shall be the testimony of at least two credible witnesses, that the diagram and notice were posted on the claim for a period of ninety days, as required by law and as contemplated in the foregoing. Thereupon it shall be the duty of the Register to transmit to the General Land Office said plat, survey, and description, with the proof indorsed as satisfactory by the Register and Receiver, so that a patent may issue if the proceedings are found regular, but neither the plat, survey, description, nor patent shall issue for more than one vein or lode.

The unity of the surveying system is to be maintained by extending over the mining districts the rectangular method, at least so far as township lines are concerned.

The contemplated surveys of the mineral lands will be made by district deputies, under contracts, according to the mode adopted in the survey of the public lands and private land claims, embracing in them all such veins or lodes as will be called for by claimants entitled to have them surveyed.

In consideration of the very limited scope of surveying involved in each mining claim, the per mileage allowed by law may not be adequate to secure the services of scientific surveyors, and hence the necessity of resorting to a per diem principle, it being the most equitable under the circumstances.

The Surveyor-General is therefore hereby authorized to commission resident mineral surveyors for different districts where, isolated from each other, and absolutely inconvenient for one surveyor promptly to attend to the several calls for surveying in such localities, the compensation not to exceed ten dollars per diem, including all expenses incident thereto. Such surveyors shall enter into bonds of $10,000 for the faithful performance of their duties in the survey of such claims as the Surveyor-General may be required to execute in pursuance of the aforesaid law and these instructions.

The *fourth section* contemplates the location and entry of a mine upon unsurveyed lands, stipulating for the surveys of public lands to be adjusted to the lines of the claims according to the location and possession and plat thereof. In surveying such claims, the Surveyor-General is authorized to vary from the rectangular form to suit the circumstances of the country, local rules, laws, and customs of miners. The extent of the locations made from and after the passage of the act shall, however, not exceed two hundred feet in length along the vein for each locator, with an additional claim for discovery to the discoverer of the lode, with the right to follow such vein to any depth, with all its dips, variations, and angles, together with a reasonable quantity of surface for the convenient working of the same as fixed by local rules: *Provided*, No person may make more than one location on the same lode, and no more than three thousand feet shall be taken in any one claim by any association of persons.

The deputy surveyors should be scientific men, capable of examining and reporting fully on every lode they will survey, and to bring in duplicate specimens of the ore, one of which you will send to this office and the other the Surveyor-General will keep to be ultimately turned over with the surveying archives to the State authorities.

The surveyors of mineral claims, whether on *surveyed* or *unsurveyed* lands, must designate those claims by a progressive series of numbers, beginning with No. 37, so as to avoid interference in that respect with the regular *sectional* series of numbers in each township; and shall designate the four owners of each claim, where the side lines of the same are known, so that such corners can be given by either trees, if any are found standing in place, or any corner rocks exist in place, or posts may be set diagonally and deeply imbedded, with four sides *facing* adjoining claims, sufficiently flattened to admit of inscriptions thereon; but where the corners are unknown it will be sufficient to place a well-built solid mound at each end of the claim. The beginning corner of the claim nearest to any corners of the public surveys is to be connected by course and distance, so as to ascertain the relative position of each claim in reference to township and range when the same have been surveyed; but in those parts of the surveying district where no such lines have as yet been extended, it will be the duty of Surveyors-General to have the same surveyed and marked, at least so far as standard and township lines are concerned, at the per mileage allowed, so as to embrace the mineral region, and to connect the nearest corners of the mineral claims with the corners of the public surveys.

Should it, however, be found impracticable to establish independent base and meridian lines, or to extend township lines over the region containing mineral claims required to be surveyed under the law, then, and in that case, you will cause to be surveyed in the first instance such a claim, the initial point of which will start either from a confluence of waters or such natural and permanent objects as will unmistakably identify the point of the beginning of the survey of the claim upon which other surveys will depend.

SEC. 5. Provides that in cases where the laws of Congress are silent upon the subject of rules for working mines, respecting easements, drainage, and other necessary means to the complete development of the same, the local Legislature of any State or Territory may provide them, and in order to embody such enactments into patents, you are directed to communicate any such laws to this office.

SEC. 6. Should adverse claimants to any mine appear before the approval of the survey, all further proceedings shall be stayed until a final settlement and adjudication are had in the courts of the rights of possession to such claim, except where the parties agree to settlement or a portion of the premises is not in dispute when a patent may issue as in other cases.

SEC. 7. Provides for such additional land districts as may be necessary.

SEC. 8. For the right of way.

SEC. 9. For the protection of rights to the use of water for mining, agricultural, manufacturing, or other purposes, for the right of way for the construction of ditches and canals; and makes parties constructing such work (after the passage of this act) to the injury of settlers, liable in damages.

SEC. 10. Homesteads made prior to the passage of this act by citizens of the United States, or persons who have declared their intention to become citizens, but on which lands no valuable mines of gold, silver, cinnabar, or copper have been discovered, are protected, so that settlers or owners of such homesteads shall have a right of pre-emption thereto, in quantity not to exceed one hundred and sixty acres, at $1.25 per acre, or to avail themselves of the homestead act and acts amendatory thereof.

SEC. 11. Stipulates that upon the survey of the lands in question, the Secretary of the Interior may set apart such portions as are clearly agricultural, and thereafter subjects such agricultural tracts to pre-emption and sale as other public lands.

In order to enable the department properly to give effect to this section of the law, you will cause your deputy surveyors to describe in their field-notes of surveys, in addition to the data required to be noted in the printed Manual of Surveying Instructions, on pages 17 and 18, the agricultural lands, and represent the same on township plats by the designation of "Agricultural lands."

It is to be understood that there is nothing obligatory on claimants to proceed under this statute, and that where they fail to do so, there being no adverse interest, they hold the same relations to the premises they may be working which they did before the passage of this act, with the additional guarantee that they possess the right of occupancy under the statute.

The foregoing presents such views as have occurred to this office in considering the prominent points of the statute, and will be followed by further instructions as the rulings in actual cases, and experience in the administration of the statute may from time to time suggest.

Very respectfully, your obedient servant,

JOS. S. WILSON, Commissioner.

To the United States Registers and Receivers and Surveyors-General.

No. 269 B.

Supplement to Circular of January 14, 1867, *in relation to Mining Claims.*

DEPARTMENT OF THE INTERIOR,
GENERAL LAND OFFICE, June 25, 1867.

Gentlemen :—In the preparation of forms adapted to the purchase of Mineral interests under the act of July 26, 1866,* it is found necessary, in connection with circular of January 14, 1867, to direct your attention to the following :—

1st. Where the rules of miners do not permit ground to be occupied, except the surface of the vein or lode, the claims presented may contain less than an acre of ground. In such cases, as we do not in regard to rates deal with a fraction, the price of five dollars is to be paid for the same; if the area exceeds that quantity, ten dollars; if more than two acres, fifteen dollars, and so on.

2d. In applications for mineral claims, it will be necessary, where a claim contains *less* than one acre, that the agreement expressed should be to pay *five dollars* for the claim.

3d. Should a party appear as an "adverse claimant," as contemplated by the sixth section of the act, you will require such person to show by proof the claim or interest he may have in the mine; and should the same be satisfactory to you, all further proceedings will be stayed until a final settlement and adjudication shall be had in the courts. But in case the adverse claimant, after proceedings have been stayed, shall fail to institute action in the courts, either pending or at their next ensuing session, with a view to the final adjustment of the claims, you will proceed with the case as if no objections had been filed.

4th. You will enter all claims under the act in separate tract books from those used for agricultural lands—dividing the books into townships and ranges, allowing about eight pages to each township.

For the present you will use the blank forms of abstracts of land sold and Register of Receipts in reporting returns, making such slight alterations in the headings as the cases may demand. Should it be found advisable in the future to have special abstracts, forms will be prepared and printed, and a supply duly transmitted to you.

You will commence a new series of numbers with the certificates—beginning with No. 1—and continue the same in regular order. As no special fee is provided for in the statute, you will be allowed one per cent. each on amount of purchase-money, as in cash sales. The moneys received for these claims will be accounted for in the Receiver's returns as cash received from sale of mineral claims.

Forms of applications, certificates, and receipts are being printed, and a supply will be sent as soon as possible.

I also append an abstract of duties prescribed in instructions of 14th January, 1867.

Very respectfully,

Register and Receiver. JOS. S. WILSON, Commissioner.

* No. 174 B.

ABSTRACT OF DUTIES PRESCRIBED IN MINERAL INSTRUCTIONS OF JANUARY 14, 1867.

Claimant—To post a *notice* on the claim giving information of his intention to apply for a patent. To file a *diagram* with the Register, together with the evidence of the rules of miners in support of the claim and its extent. After the *diagram* and *notice* have been posted ninety days, and no adverse claim filed, the claimant to apply to Surveyor-General for *survey* of the claim, deposit the amount estimated by the Surveyor-General to cover the expenses of the *survey, platting*, and *notice* with any assistant United States treasurer or designated depository in favor of the United States treasurer, to be passed to the credit of the fund created by "individual depositors for the surveys of the public lands," taking duplicate certificate of deposit, filing one with Surveyor-General, to be sent to the General Land Office, and retaining the other; and when the survey is approved and diagram thereof, together with the Surveyor-General's certificate as to improvements and character of the vein exposed, the claimant to pay to the Receiver the price of the claim.

Register and Receiver—To examine testimony filed by claimant showing the applicability of miner's rules in reference to the extent of the claim, which testimony is to be reduced to writing and filed with the claimant's application in the Register's office. Also, to examine the returns of survey approved by the Surveyor-General and filed by the claimant.

Receiver—To receive from the claimant the price of the claim on his filing with Register and Receiver the approved plat and certificate of the Surveyor-General as to the value of improvements and character of vein exposed, based on testimony by two reliable witnesses.

Register's diagram of the claim being filed by the claimant, the Register shall publish a notice in a newspaper nearest to the claim, naming the *mine, claimant, adjoining claimants, district, and county*, informing the public that application has been made for a patent. The Register will post the notice in his office for ninety days, and on the publisher's presenting his account to the Register immediately on the expiration of the ninety days, he will transmit it to the Surveyor-General; and on the receipt from the claimants of the Surveyor-General's certificate of the improvements on the claim, together with plat and other evidence of the survey approved, also the Receiver's receipt for the payment for the claim, the Register will transmit same, with proof, indorsed by Register and Receiver as satisfactory, to the Commissioner of the General Land Office for patent.

Surveyor General's duty when no adverse claim is filed, proof furnished that the *diagram* and *notice* had been posted for ninety days, and on receiving also from the Register the account of the publisher of the notice: The Surveyor-General, when applied to by the claimant for the survey of his claim, shall estimate the expense of the *survey, platting*, and *notice*, and when a certificate of deposit is filed with him by the claimant he shall order the survey to be made, and transmit the certificate of deposit to the General Land Office. When the returns of survey are made to the Surveyor-General's office, he will approve the same, hand the necessary evidence thereof to the claimant, to be filed by him in the Register and Receiver's office for examination and final preparation of patent certificate by the Register for transmission to the Commissioner of the General Land Office. The Surveyor-General will also transmit returns of the survey to the Commissioner, with the account of the Surveyor and that of the publishers of the notice, for direct payment from United States treasury to parties entitled, as in the case of payments made out of the funds deposited under the tenth section of the act of Congress approved May 30, 1862, and joint resolution of June 1, 1864.

No. 270 B.

Circular, No. 21.

From the General Land Office at Washington, relating to Agricultural Lands provided for in the 10th and 11th sections of the Mining Act of July 26, 1866, prior to the date of said act, designated as Mineral Lands, and as such excluded from survey and sale.

DEPARTMENT OF THE INTERIOR,
GENERAL LAND OFFICE, May 16, 1868.

Gentlemen :—The 10th section of the Mining Act of July 26, 1866, provides for homesteads, made prior to the passage of the act by citizens of the United States, or persons who had declared their intention to become citizens, upon lands previously reserved as mineral, and as such excluded from survey and sale, but which are properly agricultural, no valuable mines of gold, silver, cinnabar, or copper, having been discovered thereon, and which have been improved and used by settlers for agricultural purposes.

These settlers have a right of pre-emption to such land, not exceeding 160 acres, and may purchase the same at the minimum of $1.25 per acre, or enter them under the homestead law, after they become surveyed, upon the usual and proper proceedings in such cases. If the deputy surveyor returns it as agricultural, and there is no data to the contrary, and no one files an affidavit of its being more valuable for mineral than for agricultural uses, the settler will be allowed to enter it under the provisions of said 10th section. If an affidavit is filed alleging the land to be mineral, a trial must be had to determine whether it is more valuable for mining purposes than for agricultural. In such cases a day will be fixed for the hearing, giving to the claimant and to the party filing the affidavit sufficient notice to enable them to be present with their witnesses ; and when the tract had been occupied for agricultural purposes, and improved as such, before the 26th of July, 1866, the burden of proof will be upon the party seeking to establish its mineral character, and the testimony should be of a nature clearly proving the truth of such allegations, before a decision is rendered against the right of the settler to enter the land.

Should the deputy surveyor return the land as mineral, the settler will be required to furnish satisfactory proof of the error of such return prior to entering the premises claimed under said 10th section.

The return of a deputy surveyor, although entitled to respect as coming from a sworn officer, is not to be taken as conclusive in these cases, when disputed, but the matter must be investigated by the examination of witnesses, capable from experience and observation, and from previous examination, to testify understandingly in reference to the existence of minerals upon any particular tract, and whether the deposit is of sufficient extent to render it more valuable for mining than for agriculture.

When lands of the character contemplated by said 10th section have not yet been filed upon, you should satisfy yourselves as to which class they belong before taking steps looking to their disposal.

The 11th section of the Mining Act authorizes the Secretary of the Interior, after the survey of lands previously reserved as mineral, to designate and set apart such portions of them as are clearly agricultural, which are made subject to pre-emption and disposal as other public lands of the United States.

To give effect to this section, the Surveyors-General in the mining States and Territories have been instructed to require their deputies to describe in their field notes, and designate on township plats, such lands as are agricultural. After the filing of the plats in the district land offices, if no counter affidavits are presented, the tracts designated "agricultural lands" may be filed upon under the pre-emption, or taken under the homestead laws; but pre-emptors will not be permitted to prove up and enter until after such a period of actual settlement and cultivation as shall show good faith—say not less than six months from the date of settlement embraced in the filing of the declaratory statement; and if before the expiration of such time an affidavit is filed alleging the mineral character of the particular tract claimed, a trial must be had before an entry is made, to determine that question.

It is not doubted that in every township there are tracts of land more valuable for farms and gardens than for mining purposes, and the object of the law is to segregate these from the mineral and dispose of them as agricultural.

Errors of judgment may sometimes occur, but as a general rule it is believed a careful examination will enable claimants to act with safety in reference to these lands, and although they may be put to the necessity of proving their chief value to be for purposes of agriculture, by an opposing affidavit filed any time before entry, yet where reasonable precaution has been exercised, such proof seldom fails, at least as to the whole tract filed upon, and if a profitable mine were to be discovered upon a part of the premises, it would only enhance the value of the remaining portion.

Affidavits alleging particular lands to be more valuable as mineral than as arable, must apply to each of the smallest legal subdivisions. Of a quarter section, 120 acres may be mineral, and the remaining 40 arable, and the mineral character of the former is no reason why the latter should not be entered as agricultural. Nor is it sufficient that such affidavits are based upon opinion or belief. They must contain a statement of facts within the knowledge of deponents, derived from actual observation or examination, furnishing a strong presumption that the particular subdivision is mineral land, and more valuable as such than as agricultural. Mere speculation, based upon no positive knowledge, and disclosing no material facts, will not be received, and claimants ought not to be put to the trouble and expense of meeting affidavits of this character. There should be the utmost good faith required from both sides. Lands more valuable for mineral than for other purposes are not to be taken under the pre-emption or homestead laws; nor, on the other hand, are parties to be intimidated from making settlements upon, and ultimately entering under these laws, such lands as are most useful for agricultural purposes, simply because valuable mineral lands may lie in the immediate vicinity. Both classes of lands are to be disposed of under their appropriate laws, and neither interest is to be subordinated to the other to the detriment of the public welfare.

If the land officers in the various districts have reason to believe that mineral affidavits are being placed on timber land on which no mineral has been found, for the purpose of keeping the same from settlement until after the timber has been removed, they will inform the parties filing such papers that affidavits in which it is not alleged that either gold, silver, cinnabar, or copper have been found, are sufficient; and however specific and full such affidavits may be, they are not to be deemed conclusive as to the matters alleged. Any settler filing an affidavit of a contrary character, and desiring to enter the particular tract as agricultural land, is entitled to have the question examined, and on proving it to be more valuable as arable than as mineral, may file upon it under the pre-emption or enter it under the homestead law, and in due time consummate the title.

It matters not whether the precious metals are found in quartz ledges, or in placer or hydraulic mines, if the particular subdivisions of the public lands containing them are more valuable for mining than for agriculture, they cannot be entered under the pre-emption or homestead law. If placers once valuable have become exhausted so as no longer to be valuable as mines, the land may then be entered as arable.

These affidavits are to be filed with the Register and copies transmitted to this office. They are to be registered and carefully filed, but need not be recorded.

In reference to the fees authorized in pre-emption and homestead cases, and in proving up the same, you are referred to the legal provisions and instructions given in the circular from this office dated September 17, 1867.

When necessary, all witnesses must be carefully cross-examined in order to elicit the truth, and the testimony, with the papers in each case, together with the joint opinion of the district land officers, will be transmitted to this office for examination and review.

Respectfully,
JOS. S. WILSON, Commissioner.

No. 271 B.

Proofs and papers required to be filed with applications for patents under the Mining Act of July 26, 1866.

DEPARTMENT OF THE INTERIOR,
GENERAL LAND OFFICE, May 3, 1869.

Sir:—In reply to your letter of inquiry, in regard to the papers and proofs proper to be filed in the local land offices in applications for patents under the mining act of July 26, 1866, you are informed that these documents should be in the order following:—

1st. A written application, stating name of claimants, whether as individuals or an incorporated or unincorporated company, and designating the mining district, county, &c., whether the mine is of gold, silver, cinnabar, or copper; the number of feet claimed on the vein and laterally; the date of the original location; where it is recorded; whether the applicant claims as an original locator, or as a purchaser; if the latter, whether by deed or verbal contract; the nature and value of the improvements made or labor performed; whether the applicant is in actual possession at the date of the application; that he has posted diagram and notice of intention to apply for a patent in a conspicuous place on claim, giving the date of the same.

2d. With the application the claimant should file a copy of the diagram, and a copy of the notice posted on the claim.

3d. A certificate of the recorder, or officer in charge of the records, to the effect that the claim, as originally located (giving the names of the locators), appears of record on his books; that the records also show a regular chain of title from the original locators to the applicants, and that the claim was located agreeably to the mining customs in force in the district at the date of its location, should be filed, and when the same office has custody of the mining records and the mining customs, one certificate will meet both requirements. The certificate should be attested by his official seal.

A statute of the legislature of Colorado requires a copy of the records, laws, and proceedings of each mining district, relating to lode claims, to be filed in the county clerk's office, &c. Hence the county clerk of the proper county would appear to be the proper person to certify to the records of the location, and to its being made agreeably to the mining customs then in force; and as he is also *ex officio* recorder of the county, he is likewise the proper person to certify to a regular series of conveyances from the original locators to the applicants, appearing of record on his books. On receiving such certificate or certificates from the proper officer, exemplifications of the records or an abstract of title will be dispensed with. Such certificates need not cover more than one or at most two pages of an ordinary sheet of paper, and cannot be very expensive. They will be quite satisfactory in showing the true nature of the claim, and character of claimant's right to same. Copies of mining customs may also be dispensed with if the clerk certifies that the location was made in pursuance of the customs in force at the time of the location.

4th. If the applicants are an incorporated company, a certified copy of the contract or certificate of incorporation should be filed with the local officers, and in that case proof of citizenship will be dispensed with.

5th. If applicants are not a corporation, proof of citizenship, or of having filed a declaration of intention to become a citizen, must be presented, which may be in the form of an affidavit or affidavits.

6th. The claimant should make affidavit as to whether he is in the occupancy of the claim or not; how long he has occupied it; amount of money and labor expended thereon, and the nature of the improvements.

7th. After the expiration of ninety days from posting and publishing notice, the claimant should file his own affidavit and that of another disinterested party that the diagram and notices were posted in a conspicuous place on the claim at least ninety days.

If all the proofs are satisfactory to the local officers, and no adverse claimant appears, the surveyor general will proceed to make the survey and plat, and approve the same, according to instructions communicated to that officer.

8th. An affidavit of a practical miner should be filed, to the effect that the surface indications point to but one vein or lode as included within the surface ground embraced in the claim.

None of the documents required need be expensive, and ought not to be, and excepting the survey and plat, would not, according to the fees for similar documents in this district, exceed the aggregate of ten dollars.

This refers merely to the items of proof to be presented to the district land officers; to the certificates, affidavits, &c., above specified.

Any further information will be furnished you on application to the Register or Receiver, or the Surveyor-General.

Very respectfully, &c.,

JOS. S. WILSON, Commissioner.

T. H. Becker, Central City, Colorado.

No. 271½ B.

OWNER'S RIGHTS IN CANALS, &C.

GENERAL LAND OFFICE,
November 23, 1869.

If, * * * it is inquired to what extent the 9th section of the Mining Act protects property in certain water rights in California, or in a particular mining ditch or canal, the answer is, that in disposing of the public lands upon which said canal is located, the United States will, under said 9th section, maintain and protect such rights in the same as have vested and accrued by priority of possession, and which at the time of such disposal are recognized and acknowledged by the local customs, laws, and the decisions of the courts of California.

In the opinion of the commissioner, therefore, the owner's rights in the matter of the canal are primarily regulated by the customs, laws, and courts of California, and the only protection the act of July 26, 1866, can render you is in upholding the integrity of these, so far as they may constitute the foundation of any rights the owner may have in or to such when the general Government grants the lands upon which it is located, with the addition that during the time intervening between the passage of the Mining Act and the disposal of the land by the United States the owner cannot be held as a trespasser on it in respect to any rights thus secured to him by such customs and laws of California or decisions of the courts.

Respectfully, &c.,

JOS. S. WILSON, Commissioner.

No. 272 B.

Mode of proceeding in regard to mineral claims.

Persons who have no possessory rights, according to the mining laws of Colorado, not authorized to apply for patents.

DEPARTMENT OF THE INTERIOR,
GENERAL LAND OFFICE, May 7, 1869.

GENTLEMEN :—

* * * * * * * * *

If the claimants are * * * associated as a company, their united interests constituting but one claim, patentable on the expenditure of but one thousand dollars in labor and improvements, there is no question as to the right of such company to appear by an authorized agent or attorney, and no reason appears why any one of the several members may not be thus authorized.

This is the usual practice in other States and Territories, not only as to incorporated companies but in respect to those not incorporated, and as the individuals composing these associations are often widely scattered, a different rule would frequently render proceedings under the mining act impracticable.

When the interest is of such a mutual character as it is in the case of these companies there would seem to be no occasion for requiring the personal appearance at the local office of each individual of a company, and in adopting rules of practice the convenience and ability of the claimants should receive proper consideration, onerous and expensive regulations being never required in the administration of the public land system.

Mr. Sutrell further inquires whether an applicant for a patent having no possessory claim according to the mining laws and regulations of Colorado can acquire title to a claim upon which he has no improvements, and which by the mining laws of the Territory is in the peaceable possession of another, who having failed to see the notices said to have been posted and published, made no appearance as an adverse claimant until after the expiration of the ninety days

He alleges, in respect to certain applications made before you, that if notices were posted at all, they were put on the premises at the time of a deep snow, while work in the mines was suspended and the miners absent at their respective homes, the ninety days expiring before the resumption of mining operations; and that the use of the compass and chain was at the time impracticable on account of the snow on the mountains.

The mining act authorizes applications for patents by parties having previously occupied and improved their claims, according to the local customs and rules of miners in the district where the same are situated, and who have expended in actual labor and improvements thereon an amount of $1000 on each claim, and such claimants are authorized to include in their applications only those claims to which they have possessory title under and by virtue of such local customs, and they have no right to include premises to which no such possessory rights attach.

Persons having no possessory rights, according to the mining laws and regulations of Colorado, and who have not made the improvements required by the mining act, are not authorized to apply for patents, and the attempt to do so is a fraud not only against the rightful owners, but against the policy of the act itself.

Should satisfactory information of such acts be received at this office at any time before the issuing of a patent the party injured would be allowed to appear as an adverse claimant, and on making a proper showing the case would be suspended.

The time to appear as an adverse claimant in no case expires with the ninety days in which the notice is required to be published. He can in all cases appear before the approval of the survey by the Surveyor-General, as provided in the eighth section of the mining act.

Before an applicant under the act of July 26th, 1866, is allowed to make his entry, the Register and Receiver should be satisfied that he has previously occupied and improved his claim according to the mining regulations of the district, and that the diagram filed by such applicant conforms to such laws and regulations, and that he is in peaceful possession of the claim; and such reasonable proof should be required on these points as may be furnished without unnecessary inconvenience and expense.

As the laws of Colorado provide for filing all records and proceedings relating to lode claims of each mining district in the clerk's office of the proper county, it will be an easy matter for the applicant to obtain a certificate from such clerk, stating that the documents are on file or of record in his office, show the particular claim to have been located by persons (naming them) at a specified date, and to have been transferred by regular conveyances from the original locators to the applicant, if such are the facts.

The clerk may further state in the same certificate that the claim is one authorized by the mining laws of the Territory, all of which need not embrace more than a single page of cap paper, and if authenticated by the county seal it will be accepted in lieu of an abstract of title and transcript of mining regulations.

When an adverse claimant appears, he is required to file an affidavit setting out fully and distinctly the nature of his claim, and if it shows a conflicting right, determinable only by mining laws and regulations of the district, State or Territory, the case must be suspended for adjudication in the local courts. The rule as to who is to commence proceedings is not varied by the mining act from what it would be independent of the act.

The party in possession has no occasion to invoke the aid of the courts; he has all he wants, and desires no litigation. The party out of possession requires the intervention of judicial tribunals to restore him to a possession which he claims to have lost; and under the act, as well as before its passage, he is the one required to commence proceedings, and is entitled to a reasonable time to do so. As the mining laws of Colorado do not permit locations of 3000 feet on the vein, no such claim can be patented, and you will advise applicants accordingly.

Respectfully, etc.,

Jos. S. Wilson, Commissioner.

Register and Receiver, Fair Play, Colorado.

No. 273 B.

Applications under mining act of July 26, 1866—*how to be made. Diagram to accompany application. Further instructions in regard to mining claims.*

General Land Office,
September 24, 1869.

Gentlemen:—This office has received a communication from William Edmunds, of Oroville, California, stating that on 29th June last he sent to your office an application under the mining act of July 26, 1866, for a patent; that the claim was upon unsurveyed land, but was unmistakably described by approximate course and distance from the confluence of two well-known streams, and on the ground by conspicuous, natural, and artificially marked monuments; that a descriptive diagram accompanied the application, and that you returned the whole, with a note stating that he had made no application at all.

The commissioner thinks that Mr. Edmunds had made an application, though probably a defective one, and that you should have instructed him how to perfect and complete it, instead of returning the papers with the answer as stated in his letter.

No particular form of application is necessary under the mining act; it should be in writing; state the name of the applicant; the name of the lode or claim; the mining district, county and State; when and by whom the claim was located; whether the applicant has possession of it according to the local customs, and how long this possession has continued; whether he claims as locator or as purchaser; the number of feet claimed on the lode, and quantity of surface ground, and that the local rules authorize claims to that extent, with the extent and value of the improvements on the claim.

If these facts are all stated, and the paper is signed and dated, it is a good application. If any substantial omission is found in the paper, he should be instructed as to the further statements required.

The application should be accompanied with a diagram representing the claim with as much accuracy as practicable, but it need not have the accuracy of a final survey. All that is necessary in this respect is that it shall so clearly indicate and describe the claim that any one seeing it would be able to learn from it the metes and bounds of the premises claimed. The claimant should also file with the application a certificate from the mining recorder stating the date of location of claim ; names of locators ; that the mining rules of the district at the date of the location authorized claims of the size asserted by applicant; that the location was duly recorded, naming volume and page ; that the mining customs appear on record; and if the applicant is a purchaser, that a regular series of transfers appears on his records from the original locator to the applicant, if such is the fact. If the fact is not so, then the statement must be made according to the fact. This fact should be attested by the official seal of the recorder. Such a certificate, stating the facts of location, of the mining customs, and that a regular chain of title ending in the applicant appears on the mining records, will be accepted as sufficient evidence on these points.

An affidavit of possession and improvement according to the mining customs should also be filed with the application. This affidavit should be made by, say, two persons, well acquainted with the premises and the claimant. The claimant himself may be one of the affiants. It should state the length of time the claimant occupied the premises ; whether by working them as a miner, by making improvements preparatory to mining, or simply by staking off and recording the claim as required by the mining customs. In this affidavit the statement may also be made that from surface indications the premises contain but one vein or lode.

In addition to these papers a copy of the notice posted on the claim should accompany the application, so that the Register and Receiver may examine it, to ascertain whether it is sufficient. Then, if the claimant is a corporation, evidence of the fact should be filed, which is generally a certified copy of the charter, and if not an incorporated company, an affidavit of citizenship, or of having filed a declaration of intention to become a citizen, should be filed.

The papers accompanying the application, therefore, are—1st, the diagram ; 2d, the certificate of the mining recorder; 3d, an affidavit of possession and occupancy according to the mining customs, and that the premises contain but one vein or lode, according to the surface indication ; 4th, a copy of the notice posted on the claim ; 5th, a certified copy of the charter, if the claimant is an incorporated company, or an affidavit of citizenship if not an incorporated company. No proof of citizenship is necessary in the case of corporations. The affidavits should be made before an officer using an official seal, such as a judge or notary public, and the officer should be able to certify to the credibility of the witnesses.

If these six papers, the application and the accompanying five above enumerated, are drawn up with an ordinary amount of care, and are made so as to satisfy the Register and Receiver that the transaction is a *bona fide* one, the claim is in a proper state for the action of the local officers. The Register will then make the publication required by law, and the only additional proof required from the applicant is that the notice and diagram were posted on the claim for a period of ninety days.

The Surveyor-General will certify to the value of the improvements and the character of the vein exposed.

Nothing like a set form is necessary for any of these papers. Any person of ordinary intelligence can prepare them; and it matters but little whether they are drawn up skilfully or not, so they contain the substance as above stated.

The expense of these papers cannot be much, for there are but six in all, and none of them need cover more than a page of common cap paper, and others not more than half a page.

You are instructed to render the applicant and all other claimants such reasonable and proper assistance as you can conveniently furnish them to enable them to prepare their applications.

Respectfully, &c.,

JOS. S. WILSON, Commissioner.

Register and Receiver, Marysville, California.

No. 274 B.

Decision in respect to mining locations subsequent to July 26, 1866.

GENERAL LAND OFFICE,
November 6, 1869.

Sir:—Referring to a communication inquiring if ten men can "locate 200 feet each on a ledge, one or two of them buy out all the rest, and then apply and secure a patent for all the ground by showing title deeds," I reply that with respect to locations made *since* the 26th of July, 1866, the date of the mining act of Congress, a patent may issue on any claim held agreeably to the local mining rules and regulations of the district or State in which it lies, whether held by purchase or location, provided that individual locations do not exceed the maximum of 200 feet, and company locations 3000 feet in length along the lode, as limited by the fourth section of said act of Congress.

Very respectfully,

JOS. S. WILSON, Commissioner.

Thomas Lytle, Nevada City.

No. 275 B.

Sulphur springs not regarded as saline or mineral.

GENERAL LAND OFFICE,
August 25, 1869.

Gentlemen:—The testimony shows that no mine of gold, silver, cinnabar, or copper exists upon this land, but a sulphur spring is situated thereon. This office does not regard sulphur springs as saline or mineral, so as to come within the inhibition of the statutes excluding mineral and saline lands from pre-emption entry or scrip location.

Respectfully, &c.,

JOS. S. WILSON, Commissioner.

Register and Receiver, Fair Play, Wisconsin.

No. 276 B.

Extracts from the Report of Hon. Jos. S. Wilson, Commissioner, for the year 1868, *in respect to mining claims, applications for patents, &c.*

LIMITATIONS IN THE PROVISOS OF THE FOURTH SECTION OF THE ACT CONSTRUED.

The attention of this office has been called to controversies existing in some of the mining districts, arising from differences of opinion in relation to the proper construction of the mining act of July 26, 1866, some persons contending, it appears, that since its passage a company formed merely for mining purposes and locating claims can take 3000 feet on the vein, although such company or association may be composed of less than 14 individuals. It is held by this office that the manner of making locations, and the number of feet that can be taken on the same vein or lode by an individual or an association, depend upon the rules and customs of miners of the respective districts, the act of July 26, 1866, in no respect superseding or modifying these customs, except where they authorize the location of more than 200 feet on the same lode by any one person, or more than 3000 feet by any association of persons. In such cases the statute restricts and reduces locations made since July 26, 1866, to the above-named quantities, respectively, as the maximum in each case; and this is the only difference existing between the local mining regulations and the controlling act of Congress.

An individual cannot, since the date of the act, locate more than 200 feet on the same lode, nor an association more than 3000 feet, no matter how many persons may be associated together, or what the local customs may prescribe. Whether a company or association can take as much as 3000 feet, depends upon the mining regulations of the particular district, and the number of persons associated in such company.

Individuals cannot, by forming themselves into companies, locate a greater number of feet to each person than can be done by each acting separately.

They may locate as a company or an association at the rate of 200 feet to each individual embraced in it, with an additional 200 feet to the discoverer, if the local customs permit that much to be taken until 3000 feet are located, after which no additional quantity can be claimed on the same lode by the same company, whatever may be the number of its members.

In districts where the mining regulations limit locations to less than 200 feet to each individual, or less than 3000 feet to any association of persons, claimants will be restricted accordingly, such regulations remaining in full force, being unaffected by the act of Congress.

These remarks apply wholly to original locations, made in pursuance of the rules and regulations of miners in the several mining districts. They have no application to claims in the hands of purchasers, and it is not to be understood from what has been above stated that a mining claim of 3000 feet may not be owned and controlled by an association of less than 14 persons, where possession is obtained by bona fide purchases for valuable consideration, or partly by purchase and partly by location, there being nothing in the act of July 26, 1866, to prevent an association composed of any number of individuals from holding such claim, and upon proper application and proof obtaining a patent for the same.

When the mining act was first passed it was thought that among the great variety of local rules and customs, existing in a thousand remote mining districts, and known to us only as they come here in actual cases, there were probably some, authorizing the location of large claims, amounting to 3000 feet or more, by companies or associations, in consideration of the construction of improvements enhancing the value of large numbers of claims, as the building of a tunnel to drain the mines of a certain lode, or system of lodes, or the erection of any other improvements securing a common object and promoting a common interest. As such companies would not have been formed for the purpose of locating claims, and the privilege of doing so, if conferred upon them at all, would have been in the nature of a reward for having promoted the general welfare of a certain district, by the expenditure of capital and labor in works of improvement beneficial to all, the right of making such location to the extent of 3000 feet in pursuance of such supposed mining regulations was believed to be independent of the question of the size of the company, and that having rendered the service it was entitled to make the location, whether it was composed of a greater or less number of members. If the regulations of any district embraced provisions of this nature, conferring upon any company, large or small, for reasons such as have been suggested, the right of locating 3000 feet on a lode, or on each one of a number of lodes, benefited by such improvements, it is not perceived that there would be any incompatibility between them and the act of July 26, 1866, nor would the policy of the act in limiting locations appear to be more impaired by such regulations than by the unlimited right of purchase generally recognized by these local customs.

It may be that no such regulations exist, but as the customs of miners scattered through the numerous mining camps of the Western States and Territories are not to be found in any compilation, many of them never having been reduced to print, it is not surprising that misapprehension may have occurred in that respect.

As to associations or companies formed for the purpose of locating claims, however, it is very evident that they are subject to the limitations found in the provisos in the 4th section of the act, and that the restriction of 200 feet to each locator cannot be evaded by forming an association.

RULING IN RELATION TO THE APPLICABILITY OF THE MINING ACT TO "BLUE GRAVEL LEAD" CLAIMS.

The question having been presented whether the provisions of the act could be made applicable to the "blue gravel leads" found in different parts of the mineral domain, so as to entitle the holders of these claims to apply for patents, the commissioner held as follows: The mining act provides for patenting veins or lodes of quartz, or other rock in place, bearing gold, silver, cinnabar, or copper, but furnishes no definition of the terms "vein" or "lode." In geology and among miners they imply generally an aggregation of metallic matter found in the fissures of the rocks which inclose it, but are of great variety; veins differing very much in their formation and appearance. Lode is a term in general use among the tin miners of Cornwall, England, having been introduced on the Pacific coast by emigrants from the Cornish mines, and signifies a fissure filled either by metallic or earthy matter. Lead is generally used in the same sense as lode.

In Nevada the term ledge is usually employed in regulations concerning mines, and in Montana the terms lead, lode, or ledge, are similarly used. Ledge would seem to convey the idea of a layer or stratum of metal interposed between a course or ridge of rocks.

Veins may be either sedimentary, plutonic, or segregated, or of infiltration, or attrition, depending upon their peculiar formation or the mode of occurrence of the metallic deposit.

In California the ancient river channels, or what are supposed to have been such, found in various mining districts, filled with a compact blue gravel rich in gold, are called the "blue leads," and in common parlance the "blue veins." Even the shallow diggings or placers are sometimes found to occur in such regular layers or courses as to receive from the miners working them the name of veins or leads. There is also another form of deposit of all or some of the four metals named in the mining act, different from either of those mentioned above, called *contact deposit.* European miners mention still others, called in England *floors*, in Germany *stockwerke*, and a form of deposit known as *fahlbands.* These latter are, more properly speaking, ore-bearing belts, irregular in their dimensions, but presenting a degree of parallelism with each other.

Neither is the mode of occurrence designated as "contact deposit" considered as a true vein or lode. In fact, if the question were raised, neither of the forms known as contact deposit, fahlbands, or segregated veins, could be accepted as true metalliferous veins, nor could it frequently be made to appear, without expensive excavations, whether the metal in the mine, for which a patent is applied for, occurs in the form of a true vein or not. Hence, we discover that a very strict construction placed upon the terms used in the mining act would exclude from its benefits a large class of claims, even of the branch of rock mining, from the impracticability of proving the metallic deposit to occur in the form of a true vein. But there is no reason for supposing that these terms were employed according to their strict geological signification. The plain object of the law is, to dispose for money value of the mineral lands of the United States, and if the claimant is willing to pay the price named in the act, it is clearly a matter of indifference to the Government whether the metal occurs in the form of a true or false vein, or whether in the form of a vein at all. There is certainly no public policy to be subserved by favoring one class of miners and excluding others, nor has the commissioner ever heard any reason assigned why vein mines should be patented, and other deposits excluded from patent, nor any intimation expressed that such was the intention of the act. An idea may have prevailed at the time of the passage of the law, that the placers were becoming exhausted, and that their claimants did not care about buying the land or obtaining patents; or it may be that the act was drafted mainly in view of localities where placer mining constituted a very inconsiderable branch of the business, compared to rock mining, and hence, the language of the act seems to have more direct reference to vein mining than any other branch. But whatever may be the cause of the phraseology adopted, it is very evident to the commissioner that no purpose or design existed in the minds either of the framers of the bill, or of the Congress that passed it, to exclude any class of miners that chose to avail themselves of its provisions; consequently, the law should receive the most liberal construction that the language will admit of, and every class of claim that, either according to scientific accuracy or popular usage, can be classed and applied for as veins or lodes, may be patented under the law. It may be observed as an important point, that no proof is required to establish the vein formation of the deposit, the law evidently contemplating none. It requires the Surveyor-General to certify to the character of the vein exposed, but that is understood to mean that the certificate should show whether the exposed vein contains gold, silver, cinnabar, or copper, as it would frequently be impossible for the Surveyor-General, even if his knowledge of mineral veins were sufficient to render him otherwise competent, to determine whether the deposit conformed to one class of veins or the other, or whether it was a true vein at all, without extensive excavations; a requirement certainly not contemplated by the mining act.

The applicant claims a certain number of feet along the vein or lode, and as much surface ground on either or both sides of the same as is necessary for the convenient working of the mine. He may claim as many feet as the local law or mining regulations permit him to hold, not inconsistent with the act of Congress, and as much surface ground as he may need, taking care not to conflict with any other claimant. The case being presented in this form, no proof is necessary to show that the deposit appears in the form of a vein, the phraseology of the act appearing to render it evident that the claimant was not to be put to the necessity of producing such proof, the evidence called for being confined to the posting and publishing the necessary notices and diagrams, to proving the local mining customs, the location of the claim, possessory rights of the applicant, and the amount expended in actual labor and improvements; which being satisfactory, and the Surveyor-General having made proper survey and plat of the claim, with the required indorsements and certificates, a patent must issue to the applicant.

No reason is perceived why a blue gravel lead might not be presented in this form, both in the application and on the diagram and plat; and being presented, if the applicant is the *bona fide* holder of the claim, and it is clear of conflict, it will be patented to him without any proof being required as to the mode in which the deposit occurs.

To conform to the language of the act, however, the claim must call for so many feet along the lead, and a given quantity of surface ground on one or both sides of the same.

INSTRUCTIONS UNDER THE TENTH AND ELEVENTH SECTIONS OF SAID MINING ACT.

The 10th section of the mining act provides for homesteads made prior to the passage of the law by citizens of the United States, or persons who had declared their intention to become citizens, upon lands previously reserved as mineral, and, as such, excluded from survey and sale, but which are properly agricultural, no valuable mines of gold, silver, cinnabar, or copper, having been discovered thereon, and which have been improved and used by settlers for agricultural purposes.

These settlers have a right of pre-emption to such lands not exceeding one hundred and sixty acres, and may purchase the same at the minimum of one dollar and twenty-five cents per acre, or enter them under the homestead laws after they become surveyed, upon the usual proceedings in such cases. If the deputy surveyor returns them as agricultural, there being no data to the contrary, and no one files an affidavit of the land being more valuable for mineral than agricultural uses, the settler is allowed to enter under the provisions of said section. If an affidavit is filed alleging it to be mineral, an investigation is required, before the local land officers, to determine the class to which the land properly belongs. In such cases, a day is fixed for the hearing, and sufficient notice given to the claimant and the party filing the affidavit to enable them to be present with witnesses; and, when the tract has been occupied for agricultural purposes, and improved as such, before the 26th of July, 1866, the burden of proof will be upon the party seeking to establish its mineral character, and the testimony is required to be of a nature clearly proving it to be such before a decision is rendered against the right of the settler to enter the land.

Should the deputy surveyor return a tract as mineral, the settler will be required to furnish satisfactory proof of the error of such return prior to making entry on the premises claimed under the 10th section.

The return of a deputy surveyor, although entitled to respect as coming from a sworn officer, is not taken as conclusive in such cases when disputed, but the matter is investigated by the proper local land officers by the examination of witnesses, capable, from experience, observation, and previous examination, to testify understandingly as to the existence or non-existence of minerals upon any particular tract, and as to whether the deposit is of sufficient extent to render it more valuable for mining than for agriculture.

The testimony adduced and all the papers are required to be transmitted to this office, with the joint opinion of the Register and Receiver, for review and final determination.

The 11th section of the mining act authorizes the Secretary of the Interior, after the survey of the lands previously reserved as mineral, to designate and set apart such portions of them as are clearly agricultural, and tracts of the latter character are made subject to pre-emption and disposal as other public lands.

To give effect to this section, the surveyors-general in the mining States and Territories have been instructed to require their deputies to describe in the field-notes and designate on township plats the tracts which are agricultural, the designation to apply to each of the smallest legal subdivisions. After the filing of the plats in the district land offices, if no counter-affidavits are presented, the tracts designated agricultural may be filed upon under the pre-emption or taken under the homestead laws; but pre-emptors are not authorized to prove up and enter until after such a period of actual settlement and cultivation as shall show good faith, generally not less than six months from date of settlement indicated in the declaratory statement, and if before the expiration of that time an affidavit is filed alleging the mineral character of the particular tract claimed, and investigation is necessary before the entry is made to determine the question.

It cannot be doubted that in almost every township there are tracts of land more valuable for farms and gardens than for mining, and the object of the law evidently is to segregate these from the mineral, and dispose of them as agricultural. It is a matter of no legal consequence whether the precious metals are found in quartz ledges, placers, or hydraulic mines. If the particular subdivisions containing them are more valuable for mining than for agriculture, they cannot be entered as arable lands under the pre-emption or homestead statutes; yet placers once valuable, but which have become exhausted, and are no longer valuable as mines, may be entered as arable.

INSTRUCTIONS TO SURVEYORS-GENERAL IN RELATION TO DUTIES REQUIRED BY THE TENTH AND ELEVENTH SECTIONS OF THE AFORESAID MINING LAW.

Under the provisions of the 10th section of the act of Congress entitled "An act granting the right of way to ditch and canal owners over the public lands, and for other purposes," approved July 26, 1866, the public lands on which no valuable mines of gold, silver, cinnabar, or copper, have been discovered, and which had been occupied and improved by *bona fide* homestead or pre-emption settlers, are permitted to be taken up by said settlers in quantities according to legal subdivisions not exceeding 160 acres, at the rate of $1.25 per acre.

In order that the lands of that character may be known to the government and its local land officers, and that the same may be set apart as "agricultural," circular instructions have been issued to the Registers and Receivers of the United States land offices how to proceed in the ascertainment of that class of lands and their segregation from mineral lands, copies of which have been sent for the information and government of surveyors-general. It will be perceived that the instructions allude to directions having been given to surveyors-general, requiring them to cause their deputy surveyors to describe in their field-notes, and designate on township plats, "agricultural lands," as contemplated in mining circular dated January 14, 1867. In amplification of these instructions, it is found of importance to the public service that deputy surveyors should avail themselves, while executing their surveys in the field, of all trustworthy information in regard to the mineral localities falling within the sphere of their contracts, in addition to their personal and diligent observations, and to record in their field-notes sufficient descriptions of different mineral characteristics to afford draughtsmen adequate data for indicating the same on township plats, in yellow dotted shade, in respect to the out-boundaries of lands containing gold; in blue, those embracing silver; in red, such as contain cinnabar; and in green, those lands which are more valuable for copper mining than for agricultural purposes. It has accordingly become necessary that such tracts shall be designated on the township plats in a conspicuous manner as "mineral," within the out-boundaries of their respective shades as aforesaid, so that the Government officers may possess the necessary information for correctly carrying out the object of the laws in the adjudication of any conflicts that may arise in the disposal of the public lands. Such designations of "agricultural lands" and "mineral" on township plats the surveyors-general have been required to have officially represented on the approved plats of townships, sections, quarter-sections, and smaller legal subdivisions, in conformity with the data on file in their respective offices.

Timber lands on rocky hills and mountains, not known to contain any of the aforesaid minerals, will be designated as "agricultural," and, if the contrary, as "mineral."

Although gulch and creek mines are not specially named in the act of July 26, 1866, yet if the lands containing them are more valuable for mining than for agriculture, they will be reported as mineral.

Placers, once valuable, but which have become exhausted, so as no longer to be valuable as mines, will be returned as agricultural.

QUESTIONS RELATING TO AFFIDAVITS FILED UNDER THE TENTH AND ELEVENTH SECTIONS OF THE MINING LAW.

The act of 21st March, 1864, amendatory of the homestead law, and for other purposes, (United States Statutes, vol. 13, page 35), allows Registers and Receivers 22½ cents per hundred words for the testimony reduced to writing in pre-emption and homestead cases; but no authority is granted for charging a fee for simply filing an affidavit. The affidavits authorized by instructions from this office under the 10th and 11th sections of the mining act are not in the nature of declaratory statements or homestead applications. They are an expedient adopted, and the only one practicable under the circumstances, to obtain more special information than can be furnished by deputy surveyors touching the character of the various subdivisions of the public lands in what is known as the mineral domain, so that lands more valuable for mining than for agriculture may not be disposed of as belonging to the latter class; and lands really arable in character may not be withheld from settlement under the apprehension of being mineral. These two classes of land are so intermingled as to render it frequently a matter of the greatest difficulty to determine whether a particular subdivision belongs to one or the other, and the most feasible mode of coming to a reasonable conclusion appears to be by an investigation based upon the testimony of persons acquainted with the particular tracts involved.

The affidavits are further useful in enabling the Registers and Receivers to revise the lists of lands selected by agents of railroad companies before certifying to the correctness of the same, the plats and field-notes not in all cases furnishing a reliable guide, from the fact that surveyors generally are supposed to pass only along the exterior lines of the various subdivisions, and hence not always able to report accurately as to the character of the interior portions. There is consequently no fee chargeable to individuals for filing these documents, unless a trial is had, in which event the rule as to fees in other cases will be applied.

RESPECTING CITIZENSHIP OF INDIVIDUALS AND CORPORATIONS.

In reference to the question of citizenship under the mining act of July 26, 1866, when application is made by corporations organized under State or territorial laws, the commissioner has ruled to the following effect:—

It is an invariable principle in the pre-emption and homestead acts of the United States to limit the privileges conferred by these laws to citizens or persons having declared their intention to become such, and the same policy is indicated by the 1st section of the mining act. The limitation to citizenship is not repeated in the 2d section, but is necessarily implied, for the first section legalizes only the occupancy of citizens and those who have declared their intention to become such; and as occupancy must precede an application under the 2d section, it would seem to follow that if the occupancy of the applicant is not such as has been legalized by statute, it could have no standing in any proceeding under it. A proper rule of interpretation requires us to consider the several sections together and the whole as declaratory of one uniform and consistent policy; and the principle of considering together all statutes *in pari materia* warrants an examination of other enactments for the disposal of the public domain and the rule therein established, with a view of ascertaining the intention of the law-making power when in any particular statute it may not be clearly expressed. It would, therefore, be entirely too narrow a construction to hold that, because the restriction was not repeated in the 2d section, the uniform policy of the Government, for many years, was intended to be set aside in the cases provided for in that section.

These remarks apply to applicants appearing in the character of individuals, in whose cases the general principle must be adhered to and proof of citizenship furnished. This class of applicants is the only one that can take advantage of the pre-emption and homestead laws, corporations, as such, not being provided for in these acts. Yet, as corporations, at the date of the mining act and for a long time previous, had occupied and improved mining claims according to the local customs and rules of miners, and as the right to apply for a patent is, by the terms of the act, extended to any persons or *association of persons*, it would be unreasonable to suppose that it was designed to exclude them from the benefits of this law. Such an interpretation would deny its privileges to valuable and extensive mining claims, and entirely disappoint the expectations of the friends of the act. Corporations must, therefore, be permitted to share in its benefits. But "a corporation is an artificial being, invisible, intangible, and existing only in contemplation of law. Being the mere creature of law, it possesses only those properties which the charter of its creation confers upon it, either expressly or as incidental to its very existence." It can neither exercise the duties of citizenship, become naturalized, nor file a declaration of intention to become a citizen. Hence, the relations of citizenship or alienage cannot, properly speaking, be said to belong to it at all. To look beyond the mere artificial entity to the stockholders composing it, and require the citizenship of each one of a large number scattered frequently through several States and Territories to be established by proof in applications under the mining act, would involve such an amount of inconvenience and delay as practically to debar corporations from the privilege of ever making application.

The Supreme Court of the United States, in giving effect to the constitutional provision allowing *citizens* of the State where the suit is brought to be sued in the circuit courts of the United States by citizens of another State, after a variety of decisions, has at last, in the case of the Louisville Railroad Company *v.* Letson (2 Howard, 555), decided that a corporation created by the laws of a State, performing its functions under the authority of the same, and only suable there, though it may have members in others States, is *a person*, though an artificial one, *inhabiting* and *belonging* to that State, and entitled, for the purpose of suing and being sued, to be deemed a *citizen* of said State, and it is believed that an equally liberal construction should be adopted in reference to applications for mining patents by corporations. It is true that the questions in these cases before the Supreme Court pertained to State citizenship, and that the question of alienage was not involved; but when the court ceased to look beyond the mere artificial being to the natural persons composing the same, it is doubtful whether the existence of aliens among the stockholders would produce any change in the rule ultimately adopted. At all events, the necessities of the mining law would seem to require that the rule should be carried to that extent in proceedings under it. Hence, every corporation created by State or territorial laws should be treated as a citizen in all applications for mining patents, if legally competent to transact business and to acquire and hold real estate in such State or Territory.

In view of this construction, public officers of the land department have been directed to require evidence of incorporation, the usual proof of which is a certified copy of the charter or certificate of incorporation, with the signature and seal of the proper officer, and when this is presented, proof of citizenship of stockholders is dispensed with.

ON THE COMPETENCY OF WITNESSES.

The third section of the act of Congress, approved July 2, 1864 (United States Statutes, vol. 13, p. 351), provides that in the courts of the United States there shall be no exclusion of any witness on account of color, nor, in civil actions, because he is party to or interested in the issue tried. As the interest of a witness in the issue tried is no longer an objection to his competency, in the courts of the United States, the registers and receivers of the local land offices will be governed by the same rule in all proceedings before them under the pre-emption, homestead, or mining acts, and in *ex parte* affidavits filed. The weight of the evidence is, however, a matter for the consideration of the executive officers, as in all other cases where a witness may have a stronger motive to favor one side than the other. *Ex parte* affidavits may be received in applications for patents under the mining act, in proof of posting notices on claimed premises and as to other facts; reasonable care being taken by the Register and Receiver to avoid imposition by pretended affidavits or reckless or dishonest witnesses. The officers before whom such affidavits are taken should be able to certify to the credibility of the witnesses; but where this cannot be done on account of the witnesses being strangers, their character for truth must be established to the satisfaction of the local officers by other means before giving weight to such testimony.

MINERAL AND AGRICULTURAL LANDS—RAILROAD SELECTIONS.

In every case reported from the district land officers of selections made under the acts of 1862 and 1864, for the Pacific railroad, the agent of the company in the first instance is required to state in his affidavit that the selections are not interdicted, mineral, nor reserved lands, and are of the character contemplated by the grant. Upon the filing of lists with such affidavits attached, it is made the duty of Registers and Receivers to certify to the correctness of the selections in the particulars mentioned, and in other respects. They subsequently undergo scrutiny in this office, are tested by our plats, and by all the data on our files, sufficient time elapsing after the selections are made for the presentation of any objections to the department before final action is taken; and to more effectually guard the matter, there is inserted in *all* patents issued to said railroad company a clause to the following effect: "Yet excluding and excepting from the transfer by these presents *all mineral lands*, should any such be found to exist in the tracts described in this patent, this exception, as required by statute, 'not extending to coal and iron land.'" A decision is said to have been made by the Supreme Court of California, which, it is claimed, decides that an occupant of a mining claim having no title from the United States has no such standing in court as enables him to enforce the exception as to mineral lands, in patents issued to railroad companies, and may, therefore, be lawfully ejected from lands included within the general description of the tracts patented to such companies, notwithstanding the particular tract may be mineral in character, and fall within the exception. Not having seen that decision, we are ignorant as to the exact character of the ruling, but it is not understood how a person in the occupancy of mineral lands under the local customs and rules of miners, protected by the license granted in the first section of the act of July 26, 1866, could be ejected by a railroad company having no title to the land at all. The government license, it is reasonable to suppose, would constitute a sufficient defence against any one not able to show a better title. The grantee of such license is no trespasser upon the public lands, and although the license is revocable by the United States, it cannot be considered as revoked by a patent to a railroad company when such instrument expressly excepts and excludes from the grant all interdicted mineral land. Claimants authorized to apply for, and to obtain patents under the mining act have an efficient remedy in its provisions, and by taking the proper steps may obtain patents for their claims, even should they happen to be embraced within tracts patented to railroad companies, as the exceptions in such patents enable the United States to segregate the mineral lands included by distinct and separate conveyance to mining claimants. Placers more valuable for mining than for agriculture cannot be entered as pre-emption or homestead lands, nor can they be selected by railroad companies. There may be difficulties, and sometimes even hardships, connected with the system of filing affidavits to prove the mineral character of lands claimed by a railroad company, or an agricultural settler, and taking witnesses before the local land officers; but these are, in a great measure, inseparable from the subject matter; pre-emptors and homestead settlers have the same difficulties to contend with, more onerous in the new States and Territories than in the older States, from the sparseness of the population not justifying additional land offices. It has been suggested to this office that the Government should appoint a commission to segregate the mineral from the residue of the public lands; but let any one consider the vast amount of money expended by practical miners in excavations to test the value of mines, subsequently abandoned as worthless, and some idea may be formed of the time and expense such an undertaking would require, and how little confidence it would be likely to inspire. When a miner has taken possession of mineral lands under the license of the Government, and has developed their character for mining purposes, it would seem that the task of protecting his rights could not be more onerous than that which every settler is liable to encounter in defending himself against adverse claimants. The regulation of filing affidavits is simply a means of ascertaining the class to which a particular tract of land may belong, and although it may not be the best that could be devised, it is the only practical mode that has suggested itself to meet the difficulty of disposing of different classes of land mingled together in such a way as to render it frequently impossible to tell, without great labor and expense, whether a particular subdivision belongs to one or the other class.

IN REFERENCE TO THE STAY OF PROCEEDINGS FOR THE DETERMINATION OF ADVERSE CLAIMS UNDER THE SIXTH SECTION OF THE MINING LAW.

The sixth section of the mining act requires all proceedings to be stayed until a final settlement and adjudication in the courts, whenever an adverse claimant appears before the approval of the survey as provided in the third section.

The third paragraph of the instructions of June 25, 1867, requires such opposing claimant to show, by proof, the claim or interest he may have in the mine, and directs the Register and Receiver, should the same be satisfactory to them, to stay all further proceedings. It is not to be understood by this that the sufficiency of the adverse claim is to be investigated before the land officers. That is a matter that is expressly referred to the local courts by the statute. But the land officers are to be satisfied that the opposing claim is such as is contemplated by the sixth section of the mining act. They are not to suffer the forms of law to be fraudulently used by pretended claimants, having in fact no rights worthy of investigation before the courts. For instance, should it appear that the adverse claim relied upon relates to a settlement claimed under the pre-emption or homestead laws of the United States, it would at once be decided not to be such a claim as is to be referred to the judicial tribunals for determination, and upon the filing of which, the proceedings are stayed and the case suspended to await a trial in the courts; these tribunals having no jurisdiction of claims arising under the pre-emption and homestead laws. The adverse claim must be one arising under the local customs and rules of miners; such claimant is required to file an affidavit stating fully the nature of his claim, and if the facts disclosed present opposing interests under these regulations, or the local laws of the State or Territory, the proceedings must be stayed; after which it becomes the duty of the party out of possession to carry the case into the courts, not only for the reason that claimants ought not to be called upon to assume the offensive in relation to claims of which they already have possession, but because the act extends the right to apply for patents only to claimants having previously occupied and improved their claims according to the local customs or rules of miners; and although there may be cases where claimants have been fraudulently ousted of a rightful possession, and are legally entitled to patents, still, as that question is to be settled in the courts, and not in the land offices, the party out of possession is not in a condition to receive a patent until his right to possession is judicially determined.

The language of the second section, "having previously occupied and improved the same," &c., does not refer to an occupancy at some remote period. It means an occupancy continuing up to the date of the application for a patent; otherwise the mine for which a patent is asked could not be said to be one "in regard to whose possession there is no controversy or opposing claim," "as the statute requires it to be, in order to entitle the claimant to a patent." The very fact, therefore, of the applicant for a patent being out of possession, and an adverse party in possession, shows the claim to be one for adjudication in the courts before it can be disposed of in the land office. Hence it is the duty of all applicants under the mining act to state in their applications whether they are occupying the premises for which a patent is asked; and if not, whether an adverse party is in possession. If the latter is the case, the party is notified that an application for a patent has been made, in order that he may file an affidavit of his claim, and the case is then suspended for action in the courts.

RIGHTS TO THE USE OF WATER UNDER THE NINTH SECTION OF THE ACT.

The ninth section of the mining act maintains and protects the owners of water rights wherever, by *priority of possession*, rights to the use of water for *mining*, *agricultural*, *manufacturing*, or *other purposes*, have *vested* and *accrued*, and the same are recognized and acknowledged by the *local customs*, *laws*, and *decisions* of courts.

To make such a claim good under the act, the right to the use of water must have accrued—

First, by priority of possession; second, it must be recognized by the local customs; third, by the laws of the State or Territory and the decisions of the courts.

Whenever a claim to the use of water is thus recognized and acknowledged by the local customs, laws, and decisions of the courts of any State or Territory, the owner cannot be disturbed in his possession, no matter whether the land has been returned as mineral or agricultural; nor can his improvements be appropriated by other claimants under the pre-emption or homestead laws. As the right vested in the owner is an extraordinary one, differing essentially from the systems of water rights existing either under the common or civil laws, being, in fact, an anomalous system based upon the peculiar wants and condition of things found in some of the mining States and Territories, it will be necessary for the claimant to show that it has been fully adopted in the State or Territory in which the claim is situated, as the law upon the subject of water rights by enactments of the legislature or the decisions of the highest courts, and it will not be sufficient to show that such a claim has the sanction of the local customs. This office would not, by issuing patents under said ninth section, contribute to fasten upon one of the new States or Territories a system so materially affecting its local proprietary regulations without the same having been first adopted and engrafted upon the laws of such State or Territory by the proper departments of the same; and any claimant applying under said section must produce satisfactory proof of such adoption and acknowledgment. When such proof can be satisfactorily furnished, claims of this nature might be included in patents for mines, as the reasonable quantity of surface ground for the convenient working of the same, allowed by the act of July 26, 1866, where the water is used for mining purposes, according to the local customs and rules of miners, and the fact of not being adjacent to the vein or lode would not, it is believed, contravene either the letter or spirit of the act. Where these claims are embraced within lands returned as agricultural, and the water is or may be advantageously used for irrigation, they may be included in patents for agricultural lands under the pre-emption or homestead laws, as a part of the realty conveyed, being adjacent to the same and constituting a part of the legal subdivisions embraced in such patents.

The doctrine of exclusive ownership of water, by virtue of prior occupancy, appears to have been fully adopted in California by numerous decisions of the Supreme Court of that State. Whether a similar rule has been adopted in any other State or Territory by the legislature or the courts, is not known here. At all events, any owner of a water claim, in a condition to ask for a patent granting such exclusive right, is in a condition to maintain himself, for the present, without a patent, against all adverse claimants, by virtue of the protection extended to him by the act itself.

APPLICATIONS FOR PATENTS—HOW CONDUCTED.*

1. All applications for patents under the mining act should be in writing, in which should be stated the name of the applicants, and whether the claim is made by individuals, or a partnership or corporation; it should designate the mining district, county, and State, in which the claim is located; describe the character of the mine, as to whether it bears gold, silver, cinnabar, or copper; state the number of feet claimed along the

* See No. 271 B, and 273 B.

lode and laterally; the date of the original location of the claim under the mining customs; when and where it was recorded; the names of the locators; whether the applicant claims as a locator or as a purchaser—if the latter, whether by deed or verbal contract of parties in or out of possession; the nature and value of the improvements made or labor performed; whether the applicant is occupying the claim or is out of possession; and finally, whether the claim is one in regard to the possession of which there is any controversy or opposing claim within the knowledge of the applicant. The application should further state that claimant has posted a diagram in a conspicuous place on the claim, together with a notice of his intention to apply for a patent, with the date of posting such notice and diagram; and it should distinctly appear to whom the patent is to issue.

2. With the application there must be filed, first, a diagram of the claim, similar to that posted in a conspicuous place thereon, representing its boundaries and location, its length along the lode, with the surface ground necessary to the convenient working of the mine; second, a copy of the notice posted on the claim with the diagram; third, a certified copy of the mining customs of the district; fourth, a certified copy of the record of the location from the recorder's office; fifth, if the applicant is a corporation, a certified copy of the charter or certificate of incorporation; sixth, if the application is made by an individual or an unincorporated company, an affidavit or affidavits of citizenship, or of having filed a declaration of intention to become a citizen, the applicant's own affidavit will be sufficient; facts must be stated, such as place of nativity, in what court declaration of intention was filed, and the date of such declaration, with a certified copy of the same; if applicant claims to be a citizen, he must state in his affidavit the place of his birth, his residence for the past five years, and whether he has exercised the elective franchise, and where; seventh, the affidavit of claimant that he is in the occupancy of the claim, stating the length of time he has occupied the same, the amount of money and labor expended thereon, and that he knows of no adverse claim to the possession; and eighth, if claimant is in possession under purchase, a certified copy of the deed, or if the deeds are numerous, a brief abstract of title, certified by the recorder, or even a certificate from that officer that a regular chain of title, ending in the applicant, appears on his records, will answer the purpose.

3. Upon filing these papers, the Register of the land office will make the publication required in the third section of the act in a newspaper published nearest the claim, carefully stating in the notice the name of the claimant, of the mine, district, and county; also the names of the adjoining claimants, and if the claim is a relocation, the names of former claimants and claim, designating the lode, and, as near as practicable, the locality of the claim upon the lode.

The names of the adjoining claims and claimants ought never to be omitted, as that will generally be found one of the readiest means of fixing the locality of the claim. The Register will also post a copy of the notice in his office for the period of ninety days, and on the publisher's presenting his account, the Register will transmit the same to the Surveyor-General, unless the applicant has made provision for its immediate payment, in which case a duplicate receipt will be taken from the publisher, one of which to be transmitted to the General Land Office.

4. On the expiration of ninety days after posting diagram and notice, the claimant or his agent must file his own affidavit, with that of some

other person cognizant of the fact, with the Register and Receiver, that said diagram and notice were posted in a conspicuous place on the claim at least ninety days, or prove the same by verbal testimony to the satisfaction of these officers. If all the proof furnished is satisfactory to the Register and Receiver, and no adverse claim has been filed, the applicant for a patent will apply to the Surveyor-General for an estimate of the expenses of surveying or platting the claim and of making publication, if the latter has not been paid by the applicant; and on depositing the amount with any assistant United States treasurer, or designated depositary, in favor of the United States treasury, to be passed to the credit of the fund created by "individual depositors for surveys of the public land," and filing with the Surveyor-General one of the duplicate certificates of deposit taken by the claimant, that officer will order the claim to be surveyed, and transmit the certificate of deposit to the General Land Office. If an adverse claimant appears before application is made to the Surveyor-General for a survey, no action will be taken by that officer until the question as to possession is settled in the courts.

5. The survey when made must be approved by the Surveyor-General, who will also make a plat of the claim, accurately representing its boundaries, its area, and its relative position in respect to the subdivisions of the public surveys, the township and range lines being extended for this purpose according to instructions on page seven, circular of January 14, 1867, if the claim is upon unsurveyed land. In the margin of the plat the Surveyor-General will indorse his approval of the survey as in other government plats; also his certificate of the value of the labor and improvements, and of the character of the vein exposed, and will transmit papers to the local officers and to the General Land Office, as heretefore instructed.

6. The Register and Receiver will carefully examine all testimony presented, whether in the form of affidavits or parol proof, exercising the precautions heretofore recommended in reference to the former. They will also examine the returns of survey approved by the Surveyor-General, and transmit the application with all the testimony, if the same is satisfactory to them, indorsed with their approval to the General Land Office, if no opposing claimant appears before the approval of the survey, so that a patent may at once be issued.

No. 276½ B.

Proceedings to obtain titles under the mining act of July 26, 1866.

In the second section of the mining act it is provided that whenever any person, or association of persons, claim a vein or lode of quartz or other rock in place, bearing gold, silver, cinnabar, or copper, having previously occupied and improved the same according to the local customs or rules of miners in the district where the same is situated, and having expended in actual labor and improvement thereon an amount of not less than one thousand dollars, and in regard to whose possession there is no controversy or opposing claim, it shall and may be lawful for said claimant or association of claimants to file in the local land office a diagram of the same, so extended laterally or otherwise as to conform to the local laws, customs, and rules of miners, and to enter such tract and receive a patent therefor granting such mine.

The third section requires a like diagram to be posted in a conspicuous place on the claim, together with notice of intention to apply for patent. A similar notice is to be published by the Register in a newspaper nearest the location of the claim; the Register being also required to post the same in his office.

These notices are to be posted and published for the period of ninety days, after which, if no adverse interest shall have been filed, it is made the duty of the Surveyor-General, on application of the party, to survey the premises and make a plat thereof. If no adverse claimant has appeared prior to the Surveyor-General's approval of the survey, the applicant for patent is authorized to make payment to the United States Receiver of public moneys, of five dollars per acre, together with the cost of survey, plat, and notice, and furnish satisfactory evidence that the diagram and notice were posted on the claim during the aforesaid period of ninety days. Thereafter it is made the duty of the Register of the district land office to transmit to the General Land Office the plat, survey, and description, that a patent may issue thereon.

The claimant may be either an individual or an association of persons; and in pursuance of statutory provisions is required to make his application for a patent at the district land office, and file with such application a diagram of the claim.

The only mineral lands patentable under this act are those bearing gold, silver, cinnabar, or copper; and the only persons entitled to apply for and receive patents are those having previously occupied and improved their claims according to the local customs and rules of miners in the respective mining districts, and who have expended in actual labor and improvements on each claim an amount of not less than one thousand dollars, as hereinbefore indicated.

Conflicting claims to mines or mining lands cannot be adjusted in the land office, but are referred by the express provisions of the act to the courts of competent jurisdiction for determination. Hence, if a controversy exists in regard to the possession of a claim, the adverse interests must first be adjudicated before it is in a condition for patenting.

The statutory limit to the time during which an adverse claimant may appear is up to the time of the Surveyor-General's approval of the survey. If, previous to such approval, an opposing interest is presented at the district land office, further proceedings must be stayed for action in courts competent to determine the rights of the contestants, after which the successful claimant will be entitled to patent.

If no adverse claimant appears before the approval of the survey, there is no authority for suspending proceedings for patent in order to permit an adverse party to file his claim after that, provided the proceedings have been regular and free from fraud. The mining act does not state in express terms that the application must be in writing, but as official transactions are usually in writing, and much inconvenience might arise from mere verbal applications, the duty of reducing them to writing is implied and held to be necessary.

As the district land officers cannot be presumed to know whether or not an applicant for patent had previously occupied and improved his claim according to the local customs or rules of miners, or whether the diagram conforms to such customs or not, it is held proper that reasonable proof on these points should be filed with the application. This may consist of a certificate of the mining recorder, with a transcript from his records of the original location, with names of locators, and so much of the mining customs as relates to the size of locations or number of feet along the vein authorized to be taken by each locator or company. If the records contain a regular series of conveyances from the original locators to the applicant for a patent, the certificate of the recorder should state that upon diligent search he finds upon the records such regular chain of title, referring to the volumes and pages; should the certificate cover the three points of original location, mining customs, and series of conveyances, constituting a regular chain of title from the locators to the applicant for a patent, no further testimony as to previous occupancy and conformity to mining customs need be furnished.

In the event of the record not furnishing such evidence of title, from any cause whatever, the necessary facts may be established by affidavit, stating the length of time the applicant has occupied and improved the claim, the character of the improvements, and the requirements of the mining customs touching the size of locations at the time they were made. Such affidavit should also explain the absence of record evidence.

In either event, whether the proof consists of a certificate of the recorder, or an affidavit of persons familiar with the facts, the expense and trouble of furnishing it must be trifling.

The applicant should also file with his application and diagram a copy of the notice posted on the claim, that it may appear to the land officers that it meets the requirements of the statute.

If the parties applying for patent are an incorporated company, evidence of that fact being produced by filing with the application a certified copy of the charter or act of incorporation, no proof of citizenship will be required.

On the other hand, if the applicants are not incorporated, one or more affidavits will be necessary to prove that they are citizens of the United States, or have filed declarations of intention to become citizens. Such affidavits may be made by the applicants themselves, and the necessary facts should be fully set out as to place of birth, the court in which declaration of intention was filed, and the date of such filing.

The papers proper to be filed with the application are therefore, first, the diagram; second, a copy of the notice posted on the claim; third, a certified copy of the charter, or act of incorporation, or, if applicants are not incorporated, and affidavit of citizenship, or of filing declaration of intention to become citizens; fourth, a certificate of the mining recorder, or, in lieu thereof, an affidavit as to occupancy and improvement according to mining customs.

These documents being satisfactory to the Register and Receiver, no further testimony is required from the applicant until after the approval of the survey by the Surveyor-General, and the filing of the plat and survey in the district land office, when the further testimony must be furnished that the notice and diagram were posted on the claim during the period of ninety days. This proof may also be presented in the form of an affidavit, and it would be well to include in this affidavit a statement that according to surface indications, or any facts within the knowledge of claimants, or other persons familiar with the claim, the premises included in the plat and survey contain but one vein or lode, inasmuch as no patent is to issue for more than one vein or lode. Evidence as to the value of the improvements and character of the vein exposed is furnished by the Surveyor-General by indorsement upon the plat.

These proceedings, it would appear, can neither be expensive nor complicated. All the documents may be prepared by the applicants, or by any person of ordinary intelligence.

The application should state all the facts necessary to entitle claimant to apply for patent: such as having previously occupied and improved the claim according to local mining customs; having expended thereon in actual labor and improvements an amount of not less than one thousand dollars; that the mine is one producing either gold, silver, cinnabar, or copper; that applicant has posted diagram and notice in a conspicuous place on the premises as required by law; that the applicants are an incorporated company, or, if such is not the case, that they are citizens, or have filed declaration of intention to become citizens, and that a diagram of the claim is filed with the application. It should always contain a description of the premises as represented in the diagram.

OF THE EARLY PROCEEDINGS UNDER THE UNITED STATES MINING LAW.

During the first eighteen months after the passage of this enactment by Congress, delay occurred from want of familiarity on the part of the occupants of mines, and also in the local administration, in regard to the proceedings required. This inconvenience was at first unavoidable, and is not unusual in the execution of new enactments. It is now in great measure removed by the adoption of a system of rules, after a careful and thorough analysis of the subject, by which the liberal intentions of the framers of the law are being realized.

In some of the earlier cases reported it was brought to light that claims might be asserted, under new names, to old mines having expensive improvements thereon, without the knowledge of the real owners, in consequence of the notices being published and posted during their temporary absence, or, in remote and unoccupied districts, during the suspension in winter of mining operations.

The only way to prevent occasional acts of injustice in issuing patents to parties not entitled to them under the law is to require every claimant to file with his application some appropriate evidence of his possessory title under the local rules or customs of miners in the district in which his claim lies.

EFFECT OF THE LOCAL MINING CUSTOMS AND LAWS.

It was evidently the intention of the framers of the mining act not only to recognize the validity of these local mining customs and laws, and rights acquired under them, but to interfere as little as possible with them; and in administering the act this policy is steadily kept in view in this office, and patents are only issued to claimants holding the possessory right under and by virtue of such mining regulations.

In some of the States and Territories these local customs and rules of miners are enacted by the miners themselves, at miners' meetings, and observed as rules in their respective districts. In other cases the legislature of the States and Territories have passed general laws prescribing rules by which all the miners in the several districts are governed.

It has been insisted sometimes that territorial legislatures have no power to pass laws limiting mining claims, for the reason that the organic laws of such territories inhibit such legislatures from interfering in any way with the primary disposal of the soil, and that the mining act of Congress recognizes not these enactments of State or territorial assembly, but the customs of the miners themselves.

It is held by the commissioner that a State or territorial enactment regulating a more *possessory* claim, is in no way in conflict with the congressional enactment, but is in subordination to the constitutional power of Congress to deal as may seem most proper with regard to the disposal of the national domain, whether mineral or agricultural; and even if there were in fact any interference by a territorial act with the primary disposal of the soil, it was perfectly competent for Congress, by subsequent legislation, such as the mining act, to legalize the same, even though it were at variance with territorial organic law; and as the mining law extends the privilege of applying for a patent only to such as have previously occupied and improved their claims according to the local customs and rules of miners in the respective districts, the congressional enactment evidently recognizes the binding force of such rules.

With regard to the point sometimes made that the mining act recognizes only the regulations adopted by the miners themselves, and not the enactments of the territorial legislature, it is replied that the question as to how or by whom the rules or customs were passed or enacted is not at all involved.

The real point is, what are the regulations by which the miners in the several districts determine the validity of claims; what body of rules are applied to them when questions of conflict come before the local courts; and what laws are appealed to in cases where records are made or notices filed with the mining recorder, or when forfeitures are declared. The regulations controlling in such cases are the rules recognized by the mining act of Congress; and whether the miners adopted them at miners' meetings or found them in a volume of territorial statutes is a matter of entire indifference, providing they use them in determining the nature and extent of mining rights.

It has been suggested that no authority is conferred upon the territorial assembly to prescribe mining rules. Clearly no authority had previously been conferred upon miners' meetings to pass laws or rules of an obligatory character, and yet it is admitted the mining act recognizes such regulations; and certainly, if an act of Congress can impart a legal character to rules adopted by a mere town meeting, it is equally competent for Congress to give binding force to a territorial statute, even if in the first instance there had been a want of power to pass such statute.

It is not doubted that a territorial act setting apart in perpetuity a certain number of feet on every newly-discovered lode for the benefit of the public schools, adopted in one or more Territories, would be void for want of power in the territorial legislature to pass such an act; because, if not void, the United States Government would be precluded from selling the reserved portion of these lodes to whomsoever it chose to make its vendee. This would be an interference with the primary disposal of the soil, and hence void unless legalized by a subsequent act of Congress. The question as to what rules are in vogue among the miners and what is prescribed by them are matters of proof to be furnished by applicants for patents.

STATUS OF AGRICULTURAL LANDS IN MINING DISTRICTS.

Representations were made to this office that farmers, who had for years occupied and cultivated some of the finest agricultural lands, were interfered with by gold-seekers endeavoring to develop placer deposits beneath the surface of their fields; and that such farmers were deterred from erecting valuable buildings, setting out orchards, or making other improvements of an expensive and permanent character.

In view of such representations, the Register and Receiver of the proper district were instructed to the following effect: That as there are many tracts in what are called the mineral districts of no value for mining purposes, but well adapted to agriculture and horticulture, it would be a benefit to the country to promote their settlement and improvement by permanent residents, it not being the policy of the United States to keep such lands open for exploration for an indefinite period, from the mere possibility that some day or other gold, silver, cinnabar, or copper might be discovered thereon.

The local officers are instructed to endeavor to prevent unnecessary litigation and improper obstructions being thrown in the way of making agricultural entries where the tracts are more valuable for agriculture than for mining.

If a tract, say forty acres, has a mine upon it occupied and worked by the occupant in pursuance of the mining customs, there certainly can be no trouble in proving the fact, and it requires no tedious and expensive investigation to determine whether the same is subject to entry under the pre-emption or homestead law. If, on the contrary, the adjoining forty-acre tract is well adapted to farming or gardening, and has never had thereon a mine, and presents no positive indications of valuable deposits of precious metals, the facts are capable of ready proof.

A certain subdivision either has a mine upon it, and is occupied by miners in pursuance of the mining customs of the district, or it is not improved and occupied as a mine. In either case the facts may be readily and satisfactorily established by proof.

If it is occupied as a mine, or if a vein of quartz or other rock in place, bearing gold, silver, cinnabar, or copper, has there been traced, it is mineral land; but if it has no existing mine upon it, and no metalliferous vein of quartz or other rock is known to pass through or penetrate the tract, the land is not properly classed as mineral, although, contrary to present indications, gold, silver, cinnabar, or copper may at some future time be discovered upon it.

One part of a quarter section may be mineral land and another only fit for agriculture, but it does not follow from one forty or eighty acre tract having mining improvements upon it, that the other eighty cannot be entered under the pre-emption or homestead law.

Where a mine exists, the miner should be allowed such additional quantity of land as may be necessary for the convenient working of the mine, but beyond this he ought not to be permitted to interfere with the disposal of the public domain; and if the residue of a quarter section is farming land, it should be disposed of accordingly.

These questions of contest, it is supposed, generally arise upon lands claimed to contain placer deposits, but upon which no placers have yet been opened, or, if once opened, are no longer worked.

Lands containing mineral veins or lodes are usually of such marked geological structure that litigation is not likely to grow out of adverse claims on the part of agricultural settlers. Besides, under local customs vein miners are only allowed a certain number of feet on each side of the vein or lode. If beyond such allowance no other veins are found, and the land is adapted to farming, the rights of the agricultural settlers must be recognized.

The Registers and Receivers are directed to afford all proper facilities to *bona fide* settlers for obtaining titles to agricultural lands; while on the other hand they are enjoined to take care to avoid interference with the mines or mining improvements of mining occupants.

Whenever the character of a tract applied for by an agricultural settler is contested, the Register and Receiver are directed to institute an examination, requiring the applicant to serve notice upon the contestants, which may be done by posting written notices at several prominent points in the vicinity of the land, or by publishing notice in the newspaper nearest the land in dispute.

The local land offices are directed to apply to this office for any further instructions desired, and to report promptly all contested cases, that they may be disposed of without unnecessary delay.

SURVEYING INSTRUCTIONS WITH REFERENCE TO MINING CLAIMS.

In regard to surveying mineral claims in Colorado the attention of the Surveyor-General at Denver was called, under date of the 24th June last, to the fact that in certain cases claims connected with the regular public surveys are connected by broken lines of different bearings; no direct line from the nearest public corner to the beginning point of the claim having been calculated and specified in the plat or field-notes, thus rendering it impracticable for this office, in the description introduced into mining patents, to locate each claim in the particular township, section, and subdivision, which will embrace it when the public surveys are completed.

The attention of the Colorado surveying department was also called to other cases, where the claims are connected with objects wanting in permanency, such as trees, stones, and cabins, liable to disappear, and thus render it difficult, and in some cases probably impossible, to determine and identify the true corners.

The Surveyor-General was at the same time instructed to cause the draughtsman to examine the plats in the Surveyor-General's office, and endeavor to correct them so as to correspond with a sample plat then furnished for his guidance. That officer was further advised that the plats are copied into the patents, and that in certain cases it would be out of the question to do so without reducing the scale to such an extent that the claims would scarcely be visible; and he was informed it is unnecessary to represent upon the plat the line or lines from the public corner or initial point to the beginning point in the boundary of the claim, it being sufficient to indicate its bearing, and to state the distance without protracting it; that the prominent thing represented on the plat should be the lode or claim; that, in connecting it with a public corner, the nearest to the claim should be selected, and the line should be a direct, straight one, its bearings and distance being carefully and accurately ascertained; that in the field-notes the deputy should report in what township, range, section, and subdivision the claim will be located when the surveys are completed—a matter that may be easily ascertained where the surveys are so near that the claim may be connected with them.

It is required that township lines be extended over the mineral district whenever practicable; and when this is not so, the mining survey must be connected with permanent natural objects by course and distance, so as unmistakably to identify the beginning points of the respective surveys.

It is not doubted that such objects may be found in every mineral district; and this probability is rendered all the stronger from the fact that no difficulty appears to have been encountered in this respect in the general administration of the mining system. The plats received from other mining regions are full of references to mountain summits, prominent peaks, rocky points, buttes, and cañons, some of which are frequently selected as monumental points of whole districts; and by means of these permanent objects lode claims on unsurveyed lands are located with unerring precision.

FEES OF REGISTERS AND RECEIVERS IN MINING CASES.

The question having arisen as to the fees to which the Registers and Receivers are entitled for their services in acting upon mining cases, the commissioner has decided as follows :—

The fourth section of the act of March 21, 1864, "amendatory of the homestead law and for other purposes," provides that the Register and Receiver shall each be entitled to one dollar for their services in acting upon pre-emption claims, and shall be allowed jointly at the rate of fifteen cents per hundred words for the testimony which may be reduced to writing by them for claimants in establishing pre-emption or homestead rights. The sixth section authorizes an addition to the above fees of fifty per centum in the States of California, Oregon, and Nevada, and in the Territories of Washington, Colorado, Idaho, New Mexico, and Arizona.

Now, a mining claim being in fact a pre-emption, as the occupant under the mining customs is the only person privileged to purchase, and an application for a patent under the act of July 26, 1866, being analogous to a declaration of intention to enter under the general pre-emption law, it is entirely proper to apply the provision as to fees in general pre-emption cases to the special pre-emptions under the mining act. Hence, Registers and Receivers in the political divisions above mentioned, and in those formed from them, are entitled to charge applicants for mining patents, at the time of filing the diagram or making the application, three dollars, being one dollar and a half each to the Register and Receiver; and for taking the testimony, either in the form of affidavits or in writing out the answers of witnesses, they are allowed a joint charge of twenty-two and one-half cents per hundred words. In addition to this they are allowed one per cent. each on the amount of purchase money, as in other cash sales of public lands. This last allowance, however, is not paid by the purchaser, but by the United States per Treasurer's warrant.

SIZE OF CLAIMS.

A question having been made as to the authority for issuing a patent to a company for three thousand one hundred feet on the lode, the statute designating, it was assumed, three thousand feet as the maximum to be taken in any one claim, the inquiry was answered by stating that the company in question held the possessory right to a number of claims, located agreeably to the local customs and rules of miners in that district, *prior* to the passage of the mining act, and that the act is not understood as intending to interfere with locations made before its enactment.

The quartz-mining customs of the district in which the claim lies entitled each locator to one hundred feet on the vein, without limit as to the number of locators that might unite in a company. The claim referred to was located in 1863 by thirty-one locators, each taking one hundred feet.

The customs of the district permit each claimant to hold one claim by location, and as many more as he may purchase in good faith for a valuable consideration, the title of which he has recorded in the books of the county recorder within ten days after such location or purchase. Hence, while the mining customs of said district undertake to restrict monopoly in the matter of *locating* claims, no similar precaution appears to have been taken in preventing claims from accumulating in single hands by *purchase*, and this is generally true of other mining districts.

The second section of the mining act of July 26, 1866, provides that whenever any person or association of persons claim a vein or lode of quartz or other rock in place, bearing gold, silver, cinnabar, or copper, having previously occupied and improved the same according to the local customs or rules of miners in the district where the same is situated, and having expended in actual labor and improvements thereon an amount of not less than one thousand dollars, as aforesaid, it shall be lawful for said claimants to file in the local land office a diagram of said claim, and to enter the same and receive a patent therefor.

In the case referred to, the company claim to come within these provisions, and therefore to be entitled to receive a patent on complying with the other provisions of the statute. The provisos contained in the fourth section of the mining act are understood as relating to *locations* made since the 26th of July, 1866, and not understood as interfering with the right of *purchase* when the same are authorized by the local mining customs.

In the clause, "and not more than three thousand feet shall be taken in any one claim by any association of persons," in the last proviso of the fourth section, the word "taken" is understood to be used in the sense of *located;* and that clause is construed to mean that not more than three thousand feet shall be located by any association of persons in any location made since the passage of the mining act.

The first proviso limits the quantity that may be located by an individual. The last clause of the second proviso makes a similar limitation as to the quantity that may be located by any association of persons.

[Report of the commissioner for the year 1869.]

TITLE VI.

Survey of Public Lands.

No. 277 B.

Instructions to the Surveyors-General of public lands of the United States relating to their duties and to the field operations of Deputy Surveyors.

GENERAL LAND OFFICE, June 1, 1864.

1. THE SURVEYING MANUAL AND INSTRUCTIONS OF THE COMMISSIONER ARE MADE A PART OF THE SURVEYING CONTRACTS BY LAW.

By the 2d section of the act of Congress entitled " An act to reduce the expenses of the survey and sale of the public lands in the United States," approved May 30, 1862, it is provided: " That the printed Manual of Instructions relating to the public surveys, prepared at the General Land Office, and bearing date February twenty-second, eighteen hundred and fifty-five, the instructions of the Commissioner of the General Land Office, and the special instructions of the Surveyor-General, when not in conflict with said printed manual or the instructions of said commissioner, *shall be taken and deemed a part of every contract for surveying the public lands of the United States.*"

In pursuance of law, the following instructions are prescribed for your government and that of your deputies in surveying the public lands :—

2. SURVEYS TO BE EXECUTED BY DEPUTY SURVEYORS IN PERSON.

Your attention is especially directed to the last clause of the printed form of contract furnished by this office, which stipulates " that no payment shall be made for any surveys not executed by the said deputy surveyor in his own proper person." It has been the practice of deputies to take contracts for more surveying than they could perform in person, and then employ one or more compassmen with their auxiliaries to do the work. The object of the stipulation referred to in the contract is to prevent a continuance of this practice.

Deputy surveyors are required to verify by their oath that the surveys embraced in their contracts have been executed in strict conformity with instructions, the requirements of the surveying manual, and the laws of the United States. The deputy cannot consistently make this oath if the work is done by separate parties in other parts of the field from where he is operating.

That there may be no misunderstanding upon this point, you are hereby instructed not to enter into contract with any one deputy for a greater amount of surveying than it may reasonably be expected he will be able to execute in one season, under his own immediate and personal direction, with *one surveying party only ;* and deputy surveyors will be notified in advance that accounts for surveying done in violation of this rule will not be allowed.

When two deputies enter into joint contract for certain surveys, and *only one* of them goes into the field, if that one, with a single surveying party, executes all the work in person, his affidavit alone as surveyor, attached to the field notes, will be deemed sufficient, and no impediment to the payment of his account will result therefrom.

If two deputies, joint parties in a contract, *both* go into the field, each with a separate surveying party, the field notes must show clearly the particular surveying done by each deputy. The date and the name of the deputy will be stated at the beginning and end of the notes of every continuous part of such survey executed by him, so that it may be distinctly seen by whom each mile of line was run.

The following form of affidavit is prescribed, to be attached to the field notes in cases of joint surveys, in lieu of the one heretofore used, to wit:—

"I, A. B., deputy surveyor, do solemnly swear that, in pursuance of a joint contract, wherein A. B. and C. D. are joint contractors with S. G., United States Surveyor-General for ———, bearing date the ——— day of ———, 18—, I have well, faithfully, and truly, in my own proper person, and in strict conformity with the instructions furnished by the Surveyor-General, the surveying manual, and the laws of the United States, surveyed all those parts or portions of ——— as are represented in the foregoing field notes as having been surveyed under my direction; and I do further solemnly swear that all the corners of said surveys have been established and perpetuated in strict accordance with the surveying manual and printed instructions, and that the foregoing are the true and original field notes of such survey."

The separate affidavit of each deputy, in the above form, will be attached to the field notes of joint surveys.

3. OPERATIONS IN THE FIELD, WHEN TO COMMENCE.

The practice of anticipating the appropriations is deemed unwise and contrary to the spirit of the law. The surveys should not be commenced in advance of the year for which the means is provided by Congress, and no moneys can be used to pay for work done before they were appropriated. This must be regarded as an invariable rule to be rigidly observed in future.

The object of this restriction is to keep back the surveying operations to the legitimate period of time contemplated in the appropriations. These appropriations are made with reference to the current necessities of given years, and if allowed to be absorbed in advance, the purposes of Congress in providing stated sums annually to carry forward the public surveys would be defeated. In order to enable deputy surveyors to avail themselves of the whole season belonging to the fiscal year, however, they may be permitted to commence their operations as soon after the first day of May in each year as notice is received from this office that the appropriations have been made. You will be promptly notified, by mail or telegraph, as circumstances may determine, when the appropriations are passed, and no surveying chargeable to such appropriations must be done before receiving this notice.

4. CONTRACTS MUST BE APPROVED BY THE COMMISSIONER.

The first section of the act of May 30, 1862, provides that contracts for the survey of the public lands shall not become binding upon the

United States until approved by the Commissioner of the General Land Office, except in such cases as the commissioner shall otherwise especially order.

5. REVENUE STAMPS TO BE ATTACHED TO CONTRACTS AND BONDS.

The requirements of the internal revenue law make it necessary that *five separate stamps* be attached to the several parts of every contract and bond of a deputy surveyor, to wit:—

1. To the *contract*, five-cent stamp; 2. To the *affidavit* of the deputy surveyor, five cents; 3. To the *bond*, fifty cents; 4. To the *certificate* as to the sufficiency of the bond, ten cents; 5. To the *oath* of allegiance, five cents.

Surveyors-General are reminded that the sufficiency of the sureties to the bonds of deputy surveyors must be certified BY THE PROPER OFFICER OF A COURT HAVING A SEAL.

6. WHEN DESIRED BY SETTLERS, SURVEYS MAY BE MADE BY THE SURVEYOR-GENERAL AT THEIR EXPENSE IN CERTAIN CASES.

By section ten of an act entitled "An act to reduce the expenses of the survey and sale of the public lands in the United States," approved May 30, 1862, it is provided: "That when the settlers in any township or townships, not mineral or reserved by government, should desire a survey made of the same under the authority of the Surveyor-General of the United States, and shall file an application therefor in writing, and deposit in a proper United States depository, to the credit of the United States, a sum sufficient to pay for such survey, together with all expenses incident thereto, without cost or claim for indemnity on the United States, it shall and may be lawful for said Surveyor-General, under such instructions as may be given him by the Commissioner of the General Land Office, and in accordance with existing laws and instructions, to survey such township or townships, and make return thereof to the general and proper local land office: *Provided*, The townships so proposed to be surveyed are within the range of the regular progress of the public surveys embraced by existing standard lines or bases for the township and subdivisional surveys." (Sec. 10, p. 410, vol. 12, U. S. Laws.)

Applications for surveys under this law must be made to the Surveyor-General in writing, upon the receipt of which he will furnish the applicant with an estimate of how much the desired survey will cost. On receiving a certificate of deposit of a United States depositary, showing that the required sum has been deposited with him in a proper manner to pay for the work, you will contract with a competent United States deputy surveyor, and have the survey made and returned in the same manner as other public surveys are.

You are especially enjoined in all cases to state explicitly in your letters furnishing estimates to applicants, that the payment of the amount required for the survey will not give the depositor any priority of claim or right to purchase the land, or in any manner affect the claim or claims of any party or parties thereto; and that, when surveyed, it will be subject to the same general laws and regulations in relation to the disposition thereof as other public lands are.

The money should be deposited to the credit of the Treasurer of the United States on account of the proper appropriations. A separate estimate is required and a separate deposit must be made for *office work* and *field work;* one to be placed to the credit of the appropriation "for compensation of the Surveyor-General and the clerks in his office," and the other to the credit of the appropriation "for continuing the public surveys." The depositary will issue certificates in triplicate, one of which will be transmitted to this office with the contract and bond of the deputy surveyor.

The account will be adjusted and paid in the same manner as other surveying accounts. Should the amount deposited exceed the cost of survey and all expenses incident thereto, including office work, an account setting forth the fact of such excess may be rendered by the depositor, certified by the Surveyor-General, and transmitted to this office with the final surveying returns, to be reported for payment.

Where a township is surveyed under the provisions of the aforesaid act, the survey must include all the *surveyable* public land in such township.

7. SMALL ISLANDS MAY BE SURVEYED AT THE COST OF APPLICANTS.

Many applications are received at this office for the purchase of small unsurveyed islands which were omitted when the adjacent lands were surveyed. These islands are usually of too little value to justify the government in incurring the expense of survey; but where a party desires the survey made and is willing to pay the cost thereof in advance, upon the conditions set forth in these instructions, it may be done under the provisions of the tenth section of the act of May 30, 1862.

The party desiring the survey to be made must file a written application with the Surveyor-General, giving an intelligible description of the locality of the island, its distance from the main shore, the width of the narrowest channel between it and the main land, with an estimate of its area.

Upon receiving such application, made in the manner indicated, you will examine the records and data in your office, and if it appears that the island is public land and has not already been surveyed, you will furnish the applicant an estimate of the cost of surveying it, as directed under the sixth head in these instructions, stating explicitly that the depositing of the money will not in any manner affect the rights of parties in said lands, nor give any priority of claim to the depositor.

You will observe particularly that two separate deposits are to be made—one on account of the appropriation for *field work*, and one on account of the appropriation for *office work*—a separate certificate for each to be transmitted to this office with the contract and bond of the deputy surveyor.

It will be understood that these instructions relate only to isolated islands, or islands that were admitted when the public surveys were extended over the adjacent lands, and do not apply to islands falling within the regular course of current surveys, which must be included in the contracts for surveying the public lands.

As a general rule, a body of land separated from the main land by a *perpetual* natural channel may be regarded as an island for the purposes contemplated in these instructions.

8. SURVEY OF SWAMP LANDS.

Contracts with deputy surveyors must of course embrace any "swamp and overflowed" lands which, in alluvial regions, are intermingled with the arable or fast lands. Over all such lands the lines of the public surveys must be extended, as the selections in such cases are made according to the character of the *smallest legal subdivision.* If the greater part of such subdivision is "swamp and overflowed," it goes to the swamp grant; if otherwise, it is excluded from such grant, and is retained by the government.

In the survey of all lands of this mixed character, the deputies must be charged to give in their field notes a specific and full description of the land, indicating the *causes* of its being unfit for cultivation in its natural condition, with the character of the timber, shrubs, or plants growing on the tract, and the contiguity of the premises to rivers, water-courses, or lakes, naming them respectively. The swamp grant does not embrace tracts in which the inundation is casual, but only those where the overflow would totally destroy crops and prevent the raising of the same without artificial means, such as levees, draining, &c. The essentiality must be obvious to you of the requirement of full data in these respects, in order to enable the Department properly to adjust swamp and other interests.

Where the State authorities desire to have swamp lands surveyed at their expense, the same may be done in accordance with instructions on page 5 for surveys under the provisions of the 10th section of the act of May 30, 1862; but all applications for separate surveys of swamp lands must be submitted to this office, with a full report and a diagram illustrating the locality, and the approval of the commissioner first obtained.

9. CERTAIN RIVERS TO BE MEANDERED ON ONE BANK ONLY.

Rivers not embraced in the class denominated "navigable" under the statute, but which are well-defined natural arteries of internal communication, and have a uniform width, will only be meandered *on one bank.* For the sake of uniformity, the surveyor will traverse the *right bank* when not impracticable; but where serious obstacles are met with, rendering it difficult to course along the right bank, he may cross to the left bank and continue the meanders as far as necessary; but all changes from one bank to the other will be made at the point of intersection of some line of the public surveys with the stream being meandered.

The subdividing deputies will be required to establish meander corners on both banks of such meanderable streams at the intersection of all section lines, and the distances across the river will be noted in the field book.

In meandering water-courses, where a distance is more than *ten chains* between stations, even chains only should be taken; but if the distance is *less* than ten chains, and it is found convenient to employ chains and links, the number of links should be a multiple of ten, thereby saving time and labor in testing the closings both in the field and in the Surveyor-General's office.

10. WHAT LAKES ARE NOT TO BE MEANDERED.

Paragraph numbered three, on page 13 of the Manual, in regard to the meandering of lakes, &c., is modified as follows:—

Lakes embracing an area of less than *forty acres* will not be meandered. Long narrow or irregular lakes of larger extent, but which embrace *less than one-half* of the smallest legal subdivisions, will not be meandered. Shallow lakes or bayous, likely in time to dry up or be greatly reduced by evaporation, drainage, or other cause, will not be meandered, however extensive they may be.

Deputy surveyors will be allowed pay for the distance across lakes or ponds not meandered, where they are required to continue the lines of the public surveys across them ; but no offsets or lines run in triangulating will be paid for.

Where the distance across a lake or other body of water is ascertained by offsetting, it is not enough to say in the field notes "8.65 over lake and set a meander corner," but the *mode* by which the distance is ascertained must be stated and described in full.

Posts will be established by the subdividing deputy at the intersections of all the public lines with these lakes the same as if they were to be meandered.

11. CORNER POSTS AND CORNER STONES.

In loose or alluvial soil, section, quarter section, or meander posts may be driven into the ground, instead of digging holes and planting them, as required in the Manual ; but no posts will be so driven unless, from the character of the soil, they will thereby be rendered more firm and enduring.

All corner stones 14 inches long, or more, and less than 18 inches in length, should be set two-thirds of their length in the ground ; if more than 18 inches long, they should be set three-quarters of their length in the ground.

12. QUARTER SECTION CORNERS NOT TO BE ESTABLISHED IN CERTAIN CASES.

Quarter section corners are not required to be established on the *west* boundary of the *western tier of sections* in a township, nor on the *north* boundary of a northern tier of sections in a township *south of and bordering on a standard parallel or base line*. The resurvey of township, standard, or base lines by the deputy surveyor, for the purpose of establishing such quarter posts, is unnecessary and will not be paid for.

13. POSTS IN MOUNDS.

All posts in mounds will hereafter be planted or driven into the ground to the depth of twelve inches, at the precise corner point: and the charcoal-charred stake or marked stone required in the Manual will be deposited 12 inches below the surface, against the north side of the post when the deputy is running north, and against the west side when the deputy is running west, &c.

Township mounds will be five feet in diameter at their base and two and a half feet in perpendicular height. Posts in township mounds are therefore required to be four and a half feet in length, so as to allow twelve inches to project above the mound.

Mounds at section, quarter section, and meander corners, will be four and a half feet in diameter at their base and two feet in perpendicular height, the posts being four feet in length, leaving twelve inches to project above the mound.

The planting of seeds between the pits and trenches, as directed on page 11 of the Manual, is not required.

14. PITS IN LIEU OF TRENCHES.

The quadrangular trench required in connection with the construction of mounds is dispensed with. The *pits* will be continued, and should be of uniform dimensions. The pits for a township mound will be 18 inches wide, two feet in length, and at least twelve inches deep, located six feet from the post. At section corners the pits will be 18 inches *square*, and not less than twelve inches in depth.

At township corners common to *four* townships, the pits will be dug on the lines and lengthwise to them. On base and standard lines, where the corners are common to only *two* townships or sections, three pits only will be dug—two in line on either side of the post, and one on the line north or south of the corner, as the case may be. By this means the standard and closing corners will be readily distinguished from each other.

15. NOTCHING SECTION CORNER POSTS.

Posts or stones at the corners of sections in the interior of townships will have as many notches on the *south* and *east* edges as they are miles from the south and east boundaries of the township, instead of being notched on all four edges, as directed on pages 8 and 9 of the Manual.

16. MARKING LINES.

In addition to the instructions under this head on page 4 of the Manual, the following requirements will be observed, to wit:

Where trees two inches or more in diameter are found, the required blazes must not be omitted.

Bushes on or near the line should be bent at right angles therewith, and receive a blow of the axe at about the usual height of blazes from the ground sufficient to leave them in a bent position, but not to prevent their growth.

On *trial* or *random* lines, when it is necessary to lop bushes, they should be bent *in the direction of the line*, to prevent mistaking random for true lines.

17. BEARING TREES.

Where a tree not less than two and a half inches in diameter can be found for a bearing tree within 300 links of the corner, it should be preferred to the trench or pit. The *quadrangular trench* required on page 9 of the Manual as a substitute, where the requisite number of "bearing trees" is not found, is dispensed with, and a *pit* two feet square and not less than 12 inches deep is required in lieu thereof.

18. MODE OF CORRECTING BACK RANDOM LINES.

The manner of running random and true lines illustrated in the specimen field notes, marked "B," in the Manual, is hereby modified so as to conform to the directions on page 23; that is, the deputy, having run a random line, will correct back "by calculating a course that will run a true line back to the corner post from which the random started." For instance: instead of saying "west on a true line, &c.," with an *altered* variation, say "north 89° 47′ west on true line, &c.," with *same* variation.

19. ABBREVIATIONS IN THE FIELD NOTES.

The following additional abbreviations are authorized to be used in the field notes, to wit:—

For quarter section corner, use "¼ Sec. Cor.;" for variation, "va.;" for 14 inches long, 12 inches wide, and 3 inches thick, in describing a corner stone, use 14 × 12 × 3, being particular to always observe the same order of length, width, and thickness.

20. PRESCRIBED LIMITS FOR CLOSINGS AND LENGTH OF LINES IN CERTAIN CASES.

1. Every north-and-south section line, except those terminating in the north boundary of the township, must be *eighty chains* in length.

2. The east-and-west *section lines*, except those terminating in the west boundary of the township, are to be within *one hundred links* of the actual distance established on the south boundary line of the township for the width of said tier of sections.

3. The north boundary and south boundary of any one section, except in the extreme western tier, are to be within *one hundred links* of equal length.

4. The meanders within each fractional section, or between any two meander posts, or of a pond or island in the interior of a section, must close within one chain and fifty links.

5. In running *random* township exteriors, if such random lines fall short or overrun in length, or intersect the eastern or western boundary, as the case may be, of the township, at more than *three chains and fifty links* north or south of the true corner, the lines must be *retraced*, even if found necessary to remeasure the meridianal boundaries of the township.

It will be particularly observed that no changes in regard to surveying operations are made by these instructions excepting those specially stated and authorized. In every other particular the Manual and existing instructions of the Commissioner remain in full force.

Very respectfully, your ob't servant,

J. M. EDMUNDS, Commissioner.

No. 278 B.

Circular No. 22.

DEPARTMENT OF THE INTERIOR,
GENERAL LAND OFFICE, June 10, 1868.

As inquiries arise in regard to the survey of islands in lakes or rivers in districts where the office of Surveyor-General has been discontinued, the following is communicated as the proper mode of proceeding to have the same surveyed and obtain title :—

1st. Islands may be surveyed at the expense of the party applying under the provisions of the act of Congress approved 30th May, 1862, "to reduce the expenses of the survey and sale of the public lands of the United States," U. S. Statutes, vol. 12, p. 410, in the 10th section of which it is declared : "That when the settlers in any township or townships, not mineral or reserved by Government, shall desire a survey made of the same under the authority of the Surveyor-General of the United States, and shall file an application therefor in writing, and deposit in a proper United States depository, to the credit of the United States, a sum sufficient to pay for such survey, together with all the expenses incident thereto, without cost or claim for indemnity on the United States, it shall and may be lawful for said Surveyor-General, under such instructions as may be given him by the Commissioner of the General Land Office, and in accordance with existing laws and instructions, to survey such township or townships, and make return thereof to the General and proper local Land Office: *Provided*, The townships so proposed to be surveyed are within the range of the regular progress of the public surveys embraced by existing standard lines or bases for the township and subdivisional surveys."

Application for the survey should be addressed to the Commissioner of the General Land Office, and be accompanied by the affidavits of at least two reliable and disinterested parties, showing that thirty days' notice had been given the coterminous proprietors of the intention to apply for the survey of such island, stating the area, character, and situation of the island in the lake or river, with reference to the description of the section, township, and range of the public surveys, the same to be illustrated by a diagram. The width and depth of the channel, on either side between the island and the main shore, should be shown, and it should be stated whether the configuration of either shore of the mainland has materially changed since the original survey of the water front on the mainland.

2d. The applicant should designate some competent and reliable surveyor, and send to this office a statement from him, in writing, of the amount for which he is willing to execute the field work of the survey.

If, upon examination of the evidence filed in support of the application, the island is deemed a proper subject of survey, the applicant will be notified of the amount necessary to be deposited with a United States depositary to the credit of the Treasurer of the United States on account of the appropriation ——— to defray the expense of the field work of the survey, and of a separate deposit on the account of the appropriation ——— for clerk hire in the examination of the returns and the necessary protraction of plats.

Upon such deposits being made the United States depositary is required to issue certificates of deposit in triplicate, one to be transmitted to this office, upon the receipt of which, all the other requirements having been complied with, the Commissioner will issue the necessary instructions to the surveyor to enable him to execute the field work of survey in accordance with the public land system.

3d. It is proper to state that the fact of having borne the expense of survey will give no priority of claim or right, under existing laws, to purchase the land, or in any manner affect the vested interest of any party thereto, should such exist, as the island, when surveyed, will be subject to disposal according to the laws of Congress and the regulations of this office relative to the disposal of lands embraced in fragmentary surveys.

Respectfully,

JOS. S. WILSON, Commissioner.

TITLE VII.

Bounty Lands.

No. 279 B.

Bounty land act March 3, 1855. *Certificate of caveat, &c.*

GENERAL LAND OFFICE,
———, 18—

Land Warrant No. ——, for ——— acres, dated ———, in the name of ——— has been returned to this office, located by ———, as the assignee, on the ——— day of ———, 18—, at the land office at ———, upon the ———.

The said warrant purports to have been assigned by the ———, on the ——— day of ———, 18—, in the presence of ———, as subscribing witnesses, and to have been acknowledged before ———.

A caveat, dated ———, has been filed by ———, to arrest the issue of a patent in this case.

As the assignment on said warrant is, in all respects, PRIMA FACIE REGULAR, this office can take no further action in the case, until the locator, or his assignee, shall have been properly notified that the validity of the assignment under which he claims is contested by you; and, in order to enable you to bring the subject-matter to his attention, a "printed notice" is herewith inclosed, TO BE BY YOU SERVED UPON HIM, and returned to this office within ——— months from this date. Upon the receipt here of satisfactory evidence, in the form of an affidavit of the fact (on the back of said notice) of such personal service by you upon the claimant, the case will be taken up and final action had, and the result thereafter made known to you, and the claimant.

It will also be necessary for ———, to file in this office, in addition to ——— own affidavit corroborative testimony, going to show the truth of the facts alleged in the caveat, which facts, for the information of the claimant, should be specifically set forth in the blank space left for that purpose in the inclosed form of "Notice."

It must appear that the testimony is from disinterested parties; and the officer administering the oath must certify that the deponents are entitled to credit.

In default of furnishing the evidence herein called for within ——— months from this date, a patent will issue on the assignment now on file, unless before that time you, as the contestant, shall transmit to this office a transcript of a bill filed in chancery, making all concerned parties, to annul and set aside said assignment, and in that event action will be deferred until a decree is obtained, when a certified transcript thereof should be immediately sent to this office.

Very respectfully, your obedient servant,
———, Commissioner.

Accompanying letter from Commissioner of General Land Office, to ——, dated ——.

NOTICE.

——,
——,

Sir :—Bounty Land Warrant No. ——, for —— acres, issued under act of March 3, 1855, in the name of ——, has been returned to the General Land Office located in your name, at the land office at ——, on the —— day of ——, 18—, in virtue of an assignment purporting to be from ——, executed on the —— in your favor, in presence of the following witnesses: ——, and acknowledged before ——, dated ——, at ——.

This is to notify you that I have filed, in the General Land Office, a caveat under oath, in which I declare that I am the actual owner of said warrant, and that I have never sold, transferred, or assigned the same, or authorized any other person to sell or assign it for me, or in my name, and that ——. *Note.*—In this space the facts must be fully set forth.

I also hereby notify you that within —— months from this date I shall apply to the Commissioner of the General Land Office to disregard and set aside, as fraudulent and void, the assignment of said warrant to you, and will file proof of the facts annexed in the foregoing as to the invalidity of the assignment, so that if you have any good cause to show why a patent should be issued in your favor, such showing may be made at the office aforesaid, at Washington City, D. C., at or before the time above mentioned, as I shall claim an adjudication upon my application by said office on the merits of the case, and shall demand the said warrant as my lawful property. Should you not make such showing pursuant to this notice and service upon you, I shall demand the warrant, asking that your failure to answer shall be taken PRO CONFESSO in favor of such demand.

Very respectfully, your obedient servant,

——.

To ——.

TITLE VIII.

Railroad Selections.

No. 280 B.

Circular No. 15. *Grants from Congress to States and Corporations.*

Circular No. 15, of January 24, 1867 (approved January 29, 1867). In regard to selections in satisfaction of railroads and other Congressional grants; with forms for verification of lists of selections, and also of plats of survey of such roads.

DEPARTMENT OF THE INTERIOR,
GENERAL LAND OFFICE, January 24, 1867.

Gentlemen:—By the first section of the act of Congress approved July 1, 1864, Statutes 1863–64, page 335, chap. 196, it is provided that from and after the passage of *that* act, "in the location of lands by States and corporations, under grants from Congress for railroads and other purposes (except for agricultural colleges), the Registers and Receivers of the Land Offices for the several States and Territories, in the districts where such lands may be located, for their services therein, shall be entitled to receive a fee of one dollar for each final location of one hundred and sixty acres, to be paid by the State or corporation making such location; the same to be accounted for in the same manner as fees and commissions on warrants and pre-emption locations, with limitations as to maximums of salary prescribed by existing laws, in accordance with such instructions as shall be given by the commissioner of the General Land Office."

1st. Under this law the Registers and Receivers are *each* entitled to receive a fee of one dollar for each final location of one hundred and sixty acres, or any quantity approximate thereto, when the deficit is less than forty acres.

2d. When the several quantities shall have been definitely ascertained by you to enure to the grant, as hereinafter prescribed, the fees will then be due thereon.

3d. The State through its grantee, or the grantee, as the case may be, is required to file with the Register and Receiver of the proper land office descriptive lists of the tracts of land claimed as enuring under the grant, within sections of —— miles each, along the line of route on both sides thereof, to be dated and verified by the signature of the selecting agent.

For agent's certificate to be attached to each list, see Form A.

The party appearing as the agent of the grantee must file with the Register and Receiver written and satisfactory evidence, under seal, showing his authority to act in the premises.

In the preparation of the descriptive lists, the Register and Receiver will afford the agent all reasonable facilities, taking care, however, not to interrupt the current public business.

The lists must be carefully and critically examined by the Register and Receiver; their accuracy tested by the plats and records of their office. When so examined and tested, and found correct in all respects, to be a *final location;* and you will, on the payment of the requisite fees to the Receiver, so certify at the foot of each list, according to Form B.

After such lists have been examined, and you have attached your certificate thereto, the same will be consecutively numbered, commencing with No. 1, for each railroad or separate grant. Upon the payment of the fees and certification of the lists by you, the Register will post the selections in the tract book, after the following manner:—

"Selected ——, 186—, by A. B., agent for the —— Railroad Co., act ——, list No. —;" and on the plats he will mark the tracts so selected "—— R. R."

After the selections are properly posted and marked on the plats, the lists will be transmitted to this office, accompanied by the evidence of the agent's appointment.

4th. The fees will be due in all cases where the service may have been rendered *subsequent* to the passage of said act of 1864.

5th. The Receiver will account for the fees thus paid in his monthly and quarterly accounts, specially setting forth in the same the particular case or cases on which such fees had accrued, giving the name of road, number and date of the list of selections for which they had been paid.

6th. By joint resolution No. 10 of January 30, 1865, "mineral lands" are not embraced in the grants made at the 1st session of the 38th Congress, unless otherwise specially provided in the act or acts making the grants.

PACIFIC RAILROADS.

Acts approved July 1, 1862, and July 2, 1864.

7th. By section 21 of the latter act, these companies are required to pay cost of "surveying, selecting, and conveying" the lands, *in addition* to the Register and Receiver's fees exacted by the act of July 1, 1864, before mentioned. This cost of surveying and conveying is, by the decision of the Secretary of the Interior of November 8, 1866, limited to the lands granted by act July 2, 1864. Therefore, the "cost" will be assessed and collected on the lands outside of ten miles and within twenty miles from the line of the road, where the grant is under both acts.

To ascertain the cost of "surveying," which includes both *surveying in the field* and *office work*, the company will apply to the Surveyor-General of the State or Territory in which the lands are situated. Upon ascertaining the sums due for surveying and office work for the "section or sections of road" for which selections have been or are to be made, a deposit of those sums must be made, to the credit of the Treasurer of the United States, with an authorized depository. The duplicate of deposit must be filed with the Surveyor-General; whereupon he will transmit to the Register and Receiver of the proper land office his certificate of such payment having been made, specifying how much was for surveying and how much for office work as per Form C.

The Surveyor-General's certificate, together with the triplicate certificate of deposit and the evidence of the agent's appointment, must accompany the lists of selection when transmitted by you to this office.

8th. Herewith is a form of title-page to be prefixed to the Lists of Selection.

Let me here call your special attention to the necessity of *great care* in the examination and testing of these lists, so that all conflicts may be avoided and improper selections be excluded, and that the verified schedules may be absolutely accurate, thus avoiding embarrassment and delay to all concerned.

9th. Pacific Railroad act, July 2, 1864.—It is provided in section 4 that the word "mineral," when it occurs in that act, shall not be held to include iron and coal. Therefore, iron and coal lands are subject to selection by the Pacific Railroads; but all other minerals are expressly excluded from the grant, and must necessarily be so from all selections you may certify to this office. When the verified lists are received at the General Land Office, prepared and certified as above required, such definitive action as the law requires will be here taken, with a view to invest the grantee with a complete title.

These instructions will supersede those of May 30, 1866, Circular No. 9. The forms attached hereto, which are made a part hereof, will be followed in certifying to maps and lists, where the same may be applicable.

You will please acknowledge the receipt of this circular, giving the date of reception.

JOS. S. WILSON, Commissioner.

To the Registers and Receivers of the U. S. Land Offices.

DEPARTMENT OF THE INTERIOR,
Washington, D. C., January 29, 1867.

The foregoing rules are approved.

O. H. BROWNING, Secretary.

FORM FOR TITLE-PAGE.

——— OF ———
U. S. LAND OFFICE ———
———, 186—,

The ———, under and by virtue of the acts of Congress entitled "———," and under and in pursuance of the rules and regulations prescribed by the Commissioner of the General Land Office, hereby makes and files the following list of selections of public lands claimed by the said company as enuring to it, and to which it is entitled under and by virtue of the grants and provisions of the said acts of Congress, and the location of the line of route of the ——— of said company; being for the ——— section (——— miles) of the same, commencing at ——— and ending ———. The selections being particularly described as follows, to wit: ———

(A.)

——— OF ———, COUNTY OF ———, SS.

I, ———, being duly sworn, depose and say that I am the land agent of the ———, formerly the ———; that the foregoing list of lands, which I hereby select, is a correct list of a portion of the public lands claimed by the said ——— company as enuring to ———, to aid in the construction of the ——— from ———, for which a grant of lands was made by the acts of Congress approved ———; that the said lands are vacant, unappropriated, and are not interdicted mineral nor reserved lands, and are of the character contemplated by the grant, being within the limits of ——— miles on each side of the line of route for a continuous distance of —— miles, being for —— section of said road, starting from —— and ending ——.

——, [L. S.]

Sworn and subscribed before me this —— day of ——, ——.

——.

NOTE.—This affidavit may be made before either the Register or Receiver of the U. S. Land Office.

(B.)

UNITED STATES LAND OFFICE,
——, 18—

We hereby certify that we have carefully and critically examined the foregoing list of lands claimed by the ——, under the grant to the ——, by acts of Congress approved ——, and selected —— by ——, the duly authorized agent, and we have tested the accuracy of said list by the plats and records of this office, and that we find the same to be correct; and we further certify that the filing of said list is allowed and approved, and that the whole of said lands are surveyed public lands of the United States, and within the limit of —— miles on each side; and that the same are not, nor is any part thereof, returned and denominated as mineral land or lands, nor claimed as swamp lands; nor is there any homestead, pre-emption, State, or other valid claim to any portion of said lands on file or record in this office.

We further certify that the foregoing list shows an assessment of the fees payable to us, allowed by the act of Congress approved July 1, 1864, and contemplated by the circular of instructions dated January 24, 1867, addressed by the Commissioner of the General Land Office to Registers and Receivers of the United States land offices; and that the said company have paid to the undersigned, the Receiver, the full sum of ——, in full payment and discharge of said fees.

——, Register.
——, Receiver.

(C.)

U. S. SURVEYOR-GENERAL'S OFFICE,
——, 18—

I, ——, Surveyor-General for the United States in and for the ——, hereby report and certify that the —— has this day filed with me, at ——, a duplicate certificate of deposit, No. —, dated —— of the ——, to the credit of the Treasurer of the United States, showing that the sum of $—— has been deposited as cost of survey, and $—— for office work, and that the said sums are the correct amount of the cost of survey and office work for the lands mentioned and described in the list of lands, hereto annexed, to the extent of said list.

Survey, $——.
Office work, $——.

In testimony whereof, I have hereunto set my hand and official seal.

——, Surveyor-General.

Certificates for maps of the surveys and permanent location, &c.

Form No. 1. Of engineer's affidavit to map of definite location.

Form No. 2. Of president and engineer's certificate to same.

Form No. 3. Of engineer's affidavit to map of completed portion of railroad.

Form No. 4. Of president's certificate to same.

Form No. 5. Of engineer's affidavit to map of definite location where grant was made to a State or Territory.

Form No. 6. Of certificate of Governor of State or Territory to map of definite location.

Form No. 7. Of certificate of Governor to map of completed portion of railroad.

Nos. 1, 2, 3 and 4 to be used when grant was direct to the railroad.

Nos. 1, 3, 4, 5, 6 and 7 to be used when grant was made to the *State or Territory.*

(No. 1.)

——— of ———, County of ———, ss.

———, of ———, in said county and ———, being duly sworn, deposeth and says that he is the chief engineer of the ———, and has been such chief engineer since the ———; that during the period above named ——— were employed by this deponent, as chief engineer for said railroad company, as deputy or division engineers; that the said engineers, as shown by their field notes, verified under oath, did actually survey and mark upon the ground the line or route of the ——— from ——— to ———, in the sections and at the times respectively designated by dates, which are included between the flag-staffs upon and along the line of route of said railroad as delineated on this map, showing the line of the public survey in connection with the surveyed line of the route; and that the acts of said deputy or division engineers in the premises were duly approved and accepted on behalf of said company by this deponent as said chief engineer of the ———.

———, Chief Engineer.

[Revenue stamp.]

Sworn and subscribed this ——— day of ———, before me.

[SEAL.] ———, Notary Public.

The map of location *must*, as shown in the above form, in all cases show the lines of the public survey in connection with the line of route.

(No. 2.)

OFFICE OF THE ———,
———,
———, 186—

It is hereby certified that, in pursuance of the act of Congress approved July 1, 1862, entitled "An act to aid in the construction of a railroad and telegraph line from the Missouri River to the Pacific Ocean, and to secure to the Government the use of the same for postal, military, and other purposes," wherein a grant of lands is made by the ——— section to the ———, who are thereby authorized to construct a railroad and telegraph line from ———; and the act of July 2, 1864, amendatory thereof, which ——— to construct said railroad, this map shows the location of the line or route of the ——— from ——— to ———, being a part of the line or route of said railroad as definitely fixed, in compliance with said acts of Congress, and in pursuance of the resolution of the board of directors of said company, passed on the ———; and that the dates of the field work thereof are truly indicated along the line, from station to station, upon this map.

In testimony whereof, the ——— has caused the same to be signed by its president and engineer, and has attached hereunto its corporate seal at ———, on the day and year first above written.

———, President.
[SEAL.]
———, Chief Engineer.

Attest: ———, Secretary.

(No. 3.)

——— of ———, County of ———, ss.

———, of ———, in said county and ———, being duly sworn, deposeth and says that he is the chief engineer of the said railroad, from ——— to ———, being for ——— section of ——— miles, as shown by the line of route in connection with the lines of the public surveys on this map; that it has been completed and equipped as required by law, and that this line of route shows the correct location of the said railroad.

———, Chief Engineer. [SEAL.]

[Revenue stamp.]

Sworn and subscribed this ——— day of ———, before me.

[SEAL.] ———, Notary Public.

(No. 4.)

It is hereby certified that ——— is the chief engineer of the ———, and that the location of the road, as represented on this map, is correct and approved by the company; and also that the said portion of the said road has been completed and equipped in all respects as required by law.

———, President. [SEAL.]

Attest: ———, Secretary.
[SEAL.]

(No. 5.)

OFFICE OF THE ———

———

It is hereby certified that, in pursuance of the act of the legislative assembly of the ———, approved ———, entitled "———," this map shows, in connection with the public surveys, the actually surveyed line of route of the ——— from ——— to ———, as definitely fixed, in compliance with the act of Congress approved ———, and in pursuance of the resolution of the board of directors of said railroad company passed on the ——— day of ———; and that the dates of the field work thereof are truly indicated along the line, from station to station, upon this map.

In testimony whereof, the ——— has hereunto attached its corporate seal, and caused the same to be signed by the President and ———, at ———, in the day and year first above written.
[SEAL.]

———, President.
———, Chief Engineer.

Attest: ———, Secretary.

(No. 6.)

I ———, Governor of the ———, do hereby certify that this plat or map of the ——— has been duly filed in my office by the railroad company, and shows, in connection with the public surveys, the location of the line of route as actually surveyed of the ——— "from ——— to

———," as definitely fixed in compliance with the act of Congress approved———, entitled "An act ———," and with the act of the legislative assembly of the ———, approved ———, entitled "———," granting certain lands to the railroad herein named.

In testimony whereof, I have hereunto set my hand and caused to be [SEAL.] affixed the great seal of the ———.

Done at ———, this ——— day of ———.

———, Governor.

Attest: ———, Secretary of ———.

(No. 7.)

EXECUTIVE OFFICE,

———

I, ———, Governor of the ———, do hereby certify that this plat or map of the ——— has been duly filed in my office by the said ——— company, and shows that portion of the said railroad commencing at ——— and ending at ———, which has been completed and equipped as required by the act of Congress approved ———, and the act of the legislative assembly of the ———, approved ———, entitled "———," granting lands to the said railroad company.

In testimony whereof, I have hereunto set my hand and caused to be [SEAL] affixed the great seal of the ———.

Done at ———, this ——— day of ———.

———, Governor.

Attest: ———, Secretary of ———.

TITLE IX.

Indian Lands and Scrip.

No. 281 B.

Circular.

Relative to the location of half-breed Dacotah or Sioux scrip, issued under the act of Congress approved July 17, 1854.—*U. S. Stat. at Large, vol.* 10, *p.* 304.

GENERAL LAND OFFICE,
February, 22, 1864.

Gentlemen:—Questions frequently arise in regard to the location of Dacotah or Sioux half-breed scrip issued some years ago from the office of Indian affairs.

The issue was as follows: 2 for 40 acres each; 1 for 80 acres; and 2 for 160 acres each; making an aggregate for each one of 480 acres, designated thus, for example, in the first case: No. 1 A, 40 acres; No. 1 B, 40 acres; No. 1 C, 80 acres; No. 1 D, 160 acres; No. 1 E, 160 acres.

This scrip, as declared on its face, is locatable upon the following described classes of lands, viz:—

Upon the Sioux half-breed reservation, situated wholly in the St. Peter Land District, in Minnesota; being in townships 108 to 110, ranges 9 to 15.

APPLICATION OF SCRIP TO SPECIAL LOCALITIES.

1st. The scrip may be located by the half-breed upon any land within this reserve upon which, at the date of the act of July 17, 1854, he was an actual bona fide settler.

2d. Upon any land within said reservation which, at the date of said act, was not so occupied by a half-breed, or any other person who may have gone into said reservation under authority of law.

To constitute a half-breed or mixed-blood an actual and bona fide SETTLER within the meaning of the statute, it must be shown, by proof satisfactory to you, that he was an occupant by personal inhabitation within said reservation at or before the passage of the act of July 17, 1854; and in such case he will be entitled to locate his scrip, embracing his improvements, conforming to the legal subdivisions of the public surveys, unless such location interferes with another bona fide settler, when each will be allowed to take such subdivisions as will embrace his improvements.

The persons who have "gone into said Territory by authority of law," are, as the land officers at St. Peter will understand, only with such persons as, prior to the passage of said act of July 17, 1854, had entered said reservation under the Indian intercourse laws—such as licensed traders, authorized missionary teachers, and other persons in the employ of Government in connection with Indian affairs, and who inhabited the lands and made improvements thereon prior to said act.

APPLICATION OF SCRIP TO GENERAL LOCALITIES.

Besides these special stipulations in the law in regard to locations in the Minnesota half-breed reservation, the aforesaid statute enlarges the sphere of location by authorizing the location of the scrip—

3d. "Upon any other unoccupied lands subject to pre-emption or private sale."

You will understand, however, that no mineral or reserved lands can be taken by this scrip, nor can it be located upon the even-numbered, double minimum, reserved sections, nor upon any lands on which there is an actual settlement; but it may be located—

4th. "Upon any other unsurveyed lands, not reserved by Government, upon which they have respectively made improvements."

Where the half-breed for himself may make actual settlement, his improvements will be notice on the ground to any other settler, and in this respect he will stand on the same basis as a pre-emptor of unsurveyed land, and of course cannot adjust his location until after the return of the township plat to the district land office. Hereafter, and within three months, he should repair to such land office, file his scrip with his affidavit, designating specifically, in compact legal subdivisions, the tracts embracing his improvements, and should state in his affidavit the character and extent of these improvements, and file testimony of competent witnesses corroborative of his statement.

5th. When not located by the reservee in proper person, the application to locate must be accompanied by the affidavit of the agent that the reservee is living, and that the location is made for the sole use and benefit of said reservee.

The land selected in satisfaction of a certificate of scrip must of course be located in the name of the party in whose favor the scrip is issued, and the location may be made by him or her in person, or by his or her guardian or duly authorized agent. The application should be duly attested in each case by the Register and Receiver, and attached to each should be your certificate to the following effect:—

"LAND OFFICE AT ——
——1864.

"We hereby certify that the within scrip has, this —— day of —— been located on the —— containing —— acres, agreeably to the act of 17th July, 1854, and by the party duly authorized to make the location. Attest: ——, Register.
——, Receiver."

No receipt is to be issued to the locator, except in unavoidable cases, where there may be a small excess in the area of the location over the scrip, and in that case it must be paid for, and the receiver will issue his receipt, which he will number and account for, as in the case of bounty-land warrant excess. But no certificate of purchase is to be issued; the scrip and application, instead of certificates of purchase, being the instruments of title which are to be returned to the General Land Office in this class of business.

The Register, however, in the case of excess payments, will append to the application his official statement, that ——— acres of said tract (the excess) have been paid for, per Receiver's receipt No. ———.

Your proceedings in locating the certificates, and your official returns, are to be kept entirely separate and distinct from other sales and locations. At the close of each month the Register and Receiver will make a separate official return of scrip located, with all the papers on file connected with each location, accompanied by a monthly abstract.

You will observe that this scrip is not assignable, transfers of the same being held void; consequently, each certificate, as hereinbefore stated, can only be located in the name of the Half-breed; and such certificates or scrip are not to be treated as money, but located acre for acre.

No fees or commissions of any kind are allowed by this office for services of the land officers in this matter, such being an incident to their general duties; and you are, therefore, hereby interdicted from charging or receiving any compensation for such services. This scrip is, of course, not applicable to any class of Indian trust lands, but only to unreserved, unencumbered public lands.

Very respectfully, your obedient servant,
J. M. EDMUNDS, Commissioner.

Register and Receiver at ———.

No. 282 B.

Circular.

DEPARTMENT OF THE INTERIOR,
GENERAL LAND OFFICE, May 13, 1865.

Gentlemen :—Referring to the circular of November 24, 1857, relative to the location of certificates issued under the 7th section of 2d article of the treaty concluded 30th September, 1854, with the Chippewas of Lake Superior, the following instructions in regard to the location of the same are given for your guidance, in accordance with the suggestions of the Secretary of the Interior dated the 26th ultimo :—

1st. The parties, in locating their certificates, are authorized to locate, in any land district in the United States, lands open to entry or ordinary sale ; and—

2d. Upon any unoccupied public land subject to pre-emption, whether surveyed or unsurveyed. You will understand, however, that no mineral or reserved lands can be taken by these certificates, nor can they be located upon the even-numbered, double minimum, or reserved sections, nor upon any lands on which there is an actual settlement, without the written consent, duly attested, of such settler.

3d. Where the certificates may be filed for unsurveyed lands, and which are not excepted as above, the application must be accompanied by a diagram and description denoting natural objects and distances, so as to fix with certainty the exact locality wanted ; or, if a private survey of the land has been made by north and south and east and west lines, the same can be filed with the certificate and application. Such diagram and description or survey will be notice to other parties whereby conflicts may be avoided. When filed for unsurveyed lands, the party should, within three months after the return of the township plat to the District Land Office, repair to such land office, and designate specifically, in compact legal sub-divisions, the tracts embraced in his diagram and description or survey theretofore filed in said office.

4th. The land selected in satisfaction of a certificate must be located in the name of the party in whose favor the certificate is issued, and the location may be made by him or her in person, or by his or her guardian or duly authorized agent.

The application should be duly attested in each case by the Register and Receiver, and attached to each should be your certificate to the following effect:—

LAND OFFICE at ———,
———, 18—

We hereby certify that the within certificate has ——— day of ——— been located on the ——— containing ——— acres, agreeably to the 7th section of the 2d article of the treaty of 30th September, 1854, with the Chippewas, and by the party duly authorized to make the location.

Attest: ——— Register.
——— Receiver.

5th. No receipt is to be issued to the locator except in unavoidable cases where there may be a small excess in the area of the location over the scrip, and in that case it must be paid for, and the Receiver will issue his receipt, which he will number and account for as in the case of bounty-land warrant excess. But in such case no certificate of purchase is to be issued; the certificate and application, instead of certificates of purchase, being the instruments of title which are to be returned to the General Land Office in this class of business.

6th. The Register, however, in the case of excess payments, will append to the application his official statement, that ——— acres of said tract have been paid for, per Receiver's receipt, No. ———.

7th. Your proceedings in locating the certificates and your official returns are to be kept entirely separate and distinct from other sales and locations. At the close of each month the Register and Receiver will make a separate official return of certificates located, with all the papers on file connected with each location, accompanied by a monthly abstract (form B.), in which you will also give the number of the certificates filed for unsurveyed lands, and the name of the party in whose favor such certificate issued.

8th. You will observe that this scrip is not assignable, transfers of the same being held void; consequently, each certificate, as hereinbefore stated, can only be located in the name of the mixed bloods; and such certificates are not to be treated as money, but located acre for acre.

9th. No fees or commissions of any kind are allowed by this office for services of the land officers in this matter, such being an incident to their general duties; and you are, therefore, hereby interdicted from charging or receiving any compensation for such services.

These certificates are, of course, not applicable to any class of Indian trust lands, but only to unreserved, unencumbered public lands.

Very respectfully, your obedient servant,

J. M. EDMUNDS, Commissioner.

Register and Receiver at ———.

No. 283 B.

Circular. Chippewa scrip.

DEPARTMENT OF THE INTERIOR,
GENERAL LAND OFFICE,
September 18, 1866.

Gentlemen :—Referring to the circular of May 13, 1865, relative to the location of certificates issued under the seventh section of second article of the treaty concluded 30th September, 1854, with the Chippewas of Lake Superior, the Secretary of the Interior has given instructions under date of 14th inst., that these certificates are not applicable to unsurveyed lands. The circular is therefore herein modified in accordance therewith :—

1st, then, The parties, in l ocating their certificates, are authorized to locate, in any land district in the United States, surveyed lands open to entry or ordinary sale ; and—

2d. Upon any unoccupied surveyed public land subject to pre-emption, excepting mineral or reserved lands, the even-numbered double minimum, or reserved sections, and any lands on which there is an actual settlement, unless with the written consent of the settler duly attested.

3d. The land selected in satisfaction of a certificate must be located in the name of the party in whose favor the certificate is issued, and the location may be made by him or her in person, or by his or her legal representative, or duly authorized agent, the authority to be duly shown by proper instruments.

4th. The application should be attested in each case by the Register and Receiver, and attached to each should be your certificate to the following effect :—

LAND OFFICE, ———,
———, 18—.

We hereby certify that the within certificate has, ——— day of ———, been located on the ———, containing ——— acres, agreeably to the seventh section of the second article of the treaty of 30th September, 1854, with the Chippewas, and by the party duly authorized to make the location.

Attest : ———, Register.
———, Receiver.

5th. No receipt is to be issued to the locator, except where there may be a small excess in the area of the location over the scrip, and in that case such excess must be paid for, and the Receiver must issue his receipt, which he will number and account for as in the case of bounty-land warrant excess. No certificate of purchase, however, is to be issued. In such cases the application duly certified with the scrip being the instrument of title which are to be returned to the General Land Office in this class of business.

6th. The Register in the case of excess payments will append to the application his official statement, that ——— acres of said tract have been paid for per Receiver's receipt No. ———.

7th. Your proceedings in locating the certificates and your official returns are to be kept entirely separate and distinct from other sales and locations. At the close of each month the Register and Receiver will make a separate official return of certificates located, with all the papers on file connected with each location, accompanied by a monthly abstract, Form B.

8th. You will observe that this scrip is not assignable, transfers of the same being held void; consequently, each certificate, as hereinbefore stated, can only be located in the name of the mixed-bloods; and such certificates are not to be treated as money, but located acre for acre.

9. No fees or commissions of any kind are allowed by this office for services of the land officers in this matter, such being an incident to their general duties; and you are, therefore, hereby interdicted from charging or receiving any compensation for such services.

These certificates are, of course, not applicable to any class of Indian trust lands, but only to surveyed unreserved, unencumbered public lands.

Very respectfully, your obedient servant,

J. S. WILSON, Commissioner.

Register and Receiver at ——.

No. 284 B.

THE OSAGE INDIAN LANDS.

The following letter, dated November 2, from the Commissioner of the General Land Office to the Register and Receiver at Humboldt, Kansas, contains one or two points of some importance to settlers on the Osage Indian lands:—

This office has considered your communication of 17th September last, with inclosures, relative to the form of affidavit and proof required of applicants to enter Osage lands under the joint resolution approved April 10, 1869.

The joint resolution confers the privilege of purchasing the Osage lands upon *bona fide* settlers residing thereon in quantities not exceeding 160 acres to each settler, having certain prescribed qualifications as to citizenship.

Our general instructions of 3d June, 1869, require that proof of residence, settlement, and cultivation should be made in conformity with the general requirements under the pre-emption statutes. The paramount object is to ascertain that the applicant is a *bona fide* settler. A person who has made a contract to sell the lands he may acquire title to under the joint resolution cannot be regarded as a *bona fide* settler, and the affidavit required should so far conform to the usual pre-emption affidavit as to cover this point, as well as any others necessary to aid in making clear the question of *bona fides* before admitting an entry.

The inhibitions of the pre-emption statutes, limiting the privilege to those who have not had the benefit of the pre-emption right, are not the owners of more than 320 acres, and have not removed from their own land in the same State or Territory, are inapplicable under the joint resolution, while all the requirements of those statutes touching the question of good faith as a settler are applicable, in view of the limitation and restriction of the purchasing privilege to *bona fide* settlers residing on the tracts they seek to purchase. You will please conform to these requirements in the matter of proof and affidavit.

Very respectfully,

JOSEPH S. WILSON, Commissioner.

(Where a treaty with an Indian tribe reserves a certain quantity of land, to be afterwards selected by the President, and patented to an individual of the tribe, such reservation creates an equitable interest in the reservee to the land reserved, which he may sell, and upon the selection and patenting of the land the title will vest in his grantee. Creirs *et al.* *v.* Burcham *et al.*, 1 Black, p. 352.)

TITLE X.

Repayment of Purchase Money.

No. 285 B.

Circular No. 16.

DEPARTMENT OF THE INTERIOR,
GENERAL LAND OFFICE, March 29, 1867.

Gentlemen:—The following is a copy of a joint resolution, No. 27, as approved March 2, 1867, prohibiting payment by officers of the Government to any person not known to have been opposed to the rebellion and in favor of its suppression:—

Be it resolved by the Senate and House of Representatives of the United States of America in Congress assembled, That until otherwise ordered, it shall be unlawful for any officer of the United States Government to pay any account, claim, or demand against said Government, which accrued or existed prior to the thirteenth day of April, A. D. eighteen hundred and sixty-one, in favor of any person who promoted, encouraged, or in any manner sustained the late rebellion; or in favor of any person who, during said rebellion, was not known to be opposed thereto and distinctly in favor of its suppression; and no pardon heretofore granted, or hereafter to be granted, shall authorize the payment of such account, claim or demand, until this resolution is modified or repealed: *Provided*, That this resolution shall not be construed to prohibit the payment of claims founded upon contracts made by any of the departments, where such claims were assigned or contracted to be assigned prior to April first, eighteen hundred and sixty-one, to creditors of said contractors, loyal citizens of loyal States, in payment of debts incurred prior to March first, eighteen hundred and sixty-one.

Approved March 2, 1867.

The prohibition applies only to such claims as accrued or existed prior to the 13th day of April, 1861.

To give proper effect to this joint resolution, so far as it is applicable to claims for the return of purchase money on entries of land which were cancelled prior to the date mentioned therein, you are requested, as cases arise, to notify parties concerned that each application must be supported by the affidavit of the claimant, affirming that he in no way promoted, encouraged, or sustained the late rebellion; but that he was opposed thereto and distinctly in favor of its suppression.

There must also be filed in each case the affidavits of at least two persons, duly certified to be respectable and credible by the officer before whom the affidavits shall be taken, showing affirmatively that they have been personally acquainted with the applicant since the 13th day of April, 1861, and that he conducted himself during the late rebellion as a loyal citizen of the United States, and that from their acquaintance with and knowledge of him, they believe him to have been opposed to the rebellion and distinctly in favor of its suppression during the period of its continuance.

In cases coming within the proviso of said joint resolution, if any shall arise, you will require the party applying as assignee of any claim for the return of purchase money, to file his affidavit showing that he was, at the date of the assignment, a loyal citizen of a loyal State, and that said assignment was made in payment of a debt incurred prior to March 1, 1861.

These affidavits may be taken before the Register or Receiver, or any officer of the United States, or of the several States, authorized by law to administer oaths and to take affidavits, and should be certified as now required in other cases; that is to say, if taken before a State officer not having or using an official seal, they should have attached the certificate of clerk of a court of record using a seal, with appropriate revenue stamps affixed.

Very respectfully, your obedient servant,
JOS. S. WILSON, Commissioner.

Register and Receiver at ———

No. 286 B.

Circular, No. 17.

DEPARTMENT OF THE INTERIOR,
GENERAL LAND OFFICE, April 30, 1867.

Gentlemen :—Numerous applications to correct errors in entries of the public lands having been forwarded to this office without being properly supported by testimony, it is deemed advisable to collect and present in one view all the legislative enactments, of a general character, upon the subject, with such explanatory remarks as are deemed necessary.

The acts authorizing corrections of errors in entries are the following, viz :—

An Act providing for the correction of errors in making entries of land at the land offices.

[SEC. 1.] *Be it enacted by the Senate and House of Representatives of the United States of America in Congress assembled,* That in every case of a purchaser of public lands, at private sale, having entered, at the land office, a tract different from that he intended to purchase, and being desirous of having the error in his entry corrected, he shall make his application, for that purpose, to the Register of the land office; and if it shall appear, from testimony satisfactory to the Register and Receiver of public moneys, that an error in the entry has been made, and that the same was occasioned by original incorrect marks made by the surveyor, or by the obliteration or change of the original marks and numbers at corners of the tract of land, or that it has in any otherwise arisen from mistake or error of the surveyor or officers of the land office, the said Register and Receiver of public moneys shall report the case, with the testimony, and their opinion thereon, to the Secretary of the Treasury, who shall have power to direct, if in his opinion it shall be proper, that the purchaser shall be at liberty to withdraw the entry so erroneously made, and that the moneys which had been paid shall be applied in the purchase of other lands in the same district, or credited in the payment for other lands which shall have been purchased at the same office.

Approved March 3, 1819.

An Act supplementary to an act, approved on the third day of March, one thousand eight hundred and nineteen, entitled "An act providing for the correction of errors in making entries of land at the land offices."

[SEC. 1.] *Be it enacted by the Senate and House of Representatives of the United States of America in Congress assembled,* That where any mistake, in relation to the correct numbers of any tract of land, not exceeding in quantity one half section, may have been heretofore made by any purchaser of the public lands of the United States at private sale, and where one or more payments shall have been made by the person making the entry, on any tract entered by mistake, and where such payment has not been forfeited, previously to the passing of this act, for a failure to complete the payments on such tract; and where the purchaser or purchasers may not, in relation to said tract, have in any way taken advantage of the provisions of the act of the second of March, eighteen hundred and twenty-one, entitled "An act for the relief of the purchasers of the public lands prior to the first day of July, eighteen hundred and twenty," or of the act supplementary thereto, or the act continuing in force said supplementary act; and where the person or persons making the purchase has not in any way transferred his, her, or their right to the certificate of purchase, or the tract so purchased, and where no patent shall have issued for the tract so erroneously purchased; and, also, in all cases of an entry hereafter made of a tract of land not intended to be entered, by a mistake of the true numbers of the tract intended to be entered, where the tract thus erroneously entered does not in quantity exceed one half section; and where the certificate of the original purchaser or purchasers has not been assigned, or the right of the original purchaser or purchasers in any way transferred, or the patent issued for the tract erroneously entered, the purchaser or purchasers, or, in case of his, her, or their death, the legal representatives (not being assignees or transferees) may, either in the cases of entry before or after the passing of this act, and in any case coming within its provisions, file his, her, or their own affidavit or affidavits, with such additional evidence as can be procured, showing the mistake of the numbers of the tract intended to be entered, and that every reasonable precaution and exertion had been used to avoid the error, with the Register and Receiver of the land district within which such tract of land is situated, who shall transmit the evidence submitted to them in each case together with their written opinion or opinions, both as to [the] existence of the mistake and the credibility of each person testifying thereto, to the Commissioner of the General Land Office, who, if he be entirely satisfied [that] the mistake has been made, and that every reasonable precaution and exertion had been made to avoid it, shall be authorized to change the entry, and transfer the payment from the tract erroneously entered to that intended to be entered, if unsold, but if sold, to any other tract liable to entry: *Provided,* That the oath of the person or persons interested shall, in no case, be deemed sufficient, in the absence of other corroborating testimony, to authorize any such change of entry: *And provided, also,* That nothing herein contained shall affect the right of third parties.

SEC. 2. *And be it further enacted,* That either the Register or Receiver may administer all oaths to be made under the provisions of this act; and every person, knowingly, wilfully, and corruptly swearing falsely on any oath administered to him or her under the provisions of this act, shall, on indictment and conviction for such offence, before any court having competent jurisdiction to try the same, suffer the pains and penalties of wilful and corrupt perjury.

SEC. 3. *And be it further enacted*, That for every oath administered under the provisions of this act, the Register and Receiver shall be allowed the sum of twenty-five cents, and twenty-five cents for every hundred words of the evidence received and transmitted to the Commissioner of the General Land office; to be paid by the party making the application for a change of entry.

Approved May 24, 1824.

An Act authorizing repayment for land erroneously sold by the United States.

[SEC. 1.] *Be it enacted by the Senate and House of Representatives of the United States of America in Congress assembled*, That every person, or the legal representative of every person, who is, or may be, a purchaser of a tract of land from the United States, the purchase whereof is, or may be, void, by reason of a prior sale thereof by the United States, or by the confirmation, or other legal establishment of a prior British, French, or Spanish grant thereof, or for want of title thereto in the United States from any other cause whatsoever, shall be entitled to repayment of any sum or sums of money paid for or on account of such tract of land, on making proof, to the satisfaction of the Secretary of the Treasury, that the same was erroneously sold, in the manner aforesaid, by the United States, who is hereby authorized and required to pay such sum or sums of money paid as aforesaid.

Approved January 12, 1825.

The foregoing act of 12th of January, 1825, was amended February 28, 1859, so as to "authorize the Secretary of the Interior, upon proof being made to his satisfaction that any tract of land has been erroneously sold by the United States, so that, from any cause whatever, the sale cannot be confirmed, to repay the purchaser or purchasers, or their legal representatives or assignees of the purchaser or purchasers thereof, the sum or sums of money, which may have been paid therefor out of any money in the treasury not otherwise appropriated."

An Act supplementary to an act entitled "An act providing for the correction of errors in making entries of lands at the land offices," passed March third, eighteen hundred and nineteen."

[SEC. 1.] *Be it enacted by the Senate and House of Representatives of the United States of America in Congress assembled*, That the provisions of the act entitled "An act providing for the correction of errors in making entries of lands at the land offices," approved March third, one thousand eight hundred and nineteen, are hereby declared to extend to cases where patents have issued, or shall hereafter issue: upon condition that the party concerned shall surrender his or her patent to the commissioner of the General Land Office, with a relinquishment of title thereon, executed in a form to be prescribed by the Secretary of the Treasury.

Approved May 24, 1828.

These laws are plain and particular in their requirements, but few points being left to the elucidation of official instructions; and a careful attention to them will be sufficient, in most cases, to insure correctness in acting under them. It may not, however, be improper to remark—

1. That the act of 1819 is intended to afford relief to those persons whose errors in entries have been occasioned by the original incorrect

marking by the surveyor, or by the subsequent change or obliteration of those marks, or else by any other error originating either with the surveyor or the land officers. The application of the party should be made under oath, stating *particularly* the nature and cause of the error, and should be supported by the best corroborative testimony that can be procured. The case is then to be reported, with the testimony, *and your opinion thereon* to this office, for the decision of the Secretary of the Treasury.

2. The supplementary act of May, 1824, extends the provisions of the act of 1819, so as to embrace cases where the error was *not* occasioned by any act of the surveyor or land officers; and provides that in all cases of error in the entry of a tract of not more than one half section, where the right of the original purchaser has not been assigned or in any way transferred, the party making the entry (or legal representatives, not being assignees or transferees) must file an affidavit, showing the nature and particular cause of the error, that every reasonable and proper precaution had been used to avoid the error, and that the land erroneously entered had not been transferred or otherwise encumbered, accompanied by the best corroborative testimony that can be procured, for you will observe, by this act, that the oath of the party interested is not, of itself, sufficient. This evidence, with your opinions as to the existence of the mistake and the credibility of each person, will be forwarded for the decision of this office.

3. The acts of 1825 and 1859 provide for cases in which the sale of the land is invalid, in consequence of the want of title thereto in the United States from any cause whatsoever. Under these acts it has been decided, that if only *part* of the tract purchased is covered by the interfering claim, it is optional with the purchaser to relinquish the *whole* tract, or only the particular part interfered with. You will observe that, under this act, the money is to be refunded by and through the Secretary of the Treasury, and not by the receiver of public moneys. All applications to obtain the benefits of this act must be supported by your joint certificate, or that of the Surveyor-General, stating the nature of the particular interfering claim, or other circumstance rendering the sale invalid, and be accompanied by the patent, if any has been issued for the invalid sale, with a relinquishment of title, in the following form:—

"Whereas the act of Congress, passed on the 12th day of January, 1825, entitled 'An act authorizing repayment for land erroneously sold by the United States,' provides, that whenever the sale of a tract of land by the United States is void for want of title thereto in the United States, or from any other cause whatsoever, the money paid on the same shall be refunded by the Secretary of the Treasury. And whereas [a part, or the whole, as the case may be] of the within described ——— section of land, is [included in the survey of the private claim of ———, or, as the case may be]. Now know ye that, for and in consideration of the sum of ———, to me in hand paid, by the Secretary of the Treasury, I, the within named ———, hereby assign, transfer, relinquish, and surrender to the United States, all my right, title, interest, and claim of, in, and to, the land described in the within patent. Given under my hand and seal this ——— of ———, 183

Signed, sealed, and delivered, in presence of ———

4. By the act of 24th May, 1828, the provisions of the act of 1819 are so extended as to embrace patented cases. The application for relief, in these cases, will have to be reported in the manner required in those not patented under the act of 1819, and be accompanied by a certificate that

patent is surrendered to you. If the correction of the entry is authorized, you will, before the money is refunded, or the change of entry noted on your books, require the party to execute, upon the patent, a relinquishment in the following form:—

"Know all men by these presents, that, in pursuance of the provisions of the act of Congress, approved on the 24th day of May, 1828, entitled 'An act supplementary to an act entitled an act providing for the correction of errors in making entries of lands at the land offices, passed March third, eighteen hundred and nineteen,' and in order that a patent may be granted to me for the ——— of section ——— in township ———, of range ———, in lieu of the tract herein mentioned, I hereby surrender and relinquish unto the United States of America all my right, title, and interest of, in, and to, this patent, and to the land therein described. In testimony whereof, I have hereunto signed my name, and affixed my seal, this ——— day of ———, 183

Signed, sealed, and delivered, in presence of ———

At the foot of the above relinquishment, you will give a certificate, stating the precise cause of the error.

The act of March 3, 1853, provides for the correction of errors in the location of military bounty land warrants, and declares the provisions of the act 3d March, 1819, and the act of the 24th May, 1828, applicable to errors in such locations.

In all cases where patents have been issued, you will require a certificate from the county clerk, or other officer having charge of the books in which any conveyance, &c., of the land is required to be recorded to give it validity, stating that the records of such office do not exhibit any conveyance, or other incumbrance, of the land in question. The deed of relinquishment must be executed, acknowledged, and recorded in accordance with the laws of the State in which the land is situated.

Whenever the change of entry is ordered, the certificate of purchase will be cancelled, and retained in this office.

The Receiver will take a receipt from the purchaser for the purchase money of the tract erroneously entered, as if the same was refunded, which receipt will be a voucher to the receiver's credit, to be introduced into the proper monthly and quarterly accounts in the following manner, viz:—

"By this amount refunded to ———, agreeably to instructions from the General Land Office, dated the ———, being the purchase money of the ——— quarter of section No. ———, in township No. ———, of range No. ———, containing ——— acres, erroneously entered by him, and again charged to me, in the purchase of the ——— quarter of section No. ———, in township No. ———, of range No. ———."

The Receiver's receipt for the purchase money of the corrected entry is, as well as the register's certificate of purchase, to bear a new number. By this proceeding the corrected entry becomes an original transaction, and will appear as such in all your accounts.

I am, very respectfully, your obedient servant,

JOS. S. WILSON, Commissioner.

The Register and Receiver of the Land Office at ———

No. 287 B.

Form of application for repayment.

Commissioner of the General Land Office, Sir:—I hereby make application for repayment of the purchase money paid on entry of the —— of section ——, township ——, range ——, as per certificate No. ——, issued at ——, bearing date the —— day of ——, 18——, the same having been adjudged invalid and cancelled.

—— ——

State of ——, County of ——, ss.

On this —— day of —— 18——, before the subscriber, a —— in and for said county, —— personally came —— to me well known to be the person who subscribed the foregoing application, who, being duly sworn on —— oath, declare that —— ha— not sold, assigned, nor in any way encumbered the title to the tract of land described in said application.

Subscribed and sworn before me, this —— day of —— A. D. 18——.

—— ——

NOTES.

1st. If the affidavit is sworn to before a Register or Receiver, no revenue stamp is required; otherwise, if made before a clerk or notary, and if made before a justice of the peace, the certificate of the clerk of the county or county court, showing official character, must be attached, with the appropriate revenue stamps.

3d. If the application is made by an assignee or by a legal representative, it must be supported by satisfactory proof of assignment, or of the right of such representative to present the claim.

3d. Where the title has become a matter of record, a deed of relinquishment of title duly executed and recorded, with the certificate of the Recorder showing what appears upon his records touching the title, and that the same is fully restored to the United States, must be filed.

4th. Transmit to General Land Office through the Register and Receiver.

TITLE XI.

Swamp Land Selections.

No. 288 B.

The State of Iowa entitled to purchase money of swamp lands entered with cash prior to 3d March, 1857. The State is also entitled to indemnity in land for lands located with warrants or scrip, prior to that date.

ATTORNEY GENERAL'S OFFICE,
April 20, 1866.

Sir :—I have given to the legislation referred to in your letter of the 30th day of January last, relative to the "swamp grant" to the State of Iowa, careful consideration.

I am of the opinion that the State has a good legal claim ; first, to the purchase-money of the public lands therein, which were entered with cash prior to the passage of the act of March 3, 1857, and which she may be able to prove, to the satisfaction of the Commissioner of the General Land Office and the Secretary of the Interior, were swamp lands within the true intent and meaning of the act of September 28th, 1850 ; and, second, to indemnity in land, for the public lands therein which were located, with warrants or with scrip, prior to the passage of the act of March 3, 1857, and which she may, in like manner, show were swamp lands within the true intent and meaning of the statute of 1850.

In reviewing the legislation adduced by the State in support of her claim, I have diligently sought for the intention of Congress in the words of the statutes. This I have done, not only because to look elsewhere for the intent of the legislature is to violate a fundamental canon of statutory construction, but also because I have keenly felt that, in a case of this character, speculation in regard to the meaning of Congress, based upon considerations extraneous of the statute, would not advance, but only retard, the discovery of that meaning.

The act of September 28, 1850, "to enable the State of Arkansas and other States to reclaim the swamp lands within their limits," I dismiss with the remark that in my view of the present question, it is not important to determine the character and effect of the grant made by that statute. The present question arises upon the construction and effect of the two subsequent statutes of March 2, 1855 ; and March 3, 1857. If the claim of the State of Iowa is not maintainable upon these laws, it must fall. If they support it, I know no subsequent legislation which invalidates it. It is needed, therefore, to look critically into the acts of 1855 and 1857 ; and I propose now to state very briefly what, according to my legal view, is found in those laws.

The act of March 2, 1855. "An act for the relief of purchasers and locators of swamp and overflowed lands," (10 Stats., 634) contains two sections. The 1st section authorizes all persons who had made entries of public lands, claimed as of that character, with cash or warrants, before the issuing of patents for the same lands to the States, to demand their patents.

The 2d section required to be paid over to the States respectively the purchase money of such of these lands as had been sold and purchased, and provided indemnity in like amount of the public lands for such as had been located by warrant or scrip, upon due proof that any of the lands thus purchased or located were swamp lands within the meaning of the act of 1850. I think that the provisions of this act applied only to past cases of sales and locations. The phraseology employed does not embrace any other. There may be good grounds on which to contend that Congress ought, in justice to the States for whose benefit the act of 1850 was passed, to have provided a permanent measure of indemnity, embracing not only past, but also future cases of sales. However that may be, the inquiry here and now is what Congress did, not what it ought to have done; and looking at the words and the words only, of the statute for an answer to that question, I cannot discover in them the expression of an intention to give the States the money realized by the Government on sales of swamp lands within their limits, occurring subsequently to the date of the enactment.

I now come to the statute which presents the only difficulty in the case, the act of March 3, 1857. (11 Stats. 251.) Without that law the claim of the State could not be sustained. It is, to say the least of it, a most ambiguous act. This, together with the fact that your department seems always to have regarded it as adverse to the right of the State, in respect to her present claim, has caused me no little anxiety in giving construction to it. The opinion of the land office, affirmed by eminent gentlemen at the head of the Interior Department, on a question touching the interpretation of a law of this character, especially when that opinion has become a rule of action in the administration of the department, is undoubtedly entitled to great respect. I should be inclined to give it controlling effect in a case where a doubt arose which could only be resolved by the view that had received the sanction of the department. This, however, I am always to consider—that my duty, in every case submitted to me, is to give my own opinion on the question it presents. I have no right to adopt that of any one else, unless it is agreeable to my views of the law. The fact that my opinion, on a question of statutory interpretation, is disapproved by the authority of contemporaneous construction in the department whose duty it is to execute the statute, ought in every case to induce me to review the grounds of my own judgment with more than ordinary care and caution; to take time for reflection; to consider well all the opposing views; and, finally, in a proper case, to give the department the benefit of any reasonable well-founded doubt as to the proper view of the case. *Contemporanea expositio est fortissima.* But, if after this has been done, I am not able to concur in the view of the department, my duty is, as I have suggested, to give what I am requested and required to give—my own opinion on the question. That opinion, however, may or may not be adopted. It is always a question of administrative discretion whether it shall be. The department has the right to respect it, or refuse to act on it, in a proper case, without submitting the subject to the consideration of Congress. With these general observations, I proceed to state the views which I entertain in regard to the construction and effect of the act of March 3, 1857.

I cannot concur with the land office in the opinion that the right of the

State to the indemnity provided by the second section of the act of 1855, in connection with the proviso to the act of 1857, depends upon whether the selections of, as swamp and overflowed lands, were made and reported to the Commissioner of the General Land Office prior to the passage of the act of 1857. In the construction of a statute, it is an established rule, that the intention of the legislature is to be deduced from a view of the whole, and of every part, of the statute, taken and compared together. No part of it should be made void ; full sense and meaning must be given to every clause and provision. As Lord Kenyon said, in regard to a will, "One spells as it were every word, to get at the intention." If the statute contain an enacting clause, a saving clause, and a proviso, they must all be taken into view, and construed together. The saving clause is not to be rejected, unless it is directly repugnant to the body of the act, and cannot stand without rendering the act inconsistent and destructive of itself. If the statute contain a proviso, it must be held not to repeal the purview, unless flatly repugnant to, and manifestly inconsistent with the purview. The real intention must govern in every case, and prevail over the literal sense of the terms. But the intention must be such as the legislature has used fit words to express, and the spirit is to be collected from the letter. "The longer I sit here," said Sir John Coleridge, "the more I feel the importance of seeking only the meaning of a statute according to the fair interpretation of the words, and acting on that." (6 A and E., 7.)

I have endeavored to obey these canons in giving construction to the act of 1857. We have in that act an enacting clause and a proviso, so called, to be considered. The office of a proviso is to take special cases out of the general enactment, and provide specially for them. "In its abuse," says Dwarris, "it contains all unconnected matters, and disposes of whatever is incapable of combination with the rest of any clause." The meaning of this proviso, however, is equally clear, on the face of it, whether we regard it as containing what that part of an act regularly ought or ought not to contain. It would have been more regular, perhaps, if the proviso had, in this case, constituted a separate section of the statute. But that is unimportant. No different effect can be given to it from that which it would receive if it stood apart from the purview. Now, what are the provisions of the body and the proviso of the statute? The first declares, "that the selection of swamp and overflowed land, granted to the several States, heretofore made and reported, so far as the same shall remain vacant and unappropriated, and not interfered with by an actual settlement under any existing law of the United States, be, and the same are hereby, confirmed, and shall be approved and patented, to the said several States, in conformity with the provisions of the act aforesaid (1850) as soon as may be practicable after the passage of this law." There is not a word in all this provision which has any reference or relation to swamp lands which may have been purchased by private individuals, or located by warrant or scrip, prior to the date of the act, or to any right, claim, or demand of the States to, upon, or in respect to, such lands, or the proceeds thereof, or other equivalent land. It provides only for the issuing of patents to the States, and the lands for which patents are directed to be issued are swamp lands, which are vacant, unappropriated, and unsettled, and which were selected and reported to the Government as of the character of lands granted by the act of 1850, prior to the 3d of March, 1857. Under this provision, the State could maintain no claim to the moneys realized on sales of swamp lands made before or after that date, whether the lands sold were selected and reported as being of that description prior thereto or not. We come now to the proviso. It declares that the act of March 2, 1855, is "hereby continued in force, and extended to all entries and locations of land, claimed as swamp lands, made since its passage." I think no greater effect should be given to the words "hereby continued in force," than if the provision had been, that the act of 1855 is "hereby re-enacted," but that the same effect must be given to them as if that had been the language of the proviso. What, then, would have been the construction of this proviso, if it had declared the act of 1855 to be re-enacted? It is a general rule of construction, that clauses of reference, incorporating the provisions of former statutes, take effect as fully as if they had been repeated and re-enacted in the body of the latter act with relation thereto. (Dwarris on Statutes, 602.) If we give, then, the same effect to the act of March, 1855, as if it had been in terms repeated and re-enacted on the 3d of March, 1857, we find that the cases of sales and locations of lands, claimed as swamp lands, which had occurred prior to March 3, 1857, and subsequent to March 2, 1855, are fully comprehended, and then we have a substantive provision made on the 3d of March, 1857, that the purchase money of any of the lands sold, which the States may prove to be swamp lands within the meaning of the act of 1850 shall be paid over to the States, and that indemnity, in other equivalent lands, shall be given for those lands of the character mentioned, which were located by warrant or scrip. The grant was not exclusively of the purchase moneys of those swamp lands which had been selected and reported before March 3, 1857. Patents were directed to be issued for these, if they were unappropriated and unsettled. But the grant, by effect of the proviso, was of the purchase moneys of all lands claimed as swamp lands which had been sold by the government prior to March 3, 1857, and which the States could prove were of the character of lands granted by the original act of 1850. We have no right to import into the proviso, from the purview of the act, the words of limitation that are found there, than we would have to incorporate into the act of 1855 a provision that the lands purchased or located, for which the States, under that act, were entitled to indemnity, shall have been selected and reported as swamp lands to the Government before March 2, 1855.

It is fully implied in what I have said, that the provisions of the act of 1855, thus in effect re-enacted on the 3d of March, 1857, must be held to be strictly retrospective, as of that date, according to the view which I have expressed in regard to the statute of 1855.

While I affirm, therefore, the validity of the claim of the State of Iowa, under this legislation, to the purchase moneys of the public lands within her limits sold between March 2d, 1855, and March 3d, 1857, and which you may determine were swamp lands within the meaning of the act of 1850, and to indemnity in lands for the lands located with warrant or scrip during that period which you may likewise determine were swamp lands according to the true intent of that statue, I dismiss, as without legal merit, under the legislation referred to, any claim for indemnity for lands within that designation, which were sold or located subsequently to March 3d, 1857.

I am, sir, very respectfully,
Your obedient servant,
JAMES SPEED.

Hon. James Harlan, Secretary of the Interior.

No. 289 B.

Swamp land grants—how affected by the act "for the disposal of public lands for homestead actual settlement in the States of Alabama, Mississippi, Louisiana, Arkansas, and Florida."

DEPARTMENT OF THE INTERIOR,
May, 24, 1869.

SIR:—I have received your communication of the 7th inst., returning the letter of Hon. T. W. Osborne, a Senator of the United States from Florida, in relation to swamp and overflowed lands in that State.

You submit for the consideration and opinion of the department certain questions as to the extent to which the grant of lands of this description is affected by the act entitled "An act for the disposal of public lands for homestead actual settlement in the States of Alabama, Mississippi, Louisiana, Arkansas, and Florida," approved June 21st, 1866. This act declares that from and after its passage all public lands in those States shall be disposed of according to the stipulations of the homestead law of May 20th, 1862, and the act supplemental thereto, approved the 21st of March, 1864, and that the public lands in those States shall be disposed of in no other manner. My predecessor on the 5th of April, 1867, held, after careful consideration, that the act had no relation to lands where such beneficial interest had been lawfully acquired, or the status whereof had been previously so changed that they could no longer be justly considered as the property of the United States, and subject to its disposing power. Such lands as prescribed prior to the rebellion, might have been acquired by the various modes prescribed by law for obtaining title to a part of the public domain, could in view of the act, be entered only under the provisions of the homestead law; but if the status of a tract was such as to exclude it from entry or sale before the rebellion, it could not thereafter by reason of that act be entered as a homestead. In a communication of the 26th of June, 1867, the department ruled that the act does not impair any pre-existing valid rights of property, although a patent had not been issued for the lands to which such rights had attached I consider these views to be founded upon a sound interpretation of the act.

The act granting swamp lands, &c., was passed 28th September, 1850. Attorney-General Black held that the grant was, in itself, a present grant wanting nothing but a definition of boundaries to make it perfect, and to obtain that object the Secretary of the Interior was directed to make out an accurate list and plat of the lands, and cause a patent to issue therefor.

It is not necessary that a patent should issue to the State. The patent was merely the evidence of title; nothing more. Mr. Secretary Stuart, on the 2d of December, 1851, said that the grant of swamp and overflowed land was a grant *in presenti*; that when the selections were made and approved, or the patent issued, the title thereto became perfect, and had relation back to the date of the grant, and Mr. Secretary McClelland, in June, 1856, decided that land erroneously embraced in a private claim if swamp at the date of the act, would be subject to selection.

I have the foregoing opinions, although I am aware that a difference of opinion has existed as to the time when a complete and absolute title vested in the State. Parties located with warrants or scrip, or entered for cash, lands claimed as swamp prior to the issue of patents to the State, and this led to the enactment of the act March 2, 1855.

It required that patents should be issued to such purchaser or locator, notwithstanding any contrary decision of the Secretary of the Interior or other officer. It, however, provided that where a State had sold or disposed of a tract, and at the same time it had been entered or located under the laws of the United States, no patent was to issue until the State, through its constituted authorities, released its claim thereto ; but if the State did not, within ninety days after the passage of the act, return to the General Land Office of the United States a list of lands sold as aforesaid, together with the date of said sale and the names of the purchasers, the patents were to be issued immediately thereafter.

It further provided, that upon due proof that any lands purchased or located were swamp, the purchase money should be paid over to the State or States, and where the lands had been located by warrant or scrip the State was authorized to locate a quantity of like amount upon any public lands subject to entry at $1.25 per acre, or else a patent should issue therefor upon the terms and conditions above enumerated. Your decisions as to the character of the land were subject to the approval of the Secretary of the Interior. The act of March 3, 1857 (11 Stat. at Large, 25), conformed all sections of swamp and overflowed lands so far as the same remained vacant and unappropriated, and did not interfere with an actual settlement made under any existing laws of the United States. It directed such selections to be approved and patented, and continued in force and extended said act of 1855 to entries and locations of lands claimed as swamp made since its passage.

Attorney-General Speed held that the State of Iowa was entitled, under this legislation, to the purchase money of swamp lands within her limits which had been entered with cash and to indemnity, in land for such lands as had been located with warrants or scrip prior to the passage of the act of 1857, but that she had no claim on account of such lands as had been located subsequently to that date. The opinion was accepted by this department as the law of the case, and your office adjusted the account accordingly.

Upon the whole case I am of opinion that the act of 1866 does not, in any degree, interfere with your approving lists or issuing patents to the State of Florida for such as were, at the date of said act of 1850, and within its meaning, swamp or overflowed, and which were selected prior to the rebellion, and in conformity to the instructions of your office of September 28, 1850, were sold for cash or located with military warrants or scrip.

The letter from this department to you, bearing date the 13th February last (see 2 A. L. T. 39) furnishes an answer to the question you submit touching the relations which Florida sustains to the Federal Government.

Very respectfully, &c.,
J. D. Cox, Secretary.

Hon. Jos. S. Wilson, Commissioner of the General Land Office.

TITLE XII.

APPENDIX.

No. 290 B.

Circular.

Public notice to settlers on lands reserved for railroad purposes.

DEPARTMENT OF THE INTERIOR,
GENERAL LAND OFFICE, February 10, 1870.

WHEREAS, by an Act of Congress, approved 27th March, 1854, entitled "An Act for the relief of settlers on lands reserved for railroad purposes," "every settler on lands which have been, or may be, withdrawn from market in consequence of proposed railroads, and who had settled thereon prior to such withdrawal, shall be entitled to pre-emption at the ordinary minimum to the lands settled on and cultivated by them: *Provided*, They shall prove up their right, according to such rules and regulations as may be prescribed by the Secretary of the Interior."

And whereas the first section of the Act approved June 2, 1862 (12th Stat., 413), provides "That all the lands belonging to the United States to which the Indian title has been, or shall be, extinguished, shall be subject to the operation of the pre-emption Act of the fourth of September, eighteen hundred and forty-one, and under the conditions, restrictions, and stipulations therein mentioned: *Provided, however*, That when unsurveyed lands are claimed by pre-emption, notice of the specific tracts claimed shall be filed within six months after the survey has been made in the field; and on failure to file such notice, or to pay for the tract claimed within twelve months from the filing of such notice, the parties claiming such lands shall forfeit all right thereto; provided said notices may be filed with the Surveyor-General, and to be noted by him on the township plats, until other arrangements have been made by law for that purpose."

Therefore, in accordance with the instructions of the Secretary of the Interior, it is ordered that, from and after the publication of this notice for thirty days by the Register and Receiver, all settlers on *unsurveyed lands* within the lateral limits of withdrawals for railroad purposes, and who had settled thereon prior to the withdrawal, will be required, within six months after the survey in the field (or, if surveyed before said publication, within six months after publication), to file their declaratory statements with the Register of the proper local land office, and make proof and payment within twelve months from the filing of such notice.

The Supreme Court, in the case of Whitney *vs.* Frisbee, at the December Term, 1869, have sustained the views of Attorney-General Bates, expressed in opinion on page 274 of this volume (No. 256 B), and of Attorney-General Speed (see page 280, No. 261 B), in regard to the rights of pre-emption settlers prior to application to purchase and tender of purchase money.

to the local office, the settler will be required to file his notice with the Surveyor-General within six months after the survey in the field, and, upon the land office being opened and the plat filed therein, to make his proof and payment at such office within twelve months thereafter.
If a land office has not been opened, or if the plat has not been returned

2d. That where lands were *surveyed* at the date of settlement, and are within the lateral limits of withdrawals for railroad purposes, and such settlement was made prior to withdrawal, the settler will be required to file his declaratory statement, giving therein the date of settlement, within three months from the date of publication hereof by the Register and Receiver, and thereafter make proof and payment as provided by law. In the case of settlers on *surveyed lands*, which may hereafter be included within the limits of withdrawals for railroad purposes, they will be required to file their declaratory statements, in conformity with the provisions of the pre-emption laws of 1841 and 1843, and to make proof and payment as provided by law.

A failure to file and make proof and payment, as specified herein, will forfeit the claim.

These rules will become operative, and be enforced in the several land districts from and after their publication for thirty days by the Register and Receiver, and a copy of the published notice will be forwarded for the information of this office.

Acknowledge date of receipt hereof.

Very respectfully, your obedient servant,

JOS. S. WILSON, Commissioner.

Registers and Receivers U. S. Land Offices, and Surveyors-General of the United States.

No. 291 B.

Circular.

Public notice to settlers on lands not reserved for railroad purposes.

DEPARTMENT OF THE INTERIOR,
GENERAL LAND OFFICE, February 10, 1870.

WHEREAS the first section of the Act of Congress, approved 2d June, 1862, provides "That all the lands belonging to the United States, to which the Indian title has been, or shall be, extinguished, shall be subject to the operation of the pre-emption Act of the fourth of September, eighteen hundred and forty-one, and under the conditions, restrictions, and stipulations therein mentioned: *Provided, however*, That when unsurveyed lands are claimed by pre-emption, notice of the specific tracts claimed shall be filed within six months after the survey has been made in the field; and, on failure to file such notice, or to pay for the tract claimed within twelve months from the filing of such notice, the parties claiming such lands shall forfeit all right thereto; provided said notices may be filed with the Surveyor-General, and to be noted by him on the township plats, until other arrangements have been made by law for that purpose."

Therefore, in accordance with the instructions of the Secretary of the Interior, it is ordered that, from and after the publication of this notice for thirty days by the Register and Receiver, all settlers on *unsurveyed* lands will be required, within six months after the survey in the field (or, if surveyed before said publication, within six months after publication), to file their declaratory statements with the Register of the proper local land office, and make proof and payment within twelve months from the filing of such notice. If a land office has not been opened, or if the plat has not been returned to the local office, the settler will be required to file his notice with the Surveyor-General within six months after the survey in the field, and, upon the land office being opened, and the plat filed therein, to make his proof and payment at such office within twelve months thereafter.

2d. That where settlers on *unsurveyed* lands have already filed their declaratory statements with the Register of the proper land office, they will be required to make proof and payment within twelve months from and after the publication of this notice, and a failure to file and make proof and payment as specified herein will forfeit the claim.

3d. These rules will become operative, and be enforced in the several land districts from and after their publication for thirty days by the Register and Receiver, and a copy of the published notice will be forwarded for the information of this office.

Acknowledge date of receipt hereof.

Very respectfully, your ob't servant,

JOS. S. WILSON, Commissioner.

To Registers and Receivers U. S. Land Offices, and Surveyors-General of the United States.

APPENDIX TO TITLE V.

MINERAL LANDS AND MINING CLAIMS.

No. 292 B.

Right to follow lode when same "dips" under surface-ground of adjacent owner—decision under mining act of July 26th, 1866—right of courts in 6th section of act.

The adjoining claimants on a certain vein dipping at an angle of about 45°, bounded their surface-ground by dividing lines, which, in the progress of development, were found to intersect the vein at angles varying from right angles; the one on the side towards which the vein dipped bearing N. 25½° W.

The claimant on the west side of the last named line applied for a patent under the act of Congress, approved July 26th, 1866; the other protesting and asking for a stay of proceedings under the 6th section of the act that his adverse interests might be adjusted in the courts.

From the papers filed by the contestant it appeared that no controversy existed as to the respective portions of the vein claimed by the parties, nor any substantial controversy as to the parcels of surface-ground respectively claimed, but the applicant for patent occupying on the side of the division line upon which it subtended the smaller angle relatively to the course and dip of the vein was discovered in the progress of penetrating the vein in depth, to have passed beyond this line and extracting ore on the east side of it from a portion of the vein vertically under the surface-ground of the contestant, which act, in the opinion of the latter, constituted a conflict of interest between himself and the applicant for patent, and formed the basis of his proceedings as an adverse claimant. He asserted no opposing claim as defined upon the surface, but simply an "*under-ground conflict,*" as he styled it. Apparently predicating it upon the common law maxim, "*cujus est solum usque ad coelum et ad inferos.*"

The case coming before the Commissioner of the General Land Office on an application from the United States District Land Officers for instructions, the following decision was rendered.

A conflict not involving surface-lines, but pertaining wholly to matters arising beneath the surface touching the appropriation of the vein in depth, cannot be adjudicated in the courts under the 6th section of the mining-Act, for the reason that the controversy there contemplated, is one in which judicial decision would control the General Land Office in its subsequent action on the application for patent, and would lead to a modification of the grant one way or the other, so as to conform it to the decision of the court. But no such result could follow from the action of the court upon the question raised by the adverse claimants, because whatever might be determined there, the patent issued from this office would still grant "*the right to follow the vein or lode with its dips and angles and variations to any depth, although it may enter the land adjoining,*" the mining Act authorizing the grant to be made in this form, and no decision of a legal tribunal can nullify this statutory requirement.

Most assuredly a decision producing no change in the description of the premises or the parties, can in no way control the grant contained in a patent, for all its other formal parts are statutory and beyond the power of the court.

An applicant for a patent under the Mining Act may include surface-ground lying on either or both sides of the vein as part of his claim, or he may apply for a patent for the vein alone. His rights upon the vein, and in working into it, are precisely the same, whatever may be the form of his surface-ground or whether he has any or none. His end lives, and the distance between them will be the same at all depths, as upon the surface, no matter whether the position of the vein is vertical or whether it dips at a less or greater angle. This results directly from the right granted to the miner by all the local mining customs as well as by the national mining act of following the vein with all its dips, angles, and variations, and the applicants and adverse claimants alike possess this privilege by the mining resolutions of Nevada County, California.

The congressional enactment adopts in this respect the provisions of the mining customs subordinating the rights of a patentee in respect to the surface-ground to the more important rights in respect to the vein, granting the right to follow the latter with all its dips, angles, and variations to any depth, although it may enter the land adjoining and requiring the adjoining land to be sold subject to this condition.

If the vein occupied by these claimants descended vertically into the earth, no controversy would arise between them, it is presumed, in respect to the descending boundary between their claims.

The line would be a perpendicular, and at the depth of a thousand feet the claimants would still measure from such perpendicular one thousand feet in one direction and two thousand in the other, as the extent of their respective claims at the bottom of the cavity made by extracting the ore.

If then we suppose such cavity to have been already made, and that by a convulsion of nature the vein should be wrung from a vertical position to that of an angle, at which it now dips, the cavity would then in this last position represent such a one as these contestants are now authorized to make by extracting the ore from their respective portions to that depth, and the lines of such cavity would represent the lines they are now entitled to follow, either under the mining customs or the act of Congress.

If either party is guilty of trespass on the rights of the other, the courts are open to them for redress, either before or after the issuing of a patent, and such rights are neither abridged or enlarged by the patent. *Letter of Commissioner* WILSON *to Register and Receiver at Sacramento, California, dated January 7th,* 1870.

No. 293 B.

District mining regulations—validity and efficacy of State and Territorial mining laws—regulations passed at miners' meetings—force of construction of secs. 3 *and* 9 *of mining act, July* 26, 1866.

Referring to a letter enclosing the papers in the applications of the South Park G. & S. Mining Company, for patents on the "Orphan Boy," "Dr. Mary," and "Honey Comb" Lodes in Park County, Colorado, the following instructions are communicated:

The Orphan Boy Lode calls for 200 feet on the lode, with surface ground amounting in the aggregate to $1\frac{84}{100}$ acres of land.

The Dr. Mary calls for 2815.56 feet, with surface ground, and includes 145.34 acres.

The Honey Comb, 2999.70 feet on the lode, with surface ground aggregate to 155.82 acres.

It appears that the Company were informed that applicants in Colorado could not obtain title to more than 1400 feet on the vein, but they insisted that they were entitled to 3000 feet on the lode in each application, by the local regulations of Mosquito district, under which they claimed and that they held their claims without reference to territorial law, that they had never recognized the latter in holding and acquiring their mining claims, but had been in all things governed by the local customs. * * * *

In the first place it should be observed, however, that this office has never decided that an applicant in Colorado could, under any circumstances, obtain title to more than 1400 feet on the vein. The territorial act, fixing this limit, approved February 9, 1866, expressly restricts its operation to discoveries made *after* the passage of the act, and the General Land Office has never attempted to extend its provisions to a period prior to its enactment. On the contrary, a number of patents have been issued from claims in Colorado, for 1600 feet, under the act of March 10, 1864, which latter statute also affects only discoveries made after its enactment, and certainly if claims are presented here for patent based upon locations of a still earlier date, they will be tested, not by the enactment approved February 9, 1866, nor by the act of March 11, 1864, but by the regulations in force at the time the locations were made. * * * *

The proper subject of attention in this behalf, was the necessity of furnishing a duly certified record of the respective locations, with their proper dates, and a certified copy of regulations then in force in the district, authorizing such locations to be made. * * * *

It is true the act of Congress recognizes rights acquired under district mining regulations, as well as those acquired under territorial enactments, but it is also true that it does not take from territorial legislatures the power to provide these regulations, and make them uniform throughout the territory.

There were no local district customs in force in Montana when the mining act was passed, the Legislature having adopted uniform regulations as early as 1864.

The State of Nevada had, in February, 1866, adopted a general law applicable to all counties except Storey, superseding all district mining customs, which, after the first Saturday of August, of that year, were to be considered as repealed and all mining regulations were to be in pursuance of the general act.

Colorado had legislated on the subject as early as 1861, and it is well known that other Territorial Legislatures had taken similar action before July 26, 1866.

Consequently, at the time the Congressional enactment was passed, most of the mining States and Territories had general regulations upon their statute books, applicable to all districts within their respective limits, California being, probably, the only one in which the local customs adopted at district meetings were still in full force.

It would be strange, therefore, to presume that the mining act ignored such statutory regulations, and recognized only the local district mining customs.

It was for the purpose of embracing all these different regulations, whether enacted by legislatures or adopted at miners' meetings, that the act of Congress, in the 2d section, uses terms applicable to each, and including all, by providing that the diagram filed by the applicant, shall be so extended, laterally or otherwise, as to conform to the local "*laws*," "*customs*," and "*rules*" of miners; the local laws referred to, being evidently the enactments of the State and Territorial Legislatures.

The 9th section is still more explicit as to the intention of Congress respecting local regulations, where it provides for maintaining and protecting vested rights to the use of water for mining, agricultural, manufacturing, or other purposes, whenever the same are recognized and acknowledged by the "*local customs*," "*laws*," and the "*decisions of the Courts*."

The truth is, the district customs adopted at miners' meetings, would be of no legal force except for the recognition given them by the Courts and Legislatures of the different States and Territories. They were adopted as a matter of necessity to meet a condition of things for which no provision was found upon the statute books. But as the act of making rules which other persons are bound to obey, is an exercise of legislative power, which, in all law-abiding communities, can be derived only from the fundamental law—the constitutions of the States or organic acts of the Territories—and as these grant no such powers to a mere district meeting, it follows that the rules adopted by them would be wanting in legal effect, unless recognized and confirmed by the judicial and legislative powers; and that is just what has been done in mining States and Territories of the West, and in this way was derived the legal efficacy possessed by these district customs. It is folly, therefore, to assume that the intention of the mining act of Congress is to impart to such customs greater force than is given to them by the courts and Legislatures of the respective States and Territories. On the contrary, the framers of the act intended to recognize only such regulations in reference to possessory rights as had acquired the force of law through the action of the Courts and legislative assemblies, and any other construction would introduce into nearly every State and Territory two systems of mining regulations, and produce a conflict between the land department and the local courts and legislative bodies.

Park Mining Company introduced the proceedings of a miners' meeting held in the Mosquito district November 27, 1868, for the purpose of adopting rules "regulating claims in conformity to the mining laws of the United States."

The act of Congress was purposely made to conform to the local regulations existing at the time of its passage, and the Legislature of Colorado had, prior to the date of said meeting, at several successive sessions, provided regulations for Mosquito, and all other mining districts in the Territory, and that, consequently, the attempt of said meeting to provide mining regulations was contrary to the general law of Colorado, and that no rights could be acquired under its proceedings.

Unless district proceedings of a date earlier than March 11, 1864, can be produced, authorizing locations of such size as the Dr. Mary and Honey Comb, I cannot see how they can be sustained. Those sent up with the papers, purporting to have been adopted in June, 1861, limit claims to 100 feet on the lode, 25 feet on each side for surface ground, and prohibit locations of more than ten claims each way from discovery —in other words, 2100 feet. In July, 1862, these regulations were readopted, and all locations recorded for more than ten claims each way from discovery, were declared upon to pre-emption, and the person opening the same was to be entitled to all privileges of a new discoverer.

In none of these early proceedings is any authority found for locating claims of 3000 feet on the lode, nor of locating them 100 feet in width, nor for appropriating 150 acres of adjoining lands in addition thereto; and so far as appears from the papers in these cases, the only authority for all this, is to be found in the proceedings of the meeting above referred to, which was based upon a misconception, and had no power to act in the premises.

* * * * * * * * *

No rules adopted by miners' meetings after the Legislative Assembly had passed a general law upon the subject, will be recognized as valid by this office. * * * *

In order to obviate all grounds of complaint, it is deemed necessary to adhere to the rule of granting patents only on such claims in the several States and Territories as are authorized by regulations recognized as valid by their courts and legislative authorities. *Letter of Commissioner* WILSON *to Register and Receiver at Foul Play, Colorado Territory, dated January* 15, 1870.

No. 294 B.

Mill-sites on placer-mining ground aud lodes.—Grant of patents for.

A communication has been received at this office requesting information on the following points:—

1. Can a mill-site be obtained upon placer-mining ground where the same has not been worked out and abandoned?

2. Can a mill-site in connection with a lode which has been previously patented?

In explanation of the first inquiry the writer states that quartz mills are usually located in gulches in order to secure necessary water privileges, &c.; that these gulches are frequently not worked out, and, under the local usages of miners, other parties have the right to enter upon them for the purpose of mining, and it is in reference to a mill-site thus located that the first interrogatory applies; the mill owner, under the local customs, having the right to occupy the site for milling purposes and other parties for mining.

In the first place, there is no statute anthorizing the issue of a patent for a *mill-site*, as such.

Where such site is used in connection with a mine in pursuance of a local custom, a State or Territorial law, and is reasonable in extent, it may be patented with the mine as a part of the surface ground allowed for the convenient working of the same.

The fact of there being placer gold on the site would not be an obstacle in the way; but the circumstance of some individual or company having located a mining claim upon it, by taking the steps required by the mining regulations of Montana, would prevent the issuing of a patent unless the mining claim and mill-site claim were held by the same person or persons. Where this is the case the site may then be patented as a part of the surface ground of a lode claim, provided it is in fact so used or is necessary as such, and is sustained by the local regulations.

Whatever is a *bona-fide* lode claim under the local regulations may be patented under the act of July 26, 1866; and when a mill-site constituted a part of such a claim it may be included in the patent, provided there are no claims adverse to that of the patentee unadjusted.

2. Where a patent has been obtained for a lode claim and by inadvertance or misapprehension the mill-site necessary to the convenient working of the claim, and in fact constituting a part of it under the local regulation, was omitted in making application for patent, and hence not included in the claim, it may be granted in another patent on the proper application and proof being made, the transaction being a *bona fide* one and the omission in fact the result of inadvertance or misapprehension as to the rights of applicants and under the Mining Act. *Letter of Commissioner* WILSON *to Register and Receiver at Helena, Montana Territory, dated Jan* 19, 1870.

No. 295 B.

Land returned as "mineral."—How such land may be entered as "agricultural."

Where a deputy surveyor returns land as "mineral," it can then only be entered as "agricultural" by proving the return to be erroneous. * * The returns of the surveyor are not, of course, based upon underground explorations, but upon mere surface indications, and the counter testimony of the agricultural claimant would be to the effect that, according to such indications, the land is more valuable for agriculture than for mining. He is not required to prove that no mineral exists, but simply that its general appearance indicates its chief value to be for farming or gardening purposes. *Ibid. to Hon. G. W. Julian, dated February* 5, 1870.

No. 296 B.

New regulations touching publication of notice under the mining act.

In future applications the Register, before making the publication as provided in section 3 of the mining act, shall require the applicant to make a deposit sufficient to cover the expense of such publication, in favor of the United States Treasurer, as directed in the circular from this office of January 14, 1867, or enter into an agreement with the publisher that no claim shall be made against the United States for payment of such publication; and the Register will decline to publish any notice under said act until a certificate of deposit, or the agreement with such publisher, shall be filed in his office. *Ibid. to Register and Receiver, Helena, Mont., dated January* 28, 1870.

APPENDIX TO TITLE III.

PRE-EMPTION CLAIMS.

No. 297 B.

Construction concerning possession of public lands before survey.—Local laws and usages.

1. A party went into possession of public lands before survey; held the same by virtue of local usages and laws; conveyed to another such title as he possessed, but remaining in possession after conveyance, filed upon the land after survey, and applies to enter it. His grantee is also living upon the land, and also makes application to enter. To which will title issue?

2. A decree of the local court of the Territory is rendered ordering the sale, by a commissioner, of all the interests of a party in certain public lands of the United States. The sale is made, but the party against whom the decree was rendered remains in possession, and after survey files upon the land, and seeks to enter it. Will he be allowed to do so, if his right is contested by the purchaser under the judicial decree?

1. To the first inquiry is that local laws affecting the lands of the United States are not regarded in this Department except in cases where an act of Congress has confirmed them, and rendered them valid, as, for instance, in reference to mining claims. As to agricultural lands no such confirmatory act of Congress has been passed. Hence the rights of claimants under the homestead and pre-emption laws are to be tested and determined under these statutes respectively. The claimant who can bring himself, in good faith, within these enactments, and has the advantage of priority in point of time, is the one that should succeed in acquiring the government title. A conveyance made by such a claimant before entry is not recognized in this office. Of course, any transaction that would render a claimant under the pre-emption law unable to take the oath prescribed in the 13th section of that act, would necessarily defeat his application to enter, and the same result would follow to a claimant under the homestead law, who from any cause should have rendered himself unable to make and file the affidavits required by the 2d section of the homestead act of May 20, 1862.

But any failure from these causes would not enure to the benefit of any grantees of such claimants by virtue of any conveyance previously executed. Such conveyances would be treated in this office as void, and the land would again become subject to appropriation by complying with the requirements of the respective statutes.

2. The answer to the first question is in effect an answer to the second. Until a claimant has entered and paid for United States land he has no interest in it subject to sale, and no transfer of such pretended interest, either by a private or judicial sale, is binding upon the Land Department, and this is more especially the case where the sale was made before the survey of the land, and consequently before filing upon it. *Letter of Comm'r* WILSON *to R. and R. Helena, Mont., dated March* 9, 1870.

INDEX TO PART III.

D.

E.

F.

G.

S.

T.

U.

Y.

INDEX TO PART IV.

www.ingramcontent.com/pod-product-compliance
Lightning Source LLC
LaVergne TN
LVHW101439200926
848483LV00004B/403